IR

THE NEW WORLD OF
INTERNATIONAL RELATIONS

IR
THE NEW WORLD OF
INTERNATIONAL RELATIONS

Ninth Edition

Michael G. Roskin
LYCOMING COLLEGE

Nicholas O. Berry
FOREIGN POLICY FORUM

Longman

Boston   Columbus   Indianapolis   New York   San Francisco   Upper Saddle River
Amsterdam   Cape Town   Dubai   London   Madrid   Milan   Munich   Paris   Montréal   Toronto
Delhi   Mexico City   São Paulo   Sydney   Hong Kong   Seoul   Singapore   Taipei   Tokyo

Senior Acquisitions Editor: Vikram Mukhija
Senior Marketing Manager: Lindsey Prudhomme
Assistant Editor: Corey Kahn
Editorial Assistant: Beverly Fong
Associate Production Manager: Scarlett Lindsay
Project Coordination, Text Design, and Electronic Page Makeup: Integra
Cover Design Manager: John Callahan
Cover Designer: Kay Petronio
Cover Image: RTIMAGES, © Veer, Inc.
Image Researcher: Connie Gardner
Senior Manufacturing Buyer: Roy L. Pickering, Jr.
Printer and Binder: RR Donnelley–Crawfordsville
Cover Printer: Lehigh-Phoenix Color Corporation–Hagerstown

This book is not for sale or distribution in the U.S.A. or Canada

For permission to use copyrighted material, grateful acknowledgment is made to the copyright holders on pp. 366–367, which are hereby made part of this copyright page.

Library of Congress Cataloging-in-Publication Data

Roskin, Michael
    IR:the new world of international relations/Michael G. Roskin, Nicholas O. Berry.
        p. cm.
    Includes bibliographical references and index.
    ISBN 978-0-205-07949-0
    1. International relations—Textbooks.   2. World politics—1945–1989—Textbooks.
3. World politics—1989—Textbooks.   4. United States—Foreign relations—1945–1989—Textbooks.
5. United States—Foreign relations—1989—Textbooks.   I. Berry, Nicholas O.   II. Title.   III. Title:
International relations.   IV. Title: New world of international relations.
    JZ1242.R67 2012
    327—dc22

                                                                    2010052010

Longman
is an imprint of

www.pearsonhighered.com

1 2 3 4 5 6 7 8 9 10—DOC—14 13 12 11

ISBN-13: 978-0-205-07949-0
ISBN-10:   0-205-07949-0

1119807

Brief Contents

Detailed Contents

CHAPTER 5   Russia and Geopolitics   72

CHAPTER 6   Can the United States Lead the World?   94

PART III   THE GLOBAL SOUTH   111

CHAPTER 7   From Colonialism to Decolonization   112

CHAPTER 8   Eternal Warfare in the Holy Land   126

CHAPTER 9   Oil and Turmoil in the Persian Gulf   142

CHAPTER 10   **Trouble and Hope in Latin America   160**

CHAPTER 13   The Pursuit of National Security   208

CHAPTER 14   The Politics of Nuclear Bombs   222

CHAPTER 15   The Challenge of Asymmetrical Conflict   238

PART V   ECONOMIC BLOCS   253

CHAPTER 16   Europe Unifies   254

PART VI   THE POLITICS OF A NEW WORLD   301

CHAPTER 19   Diplomacy Is Still Alive   302

CHAPTER 20   The Uses of International Law   318

CHAPTER 21   The Reach of the United Nations   334

CHAPTER 22   **Finite F.E.W. (Food/Energy/Water)   350**

Preface

The new world of international relations is indeed strange and scary. Two rather stark, new questions have emerged that were heretofore little asked: Is the United States in decline, and is China's rise inexorable? While the American people and economy are resilient and will overcome the ravages of the recession that began in 2008, students of international relations must still wrestle with the prospect that a less-powerful United States may no longer be able to lead the world. The wounded U.S. economy threatens to turn protectionist, something that will constrict world trade. A deeply indebted United States had to face limits to its economic and military power.

China's rise is both awesome and worrisome. But China will hit several speed bumps, some domestic, some regional, and some global. As China turned assertive, other countries began to push back and slowly form a common front against Beijing's demands. An urgent task for U.S. policy is to define America's interests in East Asia, especially in the China Seas. Should we attempt to lead an anti-China coalition? How hard should we push Beijing to stop undervaluing its currency?

Are today's students intellectually prepared to comprehend and respond rationally to this disquieting new world? Or will they react in ignorance and anger? This book attempts to make sure students understand how the global system has changed over the course of a century or more and how it keeps changing. These are some of the challenges the ninth edition of *IR: The New World of International Relations* addresses.

NEW TO THIS EDITION

In addition to the usual updates that include recent and current developments—especially relating to the 2008–2009 financial meltdown—instructor comment prompted us to add the following to the ninth edition of *IR*:

- New Chapter 2, "IR Theories," covers realism, liberalism, constructivism, and Marxism, with criticisms of each. Although theories are found in each chapter, instructors wanted an explicit and side-by-side review of the major philosophical approaches to IR.
- To show that the problems of the Vietnam War are not ancient history, the Vietnam chapter now compares the Iraq and Afghan wars with Vietnam, namely the difficulties of conducting irregular warfare in new and artificial countries.
- To emphasize the influence of geopolitics, the two Soviet chapters are shortened into one, Chapter 5, "Russia and Geopolitics." The rise and fall of the Soviet Union provides many examples and concepts, especially on the permanent influence of geography.

- The Afghan War, the longest in U.S. history and one of the most difficult to conclude, gets a more detailed section in our Persian Gulf chapter (Chapter 9).
- The spread of nuclear weapons—especially by Pakistan, North Korea, and (perhaps soon) Iran—raises the rationality problem. Can we rely on the rationality of leaders to restrain them from using nukes? Chapter 14 on nuclear politics suggests that not all are rational.
- Beijing will do nothing that harms its economic growth, argues Chapter 17, "Asia Awakes," making Chinese foreign policy at least partly predictable. Beijing will likely calm the numerous tensions after some testy words. The chapter adds China's economic model and claims in the China Seas. Here we also introduce the problem of China's undervalued currency, explored more fully in Chapter 18.
- Two major events of 2010—the Gulf oil spill and the death of the late Norman Borlaug, father of the Green Revolution—join our chapter on F.E.W. (food, energy, water).

FEATURES

There is not yet a clear picture of what the current global system is, much less of what the next one is likely to be. Some say that we have already left the "post–Cold War system" and entered a "post–post–Cold War system," unhelpful terms that explain little. Global systems—the distribution of power and motives of a given period—matter a great deal. They structure all countries' foreign and security policies. If we accurately comprehend the system that we are in—the "structure"—then we can make shrewd and effective policies. If we misunderstand the current structure—e.g., interpret the present system as a new Cold War bipolarity—then we can make terrible mistakes. Because we emphasize international systems and what they imply, we have been called "structural realists," a term we neither embrace nor reject.

This method entails a review of IR history and geography, and that is a problem. Few young people nowadays enter college with adequate background in twentieth-century history. Ask students questions about major events in the twentieth century or strategic waterways, and you are likely to face silence. It is all news to them. But they cannot be blamed; they don't know it because they have never been taught it. Accordingly, we take it as our task to do considerable backfilling in recent history, which we arrange largely by geographic area and use to illustrate one or more concepts of international relations. Many instructors have thanked us for this approach.

Some texts in international relations pay little attention to history and even less to geography, leaping instead into the future. These are the "world-order" texts that, we think, implicitly argue the following: "The twentieth century was a horrible century that showed the worst that humans can do to each other. But it was only an episode in the maturation of humankind and has little to teach us. The twenty-first century, a time of global cooperation, ecology, and equality, is upon us. We must concentrate on it and not on the unhappy past." Such is not the view of this book.

We begin in Chapter 1 with system change and an overview of the international systems that have marked modern history. The present system still defies easy characterization. *Multipolar* does not capture the inequalities of the several "poles"; we consider *stratified, globalized, clash of civilizations*, and other models, most of them with major economic components. Chapter 1 also introduces the concepts of *power, state*, and *sovereignty*, which we believe are still fundamental to international relations.

System change has touched almost everything in international affairs, not just the obvious— the end of Cold War bipolarity between the superpowers. Unfortunately, the changes were hard to anticipate and sometimes led to violence. In the Persian Gulf, a tyrannical ruler strove to expand his realm because his previous superpower patron could no longer restrain him. Economic relations among the major industrial blocs—Europe, the Pacific Rim, America—have grown testier; fear of the Soviets no longer holds them together under a U.S. strategic umbrella. Proliferation of nuclear weapons, a minor issue during the Cold War, has become a major issue. The United Nations, previously little more than a talk shop, has developed as a crisis stabilizer. We discuss these and other consequences of system change in this book.

We believe that because system change is occurring before our very eyes, IR is more exciting and relevant than ever. In this new world there are new threats to guard against and new opportunities to take advantage of. As in earlier editions, we are trying to awaken young newcomers to the field to its fascinating and sometimes dramatic qualities, as well as acquainting them with its basic concepts and vocabulary. Toward this end, we include feature boxes titled "concepts" and "classic thought," as well as "economics," "turning point," "diplomacy," and "geography." We also include "reflections" feature boxes, which recall the authors' personal experiences or ponder issues that affect students personally and show that IR is not a distant abstraction.

Also included are the chapter-opening questions, which prime students for the main points, and the running marginal glossaries, which help students build their vocabularies as they read. Each chapter concludes with a list of key terms and further references.

SUPPLEMENTS

Longman is pleased to offer several resources to qualified adopters of IR and their students that will make teaching and learning from this book even more effective and enjoyable. Several of the supplements for this book are available at the Instructor Resource Center (IRC), an online hub that allows instructors to quickly download book-specific supplements. Please visit the IRC welcome page at **www.pearsonhighered.com/irc** to register for access.

MyPoliSciKit for IR   This premium online learning companion features multimedia and interactive activities to help students connect concepts and current events. The book-specific assessment, video case studies, mapping exercises, simulations, *Financial Times* newsfeeds, current events quizzes, politics blog, MySearchLab, and much more encourage comprehension and critical thinking. With Grade Tracker, instructors can easily follow students' work on the site and their progress on each activity. Use ISBN 0-205-07404-9 to order MyPoliSciKit with this book. To learn more, please visit **www.mypoliscikit.com** or contact your Pearson representative.

Passport for International Relations   With Passport, choose the resources you want from MyPoliSciKit and put links to them into your course management system. If there is assessment associated with those resources, it also can be uploaded, allowing the results to feed directly into your course management system's gradebook. With more than 150 MyPoliSciKit assets such as video case studies, mapping exercises, comparative exercises, simulations, podcasts, *Financial Times* newsfeeds, current events quizzes, politics blog, and much more, Passport is available for any Pearson introductory or upper-level political science book. Use ISBN 0-205-09296-9 to order Passport with this book. To learn more, please contact your Pearson representative.

Instructor's Manual/Test Bank   This resource includes learning objectives, lecture outlines, multiple-choice questions, true/false questions, and essay questions for each chapter. Available exclusively on the IRC.

Pearson MyTest   This powerful assessment generation program includes all of the items in the instructor's manual/test bank. Questions and tests can be easily created, customized, saved online, and then printed, allowing flexibility to manage assessments anytime and anywhere. To learn more, please visit **www.mypearsontest.com** or contact your Pearson representative.

PowerPoint Presentation   Organized around a lecture outline, these multimedia presentations also include photos, figures, and tables from each chapter. Available exclusively on the IRC.

Sample Syllabus   This resource provides suggestions for assigning content from this book and MyPoliSciKit. Available exclusively on the IRC.

The Economist   Every week, *The Economist* analyzes the important happenings around the globe. From business to politics, to the arts and science, its coverage connects seemingly unrelated events in unexpected ways. Use ISBN 0-205-00254-4 to order a 15-week subscription with this book for a small additional charge. To learn more, please contact your Pearson representative.

The Financial Times   Featuring international news and analysis from journalists in more than 50 countries, *The Financial Times* provides insights and perspectives on political and economic developments around the world. Use ISBN 0-205-10903-9 to order a 15-week subscription with this book for a small additional charge. To learn more, please contact your Pearson representative.

Longman Atlas of World Issues (0-205-78020-2)   From population and political systems to energy use and women's rights, the *Longman Atlas of World Issues* features full-color thematic maps that examine the forces shaping the world. Featuring maps from the latest edition of *The Penguin State of the World Atlas*, this excerpt includes critical thinking exercises to promote a deeper understanding of how geography affects many global issues. Available at no additional charge when packaged with this book.

Goode's World Atlas (0-321-65200-2)   First published by Rand McNally in 1923, *Goode's World Atlas* has set the standard for college reference atlases. It features hundreds of physical, political, and thematic maps as well as graphs, tables, and a pronouncing index. Available at a discount when packaged with this book.

The Penguin Dictionary of International Relations (0-140-51397-3)   This indispensable reference by Graham Evans and Jeffrey Newnham includes hundreds of cross-referenced entries on the enduring and emerging theories, concepts, and events that are shaping the academic discipline of international relations and today's world politics. Available at a discount when packaged with this book.

Research and Writing in International Relations (0-205-06065-X)   With current and detailed coverage on how to start research in the discipline's major subfields, this brief and affordable guide offers the step-by-step guidance and the essential resources needed to compose political science papers that go beyond description and into systematic and sophisticated inquiry. This text focuses on areas where students often need help—finding a topic, developing a question, reviewing the literature, designing research, and last, writing the paper. Available at a discount when packaged with this book.

ACKNOWLEDGMENTS

We owe a great deal of thanks to specialists who read and commented on our chapters and saved us from foolish misstatements. Ambassador Theresa A. Healy and Charles Ahlgren of the State Department made valuable suggestions for the chapter on diplomacy. Dr. Ed Dew of Fairfield University perceptively reviewed our chapters on Africa and Latin America. Physicist David Fisher of Lycoming College gave sound comments on our final chapter. Also, we thank the following reviewers for their helpful comments: Michael Grossman, Mount Union College; Allen Meyer, Mesa Community College; Caroline Payne, Lycoming College; Yury Polsky, West Chester University; Rick Whisonant, York Technical College; and David Zimny, Los Medanos College. Responsibility, of course, lies with the authors, who are happy to receive instructor comments directly for incorporation into future editions.

MICHAEL G. ROSKIN

maxxumizer@gmail.com

PART I

APPROACHES TO IR

To get an overview of *international relations* (IR) we will look at some of its basic concepts, systems, and theories. Chapter 1 explains how IR is quite different from *domestic politics*, because each *state* has *sovereignty*. In this anarchic situation, IR depends a lot on *power* and how it is distributed. The distribution of power gives rise to international *systems*, which are tricky to define and change over time. These systems are just mental constructs or models and must not be reified. Most agree there were several during the twentieth century: a failing *balance of power* system, an unstable system from World Wars I through II, and a *bipolar* Cold War system. No IR system lasts forever; all break down. An accurate definition of the current IR system is crucial to sound foreign policy, but we do not yet have a clear definition. *Multipolar*, *unipolar*, *globalized*, *clash of civilizations*, and other systems have been suggested.

A new Chapter 2 briefly introduces some of the grand or broad theories of IR: realism, liberalism, constructivism, and Marxism, with their mutual criticisms and a caution to take all with a grain of salt. Many other theories—mostly mid-range and empirical—are found throughout the book, but here we consider the big philosophical approaches that guide what kind of questions we ask and which we ask first. Most IR thinkers subscribe to one of these grand theories, sometimes blending one with another.

CHAPTER 1

Power and Systems in Transformation

Presidents Barack Obama of the United States and Hu Jintao of China meet in 2010. The two could make no progress on adjusting China's undervalued currency. In politics, conflict is the norm. (Pete Souza/Corbis)

International relations (IR) depend a lot on **power**, the ability of one country to get another to do (or sometimes not do) something. IR occurs *among* sovereign entities (see page 17), **domestic politics** *within* a sovereign entity. International laws and institutions are too weak to rely on the way we rely on domestic laws and institutions. In domestic politics, when we have a quarrel with someone, we "don't take the law into our own hands; we take him to court." In IR, it's sometimes the reverse. There is no court, and self-help may be the only option available.

Some thinkers say that IR unfolds amid **international anarchy**, but IR is not completely disorderly. Some order grows out of relative power among nations. For example, during the nineteenth century the mighty British Empire arranged much of the globe to its liking, and small, weak lands largely obeyed. Such power relationships create international **systems**, the way power is distributed around the globe. An international system is a sort of "power map" for a certain time period. If you can correctly figure out the current system—who's got what kind of power—you know where you stand and how and when to use your power. For example, if many countries have roughly equal power, it is likely a *balance of power system* (explored presently). If one country has overwhelming power, enough to supervise the globe (unlikely), it might be a *unipolar system*. The turbulent twentieth century witnessed four IR systems.

1. *Pre–World War I.* Dominance of the great European empires in the nineteenth century until 1914. In systems theory, this period exemplifies a balance-of-power system, but by 1910 it had decayed.
2. *World War I through World War II.* The empires destroy themselves from 1914 to 1945. With several major players refusing to respond to threats, the interwar period might be termed an "antibalance-of-power" system. It is inherently unstable and temporary.
3. *Cold War.* The collapse of the traditional European powers leaves the United States and USSR facing each other in a *bipolar* system. But the **superpowers** block and exhaust themselves from 1945 through the 1980s, and the bipolar system falls apart.
4. *Post–Cold War.* The collapse of the Soviet Union ends bipolarity, but ideas on the new system are disputed, ranging from *multipolar* (several power centers) to *zones of chaos* and from *globalization* to *clash of civilizations*. We will consider several possibilities.

international relations   Interactions among countries.

power   Ability of one actor to get another to do its bidding.

domestic politics   Interactions within countries.

international anarchy   No overriding power prevents *sovereign* states from conflicting.

Do not reify these periods and systems. They are just attempts to get a handle on reality; they are seldom reality itself. **Reification** is a constant temptation in the social sciences. Students often memorize neat tables to prepare for exams, but it is important to take such tables as approximate, not literal. Notice that in the previous list one period overlaps the next. The European empires did not turn off with a click in 1945; they phased out over three decades. To try to understand a confusing world, social scientists must simplify a very complex reality into theories, models, time periods, and conceptual frameworks, all of them mental *constructs* (see next chapter). The systems approach is one such framework.

CONCEPTS ■ POWER

Power is widely misunderstood. It is not big countries beating up little countries. Power is one country's ability to get another country to do what it wants: A gets B to do what A wants. There are many kinds of power: rational persuasion, economic, cultural, technological, and military. Rational persuasion is the nicest but rarely works by itself. Military power is the least nice and is typically used only as a last resort. Then it becomes **force**, a subset of power. When Ethiopia and Eritrea quarreled over their border, they mobilized their armies and got ready to use force.

Countries use whatever kind of power they have. President Obama urges Iran to put its nuclear program under international control. Tehran bluntly says no. Massive U.S. military power is unable to sway Iran's oil power. In our age, energy resources have become one of the most important sources of power. Russia, with an unimpressive army, kept Europe respectful by control of oil and natural gas exports. When Ukraine gave Russia trouble, Moscow cut the flow of gas to Ukraine. U.S. dependency on imported petroleum is the Achilles' heel of American power, one that we paid little attention to until recently. We will discuss world energy problems in the last chapter.

Sometimes, as the United States discovered in Vietnam and the Soviet Union in Afghanistan, power is unusable. The crux of power, remember, is getting the other country to do something—in the case of North Vietnam, to stop its forcible reunification with South Vietnam. Can American power really end coca cultivation in the Andes, an area where governments either cannot or will not stop the activity? U.S. military power

in 2001 beat Afghanistan's army in three weeks but could not calm or control Afghanistan. The problem, ignored by Washington for too long, is that Afghanistan is not a country but a *failed state* (see page 115) of warlords, drug lords, and Islamist fighters. After several years of fighting amid chaos, Americans tired of the war. If all your types of power—political, economic, and finally military—do not work in a particular situation, you turn out to be not as powerful as you thought.

Power cannot be closely calculated or predicted. The Soviet Union looked powerful but suddenly collapsed due to a faulty economy and tensions among its many nationalities. You often learn who's more powerful only after a war. Typically, before the war, both sides figured they were pretty powerful. The war serves as a terrible corrector of mistaken perceptions. Washington often relies too much on a bigger and better army, which does not always work. Remember, military is only one kind of power. No one—not the British, the Soviets, or the Americans, all very powerful—tamed Afghanistan.

One's power may be unsuitable to the problem at hand. Artillery and tanks may not work against religiously motivated guerrillas, who offer few good targets. Attempting to persuade another country may provoke resentment: "Who are you to tell us what to do?" Washington often gets such replies from Beijing and Tehran. Accordingly, power of whatever sort is best exercised cautiously. The question for our day is what kind of power we should emphasize—military, economic, or political?

Actually, IR thinkers use "systems" in two distinct but overlapping ways. First, there is the real system out there in the world, but it is complex, changeable, and hard to define. Second, there is the simplified system we construct in our heads that tries to describe the real system. Ideally, what's in our heads should match what's out there. Then we can conduct rational and successful foreign policies.

But if the picture in our head does not match reality, we can make terrible, expensive mistakes. For example, if decision makers who were trained for the Cold War keep operating as if the system were still bipolar, with its emphasis on controlling distant lands, they will get bogged down in chaotic places wracked by tribal and religious hatreds. Some critics charged that Soviet-specialist Condoleezza Rice, George W. Bush's national security advisor and later secretary of state, tried to treat Iraq and Afghanistan as Cold War battles. If we try to stop massacres and promote democracy around the globe, we may collide with some nasty realities in "zones of chaos." Getting the current system right means you can go with the flow of events (and sometimes manipulate them) instead of working against them.

system　Interaction of many components so that changing one changes the others.

superpower　Nation with far more power than others; able to wage all levels of warfare.

reification　Mistaking a theory for reality.

force　Application of military power.

balance of power　Theory that states form alliances to offset threatening states.

THE EUROPEAN BALANCE-OF-POWER SYSTEM

The nineteenth century exemplifies a **balance-of-power** system, which occurs during certain periods when the power of the several major nations is similar, and they arrange this power, by means of alliances, to roughly balance. If country A feels threatened by country B, it forms an alliance with country C, hoping to deter B from aggression. Later, all of them might form an alliance to protect themselves from the growing power of country D. It did not always work, but it helped to hold down the number and ferocity of wars. For a balance-of-power system to function, theorists say, it took at least five major players who shared a common culture and viewpoint and a commitment not to wreck the system. Balance of power was like a poker game in which you'd rather keep the game going than win all the money, so you refrain from bankrupting the other players. Graphically, it looks like this:

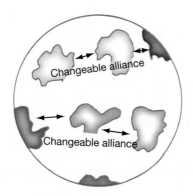

Historians see two great ages of balance of power, from 1648 to 1789 and again from 1814 to 1914. The Thirty Years War, mostly fought in Germany, pitted Catholics against Protestants and

Westphalian System set up by 1648 Peace of Westphalia that made sovereignty the norm.

sovereignty Concept that each state rules its territory without interference.

Metternichian Conservative restoration of balance of power after Napoleon.

was the bloodiest in history until World War II. By the time the Thirty Years War was settled in 1648 with the Peace of Westphalia, Europe's monarchs had had enough of bashing each other and constructed a balance-of-power system that endured until the French Revolution (1789). The **Westphalian** system also established the concept of **sovereignty** (see discussion later in this chapter).

Napoleon overturned the old system with unrestrained ambition and a mass army that conquered most of Europe. When Napoleon played poker, he tried to bankrupt all the other players (he also cheated). Gone was the restraint that had characterized the old system.

Once Napoleon was beaten in 1814, Europe's top figures met under the guidance of Austrian Prince Metternich to restore a balance-of-power system, what was called the **Metternichian** system. It worked moderately well for some decades, but only as long as monarchs restrained their ambitions and

CONCEPTS ■ SYSTEMS

A system is something composed of many components that interact and influence each other. If you can analyze the logic of a system, you can roughly predict its evolution or at least understand what could go wrong. Leaders who grasp the current international system can react cleverly to threats and opportunities. Those who do not can do great damage to their own countries.

The crux of systems is in the term "interact." If something is truly a system, you cannot change just one part of it because most of the other components also change. Systems thinking originated in biology. The human body is a system of heart, lungs, blood, and so on. Take away one component, and the body dies. Alter one, and the others try to adjust to compensate. Systems can be stable and self-correcting or they can break down, either from internal or external causes.

After World War II, systems thinking spread to many disciplines, including international relations. Thinkers—some focusing just on Europe, others on the entire globe—found that various systems have come and gone over the centuries, each operating with its own logic and producing variously stable and unstable results. Obviously, an unstable system does not last.

The strong point about systems thinking is that it trains us to see the world as a whole rather than just as a series of unrelated happenings and problems. It also encourages us to see how a clever statesman may create and manipulate events to get desired results. If he presses here, what will come out there? Will it be bad or good?

To some extent, international systems are artificial creations of varying degrees of handiwork. A system that obtains the assent of the major powers and goes with the forces of history may last a long time. A system that harms one or more major players and goes against the forces of history will surely be overturned. Systems do not fall from heaven but are crafted by intelligent minds such as Metternich and Bismarck. This brings an element of human intelligence and creativity into international politics.

Does the world form a political system? It is surely composed of many parts, and they interact. The trouble is few thinkers totally agree on what the systems were, their time periods, and the logic of their operation. Looking at the four systems of the twentieth century, some would say there are only three, because the first and second should really be merged (the second was merely the decayed tail end of the first). Others would say, no, actually there are five, adding the period of the Axis dictatorships as a separate system.

International systems thinking is inexact, not yet a science. We have still not settled on what the present system is. In this chapter, we consider several attempts to describe the current system and note that none of them is completely satisfactory. With each proposed system, ask two questions: (1) Does it exist, and (2) will it persist? That is, does the proposed system match reality, and, if so, is it likely to remain stable and last for some time?

shared the values of legitimacy and stability. This slowly eroded under the effects of nationalism in the nineteenth century—especially with German unification in 1871—until it had disappeared by World War I. There has not been a balance-of-power system since then. Some say there cannot be one again.

Some scholars reject the balance-of-power theory, pointing out that there were nasty wars when power was supposed to be balanced, for example the Seven Years War (what Americans call the French and Indian War) of the 1750s or the Crimean War of the 1850s. Balance-of-power theorists counter by saying these were relatively small wars that did not wreck the overall system.

Some writers hold that **hierarchy of power**—the opposite of balance of power—acts to preserve peace. When nations know their position on a ladder of power, they are more likely to behave. The aftermath of a great, decisive war leaves a victor on top and a loser on the bottom, and this brings a few decades of peace. Critics say balance-of-power proponents have mistaken this hierarchy for a balance that never existed. All such hierarchies are temporary and eventually over-turned as weaker states gain power and dominant states lose it.

Either way, the nineteenth-century system started decaying when two newcomers demanded their own empires. Germany and Japan upset the system with demands for, as Berlin put it, "a place in the sun." German unification (1871) and Japan's Meiji Restoration (1868) produced powerful, dissatisfied nations eager to overturn the existing system. Tremors started around the turn of the century as Germany armed the Boers who were fighting the British in South Africa, engaged Britain in a race to build battleships, and confronted France by boldly intervening in Morocco. At this same time in the Pacific, Japan attacked and beat China and Russia and seized Korea.

The balance-of-power system of the nineteenth century was no longer operative by the start of the twentieth century. Balance of power requires at least five players who are able to make and remake

> **hierarchy of power**   Theory that peace is preserved when states know where they stand on a ladder of relative power.
>
> **Bismarckian**   Contrived, unstable balance of power from 1870 to 1914.

TURNING POINT ■ BISMARCK: SYSTEM CHANGER

If someone had told Prussian Chancellor Bismarck that the unified Germany he created in 1871 would lead to two world wars and Europe's destruction, he would have been aghast. Bismarck was a conservative, yet his handiwork brought radical, systemic change. Remember, in systems you cannot change just one thing, because everything else changes too. Bismarck supervised a giant change in the political geography of Europe—German unification—but this rippled out-ward, producing a new global political system.

Before Bismarck, Germany had been a patchwork of small kingdoms and principalities that rarely threatened anybody. After unification, Germany had the location, industry, and population to dominate Europe. Bismarck thought unified Germany could live in balance and at peace with the other European powers. He was neither a militarist nor an expansionist. Instead, after unification, Bismarck concentrated on making sure an alliance

of hostile powers did not form around his Second Reich. Trying to play the old balance-of-power game, Bismarck made several treaties with other European powers pro-claiming friendship and mutual aid.

But the **Bismarckian** system was not as stable as the earlier Metternichian system (see page 6). Bismarck's uni-fied Germany had changed the European—and to some extent global—political geography. German nationalism was now unleashed. A new kaiser and his generals were nationalistic and imperialistic. They thought Bismarck was too cautious and fired him in 1890. Then they started empire building, arms races, and alliance with Austria. The French and Russians, alarmed at this, formed what diplomat and historian George F. Kennan called the "fateful alliance." Thus, on the eve of World War I, Europe was arrayed into two hostile blocs, something Bismarck desperately tried to avoid. Without knowing or wanting it, Bismarck helped destroy Europe.

Versailles The 1919 treaty that ended World War I.

interwar Between World Wars I and II, 1919–1939.

alliances. Flexibility and lack of passion are the keys here. Instead, by 1914 Europe was divided into two hostile, rigid alliances. When one alliance member went to war—first Austria against Serbia—it dragged in its respective backers. By the time the war broke out, the balance-of-power system had broken down, although many at the time did not realize it.

THE UNSTABLE INTERWAR SYSTEM

World War I, which killed some 15 million, was the initial act of Europe's self-destruction. Four empires—the German, Austro-Hungarian, Russian, and Turkish—collapsed. From the wreckage grew the twin evils of communism and fascism. The "winners"—Britain and France—were so drained and bitter they were unable to enforce the provisions of the **Versailles** Treaty on defeated Germany. The international economy was seriously wounded and collapsed a decade later.

World War I led directly to World War II. The dissatisfied losers of the first war—Germany and Austria—joined with two dissatisfied winners—Italy and Japan (Japan participated in a minor way by seizing German possessions in China and the Pacific during World War I)—while another loser, Russia, tried to stay on the sidelines.

Another connecting link between the two wars was the failure of any balance-of-power system to function, this time by design. Balance-of-power thinking stood discredited after World War I. Many blamed the cynical manipulations of power balancers for the war. This is an unfair charge, as the system had already broken down before the war. Maybe balance of power is a defective system, but the start of World War I by itself does not prove that point. At any rate, the winning democracies—Britain, France, and the United States—chose not to play balance of power, and from their decision flowed the catastrophe of World War II.

What do we call this strange and short-lived **interwar** system? It was not balance of power because the democracies refused to play. The dictators, sensing the vacuum, moved in to take what they could. We might, for want of a better term, call it an "antibalance-of-power system." Britain and France, weary from the previous war and putting too much faith in the League of Nations and human reason, finally met force with force only when it was too late; Germany nearly beat them both. Graphically, it looked like this:

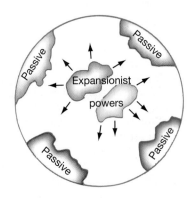

Stalin's Soviet Union also refused to play (see Chapter 5). Here it was a case of ideological hatred against the capitalist powers and the conviction they were doomed anyway. The United

States also refused to play balance of power. Isolationism plus verbal protests to Japan over the rape of China were thought to keep us at a safe distance from the conflagration (see Chapter 17). We thought we did not need a large military; we had two oceans. In 1941, both the Soviet Union and the United States learned they could not hide from hostile power.

bipolar The world divided into two power centers, as in the Cold War.

Europe destroyed itself again in World War II. Into the power vacuum moved Stalin's Red Army, intent on making East Europe a security zone for the Soviet Union. The Japanese empire disappeared, leaving another vacuum in Asia. The Communists, first in China and North Korea, then in North Vietnam, took over. The great European empires, weak at home and facing antico-lonial nationalism, granted independence to virtually all their imperial holdings (see Chapter 7). Britain, the great balancer of the nineteenth century, ceded its place to the United States. The age of the classic empires was over, replaced by the dominance of two superpowers.

THE BIPOLAR COLD WAR SYSTEM

As we shall discuss in Chapters 3 and 5, the Cold War started shortly after World War II as Stalin's Soviet Union, intent on turning East Europe into a belt of Communist-ruled satellites, proved its unfitness as a partner for Roosevelt's grand design for postwar cooperation (see Chapters 3 and 21). Many feared that Stalin was also getting ready to move beyond East Europe. By the spring of 1947, the Cold War was on, for that is when the United States openly stated its opposition to Soviet expansion and took steps to counter it.

The world lined up in one of two camps—or at least it looked that way—as there was no third major power to challenge either the Soviets or the Americans. Academic thinkers described this situation as **bipolar**. Bipolarity was a dangerous but in some ways comforting system. West and East blocs watched each other like hawks, constantly looking for opportunities to exploit in the other bloc and guarding against possible attack. It was a tense world, with fingers too close to nuclear triggers. Graphically, it looked like this:

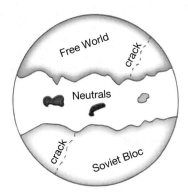

The bipolar system was seen as a "zero-sum game" in which whatever one player won, the other lost. If the Communist bloc stole a piece of the Free World, it won, and the West lost. To prevent such reverses, war was always possible (Korea and Vietnam), even nuclear war (over Cuba in 1962). Because both superpowers possessed nuclear weapons, though, they always kept their conflicts at arm's length, fighting by proxy and not directly. Both understood that a direct conflict could quickly turn nuclear, ending both the system and their dominance. They hated each other, but they were not reckless. Better, each thought, to be prince of its half of the world than run the risk of mutual wipeout. At no time did Americans tangle directly with Soviets. Still, everyone was jumpy, worried about possible gains and losses.

Some on both sides still hearken back to those days when life was simpler because you knew exactly who your friends and enemies were. The weaker allies of the superpowers, East and West Europe, mostly kept quiet and obeyed their leading power. NATO and the Warsaw Pact looked firm. Most members of each alliance had superpower military bases on their soil and accepted them as a form of protection. The comforting part about bipolarity was that you knew where you stood. For many today, life is too confusing.

If you look closely at the Cold War, however, you notice that it was never strictly bipolar. Some thinkers label it a "loose bipolar" system to account for the fact that between the two big "continents" were many "islands," neutral countries that deliberately avoided joining either camp. Both superpowers wooed these neutrals.

Was the bipolar world stable? It did not blow up in nuclear war and lasted nearly half a century, but it could not endure, for at least five reasons:

1. The bipolar system locked the superpowers into frantic *arms races* that grew increasingly expensive, especially for the weakening Soviet economy. More and more bought them less and less security, for the armies and weapons could not protect the superpowers or extend their power; their attempts to expand power collided with nationalism.

2. *Third World nationalism* arose, and both superpowers made the mistake of fighting it. Playing their zero-sum game, the two superpowers tried to get or keep peripheral areas in their "camps." They pushed their efforts into the Third World until they got burned—the Americans in Vietnam and the Soviets in Afghanistan.

3. At least one of the two camps *split*. One of the polar "continents" cracked apart, and a large piece drifted away: the Sino–Soviet dispute (see Chapter 5). Dominance breeds resentment. The other "continent" developed some hairline fractures, as NATO grew shakier (see Chapter 16).

4. The economic growth of the *Pacific Rim* countries made both superpowers look foolish. While the military giants frittered away their resources on expensive weapons and dubious interventions, Japan, South Korea, Taiwan, and other Asian rimlands turned their region into an economic giant (see Chapter 17).

5. The expensive arms race on top of an inherently defective economy and botched reforms led to the *Soviet collapse* in 1991. America, by outlasting its antagonist, in effect "won" the Cold War. The world that emerged from the bipolar system, however, is not completely to America's liking.

WHAT KIND OF NEW SYSTEM?

The two momentous events of 1991—the quick Gulf War and amazing collapse of the Soviet Union—started discussion to name and describe the new system then being born, a task not yet finished. Some of these possible systems are plausible while others are false starts, but all have a question mark after them. Do not reify them.

Multipolar?

Perhaps the most accepted model sees the world as **multipolar**—a system of several centers of power, some of them trading blocs and all of them engaged in tough economic competition. No one nation or bloc dominates. It would somewhat resemble the old balance-of-power system, but the blocs and major nations do not form new alliances. Instead, they focus on their economies, and economic growth becomes their main task, both to fight unemployment and then gain power and respect. Graphically, it would look like this:

unipolar The world dominated by one power center.

This model does not perfectly fit reality. The blocs—the European Union, the Pacific Rim, and others—cannot look after their own security; all need U.S. help. The West Europeans at first supposed they could calm the former Yugoslavia by themselves but in a few years were begging the United States to step in. South Korea, Taiwan, and Japan are powerful trade competitors with the United States, but all want free security from America. Without U.S. leadership in the world, little gets done. If trade disputes became too great, a multipolar system would break down into something else, perhaps a "resource wars" system (see pages 14–15).

Unipolar?

Some thought the great events of 1991—the Gulf War and Soviet disappearance—produced a **unipolar** system, but it was illusory. In this picture, the United States would lead in constructing what President Bush senior called a "new world order" with the Gulf War as a model: The United States leads the United Nations and the middle-sized powers to stop an aggressor. Only the United States, in this theory, now has the ability to project military power overseas, the political clout, and the vision to lead. Graphically, it would look like this:

stratified   Power distributed in layers.

The neoconservatives of the younger Bush administration adopted the unipolar view of the world and tried to implement it in Afghanistan in 2001 and Iraq in 2003. Those and other difficulties shot down the unipolar model. True, America is now the only military superpower, but economic and political factors limit its leadership. The American people and Congress are less willing to send troops and billions to far corners of the globe. Few other lands follow America into such enterprises. Some resent us. Notice how little we get our way in the world. Even much smaller powers like North Korea and Iran do not bend to our will.

Counterweight?

As the Bush 43 administration pursued a unipolar model, many European lands, Russia, China, and other countries spoke of the need for a "counterweight" to U.S. power. They saw us as domineering and too eager for war. A counterweight model would look like a unipolar model stood on its head:

Here, instead of following the United States, many other countries agree among themselves to ignore or oppose us. They would provide no support for U.S.-led causes and would sharply criticize us on everything from unnecessary use of force to economic domination. We would be labeled international bullies and politically isolated in the world. Whatever we wanted, they would oppose. In the face of massive U.S. military power, however, they would pose no security threat to us.

There are problems with this model too. The rest of the world is disorganized and cooperates on little. Some oppose the United States on one question but support us on another. And when there is a serious problem, many beg for U.S. help; they understand that only we have the power to curb dangerous aggressors and murderous civil wars. In reaction to U.S. policy on Iraq, the world tended to form a counterweight—such as Russia and China's vague Shanghai Cooperation Organization—but not a strong or consistent one.

Stratified?

A **stratified** model combines the unipolar and multipolar models and may fit reality better. It sees roughly three layers. At the top are the rich, high-tech countries. The second layer is that of rapidly industrializing lands such as China, India, and Brazil. The third layer is a "zone of chaos" dominated by crime, warlords, and chronic instability. It is startling to realize that the world's biggest single economic activity is now crime, much of it connected to the flow of drugs from the poor countries to the rich countries. Graphically, it would look like this:

duopoly   Two big powers dominate.

chimera   Mythical beast composed of several unlike parts.

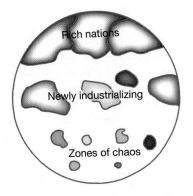

The top-layer countries can zap conventional targets with their advanced weapons, but they cannot control the chaos of the bottom-layer countries, whose terrorists, guerrillas, and drug cartels offer no good targets. Somalia, Mexico, and Afghanistan are examples of chaos that the top-layer countries would like to avoid but cannot. Many of the world's natural resources—particularly oil—are in these chaos zones, so the first layer is inevitably drawn into their difficulties. And the first layer's appetite for illicit drugs means the bottom layer gets its tentacles into the top layer.

U.S.–China Duopoly?

Some claim the new global system is a **duopoly** of power between the United States and China, the so-called G2 (Group of Two), indicating they are the only ones that really count now. G8 and G20 meetings are unimportant because, compared to the United States and China, the others are mid-sized players. The duopoly model envisions a world jointly led by the United States and China. But this so-called Chimerica is a **chimera**. The two giants do not cooperate on much, and tensions grow between them. China concentrates on its own economic growth and avoids global problems such as nuclear proliferation, peacekeeping, currency parities, and climate change. When asked to help, Beijing in effect shrugs, "None of our business." The duopoly model had an even shorter lifespan than the unipolar model (see pages 11–12).

China, based on its amazing economic rise, is not shy about showcasing its newfound power and buying friends and influence in the developing areas. It locks up resource deals (especially oil) around the world. To safeguard supply lines, it builds a navy and a "string of pearls" of friendly ports across the Indian Ocean. (Actually, this is just what Britain did in the nineteenth century.) Several developing countries tilt toward China and admire the Chinese model—an authoritarian regime that boosts economic growth.

A variation on the duopoly model is U.S.–Chinese rivalry, some of which is already appearing. If trade, currency, and Internet disputes between them increase and China stakes out territorial claims that frighten its neighbors—which it is doing—U.S.–China hostility could flare. China claims Taiwan, India's Arunachal Pradesh, and most of the South and East China Seas. These claims could persuade several other Asian lands—Japan, South Korea, Vietnam (once a U.S. enemy), Thailand,

globalization The world turning into one big capitalist market.

Australia, and India—to seek U.S. leadership to form a counterweight to China. In such a world, most countries in other regions would have no incentive to get involved.

Globalized?

Even before the Cold War ended, **globalization** began to emerge (see Chapter 18). In such a system, most countries become economic players in the world market, a capitalist competition where goods, money, and ideas flow easily to wherever there are customers. The motto of a globalized system: Make money, not war. The few countries that do not play, such as Cuba and North Korea, live in isolation and poverty. After some years, most countries want to play. Globalization can help promote worldwide economic growth. It might look like this:

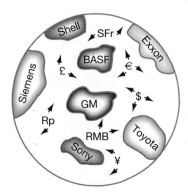

But there are many problems that limit and could end a globalized system. The worldwide 2008–2009 recession worked against globalization. Most countries—including the United States—talk free trade but do not practice it. They see their industries closing under waves of imports and respond with protectionist measures to lock out foreign goods.

Furthermore, is globalization a cause or a consequence of peace? Are the two intertwined? If so, what happens to one when the other is disrupted? Prosperity does not necessarily bring peace, as newly affluent countries demand respect, resources, and sometimes territory. As China got richer, it defined its borders more grandly, reaching far out into the South and East China Seas where there may be undersea oil.

Globalization does not seem to work everywhere. East Asia has zoomed ahead, but some countries have grown little, suggesting that sound policies and flexible cultures are key factors. China turned itself into the "factory of the world" with which few countries can compete. How many low-cost producers can the world take? Some resent the American and capitalist culture of a globalized system: "McWorld." Some think globalization is already declining.

Resource Wars?

Some thinkers warn we are moving into an "age of scarcity" marked by a scramble for natural resources, especially petroleum. Rapidly industrializing China needs ever-more resources, especially energy. To secure them, it makes exclusive deals with producing states (and never asks about their human rights record). Instead of a free market, this is a tied market that blocks the free flow of natural resources to all customers, a bit like old-fashioned colonialism. The questions of who owns the China Seas and who controls transportation corridors from the Persian Gulf and Central Asia loom larger. We may already be engaged in resource wars: the 1991 and 2003 wars with Iraq (see Chapter 9).

Related to resource wars is "resource blackmail." China has a near-monopoly of the world's rare-earth elements, crucial to many high-tech products. China can set its own price or simply refuse to export. In an age of tight energy supplies, countries with oil and natural gas deflect outside pressures with credible threats to cut exports. Saudi Arabia, resentful of U.S. complaints, finds it impossible to increase oil production. Russia, unhappy with Ukraine turning westward, temporarily shut its gas pipeline to Ukraine and to West Europe. Everyone noticed. Iran's oil income allowed it to ignore Western concern over its nuclear program. In the energy age, the weak have become powerful.

Clash of Civilizations?

The late Harvard political scientist Samuel P. Huntington in 1993 made intellectual waves with his theory that the post–Cold War world was dividing into eight "civilizations," each based mostly on religion: Western (with European and North American branches), Slavic/Orthodox, Islamic, Hindu, Sinic (Chinese-based), Japanese, Latin American, and African. Some of these civilizations get along with others, but some seriously dislike and reject others. The biggest threat: Islamic civilization, which clashes violently with Western, Slavic/Orthodox, and Hindu civilizations (see Chapter 9). Graphically, Huntington's "civilizational" theory would resemble the trade-bloc picture:

Indeed, some of these civilizations are forming trade blocs. What motivates their relations is not trade, however, but deep-seated cultural dislikes and "kin-country rallying." For example, Saudi Arabia and Iran, which both detested Saddam's dictatorship in Iraq, opposed the 2003 U.S. invasion. One should not invade a brother Muslim country. Pakistanis feel the same way about the U.S. struggle in Afghanistan. In Huntington's world, religion predicts international alignments. Most IR thinkers believe Huntington's theory contains some truth but is exaggerated.

Which, if any, of these models matches and explains international relations today? Could a combination provide a better fit? Can you come up with an accurate picture? Or will we just have to wait some years until the situation becomes clearer?

state   Country or nation, has *sovereignty*.

absolutism   Renaissance pattern of kings assuming all power.

strong state   Modern nation-state able to enforce *sovereignty*.

ARE STATES HERE TO STAY?

One may hope that the emerging international system will be an improvement, but its basic components are still sovereign **states**, and they tend to trip up plans for a peaceful, cooperative world. The concept of the modern state, nation-state, or the colloquial term "country" goes back about five centuries, when important changes rippled through West Europe. Thanks to gunpowder and cannons, monarchs got control over the nobles and amassed centralized power, a movement called **absolutism**. Economies greatly expanded with new inventions (such as printing) and the opening of trade to Asia and the Americas. The Roman Catholic Church lost temporal power as monarchs declared themselves supreme and secularized their kingdoms. To support their frequent wars, kings improved civil administration and tax collection. By the end of the horrible Thirty Years War in 1648, powerful modern states dominated West Europe.

Because they were so powerful—able to raise and fund large armies and navies—the modern **strong states** spread worldwide, for they easily conquered traditional lands. After they liberated themselves from colonial rule, the lands of Latin America, Asia, and Africa also adopted the strong state form, although some were actually quite weak (see Chapters 7 and 11).

The American and French Revolutions in the late 1700s added a new twist to the strong state: mass enthusiasm and participation. Before, the affairs of state had been confined to a handful of kings and aristocrats; subjects (rather than citizens) kept silent and obeyed. With the spread of democratic ideas, citizens felt involved and patriotic. Nationalism, originating in

CONCEPTS ■ THE STATE

States are generally defined as groups of humans having territory and government. This government, in turn, has the last word on law within its borders (*sovereignty*, which we consider presently). Only the state has a legitimate monopoly on coercion; that is, it can legally force citizens to do something. The mafia, of course, can force you to repay a debt, but it has no legal right to punish you. The Internal Revenue Service, on the other hand, can legally send you to prison for nonpayment of taxes.

Some use the term "nation-state," which adds the concept of nationality to state. Members of a nation-state have a sense of identity as a distinct people, often with their own language. Nation-states are fairly modern creations, probably not more than half a millennium old. International relations does not use "state" in the U.S. sense, such as the "great state of Kansas." In IR, in fact, the 50 American states are not states at all, because they lack sovereignty. They do not have the last word on law within their borders; the federal government in Washington does.

Most analyses of international relations take the nation-state as their starting point. State power overrides individual preferences. States can draft citizens and march them to war. Many states have a psychological hold on their citizens and inculcate and then command a sense of patriotism, not always for good ends. With this comes "we–they" thinking about foreign lands. "We" are peaceful folk simply trying to protect ourselves; "they" are plotting to harm us. U.S. and Iranian attitudes about each other are a current example. Each feels it is the aggrieved party.

Could the leading role of the state be eroding? States are not necessarily the first or last word in human organization. Throughout history, extended families, tribes, kingdoms, and empires have given way to more advanced forms of organization.

the French Revolution and Napoleonic wars, also spread worldwide, assuming dominant, even lunatic, proportions in the twentieth century (see Chapter 7).

IS SOVEREIGNTY SLIPPING?

If the new international system is to be more peaceful and cooperative than the old, states will have to give up at least part of their most basic attribute, their sovereignty. Part legal, part power, and part psychological, sovereignty means having the last word in law, able to control your country's internal affairs and to keep other countries from butting in. In a word, it means being boss on your own turf.

Sovereignty means countries can pretty much do as they wish. Pakistan in the past has worked closely with the United States but plays a double game in sometimes sheltering and sometimes fighting Islamic extremists. Washington hates this, but Islamabad decides what is in its national interest, not Washington. China's currency, says Washington, is kept too low and should rise. Beijing resists, because its low yuan gives it an export advantage. Beijing decides what is good for the Chinese economy, not Washington. In 1990 Saudi Arabia asked for U.S. troops to defend its territory against Iraq. But these soldiers could not drink a beer until they crossed into Iraq; Saudi law prohibits all alcoholic beverages (an incentive for U.S. troops to advance rapidly). Notice how sovereignty in part offsets power, in these cases, U.S. power.

Sovereignty has always been partly fictional. Big, rich, and powerful countries routinely influence and even dominate small, poor, and weak countries. Lebanon, for example, lost its sovereignty as it dissolved in civil war in 1975, its territory partitioned by politico-religious militias and Syrian and Israeli occupiers. Israel's pullout from the south of Lebanon in 2000 scarcely helped, as the territory was occupied by Hezbollah fighters, not the Lebanese army. Syria still seeks to dominate Lebanon.

In our day sovereignty has been slipping. The world community, speaking through the United Nations, told Iran that developing weapons of mass destruction was not just Iran's business but the world's business. The world felt ashamed that it did not interfere in the massacre of 800,000 Rwandans in 1994. Can mass murder ever be a purely "internal matter"? In 1999, NATO ignored Yugoslav sovereignty in trying to prevent the mass murder of Kosovar Albanians. Nations can no longer hide their misdeeds behind the screen of sovereignty. Several nations propose a new doctrine, "responsibility to protect" (R2P, see page 290), that the international community can intervene in a state that abuses its citizens. If implemented, R2P would erode sovereignty, which is why many countries dislike it.

CONCEPTS ■ SOVEREIGNTY

The root of the word sovereignty is *reign*, from the French for rule. The prefix is from the Old French for over, so a sovereign is someone who "rules over" a land (a king). Sovereignty is the abstract quality of ruling a country. The term gained currency in the sixteenth century when royalist scholars such as the Frenchman Jean Bodin, rationalizing the growth of the power of kings, concluded that ultimately all power had to center in a monarch. By the 1648 Peace of Westphalia, European states were declaring themselves "sovereign"—the last word in law—over their territories, and monarchs agreed to keep out of the internal affairs (such as religion) of other states. Although the age of royal absolutism passed, the concept of sovereignty remained, and now all states claim sovereignty.

A U.S. military policeman advises his Afghan counterpart in 2010. Some called Afghanistan a "failed state" because it could not govern much of its territory. (Reuters/Nickola Solic/Landov)

supranational   Power above the national level, as in the UN.

Supranational entities have appeared. The European Union (EU) is now one giant economic market, and many important decisions are made in its Brussels headquarters, not in its members' capitals. EU members have surrendered some of their sovereignty to a higher body. Many have given up control of their own currency—a basic attribute of sovereignty—in favor of a new common currency, the euro. Now the EU is trying to build common foreign and defense policies. The trouble here is that, if the EU goes all the way to European unification, it will not erase sovereignty but merely produce a bigger and stronger sovereign entity, one even harder to deal with. In place of many smaller states, we will face one big state. Further, the EU tends to economic protectionism, which could lead to trade wars.

REFLECTIONS ■ SOVEREIGNTY AND YOU

"You can't do that to me; I'm an American!" say many young Americans who run into trouble with the local law while traveling overseas. But they can do that to you. They can do whatever they want to you; that is their right as a sovereign state. They can cane your behind until it bleeds for spray-painting cars (which Singapore did to one American youth). They can ignore a plea from the U.S. president for leniency. It's their law, and they can enforce it any way they like. What can the U.S. embassy or consulate do for you? Suggest an English-speaking lawyer. That's all. Remember, sovereignty means they are bosses on their own turf, so when you're overseas, you have to obey their laws. Your U.S. or other foreign passport gives you no special protection.

my**poliscikit** EXERCISES

Apply what you learned in this chapter on MyPoliSciKit (www.mypoliscikit.com).

Assessment   Review this chapter using learning objectives, chapter summaries, practice tests, and more.

Menu

Flashcards   Learn the key terms in this chapter; you can test yourself by term or definition.

Flashcards

Video   Analyze recent world affairs by watching streaming video from major news providers.

Videos

Simulations   Play the role of an IR decision-maker and experience how IR concepts work in practice.

Comparative
Exercises

KEY TERMS

absolutism (p. 16)

balance of power (p. 5)

bipolar (p. 9)

Bismarckian (p. 7)

chimera (p. 13)

domestic politics (p. 4)

duopoly (p. 13)

force (p. 5)

globalization (p. 14)

hierarchy of power (p. 7)

international anarchy (p. 4)

international relations (p. 4)

interwar (p. 8)

Metternichian (p. 6)

multipolar (p. 10)

power (p. 4)

reification (p. 5)

sovereignty (p. 6)

state (p. 16)

stratified (p. 12)

strong state (p. 16)

superpower (p. 5)

supranational (p. 18)

system (p. 5)

unipolar (p. 11)

Versailles (p. 8)

Westphalian (p. 6)

FURTHER REFERENCE

Buzan, Barry, and Richard Little. *International Systems in World History: Remaking the Study of International Relations*. New York: Oxford University Press, 2000.

Calvocoressi, Peter. *World Politics Since 1945*, 9th ed. New York: Longman, 2009.

Cohen-Tanugi, Laurent. *The Shape of the World to Come: Charting the Geopolitics of a New Century*. New York: Columbia University Press, 2008.

Ferguson, Niall. *The War of the World: Twentieth-Century Conflict and the Descent of the West*. New York: Penguin, 2006.

Hiro, Dilip. *After Empire: The Birth of a Multipolar World*. New York: Basic Books, 2010.

Kagan, Robert. *The Return of History and the End of Dreams*. New York: Knopf, 2008.

Klare, Michael T. *Resource Wars: The New Landscape of Global Conflict*. New York: Henry Holt, 2002.

Lundestad, Geir. *East, West, North, South: Major Developments in International Politics Since 1945*, 5th ed. Thousand Oaks, CA: Sage, 2005.

Marks, Sally. *The Ebbing of European Ascendancy: An International History of the World, 1914–1945*. New York: Oxford University Press, 2002.

McWilliams, Wayne C., and Harry Piotrowski. *The World Since 1945: A History of International Relations*, 7th ed. Boulder, CO: Lynne Rienner, 2009.

Opello, Walter C. Jr., and Stephen J. Rosow. *The Nation-State and Global Order: A Historical Introduction to Contemporary Politics*. Boulder, CO: Lynne Rienner, 2004.

Philpott, Daniel. *Revolutions in Sovereignty: How Ideas Shaped Modern International Relations*. Princeton, NJ: Princeton University Press, 2001.

Ramo, Joshua Cooper. *The Age of the Unthinkable: Why the New World Disorder Constantly Surprises Us and What We Can Do About It*. New York: Little Brown, 2009.

Sheehan, Michael. *The Balance of Power: History and Theory*. New York: Routledge, 1996.

CHAPTER 2

IR Theories

Roosevelt and Churchill, here meeting on a British battleship off Newfoundland in August 1941, forged the Atlantic Charter even before America was in the war. Scholars debate whether this illustrates realism or liberal idealism. (AP Photo)

onfusion surrounds the term **theory**. Some students take it to mean an abstraction of little practical value. Some expect a theory to be a clear, definite formula, such as Einstein's famous "$E=mc^2$," something it rarely is in the social sciences. Actually, a theory is a device to order data, ask questions, and make sense out of a complex world. The basis of political science is **empirical** theory. Theory underlies all **rational** discourse; you cannot say much without it. Indeed, anything beyond a simple statement of fact is to some degree a theory. When you gather many facts and categorize and then generalize about them, you are beginning to theorize.

Many people suppose that they need no theory, that if they assemble enough facts, reality will be apparent. That notion itself is a theory, one of pure empiricism, which the philosopher Immanuel Kant in the eighteenth century demonstrated was insufficient. Kant saw that just gathering facts will leave you with a jumble of unrelated information. You will not know what to do with your facts; they will be meaningless. With no theory, you will not know which questions to ask and which to ask first. This is why scientists spend much time and thought developing **paradigms**, programs of how to study things.

Every chapter of this book (and most other college texts) contains theory, sometimes explicit, sometime implicit. In Chapter 1, for example, we argued that *power* counts for a lot in IR. That's a theory (that not everyone fully agrees with). Then we proposed that the world has gone through a series of *systems* that, depending on the array of power globally, explain how the world operates. That too is a theory and one that not all thinkers would place in a first chapter. In Chapter 3, we will survey U.S. foreign relations to show how *national interest* governs much (but not all) of foreign policy, another theory. In Chapter 5, Russian history will illuminate the theory that *geopolitics* also governs strategic choices. Chapter 12 explores several theories on the cause of wars.

In this chapter we explore four of the basic or "grand" theories that underlie much IR thinking. Each theory in effect proclaims, "Here is the best way to look at world politics," but it seldom proves its case entirely. This is theory in the sense of underlying assumptions or philosophies that are hard to verify with empirical evidence. Theories that can be verified—such as several of the ones in Chapter 12 on the causes of war—become less controversial because skilled researchers can either confirm or refute them. But the broad theories we discuss here are contested, precisely because they are hard to prove or disprove and are often emotional and deep-seated: "Well, that's what I think!" Some

QUESTIONS TO CONSIDER

1. Why do we need theories in international relations?
2. What is the difference between "being realistic" and realist theory?
3. What are the main features of *realism*?
4. How do realist thinkers handle ideology?
5. If IR liberals seek peace, why do they sometimes go to war?
6. What is the main argument of *constructivism*?
7. How do realists, liberals, and constructivists differ on the national interest?
8. How did Lenin adapt Marxism into an IR theory?
9. In the current situation, which is the best IR theory to use?

theory   Explanation of why things happen.

empirical   Supported by observable evidence.

rational   Able to think clearly and test ideas against reality.

paradigm   A widely accepted research model or way of studying things.

realism   IR theory that emphasizes power and national interest.

strong partisans reject and denounce other theories. Serious thinkers, however, usually admit that other perspectives have some validity.

Theories can be quite practical, as using an inappropriate theory can lead to terrible mistakes. Stalin in the 1930s foolishly followed a Marxist theory that Nazism was the last gasp of dying capitalism and would soon collapse, so Hitler would not be a threat. British Prime Minister Neville Chamberlain went to Munich in 1938 (see page 79) with the optimism of a liberal and supposing Hitler also wished peace. Then Hitler ate Europe. The neoconservatives of the Bush 43 administration embraced a neoliberal theory that the U.S. conquest of Iraq in 2003 would produce a stable democracy that would spread through the Middle East. Check your basic theoretical assumptions; they are likely the most serious flaws in any policy.

THE OLDEST THEORY: REALISM

Probably the oldest IR theory, **realism**, is still widely accepted with some variations by many academics and practitioners. Hardly anyone admits to being "unrealistic"; most like to be known as realistic because they think it means level-headed and pragmatic. But "being realistic" is not the same as realism, which is a philosophical approach to IR grounded in history and geography and consisting of several interlocking components.

Power Counts Most   Realism focuses on *power* (see page 3), a much broader concept than just military force. Power consists of the economic, political, psychological, and military tools by which A gets B to do what A wants. In the last century this came to be known as realism. Its

CLASSIC THOUGHT ■ E. H. CARR AND REALISM

British diplomat and scholar E. H. Carr (1892–1982) called the interwar period *The Twenty Years' Crisis, 1919–1939*, the title of his scathing and influential critique of the failure of the democracies to recognize world power realities. In so doing, Carr laid the groundwork for the realist school that was picked up and amplified after World War II by Hans Morgenthau in the United States.

Carr divided thinkers on international relations into two schools: utopian and realist. The utopians are optimists, children of the enlightenment and liberalism, and hold that reason and morality can structure nations' international behavior toward peace. Woodrow Wilson and his League of Nations are prime examples. Realists, on the other hand, are pessimists and stress power and national interest. This does not

necessarily mean perpetual war, for if statesmen are clever and willing to build and apply power, both economic and military, they can make aggressors back down. Implicit in this strategy is a balance-of-power theory.

Between the two great wars, Carr saw utopian fools unwilling to stand up to dictatorial beasts. The trouble with realism is that you cannot tell what is realistic until many years later, when you see how things turn out. Should you be constantly tough and ready to fight? Could that lead to too many wars, some of them unnecessary? The application of a simplified version of realism after World War II helped create and perpetuate the bipolar system of the Cold War, a dangerous system that led to a number of good-sized (but not nuclear) wars.

roots, however, go much further back. Ancient kings and empires knew all about power; most of them pursued it with single-minded determination and emphasized its military aspect. If they didn't, they figured, some other kingdom would beat them. The Old Testament and Rome's wars show shrewd appraisals of power: Conquer them or they'll conquer you. Realism can be found in Thucydides's (see page 202) famous cause of the Peloponnesian War: "What made war inevitable was the growth of Athenian power and the fear this caused in Sparta." As we will explore in the next chapter, the U.S. founders and early presidents were shrewd realists who understood that the new, weak republic had to navigate among much stronger powers.

national interest What is good for a country as a whole in international relations; often disputed.

crusade In realist thought, an ideological war unrelated to the true national interest.

Power motives, however, are often deliberately disguised with high-sounding phrases such as "defense of liberty," "just war," or "crusade to liberate the Holy Land." With Machiavelli in the early sixteenth century, if not before, thinkers were stating the obvious, that monarchs sought power, that, in fact, they *had* to. They needed sufficient power to accomplish anything, to do good or evil, or just survive. Goodness unarmed is of no use and probably short-lived.

States Are the Units That Matter   Realism also posits *states* (see page 16) as the relevant units, not individuals, groups, or transnational movements. Realists typically do not focus on specific leaders or on their motivations, which are presumed to be largely the same: safeguarding their countries. There is much variation, of course, in how they do this. Realists do not look to Stalin's warped personality to explain his takeover of East Europe; they look to the repeated invasions of Russia from East Europe (see page 73). History and geography of states are the operative factors, not individual leaders.

State-centrism came with the end of the Thirty Years War in 1648. This elevated the concept of *sovereignty* (see page 6), which included making rulers responsible for their states. For realists, this means that states are generally "unitary actors," each under the control of a sovereign. Internal splits and complexities do not much matter. Under this doctrine, the United States charged that Afghanistan, by letting al Qaeda operate on Afghan soil, was responsible for 9/11 and invaded in 2001. When Pakistan denied helping the terrorists who shot up Mumbai in 2008, India scoffed, calling the incident a Pakistani act of war. Pakistani intelligence has long and deep ties to Islamic terrorists. If the United States is ever hit by a nuclear device, Washington will waste little time looking for shadowy terrorists but will instead go straight after the country that supplied the bomb.

National Interest Trumps Ideology   Realists minimize *ideology* (see page 78) as a basis for policy; it is mostly a trick to con the gullible. Instead, realism is based on **national interest** (discussed in Chapter 3). *Feasibility* (see page 70) is the link. National interest, if pursued rationally, tells leaders how to use their power effectively. Hans Morgenthau (see box), the guru of national interest, urged nations to purse their "interest defined in terms of power." If you are preserving or enhancing your power, you are rational. If you are scattering or wasting your power in "**crusades**," you are harming your national interest and are therefore irrational. Many realists called the Vietnam and Iraq wars ideological crusades.

Not everything is a national interest. Good national leaders constantly scan the horizon looking for their country's national interests and avoiding areas that are not. The "vital national interest" is not getting conquered. To prevent that, one must have arms and allies and be willing to go to war. "Secondary interests," more distant and less urgent, may not be worth a war; some may be negotiated, others waited out. Telling the two apart requires rare intellectual ability, which Morgenthau had but many others do not. Was the 1931 Japanese conquest of Manchuria a local spat or the opening round of major aggression? The answer came in a few years when Japan began to conquer all of Asia. Is Islamic fundamentalism a vital U.S. interest or a secondary one? Should we invade distant lands to eradicate it?

Balance of Power Still Operates   Many realists (but not all) argue that balance of power (see page 5) is a natural outgrowth of the focus on power and national interest. Countries, always wary of other states encroaching upon them, will almost automatically attempt to offset hostile power by boosting their own power through arms and alliances. The balance of power is rarely aimed at peace; it is aimed at enabling states to survive and not get absorbed by other states. The Habsburg grab to take over Europe pushed Catholic France to support the Protestants. The Axis menace

CLASSIC THOUGHT ■ HANS MORGENTHAU ON NATIONAL INTEREST

A brilliant refugee scholar from Nazi Germany taught America about national interest (which we will explore more fully in the next chapter). In so doing, Hans Morgenthau (1904–1980) founded the Realist (he capitalized it) school of international relations in the United States. Many Americans, immersed in legalism and moralism, disliked the concept of national interest, which sounded like the old and evil "power politics." To Morgenthau, national interest was the only rational key to international politics. Once you understood a country's national interest, you could roughly predict its foreign policy moves. You could "look over the statesman's shoulder when he writes his dispatches;.... read and anticipate his very thoughts."

Morgenthau thought national interest was largely objective and rational because he defined it in terms of power. Intelligent leaders could figure out what they must and should do to safeguard their nation's power, and outside observers could understand why they were doing it. Said Morgenthau: "International politics, like all politics, is a struggle for power." Use your power carefully, warned Morgenthau; do not spread it too thin or fritter it away. Policies that enhance a nation's power are rational; those that diminish it are foolish. When facing the likes of Hitler and Tojo, America needed power, not legalism or moralism, Morgenthau argued. American thinkers, who

tended to stress moral goals in foreign policy (prime example: Woodrow Wilson), denounced Morgenthau's seeming amoralism.

A nation's first and vital national interest is to secure its territory; this cannot be negotiated away. Other items may be "secondary interests" about which one may, depending on circumstances, negotiate and compromise. (For Morgenthau's rules of effective diplomacy, see Chapter 19.) Vietnam, like most of the Third World, was not a vital U.S. interest; the conservative Morgenthau thought the war there was an irrational crusade that flung away America's power for no good purpose. In this way, the "amoral" Morgenthau was more moral than those who sold Vietnam as a good war.

The trouble with Morgenthau's approach is that it made no provision for the irrational aspects of national interest, which often dominate. Leaders may foolishly draw the national interest too wide and spread their power too thin, thus weakening their nation. It would be wonderful if all countries' national interests were rational; then they would be limited and predictable. Morgenthau's concept of a limited and rational national interest was actually a normative argument that countries *should* adopt such policies, for then problems could be compromised by peaceful diplomacy. At bottom, the great realist was a great moralist.

forged the Western alliance of World War II. Soviet designs forged NATO. Ideology had nothing to do with these alliances; they were formed to offset threatening power.

Starting in the late 1950s, Mao's ultrarevolutionary upheavals alienated the Soviet Union until war was possible; in early 1969 Russia and China skirmished on their Far Eastern border. Nixon had built his career as a militant anticommunist, but in the 1960s when he was out of office he read IR books that included the concept of balance of power. Nixon said in late 1971 that he sought a balance of power among the United States, Europe, the Soviet Union, China, and Japan. At this same time, a worried Mao got rational and welcomed Nixon to Beijing in early 1972. China needed U.S. power to offset the Soviet threat, and the United States needed China to offset Soviet power. Mao and Nixon abandoned their ideologies in favor of using balance of power to safeguard their respective states.

Amorality Reigns   Realism is tinged with amorality—some say deep dyed. Realists try to avoid labeling events "good" or "bad"; they look instead for what *is*. "Doing the right thing" may be wildly infeasible. Britain in late 1939 considered helping Finland repel a Soviet invasion—until the reality hit that Britain would then be at war with *both* Hitler's Germany and Stalin's Soviet Union. In mid-1941, when Hitler invaded Russia, Britain allied with the Soviet Union, although Churchill knew full well what a murderer Stalin was. Britain had little choice; for a year, it had stood *alone* against Nazi might. Power considerations trump morality. "Covert action is not to be confused with missionary work," said realist Henry Kissinger. (Actually, missionaries were often the opening wedge for Portuguese, French, English, and Americans to extend their countries' influence.) For realists, feasibility is closely connected to morality.

Criticisms of Realism

The big problems with realism are the difficulties of accurately perceiving reality and of defining the national interest. Many parade a "tough" appearance of realism without grasping the true complexities of the world out there, which may take years to emerge. So-called realist policies may turn out to be mistaken. Few have the gift of peering into the future, although many guess and use dubious *analogies* (see pages 205–206).

You can err in at least two ways: underanticipating a threat or overanticipating it. The democracies made few preparations for the Axis menace until it was almost too late. U.S. cold warriors, on the other hand, saw continuing Soviet expansion even as the Soviet economy declined at an accelerating rate. Eventually, it brought down the system. It turns out that capitalism really is better than socialism, something good American capitalists are supposed to know. All we had to do was wait. Anyone suggesting that at the time, however, would have been laughed out of Washington.

National interests are often presumed rather than analyzed. As we shall see in Chapter 4, Vietnam was overstated as a national interest. Years later, many of the war's supporters admitted that it was not. Populist demagogues, a nationalistic press, and rigid thinking in government and academia can present simplified, inaccurate pictures. Hitler's propaganda minister Goebbels explained how he got Germans to march to war: "Simple, just tell them they're being attacked." Ignorance is widespread. Few Washington officials understood the difference between Sunni and Shia Muslims and how their mutual hatred would trip up the U.S. occupation of Iraq.

Further, realist theory assumes that national leaders are rational, but many are not (see page 236). Hitler attempted to enslave Europe for a nutty race theory. Stalin shot most of his generals and colonels on suspicion of disloyalty in the late 1930s, severely weakening the Red Army before the German attack. Mao ordered two mass upheavals that killed millions of Chinese and set back China's

liberalism   In IR, presumption that countries can interact peacefully.

classic liberalism   Adam Smith's theory that an economy corrects itself without government supervision; became U.S. conservatism.

economic progress at least ten years. Iran's Ahmadinejad hears voices and sees visions. Some leaders are *paranoid* (see page 77). We had better not count on them to make rational decisions.

A major criticism of realism argues that it may have worked in earlier ages, such as the Cold War, but does not in a new world of violence by subnational groups who are quite ideological and ignore rational offers. The realists' state-centric approach does little good and much harm when the biggest problems are not state behavior but the depredations of Islamist terrorists who flit from state to state. Invading Iraq or Afghanistan does not stop them but energizes them and brings them new recruits. The terrorists understand and use this. How does the United States handle the flood of narcotics from south of the border? The Mexican state is too weak to suppress *narcotraficantes*, who own much of the police and army. Invading Mexico would do no good. State-centered realism provides no guidance in dealing with *weak* or *failed states* (see page 115).

Balance of power is another problem, one that Morgenthau recognized. How do states know when power balances? Always fearful, they amass additional power until it frightens neighboring states, which in turn must add more power. The results are arms races or even wars. It would be fine if their powers would *just* balance, but they tend to overshoot. In building security, states can increase their insecurity, something known as the "security dilemma." Balance of power may be useless in an age of *asymmetrical* warfare (see page 240). Guerrillas and terrorists do not challenge major powers with jets and tanks; they wear them down with roadside and car bombs and by turning the native populations against the occupiers.

THE LIBERAL PEACE SEEKERS

Liberalism—sometimes known as "idealism"—repudiates the previously described realist approach, which, liberals charge, leads to war. Hints of liberal idealism in IR can be found far back in history, probably as soon as humans pondered the horrors of war. Isaiah prophesied an end of war when people would "beat their swords into ploughshares and their spears into pruning hooks." During the Middle Ages, Christian thinkers argued that war should be avoided or at least limited (see the *just war theory* on page 70).

Spurts of peace seeking tend to come during or in the wake of wars. Some place Emeric Crucé and Grotius (see Chapter 20) among the founders of liberal IR theory. Both lived through and wrote in revulsion at the Thirty Years War. Prussian philosopher Immanuel Kant proposed a "league for perpetual peace" in the midst of the French revolutionary wars. Woodrow Wilson launched his League of Nations in reaction to World War I, Franklin D. Roosevelt his United Nations in reaction to World War II.

The **liberalism** we mean here is the **classic liberalism** founded by Adam Smith that dominated nineteenth-century Britain. From the Latin *liber* (free), classic liberalism urges that government keep its hands off the market and has turned into U.S. conservatism. It is almost the opposite of the modern liberalism that tries to rectify social wrongs by redistributing money from rich to poor. In IR, the old liberal thinkers claimed that, just as the free market peacefully regulates itself, so would free transactions among nations. Trade would promote peace. Two British prime ministers—realist Conservative Disraeli versus Liberal Gladstone—emblemized the debate. European unification based on trade arose after World War II with the aim of preventing war. Liberal IR theories, like realism, consist of several interlocking elements.

Liberals Are Optimists   Realists are pessimists. Countries are not inherently hostile to one another, argue liberals. The natural inclination of most countries is to get along with others. Philosophically, some compare the ferocious world of realists with Hobbes's brutal state of nature. Liberals, on the other hand, are compared with Locke's picture of the state of nature as tolerable but unstable; it just needs a little help from government institutions.

Focus on Power Is Wrong   Liberals agree with many of the criticisms of realism discussed previously, sometimes angrily. By stressing power, argue liberals, realism inclines nations to use force. Balances of power are illusory; when they break down, as in 1914, they cause global bloodbaths. Balances of power do not lead to peace; they lead to war.

Bad Regimes   Realists argue that different types of regimes and their ideologies are not the major factors. Geography is more important. They note how tsars, Communists, and Putin all pursued the same goal: safeguard Russia by keeping threats from its borders. Both Democratic and Republican administrations pursued the Cold War because they saw a geopolitical threat. Liberals, on the other hand, argue that regime type and ideology count for a lot. Any good analysis must pay them considerable attention. Fanatic or undemocratic regimes amass power beyond any reasonable need, hype nationalism, and allege foreign threats to convince populations to go to war. With democratic regimes, countries get along.

By the same token, say liberals, problem personalities can derange their entire country and damage the international system. As noted, realists pay little attention to leaders' personalities. The biggest (negative) examples for liberals were Kaiser Wilhelm and Adolf Hitler, who tried to unite Europe under German domination in World Wars I and II respectively. The problem, retort realists, was not German leaders but the power and geopolitics of a united Germany, which inclined it to dominate Europe. Liberals affirm that once we rid the world of aggressive monarchs and dictators, peace will be the norm. Democracy brings peace (which may be true; see page 346).

CONCEPTS ■ LIBERAL INTERNATIONALISM

Some liberals are willing to go to war to oust dictators and install democracy. On the face of it, this sounds like a contradiction to the liberals' search for peace. Liberal internationalists Wilson and Roosevelt argued they very much served the cause of peace, but sometimes you have to use force to first get rid of the bad guys; then you can set up democracies and peace. This doctrine can lead to a lot of wars.

Neoconservatives (see page 107) in the Bush administration, who were actually Wilsonian liberals, put this theory into practice with the 2003 invasion of Iraq, which was supposed to trigger democracy throughout the region. Liberals now debate "humanitarian intervention," whether the United States should intervene to end mass killings (see *R2P* on page 290). Some liberals argue that we must stay in Afghanistan to prevent the Taliban's horrifying mistreatment of women.

Woodrow Wilson supported the 1898 war with Spain and annexation of the Philippines. He sent U.S. forces into Mexico and Central America, and, after much hesitation, entered World War I in 1917. The way Wilson saw it, all served the cause of civilization. Franklin D. Roosevelt understood that American democracy could not survive in a world dominated by the Axis. Liberals go to war as much as realists. In some cases, realists are more cautious about war—because they ask what the national interest is—than are liberals.

Free Trade International liberals further argue that free trade among nations binds them to one another and makes war unlikely because it would hurt everyone's economy. Norman Angell's influential 1909 *Grand Illusion* argued that with Europe's economies intertwined, war was impossible. The period before World War I was a heyday of free trade, but it did not stop war in 1914. Many liberals argued that the decline of world trade during the Great Depression propelled the Nazis and Japanese militarists to power and then to war. Liberals blame the high U.S. Hawley-Smoot tariff of 1930 for prolonging and deepening the Depression and leading to World War II. They supported Roosevelt's tariff-cutting measures, the Bretton Woods agreement, and the World Trade Organization (see Chapter 18). Many liberals see *globalization* (see page 14) as a path to peace. Liberals emphasize how free trade and peace reinforce each other in the European Union, where war is now unthinkable. See, trade and treaties work.

International Law Buttressing democratic regimes and free trade is the role of international law (IL). Realists scoff at IL; some claim it does not exist. Liberals see it as a device to smooth frictions between countries and stabilize friendly relations. Accordingly, liberals favor treaties and international adjudication of disputes.

International Organization By the same token, liberals wish to participate actively in international organizations such as the UN and WTO. Some assert that the U.S. absence from the League of Nations led to World War II. The more contact and discussion, argue liberals, the more stable the peace. Realists see international organizations simply as the arenas where the major powers clash over their interests, all trying to use the organizations for their own purposes. They note that international organizations do not solve serious disputes.

Criticisms of Liberalism

E. H. Carr (see box on page 22) put IR liberals in the utopian category for supposing that reason, negotiation, and mutual advantage could stop dangerous aggressors. The epitome of this was Chamberlain, who thought he had a deal with Hitler in 1938: "peace in our time." Chamberlain was a very sensible and rational businessman; he could not understand that Hitler was not. Liberals also have trouble with rationality, assuming that the deals they offer are so overwhelming—trade, IL, peace—that every country must eventually sign up. But some obstreperous regimes such as Cuba and North Korea prefer isolation and defiance, because opening to the world would end their dictatorships.

Free trade does not come easily; it must struggle against protectionism. Liberals assume that free trade benefits all; it's "win-win." But poor countries often fear that free trade unduly benefits the rich and powerful, who will economically swallow lands just starting to climb the economic ladder. Nineteenth-century imperialism—including the Opium Wars in China—was justified as the great mechanism of free trade. Even rich countries resist totally free trade; they fear it means the export of their factory jobs to low-wage lands, a view current in the United States. The recent global recession has boosted protectionist sentiment.

The EU illustrates how free trade promotes peace, admit realists, but European unification began only after Europeans had had enough of shedding each others' blood. Finally, under U.S. protection, they accepted a series of treaties, but they were pushed into them by World Wars I and II and by American security guarantees. And notice that the Balkans required yet another bloodbath to sober up and ask for EU membership. Realism explains European unification at least as well as liberalism, claim realists.

So you don't like power, realists taunt liberals, but you are swept into the same power game as everyone else. Liberals Roosevelt and Truman created vast U.S. armed forces. They had to. Liberal President Carter, shocked by the 1979 Soviet invasion of Afghanistan, boosted the U.S. defense spending that President Reagan further expanded.

G8/G20 Group of eight/twenty leading countries.

constructivism Mental *constructs*, formed by social interaction and convention, govern thinking.

construct Idea so widely accepted that it seems to be a fact.

Democracy is a great thing and does promote peace, agree realists, but how do you install it in backward lands totally unprepared for it? Democracy failed in Russia (see Chapter 5) and is questionable in Iraq and Afghanistan (see Chapter 9). International law would be fine, too, if you could get all countries to obey it. Those who do not, "rogue regimes," still have to be dealt with by applying power. The same goes for international organizations, which quickly turn into "talking shops" that solve nothing. **G8** or **G20** meetings are just photo ops.

THE NEWEST: CONSTRUCTIVISM

The newest and perhaps currently most popular IR theory, especially in academia, is **constructivism**, which argues that subjective understandings rather than objective reality are what influence policy. People read meanings into so-called facts, but they are just mental **constructs**, established by the abandonment of old notions and acceptance of new ones through contestation and persuasion. At any given moment, you can be deceived. Constructivists are suspicious of eternal truths such as the power emphasis of realists or the peace emphasis of liberals. These are just constructs that become operative only because many think they are important. Once a construct is established, even if artificial and exaggerated, it takes on an aura of truth that, for a time, few dispute. The *conventional wisdom* (see page 330) of one era, however, may be discredited and discarded in the next. Constructivism discovered that basic views can change.

Thinking is highly conditioned by what society believes, argue constructivists. "Law," for example, becomes operative only if widely believed. Imagine a complex legal system of courts, judges, and law books but one that nobody believed or followed. Would it still be a legal system? And laws change under the impact of debate and reasoning. How can you prove that 18, not 21, is the age of maturity? (Brain science and auto-accident statistics suggest it should be 26.) Any age you pick will be a legal fiction. Law—especially international law (see Chapter 20)—is arguably the most constructed field; it works only if most people accept it. In much of the developing areas, it is considered foolish to obey the law; no one else does. Constructivism—like realism and liberalism, with which it quarrels—has several elements.

Reality Is What You Think It Is Facts, especially in the social sciences, are slippery, open to interpretations that change over time. Nation-states with sovereignty, for example, are relatively recent constructs that took over IR thinking with the end of the Thirty Years War in 1648. Before that, kingdoms were the relevant units, before that it was empires, and far enough back it was tribes and clans. In their day, each was celebrated as the highest form of human organization. Sovereignty was a shaky construct. Seldom fully observed—it never bothered Frederick the Great or Napoleon—it is now widely evaded and eroded.

You can talk yourself into mistaken national interests, constructivists point out. American expansionists, at first very few in number, picked up from European imperialists and Mahan (see page 45) the need for an American empire. They arranged a "splendid little war" with Spain in

groupthink   Janis's theory that group cohesion stifles doubt and dissent.

1898 to grab Cuba, Puerto Rico, and the Philippines and soon had the enthusiastic backing of most Americans, few of whom could find the Philippines on a map. A handful of "Anti-Imperialists" (including Mark Twain and Andrew Carnegie) opposed this, and in a few years even Teddy Roosevelt recognized that it had been a mistake, for now the Philippines would have to be defended from Japan, which, in 1942, they were not.

If Everybody Says So, It Must Be True   Constructs are highly social. Group conformity leads to what psychologist Irving Janis called **groupthink**. Instead of reasoning from facts as individuals, members of leadership teams—say, the U.S. National Security Council—are reassured that everyone agrees on the relevant facts and conclusions. Dissents and doubts are minimized because most people want to be team players, and open opposition damages careers. One of the few top advisors who warned Kennedy about Vietnam was the clear-thinking George Ball, who told JFK in 1961 that within five years there could be 300,000 American troops in South Vietnam. "George, you're crazier than hell," Kennedy replied. Ball was right but was ignored.

Constructs Are What the Other Guy Believes   Constructivists claim that they keep distant from constructs; they're too smart to get suckered into them. They see their task as ripping away (or *deconstructing*) the mental constructs of others, especially of realists. Constructivists, however, with their doubts that reality can be accurately understood, have trouble establishing what reality is. Constructivists can end up believing false constructs as much as anybody.

Power Orientations Can Be Overcome   They are just mental constructs. Realists and their power emphasis dominated Europe a century ago; now Europeans (except perhaps Russians) regard so-called realists as throwbacks to a violent age, rather like Americans. As we considered with liberalism, two bloody world wars motivated Europeans to turn from power to trade and treaties. Americans after World War II shifted from legalism to realism. "We'll give those terrorists a taste of American power," proclaimed neocons in 2001. Ten years later, U.S. generals were reflecting that we might have been creating more Taliban in Afghanistan than we were killing. Muslim militants have constructed the notion that America aims to destroy Islam. The power construct was deceptive and counterproductive when applied to Afghanistan.

Nationalism Can Be Overcome   People are nationalistic because their regimes feed them nationalist rhetoric, argue constructivists. Most government-approved history books portray a national pageant unflawed by mistakes or tragedies. Pyongyang tells North Koreans that they are a pure-blooded race the Americans aim to defile and rob. They claim that the outside world is starving and aggressive, but North Koreans—who have few other information sources—are well fed and looked after. It is not clear how many of the very lean North Koreans believe this. Hot-headed nationalists, such as Nazis and Japanese militarists, can be calmed (or killed) and turned into two of the world's biggest international cooperators. Neither were genetically power-mad nationalists; they learned it under certain circumstances. Then they unlearned it.

Yugoslavia is a case of nationalist constructs run amok. After the massacres of World War II, Tito's regime punished local nationalism, and Serbs, Croats, Slovenians, Bosnians, and others got along and increasingly even intermarried, slowly building up a "Yugoslav" identity. When Tito died in 1980, however, opportunistic state politicians whipped up destructive local nationalism

until, by the early 1990s, Yugoslavia fell apart in civil war and ethnic cleansing. There was always some disdain among nationalities,
but Yugoslavs did not have a natural hatred of each other; that was
hyped by politicians, who decreed Bosnian, Croatian, and Serbian
identities and languages. They all spoke Serbo-Croatian and still do. Yugoslavia could have gone
either way. If Tito had been followed by a strong chief and political reform, there might still be one
Yugoslavia. It did not have to fracture. (Sure, retort realists, it could have worked just fine, if only
Tito had lived another hundred years.)

relativism   Abandoning absolute
moral standards.

Liberals Are Better than Realists   Constructivists seriously dislike realists for supposing
there is an objective reality out there and that power is the way to navigate through it. But
there is a certain amount of overlap between liberals and constructivists. Both think they can
build a better, more peaceful world. The liberals would first improve institutions in the expectation that psychological change will soon follow. The constructivists would put psychological
change first.

Foreign Policy Is a Constructivist Playground   Foreign policy offers a rich field for constructivist comment. Constructivists write many brilliant books and articles demonstrating that we
are governed by fools (not hard to do). In foreign policy, they argue, meanings are seldom clear.
National interests can change 180 degrees from one era to the next. U.S. isolationists refused to
see war coming until Pearl Harbor. Then globalists accepted the Cold War *containment* theory (see
page 49) until they had to pay for it in Vietnam. Those who dissent from the prevailing wisdom are
considered radicals and gadflies and are largely ignored. Constructivists often urge policy makers
to "change your thinking" and "see things a different way," but few listen. Realists in Washington
shrug off constructivist comment as irresponsible and impractical, and few constructivists occupy
high office.

Criticisms of Constructivism

At its extreme, constructivism denies the existence of an empirically verifiable reality.
Constructivism can be super subjective and grow into what the philosophers call *solipsism*: nothing
outside of one's mind exists. Such people guiding policy could produce catastrophes. They might
propose that "if we just had another way of looking at North Korea" we could reach a peaceful
understanding with Pyongyang. The constructivist problem lies in Pyongyang, namely *its* absurd
constructs, in which it sees itself as under attack.

Mainstream constructivists do recognize that there is a world "out there" but argue that it
lacks meaning until one is constructed for it. We often fail to fathom the real world until it is
too late. Our constructs do eventually catch up with reality, but delayed and in spurts. Thus
Bush's neoconservatives sold their demonization of Iraq to most Americans. Then the 2003
invasion of Iraq revealed that it had no weapons of mass destruction or ties with al Qaeda, and
our picture of Iraq changed. The constructivists' strongest point is their emphasis that you can
talk yourself into just about anything, which may turn out to be inaccurate. Lovers and decision
makers beware.

Constructivists can slide into **relativism**, unable to label anything right or wrong because
"it all depends on the situation" and "who's to judge?" Some even object to calling Hitler,
Stalin, or Mao "mad" or "monsters." Constrained by political correctness, constructivists can

Marxism   Militant, revolutionary form of socialism.

contradiction   In Marxism, a big, incurable problem that rips the society apart.

bourgeoisie   Middle class, pejorative in Marxist usage.

proletariat   In Marxism, large class of industrial workers.

end up as amoral as realists. Realists can be wrong, but constructivists just plain cannot tell. If moral choices are muddy, policy-making will be terribly difficult. Decision makers will be dipped in doubt, fearing that whatever policy they pick could be a mistaken construct. And the opposite policy could be just as mistaken. Paralysis follows.

Constructivism returns us to a very old philosophical problem, perhaps the oldest: Where does reality reside? Out there in the "real world" or in the mind of those who perceive what's out there? Plainly, as Kant saw, you need both perspectives. Of course there is a real world, but you have to understand it correctly, and this is difficult. Realists and neocons can be too sure of themselves. They may need a constructivist tap on the shoulder from time to time, asking, "Are you sure you've got this right?"

MARXIST THEORIES OF IR

Communist and other radical regimes embraced Marxist theories, which were discarded after the Soviet collapse (if not before). In practice, even Communist countries were motivated by nationalism rather than class conflict. Still, there is something useful in Marxist IR theory, which can be seen as a warped branch of realism. **Marxism** portrays itself as the ultimate in realism, claiming that all motivations in IR, however disguised, are for the economic gain of the ruling classes. One may doubt it.

Karl Marx (1818–1883) had little to say about relations among states; he believed the big **contradictions** are *within* states, namely, between their two major social classes, the **bourgeoisie** and the **proletariat**. The upper ranks of the bourgeoisie—the "ruling circles of capitalism"—basically own and run the country, determining economic policy, foreign policy, laws, and governance, all in service to themselves. Democratic trimmings may fool the masses into thinking they have some input, argue Marxists, but they have little or none.

The chief contradiction, the one that will bring down capitalism, is between a capitalist economy that produces more and more and the impoverished workers who cannot afford to buy the growing output. This leads to *overproduction*, which leads to recurring depressions. Eventually, there will be a depression so big and a working class so angry that they will overthrow capitalism and install socialism. Marx thought he scientifically proved this in his voluminous writings, but it seems more a mental construct.

Vladimir Lenin (1870–1924), a Russian Marxist, turned Marxism into an IR theory a century ago. Marx expected a proletarian revolution in his lifetime, but it never came. Liberal English economist J. A. Hobson provided an explanation in his 1902 *Imperialism*, which argued that capitalism, plagued by *underconsumption* at home, finds new markets overseas, thus giving itself a new lease on life. Lenin, in Swiss exile, worked this up into his 1916 *Imperialism, the Highest Stage of Capitalism* to explain World War I. The capitalist-imperialist powers, scouring the globe for markets and resources, collided into each other in a scramble for colonies. The war, said Lenin, was about global dominance in which some countries are rich imperialists and others poor victims. Marx, who saw world capitalists as conniving together, not fighting, would likely have denounced Lenin's major redo of his theory.

Marx held that revolution would come first to the most industrialized lands, for they had the largest proletariat and sharpest contradictions, but Lenin also changed this. Capitalist development is always uneven, leaving some countries far behind the ones who industrialized first, especially Britain. Countries that were just industrializing, such as Russia and Spain, were "capitalism's weakest link," argued Lenin. Russia's small but growing proletariat, guided by the Bolshevik Party, would be enough to carry out a revolution that would then spread worldwide. Basically, Lenin was just grasping for any theory that would justify revolution in Russia. Mao completed this train of thought by arguing that preindustrial China, with essentially no proletariat, could base its revolution on poor peasants. Marx would not have been pleased. Presently, Marxist theories of IR contain these elements.

This Is a Material World   Causes and motives in IR reside in economics and power, not in ideas or mental constructs. People have ideas, to be sure, but they are reflections of their material conditions, argue Marxists. Capitalists celebrate the free market because it serves their interests. Muslim tribesmen rebel not because they have been talked into extremist Islam but because they are poor, marginalized, and exploited by corrupt rulers. Philosophically, Marxists are the opposite of constructivists, who suppose it's all in your mind.

Rich Capitalist Countries Still Run Much of the Globe   Marxists used to argue that capitalists run the entire globe, but plainly that is no longer tenable. Most oil-producing countries have long since nationalized their black gold and just use the oil corporations as tax collectors and marketing agents. Aramco, for example, was founded in 1933 by Standard Oil but by 1980 was wholly owned by Saudi Arabia. The biggest world buyer of oil is China's state-owned companies. China's capitalists exist by permission of the Chinese Communist Party, and they know it. Still, Marxists point out that world financial markets are very much run by and for capitalists, whose greed and deception can still plunge the world into recession.

Capitalist Countries Try to Remake the World in Their Image   Marxists make the chief culprit the United States, which promotes free-market capitalism as the ticket to global prosperity. After the Soviet collapse, a "Washington consensus" emerged that preached, "stabilize, privatize, and liberalize." Critics called this "market fundamentalism," an Ayn Rand worship of capitalism, and it effectively ended with the financial meltdown of 2008–2009, which made totally free markets seem reckless. Now some speak of a "Chinese consensus," namely, that controlled economies under state supervision are the path to stable prosperity. At any rate, the fear that capitalists will set up a purely capitalist world has receded, and very few countries want or are able to copy China. The world economy is likely to remain quite mixed.

The World Economy Is Unstable   Capitalism is still a kind of roller coaster, with giddy growth punctuated by sickening downturns. Eventually, a new Great Depression could end it. While few Marxists now predict a global economic collapse—they have predicted it too long to be believable—some foresee a series of recessions that will force governments into regulating and limiting markets. Capitalism was supposed to have collapsed long ago; the fact that it has not should be a source of great embarrassment for Marxists.

Governments Serve Capitalists   Most countries' policies serve the major centers of wealth, argue Marxists. Notice how quickly Congress bailed out giant corporations in 2008 and 2009. Washington's promotion of globalization chiefly serves big businesses. Foreign aid programs sound "liberal" but mostly flow through large U.S. firms. The Marshall Plan that rescued Europe after World War II also opened it to American corporations. Most U.S. foreign aid is "tied," that is, it can be used to purchase only U.S. products. We don't give poor countries dollars; we give them surplus American grain, which aids the U.S. agribusiness. In capitalist countries, Marxists argue, the interests of the rich and powerful dominate.

bailout Emergency loan to prevent corporation or government from collapsing.

cui bono Latin for "to whose benefit?" or "who gains?"

cultural hegemony Gramsci's theory that capitalist control of culture keeps workers unrevolutionary.

Criticisms of Marxist IR Theories

Ideas play a potent role in IR and are not just reflections of material reality, a basic Marxist contention. Many Islamist terrorists are educated and comfortable. Few are poor, but virtually all share a vision—whipped up by fiery Islamist preachers—that the West is attacking Islam and they must sacrifice themselves to save it. The fact that women and children are killed in military operations especially enrages them. Poverty does not explain the 2010 would-be Times Square car bomber, who had a job, home, and MBA. (For more on terrorism, see Chapter 15.)

Historians find little or no evidence that a struggle for colonies was at the root of World War I, in which colonies were a side show. The war was about German mastery of Europe. Britain and Germany, to be sure, were aware of Iraq's oil potential at the start of the war. Overall, colonies cost governments more to administer and defend than they ever earned, although some individual firms profited from their colonial operations. Portugal, the poorest country of West Europe, was the first and last colonial power. Its colonies kept it poor. Europeans got richer after they gave up their colonies.

The modern economy is not merely a capitalist plaything. No capitalist system is totally free and unfettered. Capitalists have unions, environmental regulations, pension funds, and government on their backs. They hate restrictions on their ability to make money, but they have to live with them. Some corporate suits go to jail for financial misdeeds. In 2010, legislation tightened controls on banking giants, especially those that got federal **bailouts**. Marxists respond, "Well, sure, they had to clean up their act to keep the system from collapsing altogether. But it still serves capitalist ends."

Capitalist control of foreign policy is an article of Marxist faith but requires closer looks. Strategic rather than economic motives usually dominate. True, in 1953 the CIA helped overthrow an Iranian regime that had seized an oil company, but it was a *British* oil company (the same one that brought us the oil spill in the Gulf of Mexico in 2010). The chief U.S. motive was to prevent the spread of communism, which Washington conflated with Iranian nationalism. The shah eventually nationalized the oil company anyway. Big oil, which is understandably pro-Arab, wields influence in Washington, but not as much as AIPAC (American-Israel Public Affairs Committee), which keeps Congress tilted well to the side of Israel. U.S. agribusiness is eager to sell to Cuba, but Miami's anti-Castro Cubans prevent it. It looks like capitalists are not as powerful as they are cracked up to be.

A residue of Marxist theory can be helpful. By teaching us to look for whose interests are served—in Latin **cui bono**—we may find unexpected patterns. And often they do not correspond

CONCEPTS ■ GRAMSCIAN MARXISM

One Marxist thinker overlapped with constructivism. Italian Communist Antonio Gramsci (1891–1937), who died in Mussolini's prisons, tried to explain why workers had not turned revolutionary, as Marx had predicted. The capitalists, Gramsci charged, by their control of education, religion, and the media, established "**cultural hegemony**" over society, brainwashing out any notions of worker solidarity or revolution and brainwashing in support of existing institutions. The capitalists' cynical constructs—what Marx called "false consciousness"—kept themselves in power and the workers down. Gramscian thought, still influential, is a partial repudiation of the strict materialism of classic Marxists.

to Marxist constructs. Marxists and other radicals, for example, denounce globalization as serving capitalist interests. The less-developed lands, according to Marxists, are deliberately kept down and poor so capitalist firms can siphon off their wealth (see *dependency theory* on page 164). But globalization has mostly benefited developing lands—with China in the lead—whose economies now grow much faster than the stagnant First World economies. The 2003 U.S. invasion of Iraq benefited only one country: Iran, which has close ties to the Baghdad regime. Although it may not deliver a complete explanation, one must, like police detectives, always ask who benefits.

> **neo-**   Revival or updating of a previous ideology or approach.

IR THEORIES: AN EVALUATION

Is it possible to operate with no theory of IR, to be purely *pragmatic* (see page 78)? Some claim it is, but that is unlikely. The brilliant Dean Acheson entered the State Department in 1941 from a top Washington law firm and served as Truman's secretary of state from 1949 to 1953. He had essentially no exposure to IR theory, which suited him just fine. "Foreign policy is answering the cables," he once snorted. But Acheson, perhaps without knowing it, subscribed to theories. He began as a Roosevelt liberal, looking forward to a postwar world of trade, nice relations, international law, and the UN. He tried to get along with the Soviet Union. By the end of 1946, however, he had lost all patience with Stalin and turned into a fierce Cold War realist, a process most of Washington was going through at that time. Doubt those who claim they have no theory.

Be aware that there are more basic theories than the four discussed here. Christian theories of IR share much with liberalism, although Reinhold Niebuhr introduced a dose of realism (see page 206). Feminist theories, some of them related to constructivism, note the prevalence of the macho values of a patriarchal society and claim they can be overcome. Older theories can be modified and revived, sometimes earning a "**neo-**" prefix, as in neorealism or neoconservatism.

So which theories of international relations should we use? From the previous brief review, it is apparent that none are wholly satisfactory. All can be criticized for failing to match reality—especially embarrassing in the case of realism. But all contribute to our methodological tool kit by teaching us to approach ideas skeptically. One must learn to doubt advocates who are so caught up in one theory they cannot reconsider data in light of alternative perspectives. It is the theory that is widely embraced but unexamined that leads to massive mistakes.

Different theories may suit different *levels of analysis* (see page 197). Realism likely lends itself to views of the globe as a whole, the ebb and flow of power among nations, and the type of *system* (see Chapter 1) that prevails at any given time. Realism may be less useful at the level of an individual country's *foreign policy* (see page 96) because national interests are easily warped and distorted. Here constructivist analysis may be more useful, one that continually reexamines the reigning conventional wisdom and asks if it still matches reality. Those who exclude liberal perspectives will have difficulty explaining European unification and the growth of international organizations. Even Marxism, by asking who benefits, can be useful.

Notice also how one theory can serve as a corrective to others. Especially useful are constructivist comments that make realists or liberals pause before they plunge deeper into a policy: "Are you sure you've got this right?" This may force policy makers to think more deeply or even "out of the box." Initially, the criticism may bounce off, as typically officeholders are very sure of themselves. But if things start to go wrong, the political opposition may seize on

---

eclectic Drawn from a variety of sources.

---

the constructivist criticism and use it to hammer current administration policy: "You were warned years ago that this was a mistake, but you refused to listen." It is the fear of losing the next election that keeps administrations attentive. In this way, last year's "far out" or "fringe" criticism can become next year's accepted analysis.

Accordingly, we urge you to be **eclectic** and tentative in your use of theories. Try one but do not wed yourself to it. If it does not explain events as they unfold, try another. When faced with a choice between theory and reality, always let reality be your guide. Be aware that the wrong theory can cloud your picture of the real world. As one of the chief planners of the Vietnam War reflected decades later: "We were wrong, terribly wrong" (see Chapter 4). Take all theories with a grain of salt and remember Oliver Cromwell's mid-seventeenth-century exhortation: "I beseech you, in the bowels of Christ, think it possible that you may be mistaken."

mypoliscikit EXERCISES

Apply what you learned in this chapter on MyPoliSciKit (www.mypoliscikit.com).

 Assessment Review this chapter using learning objectives, chapter summaries, practice tests, and more.

Menu

 Flashcards Learn the key terms in this chapter; you can test yourself by term or definition.

Flashcards

 Video Analyze recent world affairs by watching streaming video from major news providers.

Videos

 Simulations Play the role of an IR decision-maker and experience how IR concepts work in practice.

Comparative
Exercises

KEY TERMS

bailout (p. 34)
bourgeoisie (p. 32)
classic liberalism (p. 26)
construct (p. 29)
constructivism (p. 29)
contradiction (p. 32)
crusade (p. 23)
cui bono (p. 34)

cultural hegemony (p. 34)
eclectic (p. 36)
empirical (p. 22)
G8/G20 (p. 29)
groupthink (p. 30)
liberalism (p. 26)
Marxism (p. 32)
national interest (p. 23)

neo- (p. 35)
paradigm (p. 22)
proletariat (p. 32)
rational (p. 22)
realism (p. 22)
relativism (p. 31)
theory (p. 22)

FURTHER REFERENCE

Beisner, Robert L. *Dean Acheson: A Life in the Cold War*. New York: Oxford University Press, 2006.

Dougherty, James E., and Robert L. Pfaltzgraff Jr. *Contending Theories of International Relations*, 5th ed. New York: Longman, 2000.

Ekbladh, David. *The Great American Mission: Modernization and the Construction of an American World Order*. Princeton, NJ: Princeton University Press, 2009.

Freyberg-Inan, Annette, Ewan Harrison, and Patrick James, eds. *Rethinking Realism in International Relations: Between Tradition and Innovation*. Baltimore, MD: Johns Hopkins University Press, 2009.

Gallarotti, Giulio M. *The Power Curse: Influence and Illusion in World Politics*. Boulder, CO: Lynne Rienner, 2010.

Hill, Charles. *Grand Strategies: Literature, Statecraft, and World Order*. New Haven, CT: Yale University Press, 2010.

Ikenberry, G. John, Thomas J. Knock, Anne-Marie Slaughter, and Tony Smith. *The Crisis of American Foreign Policy: Wilsonianism in the Twenty-First Century*. Princeton, NJ: Princeton University Press, 2008.

Jackson, Robert, and Georg Sørensen. *Introduction to International Relations: Theories and Approaches*, 4th ed. New York: Oxford University Press, 2009.

Lebow, Richard Ned. *A Cultural Theory of International Relations*. New York: Cambridge University Press, 2009.

Lobell, Steven E., Norrin M. Ripsman, and Jeffrey W. Taliaferro, eds. *Neoclassical Realism, the State, and Foreign Policy*. New York: Cambridge University Press, 2009.

McFaul, Michael. *Advancing Democracy Abroad: Why We Should and How We Can*. Lanham, MD: Rowman & Littlefield, 2009.

Schafer, Mark, and Scott Crichlow. *Groupthink vs. High-Quality Decision Making in International Relations*. New York: Columbia University Press, 2010.

Sterling-Folker, Jennifer, ed. *Making Sense of International Relations Theory*. Boulder, CO: Lynne Rienner, 2006.

Tabachnik, David Edward, and Toivo Koivukoski, eds. *Enduring Empire: Ancient Lessons for Global Politics*. Toronto: University of Toronto Press, 2009.

PART II

THE COLD WAR COME AND GONE

The Cold War dominated the second half of the twentieth century and warped both of the main antagonists—the United States and the Soviet Union, which the Cold War helped destroy. This review of the great contest shows how the two powers reached their present situations and provides many basic IR concepts.

Chapter 3 reviews American history to illustrate the slippery and changeable concept of *national interest*. Over various periods—the independence war, manifest destiny, imperialism, World Wars I and II, isolationism, and the Cold War—U.S. national interests have changed in response to new threats and opportunities. George F. Kennan's celebrated "containment" policy, for example, may be brilliant for one era but unworkable for the next (as Kennan himself lamented). Intelligent people quarrel over what the U.S. national interest is at any given time.

Chapter 4 uses our entry into and exit from Vietnam to illustrate how national interests can easily get warped. The gap here between *political generations* is great. Vietnam illustrates *guerrilla warfare*, *feasibility*, and *just-war* theory. The writers learned that government can be, in the words of Robert McNamara, "wrong, terribly wrong," something that a younger generation had to learn anew. We also ask if our wars in Iraq and Afghanistan resemble Vietnam.

With Chapter 5 we turn to our Cold War antagonist, how Russia turned into the tyrannical Soviet Union and then back into Russia, raising questions of *geopolitics* and how geography imposes enduring national interests. What role does *ideology* play in foreign policy? Were the Cold War and Soviet collapse inevitable? We consider how *misperception* of the outside world, *hegemony* over a costly empire, a failed *détente*, and increasingly critical *elites* driven by the fear of falling behind undermined regime legitimacy. Was Soviet foreign policy largely internally or externally generated? Russia under Putin returned to authoritarianism and traditional geopolitics.

Chapter 6 brings us to U.S. *foreign policy* today. Can and should we lead this new, complex world? Should we practice *interventionism* or *isolationism*? Should *idealism* or *self-interest* guide us? Much *constrains* U.S. foreign policy: the economy, armed forces, congressional support, and a world that often does not follow us. Public opinion is *volatile*. Finally, do the institutions of our foreign policy lead to policy errors and policies by *bureaucracies*?

CHAPTER 3

America's Changing National Interests

U.S. forces fought in Korea from 1950 to 1953, a major battle in the Cold War. (Bettmann/Corbis)

Americans had a national interest even before they became a nation. As the 13 colonies evolved, they saw their interests differently from those of Britain. London wanted cheap raw materials, a closed market for British products, no undue expenses for defending the colonies, and colonial taxes to pay the defense and administrative costs of the colonies. The French and Indian War had cost a bundle and mostly served the interests of the colonists. Colonies should pay for themselves, figured London; they should not drain the royal treasury.

The American colonists wanted to sell their products to anyone, not just to Britain. They wanted to manufacture their own goods, not just buy British goods. They wanted the **Crown** to provide free security to let them expand westward. And they didn't want to pay taxes. (They still don't.) Years before 1776, American and British *national interests* (see page 42) had begun to diverge, leading straight to the Declaration of Independence.

(see page 42)

INDEPENDENCE

Colonists had come to America to live free and get rich: "Life, liberty, and the pursuit of happiness." Any government that gets in the way of these rights is bad—in this case, Britain. The writers of the Declaration of Independence in 1776 also saw an opportunity: the likely assistance of France, which had an interest in weakening Britain and gaining an American ally and trading partner. The Americans sought sovereignty, again in the words of the Declaration, to "have full power to levy war, conclude peace, contract alliances, establish commerce, and to do all other acts and things which independent states may of right do."

The founding patriots pursued America's national interests rationally—not sentimentally, as is often depicted in fiction—by several interlocking strategies aimed at getting Britain to recognize the new "United States." They knew there would be a fight, so they mobilized and equipped colonial militias. They sought both military and diplomatic support from France, Spain, and any other European power that might have a grudge against Britain. Benjamin Franklin went to Paris

Crown   Powers of the British government.

objective   Can be empirically verified.

subjective   Cannot be empirically verified; depends on intuition.

bluff   Not supporting a declared national interest with sufficient power.

to promise a U.S. alliance and trade and to try to foment a war in Europe that would tie down the British. The French, following their own national interests, saw a chance to weaken the British and provided vital aid—weapons, troops, military advisors, and even a fleet. The United States was born with French help.

The colonial war cost Britain too much, so London settled in 1782. To clinch the deal, Franklin secretly told London that the United States really sought no alliance with France, so it was easier

CONCEPTS ■ NATIONAL INTERESTS

Seemingly simple—what's good for the state as a whole in international affairs—national interest can be very tricky to apply. Intelligent people can take opposing positions over what the national interest is at a given moment. The problem arises because the term is partly **objective** and partly **subjective**.

Geography plays a role. Close to home, national interest is objective and easy to define: Stay sovereign, that is, don't get conquered, partitioned, or subverted. This is considered a "vital" (sometimes also known as a "core" or "primary") national interest. Sensing a threat, governments take security measures, such as increasing military preparedness and making defensive alliances. Security for the homeland is the irreducible minimum national interest. Historically, U.S. national interest was to get rid of outside powers on the North American continent; they were geopolitical threats.

Farther from home, national interests get subjective and sometimes "secondary," less than vital. Should we worry about the other side of the world? If we trade a lot with it, say for oil, maybe we should. If a distant aggressor threatens to upset regional peace, maybe it is an interest, but we cannot be sure. Some areas are not national interests, but it is difficult to tell. National-interest calculations are often based on estimates, analogies, and gut instinct, all of them fallible.

Who decides what the national interest is? Governing elites—the top or most influential people—do, but their judgment is often skewed by ideology; mistaken assumptions; the temper of the times; and individual, class, and regime interests. All leaders claim to pursue the nation's interest, but often they conflate their own interest—staying in power—with the national interest. Few ever admit

to having made a mistake. The worse things get, the more leaders whip up their people with nationalism under the banner of "national interest." Is Iran's nuclear program really in its national interest, or does Tehran have the dangerously warped misperception that the bomb gives it security?

What seems to be the national interest one year may be a mistake the next year. Only hindsight tells you what your national interest had been in previous years, but then it's too late. In 1965, Washington defined South Vietnam as a vital U.S. national interest. Ten years later, no one did (see next chapter). After 9/11, the Bush 43 administration defined "regime change" in Iraq as a vital U.S. national interest, and most Americans believed it. After the invasion, when no weapons of mass destruction were found but chaos broke out, Americans wondered if the war had really been in their national interest. Slippery stuff, this national interest.

One important test: Do you have the power to back up what you have declared to be your national interest? If not, refrain from declaring it a national interest. Power and national interest are closely connected. Americans sometimes state grandiose national interests with insufficient power or intention of backing them up, a dangerous policy of **bluff**. America's national interest changes from one era to another. Our national interest during the Cold War was reasonably clear: Stop the spread of communism. What is it now? Recent proclamations of the U.S. national interest include snuffing out terrorism worldwide, grabbing oil lands, promoting democracy worldwide, and settling disputes in the China Seas. Be careful of declaring too many national interests; you may lack sufficient power to follow through.

to set the colonies free. The United States double-crossed France. In pursuing vital national interests, realism—not sentiment—rules. All in all, early American foreign policy was brilliant: A weak, new country gained independence and recognition by the major European powers.

manifest destiny   Slogan calling for a U.S. continental republic.

MANIFEST DESTINY

After independence, U.S. national interests were redefined to suit the new, large, isolated nation. The weak Articles of Confederation had to be scrapped because they left us vulnerable to the European presence still in North America. The 1787 Constitution "provide[d] for the common defense" by a more centralized government that maintained an army and navy, which, for most of U.S. history, were very small. We felt threatened by the Spaniards in Florida, the French in Louisiana, the British in Canada, the Russians in Alaska, and revolutionaries in Mexico. We gained most of these territories (except for Canada) with force and/or cash.

By the 1840s Americans were convinced that they had a **manifest destiny** determined by God to claim and populate most of North America. National-interest thinking underlay each step. The United States, still small and vulnerable, did not like sharing the continent with major European powers. With most of the continent populated by Americans, we would have little to fear. Land and unlimited immigration would make America a great power. And underneath was the old contingent necessity argument: If we did not take it, someone else would.

The new technologies of the nineteenth century—the railroad and telegraph—made possible a continental republic. George Washington, even as the French Revolutionary wars raged, defined the U.S. national interest as staying out of Europe's wars. In 1793 Washington declared

CLASSIC THOUGHT ■ WASHINGTON'S FAREWELL ADDRESS

Some call George Washington the first isolationist, for when he left office in 1797 he warned against forming alliances with European powers. Actually, it was a shrewd appreciation of U.S. national interests at the time. Why get locked into Europe's habitual and sometimes pointless bloodshed? We need neither allies nor enemies but should "cultivate peace and harmony with all." Other comments from Washington's Farewell Address include the following:

> The great rule of conduct for us in regard to foreign nations is, in extending our commercial relations to have with them as little political connection as possible....
>
> Europe has a set of primary interests which to us have none or a very remote

relation. Hence she must be engaged in frequent controversies, the causes of which are essentially foreign to our concerns....

> Our detached and distant situation invites and enables us to pursue a different course....
>
> Why forgo the advantages of so peculiar a situation? Why quit our own to stand upon foreign ground? Why, by interweaving our destiny with that of any part of Europe, entangle our peace and prosperity in the toils of European ambition, rivalship, interest, humor, or caprice?

Why indeed? Washington posed tough-minded questions that every generation of American leaders should ask anew.

Continent The European mainland.

neutrality, abrogating our 1778 alliance with France. With this, we got Britain to sign Jay's Treaty in 1794 and remove its forts in our West. Neutrality also prevented a divisive issue—for or against the French Revolution—from polarizing U.S. politics.

Americans were pouring into the now French-held Louisiana territory, and France had wars enough in Europe. Jefferson's $15 million purchase from the cash-strapped Napoleon in 1803 (without congressional authorization) doubled the size of the United States. It was hard to stay neutral and carry on commerce with Europe—we wanted to sell grain to the **Continent**—and this led to the War of 1812 with Britain, in which we tried to seize Canada. Several U.S. invasion attempts were repelled, Canadians note proudly. Some historians argue that we lost the War of 1812 but never admitted it. The British burned down the Capitol and White House and left; they still do not count it as a war.

Guerrilla warfare plus $5 million in cash persuaded Spain to cede Florida to us in 1819. With the independence of Latin America from Spain and Portugal, President Monroe issued his famous 1823 doctrine that told Europe to keep out of our hemisphere and we would keep out of theirs (see Chapter 10). Threat of force against the British in Oregon (which included present-day Washington State) was mainly bluster, but it worked in 1846. American settlers

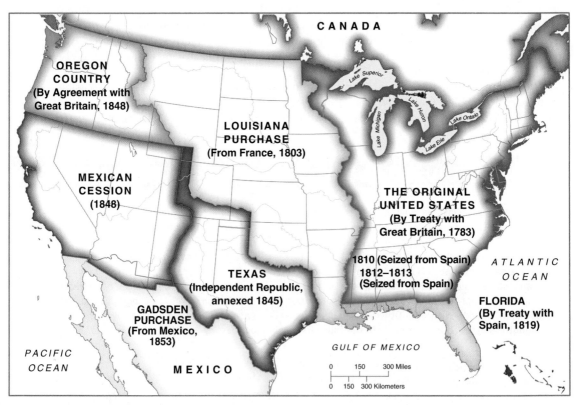

Expansion of U.S. Territory

in Texas started a war that we settled in 1848 by taking the West and giving Mexico a paltry $15 million. Cash alone, $7.2 million, bought Alaska from Russia in 1867.

strategy   Ends, ways, means.

imperialism   Spreading nation's power over other lands.

Even Union diplomacy during the Civil War—the second bloodiest conflict of the nineteenth century, after the Napoleonic Wars—was successful. Britain, whose interests in cotton almost pushed it to recognize the Confederacy, was dissuaded by Lincoln's freeing of the slaves. Britain had for decades worked against slavery worldwide, so Lincoln's move made British recognition of the South morally impossible. As the Civil War raged, France took advantage of U.S. weakness to set up a brief monarchy in Mexico. With the war over, the United States told them to scram, and they did.

Overall, U.S. foreign policy from independence through most of the nineteenth century was a spectacular success. Keeping the European powers distant, buying up their North American holdings cheap, and applying measured doses of force, the small, vulnerable United States grew into a continental republic, as planned. By the 1890s, however, the West had been won. Until then, policy goals had been clear, rational, limited, and feasible, for they focused on American interests on this continent. The next era presented policy dilemmas and goals that were not nearly as clear and limited, for they focused on the other hemisphere. In the late 1890s, America started defining its national interests to include major activity overseas, and this brought a dispute that continues to the present over exactly what U.S. **strategy** in the world should be. How should we make our way in the world?

IMPERIALISM

The causes of America's brief fling with **imperialism** are still controversial. Some see it as the continuation of a frontier spirit; once it reached the Pacific, it had to keep going westward. Imperial thinking in Washington—Captain Mahan's sea power theory (see box) and the beginning of a large, modern fleet—started in the 1880s. In 1894, America faced a sharp economic depression, prompting some to see imperial expansion as a way to gain new markets for American goods.

The triggering event of the expansion—freeing Cuba from Spanish misrule—is only part of the story. Cuban patriots had revolted against Spain in the 1870s and were brutally crushed while the United States paid little attention. In the 1890s, when Cubans again revolted, we went to war over it. In a quarter of a century, Cuba had gone from a noninterest to a national interest.

The times had changed. In the 1870s America was still nursing its Civil War wounds and filling in the West. Americans ignored foreign affairs. By the 1890s things were different. The U.S. economy had shifted from agriculture to industry. A large, iron-hulled U.S. Navy was built.

CLASSIC THOUGHT ■ MAHAN'S SEA POWER THEORY

In 1890, as the United States was expanding its fleet, U.S. Navy Captain Alfred Thayer Mahan published a book that told imperialists exactly what they wanted to hear. *The Influence of Sea Power upon History* argued that nations must expand or decline and that sea power is the key to expansion. To assure its overseas commerce, a nation needs a strong navy, which, in turn, needs colonies as "coaling stations" to service its ships. Mahan's model was the British fleet and empire. Among Mahan's followers was Theodore Roosevelt, who became assistant secretary of the Navy under President McKinley in 1897.

Social Darwinism encouraged Americans—including Teddy Roosevelt—to think of themselves as the "fittest" who were destined for world leadership over lesser (that is, colored) peoples. The European empires set an example for any country that aspired to be a "power." There was a race for colonies; we had to move fast if we wanted to grab what little was left, and the decaying Spanish empire—including the Philippines—was ripe for the taking. Germany also coveted the Philippines. The circulation wars between the new high-speed presses of Hearst and Pulitzer fanned interest in Cuba with lurid stories of Spanish brutality (especially against women). Hearst editorialized proudly: "How do you like my little war?"

By the time of President McKinley, imperialists were defining the U.S. national interest as overseas expansion, a kind of new manifest destiny. The sinking of the battleship *Maine* in Havana harbor (probably from a faulty boiler) brought the cry, "Remember the *Maine*, to hell with Spain!" McKinley did not wish war, but the country was inflamed, and the paralyzed Madrid government did not know how to get out of the mess without going to war and losing, which it did quickly in 1898.

All over America, volunteers signed up for what Teddy Roosevelt called "a splendid little war." The country had not been to war since the Civil War, and young men ached for adventure. Roosevelt went with his Rough Riders to Cuba but had earlier arranged with Admiral Dewey for the U.S. Pacific Fleet to wait at Hong Kong for a cable and then strike the pathetic Spanish fleet in Manila Bay. With little fighting, the decrepit Spanish empire collapsed into American hands. Spain officially ceded the Philippines to the United States for $20 million. Again, force and cash. In one year, 1898, the United States took Cuba (ostensibly independent but a U.S. protectorate), Puerto Rico, and the Philippines, plus Guam, Hawaii, Wake Island, and American Samoa (in 1899). Suddenly, America was an empire. (The United States had claimed Midway in 1867.)

Some Filipinos expected independence and fought the U.S. takeover. The Philippine Insurrection of 1899–1903 resembled the later Vietnam War: stubborn resistance, U.S. calls for more troops, ambushes, harsh reprisals, burning villages, and growing disgust and opposition on U.S. college campuses and in Congress. The insurrection provoked some belated rethinking: What are we doing on the other side of the globe shooting strange people who do not want us there? Is this really our national interest? The "Anti-Imperialists"—including Mark Twain and Andrew Carnegie—bitterly denounced U.S. expansion overseas.

The United States expanded its interests to include China, where American traders and missionaries had long been active. In 1899–1900, Secretary of State John Hay issued his famous Open Door notes stating that the China trade should be open to all and that China should not be broken up into European or Japanese spheres of influence. This began the U.S. policy of protecting China with words but without troops or warships. The Japanese military concluded we were bluffing and ignored U.S. protests as they invaded China. We had disconnected national interest from power. It took Pearl Harbor to reconnect them. As for Hawaii, where American settlers had already taken over, the feeling was we had better take it or Japan will. By 1900, the seeds of a U.S.–Japan war were planted.

The new U.S. Navy and merchant fleet had to be able to get quickly from the Atlantic to the Pacific. When Colombia dickered too long on a canal through its Isthmus of Panama, Washington set up an independent Panama in 1903, held off Colombia with gunboats, and bought canal rights from Panama. Again, force and cash. When several Caribbean and Central American countries were threatened with European intervention over debts, the United States intervened first, established customs receiverships to repay the loans, and thus kept the Europeans out (see Chapter 10). President Wilson sent U.S. forces into Veracruz and northern Mexico.

The abrupt shift from isolation to world power produced a backlash. The emerging academic discipline of international relations proffered legalistic and moralistic approaches to world problems.

(One thinker in this area was political scientist Woodrow Wilson.) Politicians and scholars urged conflict resolution through binding arbitration. Peace movements sprang up. Americans were not accustomed to the cynicism that must accompany being a world power. Many still are not. Expansion was easy, but it meant adding vulnerabilities and making enemies. Some question if it was ever in our national interests to expand into East Asia, which led to war with Japan.

> **isolationism** U.S. avoidance of overseas involvement.

WORLD WAR I

After war broke out in Europe in 1914, Germany tried to keep America out while Britain tried to get America in. German submarine warfare threatened U.S. shipping. President Woodrow Wilson, with the legalistic-moralistic bent of the time, won reelection in 1916 with the slogan "He kept us out of war." By early 1917, however, German submarine warfare pushed Wilson into the Great War. We had tried to stay neutral but could not.

Other forces were at work. An intercepted German telegram suggested to Mexico that it could recover lands lost to the United States in 1848. British propaganda blanketed the United States, emphasizing the barbarity of the "Huns." The ouster of the tsarist government in Russia in early 1917 now made the war look like a contest between democracy and autocracy. Wilson sold the war as one "to make the world safe for democracy." He also appreciated that the German conquest of Europe would threaten our national interest.

U.S. troops arrived when the war was two-thirds over and tipped the balance against Germany. The war ended in late 1918. But the victors, particularly Britain and France, did not share Wilson's idealistic vision of a new League of Nations to keep the peace. They wanted revenge on Germany for their terrible losses. London and Paris accepted Wilson's League as part of the Versailles peace treaty but went on to strip Germany of territory and squeeze it for impossible reparations. The U.S. Senate refused to ratify the Versailles treaty, and America, fed up with Wilson's idealism and the unreliable Europeans, slouched into **isolationism** (see Chapter 21).

ISOLATIONISM

Americans soon saw World War I as a failure. Europe was still unstable. The tricky and unreliable Europeans hadn't learned a thing from the war. Even worse, they would not pay their war debts. Americans felt they had fought and bled for nothing and must never do it again.

The United States in the interwar years had overseas interests but did not back them up; instead, it turned to law and rhetoric. Neither worked. The United States sponsored the 1921 Washington Naval Conference, which limited the number of battleships of the major sea powers. (Japan soon opted out.) The 1928 Kellogg-Briand Pact (named after the U.S. secretary of state and French foreign minister) outlawed war. Most states signed but did so in utter cynicism.

This policy of words without deeds could not conceal the fact that the United States did not have the power to do much overseas. Between the two world wars the army and navy shrank to almost nothing. The Philippines were lightly garrisoned and forgotten. The Great Depression focused Americans' attention on domestic economic recovery; the foreigners were simply trade competitors who had to be locked out of the U.S. market. In the Senate, the Nye Committee blamed U.S. involvement in the war on "merchants of death," U.S. bankers and munitions makers who brought us into the conflict. From these hearings grew the Neutrality Acts of 1935–1937, designed to keep us from ever being drawn into a similar war. Anyone who suggested we take a stand against aggression was howled down.

Atlantic Charter The 1941 Roosevelt-Churchill agreement on peace aims and basis of UN.

Lend Lease U.S. aid to Allies in World War II.

Interwar isolationism failed to recognize that the Axis powers—Germany, Italy, and Japan—threatened to create a closed, hostile world in which the United States was militarily besieged and economically isolated. U.S. national interests were massively threatened, but interwar isolationism blinded many Americans to this fact until Pearl Harbor. Then, almost too late, came sudden understanding. As Hegel observed, the owl of Minerva (symbolizing wisdom) flies at twilight.

WORLD WAR II

For a growing number of Americans, the official outbreak of World War II in 1939 (it had been on in China since at least 1937) showed that isolationism was wrong. Franklin D. Roosevelt, who had served Wilson as assistant navy secretary, always admired Wilson and slowly restored some Wilsonian idealism, one that extended U.S. national interests overseas. It showed up clearly in the **Atlantic Charter** (see box below). FDR had learned the lessons of Wilson's failure—too idealistic—and moved only a fraction ahead of Congress and public opinion to bring the United States into the war and into a world leadership role.

Roosevelt's strategy was to aid Britain without alarming American isolationists, who thought that Britain in 1940 was defeated and that the war was none of our business. (Even the U.S. ambassador to Britain, the father of John F. Kennedy, thought so.) FDR circumvented the Neutrality Acts by allowing Britain to come and get U.S. goods under a cash-and-carry policy. The United States traded 50 old destroyers to Britain for a naval base in Bermuda. With the fall of France in 1940 and Britain out of foreign exchange, **Lend Lease** simply gave war supplies to Britain and, after the 1941 German attack on Russia, to the Soviet Union. In getting these goods across the Atlantic, U.S. ships, including warships, became targets for German U-boats. The United States, in turn, depth-charged German ships in an undeclared war with Germany in the North Atlantic several months before Pearl Harbor. The Japanese attack on December 7, 1941, got both Churchill and Roosevelt off the hook. Churchill knew that Britain would now be on the winning side, and the U.S. isolationists fell silent. With U.S. leadership and supplies, the Allies won in 1945. This time the United States would play a leading world role.

Roosevelt avoided Wilson's mistakes. The United Nations Charter, separate from any peace treaty, was drawn up during the war while a common enemy cemented the alliance. U.S. military aid gave Washington great influence and induced many to accept the UN Charter. Declaring war on the Axis was the prerequisite for UN membership. Congress authorized the United Nations in

DIPLOMACY ■ THE ATLANTIC CHARTER

Meeting at sea off Newfoundland on August 14, 1941 (before America was officially in the war), President Roosevelt, who knew we would soon be in the war, and British Prime Minister Winston Churchill signed an idealistic statement of their war aims. They sought no territorial aggrandizement but wanted disarmament, self-determination for all nationalities, and freedom of trade and of the seas. The Atlantic Charter, the spiritual child of Wilson's Fourteen Points, formed the basis of the United Nations, NATO, and close U.S.–British cooperation.

1943, this time with Republican consultation and support. In San Francisco in 1945, most of the world's nations signed the Charter. As if to underscore the U.S. role, the UN headquarters was to be in New York. (For how the UN works, see Chapter 21.)

THE COLD WAR

Roosevelt slowly and cleverly repudiated interwar isolationism and revived the **Wilsonian** concept of a U.S. national interest that promoted peace and extended U.S. trade and influence overseas. The American people were ready for it, but Stalin refused to cooperate. Roosevelt thought he could charm Stalin into cooperation, but FDR died shortly before the war ended, and Stalin was impervious to charm. America, to carry out the national interests FDR had defined during the war, now had to have a massive and permanent military establishment, some of it stationed overseas.

Wilsonian   Idealistic projection of U.S. power to create a peaceful world.

Truman Doctrine   The 1947 presidential call to aid countries under Communist threat.

Marshall Plan   The 1947 call for massive U.S. aid to war-torn Europe.

containment   U.S. policy of blocking expansion of Soviet power; framed by Kennan in 1947.

The Cold War began when the Soviets quickly began breaking the agreements made at the 1945 Yalta conference (see Chapter 5). They did not hold free, democratic elections in East Europe but installed Communist regimes subservient to Moscow and kept many troops in East Europe. The United States had quickly demobilized after the war and left few troops in West Europe. As Churchill put it in 1946, the Soviets rang down an "iron curtain" to cut off East Europe. Local Communist parties plotted subversion in France and Italy, and Communist guerrillas almost won in Greece.

President Truman and his secretaries of state, George Marshall and Dean Acheson, soon grew alarmed that Moscow was closing off East Europe into brutal Soviet satellites and partitioning the peaceful, liberal world the United States had envisioned. Stalin started looking like Hitler, a dictator who had to be stopped. In the spring of 1947, Washington set forth interlocking policies of military, economic, and ideological opposition to the growth of Soviet power. The **Truman Doctrine**, **Marshall Plan**, and Kennan's "X" article (discussed on page 50)—all of which came out within weeks of each other—defined U.S. national interest for decades.

At first **containment** was relatively cheap to carry out. We had the world's greatest industrial plant and the atomic bomb. U.S. airpower overcame the 1948–1949 Berlin Blockade. We formed NATO in 1949 (see Chapter 16). Things got more complex when the Soviets exploded their first atomic bomb in 1949; we no longer had a nuclear monopoly. China fell to the Communists that same year, and in 1950 the Korean conflict began. Truman sent troops to Asia and Europe without congressional or public approval. The president's powers here have never been settled (see Chapter 6).

CONCEPTS ■ COLD WAR

The period of military and political tension between the United States and the Soviet Union after World War II was called the Cold War because there was no direct fighting between the two powers. Its dates are rather arbitrarily given as 1947–1989. Some say it started in 1946 and ended with the dissolution of the Soviet Union in late 1991. The two sides armed, sent troops into other countries, fought indirectly (as in Korea), and tried to keep their present allies and gain new ones from the enemy's camp. (See Chapters 1 and 5 for more on the Cold War.) The Cold War brought *bipolarity*, the world divided into two hostile camps.

globalism   U.S. interests extending everywhere.

Containment looked like an endless, unwinnable war with no clear goals. Americans like short, victorious wars with clear goals. Frustration and rage mounted within a U.S. public that was unused to global responsibilities and complexities: Why can't we

TURNING POINT ■ SPRING 1947

A broke and weary Britain could no longer uphold its traditional interests in the Eastern Mediterranean and told Washington so in early 1947. Communist guerrillas in Greece held much of that impoverished country, and the Soviet Union strongly pressured Turkey for territories and control of the strategic Turkish Straits. President Truman felt we had to take up the burden and articulate a new policy and new U.S. national interests. It was a massive shift to **globalism**.

Truman told a joint session of Congress on March 12, 1947, that the United States must not only aid Greece and Turkey but more generally block Communist expansion. "[I]t must be the policy of the United States to support free peoples who are resisting attempted subjugation by armed minorities or by outside pressures," said Truman. "Great responsibilities have been placed upon us by the swift movement of events."

Truman thus made official the policy that had been brewing in Washington for many months. The United States would not return to isolationism but would actively oppose the Soviets worldwide. It was a new role for the United States, a much bigger and stronger one than Wilson or FDR had envisioned: permanent and global U.S. military and political activity.

A few weeks later, at the 1947 Harvard commencement, Secretary of State George C. Marshall proposed a massive program of U.S. aid to help war-torn Europe recover. Almost unnoticed at the time, this began foreign aid as a permanent part of U.S. foreign policy. The Marshall Plan, which began in 1948, pumped some $12 billion into Europe and was a major part of the U.S. effort to contain Communist expansion. It also started West Europe on the road to economic integration (see Chapter 16).

At this same time, a quietly influential State Department official lay down the U.S. ideological line for the entire Cold War and coined the word "containment." George F. Kennan spoke Russian and had long studied Soviet behavior. Serving in our Moscow embassy, he developed a strong dislike and mistrust of the Soviet Union and Stalin. During World War II, when we were allies, few in Washington would listen to Kennan's warnings that Stalin would be aggressive and expansionist after the war. With the start of the Cold War, Washington listened to Kennan.

Kennan turned an internal 1946 cable into an article for the influential *Foreign Affairs* quarterly. "The Sources of Soviet Conduct" appeared in the July 1947 issue and portrayed the Soviet Union as relentlessly expansionist both on ideological and geopolitical grounds. The Soviets feared and hated the West and sought to subvert democratic governments, wrote Kennan under the anonymous byline "X." (As a U.S. diplomat who dealt with Moscow, he didn't want his name used, but it soon leaked.)

U.S. strategy should be "a policy of firm containment, designed to confront the Russians with unalterable counter-force at every point where they show signs of encroaching upon the interests of a peaceful and stable world," Kennan urged. If held long enough, this would "promote tendencies which must eventually find their outlet in either the break-up or the gradual mellowing of Soviet power. For no mystical, messianic movement—and particularly not that of the Kremlin—can face frustration indefinitely without eventually adjusting itself in one way or another to the logic of that state of affairs." Kennan, who died at age 101 in 2005, could note with satisfaction that his policy finally worked. U.S. policy for the more than 40 years of the Cold War was thus begun in the spring of 1947.

fight and win? Is this Cold War going to last forever? Why don't we just drop our atom bomb on those Commies? Containment had its costs, and they played into the Republican electoral victories of the 1950s and into **McCarthyism**. The Democrats set up containment and then stood accused of not doing enough to carry it out. The United States became locked into a Cold War mentality.

McCarthyism Senator Joseph McCarthy's early-1950s accusations of treason in high places.

President Eisenhower did not repudiate containment but carried it out differently and in ways more acceptable to the public. His secretary of state, John Foster Dulles, preached the "rollback" of Communism but in practice was cautious. Eisenhower ended the Korean War with a threat to go nuclear and then let Dulles announce a policy of "massive retaliation" for future Soviet-bloc aggression. Ike's secretary of defense, Charles Wilson, called reliance on nuclear weapons "more bang for the buck" that allowed us to keep draft calls down. The American public at first liked projecting strength on the cheap. Critics, however, soon decried a policy that, according to Dulles himself, took us "three times to the brink of war"—and it would be a nuclear war.

The Democrats now portrayed Eisenhower's policies as passive and rigid. Now it was the Democrats' turn to use the Cold War to win elections: Just accuse the incumbent of not doing enough. Sputnik in 1957 gave Kennedy the idea of campaigning on an alleged "missile gap" that claimed the Soviets were ahead (it turned out to be untrue). Eisenhower had let the country fall asleep as the Soviet menace grew, Kennedy charged. (Decades later, Reagan copied this line from Kennedy.) JFK narrowly won in 1960 with plans to increase defense spending, the armed forces,

Senator Joseph McCarthy in 1952, when his search for Communists in the U.S. government was at its height. (Ernie Sisto/*The New York Times*/Redux Pictures)

and missiles and to counter insurgencies with the Green Berets. Ike thought Kennedy was impetuous and mistaken. Ike was proud of having kept the United States secure at low cost with no more Koreas during his two terms.

Kennedy's can-do enthusiasm quickly met some harsh realities. The failure of the CIA-sponsored invasion of Castro's Cuba by anti-Communist exiles (see Chapter 10), planned under Eisenhower, painfully humiliated JFK in April 1961 and made him more determined to stop communism elsewhere. Kennedy's huge military buildup alarmed the Soviets; they saw it as a threat. By 1962, the United States was ahead by a ratio of 7 to 1 in strategic missiles. Khrushchev, desperate to redress the imbalance, ordered some of his older, medium-range missiles placed in Cuba, closer to U.S. targets. This led to the Cuban Missile Crisis of October 1962. Khrushchev backed down, but it could have started World War III (see Chapters 5 and 6).

The Cold War crested at that point and slowly began to subside. U.S.–Soviet relations became more flexible; several arms-control agreements were reached. The Sino–Soviet split removed the most threatening quality of the Communist movement—its unity—which U.S. policy had long tried to undermine. But the U.S. policy of containment was still deeply held as the national interest. Enshrined since 1947, it could not be modified or turned off. Established policies tend to do that; politicians and bureaucrats are used to them and do not think outside the box. Kennedy

CONCEPTS ■ MEAD'S FOUR SCHOOLS OF U.S. FOREIGN POLICY

In a much-noted 2001 book, foreign-policy scholar Walter Russell Mead delineated four schools or basic American approaches to foreign affairs that have variously combined and battled over the history of the Republic:

- *Hamiltonian*, a commerce-oriented approach that seeks to make America secure and powerful by economic means, namely, promoting domestic prosperity and trade relations. Hamiltonians, strong in business and banking, try to avoid war but will support it when pushed.
- *Wilsonian*, an *idealist* (see previous chapter) vision of peace through treaties and international law and organizations. Wilsonians, often in the church and legal communities, promote human rights and democracy and will go to war to vanquish brutal dictatorships.
- *Jeffersonian*, a hands-off caution that too much foreign involvement can hurt domestic American institutions and throw away lives and money in unnecessary wars. We can't reform the world, criticize Jeffersonians (often academics and intellectuals), and we do best when we just set an example of democracy and prosperity.
- *Jacksonian*, the view widespread among average citizens, is often ignorant and indifferent but turns to rage when America is attacked. Emotional and nonintellectual, Jacksonians are natural isolationists but once in a war demand all means for total victory and aren't squeamish about civilian deaths. They dislike the Hamiltonian and Wilsonian approaches—too brainy and complicated—and prefer simple protection of Americans' jobs and a strong military.

U.S. foreign policy and its leaders are never just one of these schools, writes Mead, but shifting combinations of them. At times, they form alliances. The first three—Hamiltonian, Wilsonian, and Jeffersonian—are elite schools; the Jacksonian is a mass view and a permanent and powerful underlying element that foreigners cannot comprehend ("Those Americans are cowboys!") and U.S. politicians cannot ignore. Of Mead's categories, which seem to dominate American foreign policy now? Why?

himself did not question containment; instead, he brought it to its logical conclusion in Vietnam (see next chapter).

During the 1960s, at the very time the United States was bogged down in Vietnam, the Sino–Soviet dispute escalated (see page 82) until finally President Richard Nixon took advantage of it with his famous visit to Beijing in early 1972. Whatever else one might say of him, Nixon was the first to realize that bipolarity and containment no longer fit the world scene and had to be replaced. (Nixon was the rare U.S. president who read books on IR.) Nixon understood that there were now more than two blocs, and the right U.S. strategy was to balance among them.

THE NEXT CHALLENGES

Clearly, U.S. national interests have changed over time. America must now adjust its national interests to two problems, one current, the other emerging: Islamist terrorism in the short term and the rise of China in the longer term. These two challenges require two different definitions of national interest. Neither of them is another Cold War, and we should refrain from returning to bipolar thinking. For the second half of the twentieth century, there was one central adversary, the Soviet Union. Islamist terrorism is decentralized and diffuse, like wisps of fog. Upset in one country, it pops up in another. Accordingly, invading every nation that is home to Muslim extremists would not crush the movement—actually, more a mood than an organization—but would stretch U.S. power too thin and create even more enemies.

The rise of a powerful China is a more subtle problem than the Soviet Union, which was a military but not an economic challenge. China is the reverse. China does not ring itself with satellites or attempt to subvert governments like the Soviet Union did. Beijing sells no ideology the way Moscow used to sell communism. Instead, it makes economic growth its guiding principle and will let nothing disrupt it. In this way, China gets respect around the world. But the Chinese are highly nationalistic and see themselves as Asia's top power. The big question for U.S. foreign policy: Would a China-dominated Asia be a threat? Or could we live with it?

We need first a clear picture of the global system (see Chapter 1), which we do not have. Is it multipolar or clash of civilizations, globalized or resource wars? How important are the "zones of chaos" mentioned in the stratified model? Are they where terrorism breeds? Is the system an unstable U.S.–China duopoly? Next, we must figure out our national interests within whatever system exists. How much do we intervene overseas? Do we have the resources for major, long-term deployments (see Chapter 6)? Should we attempt to control Middle East oil fields?

REFLECTIONS ■ KENNAN ON HISTORY

George F. Kennan, a friend of my stepfather, Ambassador Felix Cole, kindly gave me some advice before I attended graduate school. He wrote:

All I can say is that I warmly support the thought that if political science is what you wish to pursue, you start by doing your M.A., and if possible, the doctorate in political history. I have misgivings about political science

generally, as a subject, unless it is founded on serious historical study.

Kennan himself became a widely read historian. History reveals patterns of human behavior, what behavior shapes what events, and the likely consequences of those events. It is knowledge students of international relations cannot do without.

—N. O. B.

Or should we just buy oil from whomever produces it? Do we simply stop terrorists from hurting us at home or track them down worldwide? Are the China Seas any of our business? Few firm answers can be given, but *feasibility* (see page 70), always emphasized by Morgenthau, is an important guidepost.

my**poliscikit** EXERCISES

Apply what you learned in this chapter on MyPoliSciKit (www.mypoliscikit.com).

Assessment   Review this chapter using learning objectives, chapter summaries, practice tests, and more.

Menu

Flashcards   Learn the key terms in this chapter; you can test yourself by term or definition.

Flashcards

Video   Analyze recent world affairs by watching streaming video from major news providers.

Videos

Simulations   Play the role of an IR decision-maker and experience how IR concepts work in practice.

Comparative
Exercises

KEY TERMS

Atlantic Charter (p. 48)

bluff (p. 42)

containment (p. 49)

Continent (p. 44)

Crown (p. 42)

globalism (p. 50)

imperialism (p. 45)

isolationism (p. 47)

Lend Lease (p. 48)

manifest destiny (p. 43)

Marshall Plan (p. 49)

McCarthyism (p. 51)

objective (p. 42)

strategy (p. 45)

subjective (p. 42)

Truman Doctrine (p. 49)

Wilsonian (p. 49)

FURTHER REFERENCE

Ambrosius, Lloyd E. *Wilsonianism: Woodrow Wilson and His Legacy in American Foreign Relations.* New York: Palgrave, 2002.

Bacevich, Andrew J., ed. *The Long War: A New History of U.S. National Security Policy Since World War II.* New York: Columbia University Press, 2007.

Boot, Max. *The Savage Wars of Peace: Small Wars and the Rise of American Power.* New York: Basic Books, 2002.

Craig, Campbell, and Fredrik Logevall. *America's Cold War: The Politics of Insecurity.* Cambridge, MA: Harvard University Press, 2009.

Cummings, Bruce. *Dominion from Sea to Sea: Pacific Ascendancy and American Power.* New Haven, CT: Yale University Press, 2009.

Gaddis, John Lewis. *Strategies of Containment: A Critical Appraisal of American National Security Policy during the Cold War,* rev. ed. New York: Oxford University Press, 2005.

Halberstam, David. *The Coldest Winter: America and the Korean War.* New York: Hyperion, 2007.

Herring, George C. *From Colony to Superpower: U.S. Foreign Relations Since 1776.* New York: Oxford University Press, 2008.

Hogan, Michael J., and Thomas G. Paterson, eds. *Explaining the History of American Foreign Relations*, 2nd ed. New York: Cambridge University Press, 2004.

Immerman, Richard H. *Empire for Liberty: A History of American Imperialism from Benjamin Franklin to Paul Wolfowitz*. Princeton, NJ: Princeton University Press, 2010.

Kinzer, Stephen. *Overthrow: America's Century of Regime Change from Hawaii to Iraq*. New York: Times Books, 2007.

Kluger, Richard. *Seizing Destiny: How America Grew from Sea to Shining Sea*. New York: Knopf, 2008.

Kuklick, Bruce. *Blind Oracles: Intellectuals and War from Kennan to Kissinger*. Princeton, NJ: Princeton University Press, 2007.

Lears, Jackson. *Rebirth of a Nation: The Making of Modern America, 1877–1920*. New York: HarperCollins, 2009.

Leffler, Melvyn P. *For the Soul of Mankind: The United States, the Soviet Union, and the Cold War*. New York: Farrar, Straus & Giroux, 2007.

Lukacs, John, ed. *Through the History of the Cold War: The Correspondence of George F. Kennan and John Lukacs*. Philadelphia: University of Pennsylvania Press, 2010.

Magstadt, Thomas M. *An Empire If You Can Keep It: Power and Principle in American Foreign Policy*. Washington, DC: CQ Press, 2004.

Mead, Walter Russell. *Special Providence: American Foreign Policy and How It Changed the World*. New York: Knopf, 2001.

Ninkovich, Frank. *Global Dawn: The Cultural Foundation of American Internationalism, 1865–1890*. Cambridge, MA: Harvard University Press, 2009.

Nugent, Walter. *Habits of Empire: A History of American Expansion*. New York: Knopf, 2008.

Pfaff, William. *The Irony of Manifest Destiny: The Tragedy of America's Foreign Policy*. New York: Walker, 2010.

Schulzinger, Robert D. *U.S. Diplomacy Since 1900*, 6th ed. New York: Oxford University Press, 2007.

Secunda, Eugene, and Terence P. Moran. *Selling War to America: From the Spanish American War to the Global War on Terror*. Westport, CT: Praeger, 2007.

Thompson, Nicholas. *The Hawk and the Dove: Paul Nitze, George Kennan, and the History of the Cold War*. New York: Henry Holt, 2009.

CHAPTER 4

Vietnam and the Warping of National Interest

A helicopter evacuates U.S. wounded from battle in the deadly A Shau Valley. The long war turned off many Americans. (Bettman/Corbis)

The Vietnam War came up frequently as President Obama and his advisors agonized over what to do in Afghanistan. All had read and discussed how the "best and brightest" took the United States into Vietnam in the 1960s. Now Obama's best and brightest were fully aware that sending young Americans to fight for a weak and corrupt Kabul regime risked a replay of a war that became unpopular. Indeed, Obama's top diplomat on Afghanistan, Richard Holbrooke, got his start as a young foreign service officer in South Vietnam. (For similarities and dissimilarities among the Vietnam, Iraq, and Afghan wars, see page 67.) Vietnam provides lessons on what can go wrong in a military intervention and how national interests can become warped and mistaken.

Vietnam is intelligible only in the Cold War context. When the younger generation—born after the war ended in 1975—asks why we fought there, older Americans have difficulty explaining it. They form **political generations** (see box on page 58) with very different perspectives. Some of the older generation, raised in the Cold War, argue that the war made sense at the time: Continue containment; wherever communism is spreading, stop it. Eisenhower used the metaphor of "falling dominoes" to indicate what would happen if even one more country in Southeast Asia fell to the Communists. Any U.S. president who let communism expand was considered weak. The Cold War made the U.S. national interest, first defined in 1947 (see page 50), into a rigid and unexamined doctrine.

Now, after the Cold War, we can dispassionately examine the U.S. national interest in the Vietnam War and find it wanting. The fall of South Vietnam to the Communist North in 1975 signified little or nothing. The very weak "dominoes" of Laos and Cambodia also fell, but nothing else. Far from a rising tide, communism collapsed a decade and a half later in Europe, and Communist China and Vietnam turned from socialist to market-economic paths. We would have "won" in Vietnam if we had stayed out militarily and then signed up a unified Vietnam to produce athletic shoes and clothing for the U.S. market, which it now does. But neither we nor the Vietnamese Communists knew that at the time. In 1995, Robert McNamara, Kennedy's and Johnson's defense secretary, went public with what had long been on his mind: "We were wrong, terribly wrong."

QUESTIONS TO CONSIDER

1. How did the Cold War influence us on Vietnam?
2. In what ways were we ignorant of Vietnam and the Vietnamese?
3. How long did France hold Vietnam?
4. How were the French ousted from Vietnam?
5. Why did the United States inherit the problem?
6. What is the crux of guerrilla warfare?
7. Did President Johnson lie about getting us into Vietnam?
8. Was a "decent interval" really necessary for us to get out?
9. How can one say a given war is "immoral"? Aren't they all?
10. Do the Iraq and Afghan wars resemble the Vietnam War?

political generations The memory of great events imprinted on the young people who have lived through them.

protectorate Semicolony with some internal autonomy.

THE COLONIZED COLONIALISTS

The Vietnamese originated as a South China tribe that kept pushing southward. (Vietnam means South Viet.) Rice-farming lowlanders, they settled millennia ago in the Red River delta of what became known as Tonkin, roughly the northern third of present-day Vietnam. Historically, the Viets fought on two fronts, to the north against their colonial master, China, while expanding to the south, annihilating or pushing into the mountains the native peoples whom they still regard as *moi* (savages). The Viet war cry was "*Nam Tien!*" (March south). The Viets, for example, slowly penetrated and destroyed the powerful seafaring kingdom of Champa, causing the Cham people to disappear. By 1500 the Viets had taken the central third of Vietnam, called Annam ("pacified south"), and by 1800 they had occupied the southern third, later known as Cochinchina. Soon the French arrived with their own brand of colonialism. In the early nineteenth century, Viets invaded and occupied much of Cambodia until the French made them pull out.

It was ironic that the Vietnamese accused the French of colonialism, for the Vietnamese were fiercer colonialists than the French ever were. Vietnamese were always a tough, fighting, expansionist people, something Americans did not understand. In the late 1970s they revived their historical pattern, fighting China in the north while occupying Cambodia in the south.

The French, like most colonial powers, stumbled into Vietnam with no clear plan or goal. In 1626 a brilliant French priest, Alexandre de Rhodes, arrived to try to convert the Vietnamese. He devised an ingenious way to write the tonal language (sounds like singing) with the Latin alphabet instead of Chinese pictographs. This expanded literacy and Catholicism. Over the decades, French missionaries, traders, and military advisors (to warring Vietnamese factions) penetrated Vietnam piecemeal. When French citizens got in trouble, the mother country felt obliged to come to their rescue, a common pattern in imperial expansion. Between 1847 and 1883, French forces took over Vietnam, ruling Tonkin and Annam as **protectorates** and Cochinchina as an outright colony.

Of all the many peoples the French ruled in their imperial heyday, the Vietnamese were the feistiest and least willing to submit. Some never acquiesced to the French takeover and formed protests, underground parties, and revolts. The comfortable French *colons*, with their rubber plantations (Michelin) and *cercles sportifs*, were unaware that many natives hated them.

CONCEPTS ■ POLITICAL GENERATIONS

German sociologist Karl Mannheim (1893–1947) argued that great events put their mark on an entire generation who carry the attitudes formed in their young adulthood all their lives. He called this *political generations*. World War I, for example, produced a war-weary "lost generation" in Europe and the United States. The Great Depression produced people who forever craved job security and welfare measures. Vietnam made many Americans cautious about any U.S. military intervention overseas.

One theory of war—not a completely valid one— uses the political generations approach. A generation that has experienced the horrors of war is reluctant to send its sons off to another war. This inclines the country to peace. The new generation, though, which has known only peace, picks up a romantic and heroic vision of war and tends toward an assertive foreign policy that may lead to war. We might call this a "forgetting" theory: The generation that forgets what war is like is more inclined to engage in it.

THE FIRST INDOCHINA WAR

Without firing a shot, the Japanese took over Vietnam in 1940, after France had fallen to Hitler. The Vichy regime in France collaborated with the Germans, and the French colonial regime in Vietnam did the same with the Japanese. There were several Vietnamese nationalist movements, but one was Communist, led by Ho Chi Minh (see box on page 60). In 1941 Ho founded a front organization, the *Viet Nam Doc Lap Minh Hoi*, the Vietnamese Independence League, **Vietminh** for short. Ho chose the last of his many aliases to match the name Vietminh. The Vietminh gathered weapons, spied on the Japanese for the Americans, and plotted a postwar takeover.

Vietminh   Communist Vietnamese anti-French liberation movement in the 1940s and 1950s, led by Ho Chi Minh.

Dienbienphu   French strongpoint taken by Vietminh in 1954.

monolithic   Composed of one single block with no splits or divisions.

After the Japanese surrender in August 1945, Ho proclaimed Vietnam independent, even using phrases from the U.S. Declaration of Independence. Ho hoped to get U.S. support to block the return of the French. Roosevelt, in fact, had opposed letting the French back, but he died in April 1945. France, then under the provisional government of nationalistic General Charles de Gaulle, insisted on reclaiming its colonies. Paris held some unserious negotiations with Ho but insisted on keeping Vietnam subservient, making war inevitable.

In late 1946, French and Vietminh forces clashed, and the first Indochina war was on. The Vietminh used guerrilla tactics and converted peasants to their cause. The French used more or less conventional tactics and tried to get the Vietminh to come out of the jungle for a "set-piece" battle, where superior French firepower could destroy them. The Vietminh in 1951 did engage in a conventional battle and lost. Then they let the French walk into a trap of their own making: **Dienbienphu**.

To interdict Vietminh supply lines from Communist China through the jungled mountains of northern Laos, the French in late 1953 airlifted 15,000 troops into a remote valley on the Laos border and dug in. Dienbienphu was to serve as the base for patrols that would block the Vietminh. If the Vietminh attacked the large, armed camp, so much the better, the French supposed. Instead, the Vietminh hand-wheeled artillery through the mountains to surround and lacerate Dienbienphu. More than 50,000 Vietminh fought and tunneled closer, whittling down the isolated fortress. Paris begged for U.S. help, but President Eisenhower cleverly passed the issue to key senators, who rejected U.S. participation in Indochina; we had just gotten out of an unpopular war in Korea in 1953. Dienbienphu fell on May 7, 1954. It was, in the words of war correspondent and historian Bernard Fall, "hell in a

GEOGRAPHY ■ VIETNAM AND CHINA

Dean Rusk, secretary of state under Kennedy and Johnson, like many in Washington, depicted the North Vietnamese as a branch of Communist China, proxy soldiers for an aggressive, expansionist China that we had to stop. If Rusk had read a little Vietnamese history, he would have learned that most of it is a series of Vietnamese revolts against Chinese imperialism. All of old Vietnam's heroes fought Chinese domination. Geography has made Vietnam and China natural enemies.

It was, therefore, not surprising that, in 1979, just four years after North Vietnam took the south, fighting broke out on the China–Vietnam border. (The Chinese started it, and the Vietnamese pushed them back.) Other skirmishes flared. If U.S. decision makers had looked at Vietnamese geography and history—that it continually resisted Chinese domination and does so today—American policies might have been quite different. We did not like communism in any form, but we failed to grasp that it was not **monolithic** but was instead divided against itself.

Geneva Accords   The 1954 agreement
to end the first Vietnam war.

very small place." French public opinion was fed up. A new premier, Pierre Mendès-France, promised to get France out of the war. The two sides met at Geneva, Switzerland, and by July 21, 1954, reached agreement to end the war. It was a thinly disguised French defeat.

THE UNITED STATES AND THE GENEVA ACCORDS

The United States was never happy with the 1954 **Geneva Accords**, which got France out of Indochina. They seemed to surrender to communism. President Eisenhower feared other lands of Southeast Asia would be next. The United States was present at Geneva but did not sign the accords and felt little bound by them.

As provided in the Geneva Accords, about a million refugees, mostly Vietnamese Catholics, fled from North to South Vietnam while perhaps a tenth as many Vietminh fighters went the other way. Some Vietminh buried their weapons and stayed behind in the south. The demarcation line across the narrow waist of Vietnam was never intended as permanent or to lead to the establishment of a separate country in the south, the Republic of Vietnam. (The north called itself the Democratic Republic of Vietnam.) That was the Americans' doing, seemingly in violation of the accords. Because we never signed them, argued Dulles, we were not bound by them, and neither was the anti-Communist government of South Vietnam that we set up. The demarcation line was the place to draw the line against Communist expansion.

TURNING POINT ■ HO CHI MINH

Born into a nationalist, educated family in Annam in 1890, Ho Chi Minh (not his birth name) led an incredible life. He went to an elite high school but was expelled for anti-French activities. Ho got a job on a ship and worked in menial jobs in London, New York, and Paris. After World War I, the young, skinny Ho showed up at the Versailles peace conference in a rented black suit, claiming to represent Vietnam and demanding freedom from France. No leader spoke with Ho.

Ho found a better reception on the French left and became a founding member of the French Communist Party (PCF) in 1920 for the simple reason that they, unlike the Socialists, favored ending colonialism. From the beginning, Ho was a Communist because communism promised liberation for colonies. He never cared much for its complex Marxist theories.

Ho became the PCF's expert on colonialism. The Communist International (*Comintern*) soon recognized Ho's talent and in 1924 sent him for training to Moscow, and then to China and Southeast Asia as a Comintern agent. Ho led a shadowy existence one step ahead of the police as he organized an Indochinese Communist Party. Like Lenin (whom Ho met in Moscow in 1922), Ho had a gift for languages and spoke fluent French, Russian, English, Mandarin, two other Chinese dialects, and some German. Ho's small Communist Party grew at the expense of other, more moderate Vietnamese nationalist parties. The Communists would simply turn over lists of members and leaders of the other parties to the French colonial police, who arrested them.

Ho even fought alongside Americans against the Japanese. One American OSS (precursor to the CIA) veteran recalled Ho as "an awfully sweet guy" who provided accurate intelligence. The OSS gave guns and trained Ho's fighters. From 1941 until his death in 1969, Ho led his people in nearly ceaseless warfare— against the Japanese, French, and Americans. Ho, who never married, made himself a quietly charismatic "Uncle Ho" to his people. No other Vietnamese leader had a fraction of his popular appeal. With the final Communist triumph in 1975, Saigon was renamed Ho Chi Minh City. (The locals still call it Saigon.)

The Americans thought they would do a lot better than the French. First, they saw the French as demoralized losers whose rigid doctrines were especially wrong for **guerrilla warfare**. Second, the French were colonialists who could not possibly win over a subject population. One young American congressman took a special interest in Vietnam. He had visited there in 1951 and predicted a French defeat because they were trying "to hang on to the remnants of empire" against rather than with the tide of Asian nationalism. Representative and later Senator John F. Kennedy (D-Massachusetts) urged us to ally ourselves with the forces of nationalism and use them to beat communism.

guerrilla warfare Small-unit, irregular struggle based on political revolution.

Vietcong Informal name of Communist-led South Vietnamese National Liberation Front in the 1960s.

Washington thought it had the man for the job: Ngo Dinh Diem, who was both anti-French and anti-Communist, an authentic Vietnamese nationalist who would rally his people and keep the dominoes from falling. Unfortunately, Diem was a fanatic Catholic and looked down on Buddhists, the majority of South Vietnam's population. With U.S. blessing, financial aid, and military support, Diem was flown to Saigon in 1954 to found a new country called South Vietnam. At first things went pretty well. Diem took a situation of near chaos and, by adroit use of military power, shaped it into what looked like a country. He ignored, of course, the call for Vietnam-wide elections in 1956. His police rooted out Vietminh "stay behinds."

Diem made several mistakes. He ignored a program of reforms that the United States urged, including land reform to give tenant farmers a stake in the system. Paying high rents to greedy landlords drove some peasants to support the resurgent Vietminh, who now called themselves the National Liberation Front. The Diem regime dubbed them *Viet Cong* (Vietnamese Communist); they never called themselves that. Diem ignored a centuries-old tradition of village democracy by appointing as village headmen outsiders loyal to him personally. When the **Vietcong** came into the village at night to try and quickly execute these headmen, the villagers did not especially mind. Diem's rigid personality was part of the problem. He trusted only his own family, and corruption was rife.

KENNEDY'S COMMITMENT

In the late 1950s, Communist subversion grew in the South Vietnamese countryside with assassinations of government officials, ambushes, and Vietcong tax collection among the peasants. Eisenhower had been able to put Vietnam on the back burner; Kennedy could not. Eisenhower sent only a 685-man U.S. military training mission to Saigon—the number set in the 1954

DIPLOMACY ■ THE GENEVA ACCORDS

The 1954 Geneva Accords between the French and Vietminh included the following:

1. A cease fire
2. A "provisional demarcation line" across the middle of Vietnam
3. Regrouping of Vietminh forces and sympathizers to the north of this line and of the French and their sympathizers to the south of this line
4. Elections within two years in both halves of Vietnam to decide whether to unify the country and to choose who would lead.

If these provisions had been carried out, there would have been no South Vietnam. Instead there would have been elections in 1956, which Ho would easily have won—Eisenhower himself admitted that—leading to Vietnam's unification under a Communist regime, which is what happened anyway.

Geneva Accords—but made no specific U.S. commitments. By the time Kennedy was inaugurated in 1961, though, the Vietcong were gaining, and Kennedy decided to increase the U.S. presence. By the time JFK died in 1963, there were more than 16,000 U.S. soldiers in Vietnam, and several had been killed in combat. Many observers feel that the point of no return came under Kennedy and that he bears primary responsibility for the U.S. commitment.

Kennedy's decision to up the ante in Vietnam was based on several factors. First, he was a vigorous young president who had campaigned on stopping the spread of communism in the Third World. Counterinsurgency was one of his pet projects, and he geared up the armed services to intervene in the developing lands. The Green Berets, for example, were his idea. Second, early in his first year he went through the humiliating defeat of the Bay of Pigs, the invasion of Cuba by CIA-trained anti-Castro forces (see page 175). Third, that June JFK met with Soviet party chief Nikita Khrushchev in Vienna and exchanged blunt language about the spread of communism; Kennedy then felt he had to show Khrushchev that America had the will and ability to block Communist expansion. But fourth and probably most important, without U.S. help South Vietnam would soon fall, and that would hurt JFK's reelection in 1964. During the entire Cold War, American presidents feared electoral punishment if another country went Communist on their watch.

Kennedy saw Vietnam as a proving ground for the new techniques of counterinsurgency. If we could stop communism there, we could persuade the Communists not to try it elsewhere. Kennedy ordered counterinsurgency techniques applied to Vietnam. Green Beret "A teams" were sent into the hills to rally the natives. U.S. helicopters lifted troops quickly into battle and raked the enemy with machine guns. An ambitious program of "strategic hamlets" herded Vietnamese farmers into fortified villages that would keep out the Vietcong. During 1962, these measures seemed to turn the tide.

But by 1963, the war was being lost. The Green Berets made few converts. The Vietcong learned how to shoot down helicopters. And the farmers hated being removed from their traditional

CONCEPTS ■ GUERRILLA WARFARE

Widely misunderstood, guerrilla warfare is not chiefly concerned with military tactics and equipment. The word first appeared in Spain—it is Spanish for "little war"—as Spanish partisans strove to expel Napoleon's legions. The word soon spread to connote small units of irregulars behind enemy lines who use hit-and-run tactics to confuse and wear down the enemy. As such, it is an ancient type of warfare, the strategy of the underdog against the superior forces of the occupier, a branch of *asymmetrical conflict* we will explore in Chapter 15.

The crux of modern guerrilla warfare is political. Some writers call it "revolutionary political warfare" or "people's war." It really depends on your ability to get the local people to support you against an unpopular government or foreign occupier. You work closely with the people, especially peasants in the countryside, help them, organize them, redistribute land to them, provide literacy classes and political lectures, and levy taxes. You become, in other words, an underground government that displaces the official government structure. In the words of Bernard Fall: "When a country is being subverted, it is not being outfought; it is being out-administered. Subversion is literally administration with a minus sign in front." The guerrilla fights a political war while the occupier fights a military war that further alienates the local people, persuading many to support the guerrillas.

The guerrilla is also trying to persuade the foreign occupiers to give up and go home. The war, expensive to the foreigners in money and blood, forces the public and politicians on the home front to ask what good this small, faraway country is to them. Pressure mounts for a pullout. Time may thus be on the side of the guerrilla. One axiom of guerrilla warfare: The guerrilla wins if he does not lose; the occupier loses if he does not win. A "last straw" military setback may persuade the occupier to quit: such were Dienbienphu for the French and Tet for the Americans.

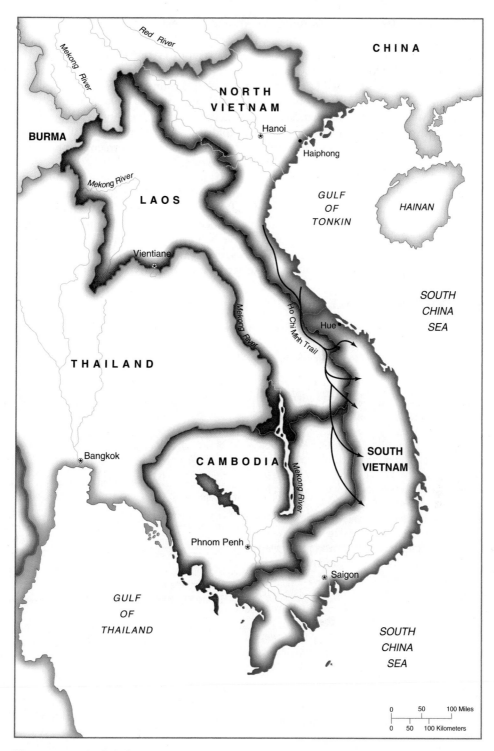

Vietnam and Vicinity

villages to labor without pay on earthworks and moats for the strategic hamlets. Soon they started welcoming the Vietcong into the strategic hamlets. Diem, sensing doom, became isolated and crazy. His murder in a coup saddened Kennedy, who himself was gunned down three weeks later.

In the spring of 1963, JFK confided to his old friend Senator Mike Mansfield (D-Montana) that he now agreed with Mansfield's argument to cut U.S. involvement in Vietnam. "But I can't do it until 1965—after I'm reelected," Kennedy told Mansfield. Mansfield recalled in 1970, "There is no doubt that he had shifted definitely and unequivocally on Vietnam, but he never had the chance to put the plan into effect." Would JFK have done it?

This question is controversial to this day. First, Kennedy told few others about this plan, not even Vice President Lyndon Johnson. Second, right up to his death, Kennedy kept emphasizing the U.S. commitment to Vietnam to stop the spread of communism. If he had been thinking of pulling out, he would have begun minimizing the importance of Vietnam. Third and most important, by 1965 the situation in South Vietnam was terrible politically and militarily. A U.S. pullout would have led to an immediate Communist victory, something no president could stand for. Kennedy may have wished to pull out of Vietnam, but circumstances, some of his own making, had locked him in.

LBJ: VICTIM OR VILLAIN?

Some writers have laid all responsibility for the war on Lyndon Johnson. True, Johnson made the decisions to escalate until, by early 1968, more than half a million U.S. troops were in Vietnam. And he made the decisions in a tricky manner. But he was not precisely a free agent. JFK had already

TURNING POINT ■ THE TONKIN GULF RESOLUTION

With the passage of the 1964 Tonkin Gulf Resolution, as in the 1964 election campaign, LBJ did not so much lie as let Congress deceive itself. First, LBJ did not tell Congress that the resolution had been drafted long before the incidents at sea ever occurred. Second, he did not tell Congress that the destroyers had been engaged in warlike activity. Third, he indicated that he would not use the resolution to go to war; it was just to make clear to the Communists that we stood firm.

This was the problem. Congress had gotten used to passing joint resolutions—which, when signed by the president, have force of law—during several Cold War crises. Strongly worded, they authorized the president to take whatever military steps were necessary. And every time, the Communists seemed to back down. Previous such resolutions included:

- Formosa Straits (1955) to keep Communist China from taking Taiwan
- Middle East (1957) to block Soviet expansion in the Middle East
- Cuba (1962) to make the Soviets back down during the missile crisis

- Berlin (1962) to prevent a Soviet takeover of West Berlin

Congress passed the Tonkin Gulf Resolution thinking it would be like the previous resolutions—a show of resolve to make the Communists back down. The words in it, however, clearly authorized the president "to take all necessary measures to repel any armed attack against the forces of the United States and to prevent further aggression." Congress had signed a blank check, and LBJ filled in the amount and cashed it.

In 1967, when a State Department lawyer told Congress that Tonkin Gulf was "the functional equivalent of a declaration of war," Capitol Hill felt it had been tricked. But the resolution was precisely that. True, Congress misunderstood the context in which they passed the resolution; they did not know LBJ had specific plans to use it to go to war. Much of Congress's hostility toward the White House during and after the Vietnam War traces back to congressional anger at having been deceived by LBJ's Tonkin Gulf Resolution, which was repealed in 1970.

committed the United States to stopping communism in Vietnam. LBJ inherited all of Kennedy's advisors, and most urged him to escalate. Most importantly, he knew the Republicans would use it against him if Vietnam fell to communism. LBJ was trapped and tried to wiggle out by lying, promising in the 1964 election that he would not send U.S. troops to Vietnam even while he planned exactly that.

Tonkin Gulf Resolution   The 1964 congressional permission for president to go to war in Vietnam.

Johnson minimized the Vietnam issue during the 1964 election, allowing him to sweep all but six states. In secret, however, he had a staff develop plans to escalate the war. The plans called for a joint congressional resolution authorizing the president to do whatever was needed, including bombing raids on North Vietnam and U.S. troops sent into the south. When these plans came out in the *Pentagon Papers* in 1971, many Americans were furious that they had been deceived. The war had been planned in advance.

The first step of the plan fell into place when North Vietnamese PT boats attacked—or allegedly attacked—two U.S. destroyers in August 1964. Neither U.S. ship was hit, and some critics charge that it was a trumped-up incident to secure passage of a joint congressional resolution. The destroyers were on a secret war mission to back up South Vietnamese vessels that were raiding the North Vietnamese coast. LBJ never told Congress about these patrols; instead, he portrayed the destroyers as peaceful victims of an unprovoked attack in international waters. This deception earned LBJ nearly complete public and congressional support.

The White House sent to Capitol Hill the joint congressional resolution that had been prepared months earlier, and Congress speedily and nearly unanimously passed the **Tonkin Gulf Resolution**. Only two senators, Wayne Morse (D-Oregon) and Ernest Gruening (D-Alaska), voted no and predicted exactly what LBJ would do with the resolution: Take the country into a major war. No one believed them, and they were not reelected.

During 1965, the rest of LBJ's plan went into action. The military draft greatly increased, and most draftees went to "Nam." The Rolling Thunder air strikes against North Vietnam soon hit every worthwhile target. At first, public opinion overwhelmingly supported the president. Yes, nodded LBJ, who followed the polls closely, "but for a very underwhelming period of time." This was prophetic, for by early 1968 majority U.S. opinion opposed the war.

The public had been promised "light at the end of the tunnel" soon, but it never came. In 1965, the very year U.S. troops arrived in large numbers, so did large numbers of the North Vietnamese Army (NVA). From 1965 on, the war became more conventional and less guerrilla. Inflated "body counts" of enemy dead made observers wonder how enemy troop strength could keep growing. Real body counts of American dead—by the war's end 60,000—appeared every evening on television news. (An estimated 1.1 million Vietnamese perished.) Vietnam was the first TV war, and its

CONCEPTS ■ WHAT IS A CIVIL WAR?

It sounds like a quibble now, but whether Vietnam was a civil war was one of the hot questions of the 1960s. The argument went like this: If Vietnam is a civil war fought within one country, it's really not much of our business. If it is an international war in which one country (North Vietnam) attacks another (South Vietnam), then it is right to help the victim.

In 1964 North Vietnam did begin quietly sending troops into South Vietnam via the "Ho Chi Minh Trail" through Laos. In retrospect, the debate was useless, for all "civil" wars have outside help and international ramifications. (By the way, what was the U.S. Civil War? Was it within one country or between two countries?)

Tet   Vietnamese new year; early 1968
North Vietnamese/Vietcong nationwide
offensive.

vividness turned many people against the war. Students grew angry, rebellious, and finally alienated. The "flower children" and their drug culture appeared at this time. Some young men ran away to Canada to avoid the draft or to desert from the U.S. Army. Massive defense spending brought an inflation that lasted through the 1970s.

Matters came to a head with the **Tet** offensive in early 1968. The American people no longer accepted an open-ended commitment; the war had lasted too long. Instead, they elected Richard Nixon, who promised to get us out with honor. Ironically, as vice president, Nixon had favored U.S. military help for the French in 1954 when Johnson had opposed it.

EXTRICATION WITHOUT HUMILIATION

President Nixon got us out of Vietnam at the same rate we had gone in. By late 1972, there were virtually no U.S. combat troops in Vietnam. Instead, "vietnamization" turned over weapons and responsibility to the Army of the Republic of Vietnam (ARVN, dubbed "Arvin" by GIs). But ARVN had never been much good. Officers were chosen for their political, religious, or personal connections. Corruption was rampant. ARVN drafted young males capriciously—they once rounded up a Japanese-American who was with the CIA—but many deserted. Morale was terrible, and ARVN often avoided engaging the enemy. Exasperated U.S. military advisors used to say of ARVN, "You can't transplant backbone."

U.S. forces had gone into Vietnam in the first place because ARVN could not handle things. What made us think they now could? President Nixon refrained from promising they could; he was merely giving them the chance. This was a major policy switch. The United States was no longer guaranteeing South Vietnam's security; now it was up to them. Could the United States have just "bugged out" quickly, in a few months? Nixon felt that abandoning an ally would have been dishonorable and would have ruined America's credibility with our allies.

The Nixon policy of "peace with honor" was actually a policy of extrication without humiliation. America should not look like it had been defeated. Nixon did not want a demoralized, beaten

TURNING POINT ■ TET

Tet, the lunar new year (taken from the Chinese calendar), was our Dienbienphu, the last straw that broke U.S. public support. In February 1968, the Communists, both Vietcong and NVA regulars, broke a truce and staged go-for-broke attacks throughout South Vietnam. The NVA took the northern city of Hue and executed thousands of civilians. A Vietcong suicide squad briefly invaded the U.S. embassy in Saigon.

Still, U.S. and South Vietnamese forces held and inflicted heavy losses on the enemy. In numerical terms, we won Tet. In psychological terms, however, the Communists achieved their goal by puncturing LBJ's optimistic reports of progress in the war. Some conservatives claim Tet could have been a turning point in our favor, that if we had stayed longer and fought harder, we could have won. But by then, few Americans wanted to.

Wide sectors of American society, including the business community, turned against the war. Senators Eugene McCarthy (D-Minnesota) and Robert Kennedy (D-New York) challenged LBJ for the Democratic presidential nomination. The unknown McCarthy, supported by an army of enthusiastic young people ("Stay clean for Gene!") almost won the New Hampshire primary. LBJ, the political pro who read the polls, knew he was finished and announced on television he would not run but would initiate peace discussions with Hanoi.

America, "a pitiful, helpless giant," in his words. The cost was high. About half of U.S. deaths in Vietnam occurred under Nixon for an essentially cosmetic rear-guard action.

Public negotiations had already begun in Paris under LBJ, but they were leading nowhere. Secretly, Nixon's national security advisor Henry Kissinger met with North Vietnam's representative to slowly hammer out an agreement. (They were jointly awarded the 1973 Nobel Peace Prize.) When Hanoi balked, a massive "Christmas bombing" in late 1972 nudged them to sign. Saigon too needed heavy arm-twisting to go along with an agreement that left them to defend themselves with only material help from the United States.

On paper, Saigon had a good chance. ARVN actually had far more soldiers and equipment than the NVA. But they lacked morale, and when the NVA made a probing attack in the mountains in

REFLECTIONS ■ IRAQ, AFGHANISTAN, AND VIETNAM

In what ways are the wars in Iraq, Afghanistan, and Vietnam similar? As the Iraq and Afghan wars stretched into the two longest in U.S. history, critics compared them to Vietnam, claiming we were again "bogged down." As usual, such comparisons show some similarities and some differences. Beware of simplified analogies (see pages 205–206).

First, the terrains were vastly different. Iraq was nearly perfect for our kind of conventional war in 2003. Recalling Vietnam, American officers joked: "We do deserts; we don't do jungles." The rugged mountains of Afghanistan favor insurgents. The Vietnam War used mostly draftees but no reservists; Iraq used no draftees but many reservists (at one point, 40 percent of U.S. forces there). Afghanistan uses some reservists. Iraq has lots of oil, Vietnam none. Afghanistan's chief product is opium.

The strongest difference is the nature of the enemy. All three wars were fought at least partly by guerrillas, but the Communists in Vietnam were united and under Hanoi's central control. Iraqi and Afghan insurgents, drawn from Sunnis, are fragmented with no one in overall control. The Vietcong could sell their nationalist ideology to other Vietnamese. Sunni fighters in Iraq cannot sell Sunni supremacy to Shia or Kurds. This is the ultimate weakness of the Sunni cause in Iraq: They can start a civil war but not win it. The Afghan Taliban face a similar problem: They are mostly Pashtun (the largest Afghan group but still less than half), and other Afghan ethnic groups do not wish to live under a regime of Pashtun religious fanatics.

There are some similarities. Anti-U.S. nationalism is the chief motivator for insurgents in all three countries: "Americans, get out of our country!" Both Iraq, invented by the British in the 1920s, and South Vietnam, invented by the Americans in the 1950s, were artificial countries whose regimes had little legitimacy. Afghanistan was never a unified country. The chief weaknesses in all three were political, not military—namely, corrupt and inept governments that enjoyed little citizen support.

All three wars were sold to Congress in panic mode over 9/11 and the Tonkin Gulf incident and passed as joint resolutions, not as declarations of war. Democratic Presidents Kennedy, Johnson, and Obama were under Republican pressure to show how tough they were. Republicans equated war with being strong on defense, security, or terrorism, and the Democratic incumbents feared not sending troops would cost them reelection. However, with no end in sight in all three cases, Congress started abandoning the president. In all three wars the United States had few allies and faced much international criticism.

The greatest similarity was in U.S. public opinion, which declined in all three wars over time and in response to U.S. casualties. Support for all started high but fell by half after a few years. Americans dislike long, inconclusive wars. Arguments widely accepted early in the wars—"stopping communism" and "war on terror"—persuaded fewer. Administrations of both parties reexamined U.S. national interests and developed timetables for withdrawal. Success was defined downward. Halfway stable-looking Iraq and Afghanistan would be good enough, and democracy was barely mentioned. As Vermont Republican Senator George Akin prescribed for Vietnam: "Declare victory and get out."

Paris Accords   The 1973 agreement
to end the second Vietnam war.

1975, ARVN units panicked. Soldiers threw down their weapons and fled southward. An ARVN rifle, GIs used to joke, had "never been fired and only dropped once." The panic—for which there was no good reason—spread, and ARVN melted away. Billions of dollars of U.S. war material fell into enemy hands. This time the U.S. Congress refused to let President Ford get the United States involved again. Instead of fighting, South Vietnamese officials clamored to be evacuated to the United States.

They paid for their cowardice. Although there was no Cambodia-style bloodbath (some 1.7 million Cambodians were killed), many Saigon officials were executed and the remainder sent to prison farms for lengthy and brutal "reeducation." More than half a million South Vietnamese fled in overcrowded coastal fishing boats, hoping to be admitted to the United States. Thai pirates raped, robbed, and murdered the "boat people" with impunity. Vietnamese who remained faced malnourished poverty as Communist bumblers wrecked the economy and turned Vietnam into one of the poorest countries in the world.

Finally, reformers in Hanoi—seeing how well the market economies of the region were doing—liberalized and welcomed foreign investment. The first to take advantage of this were the Japanese. The last were the Americans, although by the mid-1990s, they too were in on the deal. In 1995 Hanoi and Washington opened full diplomatic relations. Vietnam (like China) became partly capitalist and exported to the world market. By the 2000s, Vietnam's economy was booming with more than 8 percent annual growth, all based on foreign investment, much of it American. As Chinese wages climbed, manufacturers shifted some of their plants to take advantage of lower Vietnamese wages. Some of our athletic shoes and clothing are now made in Vietnam.

Aside from unifying their country on their terms, the Vietnamese Communists fought for an ideology doomed to failure. Even more ironic is that Vietnam has now turned to America as a counterweight to Chinese power. Historically, Vietnam always fought Chinese domination, a point virtually no Americans understood. The U.S. Navy now calls at Vietnamese ports. Vietnam and America could have had our current economic and strategic relationship decades earlier and without war.

MORALITY AND FEASIBILITY

Americans are given to moralizing about foreign policy; it is part of our religious heritage. We constantly ask ourselves, "Are we doing good or evil?" Most other countries hold such discussions to a minimum. Vietnam unleashed a torrent of moral analyses. The White House constantly assured the public that our actions were moral; many clergymen and professors argued they were immoral. Our analysis follows.

DIPLOMACY ■ THE 1973 PARIS ACCORDS

The Americans got out of Vietnam much like the French did two decades earlier, with a fig leaf to hide their shame. The 1973 **Paris Accords** resembled the 1954 Geneva Accords: The white man got out so the Vietnamese could resume the struggle for mastery of their country. There is one major difference in the two accords: In 1973 there was no "regroupment." Instead, some 150,000 NVA troops were allowed to stay inside South Vietnam. Two years later, they took the whole country.

DIPLOMACY ■ KISSINGER'S "DECENT INTERVAL"

Before he became President Nixon's national security advisor, Harvard professor Henry Kissinger confided privately that the best the United States could hope for in getting out of Vietnam was a "decent interval" of two to three years between our withdrawal and a Communist takeover, so it would not look like a direct U.S. defeat. This is what happened: two years between the Paris Accords and the fall of Saigon. There is no evidence that Hanoi agreed to any such interval; it just worked out that way.

First, the American policy of trying to block the spread of communism was not in itself immoral. Politically, economically, and morally, Communist countries were blights, some worse than others. Most have now ousted their Communist regimes, a clear indication that the system failed. The strongest anti-Communists were citizens of Communist countries. You didn't know how bad it was until you lived under it. But how could we communicate that to people who had not yet tasted Communist rule? And, as in Vietnam, how could we reach them when the local Communists had managed to capture the nationalist movement?

It was nationalism that gave communism its strength. The Vietminh beat the French because they had the force of Vietnamese nationalism on their side; the French were foreign colonizers. The Americans unwittingly stepped into the French role; we looked like new colonialists.

The Vietcong did not know or care about Marx or Lenin; they were fighting to get the foreigners out of their country. How would you feel if your country were occupied by an army of strange-looking aliens who did not understand your language and culture? Would you believe their claims that they were here to liberate you? This is how the Vietnamese saw us.

Under such circumstances, how do you save people who do not want to be saved? Making matters worse was the ineptitude of the Saigon regime; it was incapable of rallying its people. And the more the United States "helped" Saigon—with money, food, experts, and so on—the weaker it became. In place of political and moral support from the South Vietnamese, we relied on firepower, which was counterproductive. People who have seen their homes, farms, and children destroyed by artillery, napalm, or Zippo lighters hate the foreigners who have done these things. The more we fought, the worse it got. We were destroying the country in order to save it. Eventually, our moral goal was subverted by immoral means.

The Vietnam Veterans Memorial in Washington was the focus of the nation's pent-up emotions over the war. Here, veterans tearfully remember their fallen buddies. (AP Photo)

feasibility Able to do without excessive force or cost.

just war Doctrine of medieval Catholic philosophers that war under certain conditions can be moral.

Morality and **feasibility** are closely linked in international affairs. If a goal, however moral, is infeasible, trying to attain it by brute strength leads to immorality. We must ask not only what our goals are but whether they can be achieved without doing more harm than good. As we used to emphasize to the Communists, the end does not justify the means.

Are there any lessons to be learned from the Vietnam experience? We suggest the following. Note how some of them can be applied to Iraq and Afghanistan.

1. Form your national interests cautiously, with an eye to feasibility, flexibility, and long-term outcomes.
2. Pick the government you wish to help very carefully. Make sure it is incorrupt and popular.
3. Do not help too much. People have to fight for their own freedom. If we do the fighting for them, they become dependent, demoralized, and resentful. The more money you give them, the more corrupt they become.
4. Issue no visas to local citizens. Make it clear that the United States is not an escape hatch. If they lose, they will have to live under a brutal regime.
5. Make sure local nationalism is on your side, that the enemy has not captured it. If you look like foreign occupiers, you have no chance.
6. Armed forces cannot win hearts and minds. An army does one thing: destroy. Do not suppose your military might solves political problems.
7. Survey the geography to make sure it does not give your enemy advantages such as secure base areas, sanctuaries, or supply routes.
8. Remember that Americans do not like long wars and quickly lose patience.
9. Obtain the informed consent of Congress to make sure it is fully behind you. Do not attempt to sneak by with a "functional equivalent of a declaration of war."
10. Immediately increase taxes to soak up defense spending and block inflation.

CLASSIC THOUGHT ■ WAR AND PEACE

"They Make a Desert and Call It Peace"

Roman historian Tacitus showed some guilt over what Rome had done in conquering and subjugating England. The Romans did eventually bring peace, but it was a cynical kind of peace, the peace of the graveyard. Critics of the Vietnam War often recalled Tacitus's bitter remark and suggested it was what we were doing in Vietnam. Soon the perfect statement appeared:

"We Had to Destroy the Town in Order to Save It"

This quote from an American officer (a sort of unwitting Tacitus), explaining why a town in the Mekong Delta had to be leveled, was widely reported because it summarized what we were doing in Vietnam. After we finished "saving" Vietnam, what would be left?

Aquinas on "Just War"

St. Thomas Aquinas in the thirteenth century deplored war but admitted that a **just war** could exist, provided that:

1. It aimed at defending and reestablishing peace.
2. The cause itself was just.
3. Noncombatants were not harmed.
4. The means used were proportional to the ends.

St. Thomas's "proportionality" doctrine is his most important. It means you do not nuke a country over fishing rights. Some thinkers felt the U.S. war in Vietnam passed on points 1 and 2 but failed on points 3 and 4.

my polisci **kit** EXERCISES

Apply what you learned in this chapter on MyPoliSciKit (www.mypoliscikit.com).

 Assessment   Review this chapter using learning objectives, chapter summaries, practice tests, and more.

 Flashcards   Learn the key terms in this chapter; you can test yourself by term or definition.

 Video   Analyze recent world affairs by watching streaming video from major news providers.

 Simulations   Play the role of an IR decision-maker and experience how IR concepts work in practice.

KEY TERMS

Dienbienphu (p. 59)
feasibility (p. 70)
Geneva Accords (p. 60)
guerrilla warfare (p. 61)
just war (p. 70)

monolithic (p. 59)
Paris Accords (p. 68)
political generations (p. 58)
protectorate (p. 58)
Tet (p. 66)

Tonkin Gulf Resolution (p. 65)
Vietcong (p. 61)
Vietminh (p. 59)

FURTHER REFERENCE

Bissell, Tom. *The Father of All Things: A Marine, His Son, and the Legacy of Vietnam.* New York: Pantheon, 2007.

Blight, James G., Janet M. Lang, and David A. Welch. *Vietnam If Kennedy Had Lived: Virtual JFK.* Lanham, MD: Rowman & Littlefield, 2009.

Brocheux, Pierre. *Ho Chi Minh: A Biography.* New York: Cambridge University Press, 2007.

Ellsberg, Daniel. *Secrets: A Memoir of Vietnam and the Pentagon Papers.* New York: Viking, 2002.

Fall, Dorothy. *Bernard Fall: Memories of a Soldier-Scholar.* Dulles, VA: Potomac Books, 2007.

FitzGerald, Frances. *Fire in the Lake: The Vietnamese and the Americans in Vietnam.* New York: Random House, 1972.

Goldstein, Gordon M. *Lessons in Disaster: McGeorge Bundy and the Path to War in Vietnam.* New York: Henry Holt, 2008.

Halberstam, David. *The Best and the Brightest.* New York: Random House, 1972.

Karnow, Stanley. *Vietnam: A History*, rev. ed. New York: Penguin Books, 1991.

Lamb, David. *Vietnam, Now: A Reporter Returns.* New York: PublicAffairs, 2002.

Maraniss, David. *They Marched into Sunlight: War and Peace, Vietnam and America, October 1967.* New York: Simon & Schuster, 2003.

Morgan, Ted. *Valley of Death: The Tragedy at Dien Bien Phu That Led America into the Vietnam War.* New York: Random House, 2010.

Neu, Charles E. *America's Lost War: Vietnam, 1945–1975.* Wheeling, IL: Harlan Davidson, 2005.

SarDesai, D. R. *Vietnam: Past and Present*, 4th ed. Boulder, CO: Westview, 2005.

Schandler, Herbert Y. *America in Vietnam: The War That Couldn't Be Won.* Lanham, MD: Rowman & Littlefield, 2009.

Sheehan, Neil, Hedrick Smith, E. W. Kenworthy, and Fox Butterfield. *The Pentagon Papers.* New York: New York Times, 1971.

CHAPTER 5

Russia and Geopolitics

Bolshevik Leon Trotsky formed the new Red Army and used it to win the Russian civil war and invade Poland. (Bettmann/Corbis)

The rise and fall of the Soviet Union teaches much IR history, vocabulary, and **geopolitics**. The new United States faced few threats, but Russia, with no natural barriers, was open to invasion from both east and west. **Mongol** hordes erased the first Russian state by 1240. Russians are still nervous about the millions of clever, aggressive people of the East. Ivan III, the duke of Moscovy, in the fifteenth century pushed back the **Tatars** and built a new Russian state. His grandson Ivan IV, known as "the Terrible," expanded Russia by brutal means in the sixteenth century. To Russians, this "terribleness" is good; it means strong and strict in crushing both foreign invaders and any who weaken Russia from within. Russians still like rule by a single strong personality.

There are several constants in Russian/Soviet geopolitics. Landlocked Russia long struggled for a "warm-water" port that would not ice over in winter. In the early eighteenth century, Peter the Great pushed back the Turks to gain access to the Black Sea and the Swedes to gain his "window to the west" on the Baltic, where he built St. Petersburg. Peter, the first tsar to tour West Europe, was impressed by its industries and ordered them copied in Russia. He set the pattern of importation of Western technology and forced modernization from the top down. Peter, the great expansionist and modernizer of Russia, is highly honored today.

Moscow also longed for Istanbul and the Turkish Straits, both to liberate the original center of Orthodox Christianity and to secure the Straits for unhindered Russian sea traffic from the Black Sea. For this, Russia fought ten wars over two centuries with the Ottoman Empire. Exactly like the tsars, Stalin tried to gain the Straits at the close of World War II, for that would have turned the Black Sea into a Russian lake. For Russia, geopolitics is a constant.

European powers saw a Russia ripe for invasion. The Teutonic knights pushed eastward along the Baltic until stopped by the Russians under Alexander Nevsky in 1242. From 1707 to 1709, a powerful Swedish army under Charles XII battled through Russia until it gave up, exhausted. In 1812 Napoleon actually occupied Moscow. In World War I, German forces penetrated deep into Russia. In 1941, Hitler assembled the largest army in history and sent it to conquer and enslave Russia. The biggest battles of World War II occurred in the east. The Soviet Union lost 26 million citizens in that war; the United States lost fewer than half a million.

QUESTIONS TO CONSIDER

1. What has been the impact of geography on Russia?
2. Is an ideological foreign policy wise?
3. Was Stalin paranoid? What evidence is there?
4. When and how did the Soviet Union enter World War II?
5. What was the Cold War about, and when did it begin?
6. How did we perceive the Soviet Union? Were our perceptions accurate?
7. What was Soviet *hegemony* over East Europe?
8. What is the difference between *détente* and *entente*?
9. What is the theory of imperial overstretch?
10. How is Russia a continuing problem?

73

geopolitics The impact of geography on international politics.

Mongols Thirteenth-century conquerors of Eurasia.

Tatars Descendants of the Mongols (not *Tartars*).

socialism State ownership of economy to end class differences.

Lebensraum German for "living space"; theory that countries must expand to gain room for their population.

War has had a profound impact on Russia, producing at least two systemic upheavals. The Mongol conquest led to the founding of the centralized and militarized Russian state under Ivan. World War I led to the collapse of tsarism and the founding of the Bolshevik state under Lenin. Without war, evolution rather than revolution would have been Russia's probable path.

WAR AND BOLSHEVISM

Tsarist Russia early in the twentieth century had a growing economy and the beginnings of an elected parliament, the Duma. Many Russian intellectuals hated the tsarist system and turned to **socialism** and *Marxism* (see page 32). A few joined the small, underground Russian Social Democratic Labor Party. Russia's humiliating defeat in the Russo–Japanese War of 1904–1905 triggered the abortive 1905 revolution, and World War I collapsed the system. The Russian army was large but run by incompetent generals. German forces ground the Russians to a halt, and by 1916 Russia started coming apart. In early 1917, with the economy and army near collapse, a group of moderates seized power and forced Tsar Nicholas II to abdicate.

The 1917 Provisional Government—by July it was under moderate Alexander Kerensky—knew Russia could not fight Germany much longer but felt duty-bound to stay in the war so as not to betray its Western allies. America entered World War I only in April 1917 and shipped

GEOGRAPHY ■ GEOPOLITICS

Geography has a profound impact on international politics. The study of *geopolitics* began in the nineteenth century, partly to justify imperialist expansion. To think geopolitically, look at a map or globe and ask questions such as the following:

■ Should I expand my territory or just protect what I have?

■ What is the value of another area in terms of natural resources, industry, trade, protection from invasion, or a base for extending influence?

■ How easy would it be to take and hold this area?

■ If I don't take this area, who else might?

■ If this area were in hostile hands, could it be a threat?

■ What natural barriers, such as seas or mountains, help or hinder my situation?

■ Could I strengthen my situation by diplomacy and commerce, or will it take troops?

■ If I do move into this area, what new problems and enemies will I incur?

■ Will the people there welcome me or hate me?

Expansionist leaders ignore these questions until they get themselves into untenable situations, overextended and stuck in unwinnable wars. The Nazis and Japanese militarists embraced an aggressive **Lebensraum** geopolitics that destroyed their regimes. Powerful countries tend to define their geopolitical interests broadly, leading to expansionism and war. When England strove to prevent the domination of the Netherlands or Eastern Mediterranean by hostile powers, it was playing geopolitics. When the United States issued the Monroe Doctrine or took the Philippines, it was playing geopolitics. Moscow still holds traditional geopolitical views and tries to control bordering countries.

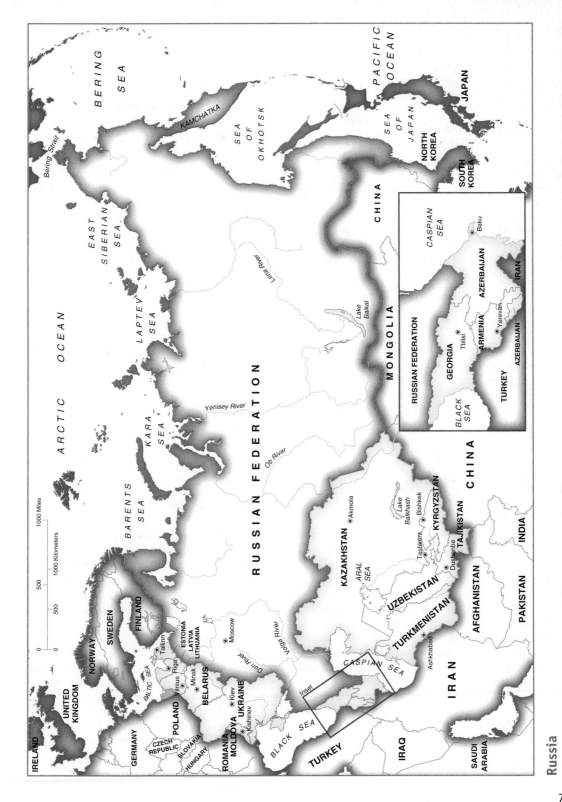

Russia

ideology Belief system that society can be improved by following certain doctrines; usually ends in *-ism*.

Brest-Litovsk The 1918 treaty dictated by Germany to get Russia out of World War I.

mobilization Getting an army ready for immediate war.

much war materiel to North Russia. At that very time, Germany arranged for Lenin to return to Russia from his Swiss exile. In November 1917, his Bolsheviks seized power, shot the tsar and his family, and began negotiations with Germany to take Russia out of the war.

Lenin's Marxist **ideology** led him to mistaken assumptions. He supposed Europe was ripe for revolution, so the Russian revolution would quickly spread. He thought the Germans would be lenient, but they demanded large areas of western Russia and an independent Ukraine. Lenin balked. Before, he had been a revolutionary trying to overthrow state power. Now, ironically, he had to preserve the Russian state. Ideology collided with reality. With Russia weak and disintegrating, in March 1918, Lenin glumly accepted the German *Diktat*. Only Germany's defeat in November (fresh American troops tipped the balance on the western front) made the **Brest-Litovsk** Treaty a dead letter and saved Russia from dismemberment.

SPREADING THE REVOLUTION

Lenin's revolution did not spread, even though War Commissar Trotsky sent his new Red Army westward into Poland. There the forces of newly reestablished Poland (it had been divided among Germany, Austria, and Russia for a century and a half) under Pilsudski pushed the Reds back and took more territory for Poland, lands inhabited mostly by Belarusians and Ukrainians that Stalin eventually got back. By the end of 1920, Lenin turned cautious and concentrated on protecting the Soviet Union and consolidating Communist—as the Bolsheviks now called themselves—power.

GEOGRAPHY ■ WORLD WAR I: THE SLAVIC CONNECTION

The causes of World War I are many, but one was the resentment of the Slavic peoples at being part of the Austro-Hungarian Empire. Serbs, Croats, Slovenes, Czechs, Slovaks, and Poles in this multinational empire stirred in the nineteenth century under the twin impulses of nationalism and Pan-Slavism, the feeling that all the Slavic peoples are related and under the benevolent protection of the largest Slavic nation, Russia. Pan-Slavism was especially important in the Balkans as Serbs, Montenegrins, and Bulgars struggled to free themselves from the Muslim Turks; they turned naturally to their "big brother," the Eastern Christian Russians. Even today, Serbs almost instinctively seek Russian protection.

Russia's imperial ambitions in the Balkans collided with those of the Austrians as both pressed southward against the weakening Ottoman Empire. In 1908 Austria annexed Bosnia, which neighboring Serbia also claimed. In 1914 Bosnian–Serb nationalists assassinated Austrian Archduke Franz Ferdinand in Sarajevo, and Vienna, in revenge, demanded a virtual takeover of Serbia. Belgrade refused, and Austria attacked.

Serbia turned to Russia for help, and the tsar ordered the **mobilization** of the huge Russian army. In the meantime, Germany gave Austria blank-check support to punish the Serbs. The German kaiser, alarmed at the Russian mobilization, also mobilized, and the little war turned into World War I. Without the Slavic connection, the war would have been a minor Balkan conflict between Austria and Serbia.

Instead of military power, Lenin urged socialists all over the world to aid the new Soviet Union. In the years 1920 and 1921, new Communist parties broke off from socialist parties and joined Lenin's disciplined, centralized international organization, the **Comintern**. All Communist parties had to obey Moscow. Communists believed that helping the Soviet Union aided socialism and so followed the most absurd twists and turns of Soviet foreign policy. For believers, communism became a secular religion with its center in Moscow.

Comintern   Short for Communist International; the world's Communist parties under Moscow's control.

Five-Year Plans   Stalin's forced industrialization in the 1930s.

paranoid   Unreasonably suspicious of others.

STALIN'S POLICY MISTAKES

Lenin died in 1924 with no designated heir. One of his last messages urged the Communist Party to reject Stalin as "too rude." By then, however, Stalin controlled the party structure, using his position as general secretary to handpick supporters for leading party positions. This enabled him to beat and exile Trotsky. By 1927, Stalin was in firm control. In 1928 he instituted the first **Five-Year Plan** of forced industrialization and the collectivization of agriculture. Brutally, the Soviet Union became a major industrial power.

Many thinkers label Stalin **paranoid**. He feared that Trotsky, expelled from the Soviet Union in 1929, still had supporters inside the Communist Party and Red Army, which Trotsky had founded. Chronically insecure, in 1934 Stalin instituted the Great Purge, which killed perhaps a million party comrades—including most of his military commanders—on suspicion of disloyalty. At this same time, Stalin had millions of ordinary Soviets—farmers who resisted collectivization, workers late to work, ethnic minorities—arrested and sent to Siberia, where most died in slave-labor projects. Altogether, more than 15 million Soviets died under Stalin's orders. This is not the working of a normal mind. (Iraq's Saddam Hussein modeled himself on Stalin.)

In foreign policy, Stalin, who had no experience with other countries, made dreadful mistakes. In 1922 the Comintern ordered the small Chinese Communist Party (CCP) to join the larger Nationalists (KMT) and influence them from within. In 1927 Chiang Kai-shek, smelling subversion, massacred the Communists, but Stalin still urged the CCP to stay with the KMT. Mao Zedong, always a CCP maverick, ignored Stalin and turned the CCP to guerrilla warfare and

TURNING POINT ■ THE NORTH RUSSIAN INTERVENTION

The Western allies were horrified at the Bolsheviks taking Russia out of the war, allowing Germany to transfer a million troops from east to west, and considered the Bolsheviks traitors and German agents. Much war materiel, most of it American, had been sent to the North Russian ports of Archangel and Murmansk, where, it was feared, it would be captured by the advancing Germans. The British and Americans sent small contingents there in 1918. Some thought the West could help the White Russian forces fighting in the civil war, but the operation was confused and accomplished nothing.

By the time the war ended in November, the North Russian ports were frozen shut. The Americans had to stay until mid-1919, and they fought minor skirmishes with the newly formed (by Leon Trotsky) Red Army. Americans and Soviets shed each other's blood early, albeit not very much. The problem, studied by diplomat and historian George Kennan, was that all the British and Americans could think about was winning the war, whereas all the Bolsheviks could think about was consolidating their revolution. Neither side could accept the other's motives as legitimate. Some say the Cold War started in 1918 in North Russia.

appeasement   A concession to satisfy a hostile country; in disrepute since Hitler.

nonaggression pact   Treaty to not attack each other.

pragmatism   If it works, use it.

ultimate victory. The roots of the Sino–Soviet conflict go back to Stalin's bad advice.

In Europe, too, Stalin misunderstood the situation. There he told Communist parties to keep their distance from "bourgeois" parties and not cooperate with them, not even with socialists. When the Depression hit Germany, the Nazi vote grew rapidly. A joint Social Democrat–Communist front could have stopped them, but Stalin rejected it on the theory that the Nazis would be short-lived. The foolish Communist slogan of the time: "After Hitler comes us." Realizing his mistake too late, Stalin ordered the Comintern to work for "popular fronts" with any and all antifascist parties. Communists then tried to explain that they were really just democrats fighting fascism. Their slogan became "No enemies on the left." Popular Front governments were briefly in power in France and Spain. Stalin's aim in the late 1930s was to get Britain and France as allies against a threatening Germany.

But London and Paris rejected Stalin's overtures. Standing together with Moscow against Hitler, the three could have prevented World War II. Instead, at Munich in 1938, Britain and France tried to **appease** Hitler by handing him Czechoslovakia. In Stalin's paranoid vision, the British and French wanted the German war machine aimed eastward, at the Soviet Union. Stalin turned the tables on them and pulled the most cynical reversal of modern history: the 1939 Hitler–Stalin **nonaggression pact**, which left Britain and France to face Germany alone. A week after the pact was signed, Hitler invaded Poland in September 1939, the official start of World War II. Stalin occupied the eastern third of Poland—that was a secret part of the agreement—thus getting back the territory Poland had taken in 1921.

THE GREAT PATRIOTIC WAR

The Hitler–Stalin Pact of 1939–1941 was strange and unstable. The blood enemies stopped cursing each other. The Soviet Union shipped much grain and petroleum to Germany. French Communists disparaged their own country's war effort. Stalin thought Britain and France would

CONCEPTS ■ IDEOLOGY AND FOREIGN POLICY

An ideology is a belief system or theory that aims to improve society. Usually ideologies end in "ism," as in liberalism, conservatism, socialism, communism, or Islamic fundamentalism. The opposite of ideology is **pragmatism**, but it is often in the service of an ideology. Even Americans have ideological motives, varying combinations of free market, democracy, and Christianity. Often ideology is not seriously believed but serves as a mask for self-interest.

Ideological foreign policies seldom last. Revolutionary countries may start out trying to export their ideology, but when it costs too much, it is minimized. Soviet foreign policy started ideological, but very quickly Marxism-Leninism became entwined with Soviet national interest. Russia was the first Communist country, so its interests were the same as communism's. That was the line Lenin and Stalin used on gullible Communists around the world. What's good for Russia is good for communism, they argued. This was ideology masking national interest.

Stalin made massive ideological flip-flops: First ignore the Nazis (early 1930s), then work against the Nazis (mid-1930s), and later make a deal with the Nazis (1939). Stalin offered ideological excuses to cover up his mistakes and keep himself powerful. Take strongly ideological foreign policies with a grain of salt. They are usually either temporary fanaticism or disguised self-interest.

be about an even match for Germany. The two sides would exhaust themselves and leave the Soviet Union as the strongest power in Europe. But in May and June 1940, the "phony war" ended as German tank columns slashed through the north of France, and aged Marshal Pétain signed a humiliating peace with the German occupiers. For a year, Britain stood alone against Nazi Germany.

Spanish Civil War The 1936–1939 conflict in which Nazis and Communists aided opposite sides.

Stalin foolishly supposed Hitler would leave him alone. The Soviets even made stiff territorial demands when they took over the Baltic states of Lithuania, Latvia, and Estonia as well as a part of Romania called Moldavia. This angered Hitler and attracted his attention eastward again, to his old first hate, the Slavic people in general and Communists in particular. In late 1940, he ordered a huge military buildup for the invasion of the Soviet Union in June 1941.

Stalin received more than a hundred intelligence reports about the attack—some from his own spies—but refused to believe them. Intelligence is worthless if you don't believe it. The British informed Stalin of the impending invasion they learned of from breaking German codes, but Stalin smelled a British trick to pull him into the war. When the invasion hit, Stalin had a nervous breakdown but emerged to rally the Soviet people. Moscow's line for years was that the Soviets knew all along what Hitler was up to and used the time to prepare. Why then were they caught so unprepared?

Hitler's Operation Barbarossa nearly succeeded. More than half a million Soviet soldiers were captured the first month. Russia is geographically tough to conquer, though. As an invader penetrates eastward, supply lines lengthen, and the front expands as Russia becomes broader. Mud and snow slow movement. German troops had no winter clothing. In November German troops neared Moscow but stalled. Winter came early, and reinforcements from Siberia held the line. By early 1943, with the Nazi defeat at Stalingrad, perceptive Germans knew they could not win. The Red Army pushed the Germans across East Europe back to Berlin. When the war in Europe ended in May 1945, the Soviets had won not by superior weapons, leadership, or tactics but by letting the foe exhaust itself in the attack and then pushing it back by means of greater numbers. It was a costly and traditional way to wage war, but it saved Russia.

DIPLOMACY ■ THE SPANISH CIVIL WAR

In the 1930s the weak Spanish Republic split in two. General Franco's conservative Nationalists rebelled against the leftist Popular Front government in 1936. The bitter civil war ended with Franco's victory in 1939 and was a curtain raiser and proving ground for World War II. Mussolini and Hitler immediately came to Franco's aid. German and Italian bombs leveled Guernica in 1937. Stalin had the Comintern recruit the International Brigades and sold the Republic tanks and artillery. Some 3,200 Americans fought for the Republic in the Lincoln Brigade; half of them perished.

The Communists, under Stalin's orders, urged centrist policies during the **Spanish Civil War**. They actually crushed Spanish Trotskyites and anarchists who wanted a proletarian revolution. Stalin's idea here was to convince the British and French—who stayed neutral while fascists murdered Spanish democracy—that the Soviets could be reliable partners in opposing fascism. Too late, London and Paris realized that Hitler and Mussolini were just sharpening their knives in Spain and that the other democracies would be next.

YALTA

In early 1945, the Big Three wartime leaders—Roosevelt, Churchill, and Stalin—met in the Soviet Crimean resort of Yalta to decide the fate of East and Central Europe. Some Republicans accused Roosevelt and the Democrats of giving East Europe to the Soviets at **Yalta**. "Yalta" became synonymous with "treason." It was sloppy diplomacy but not treason. The Soviet army had already conquered most of East Europe and was determined to keep it. No one knew how far east the Western allies would get; they could have taken more of Germany and Czechoslovakia.

The two sides at Yalta also had different notions of "democracy" for East Europe. The West meant liberal democracy, with parties competing in free and fair elections. The Soviets meant "people's democracy," the ouster of capitalists and conservatives, with power going to the "party of workers" (i.e., the Communists). The misunderstandings over Yalta were among the causes of the Cold War.

Yalta   Early 1945 agreement by Stalin, Churchill, and Roosevelt on who got what in Germany and East Europe.

Cold War   Period of armed tension between Soviet Union and West, roughly 1947 to 1989.

THE COLD WAR

The **Cold War** was the period of political and military tension between the United States and the Soviet Union that followed World War II. Its underlying cause was the Soviet takeover and communization of the nations of East Europe from 1945 to 1948. Every time Stalin installed another Communist government in East Europe, the West became angrier that he was repudiating the Yalta agreement—which called for free and democratic governments in Europe—and more fearful that he would move into West Europe.

The Cold War probably crested with the 1962 Cuban Missile Crisis, but some feel it ended with Nixon's and Kissinger's efforts at *détente* (see page 85) in the early 1970s. A few claim it then revived with the Soviet invasion of Afghanistan in 1979. Most now think the Cold War lasted until the Berlin Wall fell in late 1989.

The Cold War shows the paradox of the insecure empire. By the end of World War II, Stalin had achieved what the tsars had only dreamed about. Russia was the most powerful European nation, with a security belt across East Europe. But this alarmed the Western nations, now led by the United States, which rearmed and opposed Soviet power in every corner of the globe. Stalin's new power created a large, hostile anti-Soviet coalition. Stalin, who used to warn his subjects of "capitalist encirclement," created it. The more secure the Soviets tried to become, the greater insecurities they faced. This is called the "security dilemma."

DIPLOMACY ■ THE YALTA AGREEMENT

1. Poland would get new borders, losing territory in the east to the Soviet Union and gaining it in the west from Germany. In effect, Poland was picked up and moved over 100 miles westward.

2. The countries of East Europe would be democratic and friendly with the Soviet Union.

3. Germany would be divided into three (later four, when France was added) zones for temporary military occupation. Berlin would be likewise divided.

4. Germany would be disarmed and would pay heavy reparations for the damage it had caused, especially to the Soviet Union.

THE DECLINE OF THE SOVIET UNION

worst-casing Tendency to see enemy as stronger than it is.

During the Cold War, many American analysts and politicians feared a powerful, expansionist Soviet Union. **Worst-casing** led to overestimates of Soviet power. We now see that the Soviet giant was declining at an accelerating rate. Its army devoured one-quarter of the economy. Its empire drained it in subsidies. Its technology fell further behind every decade. Chronic shortages produced massive discontent. Hatred fumed among Soviet nationalities.

U.S. politicians, academics, and journalists failed to anticipate the collapse of Soviet power. Committed to Cold War images, few noticed that Soviet instability started after the death of Stalin in 1953. The problem is a permanent one in human psychology: how to perceive clearly. (More on *misperception theory* in Chapter 12.) By 1960, for example, the "Sino–Soviet bloc" had been replaced by the Sino–Soviet split, but our perceptions lagged behind.

After Stalin died, his lackeys competed for power. By 1955, party chief Nikita Khrushchev followed Stalin's path by naming his supporters to key positions to beat his rivals. To shake loose Stalin's influence and firm up his own power, at the 1956 party congress Khrushchev delivered a stinging, hours-long denunciation of the "crimes of Stalin" that included everything from blunders in the war to murdering party comrades. He thought he was speaking to a closed party session, but the speech soon leaked out with international consequences. All over the world, Communists who had worshipped Stalin suddenly learned that he was terrible. Many members quit. In Hungary, radical reformist Communists took over until Soviet tanks intervened. The same thing nearly happened in Poland.

In China, Mao Zedong had not been consulted about Khrushchev's speech and opposed it. Mao still used Stalin as a symbol and disliked the impulsive and reckless Khrushchev for damaging the world Communist movement. Mao repudiated Khrushchev's leadership and took China on ultraradical paths in both foreign and domestic policy. Mao called for world revolution just as Khrushchev was warning against the dangers of nuclear war. In 1960, the Soviet Union pulled all its foreign aid and experts out of China. The two called each other "revisionist," a Communist swear word. China revived old border claims going back to tsarist days, and in 1969 the two sides skirmished on their Manchurian border.

CLASSIC THOUGHT ■ KISSINGER ON ABSOLUTE SECURITY

"Absolute security for one power means absolute insecurity for all the others," wrote Harvard political scientist Henry Kissinger, who later served Nixon as national security advisor and secretary of state. Kissinger had concluded that a revolutionary country—such as France after 1789—has good reason to fear that other states will try to snuff out its revolution before it becomes a threat to them. Therefore, the revolutionary state can feel secure only by conquering all neighbors. This explains Napoleon and his compulsion to conquer all of Europe.

Kissinger thought this process explained the Soviet drive to expand its power. The Soviet Union, a revolutionary country in a world of conservative powers who hated it, could become secure only by destroying all threats. The insecurity of revolutionary states thus fuels expansionist tendencies. Perfect security is impossible, but in building its power the insecure nation makes other nations insecure, so they increase their own powers. It was a profound insight that explains arms races, Soviet behavior, and the Cold War in general.

hegemony Leading or dominating other countries.

Balkans Easternmost Mediterranean peninsula.

satellite Communist country set up by and dependent on Soviet Union.

legitimacy Citizens' feeling that government's rule is rightful.

Central Europe That part of Europe between Germany and Russia.

This split drove China toward the United States. As the Americans withdrew from Vietnam in the early 1970s, Beijing saw the Soviet Union as its biggest threat. Feelers went out, leading to President Nixon's 1972 visit to China, a plus for both sides. The Soviets had to keep a quarter of their army on the long Sino–Soviet border. China did not have to fear the two superpowers ganging up on it, but the Soviets had to worry about a U.S.–China combination. The loss of China shattered the Soviet bloc and contributed to the decline of communism. Nixon must be given credit for perceiving and using the Sino–Soviet split in his balance-of-power diplomacy.

RESTIVE EAST EUROPE

During the Cold War, East Europe was under Soviet **hegemony**. Stalin, Khrushchev, Brezhnev, and even initially Gorbachev swore they would never give up the broad belt from the Baltic through the **Balkans** that served as Russia's defensive shield, even though those **satellites** caused difficulties for Moscow from the beginning. Stalin's takeover of East Europe was the origin of the Cold War, which led to massive military expenditures and bad relations with the West. Stalin initially robbed the East European lands, but his successors had to calm them with sweetheart deals on Soviet raw materials, especially oil. Maintaining the East Europeans—who had higher living standards than Russians—was an expensive subsidy from the Kremlin. Most East Europeans disliked communism and accorded their regimes little **legitimacy**. These governments were always weak and dependent on Moscow.

Yugoslavia slipped out of the Soviet camp in 1948 when Stalin tried to make Tito his puppet. Albania departed in 1961 to pursue an ultraradical Mao-type policy. Every country of **Central Europe** rebelled at least once against communism—Czechoslovakia in 1953 and 1968, East Germany in 1953, Hungary in 1956, and Poland in 1956, 1970, and 1980–1981—and were put down with troops and tanks. Note that they did not start until 1953, because Stalin's death

CONCEPTS ■ HEGEMONY

Hegemony, from the Greek "to lead," means holding sway over other lands. Powerful countries have hegemony over weak neighbors when they can, to some degree, control their foreign and domestic policies. During the Cold War, the Soviet Union was clearly the hegemonic power in East Europe. Some argue that the United States currently exercises hegemony over Central America.

Countries practice hegemony out of fear of becoming vulnerable. Moscow calculated that it needed East Europe as a defensive shield. Washington dislikes hostile powers in the Western hemisphere. Both felt they had to extend their control and influence because, if they did not, someone else would take what they deemed vital areas. The "contingent necessity" argument is almost always a winner: "If we don't take it, someone else will." This geopolitical argument is accepted uncritically and sometimes foolishly. The trouble with hegemony is that the underdog countries detest it. Most Central Europeans hated Soviet hegemony and were unreliable allies. Some West Europeans resented U.S. hegemony. Hegemony wins few long-term friends.

East Europe

fostered the hope that things might soon get better. (Note also that there were no rebellions in the Balkans, which have long religious and historical ties to Russia.) Moscow could never regard Central Europe, Russia's supposed defensive shield, as permanently pacified. By 1989, Soviet President Mikhail Gorbachev concluded that the costs of retaining this empire were too high. He cut East Europe free, effectively ending the Cold War.

KHRUSHCHEV AND THE CUBAN MISSILES

The Cold War peaked in October 1962 when U.S. spy planes showed the Soviets building missile bases in Cuba. Nuclear war was a near thing that originated in 1957 when the Soviet Union stunned the world with the first earth-orbiting satellite, *Sputnik* ("fellow traveler"). America panicked, for it seemed to prove that the Soviets were ahead of us in missile strength. Senator Kennedy used the "missile gap" to help him win the presidency and embarked on a major defense buildup that stressed more and better missiles. Actually, the United States had always been ahead in missile strength, but it took Washington a while to realize this.

The Kremlin viewed the U.S. buildup with alarm. Soviet rockets were few, short-range, and inaccurate, and Soviet generals knew it. Khrushchev devised a quick and cheap fix: put missiles in Cuba. Besides, Castro had asked for protection. Word of the missiles leaked from Cuba, and a U2 camera plane on October 14 confirmed that Soviet missile bases were nearly finished. The president's top advisors huddled nonstop. (For more on U.S. decision making at this time, see pages 52 and 105) Kennedy chose a naval blockade because it stopped short of shooting at Russians and gave them a way out. Decades later, it was learned that the Soviets already had three dozen nuclear warheads in Cuba; if we had invaded, they would have used them, and a nuclear World War III would have started.

As the Soviet ships with oblong crates on their decks steamed toward Cuba, the world held its breath. The ships stopped and turned back, and the Kremlin offered a deal: no Soviet missiles in Cuba if Washington promised not to invade. It was a good face-saving solution, but it hurt the impulsive Khrushchev in Kremlin politics; two years later the Politburo voted him out of office for both foreign and domestic "harebrained schemes."

Who Was When: Soviet Leaders and Their Accomplishments

Party Chief	Ruled	Main Accomplishments
Vladimir I. Lenin	1917–1924	Led Revolution; took Russia out of World War I; beat Whites in Civil War
Josef Stalin	1927–1953	Forced industrialization; made pact with Hitler; beat Germany in World War II; took East Europe; made China ally
Nikita Khrushchev	1955–1964	Crushed Hungarian uprising; gained influence in Egypt; made Cuba an ally; boosted missile strength; alienated Mao's China
Leonid Brezhnev	1964–1982	Gained Soviet clients in Angola, Ethiopia, South Yemen, and Syria; achieved brief détente and then military parity with U.S.; invaded Afghanistan
Yuri Andropov	1982–1984	None—tenure too brief
Konstantin Chernenko	1984–1985	None—tenure too brief
Mikhail Gorbachev	1985–1991	Pulled out of Afghanistan; INF treaty with Reagan; attempted to reform system but only collapsed it

BREZHNEV AND DÉTENTE

President Nixon in the early 1970s took steps to relax tensions with the Soviet Union. The American people and Congress were sick of the Vietnam War; they wanted to end the draft and reduce military spending. Domestic pressures set the scene for Nixon's **détente**.

détente Relaxation of tensions between hostile countries.

republic Main Soviet/Russian civil division, like U.S. state.

Nixon visited Moscow, signed a treaty limiting missiles (SALT I), and encouraged trade with the Soviet Union. It looked like the Cold War would soon be over, but then things went wrong. Starting in 1973, the Watergate scandal paralyzed the Nixon presidency and led to his resignation in 1974. Powerful congressional voices attacked détente. The Soviets seemed to break the rules of détente. They increased missiles and troops in East Europe and picked up new clients in the Third World. They persecuted Jews at home. Many Americans, especially in the right wing of the Republican Party, believed the United States was being deceived. Détente takes two and failed because Moscow was not ready for it.

AFGHANISTAN: A SOVIET VIETNAM

In late 1979 the Kremlin ordered the Soviet military into Afghanistan for largely geopolitical reasons. The Afghan Communist regime that had taken over in a coup in 1978 was threatened with overthrow. If the *mujahedin* (Muslim holy warriors) won, they would spread their creed into the restive Soviet Muslim **republics**. Soviet control of Afghanistan would also put Russia near the strategic Strait of Hormuz, through which passes much of the world's oil.

The costs for the Soviets were high. They kept some 120,000 troops in Afghanistan; perhaps 20,000 Soviets died. Like the United States in Vietnam, there was no end in sight for the Soviets in Afghanistan. The Soviet public was told little about the war, only that it was their "internationalist duty" to defend the Soviet motherland against Afghan bandits backed by the United States.

DIPLOMACY ■ DÉTENTE

French for "relaxation of tensions," in traditional diplomatic usage détente meant that two countries moved a step away from armed hostility. That was all. It did not mean they established a new, peaceful relationship. Nixon used the term in the early 1970s, however, to suggest an era of U.S.–Soviet peace. Overused and oversold, détente became a dirty word by the 1976 presidential campaign, implying giving in to the Russians, and was never used after that.

Historian Gordon Craig and political scientist Alexander George emphasized that the move from hostility to trust takes many steps, all of them reversible. In classic diplomacy, the first step away from armed tension was *détente*. If the process went further, the two countries achieved a *rapprochement*, French for approaching each other to establish reasonable relations. If that worked, they might go on to reach an *entente*, a mutual understanding of who had what turf. And, if that succeeded, one side could offer the other a goodwill token, called in classic diplomacy *appeasement*, a term that became a swear word after Chamberlain tried to appease Hitler in 1938. Eventually, if the two countries saw a mutual advantage, they could even form an *alliance*, a pact to help defend each other.

The seventeenth- and eighteenth-century practitioners of diplomacy understood that these stages could not be rushed or skipped over. The process might stall at any stage or even go back to hostility. Nixon and Kissinger ignored the caution of traditional diplomacy by supposing that a détente was a rapprochement or entente.

inputs The ingredients of economic growth: labor, capital, raw materials, energy.

productivity How efficiently goods are produced—that is, using fewer inputs.

Returning Soviet servicemen told of a dirty war and serious morale and drug problems among the troops; dozens defected.

The Afghan war also cost Moscow friends and influence, especially in the Muslim world. Moscow's détente with the United States crashed. President Jimmy Carter declared he "learned more about the Soviets in one week" than in all previous years. He began a U.S. arms buildup, canceled grain sales to the Soviet Union, and pulled the American team out of the 1980 Moscow Olympics. The harsher international climate increased burdens on the Soviet Union and contributed to the system's collapse a few years later. The year of the Soviet pullout from Afghanistan, 1989, is also the year the Kremlin lost East Europe. With the opening of the Berlin Wall in November 1989, the Cold War was effectively over. The cause: Soviet weakness.

WHY THE SOVIET COLLAPSE?

Marx theorized that capitalism will produce a depression so big and a working class so angry that it will seize power and usher in a new system, socialism. Capitalism was doomed; socialism—meaning here state ownership of the means of production—was sure to come. Marx was right that the economy underpins everything else, but it turns out that socialism is the defective system, not capitalism.

There are two ways to get economic growth. One is by dumping more **inputs** into the system: labor, capital, raw materials, and energy. The second way is to become more efficient, using fewer inputs to produce more outputs. Only the second way yields long-term, sustainable economic growth. The Soviets boosted production but not **productivity**. On the first path, eventually inputs run out.

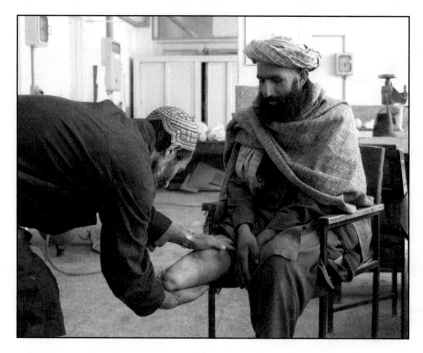

Countless Afghans lost limbs by stepping on land mines dating back to the Soviet Union's war in Afghanistan, from 1979 to 1989. (Ozier Muhammad/*The New York Times*/Redux Pictures)

With the second path, gradual gains in productivity, largely technological, can keep up forever and make the economy more efficient. As a gas company ad says, "The future belongs to the efficient."

Soviet industry turned out lots of poor-quality goods inefficiently because it was technologically backward. In a centrally directed economy, there are few plans, funds, people, or incentives to innovate and become more efficient. Some Soviet economists knew this, and under the brief Khrushchev "thaw" in the early 1960s, they suggested market-type reforms. None were implemented, and, with Khrushchev's ouster in 1964, would-be reformers laid low.

From the 1930s through the 1960s, the Soviet system grew impressively, but by the early 1970s, many of the inputs had reached their limit, and Soviet economic growth slowed, in some years to near zero. At least two Soviet elites grew worried: economists who understood how backward the Soviet system was and some generals who understood that war is increasingly high-tech and that the Soviet Union was falling behind the Americans. These two elites wanted reform and welcomed Mikhail Gorbachev to power in 1985.

glasnost Policy of media openness under Gorbachev.

perestroika Gorbachev's wish to restructure the Soviet economy.

elites The top or most influential people.

mass The bulk of the population with little interest or influence.

GORBACHEV AND COLLAPSE

Mikhail Gorbachev never intended to end the Soviet system, just reform it. But reforming Communist systems is like trying to vaccinate a balloon. Gorbachev inherited a declining Soviet economy that badly needed reform. Gorbachev did institute **glasnost** and **perestroika**, but these just made things worse. Under glasnost, citizens and the press began to complain bitterly. Especially dangerous—and totally unforeseen by Gorbachev—the many nationalities that made up the Soviet Union began to voice their suppressed feelings. Perestroika delivered little; by 1989 food shortages were serious. Constantly battling conservative forces (as had Khrushchev), Gorbachev hesitated for years and never adopted a serious economic reform plan.

CONCEPTS ■ ELITES

Political scientists call the top or most influential people in a political system its **elites**, the people with real political clout. Exactly who is an elite is hard to say, but they are a small fraction of 1 percent of the population. Political elites are not necessarily the richest people. A country may have several elites: top officeholders, business chiefs, generals, and important thinkers. Countries may have specialized elites: a party elite in China or a Muslim theocratic elite in Iran. Much of political life consists of struggles, often out of public sight, among and within elites to control the country's direction. Typically, the **masses** then follow.

Foreign policy is inherently an elite game. Often only a handful of people initiate a new foreign policy.

In the United States, it is the National Security Council with occasional consultation with top members of Congress. In the Soviet Union, it was the Politburo, the dozen or so people at the top of the Communist Party structure. In China, it is the party's nine-member Standing Committee.

Diplomats use a nation's capital as shorthand for the country's foreign-policy elite. They say "Paris" or "Moscow" instead of France or Russia. This is more accurate than saying "the Russians," as 99.99 percent of Russians have no say in foreign policy. Try to avoid "they" in reference to other countries, as it suggests all citizens have one view. Government policy may be hostile, but people in hostile countries are often friendly.

The declining Soviet economy pushed Gorbachev to genuine *détente* (see page 85); he desperately needed Western aid and trade. He first met President Reagan in Geneva in 1985. The two hit it off and built mutual trust. In late 1987, in the White House, they signed the important treaty on intermediate-range nuclear forces (INF) that got rid of a whole class of atomic weapons (see Chapter 14). The one bright spot on Gorbachev's horizon was his relationship with Reagan.

Soviet hegemony over East Europe limited this relationship. Besides, Gorbachev did not like the old-line Brezhnevite leaders who still ran East Europe. In 1988, Gorbachev told them to develop their own glasnost and perestroika. But the East European regimes lacked legitimacy, and as soon as they began to give an inch, their citizens took a mile. In partly free 1989 Polish elections, the Communist regime was trounced, and after a telephone call from Gorbachev, the Polish Communists stood aside for a Catholic prime minister. In the summer of 1989, Hungary opened its border with Austria, letting thousands of East Germans slip out to West Germany. Czechoslovakia did the same. Protests broke out in East Germany. The regime gave the order to fire on the protesters; instead, liberal Communists took over and opened the Berlin Wall in November, marking the end of the Cold War.

Gorbachev never had a sound vision of the future; he thought he could reform communism. By now a second or third elite generation, much better educated and exposed to new critical ideas, knew the system was defective. The party split between conservatives and liberals, with the liberals gaining political influence. Gorbachev at first sided with them and initiated decentralization, but halfway economic reforms undermined the system. The new market sector bumped into the state sector, creating economic breakdowns and inflation.

Gorbachev reversed himself on reforms almost annually. By 1990, Russians were fed up with him. Meanwhile, some liberal party members quit and won elections as non-Communists. In 1991, Boris Yeltsin won the presidency of Russia, by far the largest republic of the Soviet Union, in the first free election in the thousand years of Russia's history. This gave Yeltsin a legitimacy that Gorbachev lacked, for Gorbachev had never been popularly elected to anything. During the attempted coup of August 1991—carried out by Gorbachev's handpicked cabinet—Yeltsin stood firm, citizens rallied to him, the military split, and the coup plotters lost their nerve.

At the end of 1991, Gorbachev was out and the Soviet Union ceased to exist, replaced by 15 independent republics, 12 of them associated in an undefined "Commonwealth of Independent States." The red banner over the Kremlin turrets was replaced by the old Russian flag of white, blue, and red stripes. In less than three-quarters of a century, the Soviet Union was born under Lenin, grew to brutal Stalinist maturity, slowly declined under Brezhnev, and died during an attempt at rejuvenation by Gorbachev.

FOREIGN POLICY: GENERATED INTERNALLY OR EXTERNALLY?

Are foreign policies made on the basis of internal politics, needs, and demands, or as reactions to threats and opportunities from abroad? In other words, is foreign policy mostly generated internally or externally? The Soviet Union provides material for both theories.

One school of analysis saw Soviet foreign policy as the product of domestic pressures, such as elite jockeying for political power or the need for top leaders to show their people progress. If they could not deliver higher living standards, they could give Soviets the feeling of belonging to a mighty and growing empire. Some claim Soviet foreign policy was driven by ideology. Marx and Lenin foresaw the collapse of capitalism, and the Kremlin felt it must help this process along. Such approaches see Soviet foreign policy as mostly internally generated.

> **imperial overstretch**   Theory that powerful nations tend to overexpand and weaken.

Another school emphasized that the Soviet Union lived in a hostile world and was constantly reacting to events and opportunities. When it felt threatened, it built military strength. If a Kremlin client was attacked, Moscow must rescue it. If a small country turned Communist, the Soviet Union must protect it. In this view, the Kremlin's foreign policies were largely externally generated.

Internal and external factors are difficult to untangle. Why, for example, did the Soviets invade Afghanistan? Was it an ideological commitment to communism (an internal factor)? Or was it the threat posed by a hostile Afghanistan on the Soviet border (an external factor)? And what caused Gorbachev to reduce tensions with the United States? Was it Reagan's military buildup and firm positions on arms control (external factors)? Or was it the economic weakness and growing discontent inside the Soviet Union (internal factors)? Three theories of the demise of the Soviet Union illustrate the internal–external question:

1. **Imperial Overstretch.** Yale historian Paul Kennedy argued in his 1987 *Rise and Decline of the Great Powers* that major powers tend to expand until they over-expand. Imperial expenses and slower economic growth then drain them into decline. The Habsburg, British, and Soviet empires are good examples. Spending perhaps 25 percent of GDP on defense and subsidizing satellite and client states was too much for the Soviet economy, forcing Gorbachev to become flexible on arms control, Afghanistan, East Europe, and domestic economic reforms. This analysis fits into the "externally generated" school.

2. *Defective System.* Another approach, focusing on "internally generated," argues that the Soviet economic and political system was inherently defective. Communism does not work

GEOGRAPHY ■ THE SOVIET SUCCESSOR STATES

Where there used to be one Soviet Union, there are now 15 independent states, many of them still dominated by Moscow. They can be grouped into three groups of three, plus a large Central Asian group of five (the five *stans*, meaning "place of"), plus one Romanian-speaking republic.

Soviet Successor States

Slavic Republics	Russian Federation, Ukraine (no "the"), Belarus (formerly Belorussia)
Baltic Republics	Lithuania,[a] Latvia,[a] Estonia[a]
Caucasian Republics	Georgia, Armenia, Azerbaijan[b]
Central Asian Republics	Turkmenistan,[b] Kazakhstan,[b] Kyrgyzstan,[b] Uzbekistan,[b] Tajikistan[b]
Romanian-Speaking Republic	Moldova (formerly Moldavia)

[a] The Baltic states are not in the Commonwealth of Independent States
[b] Predominantly Muslim countries

privatization The selling of state-owned assets to private interests.

kleptocracy Rule by thieves.

very well; over time it runs down. At first the command economy rapidly builds a heavy-industry base, but then central planning hinders a more advanced and complex economy. People now need material incentives. The Communist Party monopolizes politics and ignores mass discontent until it boils over.

3. *Bungled Reform.* A third approach starts with what happens when Soviet elites admit that the economy really is running down. They urge reforms, but halfway reforms just make things worse. The conservative party structure stalls and sabotages reforms. The reformers seek a "middle way" between communism and capitalism, but there is none. Conflicts among the Soviet nationalities come out with unexpected viciousness. Under these circumstances, almost any reform efforts will appear bungled. In trying to fix the system, they broke it.

RESTORING RUSSIAN POWER

Capitalism in Russia did not work the way it was supposed to. **Privatization** sold state industries ultracheap to insiders who became billionaires. The system was called, half in jest, a **kleptocracy**. The Russian economy depends on exporting oil, natural gas, and other raw materials. Health standards and medical care, never very good, plummeted. Russians have few children but a high death rate. The average Russian male lives to only 60. Russia's population, now down to 138 million, declines by two-thirds of a million a year.

Russia became a *weak state* (see page 115), one in which lawlessness and corruption flourish. Democracy was tried but vanished. Wealth and power are in the hands of a few. Members of parliament, journalists, bankers, businesspeople, and ordinary citizens are routinely gunned down by *keelers*, who are rarely caught, suggesting the police are in on the deal. Said one Russian: "The only lawyer around here is a Kalashnikov."

Russians have also lost national pride. Their mighty empire, one that stood up to the Americans, first lost East Europe and then the historic Russia built by the tsars. Now it is fragmented into countries that had no names until Stalin invented them. One Russian cartoon showed Peter

DIPLOMACY ■ GEORGE F. KENNAN ON RUSSIA AND THE WEST

Diplomat-turned-historian George F. Kennan (see Chapter 3) taught America about Russia. But he also changed his mind about Russia. The deeply conservative Kennan authored the 1947 "containment" doctrine with his famous "X" article, which laid down a tough anti-Communist line that he later regretted.

In his early writings, Kennan called the Communists "snake-like" in their hostility to the West. Once out of the foreign service, Kennan reflected on the Cold War. In his magisterial *Russia and the West Under Lenin and Stalin* (1962), he began to see the rivalry more evenhandedly and even to assign some of the blame to America for ignorance and inconsistency. One of his longstanding themes is that the United States tends to conduct a "legalistic–moralistic" foreign policy instead of a realistic one. Hans Morgenthau (see page 24) argued along similar *realist* lines (see Chapter 2).

Kennan also deplored the excessive militarization of U.S. policy; he had in mind greater emphasis on diplomatic and economic forms of containment. How long would containment take? In his 1947 "X" article, Kennan suggested that, in 10 to 15 years, we would see some cracks in the Soviet edifice. He was right. In 1956, Khrushchev's de-Stalinization speech started splitting the Communist world. In 1960, China departed from the Soviet camp. In Kennan's vision, patience is more important than weapons.

the Great spanking Yeltsin for giving away the Russian empire. Putin called the Soviet breakup "the greatest geopolitical catastrophe of the twentieth century."

Russians turned, as they have historically, to strong-handed leadership. A **KGB** officer, Vladimir Putin, came from obscurity to be first appointed prime minister, then acting president, and then in 2000 elected president. After his two terms, in 2008 Putin handpicked a protégé, Dmitri Medvedev, to be a weak president while Putin made himself a strong prime minister and continued to run things. Putin, who had been head of the Russian intelligence service, the FSB, has files on who has stolen what and uses them to obtain compliance. Putin's takeover amounted to a quiet KGB coup. Most of his hand-picked **siloviki** are former KGB.

Putin still rules, but as an authoritarian, not a Stalin. He crushed the rebellious Chechens. Critical journalists were silenced, some permanently. The energy industry and main news media returned to state control. Putin faces essentially no media criticism or political rivals. Putin broke new-rich "oligarchs" and put their properties back under state control. He increased his own power and got an obedient majority in the Duma. He reined in Russia's 89 disobedient republics by carving Russia into seven big districts and naming the super-governor of each.

What does this mean for Russia's foreign policy? Already under Yeltsin there was a nationalistic hardening, one that Putin expanded. Foreign nongovernmental organizations are barred from Russia. Putin did not like them pushing for democracy or reporting misdeeds. Many Russians, including top leaders, view America as domineering and arrogant. They think we brought down the Soviet Union and then Russia (by bad economic advice). They sided with Serbia and supported its claim to Kosovo. The Kremlin sees NATO's eastward expansion and U.S. military technology as threats. Like most Europeans, Putin opposed the 2003 Iraq War. He rarely pursues policies directly hostile to America; he knows Russia is too weak. The Russian army has shrunk to fewer than 1 million and is badly fed and trained. Putin's goal is that of a KGB officer: restore Russian power. To do this, he plays the cards he has:

1. Use oil and natural-gas exports to regain influence. Where pipelines run, power follows. Russia sometimes cuts gas to Ukraine and out to Europe, warnings to energy-dependent Europe. Moscow will not recover its East European satellites, all of them now in NATO, but it can induce caution and respect in them.

2. Restore Russian pride by nationalistic moves and symbols, showing Russians and the world that they are still major players and must be respected. Putin and Medvedev travel and receive foreign leaders to emphasize Moscow's importance. Visiting is a cheap way to boost prestige and importance.

3. Keep Russia together. No region departs the Russian Federation. Any that try, like Chechnya, are crushed. Putin recentralized power in the Kremlin.

4. Control what it calls its "zone of privileged interests" of former Soviet republics. Belarus has all but re-merged into the Russian Federation. The landlocked Central Asian republics have little choice but to stay close to Moscow. In 2008, Russia "protected" South Ossetia by invading it and breaking it away from Georgia. This also puts Russian forces very near major international oil and natural gas pipelines. (See page 363 for more on "pipeline politics.")

5. Keep Ukraine and Georgia from joining NATO. Russia partially dismembered Georgia by backing its breakaway Abkhazia and South Ossetia regions. In Ukraine, Moscow supports pro-Russian parties, and Kiev now tilts toward Moscow.

6. Cooperate with the European Union but do not join it or let it take the lead. Rather, use the EU as an occasional counterweight to "U.S. hegemony."

KGB Soviet intelligence and security police.

siloviki Russian for strong men.

7. Cultivate ties with China to offset U.S. power. Hint at a Sino–Russian alliance to scare Washington. Russia sells China oil, raw materials, and weapons and buys Chinese consumer goods. Russia and China conduct joint military maneuvers to show they will not be pushed around by the United States. In the long run, however, a weak Russia may not wish to be merely a raw-materials provider to a strong China.

8. Get along with the United States but little more. Washington, busy elsewhere, pays little attention to Russia, something that does not bother Putin.

Russia's foreign policy shows continuity with Soviet and even tsarist policies, because geography determines much of national interest. If Russia pursues its interests by economic means and without threats or force, we should not worry. That would be normal IR. But Russia's power to disrupt—through arms sales, export of military technology, and cutting oil and natural gas shipments—is still dangerous.

We were naïve in assuming that Russia would quickly become democratic and capitalistic. Since the collapse of the ruble in 1998, Russia has shown economic growth but is too dependent on oil exports. Russia has low labor costs, fabulous natural resources, and resourceful people. Russia could become democratic and friendly, but not likely soon.

mypoliscikit EXERCISES

Apply what you learned in this chapter on MyPoliSciKit (www.mypoliscikit.com).

Assessment Review this chapter using learning objectives, chapter summaries, practice tests, and more.

Menu

Flashcards Learn the key terms in this chapter; you can test yourself by term or definition.

Flashcards

Video Analyze recent world affairs by watching streaming video from major news providers.

Videos

Simulations Play the role of an IR decision-maker and experience how IR concepts work in practice.

Comparative
Exercises

KEY TERMS

appeasement (p. 78)

Balkans (p. 82)

Brest-Litovsk (p. 76)

Central Europe (p. 82)

Cold War (p. 80)

Comintern (p. 77)

détente (p. 85)

elites (p. 87)

Five-Year Plans (p. 77)

geopolitics (p. 74)

glasnost (p. 87)

hegemony (p. 82)

ideology (p. 76)

imperial overstretch (p. 89)

inputs (p. 86)

KGB (p. 91)

kleptocracy (p. 90)

Lebensraum (p. 74)

legitimacy (p. 82)

mass (p. 87)

mobilization (p. 76)

Mongols (p. 74)

nonaggression pact (p. 78)

paranoid (p. 77)

perestroika (p. 87)

pragmatism (p. 78)

privatization (p. 90)

FURTHER REFERENCE

Asmus, Ronald D. *A Little War that Shook the World: Georgia, Russia, and the Future of the West*. New York: Palgrave, 2010.

Brown, Archie. *The Rise and Fall of Communism*. New York: HarperCollins, 2009.

Bugajski, Janusz. *Cold Peace: Russia's New Imperialism*. Westport, CT: Praeger, 2004.

Dallas, Gregor. *1945: The War That Never Ended*. New Haven, CT: Yale University Press, 2006.

Engerman, David C. *Know Your Enemy: The Rise and Fall of America's Soviet Experts*. New York: Oxford University Press, 2009.

Fursenko, Aleksandr, and Timothy Naftali. *Khrushchev's Cold War: The Inside Story of an American Adversary*. New York: Norton, 2006.

Goldman, Marshall I. *Petrostate: Putin, Power, and the New Russia*. New York: Oxford University Press, 2008.

Harbutt, Frasier J. *Yalta 1945: Europe and America at the Crossroads*. New York: Cambridge University Press, 2009.

Kotkin, Stephen, and Jan T. Gross. *Uncivil Society: 1989 and the Implosion of the Communist Establishment*. New York: Random House, 2009.

Laruelle, Marlène. *In the Name of the Nation: Nationalism and Politics in Contemporary Russia*. New York: Palgrave, 2009.

Leffler, Melvyn P., and Arne Westad, eds. *The Cambridge History of the Cold War*, 3 vols. New York: Cambridge University Press, 2009.

Mankoff, Jeffrey. *Russian Foreign Policy: The Return of Great Power Politics*. Lanham, MD: Rowman & Littlefield, 2009.

Munton, Don, and David A. Welch. *The Cuban Missile Crisis: A Concise History*. New York: Oxford University Press, 2007.

Plokhy, S. M. *Yalta: The Price of Peace*. New York: Penguin, 2010.

Priestland, David. *The Red Flag: A History of Communism*. New York: Grove, 2009.

Sebestyen, Victor. *Revolution 1989: The Fall of the Soviet Empire*. New York: Pantheon, 2009.

Sempa, Francis P. *Geopolitics: From the Cold War to the 21st Century*. Somerset, NJ: Transaction, 2002.

Shevtsova, Lila. *Lonely Superpower: Russia's Uneasy Relationship with the West*. Washington, DC: Carnegie Endowment, 2010.

Tsygankov, Andrei P. *Russia's Foreign Policy: Change and Continuity in National Identity*, 2nd ed. Lanham, MD: Rowman & Littlefield, 2010.

Wegren, Stephen K., and Dale R. Herspring, eds. *After Putin's Russia: Past Imperfect, Future Uncertain*, 4th ed. Lanham, MD: Rowman & Littlefield, 2009.

CHAPTER 6

Can the United States Lead the World?

U.S. President Obama meets Afghan President Hamid Karzai in 2010. The Karzai government was widely seen as corrupt, and Americans by then were tired of the war. (Jim Watson/Getty Images)

The short answer to this chapter's title question is no. At this time, the United States is unable to lead the world for four main reasons:

1. The United States has not yet figured out the world system (see Chapter 1) we operate in. The guidelines we used during the Cold War no longer work.
2. America is no longer in charge of the world economy. Economic power is shifting to Asia. Debt places doubts on the dollar's value.
3. Domestic constraints—economic, military, congressional, and public opinion—close off many paths. Money and troops for overseas interventions are stretched thin. Americans tired of Iraq and Afghanistan; they did not like being stuck in someone else's civil wars.
4. The biggest obstacle is that few allies are now willing to follow American leadership. Even traditional friends such as Britain say no to U.S requests for more troops. In world opinion surveys, many voice negative views of U. S. **foreign policies**.

World power relationships constantly change, though, and no one can predict how long the above points will be true. Let us consider the long-term tendency for U.S. foreign policy to alternate between **interventionism** and noninterventionism.

QUESTIONS TO CONSIDER

1. How did the Iraq and Afghan wars affect U.S. foreign policy?
2. Is the opposite of interventionism *isolationism*?
3. Is U.S. foreign policy cyclical? Caused by what?
4. How were the doctrines of postwar presidents similar?
5. What is the elite–mass split on U.S. foreign policy?
6. Should U.S. foreign policy be based on ideals or self-interest?
7. How important are bureaucracies in forming foreign policies?
8. Is the United States well structured for foreign policy?
9. How does unilateralism turn into isolationism?
10. What was Obama's dilemma on Afghanistan?

ALTERNATION IN U.S. FOREIGN POLICY

For some years after Vietnam, the United States shied away from another war. Washington pursued a risk-averse strategy. Even tough-talking President Ronald Reagan intervened only cautiously. When U.S. Marines on a peacekeeping mission in Beirut were blown up in 1983, he pulled them all out. The 1983 U.S. invasion of tiny Grenada had little risk.

By 1991, however, America had largely forgotten the pain of Vietnam, enabling President George H. W. Bush to boot Iraq out of Kuwait. Americans were proud of the swift victory that seemed to show the United States as the world's natural leader. The collapse of the Soviet bloc in 1989 and end of the Soviet Union itself in 1991 (see Chapter 5) gave America a sense of triumph: We had won the Cold War. By 9/11, Americans were ready for a new round of interventionism and followed President George W. Bush into Afghanistan and Iraq.

The long Afghan and Iraq wars (see Chapter 9) drained some of Americans' self-confidence. Are we still ready to intervene, or has the pendulum swung back to caution? Forty years apart,

foreign policy   The way a government deals with the outside world.

interventionism   U.S. willingness to use military force overseas.

noninterventionism   The unwillingness to use military force overseas.

the impact of the two Persian Gulf wars on U.S. foreign policy was somewhat like what Vietnam had been. The three wars started with much domestic support—about 70 percent—but fell to half that. Soon most Americans thought Iraq had been a mistake; after ten years they felt the same about Afghanistan. Economic difficulties, a declining dollar, an overstretched military, and lack of allies made Americans skeptical about other interventions.

From roughly Pearl Harbor in 1941 to Vietnam in the late 1960s, the United States practiced an interventionist foreign policy. At its high point in the 1960s, U.S. commitments nearly covered the globe to encircle what was then called the "Sino–Soviet bloc." Everything was our business, and we sent troops to dozens of countries. Mostly we were successful or, at any rate, not conspicuously unsuccessful. U.S. foreign aid and troops staved off Soviet expansion into West Europe. U.S. forces pushed back a Communist attack in Korea. CIA-sponsored coups ousted undesirable governments in Iran and Guatemala. We acted like the world's police force.

Vietnam, however, was one intervention too many. U.S. foreign policy shifted in a **noninterventionist** direction during Vietnam and was slow and reluctant to return to the sweeping interventionism of pre-Vietnam years. Then, in 1989, Soviet power collapsed; there was no more enemy. Many Americans wondered what we were doing overseas: The Cold War is over and we won, so let's go home. Even members of Congress who had been hawks during the Cold War turned noninterventionist. Strange coalitions of protesters—unionists, environmentalists, leftists, Christians, anarchists—tried to disrupt international meetings and prevent U.S. trade normalization with China. They claimed America's involvement with the outside world was wrong and harmful.

U.S. foreign policy seems to alternate between interventionism and noninterventionism at roughly generational intervals. Americans reacted to World War I by slouching into isolationism and swearing that we would never get involved in helping the ungrateful Europeans again. With German and Japanese expansionism, however, isolation was impossible, as Pearl Harbor demonstrated. The generation that fought World War II became imbued with a globalism that was more or less the opposite of the interwar isolationism. Now everything overseas mattered. We intervened more and more until we eventually got burned in Vietnam. Coming out of Vietnam,

CONCEPTS ■ INTERVENTIONISM

The great French foreign minister Talleyrand (see Chapter 19), when questioned about a policy of noninterventionism, replied: "Ah, yes, noninterventionism. A metaphysical and political term meaning approximately the same as interventionism." The cynical Talleyrand indicated that not interfering in the affairs of another country can have as great an impact as interfering.

Intervention means projecting your power into another country to make, maintain, or unmake foreign governments. As applied to U.S. foreign policy in this chapter, interventionism is a policy of using U.S. armed power overseas. When the United States sends its troops to other lands, it is pursuing an interventionist foreign policy. CIA sponsorship of a coup or insurrection is interventionism, too, but less public. When, on the other hand, Washington is unwilling to send troops or spooks (CIA operatives), it is pursuing a noninterventionist policy. There can be in-between positions; the willingness to use some forces overseas in certain circumstances might be called a moderate interventionist policy.

most wished to never get involved in anything like that again. A similar mood appeared after the 2003 Iraq War.

rally event   Dramatic incident that temporarily boosts public support.

volatile   Rises and falls quickly.

ARE AMERICANS BASICALLY ISOLATIONISTS?

Political scientist Gabriel Almond (1911–2002) observed in 1950 that "an overtly interventionist and 'responsible' United States hides a covertly isolationist longing." By the 1990s, this longing was no longer covert; leading figures of both parties opposed interventionist policies. Domestic concerns dominated politics. Allies were increasingly seen as uncooperative and unfair trade competitors. A "**rally event**" such as 9/11 can jolt public opinion into support for dramatic action, but it never lasts. Americans after 9/11 were angry and interventionist but soon wished to get out of Iraq. Political scientist John Mueller found similar patterns of declining public support for the Korean, Vietnam, and Iraq wars. After three years of U.S. casualties with no clear end, public opinion was negative on all three wars.

Public opinion on overseas activity is **volatile** and unstable, supporting a cause one year and abandoning it a few years later. In the abstract, Americans often say they support U.S. leadership in the world. In a specific situation, however, as a war lasts years and costs many soldiers and billions of dollars, Americans tire of a leadership role. In December 2009, half of Americans in a Pew poll agreed that the United States should "mind its own business internationally and let other countries get along the best they can on their own." Seven years earlier, only 30 percent had agreed with that statement.

Opinion often seems contradictory. Americans were pleased with the first President Bush's overseas successes, even as they criticized him for spending too much time on foreign policy instead of on domestic U.S. problems. The success of the quick 1991 Gulf War shot his popularity up to record levels, but within a year opinion turned negative over a brief economic recession, and he lost reelection. The U.S. public is often divided and hesitant. Before U.S. peacekeeping forces were sent to Haiti in 1994, opinion was split about whether to intervene or stay out. Americans were not eager to rush into that complex situation and were relieved when we took over quickly and easily.

There is also an *elite* versus *mass* (see page 87) split on foreign affairs. Better-educated, attentive Americans in leadership positions think that world events are important; almost all support a U.S. world leadership role. The mass public, on the other hand, generally pays little attention to overseas problems except when aroused by an attack. With little enthusiasm or understanding, they show "apathetic internationalism." A 1997 Pew Research Center survey found that 63 percent favored expansion of NATO, but only 10 percent could name even one of the three nations that were about to join (Poland, the Czech Republic, and Hungary). Elite views—through the media,

CLASSIC THOUGHT ■ SPYKMAN ON INTERVENTION

Nicholas Spykman (1893–1943), educated in the Dutch institute for colonial administration, brought with him to Yale a *geopolitical* perspective (see page 74) on world affairs. Spykman (pronounced SPEAKman) posed the classic question of U.S. foreign and defense policy in 1942: "Shall we protect our interests by defense on this side of the water or by active participation in the lands across the oceans?" In other words, to intervene or not to intervene? The answer for Spykman, one of the founders of U.S. realism, writing only days after Pearl Harbor was clear: Intervene before it is too late. The answer for our day is not so clear.

| behavioralism | Studying humans by empirical evidence, often quantified. |

education, and the pulpit—tend to gradually trickle down and become generally accepted. Criticism of wars, for example, generally starts among elites.

THE CONTINUITY PRINCIPLE

Once a basic policy has been established, it tends to endure. Presidential candidates of one party often denounce the foreign policies of incumbents of the other party. Once in office, however, the new president generally follows these policies and sometimes takes them further. Candidate Bush 43 criticized President Bill Clinton's policy of keeping U.S. troops in Kosovo; after six months in office, Bush called them "essential." He also criticized Clinton's "nation-building," but after he became president did much more of it than Clinton. Candidate Obama criticized Bush's policy of isolating Iran, but in office pushed for and got even tougher sanctions on Iran. There is more continuity than change from one administration to the next.

The continuity principle means that policies commonly associated with one president were often initiated by his predecessor. The Eisenhower doctrine of massive nuclear retaliation was implicit in Truman's actions; Eisenhower just made it explicit. Nixon's withdrawal of U.S. forces from Vietnam actually began under Johnson. Reagan's massive defense buildup actually began under Carter. Clinton's defense cutbacks actually began under Bush 41. Many trends begin earlier than is commonly thought.

CONCEPTS ■ A CYCLICAL THEORY OF U.S. FOREIGN POLICY

A **behavioral** political scientist, Frank L. Klingberg, accurately predicted in a 1952 article that the U.S. interventionism then current would end in the late 1960s. A social scientist who can predict anything deserves respect. Klingberg quantified such indicators as naval expenditures, annexations, armed expeditions, diplomatic pressures, and mention of foreign matters in presidential speeches and party platforms to discover alternating moods of "introversion" (mostly staying home) and "extroversion" (expanding U.S. power and influence outside its borders).

Klingberg's table shows that introvert periods lasted an average of 21 years, extrovert periods 27. If you add 27 to 1940, when the United States entered an extrovert phase, you get 1967, the very time that the United States tired of Vietnam and overseas involvement in general. Klingberg, of course, did not know when he wrote that Vietnam would become a major U.S. war or political issue. He merely suggested that, based on past performance, we could expect extroversion to end in the late 1960s. We can take it a few steps further. Adding 21 years (average length of introvert phase) to 1967, we get 1988. Bush 41 invaded Panama in 1989 and kicked Iraq out of Kuwait in 1991. Had we returned to extroversion? Next, adding 27 years to 1991 gets you to 2008. Did Iraq and Afghanistan lead to the end of an extrovert phase? Klingberg's theory is fascinating, but do not reify it. A higher power does not play numbers games with U.S. foreign policy. Much depends on what you count as use of force overseas.

Introversion	Extroversion
1776–1798	1798–1824
1824–1844	1884–1871
1871–1891	1891–1919
1919–1940	1940–

To be sure, there are sometimes shifts from one administration to another. Kennedy found Eisenhower's defense budget and strategy entirely unsatisfactory. He won election in 1960 in part by denouncing Ike's caution and then redid the Defense Department with major new funding. Kennedy shifted U.S. attention from Europe to the developing areas of Asia, Africa, and Latin America. Vietnam was an example of JFK's interventionism.

Why was there considerable continuity? Most obviously, the Cold War posed the same basic challenge to all presidents from Truman through Reagan; the Soviet threat could not be ignored. Next, campaign rhetoric is one thing, reality quite another. It is easy for a challenger to denounce an incumbent for not doing enough, ignoring problem areas, or failing to develop new technology. Once in the White House, though, the new president discovers that things are not so simple. President Obama pulled U.S. forces out of Iraq and Afghanistan only slowly, as a sudden withdrawal could produce even worse chaos that might envelope the whole region. What a candidate wants to do may win votes, but reality often refuses to cooperate after the election. New presidents are trapped by the policies of their predecessors.

A limiting factor is the U.S. federal budget **deficit**, which tops $1 trillion a year, much of it related to the costs of the Iraq and Afghanistan wars and the 2008 financial meltdown. The United States spends some $700 billion a year (5 percent of its GDP) on defense, roughly half of the world's defense spending. In 2010 the Pentagon made clear that military spending will have to be tightened up. **Entitlements** dominate the budget, and politicians fear voter anger

deficit   A federal budget that spends more than it takes in.

entitlements   Required federal expenditures, such as Social Security and Medicare, to large classes of U.S. citizens.

idealism   Basing foreign policy on moral, ethical, legal, or world-order principles.

self-interest   Basing foreign policy on national interest.

REFLECTIONS ■ IDEALS OR SELF-INTEREST?

Young people often wonder what they should base their foreign-policy views on, **idealism** or **self-interest**. Many learn from school and religious training a moralistic tradition that leads to idealism, aiming for the good of the world. Some are then exposed in college to the notion that foreign policy should be based on the "national interest"—looking out for the good of one's country (see Chapter 2 for the contrast between realism and liberal idealism).

Which approach is right? Either can turn into mistakes. An idealistic policy of sending "peacekeeping" forces to feed the starving in Somalia can lead to armed clashes and an ignoble retreat. The good intentions of this policy were no substitute for a hard-edged analysis of Somali politics. But a national-interest approach can be so narrow that it misses dangers that are brewing. Thinking only of self-interest, we might ignore a regime of Muslim fanatics that is distant and none of our concern. That

is the way we treated Afghanistan from 1989 to 2001. But Afghanistan sheltered terrorists who bombed U.S. ships and embassies and crashed jetliners into the World Trade Center. We should have paid more attention to Afghanistan earlier.

Idealism and self-interest are not always at odds. Sometimes the smartest thing to do is to help others, who in turn become trading partners and customers. U.S. Marshall Plan aid for Europe after World War II paid off many times over in prosperity on both sides of the Atlantic. Beware analyses that are either too idealistic or too self-interested. Are the policies feasible? What are their long-term consequences likely to be? Beware also policies that are idealistic but difficult to follow up in practice. A policy needs a certain amount of idealism, but to be accepted it must also be presented as promising a payoff. We must construct policies that merge idealism and self-interest.

constraint A limit on decision-making.

at cutting Social Security or Medicare or raising taxes. Deficits—which automatically turn into national debt at the end of the fiscal year—are made up by massive borrowing from abroad. Asked Harvard economist Larry Summers: "How long can the world's biggest borrower remain the world's biggest power?"

Presidents face numerous **constraints**; they are not free to do everything they originally thought they could. Resuming military conscription, for example, would require a major crisis and act of Congress. Americans have never liked the draft; young men during Vietnam especially disliked it. Nixon defused student anger in 1973 by ending the draft and going to the all-volunteer army (AVA), the case ever since. The AVA is highly trained and effective but relatively small. From a high of 3.5 million active-duty military personnel in 1968 (the Vietnam peak), total U.S. troops in all services fell to 1.4 million in the 1990s and is now up to only 1.5 million. As Iraq and Afghanistan dragged on, it became difficult to recruit and retain enough qualified soldiers. Some recruits had not finished high school or had criminal records; they were harder to train and discipline.

DIPLOMACY ■ PRESIDENTS AND THEIR "DOCTRINES"

During the Cold War, U.S. presidents articulated policies that journalists quickly dubbed their "doctrines." The policies were seldom that simple, and calling them doctrines tends to make them sound more clear-cut than they were. Nonetheless, they are convenient handles to help us remember who stood for what.

Notice that all these doctrines are just variations on the first, the Truman Doctrine, sometimes called the "containment" policy, from diplomat George Kennan's 1947 article (see Chapter 3). The overall goal of U.S. foreign policy did not change much: Stop communism. Only the intensity and costs changed.

President	Years	Doctrine
Truman	1945–1953	Contain the expansion of communism, presumably everywhere.
Eisenhower	1953–1961	Use nukes and spooks to prevent communist or other radical takeovers.
Kennedy	1961–1963	Respond flexibly to communist expansion, especially to guerrilla warfare.
Johnson	1963–1969	Follow through on Kennedy Doctrine by committing U.S. troops in Vietnam.
Nixon	1969–1974	Supply weapons but not troops to countries fighting off communism.
Ford	1974–1977	Continue Nixon Doctrine.
Carter	1977–1981	Make clear to Soviets that Persian Gulf is a vital U.S. interest.
Reagan	1981–1989	Sponsor anticommunist guerrillas who are trying to overthrow pro-Soviet regimes.

Today, the U.S. military is overstretched. Much of the Army's and Marine Corps's active-duty combat forces are overseas. Some soldiers—even reservists—were deployed three and four times in Iraq and/or Afghanistan. Few are available for new missions. Service abroad is hard on marriages and families. Spirited U.S. forces quickly crushed the Iraqi and Afghan regimes but then had to keep order in hostile environments. Many said their job was done and wanted to return home. The Army's top general, Eric Shinseki, now retired, warned of pursuing a "twelve-division strategy with a ten-division army."

dove   Favors peace, a noninterventionist.

Pentagon   Defense Department main building.

Joint Chiefs of Staff   Committee of top generals and admirals.

War Powers Act   The 1973 congressional time limit on president's use of troops in hostilities.

Some critics speak of the "military mind" and assume that generals are eager for war. This is far from the case; often the biggest **doves** in an administration are the **Pentagon** chiefs. It is their people, after all, who get killed. Top U.S. generals often caution and restrain presidents about deploying overseas. They know they are overstretched and how rapidly public and congressional opinion can change when casualties mount. Ignoring the warnings of the **Joint Chiefs of Staff** about Iraq, President George W. Bush and Defense Secretary Donald Rumsfeld earned the anger and resignations of several top officers.

A CONTRARY CONGRESS

The precise role of Congress in foreign affairs has never been defined. Rather, it has changed over the years, mostly declining. A nagging ambiguity came with the Constitution, which says Congress declares war but also says the president is commander in chief. Which power overrides? Must the president wait until Congress passes a declaration of war before using troops overseas? The problem had come up before, but with Vietnam it surfaced with a vengeance.

As we discussed in Chapter 4, that war was never formally declared. Instead, President Johnson used a joint resolution of Congress that empowered him to stop Communist aggression. The senators and congresspersons did not fully understand that passing (nearly unanimously) the 1964 Tonkin Gulf Resolution gave the president a blank check. Even after it was repealed, Nixon argued that the president's power as commander in chief allowed him to conduct the war and even expand it into Cambodia. Rage grew in Congress because they were essentially helpless spectators to a president's war-making whims. To try to remedy this imbalance, in 1973 Congress passed (over President Nixon's veto) the **War Powers Act**, giving the president only 90 days to use troops overseas without congressional approval.

No president, Republican or Democrat, has liked the War Powers Act. They claim it usurps their prerogative as commander in chief, and they have easily circumvented it. The president simply doesn't report to Congress that he has sent troops into "hostilities or situations where hostilities are imminent." In 1982, when President Reagan sent U.S. Marines into Beirut, he carefully noted that they were "peacekeeping" forces and thus not involved in hostilities. Congress allowed him 18 months to use the Marines for peacekeeping, even though the situation was dangerous. Congress ignored its own War Powers Act. Then in October 1983 a suicide truck bomber killed 241 sleeping Marines in their barracks, and the president ordered all troops withdrawn. At no time, however, did he admit they were in hostilities.

Several times in recent decades U.S. forces have clearly been in hostilities, but the White House never reported it as such, so the War Powers clock never started ticking. And there is

alarmism   Exaggerating dangers to
promote a policy.

nothing in the act that forces a president to report hostilities. The White House's reply will always be, "Hostilities? What hostilities?" The War Powers Act was defective, unenforceable, and probably unconstitutional (under the 1983 *Chadha* decision outlawing legislative vetoes).

In 1990, after Iraq invaded Kuwait, Bush 41 quickly sent U.S. forces to defend Saudi Arabia. He did not ask Congress for authority to do this and said the troops' mission was "wholly defensive." In January 1991, as the troop buildup peaked, Bush got from Congress a joint resolution authorizing the use of force to fulfill UN resolutions, which the United States had sponsored. Five days later, war began. Bush concealed his aims, but it is now clear that he aimed for war from the beginning. Congress went along after the plans were made and the troops deployed.

After 9/11, Bush 43 claimed broad powers and, in a highly emotional atmosphere, got congressional support (but not a declaration of war) to invade both Afghanistan and Iraq. He also asserted presidential powers inherent during an emergency to detain suspects worldwide and wiretap phone calls. Critics feared the president's claim to nearly unlimited powers warps the Constitution, and the Supreme Court agreed in some cases. Congress, however, far from checking the president in such situations, generally follows him and votes for the war funds he requests.

The Founding Fathers did not have this in mind. They gave the power to declare war only to Congress. Gradually, though, this power became irrelevant. A president can take diplomatic and military steps that lead the country into hostilities. Then, after the first shots have been fired, he demands congressional support. Congress automatically delivers it, because "our boys" are being shot at, and anyone who suggests cutting funds for the war is a traitor. In much of foreign policy, Congress is bypassed: secret funds for Nicaraguan contras, secret arms sales to Iran, secret understandings with Kuwait, Saudi Arabia, and Pakistan. Such end runs build a storehouse of congressional resentment that comes out from time to time in the form of hostile committee hearings, accusations of executive wrongdoing, budget cuts, and the blocking of administration policies and appointments (see box below). Congress has a built-in inefficiency—designed that way by the Constitution's authors—that can delay and block U.S. foreign policy. It also trips up a U.S. leadership role.

CONCEPTS ■ CONGRESS AND FOREIGN POLICY

Congress, although it generally follows the president's lead in foreign policy, can play a meddlesome or mischievous role. Sometimes it is out for revenge for having been deceived by a president. At times it delights in tripping up presidential policy, especially when the president is of another party.

To get congressional support, presidents often use either a crisis or massive pressure. Then the Congress rallies around a president and speaks of "bipartisan foreign policy." Such was the case after 9/11. Presidents often sound alarm bells and call a situation a desperate emergency. **Alarmism** can be dangerous and go too far without critical thinking. George Kennan complained that his "containment" policy was exaggerated and misapplied. A president may also enlist powerful interest groups. In 2000 Congress voted to normalize trade with China despite public, especially labor, opposition. Pressure in favor of it from big business was unusually heavy.

IS THE STRUCTURE DEFECTIVE?

National Security Council The president's foreign policy coordinating body.

As Alexis de Tocqueville observed in the 1830s, a democratic republic such as the United States will always have trouble conducting a coherent foreign policy. Democracies have to pay attention to public opinion; tyrannies do not. The need to win elections produces crowd-pleasing but oversimplified slogans and unrealistic policies. U.S. administrations appoint top officials from business, the law, and academia; many are energetic amateurs, in office only a few years. Only one secretary of state, Lawrence Eagleburger, has been a career Foreign Service Officer, and he served in the position for just a month and a half at the end of the Bush 41 administration.

The very structure of the U.S. foreign affairs community is also a problem. Big and sprawling, it often seems controlled by no one. More than a dozen federal departments and agencies focus on foreign affairs. (For the complexity of even a small U.S. embassy, see Chapter 19.) Attempting to coordinate these branches fell to the **National Security Council** (NSC), but that brought new problems (see box on page 104). Secretaries of state, nominally the nation's overseers of foreign affairs, battle over turf with secretaries of defense and national security advisors, usually losing.

The Iran-contra foul-up of the 1980s illustrated what could go wrong. Oliver North, a Marine lieutenant colonel on the NSC staff worked with nongovernmental fundraisers and "consultants" to carry out a harebrained scheme to sell U.S. weapons to Iran and use the profits to support the Nicaraguan contras in defiance of the will of Congress and U.S. laws. Who was responsible? It was hard to say. And that is one of the problems of U.S. foreign policy: Exactly who gives the orders for what? If left divided, the various departments and agencies work at cross-purposes without coordination or communication. If centralized under the NSC or the Defense Department, other agencies feel overridden and misused by partisan amateurs whose chief qualification is their friendship with or access to the president. Recent presidents have conducted foreign policy with a handful of close associates; they simply bypass the conventional structures.

Can the structure be fixed? Some have suggested requiring the national security advisor to be confirmed by and answerable to Congress, just as the secretaries of state and defense are. This would help control secret schemes, but it would give Congress more scrutiny of the White House than most presidents would wish. Presidents insist that their national security advisors are responsible only to them; this gives them flexibility and secrecy. Another proposal is to designate the secretary of state as the top and responsible person in foreign affairs. But secretaries cannot be assured of cooperation from the other branches; the Pentagon, CIA, NSC, and the new Homeland Security can ignore or fail to inform them.

After 9/11, a new structural problem became clear. The CIA, FBI, Immigration and Customs Enforcement (ICE), and state and local police barely communicated with each other. By law and by corporate culture, the CIA gathers information but does not share it with other agencies. It prepares reports only for the president and a few other top officials. The CIA had no interest or way to share with other agencies signs that al Qaeda was preparing a major strike. The CIA has massive foreign-area expertise but no law enforcement powers. The FBI, on the other hand, has great law enforcement powers but no foreign-area expertise. It would be nice if the CIA and FBI talked to each other and even better if they communicated with local police and immigration officials, the front line against terror. There is still no computer system that links all relevant agencies. The Department of Homeland Security, established in haste in

bureaucracies Career civil servants organized into various departments and bureaus.	2002, was supposed to integrate and coordinate efforts, but the FBI and CIA are not under its supervision.

The United States is not well structured to conduct a concerted, rational foreign policy. And, for deep-seated reasons, it is not likely to become so. Americans and their Congress fear a secretive, centralized system. A superagency in charge of U.S. foreign policy goes against the American grain. The uncoordinated, sprawling nature of the U.S. foreign policy community is likely to continue, and presidents who think they are in charge of policy may find that the structure is in charge of them.

DO BUREAUCRACIES MAKE FOREIGN POLICY?

One of the fads in political science, popular in the 1970s, was to analyze decisions in terms of the **bureaucracies** that carry them out and influence them. We imagine decision makers rationally discussing a problem and coming up with a logical solution. But what if the information they have been fed is skewed or incomplete? What if the bureaucrats are telling their bosses what they want to hear? Will the decision then be rational? And do the civil servants execute policy the way the decision maker wants?

Bureaucracies have lives and interests of their own, but do they really make policy? Vietnam has been analyzed in terms of bureaucratic politics. When presidents issued orders to stop the Communists in Vietnam, they didn't want any back talk about how difficult it was or that it was a

DIPLOMACY ■ NATIONAL SECURITY COUNCIL

As the United States geared up for the Cold War, Congress streamlined and partially centralized foreign and defense policymaking with the National Security Act of 1947. The act set up the Central Intelligence Agency and provided for a National Security Council composed of the president, vice president, and secretaries of state and defense.

Various presidents have used the NSC differently, some a little and some a lot. Over the decades, though, its centralized power has grown, and it has developed a large staff to assist the president. By the time of the Nixon administration, the NSC staff— which was not mentioned in the 1947 law—had become more important than the NSC itself or the regular departments.

The head of this staff is called the national security advisor, a presidential appointee not accountable to Congress. The national security advisor may have the president's ear more than anyone else in foreign policy. The president picks these advisors and their helpers mostly from academia and the military. The most famous (and probably most effective) was Harvard professor Henry Kissinger, who soon eclipsed Secretary of State William Rogers. Bush 43 relied more on National Security Advisor Condoleezza Rice than on Secretary of State Colin Powell. After 9/11, Vice President Dick Cheney and Secretary of Defense Donald Rumsfeld took the policy lead; Powell did public relations and was replaced by Rice for Bush's second term.

The NSC staff has a number of things going for it that enhance its power. First, it is close to the president, not across town. It is an information clearinghouse, receiving all State, Defense, and CIA cables and reports. It is small and thus moves faster and leaks less; the president can trust it. Many in Congress and the conventional departments are vexed that the NSC, which started as a simple policy-coordinating device, has turned into an unaccountable superagency.

lost cause. They wanted a can-do response from enthusiastic military and civilian officers. Accordingly, reports came back from the field that U.S. aid, advisors, and programs were working. The bureaucrats told presidents what they wanted to hear. Overly optimistic reporting, in this view, deepened U.S. commitments in Vietnam.

Cuban Missile Crisis   The 1962 showdown over Soviet rockets in Cuba.

This view was widely accepted until the 1971 publication of the "Pentagon Papers," a secret Defense Department history of decision making on Vietnam. The papers showed that, in general, the reports from well-informed officials were accurate and pessimistic; no one promised a short or easy war. The public relations material cranked out for the press, to be sure, was foolishly optimistic. The insider reports were coldly sober. Some of the toughest and most realistic warnings came from the CIA. There is no evidence from the Vietnam experience that bureaucrats deceived presidents.

Once the decisions had been made, however, the various bureaucracies did their utmost for the war effort. They are disciplined services and obey orders. There were, of course, the usual bureaucratic foul-ups and rivalries, but all worked in pursuit of goals laid down by the White House. By the same token, U.S. Ambassador April Glaspie was not a free agent when she told Saddam Hussein in July 1990 that the United States would not get involved in Iraq's quarrel with Kuwait. She was following a U.S. policy to stay friendly with Baghdad. Neither she nor the State Department bureaucracy was fully to blame for this blind and foolish policy. Bureaucratic politics does take place, but it does so after the stage has been set and directions given by the White House.

Some blamed "the bureaucrats" for letting 9/11 happen. The several agencies totally failed to follow up on warnings or to cross-communicate, but they were created and given their missions by Congress. The problem was that no one—not the president, Congress, or the agencies themselves—could understand that we were in a new era with new threats. Agencies designed for the Cold War were clumsy in dealing with decentralized terrorism. Once set up, agencies

CONCEPTS ■ BUREAUCRATIC POLITICS

In a widely read 1969 article, Harvard political scientist Graham Allison claimed the 1962 **Cuban Missile Crisis** unrolled the way it did because of "bureaucratic politics." The term caught on and gave birth to a new subfield. Later evidence suggested the study omitted important perspectives.

Specifically, Allison found that the crucial factor was the timing of evidence presented to the president and his advisors that the Soviets were placing missiles in Cuba. This depended on when the U2 spyplane flew. The flight was delayed a week because the Air Force and CIA squabbled over who was to pilot it. If it had flown earlier, it would have given the National Security Council time to consider other, less confrontational options. But if it had flown later, it would likely have led to one of the warlike options the military was urging

on President Kennedy. So, the timing of information gathering depended on bureaucratic politics, and that is what made all the difference.

However, tapes of Kennedy's words at the time, edited by Harvard historian Ernest May, show that at no time did JFK consider a military strike of any sort. He had recently read Barbara Tuchman's *Guns of August* and learned how World War I began as a series of misunderstood moves that escalated to total war. Kennedy was not going to let things spin out of control. Accordingly, the options that Allison thought were on the NSC table—air strikes, amphibious landings, parachute drops—were never on the table. Kennedy, from the beginning, decided he would not use them. Bureaucratic politics had little or nothing to do with his decision.

unilateralism Foreign policies without allied help or consultation.

tend to rumble on unchanged: "But we've always done it that way here." Agencies do not re-create or reform themselves; that is up to the president and Congress. By most accounts, Bush 43 alone was in charge of U.S. policy on Iraq. When he demanded evidence of Iraq's weapons of mass destruction, the agencies delivered what the boss wanted, even if it was inaccurate. Bureaucrats mostly obey.

THE UNILATERALIST TEMPTATION

Related to isolationism in U.S. history is **unilateralism**, doing things ourselves and not in concert with other countries. As we saw in Chapter 3, Washington warned against involvement in Europe, and until World War II we entered into no formal alliances, not even in World War I. We did not join the League of Nations. Sponsoring the UN and North Atlantic Treaty were major breakthroughs, for at last we were formally entangled in the world. Not all Americans like that. Some say it infringes on U.S. sovereignty. Should the UN or NATO tell us when and where to go to war? Should they be able to stop us from going to war when we deem it necessary? Should American soldiers serve under foreign generals? Should Congress pass laws and ratify treaties to please foreigners or to serve our own interests?

President Obama meets with the National Security Council in 2009. The NSC is the president's top foreign policy body. (Pete Souza/Corbis)

Bush 43 was widely accused of slipping into the unilateralist temptation, with help from the **neoconservatives**. It works like this: If we must do something in the world, we try to persuade NATO allies and UN members to support us, but we do not depend on them. We see them as timid, divided, and wrong, unable to take clear stands against evil. We must do it ourselves. Bush's unilateralism resonated with American tradition and found much public support. For example, when 178 nations signed a 2001 global climate treaty, the Kyoto Protocol, that sought to curb greenhouse gases, Bush called it "fatally flawed" and ignored it. Overall, the United States signs few treaties; the neocons say they restrict us.

neoconservative   Ex-liberal favoring use of force overseas.

Unfortunately, U.S. unilateralism turns much of the rest of the world against us, making us look like an international bully. We figure: Only we have the trained, mobile, and high-tech armed forces that can move rapidly to overthrow evil regimes in places like Afghanistan or Iraq. Allies just get in the way. In purely military terms, this may be true, but it ignores the political problems that flow from unilateral actions. It threatens to create the counterweight system we discussed in Chapter 1: The rest of the world criticizes America and refuses to follow its lead.

TURNING POINT ■ OBAMA AND THE AFGHANISTAN DECISION

The dilemma President Barack Obama faced in 2009 illustrates how events and constraints guide decisions, which are often not what you wish to do but what you must. Obama had repeatedly defined Afghanistan as a "necessary war" to block Islamist extremists from again using it to launch terrorist attacks. Both he and McCain campaigned in 2008 on increasing U.S. forces in Afghanistan.

But by the fall of 2009 the Afghan war had grown dirtier than the one in Iraq, from which Obama was slowly withdrawing U.S. forces. The top American general in Afghanistan reported the situation was deteriorating and asked for at least 40,000 more troops. Obama thought long and hard. If he pulled out of Afghanistan, Republicans would charge he was weak on defense and terrorism. If he plunged in, he could become another LBJ, ruined by an unpopular war.

After eight years of fighting in Afghanistan, many Americans were fed up with the war. Afghan President Karzai, handpicked by the Americans, "won" a rigged reelection in 2009. No one trusted his corrupt regime. Warlords, drug lords, and the Taliban ran much of Afghanistan outside of Kabul. The Taliban operated with impunity from sanctuaries in Pakistan. Strikes against them killed civilians as well. The limited aid from NATO allies was unpopular among Europeans. Afghanistan was looking a bit like Vietnam—a long, unwinnable struggle. U.S. soldiers and Marines were spread thin and exhausted from multiple deployments overseas. The U.S. federal budget was already massively in deficit from fighting the recession.

But Obama announced in November 2009 an increase of 30,000 U.S. troops in Afghanistan. Overall, in two years Obama tripled the number of U.S. troops there. But at the same time he announced that the United States would start coming home in mid-2011 as the U.S. forces gradually turned over responsibility to the Afghan military and police, who observers called uneducated, untrained, and unreliable. To withdraw immediately, however, would have meant a Taliban victory and U.S. defeat, something the Republicans would use against Obama in 2012. Every politician's overriding concern is reelection, so Obama in 2010 named a new U.S. commanding general for Afghanistan but tried to set a time limit, hoping it would not turn into another Vietnam and he into another LBJ, a one-term president.

multilateralism Foreign policies with much allied help and consultation.

Many Americans respond, "So what? Who needs them?" We do. We need them as markets and as investors. Without huge amounts of foreign investment and savings pouring into the U.S. economy, the impact of the 2008 financial meltdown would have been much worse. We used to see ourselves as the economic kingpins of the world, but with the rapid growth of China, India, and several other lands, we no longer are. The dollar, especially after 2008, is no longer king; foreigners do not completely trust it.

We cannot police the entire globe by ourselves; we are already stretched thin. We need the political support and peacekeeping forces of many countries even if they do not contribute to a shooting war. We need the cooperation of their police and intelligence services in combating terrorism and drugs. President Obama turned away from unilateralism and attempted to rebuild **multilateralism**.

TO LEAD OR NOT TO LEAD?

So, can the United States lead the world? From our discussions in this chapter, it might seem infeasible. There are many constraints: budget deficits, isolationist attitudes, an unsteady Congress, a too-small military, an incoherent structure, and an unclear strategy. But these can be reversed. The right strategy, one that understands current world realities and repairs U.S. economic weakness, can restore our role. Remember, we have gone through difficult periods before and have come out of them stronger than ever.

As we will explore in subsequent chapters, the world is chaotic, but the right application of the right kind of power—sometimes economic, sometimes diplomatic, sometimes military, but always in a coalition of partners—at the right time and place can head off many world problems before they become threats to peace and stability. If we stand back from the world scene, some of these problems will grow until they require drastic measures. Then we will wish we had taken more interest earlier on. If we do not lead, no one will.

mypoliscikit EXERCISES

Apply what you learned in this chapter on MyPoliSciKit (www.mypoliscikit.com).

  Assessment   Review this chapter using learning objectives, chapter summaries, practice tests, and more.

Menu

  Flashcards   Learn the key terms in this chapter; you can test yourself by term or definition.

Flashcards

  Video   Analyze recent world affairs by watching streaming video from major news providers.

Videos

  Simulations   Play the role of an IR decision-maker and experience how IR concepts work in practice.

Comparative
Exercises

KEY TERMS

alarmism (p. 102)
behavioralism (p. 98)
bureaucracies (p. 104)
constraint (p. 100)
Cuban Missile Crisis (p. 105)
deficit (p. 99)
dove (p. 101)
entitlements (p. 99)

foreign policy (p. 96)
idealism (p. 99)
interventionism (p. 96)
Joint Chiefs of Staff (p. 101)
multilateralism (p. 108)
National Security Council
 (p. 103)
neoconservative (p. 107)

noninterventionism
 (p. 96)
Pentagon (p. 101)
rally event (p. 97)
self-interest (p. 99)
unilateralism (p. 106)
volatile (p. 97)
War Powers Act (p. 101)

FURTHER REFERENCE

Antizzo, Glenn J. *U.S. Military Intervention in the Post–Cold War Era: How to Win America's Wars in the Twenty-First Century*. Baton Rouge: Louisiana State University Press, 2010.

Bacevich, Andrew J. *Washington Rules: America's Path to Permanent War*. New York: Metropolitan Books, 2010.

Beinart, Peter. *The Icarus Syndrome: A History of American Hubris*. New York: HarperCollins, 2010.

Berinsky, Adam J. *In Time of War: Understanding American Public Opinion from World War II to Iraq*. Chicago: University of Chicago Press, 2009.

Brooks, Stephen G., and William C. Wohlforth. *World out of Balance: International Relations and the Challenge of American Primacy*. Princeton, NJ: Princeton University Press, 2008.

Brzezinski, Zbigniew. *Second Chance: Three Presidents and the Crisis of American Superpower*. New York: Basic Books, 2008.

——— and Brent Scowcroft. *America and the World: Conversations on the Future of American Foreign Policy*. New York: Basic Books, 2009.

Calleo, David P. *Follies of Power: America's Unipolar Fantasy*. New York: Cambridge University Press, 2009.

Chollet, Derek, and James Goldgeier. *America Between the Wars: From 11/9 to 9/11*. New York: Public Affairs, 2008.

DeLong, J. Bradford, and Stephen S. Cohen. *The End of Influence: What Happens When Other Countries Have the Money*. New York: Basic Books, 2010.

Fukuyama, Francis. *America at the Crossroads: Democracy, Power and the Neoconservative Legacy*. New Haven, CT: Yale University Press, 2006.

Gelb, Leslie H. *Power Rules: How Common Sense Can Rescue American Foreign Policy*. New York: HarperCollins, 2009.

Greider, William. *Come Home America: The Rise and Fall (and Redeeming Promise) of Our Country*. Emmaus, PA: Rodale, 2009.

Halperin, Morton, and Priscilla Clapp. *Bureaucratic Politics and Foreign Policy*, 2nd ed. Washington, DC: Brookings, 2006.

Howell, William G., and Jon C. Pevehouse. *While Dangers Gather: Congressional Checks on Presidential War Powers*. Princeton, NJ: Princeton University Press, 2007.

Jentleson, Bruce W. *American Foreign Policy: The Dynamics of Choice in the 21st Century*. New York: Norton, 2010.

Leffler, Melvyn P., and Jeffrey W. Legro, eds. *To Lead the World: American Strategy after the Bush Doctrine*. New York: Oxford University Press, 2008.

Mandelbaum, Michael. *The Frugal Superpower: America's Global Leadership in a Cash-Strapped Era*. New York: PublicAffairs, 2010.

Mason, David S. *The End of the American Century*. Lanham, MD: Rowman & Littlefield, 2008.

Matlock, Jack F. *Superpower Illusions: How Myths and False Ideologies Led America Astray—and How to Return to Reality*. New Haven, CT: Yale University Press, 2010.

Norrlof, Carla. *America's Global Advantage: US Hegemony and International Cooperation*. New York: Cambridge University Press, 2010.

Nye, Joseph S. *The Powers to Lead.* New York: Oxford University Press, 2008.

Ohaegbulam, F. Ugboaja. *A Culture of Deference: Congress, the President, and the Course of the U.S.-Led Invasion and Occupation of Iraq.* New York: Peter Lang, 2007.

Preble, Christopher A. *The Power Problem: How American Military Dominance Makes Us Less Safe, Less Prosperous, and Less Free.* Ithaca, NY: Cornell University Press, 2009.

Rothkopf, David. *Running the World: The Inside Story of the National Security Council and the Architects of American Power.* Boulder, CO: PublicAffairs, 2005.

Talbott, Strobe. *The Great Experiment: The Story of Ancient Empires, Modern States, and the Quest for a Global Nation.* New York: Simon & Schuster, 2009.

Wittkopf, Eugene R., and James M. McCormick, eds. *The Domestic Sources of American Foreign Policy: Insights and Evidence,* 5th ed. Lanham, MD: Rowman & Littlefield, 2007.

Zakaria, Fareed. *The Post-American World.* New York: Norton, 2008.

Zelizer, Julian E. *Arsenal of Democracy: The Politics of National Security—from World War II to the War on Terrorism.* New York: Basic Books, 2009.

PART III

THE GLOBAL SOUTH

Virtually all conflicts are now in the *Global South* or *Third World*, most of them to some degree a legacy of *colonialism*. The developed world—Europe, North America, Japan, Australia—has been peaceful since World War II. (The Balkans may be a partial exception here, but it too has a legacy of Ottoman colonialism.) The Middle East now has by far the most conflicts, Africa the second most, and there is a sprinkling in Asia and Latin America. How this came to be is the subject of this section.

Chapter 7 reviews the dramatic transformation of the Global South with the rise and fall of 500 years of imperialism. India, South Africa, Nigeria, and Kenya illustrate the sweep of *decolonization*. South Africa is especially interesting because, even though independent, it remained structurally and psychologically colonial. South Africa also shows how the end of the Cold War deprived the two sides of their respective outside backers, forcing them into accommodation.

Chapter 8 traces the development of Arab and Israeli nationalism. Much of current Middle Eastern tension flows from the struggle of these two peoples for the same land. Many Palestinians and Israelis realize that, after six nasty wars and two Palestinian *intifadas*, they must live in separate homelands. But after many tries, peace still eludes, and militants on both sides sabotage the peace process. Some fear their war will never end.

Chapter 9 shows that mixing oil with religion in the Persian Gulf can produce a clash of arms and, some say, a clash of civilizations. The wars revealed splits in Islam, splits in the Arab world, and the power of the region to draw the United States into two wars with Iraq and likely long involvement. We pay special attention to the Afghan and Iraq wars and their aftermaths.

Chapter 10 turns us to Latin America, which we try to ignore but cannot. For a century, the United States has fought guerrillas and, more recently, drug lords there. Spanish colonialism bequeathed Latin America statism, poverty, and economic dependency. The United States has repeatedly intervened in Central America and the Caribbean, each time fostering instability. Guatemala and Cuba have been especially difficult and dangerous. The current bloodshed in Mexico illustrates the penetration of crime into politics found in much of the Third World.

Part III closes with Chapter 11, which examines why some states are rich and others poor. Literacy, technology, and values oriented toward progress are key factors. So is the population explosion in the Third World, which retards growth and fuels a great migration into the First World, raising questions of integration, jobs, official languages, and the power of market capitalism to feed the world. The rapid economic rise of several emerging markets, however, shows that, with the right policies, millions of people can climb out of poverty.

CHAPTER 7

From Colonialism to Decolonization

Nelson Mandela, released from 27 years in prison in 1990, heralded a new South Africa, one free from its colonial past. (Greg English/ AP Photos)

As we considered in Chapter 1, more than 500 years ago West Europe began modernizing and founded the strong state (see page 16). The voyages of discovery and the beginnings of **colonialism** were part of this process. Imperialism was bound to happen as monarchs competed with each other for new lands and wealth, but little Portugal led the way. Like Spaniards, Portuguese fought off centuries of Moorish rule in a vengeful spirit. They hated the fact that Arab middlemen dominated Europe's trade with Asia and vowed to go around them.

Even then, educated people knew (from the ancient Greeks) that the world was round and that Asia could be reached by going around Africa. They just did not know how far south Africa extended (farther than they thought). Portugal's Prince Henry the Navigator, who had earlier battled the Moors, was motivated by both religious hatred and economic gain. He encouraged Portuguese explorers to work their way down Africa's Atlantic coast until, finally, in 1488, Bartolomeu Dias rounded the Cape of Good Hope, so named for the riches it would bring. Quickly, little Portuguese caravels crossed the Indian Ocean and set up trading posts in India (1498), China (1514), Japan (1543), and elsewhere.

In 1492, Spain and Christopher Columbus played catch-up in trying to reach Asia by sailing west. American schoolchildren learn that Columbus's voyage was the really important one, but the Portuguese opening of both Africa and Asia was at least equal in terms of changing the world. On Africa's west coast, the Portuguese set up trading posts for slaves for the sugarcane and cotton plantations in the New World. Thus began European colonialism in Africa. Guinea-Bissau, Angola, and Mozambique were Portuguese colonies until 1975. Europe's first colonial power was also its last.

France and England soon followed Portugal, turning Africa into a series of colonies. In the late nineteenth century, Germany, Italy, and Belgium completed the process. In 1885 the leading powers met in Berlin for the "great carve-up" of Central Africa that settled competing border claims. Thus many of Africa's borders were demarcated around a table in Berlin. Only Ethiopia was not colonized (although it was occupied by Italy from 1936 to 1941).

Decolonization took more than two centuries as the European powers were forced back to Europe. The first loss was Britain's 13 colonies in North America. Next, in the 1820s,

QUESTIONS TO CONSIDER

1. What caused European imperialism? Could it have been avoided?
2. Which were the major colonial empires?
3. What was the impact of the British hold over and departure from India?
4. How did South Africa under apartheid preserve a colonial mentality?
5. What external factors forced South Africa to change?
6. Could colonialism, extensively reformed, have continued?
7. What, theoretically, would have been the best way to decolonize?
8. What happened to most African lands after their independence?

King Edward VIII, in white uniform, in 1926 visited India, then the most important part of the British Empire. Twenty-one years later, the British were out of India. (Hulton Archives/Getty Images)

came Spain's and Portugal's ousters from Latin America. Germany and Turkey lost their empires in World War I, but most of those territories were taken over by the victorious British and French under mandates of the League of Nations. Real **decolonization** did not come until after World War II, first as a trickle and then as a flood: India and Pakistan in 1947, Israel (formerly Palestine) in 1948, Indonesia (Dutch East Indies) in 1949, Ghana (Gold Coast) in 1957, then, in 1960, 17 countries, mostly British and French colonies in Africa. By the mid-1960s, all the old colonial empires had been liquidated except for Portugal's holdings. In 1975, Lisbon too gave way. After Rhodesia became Zimbabwe in 1980, South Africa stood alone as the last bastion of white rule in Africa.

LEGACIES OF COLONIALISM

The world is still suffering from what the imperial powers wrought. Some countries, especially in Africa, should not exist. Under normal circumstances, many African states would have merged into larger units or would have broken up into more natural tribal entities. But the Organization of African Unity (renamed the African Union in 2002) decided to keep the colonial borders because there was no good way to redraw them, and if states combined, many officials would lose their jobs. Thanks to the imperialists, adjacent countries have different official languages (English, French, Portuguese). What the colonialists set up, Africans have accepted, although some still dream of **pan-Africanism**, a movement to unite all of Africa.

colonialism The gaining and exploitation of overseas territories, chiefly by Europeans.

decolonization The granting of independence to colonies.

pan-Africanism Movement to unite all of Africa.

The borders the Europeans drew are a problem today, and not just in Africa. One sure sign of an artificial border is a straight line, of which Africa has many. The British typically set up borders for their colonies that took parts of neighboring lands. Then, when the British departed, the neighboring country often demanded back the original, precolonial border. In a treaty with Tibet in 1914, Britain set up the McMahon Line along the Himalayan ridge as India's border. China—both Nationalist and Communist—claimed the treaty was bogus (because Tibet was not sovereign) and rejected it. In 1962 China launched a short, victorious war with India over what it called Chinese territory. China still claims much of India's northeastern state of Arunachal Pradesh. Britain gave India borders it could not defend. Likewise, Britain took a strip of Venezuela for Guyana. Ethiopia and Eritrea are in a nearly permanent border war over what the Italians had demarcated as a boundary.

In 1923 Britain made the entire Sea of Galilee part of Palestine. Syria never accepted this border, and the dispute over it triggered the 1967 Six Day War. Iraq's borders are a permanent and current headache. Rival claims going back centuries over the exact border between Iraq and Iran contributed to their terrible war in the 1980s (see page 148). Iraq always claimed that Kuwait should have been part of Iraq and conquered it in 1990, leading to the 1991 Gulf War. The Kurds of the north of Iraq argue they never should have been incorporated into Iraq and now act as if they are independent (see page 155). We are embroiled in the Middle East today in part due to the borders Britain drew up after World War I.

The imperialists also left behind ethnic problems that lingered for decades; some continue today. Imperialists deliberately exaggerated ethnic or tribal differences to better control the natives. Belgium in Rwanda hyped differences between Hutus and Tutsis with genocidal results (see page 122). Britain invented an artificial Nigeria from coastal Christians and interior Muslims that is still wracked by religious and tribal tensions. Kenya, once thought to be

emerging economies/Global South/ Third World   Large parts of Asia, Africa, and Latin America.

GDP   Gross domestic product; sum total of goods and services produced in a country in one year; measure of prosperity.

weak state   One unable to govern effectively; corrupt and crime-ridden.

failed state   Collapse of sovereignty, essentially no national government.

GEOGRAPHY ■ LOOKING FOR A NAME

What to call the 85 percent of humankind that lives in Asia, Africa, and Latin America? French demographer Alfred Sauvy coined the term "Third World" in 1952 because it was neither the rich, industrialized First World nor the communist Second World. The term slowly caught on, but many dislike it, claiming it is impossibly broad, slightly pejorative, and now obsolete. With the collapse of the Soviet bloc, there is no more Second World; there is just "the West and the rest." American academics generally prefer the term "developing areas." The U.S. State Department uses "less-developed countries" (LDCs). Business likes "newly industrializing countries" (NICs) or "emerging markets." In 2001 Goldman Sachs coined "BRICs," for fast-growing Brazil, Russia, India, and China. We like "Global South," because it is mostly closer to the equator than the more industrialized and largely stable Global North.

The **emerging economies**, **Global South**, or **Third World**—call it what you will—is complicated and contains many exceptions. It is mostly poor, but some oil-producing and newly industrializing lands are not. Still, most Global Southeners get by on less than $1,000 a year per capita **GDP** (see box on page 115), less than a thirtieth of the industrial lands of West Europe and North America. But no peoples are doomed to poverty and, as poor countries industrialize, the gap narrows quickly. Some Asian people have climbed into affluence (Japan, Singapore) or are about to (Taiwan, South Korea). In fact, most of the world economic growth since 2008 has taken place in the developing countries.

Racial and ideological views about the Global South can also be too simplistic. For instance, the Global South is more racially diverse than is often perceived, with much of Latin America and the Muslim world having many white inhabitants. Nor are Global Southeners uniformly pro- or anti-Western. Even before the fall of the Soviet bloc and the resultant end of the Second World, most of the Global South liked to call itself "nonaligned," that is, neutral between the First World and Second World.

Many countries of the Global South are **weak states** in which crime penetrates into politics. Often, you cannot tell where politics leaves off and crime begins. Weak states are corrupt, unable to enforce their laws, and vulnerable to overthrow by revolutions and military coups. Colombia's guerrillas and drug lords are an example. Democracy is hard to establish in the Third World. One notable exception is India, which is now also scoring rapid economic growth. Neighboring Pakistan, however, is more typical: Military dictatorship alternates with tumultuous democracy, the one leading to the other, and economic growth is slow. The Third World is both economically and politically underdeveloped.

Whatever you call it cannot do justice to its variety and complexity. Some countries are making amazing progress out of poverty and toward democracy while others are stuck in decline and dictatorship. A few, such as Somalia, qualify as **failed states**. It is in the Global South that we find the "zones of chaos" mentioned in Chapter 1.

stable and integrated, has retribalized itself into Kikuyus, Luos, Kambas, Kisiis, and others. (Barack Obama's father was Luo, and Kenyans joke bitterly that Obama is the first Luo president—but not of Kenya, where Kikuyu domination prevents that.)

The worst thing about the imperialists is the poor job they did preparing their colonies for independence. Too few natives were educated to take over governing responsibilities after independence. The British did a bit better and left most of their colonies with an educated elite. Gandhi and Kenyatta, for example, went to English universities. The Belgian Congo, on the other hand, had three native high-school graduates when it became independent in 1960.

Thus it is not surprising that Africa has few democracies and several failed states, countries that only pretend to have governments. They cannot feed their people or keep order. Prime example: Somalia, where lawlessness rules. One can only speculate if Africa would be in better shape today if the imperialists had never set up their colonies. Most newly independent African countries started, on paper at least, as democracies but soon fell into either demagogic autocracy or military dictatorship, some with horrifying human rights abuses. As we will see in Chapter 11, democracy seldom takes root in poor countries. The solution: economic growth, which is happening.

The world does not know what to do with Africa. Some say the situation in much of the continent is so hopeless that we should just keep out. Africa does have success stories, although some countries show economic decline, civil war, mass murder, and an explosion of HIV/AIDS. (One

GEOGRAPHY ■ COLONIALISM

Colonialism is first a legal condition wherein a land lacks sovereignty; ultimate lawmaking authority resides in a distant capital. London controlled the laws governing India, Paris those of Indochina, and Brussels those of the Congo. Second, the natives were kept politically powerless, as the imperial power deemed them too backward and ignorant. It is startling to make a list of non-European countries that were never colonies, for the list is awfully short: Thailand, Turkey, Ethiopia, Afghanistan, and Japan. China and Iran were reduced to semicolonial status.

Colonialism often involved economic exploitation by the imperial country. The colonies supplied cheap agricultural and mineral raw materials, which the imperial country manufactured into industrial products that it sold back to the colonies. Marxists argue that colonies were captive markets that were kept poor to enrich imperialists. Actually, most colonies cost imperial governments more to administer and defend than they earned. Individual firms, to be sure, often made lush profits.

Racially, colonies were governed on the basis of skin color and according to the principle that "the lowest of the Europeans is higher than the highest of the natives." A French police officer directing traffic in Hanoi was superior to a Vietnamese doctor. A Dutch clerk in Jakarta was the social better of an Indonesian professor. Racism was woven into the fabric of colonialism, contributing much to the psychological rage felt by the leaders of independence movements: "You can't treat me like dirt in my own country!" These social and psychological factors are still alive in the minds of some Third World leaders.

Colonialism was unquestionably morally wrong, but it was also inevitable, the logical outcome of the encounter between a restless, dynamic West and a traditional Global South that looked like easy pickings. Only one traditional land held off the Europeans: Japan. Well and tightly governed, its shoguns expelled the foreigners and butchered their Christian converts. The imperial powers had no right to conquer and govern others, but they did have guns. If only Europe had stayed home! (Of course, then there would be no United States.) "Colonial" sounds nice to Americans, connoting quaint New England villages. It has a bitter ring for most other peoples. In some cases, colonialism left an anti-West chip on the shoulders of the Global South.

of the worst is South Africa, where one-fifth of adults are infected.) Overall in sub-Saharan Africa, per capita GDP has declined. (Of that GDP, 45 percent is concentrated in South Africa, the region's only industrialized economy.)

anarchic Lacking government or order.

Well-intentioned help often goes wrong. Much foreign aid is skimmed off by crooked officials. The United States attempted to bring food and order to **anarchic** Somalia but abandoned it when 18 U.S. soldiers were killed in street fighting in 1993. Taking the wrong lesson from that, in 1994 we sent no soldiers to prevent tribal massacres in Rwanda. Instead, we set up refugee camps in neighboring Congo, which made the massacres spill over into the Congo and get worse (see box on page 122). In Sierra Leone, the United Nations tried to restore peace, but its peacekeepers were disarmed and held by rebels, who stole diamonds and chopped off arms. A few U.S. troops could have stopped the death and chaos of a collapsing Liberian regime, but we did not send them. The major powers see much danger and little payoff in African peace operations, so they rarely intervene. Should they?

THE ROOTS OF AFRICA'S PROBLEMS

Nature has not been kind to Africa. Much of the soil is poor. In some times and places there is too much rain, in others too little. Insects and disease thrive; people do not. For these reasons and for most of history, Africa has been thinly populated by resilient subsistence farmers scattered in small villages. Family and survival were all that mattered, not organization or economic growth. Africa rarely developed the European type of "strong state" or nationalism (exceptions: Ethiopia and the Zulus). Almost defenseless, traditional Africa was first deranged by the Arab slave trade on the east coast and the Portuguese on the west coast before European colonialists, often with African troops, easily took over.

Many of Africa's problems trace back to Europeans, first to colonialism and then to the Cold War. In the nineteenth century, the Europeans erased much traditional culture by carving up Africa into unnatural colonies to exploit. The Europeans gave their colonies artificial borders, overcentralized administration, and no legitimacy before casting them free to become pawns in the Cold War. A few Western-trained elites—imitation Europeans—took over, most of them dedicated to self-enrichment. Africa has been misruled for centuries.

The Cold War did, however, force us to pay some attention to Africa. Support by outside powers—the United States, Soviet Union, Britain, and France—brought with it some stability. With the Cold War over and that support withdrawn, chaos has grown. Now, few care much about Africa. One U.S. government specialist on Africa, aware that his expertise was no longer in demand, sadly joked: "Africa is a dagger—aimed at the heart of Antarctica."

THE STRANGE STORY OF SOUTH AFRICA

Like much colonialism, Netherlands imperialism began as a commercial enterprise. The Dutch East India Company, needing a "refreshment station" midway on the long voyage to the Indies (present-day Indonesia), set one up at the Cape of Good Hope in 1652. Dutch farmers, or Boers, slowly pushed inland, taking all the land they wanted and subjugating the natives. During the Napoleonic wars, Britain took the Cape and later Natal province. Many Boers hated English rule and trekked (a Dutch word) to the interior to set up two small republics, the

apartheid South Africa's system of strict racial segregation from 1948 to the early 1990s.

Transvaal and Orange Free State. British imperialists—including Cecil Rhodes, founder of the Rhodes scholarships—started a war with the Boers in 1899 in order to seize their gold- and diamond-rich lands. The Boer War was no easy fight, and the British finally resorted to putting Boer families into "concentration camps," where typhoid killed some 26,000. The Boers capitulated in 1902, but their descendants, now called Afrikaners, won control of the political system and viewed themselves as the victims of British imperialism.

In 1948, the Afrikaners, a majority of the white population, won whites-only elections with their National Party and passed laws that built a thorough and complex system of racial segregation they called **apartheid** (literally, apartness). Blacks were kept separate and down. There was no such thing as a mixed neighborhood, church, school, or sports team. Blacks needed permits for jobs in urban areas, and the jobs had to be those whites did not want. Blacks were given a limited and inferior education. In the name of "influx control," blacks had to show a passbook and could be "endorsed out" of an urban or white farming area to a desolate black homeland. Eventually, it was envisioned that ten black homelands—scattered parcels of land forming 13 percent of South Africa's territory—would become independent. Blacks would be citizens of Bophuthatswana, Transkei, Ciskei, or other homelands and only temporary workers in white South Africa. This would deprive them of all citizenship rights in South Africa and make them easier to control. Blacks had no voice in their future, and protest was illegal.

As outsiders, it is inconceivable to us that human beings would long stand for such treatment. To Afrikaners, who were used to living in a racially, socially, and psychologically colonial situation, it seemed normal that the black majority would acquiesce to the fate assigned it by the white government. Because blacks were still backward and tribal, argued many whites, they would be happiest with their own people in their homelands.

South Africa is an interesting case study because its whites-only government preserved a colonialist mentality long after most colonies had won their freedom. White South Africa was sustained by Cold War rivalries. When the Cold War ended, its two main antagonists—the whites-only government and the African National Congress (ANC)—lost their outside backers and had to start talking with each other. The end of the Cold War set in motion new forces. Just a few months after the Soviet Union let East Europe break free, Pretoria freed Nelson Mandela

REFLECTIONS ■ GOLD COAST INTO GHANA

Long ago at UCLA, I knew three students from the Gold Coast, a British colony for 113 years on the bulge of West Africa. In 1957 it became Ghana, and they became Ghanaians. They were intensely proud. "Under the British," one of them told me, "we could have no feeling of patriotism for our country, because it wasn't our country. Now it's ours." The students predicted an unleashing of Ghana's energy and rapid progress now that the British overlords were gone.

Ghana's progress foundered, however. Its U.S.-educated president, Kwame Nkrumah, turned himself into a pro-Soviet dictator. "The Redeemer," as he called himself, concentrated on show projects, including statues of himself, rather than on economic growth. In 1966 the army overthrew Nkrumah in the first of several military coups. Democracy was set back; the economy stagnated and living standards deteriorated, the experience of many African countries since independence. I wonder what became of my friends and what they think now.

—M. G. R.

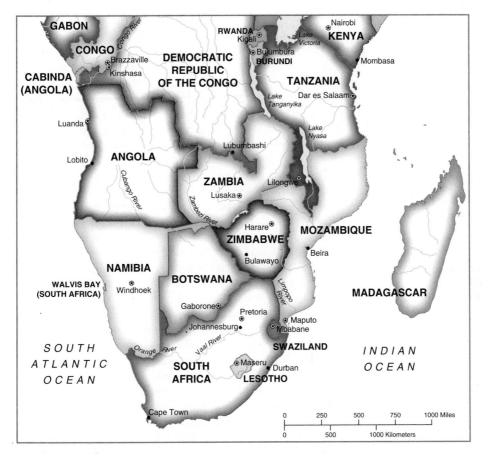

Southern Africa

from a life prison sentence. Just as the Soviet Union collapsed, the white South African regime sat down for talks on a new constitution with its former black enemies. International systems have a big impact on domestic politics. In 1994 South Africa held its first one-person–one-vote elections, which gave power to the ANC and Mandela; both the parliament and cabinet were multiracial. It was an amazing breakthrough, a sort of domestic decolonization with far less violence than had been feared.

INDIA SPLITS IN TWO

India is another important case study, for now two parts of old India—India and Pakistan—are enemies and possess nuclear weapons. As with Africa, we ask: Did the British in India make things better or worse? Before the British, India was rarely unified; it was mostly a patchwork of princely states. It was not poor but had one of the world's biggest economies. Indian intellectuals blame Britain for impoverishing India. Hindus predominated in India, but Muslims were a quarter of the population; there were tensions between the two communities.

subcontinent   Asia south of the Himalayas: India, Pakistan, and Bangladesh; sometimes called South Asia.

divide and rule   Roman and British ruling method of setting subjects against each other.

Raj   The British colonial administration of India.

partition   Dividing a country along ethnic or religious lines.

Like South Africa, the colonization of India began as a commercial enterprise. The British East India Company, chartered in 1600, set up coastal enclaves to trade for spices, silk, cotton, tea, and much else. Gradually the company took over the entire **subcontinent**. London had no plan to do this; it came about as commanders such as General Robert Clive conquered adjacent untamed areas that were security threats. By the time of the American Revolution, the East India Company ruled India on a for-profit basis. Cotton production, especially during the U.S. Civil War, soared, but the manufacturing of cloth and the profits went to England, not to Indians. India grew poorer.

The British ruled India like they ruled most of their colonies, with the classic Roman technique of **divide and rule**: By keeping them divided, you can more easily rule them. The British allowed many traditional rulers to keep their wealth and local power, thus ensuring their cooperation. A little tension between Hindu and Muslim was also useful. The 1857 Sepoy Mutiny of Indian soldiers killed many Britons and frightened London into ending the East India Company and replacing it with a colonial administration called the **Raj**.

British rule was not all bad. Relatively few soldiers and civil servants were brought in, and Indians were trained to fill the lower ranks of both the army and bureaucracy. By keeping sovereignty in London, British rule temporarily dampened conflict between Hindus and Muslims. The British introduced railroads, hospitals, the telegraph, and modern education. Without the English language, Indians would have trouble communicating nationwide, for there was no single Indian language. (Hindi is a language of northern India; southerners disliked it.) By giving Indians the tools to communicate, colonialism invented Indian nationalism. In modernizing India, the British sowed the seeds of their own departure, for the more educated and aware Indians became, the less they could stand the arrogant and exploitive British.

The Indian National Congress (INC) was founded in 1885 by educated Indians to discuss democracy and eventual independence. The present Congress Party (now in power) is thus over a century old, a factor conferring institutional stability. India's Muslims, however, feared Hindu domination—"Islam is in danger!", the cry of today's jihadis—and in 1906 founded the Muslim League to press for a separate Pakistan. The movement for self-rule thus split.

Mohandas K. Gandhi, a British-educated Indian lawyer who had sharpened his skills in South Africa for 20 years, introduced nonviolent resistance into the nationalist movement in 1918 (his inspiration: American writer Henry Thoreau). Through the 1920s and 1930s, Gandhi built a following throughout India by mounting simple, direct protests the masses could understand. He walked from village to village, wore homespun cloth (some of it spun himself), led a boycott on salt taxes, and went on hunger strikes.

In World War II, the British feared Japan would take India (some Indians went over to the Japanese), so they promised independence after the war. In 1947 Britain negotiated a hasty, messy **partition** into India and Pakistan. The lines drawn were guesswork. Under the guidance of Lord Louis Mountbatten, Pakistan was split off from India as a predominantly Muslim country. Some 14.5 million people fled their home territories—Muslims going to Pakistan and Hindus to India—in the largest population transfer in history. Perhaps half a million were killed in riots. Gandhi was horrified at the communal violence and was himself assassinated by a Hindu fanatic who thought Gandhi was soft on Muslims. The British had long warned of Hindu–Muslim violence. "Without us," they said, "you people will kill each other." This was the bottom-line argument of colonialism, but it neglects what Britain should have done to prepare India for a gradual and stable transition to independence.

India and Pakistan are a comparative case study in contrasts. Although basically the same people, India has been a (sometimes imperfect) democracy since independence, while Pakistan has been **praetorian**, oscillating between weak elected governments and military takeover. Pakistan had military coups in 1958, 1977, and 1999, and has been ruled by generals for more than half its history. India in recent years has had excellent economic growth, Pakistan has not. Many see the difference in India's **secularism** versus Pakistan's Islamic state, which intertwines government and religion. One important structural point: India has had the Congress Party to give stability; Pakistan has no equivalent.

> **praetorian** (from Rome's Praetorian Guard) Tendency for military coups and rule.
>
> **secularism** Keeping religion separate from governance.

NIGERIA: THE OIL CURSE

Nigeria, Africa's most populous nation, is a new and artificial country—like many in Africa and the Middle East—set up by the British in 1901. As in South Africa and India, the first Europeans to visit the area were Portuguese navigators. Disease kept Europeans from much activity in West Africa until malaria-fighting quinine enabled British and French explorers, traders, and missionaries to penetrate the interior in the nineteenth century.

In 1807 British Christians pressed Parliament to outlaw the slave trade. A British squadron enforced the ban in the Gulf of Guinea but was drawn ashore to suppress slavery on the coast. In 1851 the British shelled the port city of Lagos and then annexed it in 1861. As in India, Britain

GEOGRAPHY ■ THE AGONY OF ALGERIA

A colony with many European settlers is much harder to decolonize than one with few, for the settlers fight for their lands and privileged position. Such was the case with Algeria. The French arrived in 1830 to crush piracy but soon turned it into a colony where a million European *colons* dominated the Muslim majority. Algeria was even declared part of France. Algerians served in the French army but could not become French citizens.

Algerian nationalists, inspired and aided by Egypt's Nasser, began their fight for independence in 1954 with bank robberies and bombings. The French colonial structure fought back with killings and bombings of its own. Murder became nearly random.

The French army, having just lost Indochina, was determined to win. They used torture freely. When French politicians talked about ending the war, the French army began a military coup in 1958. At the last minute, retired General Charles de Gaulle was called to head a new government. The settlers and army thought he would keep Algeria French, but he led France out of Algeria with a series of referendums. With Algerian independence in 1962, a million bitter colons gave up their farms and businesses and resettled in France.

Algeria's horrors did not end. Its military regime with a socialist slant botched the economy. Unemployment soared, and millions went to France, many illegally. Islamic fundamentalists harvested mass anger and were about to oust the regime in elections in 1992. Instead, the regime repressed the Islamists, who lashed back with murder, sometimes of whole villages. The death toll since 1992: more than 75,000.

tribalism Identifying with tribe
rather than with country.

had to keep expanding its holdings to subdue hostile tribes on their borders. By 1900 Britain had two coastal protectorates and by 1903 had captured most of the Muslim north. In 1914 Britain combined its protectorates into Nigeria, named after the Niger River. Before the British, there had never been a "Nigeria."

In contrast to South Africa and India, Nigeria's independence was painless. Basically, by 1960 the British and French realized that the colonial system was over. How could they fight World War II for freedom and then deny it to their colonies? The Gold Coast in 1957 was the first (see box on page 118). In 1960, 17 colonies, mostly in Africa, were freed, and by the mid-1960s all except Portugal's colonies of Angola, Mozambique, and Guinea-Bissau were independent. Only Algeria (see box on page 121) and Kenya experienced much bloodshed on the way to freedom.

GEOGRAPHY ■ CONGO: STILL THE HEART OF DARKNESS

The Congo, called Zaire for a time, shows the very worst of what has happened to Africa. The Congo, two-thirds the size of West Europe and the personal property of King Leopold of Belgium from 1885 to 1908, was run as a tidy and profitable prison camp. To get a chilling feel of Belgian colonialism, read Joseph Conrad's *Heart of Darkness*, set in the Congo.

As most of Africa got its freedom, Congolese rioted, and Brussels hastily gave the Congo independence in 1960. The pro-Soviet Patrice Lumumba won elections, but several forces (including the CIA) plotted to kill him. He was assassinated in 1961. The Belgians had trained and prepared no one to lead, and Belgium was delighted as tribal warfare broke out and the Congo fell apart. The Belgians' game was to break off mineral-rich Katanga province in the south as a puppet state of their mining company and keep on milking it for profits. UN Secretary General Dag Hammarskjold died in a 1961 plane crash while trying to restore order in the Congo. UN intervention (and some covert U.S. operations) held the Congo together under the dictatorship of Colonel Joseph Mobutu.

The United States backed Mobutu as an anti-Communist force for stability. He hyped nationalism by renaming the country Zaire and himself Mobutu Sese Seko. One of the world's biggest crooks, he stole much of Zaire's wealth while his people grew poorer. A per-capita GDP of $300 put Congo among the very poorest countries. Mobutu stayed in power three decades by cutting his officials and supporters in on the corruption—the way it works in much of Africa, where to be a government official means to collect bribes. With the Cold War over,

the United States lost interest and stopped supporting Mobutu.

Then tribal violence spilled over from neighboring tiny Rwanda, also a former Belgian colony. Belgium had played classic divide and rule by setting up one tribe, the Tutsis, to be aristocratic masters and another tribe, the Hutus, to be underlings. As was often the case in Africa, colonialists fostered **tribalism** and tribal hatreds. After the Belgians left Rwanda in 1962, Hutu–Tutsi fighting and massacres flared every few years. One factor was population growth in an overcrowded land. The average Rwandan woman bore eight children.

The latest chapter of horror began in 1994 as Hutu *genocidaires* massacred between 500,000 and 800,000. Many Tutsis fled into Zaire and joined a rebel army led by Laurent Kabila that easily ousted Mobutu in 1997. No one, not even his own soldiers, helped the super-crook. But Kabila (assassinated by a bodyguard in 2001), who renamed the country the Democratic Republic of Congo, was worse than Mobutu; in addition to the standard corruption, civil war raged, abetted by outside armies. Rwandan and Ugandan forces fought each other over diamonds. Revenge killings by Rwandan Tutsis of Hutu refugees in eastern Congo led to approximately 3 million deaths, most from starvation and disease. The combined Rwanda-Congo death toll is estimated at 4 million, the world's worst since World War II. And the world paid little attention. The UN now has some peacekeeping forces in the Congo, but not enough to make a difference. The Congo is a failed state, due in large part to colonialism and outside intervention.

Nigerian political parties formed as early as 1923 to press for independence, and in 1947, with the chaos of India freshly on their mind, the British began to prepare for it. They set up a federal system with three regions—the Northern for the Muslim Hausa-Fulani and the Western and the Eastern for the mostly Christian Yoruba and Igbo, respectively. Parties, as is usually the case in Africa, formed along tribal lines; there was no equivalent to an Indian Congress Party. In 1954 Britain made the federation self-governing and in 1960 made it independent. In short, the British did a much better job in Nigeria (and in most of Africa) than they had done in India.

That, alas, did not lead to a peaceful or democratic Nigeria, which fell into *praetorianism* (see page 121). Nigeria has had seven coups and been ruled by generals for two-thirds of the time since independence. The breakaway tendencies of its tribal and religious groups are too strong. Especially dangerous is tension between Muslim northerners and Christian southerners. When chaos threatens, the army takes over and may do so again. A 1966 coup attempt by Igbo officers led to Muslim riots against Igbos, which in turn led to the terrible Biafra War of 1967–1969, in which Igbos declared an independent country called Biafra in the Niger Delta. Underlying the war was the knowledge that major oil reserves lay under the Delta. The Delta, its farming and fishing ruined by the oil industry, is still the scene of permanent insurrection.

Oil is the great prize that has both held Nigeria together and ruined it. Nigeria's presidents, whether civilian or military, keep state governors (there are now 36 states) halfway obedient by

GEOGRAPHY ■ BAD WAY IN ZIMBABWE

Zimbabwe also shows what can go wrong in Africa and how easy it is to turn a country into a corrupt, impoverished dictatorship. Gold and diamond king Sir Cecil Rhodes set up Rhodesia on a commercial basis in the 1880s, but in 1923 Britain took it over as two colonies, Northern Rhodesia and Southern Rhodesia. The north, with few European settlers, became independent Zambia in 1964 and, after some corrupt and despotic rulers, has a fairly elected government.

Southern Rhodesia, with many settlers, was not as easy. Its white rulers, fearful of a black government, declared independence from Britain in 1965 under a white minority government that imitated South Africa's apartheid structure. Soon guerrilla fighting broke out, and an international embargo tried to isolate the Rhodesian economy. In 1980, the exhausted white government finally handed over power to Robert Mugabe, who revived the ancient name of Zimbabwe.

President Mugabe, bright and well-educated, won election in 1980 and stayed in power, along with his party, the Zimbabwe African National Union (ZANU), which is based on the majority Shona tribe and uses violent election tactics. As is standard in Africa, politics is tribal. Mugabe's forces killed thousands of the minority Ndebele tribe. Most of the country's good farmland was owned by a tiny white minority. Mugabe denounced them and ordered their lands taken but gave them only to the army and his political supporters. Many of the remaining whites departed, taking their skills with them. Mugabe's mismanagement brought hyperinflation, 80 percent unemployment, hunger, and disease. Store shelves are bare. Many Zimbabweans flee into neighboring South Africa, which tries to keep them out. South Africans, fearing poor Zimbabweans will take their jobs, riot against them.

The opposition Movement for Democratic Change (MDC), centered in urban and Ndebele areas, could win elections—if a fair count were permitted. Instead, the MDC suffers arrest and murder; outside observers call elections rigged. The 2008 elections were deliberately stalled during counting, and Mugabe, then 84 and clearly out of touch with reality, refused to admit defeat. Still seeing himself as the revolutionary savior of his country, he claimed he was doing a great job and Zimbabwe's economy was in fine shape.

The decline of Zimbabwe under a demented dictator poses a big question: Must the outside world under the traditional doctrine of sovereignty (see page 17) keep its hands off Zimbabwe's internal affairs, or should it intervene to stop the madness?

clientelism Distributing funds in exchange for political support.

BRIC Short for Brazil, Russia, India, and China—important emerging economies.

passing out millions in petroleum revenues, the sort of **clientelism** widely practiced in the Middle East. Much of the oil money goes into private pockets rather than for development, which is why most oil-rich countries are poor, corrupt, and undemocratic. As we shall explore more fully in Chapters 9 and 11, the "oil curse," by concentrating wealth into the hands of a few, blocks democracy.

The Niger Delta, where the oil is produced, is undergoing a low-level war that could turn high-level. Local people, who get little from the oil revenues, have had their fishing and farming destroyed by pollution. Parts of the Delta look like stage sets for Dante's *Inferno*. Heavily armed gangs posing as liberation fronts have knocked out a third of Nigeria's oil production and threaten all-out warfare. This matters more than you think, as Nigeria is the fifth-largest oil supplier to the United States. Without Nigerian oil, gasoline prices would soar again.

THE ASSERTIVE EMERGING COUNTRIES

From the previous section, one might assume that the Global South in general and Africa in particular is doomed to failure. That is not at all the case. Today an increasing number of emerging lands have much faster economic growth than the advanced countries (see Chapter 11). Sub-Saharan Africa, long ignored, is growing at several percent a year. A resource-hungry world discovered that Africa has major mineral deposits and untouched agricultural potential and is investing heavily. If the Europeans hesitate to start projects in Africa, China plunges in and is now Africa's biggest trading partner. The **BRICs** are rising rapidly; Turkey, Indonesia, and South Africa are now often included with them. Princeton economist and Nobel Prize winner Paul Krugman pointed out that no one has been able to predict the next country or region of rapid economic growth; it always surprises us.

As their economies grow, the emerging countries assert their own international perspectives and policies. Although several major powers court them, they do not follow the United States or anyone else. Turkey and Brazil, for example, negotiated with Iran to monitor its nuclear program. Washington, fancying itself the leader in these matters, did not like Ankara's and Brasilia's initiatives, but they could talk with Tehran when Washington could not, precisely because they were all emerging countries and had not demonized each other. Turkey (see page 157) now sees itself as a leader of the Middle East and well positioned to mediate with Iran. Brazil has eclipsed Mexico to become Latin America's leading economy. Under its "friends with all" foreign policy, Brazil cultivates ties with China and Iran. China, now the world's second-largest economy, ignores U.S. demands to get tough with North Korea. Beijing argues that quietly negotiating with Pyongyang gets farther than tough public threats.

Washington is not happy with such assertive policies from the emerging lands, but there is nothing it can do about it. The Bush 43 administration tried to "lead" the emerging countries and was rebuffed. The Obama administration reoriented policy to treat the newly important lands with respect; President Obama's 2010 national security strategy noted, "Emerging powers in every region of the world are increasingly asserting themselves." Obama had a personal connection with an important emerging country, Indonesia, the world's largest Muslim nation and third-largest democracy. From age 6 to 10, Obama lived and went to school in Jakarta. One of the great trends of our day is the rapid development of the Third World. The rise of these countries is transforming global politics in a *multipolar* direction (see page 10) that Washington must take into account.

my**poliscikit** EXERCISES

Apply what you learned in this chapter on MyPoliSciKit (www.mypoliscikit.com).

Assessment   Review this chapter using learning objectives, chapter summaries, practice tests, and more.

Menu

Flashcards   Learn the key terms in this chapter; you can test yourself by term or definition.

Flashcards

Video   Analyze recent world affairs by watching streaming video from major news providers.

Videos

Simulations   Play the role of an IR decision-maker and experience how IR concepts work in
Comparative   practice.
Exercises

KEY TERMS

anarchic (p. 117)
apartheid (p. 118)
BRIC (p. 124)
clientelism (p. 124)
colonialism (p. 114)
decolonization (p. 114)
divide and rule (p. 120)

emerging economies (p. 115)
failed state (p. 115)
GDP (p. 115)
Global South (p. 115)
pan-Africanism (p. 114)
partition (p. 120)
praetorian (p. 121)

Raj (p. 120)
secularism (p. 121)
subcontinent (p. 120)
Third World (p. 115)
tribalism (p. 122)
weak state (p. 115)

FURTHER REFERENCE

Adelman, Howard, and Astri Suhrke, eds. *The Path of a Genocide: The Rwanda Crisis from Uganda to Zaire.* Rutgers, NJ: Transaction, 1999.

Ansprenger, Franz. *The Dissolution of the Colonial Empires.* New York: Routledge, 1989.

Brendon, Piers. *The Decline and Fall of the British Empire, 1781–1997.* New York: Knopf, 2009.

Cocker, Mark. *Rivers of Blood, Rivers of Gold: Europe's Conquest of Indigenous Peoples.* New York: Grove, 2001.

Fernández-Armesto, Felipe. *1492: The Year the World Began.* New York: HarperCollins, 2010.

Howe, Stephen. *Empire: A Very Short Introduction.* New York: Oxford University Press, 2002.

Huband, Mark. *The Skull Beneath the Skin: Africa After the Cold War.* Boulder, CO: Westview, 2001.

Jones, Bruce D. *Peacemaking in Rwanda: The Dynamics of Failure.* Boulder, CO: Lynne Rienner, 2001.

Lemarchand, René. *The Dynamics of Violence in Central Africa.* Philadelphia: University of Pennsylvania Press, 2009.

Love, Janice. *Southern Africa in World Politics: Local Aspirations and Global Entanglements.* Boulder, CO: Westview, 2005.

Lyman, Princeton N. *Partner to History: The U.S. Role in South Africa's Transition to Democracy.* Herndon, VA: U.S. Institute of Peace, 2002.

Mandela, Nelson. *Long Walk to Freedom.* Boston: Little, Brown, 1994.

Meredith, Martin. *The Fate of Africa: From the Hopes of Freedom to the Heart of Despair; A History of Fifty Years of Independence.* New York: PublicAffairs, 2005.

Turner, Thomas. *The Congo Wars: Conflict, Myth and Reality.* London: Zed Books, 2009.

Wrong, Michela. *I Didn't Do It for You: How the World Betrayed a Small African Nation.* New York: HarperCollins, 2005.

CHAPTER 8

Eternal Warfare in the Holy Land

Clashes between Israeli security forces and Palestinians are inevitable as Israel's occupation of the West Bank stretched past 40 years. Here, a Palestinian tries to get past an Israeli border police officer to get into Jerusalem's Al Aqsa Mosque for Friday prayers in 2000. (AP Photos)

Americans are natural optimists, so it is sad to contemplate that there may be no peace in the Middle East. Looking at the six wars over six decades, the mistrust, the maximalist demands of both sides, and the long history of a stalled "peace process," pessimism may be justified. Few Israelis or Palestinians are ready for genuine compromise. Many on both sides demand the whole of historic Palestine. How did two peoples become attached to the same land? History and religion created two communities from which a national consciousness grew that was fixated on the same territory of **Palestine**. Thus two strong *nationalisms* evolved at odds with each other and still block peace efforts. Can they be overcome?

THE MAKING OF JEWISH NATIONALISM

Jewish peoplehood is rooted in the Holy Land and Scripture. The ancient Hebrews were conquered by Assyria, Persia, Alexander the Great, and Rome. They became a dispersed people but preserved a sense of their nationhood through the Old Testament.

QUESTIONS TO CONSIDER

1. What is nationalism, and where did it come from?
2. How did Israelis and Arabs become nationalistic?
3. How and why did the British help set up the Arab–Israel dispute?
4. How many wars has Israel fought? When were they, and what was their underlying cause?
5. What strategy did Kissinger use to end the 1973 war? Is there a message in this for current peace attempts?
6. Is the conflict a clash of religions or just about land?
7. What role can the United States play in the peace process?
8. Can there eventually be Arab–Israeli peace? How?

Scattered throughout the Roman Empire and beyond, over the centuries millions of Jews converted to other religions—sometimes by force—and assimilated into local life. Mixing went the other way, too, and in Israel today one can meet Jews who look like Germans, Spaniards, Russians, Turks, Arabs, Indians—you name it. The connection between people and land is less racial than psychological. Jewish life in Europe ranged from tolerable to horrible. Jewish life in Arab lands was generally better, as Islam historically tolerated Christian and Jewish minorities. Nationalism in the nineteenth century awakened Jews much as it did colonial peoples. Every people, nationalism taught, must have their own country. Jews in the late nineteenth century began devising their own nationalism, **Zionism**.

A key event in Zionism was the Dreyfus Affair of the 1890s, in which a Jewish French officer was convicted on fake evidence of spying for Germany. France, a society badly split since the Revolution, split again as reactionaries reviled Jews and liberals defended them. An assimilated Jewish journalist at Dreyfus's trial, Theodor Herzl, was horrified by the anger and violence that appeared in France and concluded that Jews could be safe only with their own country. In 1896 he published *Der Judenstaat* (The Jewish State) and became the principal advocate and organizer of modern political (as opposed to religious) Zionism. In 1897 he organized the first Zionist Congress

Palestine   Ancient Holy Land, part of Fertile Crescent bordering the Mediterranean, Egypt, and Lebanon.

Zionism   Jewish nationalism focused on gaining and keeping Israel as a Jewish state.

Ottoman   Turkish empire in Balkans and Middle East from fourteenth century to World War I.

nationalism   A people's sense of identity and unity, often exaggerated and focused against foreigners.

and predicted that within 50 years his dream of a Jewish state would be a reality. He was off by only one year, for Israel was proclaimed a state in 1948.

Aiding recruitment for Herzl's new movement were conditions in Russia, which at that time included eastern Poland, the area of heaviest Jewish population. The tsarist government encouraged *pogroms* (anti-Jewish riots) to deflect mass discontent onto Jews. Many Jews emigrated to West Europe and America, but a few, imbued with Zionism, settled in Palestine.

In 1900 Palestine was a sleepy part of the **Ottoman** Turkish empire, its small population mostly Arab. Zionist immigrants intoned, "The land without a people shall have a people without a land." They barely noticed the local Arabs. The young Zionists were secular (some were even atheists), socialist, and pioneering. Jewish nationalism was their religion, and working the soil was their worship. Most Israelis got religious only recently.

The Zionists were few in number but well organized. A Jewish National Fund raised money abroad, and a land development company bought land and trained young Jewish settlers who set up *kibbutzim* (communal farms) and *moshavim* (cooperative farms). The pioneers drained swamps and irrigated deserts. Hebrew was revived as a spoken language, no longer just for prayer. In 1903 Tel Aviv ("Hill of Spring") was founded as a modern Jewish city, just north of the Arab port of Jaffa.

CONCEPTS ■ NATIONALISM

Nationalism is the sometimes angry belief in the independence and greatness of one's people. It often includes resentment or hatred of alien rulers or threatening foreigners: "No foreigners will push us around!" It is the strongest and most emotional of the world's ideologies. Most of the world's peoples—including Americans—are nationalistic, some a little and some a lot.

The modern concept of *nationality* began with absolutist monarchs in the seventeenth century who tried to replace local consciousness (e.g., Burgundian) with national consciousness (e.g., French). **Nationalism**, however, didn't rise until the French Revolution, which, because it was based on "the people," gave the French an exalted view of themselves as Europe's leaders and liberators. (To get a feel for the emotional power of nationalism, listen to the French national anthem, "La Marseillaise.")

Wherever Napoleon's arrogant legions conquered, they awoke nationalism among other Europeans.

Nationalism teaches that it is deeply wrong to be governed by foreigners. French occupation gave life to Spanish, German, and Russian nationalism. (To see how a francophile Russian learns to hate the French and become a Russian nationalist, read Tolstoy's epic *War and Peace*.) During the nineteenth century, one European land after another awakened to demand its own nation. The European empires inadvertently spread nationalism overseas. By administering different peoples as one unit and educating them in a common language and culture, the colonialists taught the "natives" to think of themselves as one people and to resent being governed by foreigners. The more recently a country has been a colony, the more nationalistic it tends to be, for its grudges against foreigners are still vivid. Especially explosive is nationalism entwined with religion, as in India, Pakistan, ex-Yugoslavia, Afghanistan, and the Middle East.

THE MAKING OF ARAB NATIONALISM

Arab nationalism is also rooted in religion, in the **Islam** that exploded out of Arabia in the seventh century. Muhammad believed he was the last prophet of Allah (Arabic for God). His recitation of God's words formed the *Koran*, or holy book. Arabic thus became the liturgical language of **Muslims** (meaning those who surrendered to the will of God). As Islam spread, so did the Arabic language and culture. Arabic and Hebrew are related Semitic languages.

Islam   Faith founded by Muhammad in seventh-century Arabia.

Muslim   Adherent of Islam, also an adjective.

caliphate   Muslim empire.

Arab invaders spread the new faith like wildfire, and in a few decades Islam blanketed the present Middle East, Persia, Central Asia, Western India, North Africa, and Spain. They also founded **caliphates**, which culturally were far ahead of Europe, then stuck in the Dark Ages. Thanks to Arabic translations, the ancient Greek classics revived and spread into Christian Europe. Medicine, the arts, and commerce flourished under Arab empires.

These caliphates crumbled over time. The Christian crusades and a brutal Mongol invasion in the thirteenth century weakened Arab civilization. No longer able to expand, it atrophied. Portugal opened the sea route around Africa to Asia, bypassing Arab traders. Islam turned from a tolerant and flexible faith to a narrow and reactionary one. By the time the Ottoman Turks, themselves Muslims, expanded through the Middle East in the sixteenth century, there was little Arab resistance. The Arab lands fell into the "sleep of centuries" as backwater provinces of the Ottoman Empire.

DIPLOMACY ■ PROMISES, PROMISES

Desperate in World War I, Britain made promises to win allies and paid no attention to how the promises overlapped and contradicted each other, leading to angry conflict later.

1. *The McMahon–Hussein Letters*: The British boss of Egypt, Sir Henry McMahon, exchanged ten letters with Sherif Hussein in 1915–1916 to encourage the Arabs to revolt against the Turks. McMahon agreed with Hussein that there should be an Arab land, but he left the borders vague. Hussein wanted the entire Arabian Peninsula and Fertile Crescent (including Palestine). McMahon hedged, but the Arabs thought they had a deal.

2. *The Sykes–Picot Agreement*: At the same time, Britain, France, and Russia secretly agreed to carve up the Ottoman Empire after the war. The Arabs could have the Arabian Peninsula, but Britain and France would divide the Fertile Crescent, the British in Palestine and Mesopotamia and the French in Syria and Lebanon. The Bolsheviks published the agreement to show how dastardly the imperialists were. Sykes–Picot was clearly at odds with the McMahon–Hussein understanding.

3. *The Balfour Declaration*: In the fall of 1917, the British cabinet, to win worldwide Jewish support for the war effort, issued a declaration named after the foreign secretary:

   His Majesty's Government view with favour the establishment in Palestine of a national home for the Jewish people, and will use their best endeavours to facilitate the achievement of this object, it being clearly understood that nothing shall be done which may prejudice the civil and religious rights of existing non-Jewish communities in Palestine.

Notice that the declaration promised no Jewish state, just a "national home," and that it looked out for Arab rights as well. Nonetheless, it seems to be at odds with the preceding two agreements. To how many people can you promise the same land?

mandate   League of Nations grant of semicolonial power to Britain and France over former German and Turkish possessions.

In the nineteenth century, however, Europe's nationalism also rippled into the decaying Ottoman Empire. Arab officers in the Ottoman army resented not being treated as equals with Turkish officers. Some formed conspiratorial cells aiming for Arab independence. An "Arab awakening" began with a literary revival in Lebanon in the mid-nineteenth century, much of it led by Arab Christians. Half-forgotten classics spoke of the glory of Arab culture and history.

The first Arab Congress met in Paris in 1913 to seek Arab self-rule within the Ottoman Empire. Istanbul refused. On the eve of World War I, Arab nationalists saw that they needed a powerful ally to free them from the Turks. Like the Zionists, the Arab nationalists lined up British power for their own nationalist ends. Britain in World War I launched both Zionist and Arab nationalist movements into a contest for land.

WORLD WAR I AND THE MANDATE

Turkey allied with Germany in World War I. Istanbul knew that Britain, France, and Russia coveted pieces of the Ottoman Empire. A British officer, T. E. Lawrence, organized the Arab revolt of 1916 to oust the Turks from the Fertile Crescent and expand the British Empire. But the Arabs in this revolt, led by Hussein, sherif of Mecca and Medina, thought they were fighting for Arab self-rule. Britain meanwhile encouraged the Zionist movement as a means of mobilizing Jewish opinion in the United States and Russia to support the war effort.

Britain soon torpedoed Arab aspirations. Britain and France divided the Fertile Crescent and ignored Arab protests. In 1922, the new League of Nations, which Britain and France dominated, gave them **mandates** over the region. The British did, for a while, honor the Balfour commitment to let Jews have a national home in Palestine, and from 1919 to 1931 an average of 10,000 Jews entered annually, not a major influx. Angered at British betrayal and fearful that Jewish immigration would take over the country, Palestinian Arabs rioted against Jews in 1920 and 1921, leaving more than 100 dead. This began the violent confrontation between the two communities.

In the 1930s, anti-Semitic regimes in Germany and Poland accelerated Jewish immigration to Palestine. Jewish organizations bought more land, and this led to a 1936–1939 civil war between Arabs and Jews in Palestine. A Jewish self-defense force, the *Haganah*, was organized; it later became the core of the Israeli army. Kibbutzniks tilled the soil by day and fought off Arab attacks by night.

By 1938 there were 413,000 Jews in Palestine, still a minority because the Arab population had grown, too. By 1939, Britain knew that war was coming and that Germany desired the region's strategic position and petroleum. Hitler indeed sent two armies toward the area, one through Russia into

GEOGRAPHY ■ BRITAIN INVENTS JORDAN

The original League of Nations mandate on Palestine included present-day Jordan as well. In 1921 the British split off Transjordan ("the land beyond the Jordan River") and gave it to one of Hussein's sons as a reward for his help in the war. The British advised Transjordan's king, subsidized him, and equipped and trained his army, the Arab Legion. In 1948, as the British pulled out of Palestine, the kingdom was renamed Jordan. Some Israelis argue that Jordan's origins as part of Palestine mean that Palestinians already have a state—on the other side of the Jordan River. No Palestinians buy this argument.

the Caucasus and another across North Africa into Egypt. German agents encouraged the Arabs (and Iranians—see Chapter 9) to revolt against the British. Britain was scared and tried to calm the Arabs.

white paper Major diplomatic policy statement.

In 1939 Britain issued a **white paper** that severely restricted Jewish immigration; only 75,000 more would be allowed over the next four years. This calmed the Arabs but betrayed the Zionists. Britain closed the immigration door precisely when Europe's Jews needed a refuge. Still, the Jews of Palestine had to support the British. Said Zionist leader David Ben Gurion: "We will fight the White Paper as if there were no war and fight the war as if there were no White Paper."

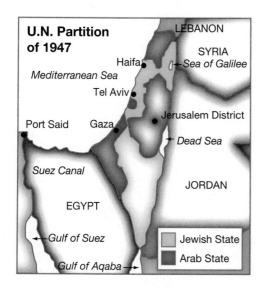

Shifting Middle East Maps

Holocaust Nazi genocide of Jews.

Sinai Campaign The 1956 war in which Israel took Sinai.

The war turned Zionism from a romantic dream to a tough demand for a Jewish state. As Jews desperately sought to leave Europe, there was practically no place that would take them. The British barred them from Palestine. Some Zionists, including two who later became prime ministers of Israel (Menachem Begin and Yitzhak Shamir), in rage and frustration turned to terrorism against the British mandate: "The Nazis kill us, and the British won't let us live."

The liberation of the Nazi death camps in 1945 clinched the Zionist argument, an argument made since Herzl: Jews would never be safe until they had their own country. The Nazis had exterminated some 6 million Jews while the world paid little attention. The survivors demanded to be let into Palestine, and Zionists demanded a Jewish state. Jewish terrorists in Palestine murdered British soldiers. To fight for a Jewish state was the highest morality; anyone who got in their way was immoral. Israelis developed a mindset to never again trust their fate to others—no one gave a damn during the **Holocaust**—and to this day Israelis dislike outsiders proposing "peace plans" that risk their security.

THE 1948 WAR

Britain's position in Palestine became untenable after World War II. Broke and exhausted, Britain in 1947 threw the problem to the new United Nations. A UN commission recommended partitioning Palestine into a checkerboard of Arab and Jewish areas with a neutral Jerusalem (see maps on page 131). The UN General Assembly voted for the plan 33 to 13, with 10 abstaining. Both the United States and the Soviet Union and their allies voted for the plan, but all of the Middle Eastern states voted against. Moscow saw it as a way to get Britain out of the Middle East and enhance its own role.

The Jews, at this point about a third of Palestine's population, accepted partition, but the Arab states and the Palestinian Arabs rejected it. Arabs, denying Israel's right to exist, saw no reason to compromise. On May 14, 1948, as the British mandate ended, Ben Gurion proclaimed the State of Israel, and five Arab armies—those of Egypt, Syria, Iraq, Jordan, and Lebanon—moved in to grab a piece of Palestine.

The Arabs got a shock. The Haganah fielded an army of 40,000, half of them World War II veterans, and scrounged up war-surplus weapons or made their own. Their best weapon was high morale born of desperation. If they lost, the entire Jewish population would be "pushed into the sea." Israeli military doctrine is based on *ayn brayra*, no alternative.

With the exception of Jordan's British-officered Arab Legion, the Arab armies fought poorly. No Arab country wanted a separate Arab country of Palestine. Israel beat all but the Jordanians, who occupied and held what is today called the West Bank plus East Jerusalem with the Old City and most holy sites. Israel held West Jerusalem.

Under UN auspices (see Chapter 21) in 1949, Egypt, Syria, Jordan, and Lebanon agreed to truces with Israel but not to peace. Israel now held 80 percent of the Palestine mandate. Some 700,000 Palestinian Arabs fled Israel; their property was declared "abandoned" and seized. The permanent core of the Arab–Israel conflict has been and still is the Palestinians.

THE 1956 WAR

The 1956 war, also known as the Suez Crisis and **Sinai Campaign**, again illustrates the role of outside powers in starting and ending Arab–Israeli wars. Britain and France attacked Egypt, and the United States and USSR pressured them to clear out.

Egyptian President Gamal Abdul Nasser was a new breed of Arab leader. Egyptian army officers, humiliated at defeat by the Israelis, blamed the corrupt monarchy, and under Colonel Nasser's leadership overthrew King Farouk in 1952. Nasser saw himself not simply as an Egyptian nationalist but as the leader of a pan-Arab movement. He supported the Algerian nationalists against the French and opposed the U.S.- and British-backed Baghdad Pact, which sought to keep Soviet influence out of the Middle East.

Tiran Strait   Narrow entrance from Red Sea to Gulf of Aqaba.

Six Day War   The 1967 war in which Israel took Sinai, West Bank, and Golan Heights.

Events unrolled quickly as each side enraged the other. It began with Palestinian refugees. In the Gaza Strip, under Egyptian control since 1948, some Palestinians became *fedayeen*, "self-sacrificers," who made raids into Israel. They were armed and trained by Egypt as part of Nasser's policy of using conflict with Israel to arouse and unify all Arabs under his leadership. Israel retaliated with major raids on Egyptian posts in the Gaza Strip. Nasser angrily sought arms. The United States and Britain refused, but the Soviet Union was happy to sell enormous quantities. With Soviet weapons, Nasser built up his forces in the Sinai facing Israel, and Israel grew nervous.

Disappointed that Nasser was turning to the Soviets, the United States and Britain withdrew their offer to help fund construction of Egypt's dream, the Aswan Dam on the Nile. Angered by this withdrawal, Nasser nationalized the British- and French-owned Suez Canal on July 26, 1956. It was a vestige of colonialism, he argued, and now Egypt needed its revenues to build the Aswan Dam. Enraged by Nasser's canal takeover, Britain and France quietly colluded with Israel to take the canal back. Israel would strike first, and they would come in to "protect" the canal.

On October 29, 1956, Israeli forces streaked through the Sinai toward the Suez Canal. London and Paris issued ultimatums to both sides to withdraw ten miles from the canal. Then they invaded and seized the canal zone on November 5. The 1956 war ended with Israel in possession of the Sinai and Britain and France in possession of the canal. Nasser was beaten but not defeated. President Eisenhower was angry that London and Paris moved on Egypt against U.S. advice. This last gasp of British and French imperialism would only push Arab nationalists closer to the Soviets, Ike reasoned. The United States supported a UN resolution to oust the invading forces and used economic pressure to get the British and French to withdraw from Suez, which they did in December.

Israel took more persuading. Ike threatened economic sanctions and promised to get Egypt to open the **Tiran Strait** to Israeli shipping. With a UN Emergency Force (UNEF) to patrol the Sinai, Israel pulled out in March 1957. In the Sinai Campaign, as in subsequent wars, the victors had not won, and the war settled nothing.

THE SIX DAY WAR

One result of the 1956 war was that Egypt and Syria became Soviet clients. Fedayeen again raided, and Israel retaliated. In 1963, Israel began a project to divert water from the Jordan River (a creek in U.S. terms), angering Syria and Jordan. Regional tensions mounted. By spring 1967, events took hold of Nasser and pushed him toward war. He may have been bluffing; the Israelis called it. Nasser declared he was ready for war with Israel, and Israelis took the threat literally. This was in part the clash of two cultures: Arabs are given to exaggerated rhetoric, Israelis to straight, blunt talk.

Much of the blame for the **Six Day War** rests on Syrian and Soviet lies. Syria held the Golan Heights overlooking Israel's lush Upper Galilee and shelled Israeli farmers; in response, Israeli jets hit Syrian gun positions and shot down six Syrian MIGs. Damascus lied, saying that Israel was massing troops in the Galilee to attack Syria. What, Damascus demanded, was Nasser, the great hero of the

preempt   To strike first on the eve of war.

Arabs, going to do? Syria was goading Nasser into a strong response. Israel denied any such intent and invited the Soviet ambassador to take a look; in this small valley, troops are easily visible. The ambassador declined but repeated that Israel was preparing to invade Syria.

Nasser now had to show he would aid Syria. He ordered UN forces out of the Sinai, where they had served as truce observers since 1957. Then he closed Tiran to Israeli shipping and ordered a troop buildup in the Sinai. On May 30, 1967, he signed a defense pact with King Hussein of Jordan; he already had such an agreement with Syria. The cautious Hussein had previously stayed clear of involvement with Nasser and had not threatened Israel.

Israel was thus surrounded by hate-filled Arabs screaming "war." Israel's narrow neck between Jordan and the sea was less than ten miles wide in places. Israel's attitude grew out of its geopolitical situation: Either we **preempt** or we're doomed. Israel quietly began mobilizing reservists. On June 4, Jerusalem learned that the United States would not force open the Tiran Strait as it had pledged in 1957. America was bogged down in Vietnam. Israel felt endangered and abandoned and, on June 5, preempted.

The results were quick and breathtaking. Using tactics from U.S. military courses, Israeli jets first destroyed Egyptian warplanes on the ground and then Egyptian armor. Israel streaked across the Sinai and reached the Suez Canal on June 8.

Jordan began shelling Israel and gave the Israelis the excuse they had been looking for since 1948 to take the Old City of Jerusalem, which they did with three battalions. Jerusalem was declared reunified and forever the capital of Israel, an intensely emotional symbol. Israel also took the entire West Bank. The Golan Heights were the hardest for Israel: uphill against Syrian bunkers from June 8 to 10. To this day, Israelis swear they will never relinquish the strategic Golan position; they incorporated it into Israel in 1981.

The Israelis in 1967 knew time was short. The superpowers saw the danger of the war expanding. Moscow threatened to intervene as its clients' armies collapsed, and Washington told Jerusalem to wrap it up fast. The Six Day War was short because of the superpowers.

The three Arab countries lost 14,000 soldiers, Israel only 700. It looked like a brilliant victory, but again the war settled nothing. Israel had not taken an Arab capital or heartland; the superpowers saw to that. There was no pressing need for the Arabs to "sue for peace" as in classic diplomacy. Instead, they announced in Khartoum that September: "no negotiation, no recognition, no peace." The United Nations passed the evenhanded Resolution 242, the basis of peace plans ever since, that asked Israel to withdraw and the Arabs to accept Israel's existence on peaceful terms. Both sides ignored 242, each claiming it could not trust the other side. The stage was set for the 1973 war.

Israel, in the flush of victory, also acquired a major problem. The recently seized West Bank and Gaza Strip contained 1.3 million Palestinians (now grown to more than 3 million), most of them refugees from the 1948–1949 war or their descendants. Israel would now have to govern the people it wanted to get rid of in 1948.

THE 1973 WAR

Egyptian President Anwar Sadat, who took over upon Nasser's death in 1970, believed that Israel's occupation of the Sinai, Golan Heights, and West Bank had to be challenged, partly to overcome the defeatist psychology of Arabs and the victorious psychology of Israelis and partly to make the superpowers take an active interest.

On October 6, 1973, Egyptians and Syrians struck a surprised Israel. More than 2,000 Soviet-made Syrian tanks penetrated the lightly held Golan Heights. Israel repelled them in the biggest tank battle in history. Meanwhile, Egyptian forces crossed the Suez Canal and broke through Israel's lightly held Bar Lev Line and into the Sinai. In a bold gamble, Israeli General Ariel Sharon—later prime minister—crossed his forces to the west side of the canal and cut off the Egyptians on the east.

> **October War**   The 1973 Arab–Israeli war, also called Yom Kippur or Ramadan War.
>
> **logistics**   The supplying of an army.

At this point, the United States and USSR, after desperately resupplying their clients, tried to enforce another UN cease-fire. Moscow threatened to send troops to aid the Egyptians. President Nixon then put U.S. forces on worldwide alert to deter Soviet intervention. U.S. delay in resupplying Israel stopped Israel's further advances. As before, outside powers exercised great influence.

The war, known as the **October War**, jolted the world. Arab oil exporters embargoed oil shipments to pro-Israel countries (the United States and Netherlands) and quadrupled the price of petroleum. This kicked up world inflation for years. Militarily, the world's armies took careful note, for the war demonstrated that small, guided missiles could knock out jets and tanks. The Arabs had shown that Israel was not invincible. Heavy Israeli losses (2,500 dead to 8,000 Syrian and 8,000 Egyptian deaths) made Israel worry about a long war.

The psychological change enabled Anwar Sadat to amaze the world. In 1977 he accepted Israel's invitation and flew to Jerusalem for face-to-face talks with Israeli Prime Minister Menachem Begin. Sadat spoke to Israel not as a loser but as an equal. This led to the Camp David talks at the president's Maryland retreat in 1978. President Carter mediated and cajoled Begin and Sadat into the first Arab–Israeli peace treaty, completed in 1979. Each side emerged with something. Sadat got the Sinai back and more U.S. aid to head off food riots by Egypt's poor. Begin got an opportunity to split Israel's Arab enemies—Egypt was expelled from the Arab bloc—and increased U.S. financial support.

DIPLOMACY ■ LOGISTICS AND PEACE

The 1973 war showed that modern warfare consumes munitions at a prodigious rate. War becomes highly dependent on **logistics**. Said Israel's defense minister in 1973: "We are firing shells this afternoon that we did not have in the country this morning." They got them by a U.S. airlift across the Atlantic with aerial refueling. U.S. airlift capacity allows it to project power like no other country.

U.S. Secretary of State Henry Kissinger was no specialist on the Middle East, but he had written books on the balance of power. When Israel was losing, the United States had to resupply it. But Kissinger knew that another Israeli victory would not lead to peace; it would be a repeat of 1956 and 1967. So Kissinger discreetly held up resupplying Israel, which soon did not have the munitions to move further. Neither side won or lost in 1973; they psychologically balanced.

In "shuttle diplomacy," Kissinger jetted repeatedly among Cairo, Jerusalem, and Damascus, securing truces that held. In both the Sinai and Golan, he mapped out strips of no-man's land flanked by strips thinly patrolled by each side, backed up by strongly held zones. The idea was to separate their main forces. The belligerents signed. The agreement formed the basis of a peace treaty between Egypt and Israel. Based on the idea that power should balance, Kissinger produced a brilliant piece of diplomacy.

PLO   Palestine Liberation
Organization, mainstream resistance
party that formerly ran *PA*.

intifada   Arabic for uprising; includes
suicide bombings.

THE RISE OF PALESTINIAN NATIONALISM

The 1978 Camp David agreement left the underlying problem unsettled, and it led to another war. Israel pledged to accept "Palestinian autonomy," but nothing came of it. Land seizures for new Israeli settlements in East Jerusalem and the West Bank increased; now more than 500,000 Israelis live there. Palestinian nationalism grew, mostly under the **PLO**, headed by Yasser Arafat. Palestinians had been treated badly by the British, the Israelis, and other Arab countries, who used them for their own purposes. Everywhere they were homeless and foreigners. No Arab country wanted them in large numbers. In a colossal irony, the Palestinians became like Jews, a dispersed and sometimes suspect people with no national home. And like Zionists, Palestinians concluded they needed their own country.

Israel's takeover of the West Bank and Gaza Strip in 1967 ended any illusions about Egypt or Jordan "protecting" the Palestinians. This also allowed Palestinians to work in Israel and view for the first time their ancestral land, but as noncitizens. Israelis treated them with disdain, and there was little contact between the two communities. The hatred got worse.

A number of factors led to two bloody **intifadas**. The fate of Palestinians has dangled unresolved for decades. They still have no country of their own. Israeli settlements, roads, and security fences in the West Bank continue to grow, taking more Palestinian land and hacking the territory into small pieces. The Palestinian birth rate is one of the world's highest. In a century, the number of Palestinians has grown from half a million to 5 million, many of them in other countries. Coupled with a ruined economy, this produces armies of unemployed, angry youth. Muslim extremism has grown across the Middle East, inspiring some youths to become terrorists and suicide bombers. Every act of Palestinian terrorism produces brutal Israeli reprisals—demolition of homes, "targeted assassinations," and tough occupation restrictions—that inflame more Palestinians. Another intifada is waiting to happen.

THE 1982 WAR

In 1975, Lebanon fell apart in a civil war between Christians and Muslims, and this allowed the PLO to set up a state within a state, "Fatahland," in southern Lebanon. A dozen Lebanese religio-political militias battled, some of them backed by Syria, which took over eastern Lebanon, an area it had long claimed. Israel invaded Lebanon in June 1982 to knock out

Arab–Israeli Wars		
Year	Name	Result
1948–1949	Israeli Independence	Israel founded in most of Palestine.
1956	Sinai Campaign	Israel beats Egypt, takes Sinai.
1967	Six Day War	Israel takes Sinai from Egypt, West Bank from Jordan, Golan Heights from Syria.
1973	October War	Israel repels Egypt and Syria.
1982	Lebanon Incursion	Israel invades southern Lebanon.
2006	Hezbollah War	Israel in Lebanon again.

Palestinian bases and help put Christians back in power, but the Israeli army bogged down fighting Muslim militias.

    U.S. "peacekeeping" forces arrived but soon began supporting the Christians. Misguidedly, we took sides in a civil war. A **Hezbollah** truck bomb killed 241 sleeping U.S. Marines, and we withdrew. Israel pulled back but kept a roughly nine-mile-deep "security zone" in southern Lebanon. Hezbollah fighters bombed and ambushed the Israelis weekly until they withdrew entirely in 2000. In 2006, Hezbollah kidnapped two Israeli soldiers, and Israel responded with another invasion that did massive civilian damage. Some count it as the sixth Arab–Israeli war. Hezbollah boasts that it is the only Arab force to ever beat the Israelis.

> **Hezbollah** ("Party of God") Iranian-sponsored Lebanese Shia militia.
>
> **rejectionist** Someone who rejects compromise peace.

IS THERE HOPE?

War is easy; peace is hard. Peace negotiations, opposed by **rejectionists** on both sides, can quickly collapse. In a climate of tension and frustration, extremists fuel a downward spiral. Four Arab–Israeli wars (1956, 1967, 1982, and 2006) were triggered by terrorist attacks on Israel. Palestinian militants say only violence works, because Israel seizes their land and ignores their rights. And

DIPLOMACY ■ OBAMA: RETURN TO EVEN-HANDEDNESS?

The United States preserved a sort of even-handedness in dealing with Israel and the Arab countries for the first few decades of Israel's existence. Truman recognized Israel immediately, but the Arab-leaning State Department warned against alienating the Arab states, which were important both for oil and for which side they took in the Cold War. Eisenhower was angry at the 1956 British-French-Israeli attack on Egypt and told them to clear out. Johnson sympathized with Israel in the 1967 war but was too bogged down in Vietnam to get involved.

    Although American Jews mostly vote Democrat, it was Republican presidents who tilted sharply toward Israel. Nixon saw Israel as an anti-Soviet ally in the Cold War and delivered a credible deterrence threat that persuaded Moscow not to intervene in the 1973 October War, when he airlifted U.S. munitions to a desperate Israel. Bush 41, an oilman with many Arab connections, was even-handed, but his son praised and supported Israel fulsomely, seeing it as a democratic ally in a hostile and unstable region. Critics feared the Bush 43 tilt harmed America's honest-broker role and tacitly let Israel expand its West Bank settlements.

    President Barack Obama, on the other hand, improved ties with Arab countries and warned Israel against expanding its West Bank settlements. According to the White House, these moves were just to restart the peace process; they were not anti-Israel. U.S.-sponsored peace talks between Israelis and Palestinians resumed in 2010 amid very low expectations and indeed got nowhere. The Israeli right wing, which includes Prime Minister Benjamin Netanyahu, did not conceal its opposition to the Obama policies. The two met in 2010, but it was little more than a photo-op. Some called it the worst U.S.-Israel relations in half a century. Much was symbolic, as when Israel announced an expansion of Jewish settlements in formerly Arab East Jerusalem just as Vice President Biden was visiting to promote talks. It looked like an impolite Israeli rejection. Washington has minimal contact with Israel's right-wing foreign minister, Avigdor Lieberman, who advocates making the West Bank entirely Israeli. To many it looked like Washington and Jerusalem were pulling apart, but historically it was more a return to U.S. even-handedness.

Israel built a massive separation barrier, seen here in Jerusalem, to keep out Palestinian suicide bombers. Some thought the wall would become a permanent border. (Richard Wainwright/Corbis)

Israeli militants say they are entitled to retaliation because the Arabs want to kill them all. Down and down the spiral goes.

Cooler heads on both sides know that they must strike a deal, but both are constrained by fears of what could go wrong and by their own militants. Israel cannot govern millions of angry Palestinians on the West Bank without becoming an authoritarian police state. Israelis fear, however, that a Palestinian state would be a terrorist training camp fixated on recovering all of historic Palestine. Many Palestinians still wish to destroy Israel.

Constantly expanding Israeli settlements in the West Bank are major obstacles. Settlers are lured by a mixture of religion and affordable housing. Rightist Israelis claim these areas are theirs by biblical right, that they have been paid for in blood, and that turning them over to Israel's sworn enemies would be suicidal. Liberal and leftist Israelis say that giving up these settlements for a lasting peace would be worthwhile.

Moderate Palestinians know they must come up with a Palestinian state soon without conceding too much, or extremists will spark a new war, giving Israel the excuse to "transfer"—an euphemism for expel—thousands of Palestinians out of the West Bank and take over most of it. Israel's foreign minister openly speaks of the "transfer" option. Rejectionists on both sides are happy to block the peace process. The 2000 intifada exploded when a right-wing Israeli ex-general (and later prime minister), Ariel Sharon, defiantly visited Jerusalem's top Muslim holy site. Thousands died, mostly Palestinian youths, many of whom volunteered for suicide bombings. Among both Palestinians and Israelis, many cheer the *failure* of peace talks, arguing they give away too much to the other side.

In 2006 Israel completed a long fence to keep Palestinian suicide bombers from reaching Israel. In 2005, Sharon ordered some 8,500 Israeli settlers out of the Gaza Strip; many resisted. These moves marked an Israeli unilateral solution. Jerusalem in effect says, "Look, Arabs won't negotiate and can't stop violence, so we'll do what we must to make Israel secure." But the wall did not stop Hamas and Hezbollah rockets and infiltrators. In 2006, after Hezbollah kidnapped two Israeli soldiers, Israel fought Hezbollah in Lebanon for a month but withdrew inconclusively. Hezbollah fired some of its

12,000 Iranian-supplied rockets into Israel and crowed that it had won. At the end of 2008, rockets fired by Hamas militants in Gaza triggered Israeli air and ground strikes that killed 1,300 Palestinians, most of them civilians.

Peace in the Middle East does not seem to be making headway. Israeli Prime Minister Itzhak Rabin and Palestinian leader Yasser Arafat in 1993 pledged on the White House lawn to work for peace, but in 1995 an Israeli rejectionist gunned down Rabin at a peace rally. Egypt and Israel signed a peace treaty in 1979, Jordan and Israel in 1994, but these led only to "cold peace" with little contact, commerce, or good feeling. Both treaties happened because, at a certain point, the two sides had more to gain than to lose by ending the state of war. Both treaties were sponsored by the United States, which delivers major foreign aid to all three countries. Israel gets some $3 billion in U.S. aid annually, Egypt some $2 billion. If the United States cut its gifts of grain to Egypt, food riots would break out. Aid gives some leverage.

two-state solution   One Israel and one Palestine living side-by-side in peace.

Fatah   Yasser Arafat's armed party that dominated *PLO*.

Palestinian Authority   (PA) Quasi-government of Palestine.

Hamas   (Arabic for "zeal") Armed Palestinian Islamist party, founded in 1987.

Muslim Brotherhood   Original modern Islamist movement, founded in Egypt in 1928.

Israel–Palestinian talks earlier seemed to point to a **two-state solution** (first recommended in 1937), but three big issues always blocked a deal: (1) Israel must give up many—perhaps most—of its settlements in the West Bank to make a territorially coherent Palestinian state. Many Israelis, including Prime Minister Netanyahu, refuse and keep expanding the settlements. (2) Palestinians want the right of return, to go back to the homes and farms they fled in 1948. Israelis fear they would soon be swamped and reject the notion. (3) Palestinians also insist on sovereignty over East Jerusalem. Israelis proclaim all of Jerusalem eternally theirs and redo whole districts, pushing out their Palestinian residents. Peace between Palestinians and Israelis could produce an economic boom in the region. If they cannot compromise, there will likely soon be another war. At present, nothing points to peace.

DIPLOMACY ■ CAN EXTREMISTS TURN PRAGMATIC?

Militant Palestinian organizations have evolved, slowly and grudgingly, from passion to practicality. The PLO, founded in Egypt in 1964, began with fiery radio rants calling for the destruction of Israel—one reason Israel preempted in 1967. Meanwhile, Yasser Arafat developed his **Fatah** into a guerrilla force and with it took over the PLO in 1969. The PLO became a Palestinian government in exile successively in Jordan, Lebanon, and Tunisia, always hunted by the Israelis.

In 1988, King Hussein dropped Jordanian claims to the West Bank, indicating it should become a Palestinian state. The 1991 Gulf War (see next chapter) left the PLO broke and isolated, and the PLO moderated, turning from raids to diplomacy. Arafat—not always backed by more militant Palestinians—accepted the existence of Israel and began off-and-on negotiations with it. Norwegian mediation brought the Oslo Accord in 1993, which, among other points, created the **Palestinian Authority** (PA). The PA now controls the Gaza Strip and parts of the West Bank but is not yet a state. Arafat was PA president until his death in 2005.

Arafat longed to overthrow Israel, but he could not and so was forced to become more pragmatic. **Hamas**, related to the **Muslim Brotherhood**, swore to destroy Israel and carried out suicide bombings. Hamas became bigger than the corrupt and ineffective PLO by delivering charity, schooling, and health care. Hamas won the 2006 PA parliamentary elections and took over the PA government. After Israel pulled out of the Gaza Strip, Hamas took it over and shot rockets into Israel, which retaliated by a blockade and brief invasion in late 2008. In 2010, Israel boarded a Turkish charity ship trying to run the Israeli blockade of Gaza, killing nine. The big question: Will fierce Israeli reprisals and economic hardship force Hamas, which is dedicated to the destruction of Israel, to abandon its goal and negotiate? Or will it make things worse?

LESSONS OF THE ARAB–ISRAELI CONFLICT

1. Nothing gives an eternal claim to land. The belief that history or the Bible or God gives territories to certain people leads to war without end.

2. People have long memories, especially of injustice. The Israelis remember the Holocaust, and the Palestinians remember their lost homeland. For peace, memories must fade.

3. Outside powers start conflicts. British, U.S., and Soviet arms, money, and policy set up Middle East wars.

4. Terror begets terror. All sides have practiced terrorism, which guarantees terrorist responses and blocks peace.

5. One war leads to another. A clear causal line connects World War II, 1948, 1956, 1967, 1973, 1982, and 2006.

6. Do not lie or bluff about war. Your adversary may take it literally.

7. You cannot ignore inconvenient people. Neither Israelis nor Palestinians will disappear.

8. A few extremists can upset the peace process. If hardliners guide events, there will be no peace.

9. A committed outside mediator is essential for the peace process. The United States must play this role.

10. We are entitled to despair but better not. Abandoning peace efforts would strengthen extremists, leading to new wars that could hurt us.

mypoliscikit EXERCISES

Apply what you learned in this chapter on MyPoliSciKit (www.mypoliscikit.com).

Assessment   Review this chapter using learning objectives, chapter summaries, practice tests, and more.

Menu

Flashcards   Learn the key terms in this chapter; you can test yourself by term or definition.

Flashcards

Video   Analyze recent world affairs by watching streaming video from major news providers.

Videos

Simulations   Play the role of an IR decision-maker and experience how IR concepts work in practice.

Comparative Exercises

KEY TERMS

caliphate (p. 129)

Fatah (p. 139)

Hamas (p. 139)

Hezbollah (p. 137)

Holocaust (p. 132)

intifada (p. 136)

Islam (p. 129)

logistics (p. 135)

mandate (p. 130)

Muslim (p. 129)

Muslim Brotherhood (p. 139)

nationalism (p. 128)

October War (p. 135)

Ottoman (p. 128)

Palestine (p. 128)

Palestinian Authority (p. 139)

PLO (p. 136)

preempt (p. 134)

FURTHER REFERENCE

Bickerton, Ian J., and Carla L. Klausner. *A Concise History of the Arab–Israeli Conflict*, 6th ed. Upper Saddle River, NJ: Prentice Hall, 2010.

Carter, Jimmy. *Palestine: Peace Not Apartheid.* New York: Simon & Schuster, 2006.

Cohen, Stephen P. *Beyond America's Grasp: A Century of Failed Diplomacy in the Middle East.* New York: Farrar, Straus & Giroux, 2009.

Dockser Marcus, Amy. *Jerusalem 1913: The Origins of the Arab–Israeli Conflict.* New York: Penguin, 2008.

Gelvin, James L. *The Modern Middle East: A History,* 2nd ed. New York: Oxford University Press, 2007.

Gunning, Jeroen. *Hamas in Politics: Democracy, Religion, Violence.* New York: Columbia University Press, 2010.

Haas, Richard and Martin S. Indyk, eds. *Restoring the Balance: A Middle East Strategy for the Next President.* Washington, DC: Brookings, 2008.

Hirst, David. *Beware of Small States: Lebanon, Battleground of the Middle East.* New York: Nation, 2010.

Kennedy, Hugh. *The Great Arab Conquests: How the Spread of Islam Changed the World We Live In.* New York: Perseus, 2007.

Khalidi, Rashid. *Sowing Crisis: The Cold War and American Dominance in the Middle East.* Boston: Beacon, 2009.

Kimmerling, Baruch, and Joel S. Migdal. *The Palestinian People: A History.* Cambridge, MA: Harvard University Press, 2003.

Krämer, Gudrun. *A History of Palestine: From the Ottoman Conquest to the Founding of the State of Israel.* Princeton, NJ: Princeton University Press, 2008.

Lesch, David W. *The Arab–Israeli Conflict: A History.* New York: Oxford University Press, 2007.

LeVine, Mark. *Impossible Peace: Israel/Palestine since 1989.* New York: Palgrave, 2008.

Lewis, Bernard, and Buntzie Ellis Churchill. *Islam: The Religion and the People.* Upper Saddle River, NJ: Wharton Press, 2009.

Meital, Yoram. *Peace in Tatters: Israel, Palestine, and the Middle East.* Boulder, CO: Lynne Rienner, 2005.

Miller, Aaron David. *The Much Too Promised Land: America's Elusive Search for Arab–Israeli Peace.* New York: Bantam, 2008.

Milton-Edwards, Beverley, and Stephen Farrell. *Hamas: The Islamic Resistance Movement.* London: Polity, 2010.

Morris, Benny. *One State, Two States: Resolving the Israel/Palestine Conflict.* New Haven, CT: Yale University Press, 2009.

Muasher, Marwan. *The Arab Center: The Promise of Moderation.* New Haven, CT: Yale University Press, 2008.

Oren, Michael J. *Six Days of War: June 1967 and the Making of the Modern Middle East.* New York: Oxford University Press, 2002.

Rogan, Eugene. *The Arabs: A History.* New York: Basic Books, 2009.

Ross, Dennis, and David Makovsky. *Myths, Illusions, & Peace: Finding a New Direction for America in the Middle East.* New York: Viking, 2009.

Segev, Tom. *1967: Israel, the War, and the Year that Transformed the Middle East.* New York: Holt, 2008.

Shindler, Colin. *A History of Modern Israel.* New York: Cambridge University Press, 2008.

Shlaim, Avi. *Israel and Palestine: Reappraisals, Revisions, Refutations.* London: Verso, 2009.

Thomas, Baylis. *The Dark Side of Zionism: Israel's Quest for Security Through Dominance.* Lanham, MD: Rowman & Littlefield, 2010.

Tyler, Patrick. *A World of Trouble: The White House and the Middle East—from the Cold War to the War on Terror.* New York: Farrar, Straus & Giroux, 2009.

Wasserstein, Bernard. *Israelis and Palestinians: Why Do They Fight? Can They Stop?* 3rd ed. New Haven, CT: Yale University Press, 2008.

Zertal, Idith, and Akiva Eldar. *Lords of the Land: The War for Israel's Settlements in the Occupied Territories.* New York: Nation Books, 2007.

CHAPTER 9

Oil and Turmoil in the Persian Gulf

Repelling a Taliban attack in 2010, an American soldier throws a grenade. At its peak, 100,000 U.S. troops fought the ten-year-long war. (Patrick Baz/Getty Images)

The Persian Gulf, currently the world's most explosive region, exemplifies the "zones of chaos" mentioned in Chapter 1. The United States is deeply involved in the region and probably will be for a long time. The initial U.S. victories in Afghanistan in late 2001 and Iraq in spring 2003 were quick and brilliant, but occupation of both became long and messy with no easy way to get out. Most Americans agreed that the two regimes were odious and deserved to be ousted, but few knew much about Afghanistan and Iraq or the complexities that would result from occupying the two lands. Americans, as in Vietnam, do not like long, inconclusive wars, and both wars became unpopular.

Most Americans would like to keep out of the Middle East, but its oil, politics, and even religions draw us in. Islam is not just a religion; it is a distinct civilization that does not easily bend or compromise with the modern world. Islam has always divided the world into the *dar es-salaam* (house of peace, meaning the Islamic world) and the *dar al-harb* (house of war, the non-Muslim world). Muslim fundamentalists still see the world this way: us versus them.

In the Gulf, religion and nationalism fuse into a political tool with which to push out foreigners: first the British, later the Russians, now the Americans. If this were Tierra del Fuego, it might not matter, but the Gulf region contains over half of the globe's proven petroleum reserves. Another large reserve is around the **Caspian** Sea. Neither of these is a stable area.

QUESTIONS TO CONSIDER

1. Why is the Persian Gulf region so important?
2. What are the strategic waterways of the region?
3. What is Huntington's civilizational theory?
4. How are Iran and the Arab countries different?
5. Why did Iran erupt in Islamic revolution?
6. What were the first, second, and third Gulf wars about?
7. Why did Saddam use chemical weapons in the first but not the second or third Gulf wars?
8. How did U.S. diplomacy blunder in Iran and Iraq?
9. Is revolution likely in the Arab world?
10. Would you be willing to fight to keep Gulf oil flowing?

IRASCIBLE IRAN

Iran is Muslim but not Arab. It is heir to the much older civilization of Persia and speaks the Indo-European tongue of Persian (Farsi). Arabs conquered Persia in 642 A.D. and converted Persians from Zoroastrianism to Islam, but in 1501 Iran adopted the **Shia** offshoot in contrast to the **Sunni** Islam of most Muslims. Sunnis consider Shias heretics and do not trust them.

In the nineteenth century, **Persia**, then in decline, became the prey of outside powers. The Russians in the north, who were rounding out their empire in the **Caucasus** and **Central Asia**, gained economic concessions and territory from the corrupt Qajar **shahs**. The British, pushing

Caspian   Large inland sea between Caucasus and Central Asia.

Shia   Minority branch of Islam but Iran's state religion.

Sunni   Mainstream Islam.

Persia   Old name for Iran.

Caucasus   Mountainous region between Black Sea and Caspian Sea.

Central Asia   Ex-Soviet area between Caspian Sea and China.

shah   Persian for king.

sphere of influence   Area where a major power held sway.

populist   A crowd-pleasing politician, claims to represent "the people" against elites.

nationalize   To seize private firms for the state.

up from India, did the same. In 1907, the two powers divided Persia in a treaty that assigned each **spheres of influence**, in which they dominated and controlled trade. Persia, like China, was reduced to semicolonial status. Persians hated it and vented their anger from time to time on foreign diplomats. Iranians still feel they have been used and exploited for a century and that now it's their turn to get back at the foreigners.

The Persian government attempted to balance the British against the Russians, then Germany against both, so as to give Persia a little freedom and independence. This pattern of playing stronger outside powers against each other continues, a rational response for a weak country trying to preserve its independence.

In 1908 the British first discovered oil in Persia and got an exclusive concession to develop it, paying a paltry 16 percent royalty to Persia. The Anglo-Iranian Oil Company (AIOC) was powerful and owned much of the Iranian economy, which made Iranians hate it. Early in the twentieth century, many Persians sought democracy and constitutional monarchy. They were ignored by the British and the corrupt rulers of Tehran; this deepened their hatred of the British. In 1925 a vigorous but illiterate cavalry officer, Reza Khan, proclaimed himself shah. Never popular or democratic, Reza Khan ruthlessly modernized his country—which he renamed Iran, Persian for "Aryan," a word later beloved of Nazi ideologists.

When the Hitler regime looked for openings in the Middle East, it found a willing ally in Reza, who thought he could use the Germans to dislodge the British. Instead, the British exiled the shah. When the Soviet Union entered the war in 1941, it invaded northern Iran while the British took the south, just as the 1907 treaty specified. Iran became a major conduit for U.S. supplies into the Soviet Union during the war. Both agreed to exit Iran within six months of the end of the war. Stalin did not and even set up Soviet puppet states in the north of Iran. Some historians peg Stalin's attempt to seize part of Iran as the opening round of the Cold War.

In 1951, an elected **populist** prime minister, Muhammad Mossadeq, **nationalized** the AIOC and forced the young shah, son of Reza Khan, to flee to Rome. Especially hurt were the British, the owners of the AIOC, who turned to Washington for help. President Eisenhower, fearing Communist influence, in 1953 sent Kermit Roosevelt of the CIA to Tehran with $1 million in a suitcase. Hired mobs encouraged anti-Mossadeq and pro-shah protests. Mossadeq fell, and the shah returned but was never very popular.

The shah built a corrupt dictatorship, controlling oil revenues, parliament, and all mass communications. He suppressed both leftists and Islamic fundamentalists with secret police, the dread SAVAK, which arrested and tortured opponents. The United States deliberately did not notice any of this, seeing the shah as a pillar of stability and a friend in an important part of the world. The shah sought military strength, and Washington was happy to sell him weapons. Much of Iran's oil income went for arms, a point that angered many Iranians. The major U.S. presence in Tehran—diplomatic, military, and private business—offended some Iranians, especially devout Muslims. Ayatollah Ruhollah Khomeini, a top Muslim cleric who took power after the shah's overthrow, later used this feeling that Americans were "unclean" to fuel opposition to the United States.

Both the Americans and the shah believed that petroleum revenues would fund Iran's modernization. The shah instituted a "White Revolution" (a revolution from the top down, instead

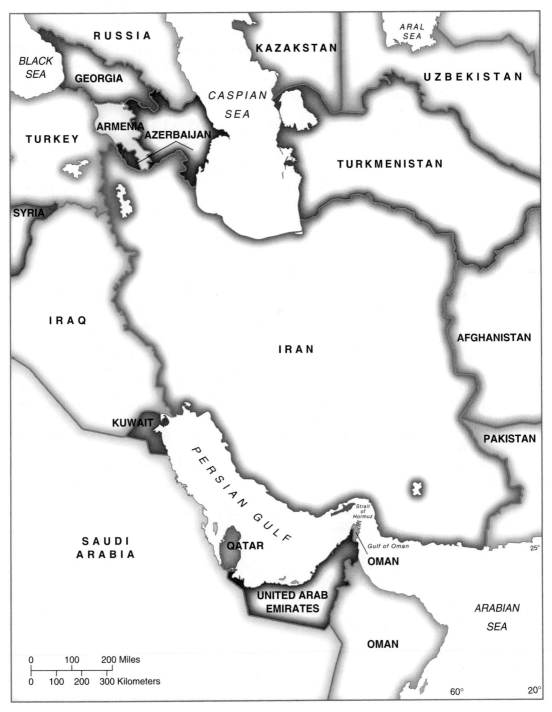

The Persian Gulf and Caspian Sea

OPEC Organization of Petroleum Exporting Countries; cartel aimed at keeping price of oil up.

of a "red" revolution from the masses up) that divided landholdings and gave them to poor peasants. But many Iranians opposed the land reform, especially Muslim charitable foundations that lost much of their lands. Rioting broke out in opposition. Political development was zero. Economic growth without channels of mass participation in politics—parties, parliament, elections, and so on—means that mass discontent can manifest itself only in violent and revolutionary ways.

The Ayatollah Khomeini especially attacked the shah and, in 1964, was exiled to neighboring Iraq. Khomeini kept up his drumfire of hatred for the shah and charged that SAVAK had murdered his son. The shah put pressure on Iraq, which expelled Khomeini to France in 1978. From his suburban Paris home, Khomeini made bitter anti-shah sermons that were telephoned to and recorded in Iran. Cassettes were then distributed nationwide and played in mosques, overleaping the shah's control of mass communications. Cheap cassette players thus helped bring him down.

What really hurt the shah was too much money. He hammered the Western oil companies for a better deal—eventually getting a 75 percent split for Iran—and was a founding member of **OPEC**. The shah took advantage of the 1973 Arab–Israeli war to take over the foreign interests in Iran's oil consortium and quadruple oil prices. The shah did exactly what Mossadeq did but 20 years later. He argued (correctly) that the producing states had been paid too little. Now a flood of oil revenue washed into Iran, and the shah pursued a grandiose vision of Iran as a major industrial and military power. Some Iranians—often the more corrupt, including the shah and his friends and relatives—got rich fast; jealousy flared. Poor rural people migrated to the cities in search of work and a better life. Instead, many found unemployment, inflation, and corruption. Religious to begin with, they got sympathy and support at the local mosque, where they also picked up anti-shah messages. By the late 1970s, the shah had little popular support.

In 1978, major demonstrations shook Iran. Police and troops fired on protesters, enraging them even more. Soldiers began to side with the crowds. The shah, sensing he was doomed (and dying of cancer), departed in January 1979, and two weeks later the Ayatollah Khomeini returned to the cheers of millions.

The ayatollah's support was a loose coalition of anti-shah groups: Islamic fundamentalists, Communists and other leftists, **secular** intellectuals, and convinced democrats. One by one, sometimes by firing squad, the ayatollah got rid of all but his Islamist supporters. The takeover of the U.S. embassy was an internal power play to bump Iranian moderates from leadership.

GEOGRAPHY ■ THE STRAIT OF HORMUZ

The entrance to the Persian Gulf at its narrowest is 35 miles wide. Two ship channels used by supertankers are two miles wide each, one for westbound and one for eastbound vessels. Through this strait pass an average of 15 supertankers a day carrying some 20 percent of the world's oil supply, much of it to East Asia. Closing the Strait of Hormuz would wreak havoc on the world economy.

It would have been easy for Iran to close in the first Gulf War in the 1980s, by planting mines in the ship channels or firing missiles. After a few hits, shippers would not be able to pay insurance premiums. But the Iranians refrained because they exported all their oil by ship through it; their Arab adversaries could still export by pipeline to the Mediterranean and Red Seas. The finger of land on the southern side of the strait belongs to Oman, a U.S. ally.

Within a year, the **mullahs** had built a dictatorship far bloodier and more thorough than the shah's. One of the last cries of an anti-shah group that had supported Khomeini: "In the dawn of freedom, there is no freedom." Iranians discovered how revolutions end badly.

THE FIRST GULF WAR

Iran's neighbor to the west, ancient Mesopotamia, is a new country that the British named Iraq only in 1922. For centuries it was three provinces of the Ottoman Empire. British forces from India conquered Mesopotamia in World War I, and in 1921—owing a debt to the Hashem family of Arabia that had helped Britain oust the Turks—placed a Hashemite prince on the throne of Iraq (and his brother on the throne of newly created Transjordan, carved out of its Palestine mandate). In 1932 Iraq became independent but, when it tilted toward Germany in 1941, the British occupied it until 1947. British imperialism rankled nationalistic Iraqi army officers. In 1958 they executed the royal family and top officials and moved Iraq sharply away from the West and toward the Soviet Union. Saddam Hussein, who began as a revolutionary assassin, became dictator of Iraq in 1979.

There has been bad blood for centuries between the peoples of present-day Iran and Iraq, especially over the border where the Shatt al Arab flows into the Persian Gulf (see box on page 148). In the early 1970s, Iran and Iraq came close to war until Iraq backed down and settled the border in Iran's favor in 1975. Iraq was always unhappy with this settlement, however, and claimed it was coerced into signing.

mullah Islamic cleric.

civilization In Huntington's theory, a major and distinct cultural area, based largely on a religion.

Islamism The Muslim faith used in a political way, sometimes called "Islamic fundamentalism."

CONCEPTS ■ HUNTINGTON'S "CIVILIZATIONAL" THEORY

The real divisions in the post–Cold War world are not between nations or trade blocs but between **"civilizations"** based largely on religion, argued Harvard political scientist Samuel P. Huntington (1927–2008). In a controversial 1993 article, Huntington saw seven major civilizations: Western (with North American and European branches), Slavic/Orthodox, Islamic, Confucian, Hindu, Japanese, and Latin American. Within a given civilization, nations share the same values and can empathize with each other; conflicts are generally limited. Between civilizations, understanding is more difficult, and conflicts can be big and nasty.

The greatest conflict, asserted Huntington, is where Muslim civilization meets other civilizations. "Islam has bloody borders," he argued. Examples include Israel versus the Arabs, Russians versus Chechens, Armenians versus Azeris, Muslim Bosnians and Kosovars versus Serbs, Christians versus Muslims in Lebanon, India versus Pakistan, and Islamic terrorism aimed at U.S. and other Western targets.

Furthermore, within Islam there is currently a struggle over who will govern Muslim countries, moderates versus fundamentalists. Already fundamentalists—sometimes known as **Islamists**—impose *sharia* (Muslim law) as the law of the land in Iran and Sudan. If Algeria held free and fair elections, Islamists would win, which is why Algeria cancelled elections in 1992. The Muslim Brotherhood, the father of many Islamist movements, showed its strength in Egypt's 2005 elections. The radical Hamas (related to the Muslim Brotherhood) won the 2006 Palestinian parliamentary elections. Saudi Arabia and Pakistan could fall to Islamists. In the 2003 war, Muslims worldwide rallied to Iraq, and U.S. occupation stirred Muslim hatred.

The Shatt al Arab forms a boundary between Iraq and Iran. ▶

(NYT Graphics)

When Iran turned Islamist in 1979, it encouraged Iraq's Shia majority to rise up and spread Islamic revolution. Saddam Hussein thought Iran was weakened by revolution and would be easy pickings, as it had no more U.S. protection. In September 1980, Iraq tore up the 1975 treaty and attacked, but the Iraqi invasion roused Iranian nationalism, and the country rallied behind Khomeini. Young Iranians joined the *Pasdaran* (Revolutionary Guards) and threw their lives away in human wave attacks against the Iraqis. Many carried little portraits of Khomeini and plastic keys, symbolizing admission to heaven. Losses were staggering. Possibly half a million died, two-thirds of them Iranians. Iran had the advantage in numbers and courage—they were much more willing to die in combat than Iraqis—but Iraq had the advantage in weapons.

Several factors finally ended the war after eight terrible years. Economics tilted against Iran, which could not export nearly as much oil as Iraq. Iraq also received large loans from conservative Gulf monarchies afraid of Islamic revolution. Iraq could buy weapons nearly everywhere; Iran could not. U.S. satellite photos showed Iraq where Iranian troops were deployed. (Yes, we helped Saddam.) On the battlefield, Iraq's poison gas panicked Iranian troops into retreat. In 1988 Iran finally agreed to

GEOGRAPHY ■ THE SHATT AL ARAB

Iraqis proudly note that the 120-mile-long waterway formed by the confluence of the Tigris and Euphrates is called the Shatt al Arab, the River of the Arabs. The lowest 40 miles of the Shatt form the boundary between Iraq and Iran. The question is where the border should run. Baghdad claims the whole river, right up to the eastern shore, giving it control of all river traffic. Tehran claims that the border follows the deepest channel of the river (called, in German, the *thalweg*), giving Iran direct access to the open sea from its oil ports of Khorramshahr and Abadan.

In an 1847 treaty, the Ottoman Empire got the entire river, but Iran always tried to get more rights around its ports. A 1937 treaty gave Iran a five-mile area around Abadan but otherwise secured the Shatt for Iraq. In 1969 Tehran denounced the 1937 treaty as British imperialism and moved to enforce the thalweg as its border. To put pressure on Baghdad, Iran helped the rebellious Kurds of northern Iraq. A strong Iran allied with the United States could prevail in those days, and in 1975 Iraq agreed in a treaty to a deepest-channel boundary. Iraq claimed the treaty was forced upon it and broke the treaty by invading Iran in 1980. Another Iraqi war aim: The area on the eastern bank of the Shatt—called Arabistan by Iraq—is partly peopled by Arabs, whom Baghdad felt should belong to Iraq.

UN Security Council Resolution 598, which brought in UN mediation to end the fighting. Khomeini, then 85, said he would rather "drink poison" but had to agree to save the Islamic Republic.

THE SECOND GULF WAR

Washington was so blinded by hatred of Iran that it failed to notice the menace of Iraq under the dictatorship of Saddam Hussein. Washington said few words against Iraq's use of poison gas—including on its own Kurds—but in 1984 reestablished diplomatic ties with Baghdad on the theory that increased contact, including arms sales, would make Iraq cooperative. During the 1960s and 1970s, Iraq had been a Soviet client state, and we were proud to have "won" Iraq away from Moscow. In addition to building the fourth-largest conventional army in the world, Iraq quietly purchased equipment to produce poison gas and medium-range missiles and work on nukes. Germany was the biggest supplier, but some of the technology was American.

Saddam had certain points to complain about. Kuwait and Saudi Arabia, U.S. client states, pumped oil in excess of OPEC quotas, keeping prices down; Iraq wanted prices higher. Iraq had never fully accepted Kuwait as an independent state; Baghdad claimed that under the Ottomans Kuwait had been part of Basra province. Iraq and Kuwait shared the large Rumaila oilfield, but Iraq charged that Kuwait was pumping far more than its share. Baghdad also argued that Kuwaiti and Saudi loans during the war with Iran should be forgiven; after all, Iraq had turned back Iran's Islamic revolution. But underneath Saddam's complaints was his drive to control the Gulf's oil to enlarge his military machine and make Iraq the regional superpower. Saddam was the new Nasser, the self-appointed hero who would unite and lead the Arabs.

DIPLOMACY ■ WHAT DID THE UNITED STATES KNOW, AND WHEN DID IT KNOW IT?

Could the United States have warned the shah that his rule was decaying in the 1970s? Perhaps with the right reforms he could have headed off revolution. We did not tell him because we did not know—in fact, did not want to know. The CIA station in our Tehran embassy agreed not to contact the anti-shah opposition, an important CIA function. SAVAK was supposed to pass on information to the CIA but did not—the shah's regime refused to admit there were problems—so embassy reports failed to notice the rise of anti-shah feeling.

Diplomats are not free agents; they must obey a command structure just like military officers do. In 1977 the shah visited Washington, and in 1978 President Carter visited Tehran. The presidential message from both visits: The shah is our friend and is making major improvements. That was the word, enforced by the U.S. ambassador, and American diplomats dared not challenge it. The result was inaccurate and overly optimistic reporting. In an important gap, the CIA did not learn the shah was dying of cancer.

Few American diplomats spoke Persian. Only a few Americans in diplomatic missions speak the local language. The U.S. Foreign Service is the only one that does not require fluency in a foreign language. When Iranian radicals seized our Tehran embassy in 1979, only six of the 53 hostages could speak Persian, an unusually high percentage because the embassy had already been reduced to a skeleton crew.

The shah's government put on a good public relations smokescreen that made influential Americans think all was well in Iran. Iranian Ambassador Ardeshir Zahedi showered Washington with lush parties and gifts. Professional PR people—including the wife of one senator—churned out upbeat news and views about Iran for fat fees. Only a handful of U.S. academic specialists saw the decay in Iran and predicted collapse.

Kurds Nationality inhabiting area where Iraq, Iran, and Turkey meet.

To Saddam's surprise, the United States strongly opposed his invasion of Kuwait on August 2, 1990, ten years after he invaded Iran. Soon U.S. troops arrived to defend Saudi Arabia, which they thought might be Saddam's next target. In October, President George H. W. Bush, without consulting Congress, ordered the buildup for war. Washington assembled a large international coalition that included Europeans, Arabs, and Asians. U.S. power decided the war, but the allies were politically essential to show that this was not U.S. imperialism but the will of the UN and most of the world. The Soviet Union backed U.S.-sponsored resolutions in the UN Security Council, and China refrained from vetoing them. Bush 41 lined up the world against Saddam.

The situation favored the United States. Bases, ports, and airfields were ready in Saudi Arabia. The United States had time—almost half a year—to get its forces in place. The U.S. military had always hated the incremental pace of the Vietnam War; the Gulf War was an overwhelming, quick attack. The open terrain left Iraq with few hiding places. In January 1991, massive air attacks—many with cruise missiles, stealth jets, and smart bombs—quickly knocked out Iraq's air defenses, communications, electricity, and bridges. Saddam Hussein appeared unfazed and welcomed the upcoming "mother of all battles." He hurled his inaccurate SCUD missiles at Saudi Arabia and Israel, hoping to goad Israel into entering the war, thus breaking the Arab countries from the coalition. After 38 days of air attacks, U.S.-led ground forces sliced into southern Iraq, and in 100 hours of fighting, Saddam's divisions melted away in surrender or hasty retreat. Arab forces were given the honor of liberating the plundered Kuwait City. The United States lost some 150; Iraq lost unknown thousands.

One question about this war is why Saddam did not go chemical. Iraq had used a lot of poison gas against both Iran and Iraqi **Kurds** in the previous Gulf war. Why not in 1991? Some Iraqi missiles had chemical-warhead capability. Only one answer fits: Both the United States and Israel would have responded with nuclear weapons. Bush 41 delivered a credible deterrent threat that Iraqi use of poison gas would provoke a terrible U.S. response. Saddam wanted Israel to enter the war but not with nukes. In effect, deterrence took place in the middle of the second Gulf war: A chemical power does not use gas against a nuclear power. Nukes deterred gas. (For more on deterrence, see Chapter 13.)

The real problems came with victory. Should coalition forces keep going to Baghdad and depose Saddam? Many U.S. officers wanted another four days to finish off Saddam, and later some regretted that we hadn't taken Baghdad in 1991, saving us a war in 2003. Then-Secretary of Defense Dick Cheney argued against it, noting (1) UN Resolution 678 merely called for expelling Iraq from Kuwait, nothing more; (2) our Arab allies strongly opposed it; (3) Iraq would be in

GEOGRAPHY ■ THE BAB AL MANDAB

Another maritime chokepoint in the region is the narrow southern entrance to the Red Sea, the Bab al Mandab, Arabic for "gate of tears." There, at the southwestern tip of the Arabian Peninsula, is the radical Arab country of Yemen, now home to al Qaeda militants. On the African side of the strait is Eritrea, which broke away from Ethiopia, and the French-run territory of Djibouti. Control of either coast gives radical forces the ability to close the Bab, cutting off most ship traffic through the Suez Canal. This ship traffic is not as important as it used to be, for supertankers are too big to pass through Suez; they have to go all the way around Africa to reach Europe and America.

chaos, which we would have to fix; and (4) Iran would be strengthened. Ironically, precisely these points came true after the 2003 war.

Besides, the White House figured that Iraqis would soon overthrow Saddam anyway. Restive Shias in the south and Kurds in the
north, on U.S. urging, rose against the Baghdad regime, but Iraq's
security forces were intact and brutally murdered hundreds of thousands of suspected opponents.
Kurds fled to the mountains on the Turkish and Iranian borders, barely kept alive by international
relief efforts. In vain, Washington pursued a "dual containment" policy of trying to isolate both
Iraq and Iran, but America's partners ignored it.

A moral dilemma appeared concerning Iraq's children, whom Saddam paraded to visitors as
malnourished and without medicines. Actually, Iraq had plentiful revenues to buy food and medicine under a UN-supervised oil-for-food program, but Saddam used the children for propaganda
while he bought military equipment and built dozens of luxurious palaces for himself. The UN
program faltered in disagreement over what were "humanitarian goods" as opposed to "dual-use
technology" that might be used to produce weapons of mass destruction. Iraq played cat-and-
mouse with UN weapons inspectors until they left in frustration.

al Qaeda   (Literally, "the base")
Osama bin Laden's *Islamist* terrorist
organization, perpetrators of 9/11.

THE THIRD GULF WAR

Within days of 9/11, President George W. Bush decided we must overthrow the fanatic Islamist
Taliban regime of Afghanistan for harboring **al Qaeda** and its chief, Osama bin Laden. In late
2001, using a few U.S. Special Forces working with local anti-Taliban Afghans, we ousted the

DIPLOMACY ■ A GREEN LIGHT FOR AGGRESSION

The United States had trouble grasping the aggressive
and dangerous nature of the Saddam regime in Iraq.
Some argue that State Department Arabists, trained
to promote only good relations with Arab countries,
could see no evil in Saddam. The United States
thought the Iraq–Kuwait dispute was about borders
and oil rights. When Saddam made threatening demands on Kuwait in July 1990, U.S. Ambassador April
Glaspie, fluent in Arabic, had a nice chat with him,
urging him to settle their border dispute peacefully
but adding that the United States would not get involved. Then she left on vacation. But Glaspie did not
act on her own; the conciliatory policy came from the
White House. Saddam took the message as a green
light from Washington to invade Kuwait.

The real problem was Washington's lopsidedly
anti-Iran policy that looked the other way when Iraq
invaded Iran and used poison gas. Only after the
war, when UN inspectors uncovered the magnitude
of Iraq's nuclear and chemical weapons programs,

did it finally sink in that we had favored a murderous
aggressor who planned to seize the entire region.

Would a U.S. warning to Saddam in July 1990
have made a difference? To deliver a credible deterrence threat, we would have needed U.S. forces on
the ground in Kuwait and Saudi Arabia, and the two
countries would not allow that. Fearful that a U.S.
military presence would provoke radical elements—
Palestinians and local Islamists—Kuwait and Saudi
Arabia wanted U.S. protection "over the horizon,"
that is, on ships and not on shore. Only after the
invasion, when Saudi princes worried that they
would be next, did they "invite" (at Washington's
urging) U.S. forces. Kuwaiti and Saudi fears had
made it impossible to deliver a credible deterrence
warning to Saddam. Even if Ambassador Glaspie had
tried, she would not have been believed. You cannot
deter aggression with words alone. (For the relationship between diplomacy and military strength, see
Chapter 19.)

weapons of mass destruction (WMD) Nuclear, chemical, or biological arms; "nukes, gas, bugs."

jihad Muslim holy war to defend the faith.

Taliban, but bin Laden escaped to neighboring Pakistan. It was a spectacular U.S. success, one supported by most of the world.

Bush 43 also decided to oust Saddam in Iraq, and during 2002 he made his decision clearer. This time most of the world opposed us, viewing with skepticism U.S. claims that Iraq had **weapons of mass destruction** and sponsored terrorism. No WMD were found, and that was our main reason for war. Apparently UN weapons inspectors had indeed supervised demolition of Iraq's WMD by the mid-1990s. Why then did Saddam play cat-and-mouse games with inspectors and not openly reveal that he had no WMD? Postwar analysis showed Saddam still feared Iran and wanted Tehran to think he had WMD. He figured that Bush 43 would not invade because Washington still needed Iraq to block Iranian expansion, which is why Bush 41 left him in office in 1991—a true point. Saddam's reasoning in 2003, however mistaken, was rational. Bush's was not. "Sometimes," Bush 43 said, "you have to go with your gut."

In contrast to 1991, Saudi Arabia in 2003 did not permit us to attack from its soil. Only Kuwait and some small Gulf states let us base there. Only Britain sent substantial forces. Even our old ally Turkey did not help. America was at odds with most of the world. In March 2003 U.S. armor raced up the Tigris and Euphrates valley to take Baghdad in three weeks. In two more weeks, all of Iraq was ours, and Bush declared major combat over on May 1. Iraq, however, never surrendered or signed a cease-fire; Iraqi soldiers and security police just melted away, some to fight another day. Saddam hid, but U.S. forces captured him in late 2003. An Iraqi court tried and hanged him in 2006, but this did not calm Iraq.

Looting and lawlessness broke out immediately after the U.S. conquest, something we had not anticipated. Electricity, water, and oil production stopped. We neglected to send military police, civil affairs specialists, and engineers until weeks later. Initially most Iraqis welcomed us, but without security or jobs, many soon resented us. U.S. officials disbanded the Iraqi army and police, something we soon regretted. Resistors—most of them Sunni Arabs—shot and bombed U.S., UN, and Shia Iraqi targets, trying to make Iraq ungovernable. More than 4,400 Americans were killed in Iraq. Some foreign Islamic terrorists (mostly Saudi) who craved **jihad** slipped into Iraq. The Middle East was angrier than ever.

Postwar policy in Iraq was initially given to the Defense Department, which supposed that U.S.-sponsored Iraqi exiles would be welcomed and quickly form a federal democracy that in turn would inspire democracy throughout the region. But Iraq, after decades of brutal dictatorship that had crushed all independent voices, was politically fragmented, and its main groups—Shias in the south (62 percent of the population), Sunni Arabs in the center (under 20 percent), and Kurds in the north (about 20 percent)—fought civil wars within civil wars. We turned nominal sovereignty back to Iraq in the middle of 2004, and Iraq held three elections in 2005—one for an interim government to draft a constitution, a second to approve the constitution, and a third to elect a regular government.

DIPLOMACY ■ STATUS QUO ANTE BELLUM

The Latin phrase *status quo ante bellum* (the situation before the war) provided a formula for ending the first two Gulf wars. It means restoring things to the way they were before the war. In 1988, Iraq could accept the border that split the Shatt al Arab, and Iran could agree to ask for no more. In 1991, Iraq had to accept the borders and independence of Kuwait. Every country except Iraq found the status quo ante bellum in the Gulf acceptable.

A Marine in front of a Humvee that was destroyed by a homemade bomb in 2005 in Ramadi, Iraq. (Capt. Rory Quinn/U.S. Marines/*The New York Times*/Redux Pictures)

Experts warned that Iraq was not ready for democracy, and Iraqis had trouble forming a stable government. In 2007, a "surge" of U.S. forces and rallying of Sunnis to the government calmed things somewhat and gave hope that a kind of democracy could take hold. By then, however, most Americans were fed up with Iraq. President Barack Obama, as promised, began withdrawing U.S. forces in 2009. In 2010 Iraqis elected a parliament split between Shia parties and a secular (but heavily Sunni) party. The two dickered for nine months before forming a shaky coalition, but the leading party in it is Shia and has strong ties to Iran. The situation is far from peaceful or settled.

AN ARAB EXPLOSION?

Many observers agree that revolutionary potential simmers in most Arab countries, but that has been the case for years. It is not clear if there has ever been an Arab revolution. Egyptian, Libyan, Syrian, and Iraqi regimes proclaimed themselves revolutionary, but they took power by *coup* (see page 163). Conservative Gulf monarchies and authoritarian regimes in Egypt, Syria, and elsewhere rule by security police, obedient parliaments, and rigged elections that give them shaky legitimacy. Most rulers have been in office decades, arguing that only they can keep order. Their deaths could open up splits and succession struggles. Rich oil lands buy citizen support through lavish subsidies, but they depend on high oil prices.

Several changes are hitting the Arab world. Its population has doubled in 30 years, producing a "demographic bulge" of young people that slow-growing economies cannot begin

Taliban (Pashto for "students")
Sunni extremists who ruled
Afghanistan 1996–2001 and now
threaten Afghanistan and Pakistan.

to employ. The Middle East and North Africa have the world's highest unemployment. In 1996 a new satellite TV station, Al Jazeera, opened in Qatar and quickly became the most-watched in the Arab world. Al Jazeera's coverage of Palestinian suffering, the U.S. wars in Iraq and Afghanistan, and problems in the Arab world created a critical pan-Arab viewership. Recovery of Palestine has become a sacred Arab cause, one not amenable to compromise. Islamic fundamentalism—more properly known as *salafiyya* (see page 247)—has spread. Al Qaeda is a salafi movement, one of several that seek to overthrow existing Arab regimes because they are corrupt, insufficiently pious, and pro-American.

There are some hopeful signs as well. Education levels—spurred in part by Gulf branches of U.S. universities—are rising sharply, especially among women. *Fertility rates* (see page 186) are half what they were a generation ago. Democracy is making slow and halting progress as regimes allow more elected offices. Turkey, a Muslim but not an Arab country, demonstrates that democracy can work in the Middle East and that moderate Islamist parties can be effective and popular. Many Arabs fear that a salafi takeover could be murderous and repressive. They notice that al Qaeda's chief victims have been Muslims. Al Jazeera, cell phones, and computers connect and inform people as never before. The Gulf emirates have become modern business centers. Some see a race in the Arab lands between modernization leading to democratic stability and tumult leading to revolution and extremism. Few are taking bets.

THE AFGHAN WAR

By the time you read this, Afghanistan—which could count as the fourth Gulf war—will have become America's longest war. Afghanistan—a jumble of tribes, languages, and clans afflicted by what one American called "valleyism"—always resisted central government, even by Afghans. Foreign occupiers were harassed until they retreated. The British, seeking to secure the northern border of India, invaded Afghanistan three times—1839, 1878, and 1919—but were pushed out by savage tribes each time. Kipling called Anglo-Russian rivalry in Central Asia the "Great Game," the setting for his novel *Kim*. The Soviets invaded in 1979 and gave up a decade later (see page 85). Some call Afghanistan the "tomb of invaders." Others call it a *failed state* (see page 115) because it has little central government.

U.S. inattention contributed to the current problem. The U.S. CIA (along with Saudi Arabia and Pakistan) contributed money and weapons to the Islamist uprising against the Soviet-backed Afghan regime in the 1980s. All suffered *blowback* (see page 244) when their Islamist clients turned on them. After the Soviets withdrew in 1989 (the same year they let East Europe go its own way), Washington walked away from anarchic Afghanistan, where a dozen groups murdered with impunity and battled for control. Pakistan's ISI (Inter-Services Intelligence), seeking some stability to its north, founded and funded the **Taliban**, a movement that began in extremist *madresas* (schools) in Pakistan. In 1996 the Taliban took over most of Afghanistan, and at first most Afghans, sick of the carnage, welcomed the Taliban, who administered a rough justice based on *sharia* (see page 247). The Taliban enforced an extreme version of Islam that banned music, educating women, shaving, and flying kites.

The United States paid attention to Afghanistan only after Osama bin Laden, who had earlier fought the Soviets there, set up al Qaeda headquarters in Afghanistan in 1996 and began plotting terrorist attacks on U.S. targets, culminating in 9/11. After the Kabul regime refused to hand over bin Laden, President George W. Bush dropped U.S. Special Forces to link up with anti-Taliban holdouts and call in air strikes. Lukewarm Taliban supporters changed sides, and the obnoxious regime was quickly overthrown in late 2001. But bin Laden and his helpers got away, over the border into the uncontrolled tribal areas of northwest Pakistan.

As Congress cheered, Washington installed Hamid Karzai as Afghanistan's president and assumed the job was done. America invaded Iraq in 2003 (see page 152) and had few resources for or interest in Afghanistan, where Karzai governed poorly. He was dubbed the "mayor of Kabul" as his writ barely extended beyond the capital. NATO forces focused on nation building but made little headway against corruption, warlords, and the opium trade. In 2010, the Afghan police and army still were largely illiterate, untrained, and unreliable. Average Afghans lived without justice, jobs, security, or democracy. Many say the Taliban are less corrupt than the government and deliver welfare. The Taliban, which is mostly **Pashtun**, operates safely in the Pashtun areas of Pakistan. A point often missed: The Taliban is also a Pashtun national liberation movement as well as an Islamist movement. After 2001, the Taliban regrouped and infiltrated back into Afghanistan; there are not nearly enough U.S., NATO, or Afghan forces to stop them. President Bush ignored the problem, but President Obama could not.

The problem spills over from Afghanistan to Pakistan. The Pakistan branch of the Taliban operates in wide areas of Pakistan, which has nuclear weapons. Some fear that **loose nukes**

Pashtun   Largest ethnic group of Afghanistan and second largest of Pakistan. Language: Pashto.

loose nukes   Nuclear weapons outside of government control.

GEOGRAPHY ■ THE MISUSED, ANGRY KURDS

There are at least 25 million Kurds, but they never had their own country. Instead, most live in Turkey with smaller numbers in Iraq, Iran, and Syria where their borders converge. The Kurds of northern Iraq now act like a separate country at odds with Baghdad. Fighting over the oil city of Kirkuk—the Kurds say it's theirs, Baghdad says it isn't—could blast Iraq apart. Kurds are mostly Sunni Muslims but are not Arabs, Turks, or Persians, and they speak several dialects all their own. They often fight among themselves and do not form a united front. Fierce mountain warriors, the Kurds first appear in history harassing Alexander's invading Greeks. The most famous Kurd was the chivalrous Saladin (1138–1193), who beat the Crusaders.

With nationalism stirring the Middle East in the late nineteenth century, the Kurds too started thinking of their own nation and rising up against Baghdad, Tehran, Istanbul (old capital of the Ottoman Empire), and later Ankara (new capital of modern Turkey). Turkey brutally crushed the insurgency of the Kurdish Workers Party (PKK), a conflict that claimed some 37,000 lives in the late twentieth century and still simmers. Turkey urges its Kurds to assimilate; many have.

Since the 1960s, the Kurds' struggle has focused on northern Iraq, which includes the oilfields of Kirkuk. Baghdad repeatedly tried to crush Kurdish armed resistance, but the tough Kurds held out. In the early 1970s, Iraqi Kurds got help through Iran. The shah, along with Israeli and U.S. covert branches, supplied arms. The shah wanted to put pressure on Baghdad to secure Iran's rights to the Shatt al Arab. The Israelis wanted to weaken an enemy and had stocks of Soviet weapons captured in the 1967 war. And Iraq had become a Soviet client state—which broke relations with Washington in 1967—so the CIA wanted to undermine Iraq.

Then, in a cynical betrayal, when the shah got the border he wanted in a 1975 treaty, he cut off the Kurdish fighters in Iraq and let Baghdad do its worst. With the Iran–Iraq war, Tehran again encouraged Iraq's Kurds to rise up. Some Kurds believed an Iranian victory would give them their best chance for independence. Baghdad used poison gas to kill some 50,000 of Iraq's own Kurdish citizens. In 1991, the United States encouraged Iraq's Kurds to rise against Saddam Hussein but did not help them when they did. Small wonder the Kurds feel betrayed. A Kurdish saying: "The Kurds have no friends."

could fall into terrorist hands. Pakistan's powerful ISI still sponsors terrorists and guerrillas to fight India over Kashmir. U.S. military documents leaked in 2010 confirmed what was long suspected, that the ISI works both sides of the street in its contacts with the Afghan Taliban. The Pakistan army does not do all it can in the wild North-West Frontier Province and the even wilder Federally Administered Tribal Areas, where both the Taliban and al Qaeda operate semi-openly. U.S. forces are barred from Pakistan. U.S. drone strikes there are sometimes effective but create local rage. Once U.S.–Pakistani ties were close, but now a majority of Pakistanis hate the United States. Because Afghanistan and Pakistan are closely linked, Washington referred to the problem as "Af-Pak," and Obama placed Ambassador Richard Holbrooke (1941–2010) in charge of it.

Rigged 2009 Afghan elections kept Karzai in power but triggered criticism that U.S. and NATO forces were fighting for a corrupt, illegitimate regime. Critics argued that sending more troops to Afghanistan made more Afghans hate us and aided the Taliban cause. Although they aim to help local civilians, U.S. forces inevitably kill some. Aircraft, including drones, cannot distinguish civilians from fighters. U.S. generals realize that the problem is basically political, not military, and that we cannot stay in Afghanistan forever. In the face of an unstable future, Obama increased U.S. forces in Afghanistan and named new U.S. commanding generals while trying to get moderate elements among the Taliban to make a peace deal with the Kabul government. Obama aimed to start withdrawing U.S. forces in 2011; many Americans were ready to do it earlier.

WAR WITH IRAN?

Iran exchanges angry words with the United States and Israel. Iranian arms, money, and advice flow to Shia militias in Iraq, who use them against Americans and Sunni Muslims, and to militants in Lebanon and Gaza, who use them against Israelis. President George W. Bush warned Tehran not to develop nuclear weapons and threatened "regime change," the words used before the 2003 U.S. invasion of Iraq.

President Obama offered an open hand if Tehran would unclench its fist, but Iranian President Ahmadinejad accelerated Iran's "peaceful" nuclear program—which could soon build bombs—and wants to "wipe Israel off the map." War with Israel and/or the United States is not out of the question. In 1981 Israel bombed an Iraqi nuclear reactor and in 2007 a Syrian reactor (set up with North Korean help) to head off a threat early. The 1991 war revealed that Iraq had a substantial nuclear program. When threatened, Israel *preempts* (see page 134).

War, however, is not inevitable. Several factors work against it. U.S. forces in 2010 were already overstretched in Iraq and Afghanistan, and Pentagon chiefs warned that we were in no position for another war. Shia Iran has essentially no allies because Sunni countries do not follow its lead and many oppose it. Iran might not need a bomb to deter: It could retaliate against an attack by closing the Strait of Hormuz—Asia gets most of its oil through Hormuz—plunging the world into recession.

Iran is split between fanatics and moderate conservatives, who have turned critical of Ahmadinejad and accused him of governing through the elite Revolutionary Guard like a military dictator. Ahmadinejad's lavish subsidies botched Iran's economy, but he "won" a rigged reelection in 2009. He, however, is not Iran's top ruler; Ayatollah Khamenei has the final say on all important decisions.

We should also remember that many Iranians are pro-democracy and pro-American. They massively protested Ahmadinejad's 2009 reelection, and many were killed or jailed. In the right circumstances, Iranians could overthrow their unpopular regime. Both Tehran and Washington know there is money to be made in oil, especially in the pipelines that will bring Central Asia's oil to the world market. (The United States sponsored a pipeline through Turkey, but the best route is through Iran. Russia's pipeline runs through Chechnya—one reason it crushed Chechen rebels.) Some remember that when the United States and Iran were partners, Iraq did not dare attack Iran. Mutual benefit could make us partners again.

LESSONS OF FOUR GULF WARS

1. You don't have to be a major power to have a major war. Even Global South countries can build large armies and buy arms.
2. The economy is as important as your army. In the 1980s, Iraq could outlast Iran because it had more money.
3. Arms sellers are happy to supply aggressors. Iraq bought just about anything it wanted on the international arms market.
4. War is increasingly electronic. The ability to paralyze communications and the use of "smart bombs" and drones give us a tremendous edge.
5. Deterrence works. Saddam used chemical weapons on Iranians and Kurds but not on Americans or Israelis. Fear of nuclear retaliation deterred him.
6. Governments control media coverage of wars. We saw essentially nothing in the 1991 war and only narrow-angle "embedded" coverage of small units in the 2003 war.
7. The aftermath of a war is as important as the fighting. Is a dictator still in power? Are we prepared to run a chaotic country and rebuild it with our dollars? If you cannot follow through, do not go in.
8. The political effects of a war are as important as military victory, especially if occupation makes us new enemies in the country, the region, and worldwide.

DIPLOMACY ■ "THE ENEMY OF MY ENEMY IS MY FRIEND"

Of Arab origin, the logical dictum "the enemy of my enemy is my friend" illustrates national-interest thinking. Israel and Turkey, for example, developed cordial ties, even though Turkey is Muslim, and Arab governments howled in protest. Turkish elites are largely secular, especially top army officers, and Turkey has territorial and river quarrels with Syria and Iraq. Turkey logically turned to another country with the same enemies, Israel. National interest can trump ideology and/or religion. Score one for the realists (see Chapter 2).

But in 2002 Turkey elected an Islamist government (reelected in 2007) and revived its Muslim roots. Seeing that Turkey would never be admitted into the EU, Ankara redefined itself as leader of the Middle East (which it had been until World War I), improved ties with Arab countries and Iran, and grew cool to Washington. In contrast to the 1991 Gulf War, in 2003 Turkey did not permit U.S. forces to invade Iraq from Turkey. Ankara turned angry at Israel, especially after Israel's 2010 violence against a Turkish charity ship attempting to run Israel's blockade of Gaza.

In another Middle Eastern example, Iran under the shah had close relations with the United States and unofficial but good relations with Israel. Iran, the United States, and Israel had Iraq as a common enemy. But the ayatollahs made Islamic revolution Iran's chief concern and demonized the United States and Israel. Both Ankara and Tehran, based on their new ruling elites, had redefined their national interests. Score two for the constructivists.

9. If you do not understand the complexities of a country, be cautious about occupying it. With little knowledge of Iraq's and Afghanistan's languages, religions, politics, and geography, we put ourselves into someone else's civil wars.

10. The United States, like it or not, is involved in the Gulf. The region's instability, our oil dependency (see Chapter 22), and Pakistan's nukes drag us in.

mypoliscikit EXERCISES

Apply what you learned in this chapter on MyPoliSciKit (www.mypoliscikit.com).

Assessment   Review this chapter using learning objectives, chapter summaries, practice tests, and more.

Menu

Flashcards   Learn the key terms in this chapter; you can test yourself by term or definition.

Flashcards

Video   Analyze recent world affairs by watching streaming video from major news providers.

Videos

Simulations   Play the role of an IR decision-maker and experience how IR concepts work in practice.

Comparative
Exercises

KEY TERMS

al Qaeda (p. 151)
Caspian (p. 144)
Caucasus (p. 144)
Central Asia (p. 144)
civilization (p. 147)
Islamism (p. 147)
jihad (p. 152)
Kurds (p. 150)

loose nukes (p. 155)
mullah (p. 147)
nationalize (p. 144)
OPEC (p. 146)
Pashtun (p. 155)
Persia (p. 144)
populist (p. 144)
shah (p. 144)

Shia (p. 144)
sphere of influence
   (p. 144)
Sunni (p. 144)
Taliban (p. 154)
weapons of mass destruction
   (WMD) (p. 152)

FURTHER REFERENCE

Allawi, Ali A. *The Crisis of Islamic Civilization.* New Haven, CT: Yale University Press, 2009.

Axworthy, Michael. A *History of Iran: Empire of the Mind.* New York: Basic Books, 2008.

Bayandor, Darioush. *Iran and the CIA: The Fall of Mossadeq Revisited.* New York: Palgrave, 2010.

Cockburn, Patrick. *Muqtada: Muqtada al-Sadr, the Shia Revival and the Struggle for Iraq.* New York: Scribner, 2008.

Cole, Juan. *Engaging the Muslim World.* New York: Palgrave, 2009.

Duelfer, Charles. *Hide and Seek: The Search for Truth in Iraq.* New York: Public Affairs, 2009.

Ehrenberg, John, J. Patrice McSherry, José Ramón Sánchez, and Caroleen Marji Sayej, eds. *The Iraq Papers.* New York: Oxford University Press, 2010.

Esposito, John L. *The Future of Islam.* New York: Oxford University Press, 2010.

Filkins, Dexter. *The Forever War*. New York: Knopf, 2008.

Gause, F. Gregory, III. *The International Relations of the Persian Gulf*. New York: Cambridge University Press, 2009.

Giustozzi, Antonio, ed. *Decoding the Taliban: Insights from the Afghan Field*. New York: Columbia University Press, 2009.

Haass, Richard N. *War of Necessity, War of Choice: A Memoir of Two Iraq Wars*. New York: Simon & Schuster, 2009.

Hardy, Roger. *The Muslim Revolt: A Journey Through Political Islam*. New York: Columbia University Press, 2010.

Jervis, Robert. *Why Intelligence Fails: Lessons from the Iranian Revolution and the Iraq War*. Ithaca, NY: Cornell University Press, 2010.

Junger, Sebastian. *War*. New York: Grand Central, 2010.

Kepel, Gilles. *Beyond Terror and Martyrdom: The Future of the Middle East*. Cambridge, MA: Harvard University Press, 2008.

Kilcullen, David. *The Accidental Guerrilla: Fighting Small Wars in the Midst of a Big One*. New York: Oxford University Press, 2009.

Lacey, Robert. *Inside the Kingdom: Kings, Clerics, Modernists, Terrorists, and the Struggle for Saudi Arabia*. New York: Viking, 2009.

Lennon, Alexander T. J., ed. *The Epicenter of Crisis: The New Middle East*. Cambridge, MA: MIT Press, 2008.

Nasr, Vali. *The Rise of Islamic Capitalism: Why the New Muslim Middle Class is the Key to Defeating Extremism*. New York: Simon & Schuster, 2010.

Peters, Gretchen. *Seeds of Terror: How Heroin Is Bankrolling the Taliban and al Qaeda*. New York: St. Martin's, 2009.

Pollack, Kenneth M. *The Persian Puzzle: The Conflict Between Iran and America*. New York: Random House, 2008.

Pope, Hugh. *Dining with al-Qaeda: Three Decades Exploring the Many Worlds of the Middle East*. New York: St. Martin's, 2010.

Ricks, Thomas E. *The Gamble: General David Petraeus and the American Military Adventure in Iraq, 2006-2008*. New York: Penguin, 2009.

Roskin, Michael G., and James J. Coyle. *Politics of the Middle East: Cultures and Conflicts*, 2nd ed. Upper Saddle River, NJ: Prentice Hall, 2008.

Roy, Olivier. *The Politics of Chaos in the Middle East*. New York: Columbia University Press, 2009.

Walzer, Michael, and Nicolaus Mills, eds. *Getting Out: Historical Perspectives on Leaving Iraq*. Philadelphia: University of Pennsylvania Press, 2009.

Wawro, Geoffrey. *Quicksand: America's Pursuit of Power in the Middle East*. New York: Penguin, 2010.

West, Bing. *The Strongest Tribe: War, Politics, and the Endgame in Iraq*. New York: Random House, 2008.

Woodward, Bob. *Obama's Wars*. New York: Simon & Schuster, 2010.

Zaeef, Abdul Salam. *My Life With the Taliban*. New York: Columbia University Press, 2010.

CHAPTER 10

Trouble and Hope
in Latin America

Buoyed by scientific farm techniques, massive soybean production turned Brazil into a food export giant. (Werner Rudhart/Corbis)

"Brazil is the country of the future and always will be," Brazilians used to jest. They aren't joking anymore: Brazil has, surprisingly, arrived. Latin America's only Portuguese-speaking country, Brazil is now the continent's economic and political leader. Sometime this decade it will become the world's fifth-largest economy, ahead of Britain and France. For a century, Brazilian demagogues alternated with military coups, but now Brazil has settled into stable democracy. Brazil's last coup was in 1964; when the generals left office in 1985 they warned that, in case of tumult, they would be back. But Brazil modernized out of *praetorianism* (see page 121).

Current and previous Brazilian presidents like to call themselves leftists, but they use capitalist growth to pay for modest welfare programs, a mix that pleases most Brazilians. Brazil, with a large, educated middle class and per capita GDP of over $10,000, is now a magnet for investment and model for other Latin American countries. Brazil's nice balance between exports and domestic consumption could teach export-dependent China something.

Many Americans are unaware that Latin America, thanks to high demand for raw materials and sound economic policies, now enjoys good economic growth of around 5 percent a year. Americans tend to ignore the countries to their south. Many cannot distinguish among **Latin America**, **South America**, and **Central America**. We pay far more attention eastward across the Atlantic and westward across the Pacific than to our hemispheric neighbors. But they are important both to our future and to world stability in general. One could even propose U.S. policies that pay more attention to our south (and maybe even a little to our north, to Canada) than to east and west.

Parts of Latin America, to be sure, are still examples of the zones of chaos that trouble much of the Global South. Income inequality is the world's worst. Crime rates—including murder and kidnapping—are among the world's worst as well. Drug lords in several Latin American countries buy politicians, judges, police, and the military; the ones they cannot buy, they kill. America is addicted to illegal drugs, most of them from south of its border. (We should actually say "North America," for the rest of the hemisphere is also America, and referring to the United States simply as "America" annoys many Latin Americans. They're Americans, too.) Marijuana, cocaine, and heroin flow in from the south in ever-shifting patterns. Eradicated in one country, the trade moves to another. Break one drug cartel, and others take its place. Cut the growing of coca (used by **indígenas** for centuries), and farmers plant opium poppies. With North Americans' appetite for cocaine undiminished

Questions to Consider

1. Why do Americans ignore the rest of the Americas?
2. How did Spanish differ from English colonization?
3. Is it fair to call Central America a U.S. sphere of influence?
4. Should we be prepared to intervene in Latin America?
5. Can we stamp out drug cultivation in the Third World?
6. What would be the best way to get communism out of Cuba?
7. Should we turn our attention southward, instead of east and west?
8. Is Mexico becoming democratic? How can you tell?

Latin America   All countries south of the United States.

South America   Continent south of Panama.

Central America   Countries between Mexico and Colombia

indígena   Preferred Latin American term for Indian.

cocalero   Farmer who produces coca leaf.

narcotraficante   Drug trafficker.

interdiction   Cutting the flow of something.

statism   Government owns and runs major industries.

entrepreneurialism   Starting your own business; private enterprise.

and profits enormous, **cocaleros** are happy to grow the leaf (and get $5 a kilo, several times what they get for any other crop) and **narcotraficantes** to process and smuggle it. It is a business, obeying the laws of supply and demand.

Eradication and **interdiction** have not worked. Andean cocaine production is undiminished, and drugs are plentiful and cheap on the U.S. market. For every kilo intercepted, perhaps 20 get through. Cracking down on U.S. drug users has simply doubled our prison population without denting the problem. Vigorous drug suppression programs in Bolivia and Peru—aerial spraying, crop burning, destruction of processing camps, and paying farmers to grow other crops—temporarily cut drug production there, but it returned. The trade also moved to Colombia, which now produces 90 percent of the cocaine and 60 percent of the heroin used in the United States. Cultivation has branched out into African countries. The real problem is U.S. drug users, found in every walk of life and every town (and on your campus). In the words of Pogo: "We have met the enemy, and he is us."

Can we stop the flow of drugs? In recent years, $3 billion in U.S. aid has gone to Colombia, whose jungled *cordilleras* are hard to control. Marxist guerrillas, who fund themselves by taxing drug traffickers (as does the Taliban in Afghanistan), still control parts of Colombia. In recent years the Colombian army has scored major successes, and the guerrillas have lost many of their fighters and commanders. This has done essentially nothing, however, to curb the flow of drugs.

Internal warfare is the norm in Colombia: 300,000 died in *La Violencia* from 1945 to 1965; another 35,000 have died since 1990. The countryside has never been safe from guerrillas and bandits. In Colombia, the two merge, and many "revolutionaries" are in it for the money. Bombings, assassinations, and kidnappings still occur—some criminal, some political. Right-wing death squads, tied to the Colombian military, murder with impunity. (In Peru, more than 69,000 died in guerrilla warfare from 1980 to 2000 under similar circumstances.) Many Colombian judges and journalists have been killed. Colombia is not just a drug problem but exemplifies the *weak state* (see page 115) that cannot keep law and order.

ECONOMICS ■ STATISM

Spain brought with it **statism** (borrowed from the French kings): the government as number-one capitalist, owning and supervising the big parts of the economy, which in colonial times meant gold and silver. More recently statists argued that if railroads, steel mills, or telephone networks needed to be built, government must do it, because only government has the plans and money to carry out big projects. Some statists still argue that they have no capitalists willing and able to make major investments.

Culturally, Latin America had little **entrepreneurialism** and so, until recently, was largely statist, which led to slow growth, unemployment, bloated bureaucracies, corruption, and a chronic dependence on foreign capital, thus leading to *dependency* (see pages 164–166). Over the past few years, many Latin American countries moved from statist to private industries, and, with surging global demand for raw materials, show excellent growth.

SPAIN COLONIZES THE NEW WORLD

creole Spaniard born in the New World.

mestizo Person of mixed Indian-Spanish descent.

coup Extralegal seizure of power, usually by military.

How did Latin America fall into such a condition? As in Africa, the roots of the problem go back to European colonialism. The Spaniards plunged eagerly into the New World for "glory, God, and gold," in the words of American historian Paul Wellman. More than 80 percent of Indians soon died of smallpox, against which they had no immunity. Spain had just finished eight centuries of pushing out the Moors and treated the Indians the same: Crush their kingdoms and cultures and utterly dominate them. They did not displace the Indians but enslaved and impregnated them, producing a feudal-type hierarchy: a small **creole** class of officials and landowners at the top, a larger class of **mestizos** to do the work, and many impoverished and isolated Indians. The economy was based on extracting gold and silver or on plantations.

Inspired by the U.S. and French revolutions, the Spanish and Portuguese colonies won independence in the 1820s. Their idealistic constitutions—modeled on the U.S. and French revolutionary constitutions—failed almost immediately in the face of their feudal social structures. Latin American countries had the trappings of power—presidential palaces, lots of bureaucrats (far too many), and armies—but lacked the economies or educated citizenries to sustain democracy. A small elite dominated politics. The central government's writ did not extend far from the capital. Corruption was the norm. Amid frequent instability, army officers pulled **coups** and took over governments. Bolivia had more than 190 coups since independence in 1825.

CENTRAL AMERICA AND THE CARIBBEAN

Although little noticed by most Americans, the Caribbean basin is important to the United States: It is weak, near, and strategic. There are many reasons for its weakness. The class structure typically divides the country into a few very wealthy families and many very poor ones. Political institutions are fragile and usually do the bidding of the wealthy class (i.e., make sure they stay wealthy). The economy largely produces raw materials and until recently has grown slowly, but populations grow fast—some Central American countries grow faster than 3 percent a year—and the region has far more people than jobs.

The region has been subordinate to the great powers from the first penetration by Europeans in the late fifteenth century. The Europeans saw the strategic and economic importance of Central America and the Caribbean. Imperial competition—by French, Spanish, British, and Americans, and later by Cubans and Soviets—thwarted democracy and economic development. Central America is the victim of its geopolitics.

Columbus's discovery of the New World began in the Caribbean (he thought that he was in Asia) and gave Spain dominance in the region. Spain wanted (1) control of trade routes, (2) control of land for settlement, (3) the gold and silver of the New World, and (4) conversion of the natives to Catholicism. Under the Habsburgs (who also held Austria), Spain battled for predominance in Europe and needed the gold and silver of the New World to pay for its huge armies. Mexico was Spain's richest colony.

To control trade and land, Spain established colonies, forts, and harbors. Balboa crossed the Isthmus of Panama to the Pacific in 1513. Six years later, Cortes left Cuba to conquer the Aztec empire

dependency Economic subordination of poor countries to rich ones.

in Mexico. The few areas that Spain did not colonize, the English (Jamaica and Belize), French (Martinique), and Dutch (Netherlands Antilles) did. The Caribbean became a battleground among colonial powers. Caribbean piracy got its start with English "letters of marque," royal licenses to capture Spanish ships for private profit. (Notice that the U.S. Constitution lets Congress issue letters of marque.) The French fleet in the Caribbean provided essential help to the North Americans in their war of independence. Central America freed itself from Spain in 1821 and tried to consolidate as the Central American Confederation, but it fell apart in 1839.

ECONOMIC DEPENDENCY

Under these circumstances, Latin America became economically tied to outside powers—Britain in the nineteenth century and the United States in the twentieth. During the Cold War, Latin American leftists subscribed to **dependency** theory (*dependencia* in Spanish) as an article of faith: The big, bad United States keeps Latin America poor. The United States controls the economies of weaker countries through local middlemen who do the bidding of U.S. corporations, argue dependency theorists. The poor country must sell its agricultural and mineral products cheap and buy high-priced U.S.-made goods. This continually siphons off the wealth of the poor country and keeps it poor.

Marxists added a sinister twist to dependency theory: When the United States doesn't get its way, it uses dirty means, such as encouraging rigged elections and military coups. In a pinch,

Central America and the Caribbean

the United States **intervenes** directly, as in the Caribbean and Central America early in the twentieth century and in Panama in 1989. If radicals try to break the dependent relationship—Arbenz in Guatemala, Castro in Cuba, Allende in Chile, or Chávez in Venezuela—Washington brings great political, economic, and even military pressure to oust them.

intervene   One country reaches into the affairs of another.

capital flight   Sending your money out of the country instead of reinvesting it there.

There is some truth to dependency theory, but it overlooks basic economic points. The Spanish set up extractive economies (mines and plantations) and feudal class structures that created capital only for export. Now local capitalists, worried about losing their money, stash it abroad, what is known as **capital flight**. Dependency thus occurs naturally because the host country does not generate capital for its own investments; in part, this is due to its statist economy, which discourages local capital formation. Where local capitalists fail to invest, foreign capitalists may.

CONCEPTS ■ INTERVENTION

In Chapter 6 we defined "interventionism" from the standpoint of U.S. foreign policy. What is it like to be on the receiving end? Latin America provides some case studies. Intervention in this sense is one country reaching into another to make or unmake governments. States intervene to control the foreign and sometimes domestic policies of other governments and to gain allies for themselves and deny them to their adversaries.

Intervention is usually a lot cheaper and more subtle than war. It can include bribes to government officials, foreign aid, secret subsidies to political parties, destabilization campaigns, encouragement to coup-plotters, arms shipments, proxy armies, and, if nothing else works, invasion. The United States has been more likely to send its own troops into the Caribbean area and to use more subtle means farther south. Here are some of the major U.S. interventions in Latin America.

Year	Country	U.S. Action
1846–1848	Mexico	Defeat Mexico, take vast territory
1898	Spain	Take Puerto Rico, dominate Cuba
1903	Panama	Break Panama away from Colombia
1912–1933	Nicaragua	Marines occupy to keep order
1915–1934	Haiti	Marines occupy to keep order
1916	Mexico	Pershing pursues Pancho Villa
1916–1924	Dominican Republic	Marines occupy to keep order
1954	Guatemala	CIA overthrows reformist regime
1961	Cuba	Failed invasion by proxy army
1964	Brazil	Encourage coup against leftist regime
1965	Dominican Republic	Occupy to squelch rebellion
1973	Chile	Encourage coup against leftist regime
1981–1986	Nicaragua	Supply anti-Communist rebels
1989	Panama	Invade to capture dictator
1983	Grenada	Invade to oust Communist regime
1994	Haiti	Invade to oust rightist dictator

exploitation   Paying producers less than they deserve.

demagoguery   Politics through the manipulation of votes by extravagant promises.

Monroe Doctrine   The 1823 U.S. proclamation to keep Europe out of the Western hemisphere.

Roosevelt Corollary   The 1905 U.S. warning to Europe not to use local debts to breach *Monroe Doctrine*.

Economic growth has greatly lessened dependency, and you get growth by participating in the world economy, not by hiding from it. Brazil's two most recent presidents, Cardoso and Lula, abandoned dependency theory in favor of capitalism and foreign investment, and Brazil boomed, especially in agriculture, until it was not dependent on anyone (see page 164). Many Latin American intellectuals, impressed by capitalist growth, stopped worrying about capitalist **exploitation**.

Venezuela, in contrast to Brazil, slid back into the common Latin American tendency to **demagoguery**: Denounce the Yankees and nationalize industry. Hugo Chávez, a former paratroop officer who earlier attempted a coup, has been twice elected Venezuela's president with populist promises to uplift the poor. American corporations have siphoned off Venezuela's oil, charged Chávez, but we Venezuelans will seize it and use it to end poverty. The huge run-up in oil prices enabled Chávez to fund ambitious programs, but oil is not a solid basis for growth; its price fluctuates, and the oil runs out. Oil employs few, concentrates wealth into the ruler's hands, limits economic growth, and blocks democracy. By 2010, facing big deficits and shortages, Chávez was in trouble.

For most of our history, the United States simply paid little attention to Latin America. We seem to have a cultural blind spot for our hemispheric neighbors. Only security concerns prompted U.S. interest: European penetration after Spain's ouster (the **Monroe Doctrine**), German penetration before World War I (the **Roosevelt Corollary**), and Soviet penetration during the Cold War. Security rather than economics is the chief U.S. motivation: no threat, no interest.

DIPLOMACY ■ FROM MONROE DOCTRINE TO ROOSEVELT COROLLARY

The United States welcomed Latin America's independence in the 1820s. It removed potentially hostile empires from our hemisphere and reminded us of our own independence struggle. The United States wanted to make sure other European powers did not try to take Spain's place. In 1823 President Monroe issued his famous doctrine telling Europe that the United States would not become involved in European affairs but that "we should consider any attempt on their part to extend their system to any portion of this hemisphere as dangerous to our peace and safety." No European power should recolonize the newly independent lands. Once you're out, you're out for good.

In mathematics, a corollary is a statement that logically flows from a previous proof. The term came with President Theodore Roosevelt's 1905 warning

to European powers. If Monroe told the Europeans, "No more colonies in our hemisphere!" we had the right and duty to prevent them from establishing colonies by indirect means. Much of Central America and the Caribbean had become deeply indebted to European banks, and European powers claimed the right to seize the little countries' customs houses and collect tariffs until the debts were paid. This "customs receivership" was a breach of the Monroe Doctrine, Roosevelt reasoned. It would put European (especially German) gunboats in our lake. So Roosevelt told the Europeans: We will collect any debts for you; you keep out. The paternalistic Roosevelt Corollary gave the United States an unlimited right to intervene directly in the region for a generation. To many natives of the region, it looked like U.S. imperialism.

THE PATTERN OF U.S. INTERVENTION

The United States has been intervening in Latin America since before the war with Mexico in 1846–1848, which gained us the Southwest and for which we paid Mexico $15 million (remember: force and/or cash). A pattern emerged. Americans came to think of Latin American lands as weak, comical countries. They were not our equals; their sovereignty was nominal. If they threatened U.S. interests and investments, small armed expeditions would correct them. They were like children who needed a spanking from time to time.

Earlier, there was great-power rivalry in Central America and the Caribbean. The United States, Britain, and France had a strong interest in building and controlling a canal to link the oceans. In 1846, President Polk signed a treaty with Colombia, which then included Panama, to develop a canal. Competition with Britain for a similar treaty with Nicaragua led to the 1850 Clayton-Bulwer Treaty, which envisioned U.S.–British cooperation in building a Nicaraguan canal.

U.S. investments in the region grew. An American adventurer, William Walker, gathered a private army and took over Nicaragua from 1855 to 1857 but was defeated by U.S. railroad tycoon Cornelius Vanderbilt, a rival for control of one of the main routes between the two

TURNING POINT ■ GUATEMALA: THE WORST CASE

Guatemala is perhaps the worst example of U.S. intervention and how it can go wrong. Guatemala was a true "banana republic"; the United Fruit Company ran much of its economy and owned huge banana plantations. United Fruit was a state within a state that no Guatemalan government dared touch but that many Guatemalans resented. In 1944 a coalition of students, liberals, and army officers ousted the dictatorship and set up a democracy dedicated to major reform. Leftists and Communists from all over Latin America—including an Argentine medical school graduate, Ernesto ("Che") Guevara—came to participate.

A showdown came in 1952 when the government of President Jacobo Arbenz passed an agrarian reform act that targeted United Fruit. Most of the company's gigantic holdings were expropriated for redistribution to landless peasants. In compensation, United Fruit got a paltry $1,185,000—$2.91 an acre—which is what the company had listed its land at for tax purposes. United Fruit cried "communism," and Washington heard.

Secretary of State John Foster Dulles and his brother, CIA Director Allen Dulles, plotted the overthrow of the Arbenz government in 1954. An exiled Guatemalan colonel, with arms and funds from the CIA, recruited a fake "army" of 140 in Honduras. The CIA broadcast imaginary news of battles and rebel victories. Light bombers staged strafing runs to make it look like a big invasion. Arbenz ordered the army to issue weapons to citizens, but it refused and stood aside as the rebel "invasion" ousted Arbenz. With fewer than 20 dead, the United States toppled a government that had considerable popular support.

The 1954 Guatemalan coup was celebrated as a CIA triumph, but it meant the end of reforms and the beginning of a bloodbath. Leftist guerrillas tried terrorism against the military regime, which retaliated by indiscriminate killing of anyone suspicious. Some 200,000 Guatemalan Indians, priests, teachers, and labor leaders were murdered over the decades. One military regime overthrew another, until finally, in 1985, reasonably democratic elections produced a civilian government. Since then, democracy has gained strength, and a peace treaty was signed with the guerrillas in December 1996.

Another consequence of 1954 was the lesson learned by Arbenz's leftist supporters. Some gathered in Mexico City to discuss what had gone wrong. What is needed, they decided, is not reform but revolution, especially replacement of the old army with a new, revolutionary one. Discussants included Che Guevara and Fidel Castro. In 1956, their band landed in Cuba for three years of guerrilla warfare. When the CIA tried to replicate its Guatemala triumph in Cuba in 1961, it failed.

oceans. U.S. investments in the region's coffee, banana, and sugar plantations and the related docks, railroads, and telegraph lines steadily grew. Increasingly, the United States saw the Caribbean as an American lake and Central America as a natural sphere of influence. The 1898 Spanish–American War (see Chapter 3) confirmed this attitude for many Americans. Much to American displeasure, a French company under Ferdinand de Lesseps (who had built the Suez Canal) had obtained rights from Colombia in the 1870s to build a canal across the Isthmus of Panama. Americans were not too sad that yellow fever and bankruptcy stopped the French effort.

President Theodore Roosevelt picked up where the French left off. He offered Colombia $10 million plus $250,000 a year in rent, but Colombia held out for more. Some Panamanians resented Colombian delay on the canal, and with support from Washington they rebelled and seceded from Colombia. Roosevelt sent the cruiser *Nashville* to enforce the breakup of Colombia. The United States invented Panama in 1903. Its canal zone was to be run "in perpetuity" by the United States as "if it were the sovereign of the territory."

Under the Roosevelt Corollary (see box on page 166), U.S. troops intervened repeatedly throughout Central America and the Caribbean. The governments of the region were "irresponsible," argued Washington, and the United States had the duty to "preserve order" and keep out other powers. The reasons for U.S. military intervention were many: nonpayment of debts, revolutions, threats to U.S. property, and leaders the United States disliked. The Marines would land, occupy the cities for a few years to set things right, and leave.

They never, of course, really solved the problems and often left them worse. Typically, the Americans would train a local army and install its leader as president, confident that he would preserve order and remain friendly to U.S. interests. This led to corrupt military dictatorships but produced an illusory order that was often just a buildup to serious revolution.

REFLECTIONS ■ THE TAKING OF SWAN ISLAND

In late summer 1960, I was an explosive ordnance disposal diving officer on a U.S. minesweeper south of Cuba. Suddenly the chief of naval operations in Washington ordered us to Swan Island, about 125 miles north of Honduras and claimed by both the United States and Honduras. We were to seize the island, capturing or killing the armed "Honduran leftist students" who had invaded hours before.

As our small ship steamed at flank speed toward Swan, the captain called me into his cabin. "When we get there, take your diving team and some explosives and make an underwater attack on the students' ship," he ordered. "Sink it." Our three-man team suited up and readied our explosives.

But as we approached the flat, scrub-pine-covered island, there was no students' ship. An armed landing party went ashore to find that the students had left a couple of hours earlier. They had run up the Honduran flag at the U.S. Steamship Company communications center—the only installation on the island—drank a case of beer, found the place dull, took down their flag, and left. We guarded Swan for three weeks until relieved by another minesweeper.

Only later did we learn that "U.S. Steamship" was a front for the CIA, a communications center for the U.S.-sponsored Bay of Pigs invasion a few months hence. What did I learn? First, people often play small roles in world events without being fully aware of what is going on. Second, legitimate orders from official authorities make subordinates willing to carry them out. My team was set to blow up that ship and anyone unfortunate enough to be on it, no questions asked.

—N. O. B.

Fidel Castro visits adoring Cubans in 1964. (Jack Manning/*The New York Times*/Redux Pictures)

During World Wars I and II, the United States kept German influence out of Central America and during the Cold War fought Soviet influence in the region. The problem was that this pushed the United States to stand by reliable anti-Communist dictators rather than take a chance with democratic reformers who might let Communists in the back door. During the Cold War, a panicky Washington tended to see reformists as Communists and to intervene against them.

CUBA LEAVES THE U.S. SPHERE

Cuba had been solidly in the U.S. sphere since the Spanish–American War in 1898. From then until Fidel Castro rolled into Havana on New Year's Day, 1959, Cuba was a virtual U.S. protectorate, a market for U.S. goods, a place of investment for U.S. capital, and a playground for Americans. Some Cubans resented this status and rallied to Castro's cry "*¡Cuba sí, Yanquis no!*" Castro kept his Communist views to himself as he led a guerrilla war against the corrupt Batista regime in the Sierra Maestra of eastern Cuba. Castro's victory brought a brief period of joy, but soon Castro clamped down his own dictatorship—a far more thorough one than Batista's—and turned to the Soviet Union for arms and financial aid. By nationalizing U.S. industries in Cuba, Castro deliberately angered the Eisenhower administration, which broke diplomatic relations.

Castro's aim was the communization of Cuba and the spreading of its revolution. Cuban arms, agents, and influence turned up throughout the region. The entire Cuban upper class and much of the middle class—close to three-quarters of a million Cubans—left for Miami, which suited Castro just fine. Their departure cleared out opposition to his rule and opened up positions for young, loyal revolutionaries. Within two years, Cuba was a Communist dictatorship.

TURNING POINT ■ THE BAY OF PIGS, 1961

When the Eisenhower administration became aware that Castro was turning Cuba into a Soviet client, it had the CIA assemble and train an army of 1,400 Cuban exiles. The model was the 1954 takeover of Guatemala (see box on page 167). But Castro and his officers had studied the lessons of Guatemala. Castro got completely rid of the old Cuban army—some by firing squad—and replaced it with his own revolutionary army, which he personally headed. Castro's "neighborhood committees" allowed no organized opposition.

The CIA plan called for the exiles to train in Honduras for several months, then stage an amphibious landing supported by U.S. air cover in unmarked planes. The CIA believed the landing would provoke a popular uprising against Castro. After the exiles consolidated a beachhead, the United States would recognize and aid them. President Kennedy adopted the plan but canceled direct air support, thinking the world would view it as a U.S. invasion.

Everything went wrong. The landing site was poor, a beach on Cuba's south called the **Bay of Pigs**, which was easy to contain. There was no uprising; Cubans either supported the regime or kept quiet. The invaders of April 1961 were pinned down on the beach; most surrendered. The United States ransomed them back for machinery and medicine. Kennedy was humiliated. He had lost his first tussle with communism in the Third World. The fiasco contributed to his resolve not to lose in South Vietnam.

Bay of Pigs   The failed 1961 CIA-backed attempt to invade Cuba and overthrow Castro.

How did Castro get away with building a Communist regime a mere 90 miles from U.S. shores? In earlier decades, this would not have been possible; U.S. Marines would have intervened. But the situation had changed. Direct intervention had become unfashionable. The United States thought that it could depose Castro with a small exile army, as it had done with a too-reformist regime in Guatemala in 1954.

Castro's revolution and America's failure to dislodge him jolted the Kennedy administration into action. Such a thing must never be allowed to happen again. The United States

DIPLOMACY ■ THE CUBA PROBLEM

Long after the Cold War ended and Cuba lost its Soviet patron, the United States still glared at the Castro brothers—and they glared back. What to do with this troublesome little island? At the very time that Washington tried to coax Vietnam and North Korea into joining the world, we stayed with a policy of isolating Cuba.

Most of the powerful and passionate Cuban American voting bloc in Florida opposes anything that appears to be giving in to Castro—from reestablishing trade to allowing Americans to visit Cuba. Knowing how important it is to win Florida, both parties generally give the Miami Cubans what they want: no recognition of or trade with Cuba. U.S. laws penalize foreign companies doing business with Cuba, but the rest of the world just ignores the unenforceable laws.

Others—including a growing number of Cuban Americans—think that the way to end the regime is to bring Cuba out of its shell by trade and contacts. Exposing Cubans to a better, freer life would undermine the Communist dictatorship. Much of Cuba's wretched economy already depends on dollars from relatives in Miami, a point recognized by Castro's successor, his brother Raúl. An uprising is unlikely; Cuba still has secret police, and many Cubans still appreciate the education, jobs, health care, and equality for Cuba's large lower class, many of whom are of African descent. Isolating Cuba keeps its authoritarian regime in power.

CONCEPTS ■ "TORN" COUNTRIES

Harvard political scientist Samuel Huntington (see pages 15 and 147) called countries "torn" when they are pulled between a modernizing elite that wants to join Western civilization and traditional masses that resist. One example is Mexico, where energetic, well-educated younger professionals want to remake Mexico into a modern and capitalistic North American country. Many Mexicans, especially leftists, fight the idea, seeing Mexico's future in socialist help for the poor. Another example is Turkey, torn between secular modernizers who want to join Europe and traditionalists who want to return to Islam and lead the Middle East.

developed the Green Berets and an ambitious foreign aid program called the Alliance for Progress to counter revolutions. Castro may have won by stealth in Cuba, but his revolution would not spread, vowed Washington. President Johnson applied the Cuba analogy—a poor one—to the Dominican Republic in 1965 and sent in U.S. forces "to prevent another Cuba."

Kennedy understood that reforms were badly needed in order to head off revolution. "Those who make peaceful revolutions impossible will make violent revolutions inevitable," he said. In Central America, revolution brewed as some people got rich while others grew poorer. The spread of commercial export crops—coffee, cotton, sugar, tropical fruits—diminished the acreage devoted to foodstuffs such as beans and rice. Commercial farmers made more money, but peasants went hungry. When they got hungry enough, some supported rebels; others flocked northward to work in the United States.

MEXICO: DRUGS AND DEMOCRACY

American media and academics pay great attention to China and Afghanistan but little to our number-one problem: Mexico (which, by the way, is a *North* American country). Our cultural blindness to things Latino may underlie the problem. Mexico is the only place on earth where you can walk from the Third World into the First. Poverty and unemployment push many Mexicans to make that dangerous walk. Mexico's population has grown rapidly—from 20 million in 1940 to 112 million now—but its economy grows only fitfully.

Mexico is a *zone of chaos* (see page 13) on our border, an endless source of drugs, crime, corruption, instability, and undocumented workers. Most of America's illicit drugs flow through Mexico; those who try to stop them are killed. The influence of *narcotraficantes* extends through Mexico's army, police, and courts. Mexico is now engaged in a murderous struggle with its drug cartels; thousands are killed each year, including police, soldiers, judges, journalists, and innocent bystanders.

CONCEPTS ■ SPHERE OF INFLUENCE

Related to *hegemony*, a sphere of influence is where a major power molds the policies of another state without directly controlling its government. Threats and bribes keep local rulers submissive to the powerful state. Major powers create and maintain spheres of influence for their security, economic well-being, and sometimes for prestige. The term grew up in the China trade, where the European imperial powers divided up coastal areas in the nineteenth century into their "spheres of influence," understandings of who dominated where.

PRI   Mexico's long-dominant party.

NAFTA   North America Free Trade Agreement, which links the United States, Canada, and Mexico.

maquiladora   Assembly plant.

Some claim that Mexico is or soon could be a *failed state* (see page 115), but the battles with the *narcotraficantes* show that Mexico still has a functioning government. Mexico, like many Latin American countries, is a *weak state* (see page 115) but not a failed one.

Mexico had a major revolution from 1910 to 1917. In 1929, the winning generals formed the Institutional Revolutionary Party (**PRI**), which won 14 elections in a row, most of them rigged. Billing itself as a leftist party of the people, PRI became statist, bureaucratic, and corrupt. Mexico's presidents (who hold single six-year terms) until recently simply named their successors, and the PRI machine delivered their election by suppressing any opposition, handing out gifts, and ordering whole towns to vote PRI. Businesses and banks transferred huge sums to PRI. Until PRI lost free and fair presidential elections to the National Action Party (PAN) in 2000, Mexico was not a democracy.

Mexicans became more middle class, educated, and critical. Many business and government people have degrees from U.S. universities, including PhDs in economics. Much of Mexico's statist economy has been privatized, but not oil. Pushing in this direction was Mexico's accession to **NAFTA** (see Chapter 18), which opened its borders to free trade with the United States and Canada. **Maquiladoras** near the U.S. border assemble products—including wide-screen televisions—out of parts from many sources for export. Mexico's economy—long plagued by unemployment, inflation, currency collapse, and crooked banking—has grown to $14,000 per capita, setting the stage for stable democracy.

Mexico's presidential elections of 2000 showed what happens when a country becomes middle-income and educated. Many Mexicans were fed up with PRI dominance and understood that democracy needs alternation in power. PRI turned from handpicked candidates to open and hotly contested primaries. Despite PRI's usual tricks—in Yucatán, it handed out thousands of washing machines (no doubt campaigning for a clean election)—Vicente Fox of the free-market PAN won the election. In 2006, PAN's Felipe Calderón won and continued the trend toward markets and growth despite having to wage open warfare with drug cartels.

CONCEPTS ■ FREE AND FAIR ELECTIONS

Like most of the Global South, Mexico for a long time had no free and fair elections. The problem goes a lot deeper than secret ballots and accurate counting—the things outside observers look for. The problem is the dominance of the powerful over a population not aware and organized enough to voice its wants and needs. The root cause is a poor country with too few educated people. With few exceptions—India is the biggest one—poor countries do not have democratic elections.

Instead, those who have power use it to make sure they stay in power. They prohibit or hassle opposition parties—sometimes by murder—until they are ineffective. They deny them access to the mass media, chiefly through government control of television. They distribute gifts, favors, and jobs to their supporters, who vote early and often. They tell the poor and ignorant that they have ways of learning how they cast their ballots. In much of the world (including Russia), elections are rigged well in advance of election day. American efforts to promote electoral democracy in such lands are poorly conceived. The solution: a large, educated middle class. When Mexico and Brazil got one, they became democracies.

WHAT CAN WE DO?

Practically all of Latin America turned to democracy in the 1980s (exception: Cuba), although Venezuela slid back part way to authoritarianism. With the Cold War over, Central American massacres subsided in favor of elected governments. What can and should the United States do to encourage Latin America's steps to democracy and prosperity? We should first learn from history

REFLECTIONS ■ WE BUILD A HOUSE IN HONDURAS

In the early 1990s, Honduras had a per-capita GDP of less than $800 with a population increasing by more than 3 percent a year. Honduras needed all the low-cost housing it could get. With as much to learn about Honduras as I did about building a house, I joined a Mennonite Church housing team on a demonstration project in a new settlement outside of San Pedro Sula. The Mennonites—including an architect, a mason, and a contractor—concentrated on teaching the Hondurans to build houses themselves using local materials. We built a house in eight days for less than $1,000.

I was surprised to find that even poor Hondurans were far more politicized, energetic, and assertive than I had expected, in spite of massive poverty and malnutrition. Even a squatter shanty town that we visited had an appointed representative who successfully bargained with the local authorities for land for the entire community. Things are looking up in Central America. Honduras now has a per capita GDP of more than $4,400 and a 2 percent population growth rate.

—N. O. B.

This Honduran family survives in flood and mud under one small roof. The light-colored hair of the younger children is more likely from malnutrion than from ancestry. (Gustavo Amador/Corbis)

CLASSIC THOUGHT ■ POOR MEXICO!

¡Pobre México! Tan lejos de Dios, tan cerca de los Estados Unidos. "Poor Mexico! So far from God, so close to the United States," said Mexican President Porfirio Díaz (1830–1915), reflecting the widespread Mexican view that just being next door to the United States ensures U.S. domination.

Díaz witnessed the U.S. invasion of 1846–1847, which seized the northern half of the original Mexico in 1848. The sad exclamation also reflects considerable Mexican jealousy of their rich, well-run neighbor. Many Latin American intellectuals share the sentiment.

Mercosur   Free trade agreement of southern part of South America.

FTAA   Proposed Free Trade Area of the Americas.

that U.S. intervention, even indirect, often makes things worse, leading to dictatorships and bloodbaths. Military intervention can turn long and frustrating. U.S. Marines in Nicaragua hunted nationalist guerrilla Augusto César Sandino from 1927 to 1933 and never caught him.

The long-term and only effective solution is economic growth, which requires rule of law, sound policies, participation in the global economy, and rolling back statism. The rise of several Latin American economies illustrates that poor countries need not stay poor forever. After a few years, NAFTA had a positive impact on the Mexican economy. Some feared NAFTA would send Americans jobs to Mexico, but it did not. The limiting factor in Mexican economic growth—and that of many other countries—is China, whose labor costs undercut almost everybody's. Mexico lost factory jobs to China. (Recently China has been losing some to Vietnam.)

Mercosur (Southern Market) for several years boosted growth in Argentina, Brazil, Uruguay, Paraguay, Chile, and Bolivia until Argentina's currency collapsed in 2002. One hemispheric vision urges merging NAFTA with Mercosur to make a Free Trade Area of the Americas (**FTAA**), which would cover almost all the hemisphere. Today's generation may rediscover Latin America and participate in its economic growth. One advantage: You need learn only one language, Spanish, to cover most of the continent. Add Portuguese—whose written, but not spoken, form is very similar to Spanish—and you can chat from Texas to Tierra del Fuego.

mypoliscikit EXERCISES

Apply what you learned in this chapter on MyPoliSciKit (www.mypoliscikit.com).

Assessment   Review this chapter using learning objectives, chapter summaries, practice tests, and more.

Menu

Flashcards   Learn the key terms in this chapter; you can test yourself by term or definition.

Flashcards

Video   Analyze recent world affairs by watching streaming video from major news providers.

Videos

Simulations   Play the role of an IR decision-maker and experience how IR concepts work in practice.

Comparative
Exercises

KEY TERMS

Bay of Pigs (p. 170)
capital flight (p. 165)
Central America (p. 162)
cocalero (p. 162)
coup (p. 163)
creole (p. 163)
demagoguery (p. 166)
dependency (p. 164)
entrepreneurialism (p. 162)

exploitation (p. 166)
FTAA (p. 174)
indígena (p. 162)
interdiction (p. 162)
intervene (p. 165)
Latin America (p. 162)
maquiladora (p. 172)
Mercosur (p. 174)
mestizo (p. 163)

Monroe Doctrine (p. 166)
NAFTA (p. 172)
narcotraficante (p. 162)
PRI (p. 172)
Roosevelt Corollary (p. 166)
South America (p. 162)
statism (p. 162)

FURTHER REFERENCE

Ai Camp, Roderic. *The Metamorphosis of Leadership in a Democratic Mexico.* New York: Oxford University Press, 2010.

Barshefsky, Charlene, and James T. Hill, eds. *U.S.-Latin American Relations: A New Direction for a New Reality.* New York: Council on Foreign Relations, 2008.

Bowden, Mark. *Killing Pablo: The Hunt for the World's Greatest Outlaw.* New York: Grove/Atlantic, 2001.

Crandall, Russell. *Gunboat Diplomacy: U.S. Interventions in the Dominican Republic, Grenada, and Panama.* Lanham, MD: Rowman & Littlefield, 2006.

———. *The United States and Latin America after the Cold War.* New York: Cambridge University Press, 2008.

Diamond, Larry, Marc F. Plattner, and Diego Abente Brun, eds. *Latin America's Struggle for Democracy.* Baltimore, MD: Johns Hopkins University Press, 2008.

Hufbauer, Gary Clyde, and Jeffrey J. Schott. *NAFTA Revisited: Achievements and Challenges.* Washington, DC: Institute for International Economics, 2005.

Jonas, Susanne. *The Battle for Guatemala: Rebels, Death Squads, and U.S. Power.* Boulder, CO: Westview, 1991.

LaFeber, Walter. *Inevitable Revolutions: The United States in Central America,* 2nd ed. New York: Norton, 1993.

LeoGrande, William M. *Our Own Backyard: The United States in Central America, 1977–1992.* Chapel Hill, NC: University of North Carolina Press, 1998.

Musicant, Ivan. *The Banana Wars: A History of United States Military Intervention in Latin America from the Spanish-American War to the Invasion of Panama.* New York: Macmillan, 1990.

Paterson, Thomas G. *Contesting Castro: The United States and the Triumph of the Cuban Revolution.* New York: Oxford University Press, 1994.

Peeler, John. *Building Democracy in Latin America,* 2nd ed. Boulder, CO: Lynne Rienner, 2004.

Ruiz, Ramón Eduardo. *On the Rim of Mexico: Encounters of the Rich and Poor.* Boulder, CO: Westview, 1998.

Smith, Peter H. *Democracy in Latin America: Political Change in Comparative Perspective.* New York: Oxford University Press, 2005.

———. *Talons of the Eagle: Latin America, the United States, and the World,* 3rd ed. New York: Oxford University Press, 2007.

Stone, Samuel. *The Heritage of the Conquistadores.* Omaha, NE: University of Nebraska Press, 1991.

CHAPTER 11

Development in Rich and Poor Countries

Indian specialists staff help lines 24/7 for U.S. customers. Many such support jobs moved overseas to save on wages. (Brian Lee/Corbis)

Why are some countries rich and others poor? The richest fifth of humankind takes four-fifths of the globe's income; the poorest fifth gets 1 percent and lives on less than $1.25 a day, the World Bank's definition of "absolute poverty." A third of the world's population lives on less than $2 a day, what the World Bank calls "moderate poverty." And these figures are a big improvement over 20 years earlier. Why are some countries' economies growing rapidly and others slowly? There are two broad explanations for these gaps, one focusing on external causes, the other on internal.

Among others, Marxists and Third World radicals favor the external explanation. As we considered in Chapter 2, English economist J. A. Hobson argued that capitalism's spread around the world, the nineteenth-century empires, had given it a new lease on life. By exploiting their colonies—cheap labor to produce cheap raw materials and captive markets for their products—capitalist economies were able to last much longer than Marx had expected. Lenin popularized these views in his 1916 pamphlet *Imperialism, The Highest Stage of Capitalism*. The capitalist empires enrich themselves at the expense of their colonies, which get poorer.

The evidence does not support this view very well. In some cases, individual firms got wealthy from the colonial trade, but, overall, colonies cost the imperial government more to administer and defend than they earned. Colonialism was more a prestige item than economic calculation. The four richest countries of Europe—Norway, Sweden, Luxembourg, and Switzerland—never had colonies. The fifth-richest country, Germany, lost all its colonies in World War I. France enjoyed an economic resurgence after it gave its colonies their independence in the early 1960s. The poorest country of West Europe, Portugal, was both the first and last colonial empire; its five centuries of empire drained it rather than the other way around. Economists long advised the European powers to get rid of their colonies because they were money-losers.

Even after decolonization, though, the view lingers in updated form. Radicals argue that the poor countries, which have only their raw materials to export, get low prices for them from the rich countries. This drains the developing countries' wealth and keeps them tied to the big capitalist

1. What is the relationship between democracy and economics?

2. Is world poverty the result of imperialism?

3. How does psychology contribute to backwardness?

4. What factors made the West the first to modernize?

5. What moral case can be made against imperialism?

6. Is the earth's population increasing at a dangerous rate?

7. What explains the massive migrations of our day?

8. Why has the Global South tended toward socialism and statism?

9. How does a country get rapid economic growth?

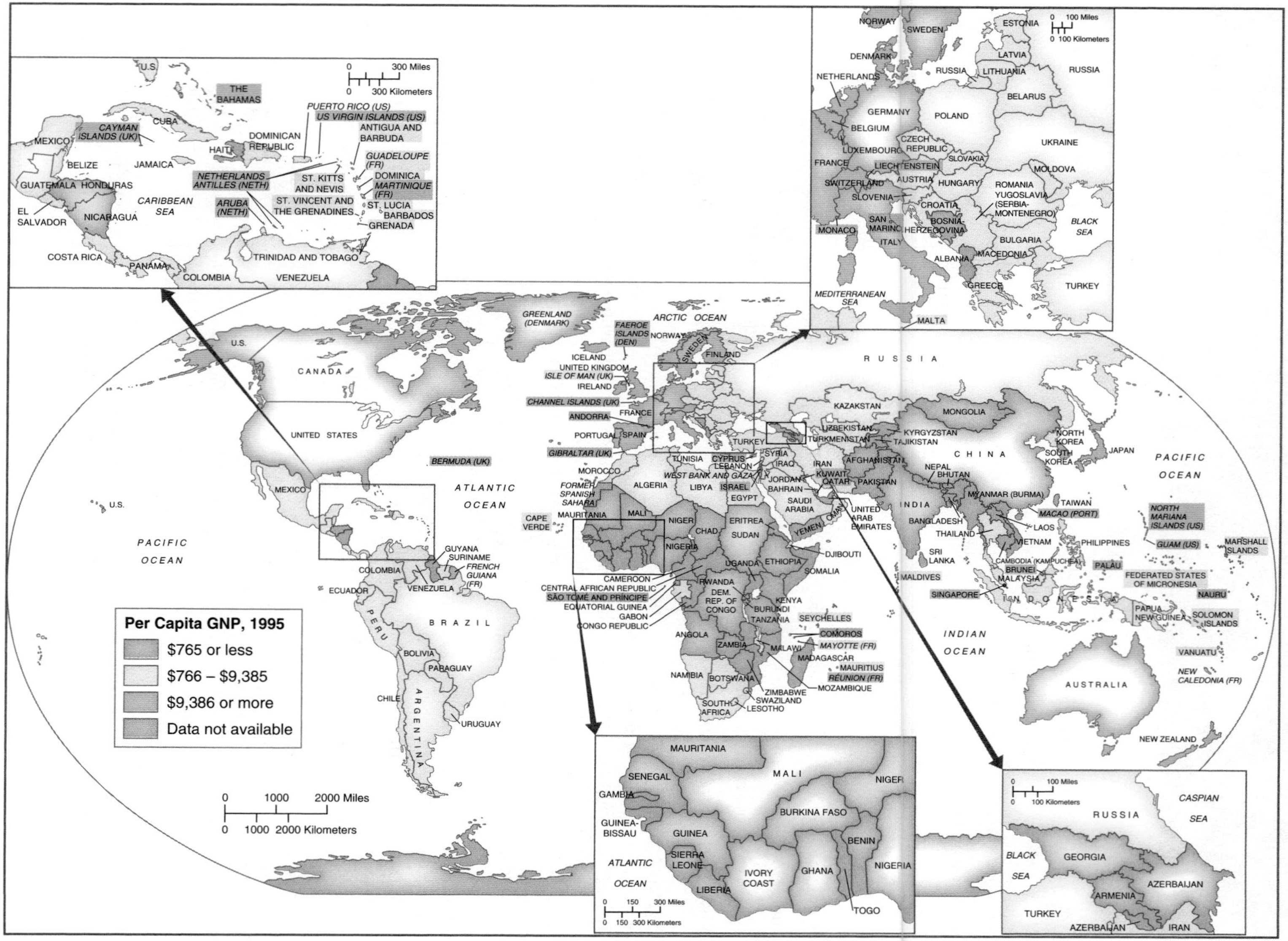

The World by Wealth

Per Capita GNP, 1995

$765 or less
$766 – $9,385
$9,386 or more
Data not available

countries and as poor as ever. Instead of colonialism, developing countries now suffer from **neocolonialism** (see box on page 182), say critics. This situation is not necessarily the result of a capitalist plot, however. If a country's chief product is in oversupply, it will earn little from it. One solution is to diversify; Brazil has done this and is now nobody's neocolony. Another solution is to form a cartel like OPEC to limit production and keep up prices. The oil-exporting countries turned the tables on the capitalist oil-importing countries and exploited them. And why did Japan—with no natural resources, ruined and defeated in war, and occupied by the Americans—not turn into a neocolony of the United States?

neocolonialism   Rich-country dominance by indirect, economic means.

culture   The sum total of a group's learned behavior.

Protestant ethic   Weber's theory that religion first ignited capitalism.

The internally caused view, often favored by conservatives, argues that **cultural** problems retard the poor countries. Lack of natural resources is rarely the problem. Some of the most resource-poor countries have turned into economic dynamos based on their human resources (Japan and Taiwan), while resource-rich countries have stagnated (Nigeria and Burma). Human inventiveness and sound economic policies are far more important than natural resources. Growth needs a psychology that you can and should work hard to improve your situation. This is weak in traditional societies, where people have for centuries tilled the soil, asked for little, and died young. Political and religious structures often teach obedience to inherited authority and fatalism.

"Modern" and "traditional" are heavily cultural. Modern minds do things right, quickly, and often; they adapt to high productivity and high technology. Even if they start poor, modern-thinking people soon produce prosperity. Traditional people see little need to hurry, do things carefully, or grow economically. "Time is money," says the modern person. "*Mañana*," says the traditional person. Many of these cultures are rapidly changing; witness the current rise of several countries from traditional and poor to modern and prosperous.

CLASSIC THOUGHT ■ PROTESTANT ETHIC

One of the efforts of the great German sociologist Max Weber (1864–1920) was to refute Marx, who had argued that economic conditions give rise to new thoughts. For example, Marx said the North German princes and merchants were already profiting from capitalism when they turned Protestant to escape Catholic restrictions on their profits.

Weber said no: First came Protestantism, then came capitalism; the former gave rise to the latter. Protestants—particularly Calvinists—felt they had to prove themselves in this world, not just wait for their rewards in the next. Consequently, the **Protestant ethic** emphasized hard work and conspicuous individual achievement, explaining why people started amassing capital beyond their immediate needs: "Look at me. I'm a big success." Capitalism, the philosophy of economic growth without limit, argued Weber, has a religious basis.

Weber's theory of a Protestant catalyst for capitalism remains unproven. The earliest capitalists were Catholic banking houses in North Italy and South Germany. Recent historical research shows that between 1300 and 1900 the populations of German-speaking Catholic and Protestant cities grew at the same rate, suggesting that their economies were growing at about the same rate. And how do you explain Asia's growth? Some argue that a Confucian ethic is the functional equivalent of a Protestant ethic: Work hard and reinvest your money. Any culture can develop such an ethic, but not all have.

GDP   Gross domestic product; sum total of goods and services produced in a country in one year; measure of prosperity.

WHY DID THE WEST RISE?

One approach to the question of economic growth is to ask why some countries first began what economist Robert Heilbroner called "the great ascent." Europe during the Middle Ages was a traditional society, far behind Arabs, Indians, and Chinese in wealth, education, science, and commerce. For most of history, what we now call the developing areas produced some 80 percent of the global GDP. But by the sixteenth century, certain areas of Europe were growing until, by the twentieth century, the developed countries were producing some 60 percent of the world's GDP. Now, interestingly, the balance is shifting back, with Asia assuming its old predominance.

The reasons for Europe's modernization are several and interlocking, but many historians credit the quality of thought that flowed from the Italian Renaissance starting in the early fourteenth century. Painting improved as artists discovered perspective and shadow. Leonardo da Vinci bridged the worlds of art and science; for a renaissance man, there was no difference. Galileo

CONCEPTS ■ PER-CAPITA GDP

The standard way to measure and compare economies is the per-capita gross domestic product (GDPpc). Every time a car rolls off an assembly line or you get a haircut, the **GDP** increases by whatever those items are worth. The older expression, gross national product (GNP), is now used to designate all income, including from overseas, whereas GDP is considered the more precise measure. The "per capita" is arrived at by dividing the country's GDP by its population. The per cap, now usually expressed in purchasing power parity (PPP, see page 292), gives the most widely used comparison of how well people live.

GDP is not a complete measure or easy to calculate, for some economic activity is off the books, such as the underground economy and unpaid work. Because it is an average, GDPpc does not show inequality of income, which may render averages meaningless. (Old joke: Bill Gates enters a room and suddenly on average everyone there is a millionaire.) Nigeria's $2,300 average conceals the fact that much of it—namely, its oil revenues—goes into just a few pockets. Many people suppose the best economies are the most equal ones, but rapid growth creates inequality, as some people climb the income ladder sooner than others. China's rapid growth is accompanied by surging inequality of incomes.

Many would like to shift to measures that go beyond material aspects to capture overall quality of life. The UN's Human Development Index (HDI) attempts this by combining life expectancy, average income, and education level. But should each of these three measures count equally as one-third of the index? Further, the HDI shows all the advanced countries bunched up at the top, so it is not useful to distinguish one from another. And it mostly tracks GDPpc.

Some would include protection of the environment as an important measure. GDP is indifferent to breathable air, drinkable water, or climate change: Just crank out more stuff. China's fast GDP growth came at a terrible cost to its environment. Some would include security of jobs and incomes and economic sustainability in an index. GDP takes no account of *bad* investments, such as those that brought on the 2008–2009 financial meltdown. In GDP-land, all investments are good. Nobel Prize winner Joseph Stiglitz noted, "There is no single indicator that can capture something as complex as our society." But he added, "If we have the wrong metrics, we will strive for the wrong things."

GDP, imperfect as it may be, is still the best measure of overall economic activity we have, but do not confuse it with human wellbeing or happiness. Tiny Bhutan, high in the Himalayas, proposes a "gross national happiness" index constructed from 72 variables. Can national happiness be calculated?

discovered laws of physics and engineering that we use today. Printing with movable type opened up mass literacy. Commerce increased as trading networks covered Europe. People grew restless and oriented to change and improving their lives; a new dynamic was unleashed upon the world.

modernization theory   Economic growth modernizes whole society.

Starting in France, monarchs began to centralize and increase their power, leading to absolutism. Competing with other monarchs, they funded expeditions and imperial expansion to gain territories to exploit. Columbus's discovery took place in a different context from the earlier Viking discoveries of America. The Vikings had no demanding monarch behind them, no desire for an empire, and no printing press to spread news of their find. The voyages of discovery did not trigger the modern age but were an expression of it.

A new culture of money and material progress appeared. In traditional societies, people saw little reason to amass money beyond their immediate needs. Working hard to get rich was impossible and therefore not attempted; wealth and status were inherited. Tradesmen sought a good living for their families but saw no reason to expand beyond that. In certain parts of Europe, however, in about the fifteenth century, a capitalist mentality appeared. It became good and respectable to amass as much wealth as possible, more than you or your family could spend. Instead of steady-state attitudes, people began to think in terms of growth without limit: "Invest and grow; then reinvest and grow some more." This mentality, now abundant in East Asia, is still lacking in some developing lands, and without it there can be no self-sustaining economic growth.

Why this shift occurred has never been settled. Max Weber (see box on page 179) claimed it was triggered by Protestantism, but other thinkers peg it to technological change and innovation, improved transportation and communication, the consolidation and centralization of kingdoms, or the opening of trade routes. Watt's steam engine in 1775 and Cartwright's power loom in 1785, for example, launched the Industrial Revolution in Britain. But earlier civilizations—the Roman, Arab, and Chinese—were technologically and organizationally advanced but did not produce self-sustaining economic growth. These empires had the ingredients for takeoff, but they petered out.

Other thinkers emphasize cultural factors, specifically the rise of Protestantism that challenged the steady-state attitudes of the medieval Catholic faith. The Catholic Church was

CONCEPTS ■ MODERNIZATION THEORY

Economics and politics are clearly related. What is called **modernization theory** has found a dividing line around $5,000 to $8,000 per capita GDP (see box on page 180). Below that, few countries are democratic, and attempts to found new democracies usually fail amid demagoguery and military coups. Above that level—what are called "middle-income countries"—most countries are democratic and do not slide back into authoritarian rule. (India, poor but democratic, is the massive exception to this division.)

The reason seems to be that poor countries have only a small middle class; their societies are divided into a few rich and many poor. The middle class, which grows as a country gets richer, is educated and moderate and dislikes dictatorships. As one scholar put it: "No bourgeoisie, no democracy." Taiwan, South Korea, Brazil, and Chile turned from authoritarian dictatorships to democracies after their economies had grown. This leads to the question of how to make economies grow.

not growth-oriented; it taught people to accept their place in life. Lending money at interest was deemed immoral and was prohibited, a major impediment to economic growth. Protestantism rejected such restrictions and brought economic growth (see box on page 179), especially to England and the Netherlands.

Whatever the causes, the West pulled ahead and conquered or converted the rest of the world. European arms and military organization made short work of Arab, Asian, and African states. Colonial administrators carved up the globe and attempted to remake it to Western tastes. Western dynamism and expansionism—or, if you prefer, greed—took over most of the globe.

A few non-European lands engaged in "defensive modernization"; they tried to adopt enough of the West's technology to stave off the imperialists. Japan adapted European ways wholesale (see Chapter 17) to beat the West at its own game. The Ottoman Turks and Chinese empire adopted European weapons but were picked apart. That's the trouble with halfway modernization. You cannot adopt just one facet of Western civilization—such as the military—and leave the rest of your system traditional. It will not work, for you need Western education, economics, and nationalism to make your military arm work right. You have to become as modern as those who would conquer you.

The Global South resisted—and in a few cases is still resisting—becoming modern. Some developing countries dislike the implication that everything they stand for and live by—their religion, values, and culture—is inferior. They usually try to preserve their culture while adopting Western technology. It is a difficult combination. The countries of the Persian Gulf attempted to stay Islamic while building a high-tech petroleum economy. The result, as we considered in Chapter 9, was instability and breakdown. Islam especially resists Western culture, for Islam sees itself as morally superior to the West's crass materialism.

There are no purely traditional countries left in the world; all are unstable combinations of modern and traditional, creating massive problems that some people would like to fix by returning to a rural idyll where all live as organic farmers. This is not possible; populations are too big and expect growing living standards. It can be a recipe for misery and starvation, as in Cambodia under the back-to-the-village Khmer Rouge murderers. No, once you have started the "great ascent," you cannot go back. You cannot even pause.

THE POPULATION EXPLOSION

For most of human history, the population grew very slowly, with high birth rates offsetting high death rates. The world's population reached 1 billion only around 1830. During the nineteenth century, it gradually accelerated, reaching 2 billion around 1930. Then it grew faster, hitting

CONCEPTS ■ NEOCOLONIALISM

In the parlance of radicals, neocolonialism is the indirect continuation of colonialism by economic means. France, for example, freed its many African colonies, but there are more French people in them than ever, helping the African lands with their economy, education, and defense. Radicals call this neocolonialism, but many poor African countries found they needed continued French help. Only France pays much attention to Africa. In Latin America, one version of neocolonialism is called *dependency* (see pages 164–165).

3 billion around 1960 and 5 billion in 1987, the sort of exponential growth the English econo-mist Thomas Malthus predicted (see box on page 354). It is now 7 billion and is expected to top 9 billion by 2050.

The world's population is increasing 1.2 percent a year, but most of this is in the developing lands. The population of the industrialized countries increases about 0.7 percent a year, less-developed countries increase 1.4 percent, and least-developed countries increase 2.4 percent, a problem rate. If a country's GDP growth is 2.4 percent but its population growth is also 2.4 percent, it enjoys no per-capita increase and remains poor. But as a poor country gets a little richer, with a per cap of $1,000 to $2,000, its *fertility rate* (see page 186) starts to drop. When it reaches a per cap of $4,000 to $10,000, it usually falls to just replacement level. Slower population growth accompanies faster economic growth.

Rapid population growth is a kind of overshoot. Traditional societies had high birth rates and high death rates. They needed the former to compensate for the latter and to stay in rough balance. A quarter to half of babies died soon after birth, as did the mothers, and people lived only to 30 or 40. Simple public health improvements—sewers, clean water, washable cotton underwear—boost life spans. With inoculations, visiting nurses and midwives, and adequate diet, people attain near-modern levels of health. Life expectancy in the Third World increased an amazing 22 years from 1960 to 1995. Their death rate has dropped, but they are used to high birth rates and still expect many babies to die. They like lots of male children, for males earn more to support them in their old age. Their religion may forbid birth control. As their birth rates exceeded their death rates, their populations exploded.

Population growth is slowing everywhere as societies move from traditional to modern. From 1950 to 2000, the developing areas' fertility rate fell by half, from six to three. In Singapore, Hong Kong, Taiwan, and South Korea it's not much above one (2.1 is replacement rate—see page 186). The world's population is predicted to peak at around 9.2 billion by mid-century and then stabilize. After a while, people recognize that there is no need for so many babies, for practically all of them live, and government welfare measures help the elderly. People live in cities, in small apartments, where children are more of a burden than they are on a farm. Industrialized countries have low birth and population-increase rates. Europe and Japan even have shrinking populations. The solution to the world's population increase is to get the developing countries to industrialize quickly. The most effective way to curb the number of babies per woman is to educate girls: the more schooling, the fewer babies. Some claim that drastic curbs on births—as practiced in China—are necessary, but modernization brings the birth rate down without coercion.

REFLECTIONS ■ THE PSYCHOLOGY OF BACKWARDNESS

I had studied about transitional countries in the abstract but didn't understand them until I got a pocket calendar in Belgrade, where I was studying. A Balkan country, Yugoslavia at that time (1963–1964) was still partly traditional, with one foot in Europe and one in the Middle East. Many of its people lived in the old ways. The calendar puzzled me for several days until I found the problem. The calendar was one day off; its makers had made 1963 (and not 1964) a leap year. And then I realized that backwardness is a cultural or psychological problem, a lack of paying attention, of not doing things right the first time. American students are not immune to this problem.

—M. G. R.

migration   Resettling from one country to another.

remittance   Money sent back home.

Countries with determined leadership can bring their birth rates down. China, with 1.35 billion citizens, holds its annual increase to 0.6 percent, very low for the Global South. The methods for this are not pretty: compulsory abortions, female infanticide, and punishment for parents who produce three children. Saudi Arabia, a strictly Muslim country, had an amazing population growth of 7.9 percent a year in the 1980s, dropping to a moderate 1.8 percent by 2009. It is full of unemployed and angry youths, many of whom turn to Islamic radicalism.

Population growth by itself need not spell doom—if there are enough jobs. But where unemployment is already high, as in most of the developing lands, jobless young men turn to violence and revolution. Mexico, Brazil, and Egypt each need to add a million new jobs a year just to keep even. An expanding population may fuel dictators' dreams of aggrandizement: Syria and Iraq in recent decades had rapid population growth.

THE GREAT MIGRATION

Jobs are the reason Global Southerners immigrate to the North. Legally and illegally, by planes, boats, and foot, citizens of poor countries seek jobs in rich countries. Hundreds die trying every year. Millions of Pakistanis, Indians, and Caribbean islanders in Britain; North Africans and those from farther south in France; Turks and East Europeans in Germany; and Mexicans, Caribbean islanders, and Asians in the United States illustrate the universality and magnitude of the new **migration**. Most rich countries try to limit them. The United States annually takes in more than 1 million legal immigrants plus many illegal ones.

Can you blame the immigrants? Typically, they flee unemployment and dismal prospects. Even the dirtiest, lowest-paid jobs in the First World pay ten or more times what migrants can make at home. Their **remittances** to relatives back home are three times bigger, more efficient, less corrupt, and steadier than foreign aid. And there are jobs in the First World, whose aging workforce cannot staff its agricultural and industrial base. Many citizens of rich countries refuse to take low-end jobs; they prefer to live off welfare.

Is there anything wrong with poor immigrants taking the lowliest jobs? Is it not a replay of how many of our ancestors arrived in the United States? They too were in a push–pull

ECONOMICS ■ THE RULE OF 70

How long does it take a quantity to double, figuring in the effects of compounding? If you know its annual growth rate, divide that into 70 for the number of years it will take to double. West Europe's population increase of a very low 0.2 percent a year means—if that rate holds—it will take 350 years for its population to double. The United States, with a moderate 0.7 percent, will double in 100 years, not counting immigration. Africa, however, with a natural increase of more than 3 percent, could double in less than 25 years (depending on the impact of AIDS). The average Rwandan woman bore eight children, which produced a 3.4 percent annual growth rate and made Rwanda the most densely populated country in Africa, which contributed to the genocide of the 1990s. You can use the same rule going the other way: If a country took 11 years to double its per-capita GDP, it had an average annual percentage increase of 6 percent.

Guatemalans cross into Mexico on their way north for a better life. (Luis J. Jimenez/*The New York Times*/Redux Pictures)

situation: Poverty and limited opportunities pushed them out of the old world; prosperity and unlimited opportunities pulled them to the new world. A century ago, however, the immigrants to America were mostly Europeans and assimilated rather quickly to U.S. culture. After two generations, they looked, spoke, and thought like other Americans. The new immigrants are mostly non-European and do not easily assimilate into the host country's culture; the gap is too big. Pakistanis in England, North Africans in France, and Turks in Germany tend to ghettoize themselves and become more religiously Muslim than they ever were in their homelands. Some Spanish speakers in the United States don't learn English, and parts of the United States have become bilingual Spanish–English—a point that bothers Americans who fear for the nation's unity.

America has it relatively easy, for it is used to immigrants. The European host countries, however, are unused to waves of immigration, especially from outside of Europe. They were never immigrant societies; until recently, they exported people. The result of this meeting of unlike cultures is nasty racism and efforts to stop further immigration. Most European countries have anti-immigrant movements or parties, many with fascist undertones, such as the French National Front, German National Democrats, and Austrian Freedom Party, led by people who whip up racist fears to win votes. In the high-unemployment areas of Germany, young skinheads take out their frustrations in neo-Nazi movements and foreigner-bashing.

political asylum   Permission to remain in host country for those fleeing persecution.

fertility rate   Average number of babies per woman.

Immigrants have become a global political issue. French, German, and American authorities bundle illegal aliens onto planes to send them back home. Some of them beg for **political asylum**—they say they are persecuted at home—but most countries shrug them off as "economic refugees" and expel them. The United States now looks at them as potential terrorists. If we do not treat illegal immigrants firmly, many argue, it would encourage millions more to come. The world does not love refugees.

What can be done? The answer is industrialization in the home country, which has at least two demographic effects: It keeps people at home in jobs, and it lowers the fertility rate. Instead of trying to prop up its old industries, the rich countries should be exporting them to the devloping lands, which use their natural advantage in low labor costs to move into the industrial age. One way to promote this is to eliminate tariffs on the products of the poorest countries. The 17 percent U.S. tariff on African-made textiles and clothing—now repealed—throttled African growth. Now Africa, with farmland and minerals, is growing. Biggest investor in Africa: China.

Europeans, Japanese, and Americans lavish $1 billion a day on their farmers in taxpayer subsidies. This undercuts Third World growers who cannot sell their products. What the rich world gives in foreign aid it takes away in the harm done to Global South agriculture. Proposals to cut these odious subsidies meet with staunch refusals in Europe, Japan, and even the free-market United States.

ECONOMICS ■ UNEVEN POPULATION GROWTH

World population growth is highly uneven—in some places too much, in others too little. In the former countries, generally poor, it means not enough jobs. In the latter countries, generally rich, it means not enough workers to support an aging population on social security. One solution—already being practiced—is migration.

One key measure is the **fertility rate**, the number of babies per average woman. (This is not the same as the birthrate or rate of population increase.) The replacement fertility rate is 2.1—enough to replace both parents plus a little for those who die or have no offspring. If below replacement, a population shrinks over time; if it is higher, it grows. The following table shows UN fertility rate estimates for 2005–2010.

The average North American and West European woman has between one and two children, the average Global South woman three; their mothers had six. (The world champ, Mali at 7.3, is threatened by hunger.) Over 30 years, Third World fertility rates have fallen by about half and could eventually fall below replacement. Citizens of the rich countries live long on good pensions. Some countries, especially Germany and Japan, are running out of working-age people, whose taxes fuel their retirement systems. Migration from poor to rich countries is therefore not only natural but a fiscal necessity.

UN Fertility Rate Estimates, 2005–2010

Europe	1.45
North America	2.0
Latin America	2.37
Asia	2.34
Africa	4.67

SOCIALIST VERSUS MARKET PATHS

market economics Capitalism.	
offshore To move production overseas.	

Until recently, much of the Global South approached development with a socialist twist. Many leaders saw colonialism and capitalism as one and the same: unfair, exploitive, and inhuman. The first generation of leaders typically studied in Europe, where they picked up then-fashionable socialist views and returned to their native lands determined to build a better, more-just system by means of state ownership and supervision.

The results were catastrophes. Socialism in the Soviet Union and East Europe merely worked badly. In the Global South, it yielded results ranging from genocide under Communist regimes (Cambodia and Ethiopia) to tyranny and economic decline under "third-way" regimes that were partly socialist (Zimbabwe and Burma). The countries that follow a market path, although riddled with problems, show more rapid economic growth and greater personal freedom. There are no examples of successful Third World socialist economies.

Eventually, reality hit home. Everything Third World socialists hated—capitalism and trade—turned out to be the ticket to rapid economic improvement. A new generation of leaders let market sectors rise with generally good results: higher food production, living standards, and economic growth. Socialism was out, free markets in, even in Communist China. The collapse of communism in East Europe and the Soviet Union came just as most Global South countries were changing their attitudes on economic development. The socialist and statist presumptions that had been popular in the 1950s and 1960s found few defenders by the late 1980s. Worldwide, the new catch phrase was "**market economics**."

ECONOMICS ■ IS MY JOB SAFE?

No, your job is not completely safe, even a specialized, high-tech job. We now import not only clothes, shoes, and toaster ovens from the Global South but also services. Economists used to say that free trade is both morally and economically the right thing to do, but recently some worry about "outsourcing jobs" and "**offshoring**" America's technological and industrial base. It was one thing when we outsourced making shirts, another when we outsource high-tech jobs.

Classic free-marketers argue that if we kept factory jobs in the United States, many would be staffed by Global South immigrants willing to work long and hard for low wages. Much of America's Sun Belt industry already depends on workers—many of them illegal—from south of the border. By moving some jobs to the emerging economies, we reorient ourselves to higher-tech, higher-paying jobs, and we give the developing lands a chance to climb the economic ladder. Typically, the first rung on this ladder is textiles and clothing. We also turn developing countries into trading partners for U.S. goods and services. That's the good part.

But the export of jobs did not stop with manufacturing; it moved into areas people thought could never be offshored. Instant digital communication means that, for a fraction of U.S. costs, radiologists in India read X-rays for U.S. hospitals, Indian engineers develop new software, and Indian lawyers do research for U.S. law firms. Some skilled and educated Americans lose jobs even as their bosses profit from the cheap overseas labor—one of the causes of the growing gap in U.S. incomes. The Democrats played this card in the 2008 elections but kept vague what they would do about it. Undertakers may have the only American job that is not exportable.

ECONOMICS ■ DOES FOREIGN AID WORK?

Some people would like to see a massive increase in foreign aid—with the United States in the lead—to developing countries. True, U.S. foreign aid—about one-tenth of 1 percent of our GDP—is low; West Europe and Canada give about three times as much as a percent of GDP. Much of U.S. aid is in surplus grain, which both supports American farmers and feeds the starving but does little to develop Third World economies. Americans have never liked foreign aid, believing it is a waste of money.

The first big U.S. foreign aid program, the Marshall Plan, lifted West Europe after World War II, but later efforts in the developing areas show no correlation between aid and economic growth. Some countries received a lot of aid but grew poorer; others received little but grew impressively. Corruption skims off much aid. British economist P. T. Bauer called aid "an excellent method for transferring money from poor people in rich countries to rich people in poor countries." Bauer also coined the term *kleptocracy* (see page 92) to emphasize that much aid for countries without rule of law or sound economic policies disappears into private pockets. With both of those items in place, poor countries attract foreign investment and grow rapidly without aid. No rock concert has ever aided Africa; self-promotion is not the same as results.

Researchers have found no consistent way to produce economic growth. Markets can help, but only when certain policies are followed. Capitalism sounds like a simple system: Governments step back and let private industry and initiative produce and sell what the market wants. Actually, capitalism is complex and requires government to create favorable conditions and reasonable regulations. The fastest-growing emerging economies generally follow these policies:

1. *Prices:* Let prices find their own level. Subsidies or fixed prices create distortions in supply and demand and retard growth. Free prices are signals, telling producers what and how much to produce. Do not block these signals.

2. *Currency:* Do not print too much money or set fixed exchange rates. One telltale sign: If you can get 20 percent more on the black market for your dollars than you can in a bank, the exchange rate is distorted.

3. *Education:* Invest in people. A healthier and better-educated workforce means faster productivity growth and attracts more foreign investment. The real payoff is in good elementary and secondary education, not college.

4. *Trade:* Open your economy to the world. Welcome foreign investment and technology and make products for the global market, not just your home market. Says Columbia University economist Jeffrey Sachs: "There is not a single example in modern history of a country

CLASSIC THOUGHT ■ SOCIALISM WHEN YOU'RE YOUNG

Latin Americans like to repeat this old wisdom: "If you're not a Communist when you're 20, you have no heart. If you're still a Communist when you're 40, you have no head." They mean that young people are supposed to be idealistic, critical of the present unfair society, and eager to help the poor. After they've been out in the world and learned how hard it is to change things and how great dreams turn sour, people abandon socialist visions. Aging wises you up.

successfully developing without trading and integrating with the global economy."

5. *Governance:* Promote rule of law. Government must not choke off growth by regulations and corruption, but it must enforce contracts, protect private property, and keep dealings **transparent**. Several fast-developing economies tumbled when their "**crony capitalism**" was unmasked.

transparency   Business and political transactions open to public view.

crony capitalism   Corrupt, secretive favors among government officials and businesspeople.

Some thinkers were unduly pessimistic about economic growth in the Global South. The number of desperately poor is down. Since 2005 the emerging economies account for over half of world GDP and are growing much faster than the economies of the advanced countries, which are having trouble recovering from the 2008–2009 recession. Asia is resuming its share of the world economy that it held until two centuries ago. Asia fell behind because it missed the Industrial Revolution; it is now zooming ahead because it has joined the Industrial Revolution.

Britain—where the Industrial Revolution began—took about 60 years, starting in 1780, to double per-capita income. The United States, starting in 1840, took 50 years to do the same. Japan after 1885 needed only 35 years. Turkey, beginning in 1957, did it in only 20 years. Brazil

ECONOMICS ■ THE BURMESE WAY TO CATASTROPHE

Burma—whose dictators renamed it Myanmar—serves as a negative example of economic development and of Third World "socialism." Burma, once the world's leading rice exporter, experiences food shortages. With abundant natural resources—rich agriculture, teak forests, and petroleum—Burmese grew poorer. Most of Burma's economy, however, is off the books, in the black market and smuggling. To avoid confiscatory taxes, Burmese smuggle their gems, hardwoods, rubber, and heroin out to Thailand and Malaysia.

How did it get this way? In 1962, General Ne Win (who worked for the Japanese in World War II) seized power in a coup and kept it. A single party, the Burma Socialist Program Party, consisting mostly of army officers, preached the "Burmese Way to Socialism" but lived well off corruption and the state-owned economy. Chinese and Indians were expelled, and they were Burma's merchants and technicians. The generals also isolated Burma, letting in few foreigners, even to deliver aid after the devastating 2008 hurricane. Burma long waged antiguerrilla campaigns against minority Karens, Shans, Chins, and Kachins who wanted to break away from Burma.

Burmese mostly live passively with the decline but every few years protest massively against corruption and repression. Police and soldiers have gunned down thousands. The military dictatorship refuses to step down even after losing free elections in 1990. Instead, the junta keeps the winning presidential candidate, Aung San Suu Kyi, winner of the Nobel Peace Prize, under permanent house arrest.

In protest, the West imposes economic sanctions on Burma, which have not budged the junta but help keep Burmese poor. While the West kept out, China, which ignores human rights abuses, plunged in. China is now investing $3 billion in a pipeline to transport Persian Gulf oil through Myanmar into China, shortening the previous tanker route through the Straits of Malacca. Some critics claim that isolating Burma does no good but that loosening sanctions would open it to economic growth and political change. (Note how the same argument is used with Cuba, page 170. Is it true?) Starting in 1993, Burma relaxed economic controls a little, and the economy has grown to a per cap of $1,100 in 2009, still miserable but an improvement. Burma may yet see freedom.

demonstration effect   One country copying another's success.

informal economy   Transactions off the books, the black market.

after 1961 took only 18 years. South Korea, starting in 1966, needed just 11 years. And China, starting in 1977, did it in 10 years and continues to grow rapidly. Why the acceleration? The old industrialized countries had to invent technology; the emerging economies just import it and use it with their cheap labor to undercut the rich countries.

One of the pluses of the post–Cold War era is that two superpowers no longer compete for clients in the Global South. All manner of horrors and nonsense went on as part of the zero-sum mentality that posed the Third World as a strategic prize. Both superpowers aided and armed dictators, guerrillas, death squads, and political police. They sponsored attention-getting foreign aid programs that contributed little to economic growth. Much aid was skimmed off by corruption.

The path out of poverty is increasingly understood. Most of the developing lands have accepted the previously-described policies for economic development. When one country follows such policies and succeeds, it creates what economists call a **demonstration effect**, which encourages copying by other lands. As economist Paul Krugman points out, no one has successfully predicted the next lands of rapid growth; it's always a surprise. Latin America, ignored for decades, is now growing faster than the U.S. economy. India, written off for years as hopeless, in 1991 abandoned its statist economic policies in favor of private enterprise and zoomed ahead, especially in information technology.

ECONOMICS ■ THE BLACK MARKET AS MODEL

In 1987, a book by a Peruvian economist shook Latin America and reverberated through the Third World. Rejecting the standard socialist or statist models for economic growth, Hernando de Soto suggested as a model the most dynamic and innovative sector of developing economies: the black market. His controversial book, *The Other Path: The Invisible Revolution in the Third World*, said that slow growth in Latin America is the fault of an oversized bureaucracy that strangles everything in red tape. These societies aren't even capitalist; they are leftovers of a precapitalist colonial system that fosters corruption and inefficiency.

De Soto gave some examples from Peru. It took 289 days to register a small business with the government. A group of minibus drivers needed 26 months to get a license. To homestead state land in order to build a small house, it took three and a half years and cost more than most Peruvians could possibly pay. And Peru wondered why its economy didn't grow faster.

While the official economy chokes on regulations, the **informal economy**—making up over 40 percent of Latin American economies—thrives. Here people simply ignore laws and regulations and work for themselves, producing according to supply and demand. Instead of trying to stamp out the black market, de Soto suggests, countries should encourage it to spread. If you think about it a minute, a black market is just a free market trying to wiggle out from under economic controls.

More recently, in *The Mystery of Capital*, de Soto discovered another bar to economic growth: inability to get loans. The trick to capital growth, he finds, is being able to use your property as collateral for loans. Squatters do not own the land they build their shanties on, so they cannot use their homes to secure loans with which to start and expand businesses. The solution: Give them clear title to their land. De Soto has the gift of looking at things most mainstream economists ignore.

As the rapid growth of the emerging economies became clear, a curious reversal took place in the rich countries. From scoffing at poor lands, the advanced countries started fearing them: "Hey, they're taking our jobs!" There is little to fear. Ultimately, everyone gains. The Third World climbs out of poverty, and First World consumers gain by the cheap products from the developing lands. Many Europeans and Americans worry about losing factory jobs, but most of them upgrade their skills and move into higher-paying jobs. And it is much better to have a rich trading partner than a poor one. (For more on this, see Chapter 18.) In terms of percent of world GDP, countries such as China and India are just rebounding to where they used to be two centuries ago. We should not hinder them.

mypoliscikit EXERCISES

Apply what you learned in this chapter on MyPoliSciKit (www.mypoliscikit.com).

 Assessment   Review this chapter using learning objectives, chapter summaries, practice tests, and more.

Menu

 Flashcards   Learn the key terms in this chapter; you can test yourself by term or definition.

Flashcards

 Video   Analyze recent world affairs by watching streaming video from major news providers.

Comparative
Exercises

 Simulations   Play the role of an IR decision-maker and experience how IR concepts work in practice.

Videos

KEY TERMS

crony capitalism (p. 189)	informal economy (p. 190)	offshore (p. 187)
culture (p. 179)	market economics (p. 187)	political asylum (p. 186)
demonstration effect (p. 190)	migration (p. 184)	Protestant ethic (p. 179)
fertility rate (p. 186)	modernization theory (p. 181)	remittance (p. 184)
GDP (p. 180)	neocolonialism (p. 179)	transparency (p. 189)

FURTHER REFERENCE

Bates, Robert H. *Prosperity and Violence: The Political Economy of Development*, 2nd ed. New York: Norton, 2010.

Beattie, Alan. *False Economy: A Surprising Economic History of the World*. New York: Penguin, 2009.

Clark, Gregory. *A Farewell to Alms: A Brief Economic History of the World*. Princeton, NJ: Princeton University Press, 2007.

Collier, Paul. *The Bottom Billion: Why the Poorest Countries Are Falling Behind and What Can Be Done About It*. New York: Oxford University Press, 2007.

Cooper, Phillip J., and Claudia María Vargas. *Sustainable Development in Crisis Conditions: Challenges of War, Terrorism, and Civil Disorder*. Lanham, MD: Rowman & Littlefield, 2007.

Easterly, William. *The White Man's Burden: Why the West's Efforts to Aid the Rest Have Done So Much Ill and So Little Good*. New York: Penguin, 2006.

Harding, Jeremy. *The Uninvited: Refugees at the Rich Man's Gate*. London: Profile Books, 2000.

Harrison, Lawrence E. *The Central Liberal Truth: How Politics Can Change a Culture and Save It from Itself*. New York: Oxford University Press, 2008.

_____ and Samuel P. Huntington, eds. *Culture Matters: How Values Shape Human Progress*. New York: Basic Books, 2000.

Hirsi Ali, Ayaan. *Nomad: From Islam to America. A Personal Journey Through the Clash of Civilizations*. New York: Simon & Schuster, 2010.

Hoffmann, Stanley. *Chaos and Violence: What Globalization, Failed States, and Terrorism Mean for U.S. Foreign Policy*. Lanham, MD: Rowman & Littlefield, 2006.

Hubbard, R. Glenn, and William Duggan. *The Aid Trap: Hard Truths About Ending Poverty*. New York: Columbia University Press, 2009.

Lancaster, Carol. *Foreign Aid: Diplomacy, Development, Domestic Politics*. Chicago: University of Chicago Press, 2006.

Legrain, Philippe. *Immigrants: Your Country Needs Them*. Princeton, NJ: Princeton University Press, 2007.

Mokyr, Joel. *The Enlightened Economy: An Economic History of Britain, 1700–1850*. New Haven, CT: Yale University Press, 2010.

Moyo, Dambisa. *Dead Aid: Why Aid Is Not Working and How There Is Another Way for Africa*. New York: Farrar, Straus & Giroux, 2009.

Naím, Moisés. *Illicit: How Smugglers, Traffickers, and Copycats Are Hijacking the Global Economy*. New York: Doubleday, 2005.

Rapley, John. *Understanding Development: Theory and Practice in the Third World*, 3rd ed. Boulder, CO: Lynne Rienner, 2007.

Sachs, Jeffrey D. *Common Wealth: Economics for a Crowded Planet*. New York: Penguin, 2008.

Seligson, Mitchell A., and John T. Passé-Smith. *Development and Underdevelopment: The Political Economy of Global Inequality*, 4th ed. Boulder, CO: Lynne Rienner, 2008.

Thirlwall, A. P., and Penélope Pacheco-López. *Trade Liberalisation and the Poverty of Nations*. Northampton, MA: Edward Elgar, 2009.

Thurow, Roger, and Scott Kilman. *Enough: Why the World's Poorest Starve in an Age of Plenty*. New York: PublicAffairs, 2010.

Yunus, Muhammad. *Creating a World Without Poverty: Social Business and the Future of Capitalism*. New York: PublicAffairs, 2008.

PART IV

THE ETERNAL THREATS

Alas, wars are still very much with us, although their number has declined in recent years. Attempts to wish war away leave us unprepared for a harsh reality. Technology has historically brought new threats; now weapons of mass destruction proliferate and could be used.

Chapter 12 examines some of the suggested causes of war, whether it is inherent in humans, a product of the states they live in, or a result of a chronically insecure international system. Thucydides' theory that fear causes wars is still highly relevant. China's rapid growth has reawakened the theory that "rising powers" cause wars.

Chapter 13 considers how states seek security, although none can attain absolute security. Some insecurity is to be expected and tolerated. Typically states counter threats by defense, deterrence, détente diplomacy, disarmament, or some combination of these four "Ds."

Chapter 14 discusses why the Bomb is probably here to stay. Nuclear weapons have too many political functions for governments to scrap them. India, Pakistan, and North Korea got a lot more respect after they exploded their first nukes. Nuclear proliferation, however, especially by extremist regimes, suggests that eventually these weapons could be used.

This brings us to the new problem of *asymmetrical conflict*, sometimes simplified to "terrorism" but which long precedes 9/11. We discuss the causes and consequences of asymmetrical warfare with special reference to the Middle East in Chapter 15.

CHAPTER 12

The Causes of Interstate Conflict

London suffered massively from German bombing in World War II, what Britons called the "blitz." (William G. Vanderson/Hulton Archives/ Getty Images)

Thinkers have been pondering the causes of war for centuries, usually with an eye to preventing future wars. Many theories of war have been advanced; none is wholly satisfactory. It is likely that any given war has a mixture of causes, and no two mixtures will be the same. As always in the social sciences, **causality** is hard to prove.

Did humans always practice war? It depends in part on how you define war. Archeological evidence indicates primitive hunter-gathers practiced plenty of violence against other humans. Hunter-gatherers and later nomadic herders owned no territory but, when population pressure mounted, they fought over hunting lands, cattle, pasture, and water. With no law ruling the land, spears were the only way to get back a stolen cow. Their conflicts, however, were usually episodic and loosely organized vendettas among families and clans. (Also unable to use legal methods, drug cartels operate on a similar self-help basis.)

Many scholars think that organized warfare required the founding of cities and their close offshoot, civilization. (The root of "civilization" is Latin for "city.") These produced states, kings, a warrior class, and a reason for fighting other kingdoms: territory. More territory brought a state more food and more people and thus more power to both resist attack and to expand. States, power, and war were likely born triplets.

QUESTIONS TO CONSIDER

1. Are humans naturally warlike?
2. What are *micro* and *macro* approaches to the causes of war?
3. What were Clausewitz's warnings about war?
4. What is the "levels-of-analysis" problem?
5. Are wars growing out of conflicting cultures now likely?
6. Does capitalism cause wars or peace?
7. Does a balance of power lead to peace? Or does a hierarchy of power?
8. What evidence supports the "previous-war" theory?
9. How may analogies be misused in IR?

MICRO THEORIES OF WAR

Micro theories are rooted in biology and psychology. In the biological view, humans are essentially animals. As Hobbes put it, "Man is to man a wolf." Actually, that is unfair to wolves, which are usually pretty nice to other wolves. Few animals are uniformly aggressive, but they may become so when attacked. Carnivorous mammals such as lions have to be trained by their mothers to hunt and kill. Man's closest relatives, the primates, are mostly peaceable and sociable.

Some attempt to explain war as the result of genetic human aggressiveness. Millions of years of evolution have made humans fighters—to obtain food and defend their families and territory. From the beginning, extended families and clans formed hunting bands of males, which created male bonding and carried over into fighting other bands of humans. Novelist and radical critic Norman Mailer proposed that Americans' love of hunting underlay the Vietnam War, but few accepted the simplistic connection. The bonding spirit of a football huddle and an infantry squad are quite similar. Thus one cure for war, some suggest, is getting young males to bash themselves silly on the sports field to slake

causality Proving that one thing causes another.

micro Close-ups of individual and small-group behavior.

their thirst for violence. There is no evidence that sports can replace war. Aggressive behavior in lacrosse does not necessarily transfer into killing others.

Recent research suggests that young soldiers, far from being natural killing machines, have to be carefully trained and encouraged to kill. The natural instinct in battle is to run away. To prevent this, armies invented sergeants. Now, after deployment to Iraq and Afghanistan, some American soldiers get drugs and counseling to stave off mental breakdowns. Warfare does not come naturally.

Most anthropologists reject biological determinism, arguing that primitive peoples exhibit a wide variety of behavior—some are aggressive and some are not—that can be explained by culture and circumstances. Some cultures, from their religion and early history, tend to be warlike. Circumstances, such as a drought, may push peaceful pastoralists into the territory of another tribe and lead to fighting. The Plains Indians of North America, with no defensive barriers, had to be ready to fight for their hunting grounds. The cliff dwellers of the Southwest just pulled up their ladders. Today's few remaining hunter-gatherers—such as the San people of Southern Africa, whose DNA is closest to that of original humans—are quite amiable. When they encounter other bands in their perpetual search for food, they share information about game and water and arrange marriages (to guard against inbreeding) and go on their way. Fighting is rare.

Psychological approaches are related to biological ones; both assume the causes are deep within individuals. Psychological studies explore the personalities of both leaders and followers, what made them that way, and why they are willing to turn to violence and war. Studies of the 2003 Iraq War are incomplete if they do not include the state of mind of Saddam Hussein and of America after 9/11, which was a psychological shock that had to be avenged. Westerners are still puzzled over what makes Osama bin Laden and his followers Islamic fanatics who hate us more than they love life. Clearly, there are vast psychological and cultural gaps in our understanding (see Chapter 15 for more on this). If the problem is really rooted deep in human psyches, understanding it will not necessarily lead to curing it. An old slogan proposes "no world peace without mental health," but how are you going to get Napoleon, Hitler, and bin Laden to come in for their meds and therapy?

Biological and psychological theories offer some insights but fall far short of explaining wars. If humans are naturally aggressive, then all nations should be constantly at war. But most nations most of the time are at peace. How is it that countries can fight a long series of wars—the ten Russo–Turkish wars over 200 years around the Black Sea or the six Arab–Israeli wars over 60 years—under different leaders who surely must have been psychologically distinct? Biological and psychological approaches may offer insights into some of the *underlying* causes of war but not the immediate causes. For this we turn to state-level and macro theories.

STATE-LEVEL THEORIES OF WAR

Here we move the camera back from the close-up of micro-level analyses of individuals and small groups to the wider view of whole countries. This "state-level analysis" looks at nation's political structures, economies, and cultures. Marxists argued that capitalism pushes countries to war because the very rich and their helpers invariably control the government and dictate policy. When the capitalists run out of markets in one country, they expand to others, giving rise to empires and wars as the several capitalist powers bump into each other around the globe. This, wrote Lenin, caused World War I. Evidence shows that competition for colonies played little or no role in the march to war in 1914. In 1885, for example, the European powers met in Berlin to amiably carve up Africa.

Liberal idealists (see Chapter 2) such as Norman Angell argued before World War I that the economies of most countries had become so prosperous and interdependent that they could not possibly go to war with each other. In this view, it is precisely the free market of capitalism that leads to peace. This made good sense during most of the nineteenth century, when world trade grew and peace prevailed. World War I then busted both to pieces. Globalization (see Chapter 18) carries an updated version of the view that trade and capitalism bring peace.

reactionary Extremely conservative; seeks returning to old ways.

level of analysis Where you suppose causality resides: in individuals, states, or the international system.

For Woodrow Wilson, it was undemocratic regimes that cause war, specifically the **reactionary** monarchies of Germany and Austria-Hungary in 1914. Once they were destroyed and replaced with democracies, there would be peace. This is an early version of the "democratic peace" theory (discussed on page 346): Democracies do not go to war with other democracies. It seems to be true, but getting democracy to grow where it has never grown before is no easy matter, as we learned in Iraq and Afghanistan. Germany's democracy of the 1920s collapsed into Hitler's hands in the 1930s. The fall of the Soviet Union brought an attempt at democracy but led to the authoritarianism of Putin.

State-level analysis can also include the country's culture. Are some cultures inherently hostile? (See the following box.) Did Germans and Japanese have a national superiority complex that encouraged them to conquer their respective continents? Are Americans domineering and self-righteous "cowboys" who think they can remake the globe in their image? One problem with "culture" as an explanation is that it can change quickly and thoroughly in response to events. Germans and Japanese are now pacifistic, often unwilling to support the United States or send troops into any kind of combat. Before World War II, people said Jews could not fight and made poor soldiers. Now many complain that Israelis automatically turn to military solutions and oppose peace.

CONCEPTS ■ WALTZ'S THREE LEVELS OF ANALYSIS

In 1959 Kenneth Waltz published a minor classic, *Man, the State, and War*, which delineated three "**levels of analysis**" that are often confused but should be separated for the sake of clarity. The first level, "man," supposes individual humans cause wars. Evil, mentally ill, or power-hungry people, especially national leaders, start wars to enhance their powers or their egos. Some posit humans as biologically aggressive. Studies of Hitler as the cause of World War II are first-level analyses. Such explanations are popular but lack rigor. How could one man start a giant conflagration? Only if he had control of state power. How did he get such power, and why did the state, say, Germany, follow him?

This bumps the level of analysis up to the "state" level in which we look at whole countries, their societies, and their economies. With second-level analyses, it is bad states that cause wars. The particular form of "bad" varies from thinker to thinker. Marxists see capitalists as the problem. Economic slowdowns force capitalist states into overseas expansion and war with other lands. Americans, on the other hand, blamed Communist states for causing wars in Korea, Vietnam, and Afghanistan. Always insecure, the Soviet Union was driven to expand and wipe out its capitalist rivals. Woodrow Wilson saw nondemocratic governments as the problem, such as Kaiser Wilhelm's Germany, a state that was geared up for World War I. Replace these with democracies, he declared, and peace will prevail.

Any explanation offered in these first two levels, Waltz argued, is incomplete. We really have to take it up to the third level of analysis, the international system. Most of these systems (which we explored in Chapter 1) are anarchic; that is, there is no overriding force or power to make countries obey. Simply put, there are wars because there is nothing to stop them. Evil personalities or expansionist states may be the *specific* cause of a given war, but this cause becomes operative only in a *context* of international anarchy. Studies become muddy when they use the insights of one level of analysis to explain something at another level. IR thinkers have been using Waltz's levels of analysis ever since, and so shall we.

MACRO THEORIES OF WAR

Moving the camera back until it takes in the entire globe leads us to **macro** theories, which are rooted in history and political science and are often related to the *realist* approach we discussed in Chapter 2. They focus on the power of states without looking too much into state structures, economies, and cultures the way state-level analysis does. Instead, they tend to treat states as billiard balls colliding on a pool table. The internal structure of the balls is seldom decisive, as states move according to the *external* forces that bump them. The first thing states do, as we shall explore in the next chapter, is defend themselves. A state can be democratic, dictatorial, Islamist, or vegetarian, but if attacked most will fight. A possible exception here might be Czechoslovakia in 1938 and 1939, which allowed itself to be taken by Hitler without a shot fired. But Britain and France had abandoned a brother democracy at Munich in 1938, leaving Czechoslovakia alone and defenseless.

macro Big, panoramic view of state interactions.

Another rather basic tendency of states is to expand when and where they can. If they have little power, of course, they do not attempt to expand but hunker down and try to avoid trouble. States with considerable power, however, tend to use it, as in the Germans' medieval push to the

CONCEPTS ■ ISLAMIC WARS?

Cultural explanations of war and conflict got a boost with Huntington's 1993 article "Clash of Civilizations" (see pages 15 and 147). Several analysts of turmoil in the Middle East hold that its underlying element is a broad and deep Muslim cultural antipathy toward the West. Even a Danish cartoon could set off Muslim riots in 2006. Muslim countries, showing what Huntington called "kin-country rallying," opposed the 2003 U.S. invasion of Iraq. The cultural approach argues that Islam and Christianity were born enemies, for Islam teaches that it is God's successor to Christianity and will triumph worldwide.

In the seventh century, Islam's first conquests and conversions were of the Christian lands of the Byzantine Empire and North Africa. Islam and Europe have been enemies for centuries—consider the Moorish conquest of Spain (and invasion of France), the Crusades, the Ottoman conquest of the Balkans (and two sieges of Vienna), and European imperialist takeovers of the Middle East.

For several and complex reasons, Muslim civilization stagnated while an energized Europe, starting around 1500, moved ahead. Russia and Austria slowly pushed back the Ottoman Empire in the Balkans in a series of wars. Be careful of calling Muslim–Christian wars religious or cultural. Much of the motivation was material—fighters seeking lands and booty and emperors seeking to expand their empires—with religion as the excuse. A possible exception to this might be the First Crusade (1095–1099), which was motivated by Christianity but did many un-Christian acts along the way.

War seen in this manner is a grudge match between cultures in which the loser of one century seeks revenge the next. This theory is much too simple, because at any given time many Muslim lands are at peace and even aligned with Christian countries, while some Muslim states fight bitterly with each other. In 1991 some Muslim countries supported the U.S.-led war against Iraq. Why? In 1991 we were liberating a Muslim country, Kuwait; in 2003 we weren't. Islamic states, like all states, form their policies according to their national interests at that moment. Change the situation and their policies change, even if their "culture" stays the same.

If Muslims hate the West, why do so many of them immigrate to Western countries? Some analysts point to specific issues—for example, the U.S. occupation of Iraq and support for Israel and for local authoritarian regimes such as Egypt and Saudi Arabia—as the root of Muslim opposition. If Washington changed its policies, they argue, Islamic hatred would subside. (New regimes, however, could be worse.) One big danger: If we act on the "culture war" theory, we make it come true, possibly creating enemies where we had none.

east, the Americans' "manifest destiny," the growth of the British and Japanese empires, and the Soviet takeover of East Europe. Only countervailing power may stop the drive to expand. One country, fearing the growth of a neighbor, will strengthen its defenses

escalation Tendency of a war to grow bigger and fiercer.

or form alliances to offset the neighbor's power. The 1949 formation of NATO to stop Soviet power is an example. Likewise, the more recent tendency of many countries to oppose U.S. policies (the counterweight system discussed in Chapter 1) is a natural reaction against a superpower that tells others what to do. Notice that such foreign policy moves have little to do with leaders' psychologies or cultural differences, and macro approaches do not much bother with them.

CLASSIC THOUGHT ■ THE CRUX OF CLAUSEWITZ

The Prussian philosopher of war, Carl Maria von Clausewitz (1780–1831), has been widely ignored in our time. Although his massive *On War*, essentially his notes edited by his widow, is difficult to read and full of seeming contradictions, Clausewitz's lessons are valid today. At the risk of oversimplifying, we think this is the crux of his thinking:

1. Wars tend to **escalate**. Why? Both sides want to win, so they continually increase their efforts. The war takes on a life of its own, growing bigger and more ferocious. Don't suppose you can always keep wars small and under rational control.

2. A war that escalates to "absolute war" would have no purpose, so put limits on how far a war can escalate.

3. Restrain war by making sure it has clear and doable political goals. Thus Clausewitz's famous dictum, "War is the continuation of policy by other means." If you don't have such goals, don't go to war.

4. Politics is in command. The general must advise civilian authorities, especially on questions of feasibility, but the setting of political goals is not his job. He should make sure there are feasible political goals and that the civilian authorities understand the heavy costs involved.

5. Win the war by breaking the enemy's "center of gravity," without which he cannot resist. That probably means destroying his main forces.

6. Territory is not so important. If, say, you capture the enemy's capital but his main forces are intact, you are still in trouble. (Example: Napoleon takes Moscow, but the Russian army is unbroken.) Terrain matters only if it helps you crush the enemy. Don't take a hill for the sake of taking a hill.

7. Do not think you can do war cheaply or easily. If you hold back in intensity, you merely give the enemy a better chance.

8. Likewise, do not think you can avoid the horror of battle (*die Schlacht*, cognate to slaughter). Don't kid yourself that you might win by clever maneuvers and bluff.

9. Therefore, "First, be very strong." It sounds obvious, but many in the White House, State Department, and Congress think a "show" of force will suffice.

10. A "remarkable trinity" of people, government, and army makes the enterprise work. Weakness in one element may doom the effort. (Example: A U.S. public that no longer supported the war in Vietnam.) Don't go to war unless you're solid in all three.

To remember Clausewitz's points, think of all the things we did wrong in the Vietnam War. Clausewitz warned against every one of them. Political goals? Feasibility? Costs? Enemy's center of gravity? Escalation? Trinity? Clausewitz's detractors misread him as a bloodthirsty warmonger. He is saying that war has a logic of its own that you ignore at your peril.

asymmetric   Out-of-balance, as when one country has more power than another.

Why should states wish to expand? Why do they not simply build sufficient power to fend off invaders but stay home? That would be the ideal, extolled by realist thinkers such as Hans Morgenthau (see page 24). Unfortunately, states are plagued by insecurity. They survey the world around them and perceive threats or opportunities. They might behold a weak neighbor who could soon be taken over by a stronger state, bringing a hostile power to their own borders. So they adopt the (flawed) reasoning, "If we don't take it, someone else will." The United States expanded from sea to shining sea on that basis and then took the Philippines and Hawaii. States may practice outright conquest or merely gain *hegemony* (see page 82). Either way, expansion often leads to collision with other powers that are also expanding. In Manchuria in 1904, an expanding Russia bumped into an expanding Japan, which started the Russo–Japanese War. Later, U.S. power collided with Japanese power in Asia and the Pacific.

Much international behavior can be explained by the aphorism *Si vis pacem para bellum* ("If you want peace, prepare for war"), which underlay U.S. policy during the Cold War. Better an arms race than military weakness, which would tempt an aggressive adversary and thus lead to war, was the thinking in Washington. Another aphorism is "The enemy of my enemy is my friend" (discussed on page 157). Within five years of the end of World War II, recent enemies Germany and Japan were U.S. allies, because all faced expansionist Communist power. Typically, when the threat ends, the alliance fades (see Chapter 16). Political leaders, claim macro (and realist) theorists, have an almost automatic feel for national interest and power and move to enhance them.

POWER ASYMMETRIES

Most countries seek sufficient (sometimes excessive) power, but does this lead to war or peace? There are two macro theories about this. The *balance of power* theory (discussed in Chapter 1), the oldest and most commonly held theory, says that peace results when several states, improving their national power and forming alliances, balance one another. Would-be expansionists are blocked. Under **asymmetric** conditions, war is more likely. According to balance-of-power theorists, the two great periods of relative peace—between the Peace of Westphalia in 1648 and the wars that grew out of the French Revolution (1792–1814), and again from 1815 to the start of World War I in 1914—have been times when European alliances balanced each other. When the balances broke down, there was war.

Fighting in Bosnia calmed in 1995 only after power there roughly balanced. When the Serbs were winning, they had no incentive to settle; when they were on the defensive, they had a strong incentive to stop the fighting. Many thinkers consider the Cold War a big and durable balance-of-power system that explains why there was relative peace—at least no World War III—for more than four decades.

Other analysts reject the balance-of-power theory in favor of a *hierarchy of power* theory (also discussed in Chapter 1). First, because calculations of power are so problematic, it is impossible to know when power balances. Second, the periods of peace, some writers note, occurred when power was asymmetric, when states were ranked hierarchically in terms of power. Then every nation knew where it stood on a sort of ladder of relative power. It is in times of transition, when the power hierarchy is blurred, that countries are tempted to go to war. After a big war with a decisive outcome, there is peace because then relative power is clearly known. If this theory is correct, then trying to achieve an accurate balance of power is a mistake that will lead to war because obstreperous states will think they have a good chance to win.

MISPERCEPTION

Weaving micro and macro approaches together, some thinkers have focused on "image" or "perception" as the key to war, a view that overlaps with the constructivist approach discussed in Chapter 2. Both psychological and power approaches have something to contribute, but they are incomplete. It's not the real situation (which is hard to know) but what leaders perceive that makes them decide for war or peace. They often misperceive, seeing hostility and development of superior weaponry in another country, which sees itself as acting defensively and as just trying to catch up in weaponry.

At one of the last remnants of the Cold War, a North Korean border guard glares at the camera. The Korean War was never settled and could break out again. (Pierre Bessard/Redux Pictures)

John F. Kennedy misperceived the Soviets as enjoying a "missile gap" over the United States; he greatly increased U.S. missile efforts. It turned out that the Soviets were actually behind the United States, and they perceived the new American effort as a threat that they had to match. The misperceptions led to the 1962 Cuban Missile Crisis, the closest we came to World War III.

The history of U.S.–China relations (see Chapter 17) is a roller coaster of exaggerated images alternating between a "little brother" China that we had to save from the Japanese, followed by an aggressive Communist China that had to be stopped by war in Korea and Vietnam, and then a friendly China and ally against Soviet power. Korea in 1950 offers two good examples of misperceptions. As UN forces under General Douglas MacArthur pushed back the North Koreans to their border with China, Beijing grew convinced we intended to keep going into China, never the U.S. intention. Beijing put out clear warnings to keep well back from the Yalu River, but MacArthur misperceived China and could not imagine it would enter the war. He was taken by surprise when China did and pushed back UN forces.

misperceive To see things wrongly.

When the Communists built the Berlin Wall in 1961, we misperceived it as a first Soviet step to take all of Berlin. We thundered back that we would not let them take West Berlin, which the

CONCEPTS ■ MISPERCEPTION

How do we know in IR that what we perceive is accurate? The world "out there" is extremely complex, often defying our attempts to simplify it into intelligible form for our limited brains. News and intelligence reports are often skewed. Thus we often **misperceive** what is happening in other countries, seeing them as either better or worse, more aggressive or more peaceful, weaker or stronger than they actually are.

Often we learn only later that we have been mistaken. Chamberlain in 1938 at Munich misperceived Hitler as a reasonable man who wished peace. The United States misperceived Iraq in 2003, supposing that

it had weapons of mass destruction. Many specialists on the Soviet Union misperceived it as being a strong, stable system; they were surprised at how fast it collapsed. Anyone, including experts and top decision makers, can be caught up in misperceptions.

Wrote Catholic theologian Thomas Aquinas in the thirteenth century: "That which is perceived, is perceived in the manner of the perceiver." (You get extra credit if you learn it in the original Latin: *Quidquid recipitur ad modum recipientis recipitur.*) You see what you are trained to see. St. Thomas's insight is old but still valid, especially in IR.

Soviets perceived as a first U.S. step to invading East Berlin. Both sides were extremely nervous. Some scholars claim the 1961 Berlin Wall crisis was actually more dangerous than the 1962 Cuban Missile Crisis (see page 84). A Soviet or American tank gunner at Checkpoint Charlie in August 1961 could have started World War III.

In misperception or image theory, the psychological and real worlds bounce against each other in the minds of political leaders. They think they are acting defensively, but their picture of the situation may be distorted. For a long time, it is interesting to note, no country has ever called its actions anything but defensive. The Americans in Vietnam saw themselves as defending the free world; the Russians in Chechnya saw themselves as defending their country. In its own eyes, a nation is never aggressive. A country—under the guidance of its leaders, its ideology, and its mass media—may work itself into a state of fear and rationalize aggressive moves as defensive. Under rabidly nationalistic leadership, most Germans and Japanese in World War II saw themselves as defending their countries against hostile powers. Serbian dictator Slobodan Milošević played the Serbian nationalist card and got most Serbs to believe they were threatened with subjugation or even genocide. Once convinced that they are being attacked, normally peaceful people will commit all manner of atrocities.

North Korea, locked in isolation and hysteria, looked at the U.S. conquest of Iraq and feared it would be next. In 2002, Bush 43 had indeed called Iraq, Iran, and North Korea the "axis of evil." Be careful what you say to a domestic audience; it goes around the globe within minutes and can be heard as something quite different. What most Americans dismissed as a figure of speech to rally domestic opinion, Pyongyang perceived as a real threat. In turn, Pyongyang tested a nuclear bomb and long-range rockets, thinking that would deter the Americans. Washington, in turn, perceived North Korea as threatening to attack America. Wars have started over mutually reinforcing perceptions such as these.

Mutual misperceptions of Muslims and Americans have reached dangerous heights. Many Americans perceive Muslims as fanatics and terrorists. Most Muslims perceive Americans as arrogant and imperialistic. We saw ourselves as liberating Iraq, whereas many Muslims saw us as conquering Iraq, intending to keep it for its oil. There is no quick fix for these misperceptions. U.S. programs to improve "communications" with the Arab world have little impact. Arabs now get much of their news from independent satellite stations such as Al Jazeera, which are highly critical of U.S. policy. Arabs and Americans utterly misunderstand each other, making U.S. leadership in that part of the world unlikely.

A subset of misperception theory might be termed "the fear factor." Depending on their geographical and political situation, many countries are dominated by fear, sometimes justified, sometimes exaggerated. They believe other nations are out to harm them, possibly to conquer them. Hence they arm and form alliances in ways that often increase tensions and fear. The United States feared

CLASSIC THOUGHT ■ THUCYDIDES ON FEAR

One of the earliest thinkers on the causes of war was a cashiered Athenian general who had time to reflect and write about the Peloponnesian War, which devastated ancient Athens. Thucydides' insight still has not been topped: "What made war inevitable was the growth of Athenian power and the fear this caused in Sparta."

Athens had become an imperial power, gaining hegemony over many other Greek city-states. Sparta and some other city-states grew worried. Sparta

wished no war but observed the growth of Athenian power and how Athens used it ruthlessly; for example, it massacred the defiant Melians who refused to submit to Athenian domination. "We could be next," thought the Spartans, so they organized an alliance against Athens. The Athenians, in turn, feared this alliance as a threat. In a climate of mutual fear against the other side's presumed—or possibly real—drive for hegemony, war became inevitable.

Iraq had weapons of mass destruction and was building more when it invaded in 2003. Command pressure reached down into the working levels of U.S. intelligence agencies and required them to produce data confirming the leaders' worst fears. Rumors were accepted as facts.

arms race Competition between rival countries to build more weapons.

Misperception and fear can go the other way, too. Sometimes states are not sufficiently attentive and fearful. They love peace so much they shrug off threats. British and French leaders between the two World Wars were timid. With their staggering losses in World War I in mind, they failed to see the Hitlerian threat until it was almost too late. The United States did no better; it took Pearl Harbor to jolt America into realizing that it could not isolate itself. Israel in 1973 convinced itself that Egypt could not and would not strike across the Suez Canal.

THE POWER DILEMMA

All except pacifists agree that a state must have sufficient power. The world is dangerous, and going unarmed invites attack. But if you have too much power, you create fear among other states, who themselves arm and ally to offset your power. Some call this the *security dilemma*, in which your search for security ends up making you less secure (see Chapter 13). At a minimum, an **arms race** ensues, sometimes ending in war. The trick is to get the "right" amount of power, but this is exceedingly hard to calculate. Because many states are chronically insecure, they *worst-case* (see page 81) and build more military power than they really need. Better too much than too little, they reason. As we discussed in Chapter 5, such was the case with the chronically insecure Soviet Union, which unintentionally created a ring of enemies around itself, thus heightening its insecurity.

CONCEPTS ■ THE PREVIOUS-WAR THEORY

One obvious cause of war is the previous war. This explanation looks simple but is actually a shorthand way of stating something more complex: Any given war leaves behind regional imbalances, thirsts for revenge, and elite calculations that often lead to another war. Other factors, to be sure, help determine if a new round of war actually takes place.

As Australian economic historian Geoffrey Blainey points out, a really thorough, crushing defeat tends to keep the losing power in its (lowly) place for a long time. Examples are Paraguay following the War of the Triple Alliance (1865–1870), Bolivia following the Chaco War (1932–1935), and Germany and Japan following World War II. Nothing aggressive—or even much defensive—has been heard from then since.

The Arab–Israel wars are examples of the opposite, as none of their wars was decisive. In reverse historical order: Israel's 2006 Lebanon incursion was a continuation of its 1982 Lebanon invasion, which grew out of the business left unfinished by the 1973 war, which grew out of the imbalances left by the

1967 war, which was a bigger version of the 1956 war, which was a continuation of the 1948 war, which was a direct result of the Holocaust during World War II, which was just a second act of World War I, which grew out of the wars of German unification, which were a result of the Napoleonic conquests.... One can follow the chain back a very long time. Schematically, it looks like this:

WWI » WWII » 1948 » 1956 » 1967 » 1973 » 1982 » 2006

The previous-war theory leads to a couple of conclusions: (1) There are few really decisive wars that settle things once and for all. A war may settle matters for the losing country for a while—Germany and Japan after World War II—but regional power vacuums left by their defeats brought Communist power into East Europe and East Asia, which led to the Cold War, Korea, and Vietnam. (2) Preventing one war may also prevent a string of subsequent wars. You will not know, of course, which wars you have prevented.

legitimate In Kissinger's theory, IR system in which states accept each other's right to exist.

revolutionary In Kissinger's theory, IR system in which major state seeks to overthrow others.

Many IR scholars detect the origin of the problem not in power but in the type of international system that prevails at a given time. If it is tense, countries will arm. If it is relaxed, countries will keep few arms. After Napoleon, Europe faced few threats from other European powers until Germany unified in 1871 and turned expansionist late in that century. Unthreatened, Europe generally relaxed and enjoyed three generations of peace and prosperity. Now, after the collapse of the Soviet Union, Europe again faces no threats from another European power. (It still has to contend with terrorism that originates in the Middle East and North Africa.) Europe shrinks its armies and chastises the United States for being trigger happy. The context creates the psychology.

The trick then, as Henry Kissinger wrote in his 1954 Harvard doctoral dissertation, is to artfully construct a "**legitimate**" world system—one in which no country threatens another. Metternich did this in Europe after Napoleon was finally packed off to a remote island in the South Atlantic. A "**revolutionary**" world system—one in which types like Napoleon and Stalin threaten everybody—automatically brings tensions and wars that cannot be wished away by good will. In these conditions, states are driven to accumulate power, sometimes too much.

CONCEPTS ■ DO RISING POWERS CAUSE WARS?

Some realist thinkers (see Chapter 2) argue that rising new major powers always collide with other powers, leading to wars. This is true of the Athenian, Roman, Arab, Habsburg, British, German, and Japanese empires, and even the United States. The world did not politely make way for their rise; each had to fight their way up in a series of wars. Some now argue that a rising China will collide with other powers, and China has already fought with the United States in Korea and briefly with India, Russia, and Vietnam. China claims its is a "peaceful rise," one without war, but still asserts major claims to nearby territories and seas.

The rising-powers theory is valid but only when there is a major *territorial* quarrel involved: Who will get what? The Athenian alliance fought the Spartan alliance over colonies in Italy. Rome fought Carthage over Spain. The Habsburgs waged the Thirty Years War over who would dominate Europe. Britain fought France, first over English holdings in France, then over North America. The expanding United States warred with Mexico and Spain to gain, respectively, the Southwest and the Philippines. Germany and Japan fought to grab, respectively, Europe and Asia. The Cold War started over the Soviet taking of East Europe.

If there are no territorial disputes, collisions among rising powers are few or none. Spain and Portugal agreed to divide the barely discovered New

World in the 1494 Treaty of Tordesillas. Mediated by the pope, it drew a line 370 leagues west of the Cape Verde islands and gave Portugal lands to the east of that line. Likewise, Spain and Portugal did not fight over who had what in Asia. Spain had the Philippines, and Portugal had Goa, Timor, Macau, and the Japan trade.

The infant United States fought Britain first over independence and then over shipping (1812), but Britain welcomed the rise of a powerful United States in the late nineteenth century, seeing it as a partner. Britain did not resist the United States replacing it in trade with Latin America, and the United States was unbothered by British dominance in Asia. Britain, France, Germany, Portugal, and Belgium used diplomacy to settle the "scramble for Africa" by carving it up around a table in Berlin in 1885.

This suggests that the rising-power problem can be avoided by settling early and calmly who is to get what. With China, for example, an international conference could determine how far China's maritime boundaries extend into the South and East China Seas. Who will possess the Diaoyutai (Japanese: Senkaku), Spratly, and Paracel Islands? Undersea oil and natural gas around them could be jointly developed. In 2010, however, Beijing angrily rejected a U.S. call for such a conference. China's rise may not be peaceful.

THE DANGER OF ANALOGIES

Human intelligence is finite; it cannot start every thought from scratch. Instead, we rely on **analogy**, even though analogies can be terribly mistaken. Analogies pervade our thinking, structure our organizations, and are drummed into us in school. Indeed, in studying IR you are in effect assembling a tool kit of analogies to apply to present situations. Unfortunately, no two cases are identical; the elements of *dysanalogy* often outweigh those of analogy.

> **analogy**   A previous situation that (you think) explains a present one.

The history of IR is replete with analogies, often false ones. The Germans in 1914 marched happily off to war, thinking it would duplicate their quick victory of 1870–1871 in the Franco–Prussian War. Indeed, almost everyone thought conflict in 1914 would be short, because they made an analogy with the most recent conflict, the quick Russo–Japanese War of ten years earlier. Only a few saw that machine guns and barbed wire would force armies to dig trenches, and fighting would stall for years. Generals, it is often said, refight the last war.

In 1951, Dean Rusk, then an assistant secretary of state, used an analogy of the Japanese puppet state of Manchukuo (see page 280) to explain to Congress why we had to fight Communist China in Korea: "The Peiping [Beijing] regime may be a colonial Russian government—a Slavic Manchukuo on a larger scale." We now see that China was never a Soviet puppet state. Recently, new analogies have been offered: (1) 9/11 was like Pearl Harbor, and (2) we have entered into a conflict with radical Islam that is like the Cold War: long, ideological, and requiring numerous U.S. military interventions. Are either good analogies?

Now one hears analogies between South Vietnam and Afghanistan. There are, to be sure, points in common: Both were weak states and would have been failed states without U.S. troops and money. Both were run by unpopular U.S.-appointed presidents (Diem and Karzai) who rigged elections and gave top jobs to relatives and friends. Corruption was high and government legitimacy low in both lands (the two problems are related). Their military forces were unreliable; many

DIPLOMACY ■ "NO MORE MUNICHS"

One of the most overused and misleading analogies of all time has been "Munich," the 1938 meeting in which Britain and France tried to appease Hitler by giving him a piece of Czechoslovakia. "No more Munichs" was used for decades in Washington and contributed to U.S. intervention in Vietnam. Even President Bill Clinton's Secretary of State Madeleine Albright, the daughter of a Czech diplomat, said in the late 1990s that the formative experience of her life was Munich, and she continued to apply its lessons.

The Munich analogy was seriously misapplied to Vietnam in the 1960s. In the first place, the United States did not even participate in the Munich conference and did not give Hitler anything. London and Paris take the blame for the Munich fiasco. More importantly, communism was a far more complex foe than Hitler, requiring very different strategies. Communist

countries were divided among themselves, and after 1953 there was no Stalin to hold them together. China was not a puppet of the Soviet Union, and Vietnam was not a puppet of China. Third, Hitler was in a hurry; Communist leaders, believing history was on their side (it was not), took their time. Fourth, in 1938 Britain and France were militarily weak and dominated by war-weary leaders, very unlike Washington in the 1960s.

Few now admit to ever having used the Munich analogy, but the one that replaced it may be no more accurate: "No more Vietnams." Vietnam may provide faulty analogies for unlike situations in Colombia, ex-Yugoslavia, Afghanistan, and Iraq. Vietnam was like Vietnam, unique, one of a kind. Be skeptical when someone tells you a current situation is "like" an earlier one. Ask: "Do the elements of analogy outweigh the elements of dysanalogy?"

CONCEPTS ■ THE PACIFIST FALLACY

Pacifists deem any use of arms immoral. American Protestant theologian Reinhold Niebuhr wrestled with this problem during World War II, when some American Christians took the pacifist view that we should keep out of war. Niebuhr concluded that pacifism is a type of heresy because it requires Christians to do nothing in the face of evil; you just stand there and let the murders continue.

Pacifism is still around. Some people were morally outraged over U.S. actions in the Persian Gulf, Bosnia, and Kosovo. This is a "politics of conviction," a rigid and simplistic rejection of force no matter what the situation. The opposite is a "politics of responsibility" that asks, "If I don't act, what will happen? Would my military intervention make things better or worse?" If you proclaim your country will never intervene militarily, you notify the world's dictators and extremists that they can murder with impunity.

The opposite of pacifism is bellicosity, an eagerness for war, and it is still around too. Some people suppose that the answer to most foreign policy challenges is the threat or use of force. Munich is their favorite analogy. Such policies get us involved in unwise wars that are not in the national interest. The regime uses patriotism to mask blunders, and the country gets stuck in a long conflict, unwilling to admit the war was a mistake. Once the **casualties** have started, the **"sunk costs"** argument claims that previous losses morally require us to stay in the war, otherwise our boys have died in vain. On that basis, you can stay in any war forever. There is no simple answer on the choice of war or peace in a given situation; you can err in either direction. In either case, beware of emotionalism and simplified analogies.

---

casualties   Killed plus wounded.

sunk costs   Previous losses justify continuing the war.

deserted. The local population did not snitch on the Viet Cong or Taliban, which dominated many provinces. Both had base areas in adjoining countries and easily infiltrated supplies and fighters. Congress approved both wars in panic mode by joint resolution rather than the constitutional way, with a declaration of war. U.S. firepower—especially air power—killed many civilians and alienated much of the population. The U.S. public soon turned negative on both wars.

But there are important differences. The Viet Cong and North Vietnamese were under the central control of Hanoi and fought for a unified Vietnam. The Afghan fighters are unruly and decentralized—each band obeys different leaders—and most fight for Pashtun rule. Vietnamese had the same ethnicity and language; Afghanistan has many ethnic-linguistic groups, which do not get along. Hanoi had the help of two nuclear powers, the Soviet Union and China. The Taliban are supported by no major powers and finance themselves through the opium trade. Shia Iran does not aid the Sunni Taliban. The Taliban's base area in northwest Pakistan is insecure; Pakistan could take it back. The real stakes in Afghanistan are over who will win in Pakistan and get its nuclear weapons. So, is Afghanistan "like" Vietnam? Or is Afghanistan more complex and dangerous? Both may be quagmires, but in different ways.

mypoliscikit EXERCISES

Apply what you learned in this chapter on MyPoliSciKit (www.mypoliscikit.com).

 Assessment   Review this chapter using learning objectives, chapter summaries, practice tests, and more.

Flashcards Learn the key terms in this chapter; you can test yourself by term or definition.

Flashcards

Video Analyze recent world affairs by watching streaming video from major news providers.

Videos

Simulations Play the role of an IR decision-maker and experience how IR concepts work in

Comparative
Exercises practice.

KEY TERMS

analogy (p. 205)

arms race (p. 203)

asymmetric (p. 200)

casualities (p. 206)

causality (p. 196)

escalation (p. 199)

legitimate (p. 204)

level of analysis (p. 197)

macro (p. 198)

micro (p. 196)

misperceive (p. 201)

reactionary (p. 197)

revolutionary (p. 204)

sunk costs (p. 206)

FURTHER REFERENCE

Art, Robert J., and Kenneth N. Waltz, eds. *The Use of Force: Military Power and International Relations*, 7th ed. Lanham, MD: Rowman & Littlefield, 2008.

Baum, Matthew A., and Tim J. Groeling. *War Stories: The Causes and Consequences of Public Views of War*. Princeton, NJ: Princeton University Press, 2009.

Bell, David. *The First Total War: Napoleon's Europe and the Birth of Warfare as We Know It*. Boston: Houghton Mifflin, 2008.

Blainey, Geoffrey. *The Causes of War*, 3rd ed. New York: Simon & Schuster, 1988.

Bobbit, Philip. *The Shield of Achilles: War, Peace, and the Course of History*. New York: Knopf, 2002.

Cashman, Greg, and Leonard C. Robinson. *An Introduction to the Causes of War: Patterns of Interstate Conflict from World War I to Iraq*. Lanham, MD: Rowman & Littlefield, 2007.

Chua, Amy. *Day of Empire: How Hyperpowers Rise to Global Dominance—and Why They Fall*. New York: Knopf, 2009.

Gabriel, Richard A. *Empires at War: A Chronological Encyclopedia*, 3 vols. Westport, CT: Greenwood, 2005.

Gray, Colin S. *War, Peace and International Relations: Introduction to Strategic History*. New York: Routledge, 2007.

Hanson, Victor Davis. *The Father of Us All: War and History, Ancient and Modern*. New York: Bloomsbury, 2010.

Kagan, Donald. *On the Origin of War and the Preservation of Peace*. New York: Doubleday, 1995.

Kahler, Miles. "Rumors of War: The 1914 Analogy." *Foreign Affairs* 58 (Winter 1979/80): 2.

Kupchan, Charles A. *How Enemies Become Friends: The Sources of Stable Peace*. Princeton, NJ: Princeton University Press, 2010.

MacMillan, Margaret. *Dangerous Games: The Uses and Abuses of History*. New York: Random House, 2009.

Mandelbaum, Michael. *The Fate of Nations: The Search for Security in the Nineteenth and Twentieth Centuries*. New York: Cambridge University Press, 1989.

Michalak, Stanley. *A Primer in Power Politics*. Wilmington, DE: Scholarly Resources, 2001.

Roberts, Andrew. *The Storm of War: A New History of the Second World War*. New York: HarperCollins, 2011.

Volgy, Thomas J., and Alison Bailin. *International Politics and State Strength*. Boulder, CO: Lynne Rienner, 2002.

Waltz, Kenneth N. *Man, the State, and War: A Theoretical Analysis*, rev. ed. New York: Columbia University Press, 2001.

CHAPTER 13

The Pursuit of National Security

Airborne Warning and Control System (AWACS) planes give U.S. forces a high-tech edge. Here, a Navy AWACS lands on the *Independence* in the Persian Gulf. For more about the link between technology and security, see page 210. (Tom Stoddart/Getty Images)

At first, the end of the Cold War seemed to lessen the **security** problems of the major powers, but in a decade 9/11 brought new threats in unexpected ways and demonstrated that countries, even rich and powerful ones, must always be on guard. For some states, security problems have actually gotten worse after the Cold War bipolar system ended. With bipolarity, the two superpowers tried to supervise much of the globe and keep their client states on a leash. Now the leashes are broken, and several states seek weapons of mass destruction (WMD).

QUESTIONS TO CONSIDER

1. Why is there still so much international insecurity?
2. What is the relationship between technology and security?
3. If deterrence worked during the Cold War, could it work now?
4. Under what circumstances can détente diplomacy work?
5. How did *appeasement* become a dirty word?
6. Is disarmament really impossible?
7. What is the difference between deterrence and defense?
8. Would a national missile defense make America secure?

There are also some positive trends. There are fewer international wars after the Cold War, as Moscow's client states no longer get generous loans for massive shipments of Soviet arms. Russia is still happy to supply weapons, but now the buyers have to pay for them. Unfortunately, internal wars did not disappear but grew when the Cold War ended; they peaked in 1993 and still number over a dozen. As we will analyze at the end of this chapter, internal security depends on good government and foreign assistance. Internal wars are usually the fight of a minority that feels discriminated against to break away and become a separate country.

International wars still present the greatest danger to national security. In an age where nuclear, chemical, and biological WMD proliferate and where disputes still smolder over boundaries, ethnic and religious power, resources, refugees, human rights, and trade, security remains high on every state's agenda. Almost all states try to get international organizations, such as the UN, the African Union (AU), the Association of Southeast Asian Nations (ASEAN), or the Arab League, to resolve disputes that endanger security. If the causes of the conflict are deep and serious, however, international forums are of little help. (See Chapter 21 for the UN role in national security.)

As we discussed earlier, states tend to form alliances to help with their security problems. As we shall see in the case of NATO, alliances rise and fall with the security threat (see Chapter 16 for more on this). Alliances pool the resources of members to gain strength either to defend against an attack or, even better, to deter an attack before it happens. Thus, of four basic strategies to preserve security, **defense** and **deterrence** rank first and second, followed by **détente diplomacy** and **disarmament**. Alone or in combination, states utilize these four strategies. Technology has always influenced their strategies.

security What a country does to safeguard its sovereignty.

defense Blocking an enemy's attack.

deterrence Dissuading attack by showing its high costs.

détente diplomacy Attempts to relax tensions between hostile countries.

disarmament Elimination of existing weapons.

revolution in military affairs Electronic, high-tech warfare.

TECHNOLOGY AND SECURITY

A nation's security has always depended on the type and level of military technology existing at a given time. Change the technology and you change what a country must do to secure itself. (See the box on the fall of Constantinople on page 211.) In early-modern Europe, cannons meant that large, sovereign kingdoms absorbed small, medieval principalities. Castle walls could now be broken. Gunpowder (among other ingredients) ushered in the modern age and created two new military branches, artillery and infantry. Canons cracked stone walls so the infantry (from *infante*, boy) could rush through. State power now depended on a large population and a robust economy. Rivalries between monarchs stimulated expansion and conquest abroad, including Asia and the Americas.

In our own age, nuclear weapons and technologies of communications and transportation have had profound effects, especially on wars. It was called the **revolution in military affairs** (RMA). War is increasingly electronic—drone aircraft, precision guided munitions, global positioning systems, communication networks, computers—as shown in the Gulf wars (see Chapter 9). Some argue that all the United States has to do is keep about a 20-year technological lead and it will never be attacked, a dangerous assumption. We learned on 9/11 how our own technology—fuel-laden jetliners—could be used against us.

CONCEPTS ■ SECURITY

Since the first organized states came into contact with other states, security has been the chief interest of rulers and remains the overall prime national interest. Governments go to great lengths to protect their people and preserve their territories and themselves. Security—closely related to sovereignty—means keeping the state whole—its government, its people, and its territory. There are at least six general approaches states adopt:

1. *Live and let live.* This is the best way, provided you live in a peaceful world and have nice neighbors. Small island nations sometimes pursue this strategy.

2. *Bystanding.* If you have aggressive neighbors, you may try to stay neutral, as Sweden and Switzerland did in both world wars.

3. *Bandwagoning.* A weak country may decide the safest path is to join a stronger country and let it lead. Thailand, surrounded by Japanese forces, reluctantly joined Japan in World War II, and Saudi Arabia for a while followed the lead of Egypt's Nasser in the 1960s.

4. *Buck-passing.* Similar to bystanding, a buck-passing country passes responsibility to a powerful hegemon, the way most of West Europe let the United States bear heavy Persian Gulf burdens.

5. *Balance of power.* As we discussed in Chapters 1 and 12, nations often decide to pool their power to offset a threat, as NATO did toward the Soviet Union.

6. *Hegemony.* A strong country becomes the dominant power, arranging things as it sees fit and letting weaker powers bystand or buck-pass. The United States may have moved into this strategy after 9/11.

Remember, there are no sure-fire strategies. Much depends on your relative strength and the situation you face. Whatever you do can become obsolete or make things worse. Flexibility is the key.

Technologies also drive the strategies that states use to protect themselves. As with the walled city, the existence of the nation-state depends on its ability to protect itself. When it no longer can, the nation-state could slide into history, like the walled city. Protection in the nuclear age means integrating into the global system and establishing good government at home. The four strategies mentioned earlier—defense, deterrence, détente diplomacy, and disarmament—are based on certain assumptions about the relations between states. Each has evolved along with technology. Each uses a different process to secure the state, and none is totally effective. Some measure of insecurity is normal in international politics.

DEFENSE

Defense makes an opponent's offense ineffective. Offense seeks to weaken a state and break its political will; defense strengthens a state and upholds its will. Whatever military technique the offense uses, the defense tries to counter. If a defense is strong and an aggressor knows it beforehand, defense may also serve as a deterrent. Think of defense as a shield. The assumption behind defense is that the world is dangerous and hostile powers might attack you. Agreements are unlikely to restrain them. Deterrence may not be credible. Diplomacy works only when backed up by arms. If an aggressor thinks he'll win, the chances of war are high.

Defense first serves as a deterrent warning: Attack me and you'll pay for it! If that fails, it preserves the state by blunting the attack and then possibly counterattacking to overthrow the attacker, as the Allies did to Nazi Germany and Imperial Japan in World War II. The difference is that deterrence prevents an attack by threatening high costs from retaliation, whereas defense prevents an attack by showing the attacker he won't win. Defense and deterrence overlap.

At least two problems come with every country's defense strategy: (1) Does it have enough? (2) Is it the right kind? Terrible mistakes are made on both counts. For the first question, a country must ask, "What is my strategic situation?" West Europe today, facing few security threats (but one of them is terrorism), can spend little on defense and have small armies. To counter terrorism, you need good police work rather than large armies. Indeed, West Europe long depended on the United States to defend it during the Cold War; now Europe has to do even less. At least that's the way most Europeans see it. Canada decades ago decided that maintaining a large army was infeasible and unnecessary—the United States would always defend it—so it has only a small (but well-trained)

TURNING POINT ■ THE FALL OF CONSTANTINOPLE

The English and French fought the famous battle of Agincourt in 1415 without firearms, but the technology of war quickly changed. In 1453, Sultan Mehmed II of the Ottoman Empire, then 21 years old, eradicated the last vestige of the old Byzantine Empire, the city-state of Constantinople, with a new weapon—70 large cannons or bombards, the heaviest weighing 19 tons and capable of firing a 1,500-pound stone ball over a mile. Forty days of bombardment leveled towers and penetrated the city's walls to allow a successful land and sea assault. Emperor Constantine XI died defending his city. Walls that had protected the Byzantine capital for centuries fell before a new technology of war. Cannons were the beginning of the end of impregnable fortifications. Quickly, all of Europe's monarchs acquired their own cannons and began building new types of fortifications.

Blitzkrieg German for "lightning war"; quick armored attack.

strategic bombing Air raids deep inside enemy's territory to destroy his war capacity.

army dedicated chiefly to peacekeeping operations, which it does well. Canada's choice is rational for its circumstances and has won Canada much international respect.

If you face a serious threat with no major ally to protect you, however, you'd better arm. France waited until too late to rearm and was overrun by German forces in 1940. Britain was barely saved by the English Channel. Goering talked Hitler into first smashing Britain with air power before a German amphibious invasion, and this gave the British time to rebuild and gain a powerful ally, the United States. The British also had a new technology, radar, which let them scramble their Hurricanes and Spitfires to meet German bombers.

Second, you must constantly ask if your troops and weapons are of the right kind to meet a likely attack. Generals, it has long been said, prepare for the last war. In one or two decades, technology can totally change the battlefield. The tank, used at the very end of World War I, attracted little attention in the British and French armies. British strategist Basil Liddel Hart and French Colonel Charles de Gaulle wrote on armored warfare, but mostly German officers read their works. By 1939 Germany had totally reconfigured its forces around armor and the **Blitzkrieg** doctrine. Its neighbors, who did not, were quickly smashed. Polish cavalry heroically charged German *Panzers* in 1939 with predictable results.

One key question strategists must ponder: Does current war technology favor the offense or the defense? Mistakes here can be catastrophic. As we discussed in Chapter 12, Europeans before

CONCEPTS ■ ILLUSORY WEAPONS

Rather consistently, finds mathematical physicist Steven Weinberg, generals become attached to weapons not because they are effective but because they look impressive. Armored knights on horseback looked awesome, but historically they were more often defeated by archers or pikemen (especially, as the Swiss discovered, if the pike had a hook on it). The mounted knights were great for tournament spectacles but not for winning battles.

In 1905 Britain launched the first battleship, the *Dreadnought*, whose size, speed, and armor made it breathtaking and allegedly invincible. A jealous Germany challenged Britain by building its own dreadnoughts, so Britain built even more. The "dreadnought crisis" was an arms race that heightened tension between the two countries. In World War I, battleships did little and battled each other only once, in the inconclusive 1916 Battle of Jutland. The real naval weapon of World War I, little noticed at first, was the submarine, which nearly cut off Britain's supplies. In World War II, battleships were still highly admired, although they counted for little; now aircraft carriers mattered.

In World War I, airplanes—flown by dashing young men with white scarves—captured the generals' imagination, and they developed theories of "victory through airpower." In World War II the Germans, British, and Americans practiced **strategic bombing** that destroyed whole cities but knocked no one out of the war. The money and lives would have been more effective elsewhere in the war effort. The U.S. postwar Strategic Bombing Survey revealed that bombs scarcely damaged German industry; most either missed entirely or hit civilian targets. Hiroshima and Nagasaki came *after* the Japanese had lost on land and sea.

Now nuclear weapons have given us another military illusion, writes Weinberg. They are almost perfectly unusable but make countries feel important and safe. He calls missile defense another folly; it gives the illusion of security but has not been able to hit an incoming missile except in carefully staged tests. Weapons systems that promise invincibility or security are often mistaken wastes, warns Weinberg.

World War I, looking at recent wars (Franco–Prussian and Russo–Japanese), thought war now favored the offense: Attack quickly with bold thrusts and you'll win a short war. Instead, the machine gun and barbed wire gave the advantage to the defense, and World War I bogged down in the trenches for four horrible years. The tank then gave the advantage to the offense in World War II; it went around or smashed through fixed fortifications (see box on page 214).

Strategic Defense Initiative
Defensive missiles to protect the United States from incoming missiles.

national missile defense   Revival of SDI proposed by Bush 43.

Currently, most suppose technology favors the offense, as U.S. forces demonstrated in two wars against Iraq. But a foe with good electronic countermeasures could turn the tables on a high-tech offensive. Furthermore, guerrilla warfare and terror tactics work around high-tech armies, so-called *asymmetrical warfare* (see Chapter 15). Technology cannot solve all security problems.

In the early 1980s, some U.S. scientists and strategists argued that a defense against missiles could soon be developed. They did not trust the Soviets to keep their arms control agreements. This was the beginning of the **Strategic Defense Initiative** (SDI) or "Star Wars," announced by President Reagan in 1983. Critics charged that the complex system—which would have to hit missiles and their warheads in flight—either wouldn't work or, if it did work, would destabilize nuclear deterrence by giving one side a shield to hide behind while it launched a first strike.

The end of the Cold War took the urgency out of SDI, but research continued. Iraq's Scud missile attacks in the Gulf War reawakened concern, and in 1993 President Clinton ordered research on theater missile defense (TMD) to protect our forces from short-range missiles. Republicans in Congress pressed for **national missile defense** (NMD) protecting all 50 states, and Clinton ordered NMD research. Proponents of NMD in the Bush 43 administration argued that "axis of evil" states with missiles and nuclear warheads—North Korea and Iran—would soon be a threat.

Critics charged NMD would set off a new arms race. Russia, China, and even U.S. allies in Europe denounced NMD. It broke the 1972 Anti-Ballistic Missile (ABM) Treaty, which prohibits defense against missiles, a U.S.-inspired idea that mutual vulnerability keeps nuclear deterrence stable. At first Moscow had been skeptical of this idea, but Nixon and Kissinger sold the Russians on it. Breaking a treaty is a serious matter, but the Bush 43 administration said the treaty was obsolete and U.S. security concerns had changed. An NMD shield could also protect Japan, North Korea's close target. Russia and China warned of a "spiraling arms race." To counter a potential Iranian missile threat, Bush proposed U.S. missile bases in the Czech Republic and Poland. Moscow angrily charged that the bases would be aimed against Russia. The Obama administration scrapped the plan in favor of a seaborne defense.

NMD has weak points; early tests failed. Critics accuse proponents of missile defense of having a "Maginot Line mentality," building a false sense of security. Simple mylar decoys would confuse and overwhelm NMD. A rogue state or terrorists would more likely deliver a nuclear device by shipping container. The true limiting factor: With two wars and a massive budget deficit, the United States could not afford the expensive program.

DETERRENCE

Deterrence is based on the assumption that hostile governments are rational and make cost-benefit calculations—something you cannot always assume. A rational enemy will not attack if the costs outweigh any benefits. Deterrence is the ability to impose costs and let the enemy know it in advance. Such capability comes from the size, skill, and weaponry of one's armed forces. Britain, for example, deterred all serious plans of invasions after 1066—except for the Spanish Armada—

credibility Being considered trust-worthy or believable, the crux of deterrence.

Maginot Line French fortifications facing Germany before World War II, easily circumvented.

by having the naval capability to destroy the invasion fleet. The Spanish Armada disaster in 1588, due partly to storms, added **credibility** to British deterrence.

The problem with conventional deterrence is that, if a state can defeat an attack, why not attack the threat first and knock it out before it can hurt you? In this way, a deterrent capability can lead to war. It is expensive to maintain the military superiority necessary for deterrence over a long time. Why not use it? The English, for example, both before and after the Armada, raided and plundered the Spanish empire and its ships. Spain couldn't deter them. Conventional deterrence depends on superiority and restraint. Deterrence really becomes operative in the nuclear age, because now nuclear powers can inflict huge damage on an attacker—and the potential attacker knows it.

Nuclear weapons allow even the weaker side to impose unacceptable costs and thus deter attacks. Deterrence theorists argue that World War III was prevented, even during the worst crises of the Cold War, because neither side could rationally calculate that it would bring benefits greater than costs. Protecting a state by deterrence relies on preventing a potential aggressor from beginning policies that lead to war. The logical conclusion that nuclear war is obsolete is one of the revolutionary effects of nuclear weapons. Nuclear technology produced a major turning point in world history. (See Chapter 14 for more on nuclear proliferation.)

Deterrence really came into its own in the nuclear age, because no one could make a rational calculation in favor of starting a nuclear war. Nuclear deterrence carries an inherent credibility. Governments will likely use any weapon to prevent their state's extinction. Nuclear weapons also cost less than large numbers of conventional armaments. They induce caution in even the most aggressive leaders. States with nuclear weapons or those under another state's nuclear umbrella through a military alliance seem almost immune from attack.

These advantages of nuclear deterrence, paradoxically, are also its weaknesses. If a government that is attacked by conventional forces engages in nuclear retaliation, does it not invite a nuclear attack on itself? This is called "counter-retaliation." A conventional attack puts the onus of making the war nuclear on the victim. Because the use of nuclear weapons risks the survival of the state, would "first use" of the weapon be credible? Some theorists say no. They advocate sufficient conventional forces to repel an attack. But, as we considered, large conventional forces sufficient to defeat an attack can tempt a country to use them. Like the English navy against Spain,

TURNING POINT ■ THE MAGINOT LINE

Germany trounced France in 1870–1871 and nearly won again in World War I. In 1929, France began constructing a series of fixed fortifications running from the Swiss to the Belgian borders. Called the **Maginot Line** after French War Minister André Maginot, its elaborate concrete bunkers and tunnels made France feel secure with only a small army. Paris supposed the Maginot Line would deter a German attack, and if Germany attacked anyway, the Line would serve as an impregnable defense. They were wrong on both counts.

The Maginot Line failed in 1940 and discredited defensive weapons and strategies for more than four decades. Germany outflanked the Line by its *Blitzkrieg* attack through Belgium and Luxembourg and penetrated weak points. Moral: Fixed fortifications don't work. Israel relearned this when Egyptian forces breached its Bar Lev Line on the Suez Canal in 1973.

large conventional forces could be used to attack without the fear of nuclear retaliation.

rogue state   Aggressive, risk-taking regime unbound by rules or agreements.

coercive disarmament   Methods of compelling a foe to give up weapons.

In recent years, international peacekeeping forces seek to deter both sides in regional conflicts. U.S. peacekeepers, for example, were in ex-Yugoslavia for several years to deter Serbia from forcibly annexing what it regards as its provinces. (For the growth of peace-keeping, see Chapter 21.)

Can deterrence work after the Cold War, this time against **rogue states**? Some say it already did, in both Gulf wars. In 1991 Iraq had chemical warheads but chose to fling only its ineffective high-explosive warheads at Israel and the U.S.-led coalition forces. Saddam knew what would hit Iraq if he went chemical. The Bush 43 administration feared Saddam would use WMD in 2003, but it turns out he didn't have any. Saddam had let us think he did, apparently to deter *Iran* from attacking Iraq. Instead, Bush became more and more convinced that we had to invade Iraq to take out Saddam's (nonexistent) WMD. Actually, we had strong-armed Iraq into giving up its WMD long before the 2003 war, but we did not know we had succeeded. This type of deterrence—called **coercive disarmament**—might in some cases make invasion unnecessary.

The *revolution in military affairs* (see page 210) has enhanced U.S. deterrence capability against most types of attacks. Powerful computers and sensors can find targets and guide muni-tions. New, high-tech weapons systems give the United States—whose military spending equals the rest of the world combined—a distinct advantage, as Iraq learned in both Gulf wars. It is bad news for potential foes; therefore, it deters. But such deterrence requires clear targets. A decentralized foe such as guerrilla forces or terrorists offers few good targets and may thus not be deterred.

Nuclear or conventional deterrence rarely stands alone as the strategy to preserve security. Even during the height of the Cold War, from 1947 to the late 1960s, the two enemy blocs talked

CONCEPTS ■ DETERRENCE

To deter is to stop a foe from doing something it is not yet doing. A can deter B from doing X by issuing this threat: "If you do X, I will do Y." B must perceive the costs of A doing Y as far greater than the benefits that might come from doing X. Deterrence presumes that B is rational. No rational animal will do X if it brings more costs than benefits. It also presumes that A can see B's cost-benefit calculations accurately.

A homey illustration: When Nick Berry's wife drops a sausage on the kitchen floor, she yells "No" as their dog rapidly approaches the sausage. The dog is not deterred; she grabs the sausage and runs. The dog knows that the wife does not strike animals or anything else. The only cost the pet will incur is a vocal "Bad dog!" The sausage is worth far more than that. However, when Nick drops a sausage, his "No!" stops the dog short. The dog knows

that Nick does strike, a cost not worth the sausage. The parable suggests that advanced levels of rationality are not necessary to deter; cocker spaniels are not notably rational, but they can fear.

Deterrence depends on four Cs:

1. Communication: A must deliver the threat before B decides to act.

2. Capability: A must be perceived as able to carry out its threat and inflict costs.

3. Credibility: B must perceive A as actually doing Y if B does X. A must not be seen as bluffing.

4. Calculation: B must reckon the benefits of X as less than the costs on itself if A does Y.

to each other. Arms control, trade, and cultural and educational exchange agreements helped calm things. Détente diplomacy eventually created and confirmed the end of the Cold War and could do the same in current regional conflicts.

DÉTENTE DIPLOMACY

As we considered in Chapter 5, *détente* means a lessening of tensions, a backing away from warlike positions held by hostile nations. The word originated in medieval warfare, when the crossbow was a fearsome weapon. Once tensioned, its bolt (small arrow) could penetrate a knight's armor. If it wasn't shot, though, it had to be "detensioned," or cranked down. *Détente* is French for detension. It does not mean the two countries have reached an *entente* (see page 85) with each other; it just means war is less likely.

Two things are needed for détente diplomacy. First, the parties to the dispute must have more interests in common than in conflict. This means that a negotiated settlement will bring more benefits than costs compared with other alternatives. Some of the other alternatives are unpleasant: continued deadlock, submission, escalation of threats, and use of force aiming at military victory. The parties may find détente a much better alternative, as did the United States and Soviet Union starting in the 1960s.

Détente diplomacy depends on the parties' abiding by the terms of their agreements. States generally comply with agreements that are in their interests. Why else would they enter into agreements in the first place? If a state violates its agreements, few do business with it. Serious violations by one side bring serious violations by the other, and soon there is no agreement left.

CONCEPTS ■ DO WMD DETER OR PROVOKE?

Countries acquire arms to defend or deter, but the 2003 Iraq War demonstrated that weapons of mass destruction may be worse than worthless. Under what circumstances would you really use them? Do they deter an attack or provoke one? If the Iraq War pushed countries that have been developing nukes, bugs, and gas to rethink and abandon these programs—as Libya did—it may have served a worthwhile purpose. (Libya, internationally isolated since its agents blew up Pan Am 103 over Lockerbie, Scotland, in 1986, was also under severe economic pressure to mend its ways.)

Saddam clearly had chemical weapons in the 1980s—he used them against Iran—but concluded (rationally) in 1991 that they were useless against the United States. If Saddam used them, he would have confirmed to the world the Bush 41 accusations, and Iraq would suffer horrifying damage in return. Iraq's WMD were a multimillion-dollar program that had to end with disposal of them.

The Iraq experience suggests that less-powerful countries *lose* security by trying to catch up with a superpower in WMD. Whatever their programs yield in terms of warheads, these countries are still vastly weaker than the United States and are unlikely to use their bugs and gas and certainly not their nukes. If they use them, they risk total destruction. Making a hole in Manhattan is simply not worth losing your entire country. One hopes North Korea understands this.

Any indication of WMD in the hands of aggressors likely provokes other countries more than it deters them. That is precisely what happened with Saddam— even if he didn't have WMD. With every fragmentary (and, it turns out, inaccurate) evidence of Iraqi WMD, Bush 43 became firmer in his resolve to eliminate them. Bush was not afraid; he was enraged. WMD can get you into precisely what you were trying to deter: a hopeless war and overthrow of your regime.

President Ronald Reagan met with Soviet President Mikhail Gorbachev at Geneva in 1985. The good personal chemistry led to major arms reduction agreements. (Bettmann/Corbis)

Collapse of the agreement probably means renewed tensions, something the signatories may wish to avoid, so most states keep their agreements. When North Korea abandoned its agreement not to build nuclear weapons, its hopeful trade, aid, and technical agreements with South Korea, Japan, and the United States died. Pyongyang's bellicose behavior isolates it.

Three tendencies have spurred the use of détente diplomacy. First, nuclear weapons and their rapid delivery systems have made the use of force dangerous and unstable, so it's best to calm things before they turn nuclear. India and Pakistan, contending over Kashmir, conduct occasional détente diplomacy under the shadow of mutual nuclear deterrence.

Next, world trade is growing, and most countries want to participate in it. Lower tensions between states lead to more trade, and détente diplomacy is the way to do this. Destitute North Korea needs détente to save its economy, as does the stagnant Iranian economy.

Finally, spy satellites, electronic eavesdropping, seismology, and downwind air samples—euphemistically called "national technical means of verification"—make violations of agreements, especially on arms control, difficult to hide. In 2006, North Korea's first test of a nuclear device could be heard through earth rumbles and confirmed by air samples. Technology provides more confidence that treaties will be observed.

Diplomatic agreements can enhance a state's security. All agreements have a similar format: Party A will do X (or not do Y), and in exchange party B will do S (or not do T). Agreements promote stability and ban aggression. Most spell out procedures for resolving conflicts over the interpretation of the agreement. Agreement can create momentum for more agreements, becoming "confidence-building measures." Because diplomacy is inexpensive (compared with threats and military measures), benefits relative to costs are usually exceedingly high.

appeasement   A concession to satisfy a hostile country; in disrepute since Hitler.

Détente diplomacy does not always work. If common interests are actually far less than conflictual interests or one side has no intention of keeping its word, making agreements would be a major mistake. Agreements would not restrain the behavior of the other party. One side is duped into a false sense of security, which leads to unpreparedness for attack or threats. Hitler was clever with fake détente diplomacy (see box below). A country like North Korea, self-isolated and paranoid, is difficult to coax into mutually beneficial compliance.

Faced with a threat, most countries will try détente diplomacy along with defense and deterrence. It does not come with a guarantee, but India and Pakistan, Russia and Japan, Turkey and Greece, and other historic rivals have sometimes been open to détente diplomacy (see Chapter 20). If a détente process works really well, it could lead to disarmament and enhanced state security with fewer arms.

DISARMAMENT

The assumption behind disarmament is that "arms cause wars." Proponents of disarmament agree with anthropologist Margaret Mead that war is learned behavior and can be unlearned. And arms are the centerpiece of war behavior and of the whole military mentality.

True, those who manufacture arms and those skilled in their use have a vested interest in war preparations. Both occupations would disappear if war did not exist. The mere presence of arms creates the possibility of war. Arms repress humans' cooperative nature. Weapons in the hands of one state are seen as threats by other states, so they too will arm. Arms races lead to war. Nuclear weapons make war too devastating to contemplate. Disarmament, by eradicating the expectation and tools of war, prevents wars. Humanity will turn to peaceful methods, preferably multilateral diplomacy in the United Nations and international law. Military spending can go for human needs. The theory of disarmament is related to liberal theory, discussed in Chapter 2.

DIPLOMACY ■ APPEASING HITLER

The prototypical failure of détente diplomacy was that of Britain and France toward Germany in the 1930s. British and French leaders thought that Hitler had plausible claims against the inequities of the Versailles Treaty and might be allowed to incorporate Germans outside Germany—such as Austria and the Sudetenland—into the Third Reich. They thought that **appeasement** would bring peace and stability to Europe. Hitler said he only wanted justice and national self-determination and hid his real goals—German power and mastery of Europe.

At the Munich summit in the fall of 1938, British Prime Minister Neville Chamberlain and French Premier Edouard Daladier allowed Hitler to take over the German-speaking area of Czechoslovakia, the Sudetenland, whose mountains contained Czechoslovakia's defenses. It was a con. The next spring, Germany took all of a defenseless Czechoslovakia, exposing the enormity of Hitler's deception.

Britain and France would have actually enhanced their national security by standing firm in 1938. Thus emboldened, in the fall of 1939 Hitler attacked Poland. Ever after, politicians have used appeasement to denounce opponents as weak in the face of aggression. John McCain used it against Barack Obama, who said he would talk with Iran. If that worked, it would be détente diplomacy. If it failed, it could look like appeasement.

The weaknesses of this theory are evident. To paraphrase James Madison, who said that if people were angels, governments would not be necessary, we add that neither would wars. Common views of human nature are pessimistic for good reason. There's always a North Korea. Humans tend to resort to fighting. In a situation where both A and B want X and only A is armed, who will get X? If both A and B are disarmed, what about C, D, and E? Because armed states have an advantage over disarmed states and there are vital interests that can be attained only by armed force, disarmament would only lead to insecurity, especially in the nuclear age.

Accordingly, there have been no general disarmament treaties. More modest attempts at disarmament have been more successful. Treaties focusing on the elimination of weapons in a particular geographical area are common and effective. These include the U.S.–British (for Canada) 1817 Rush–Bagot Treaty, which essentially demilitarized the Great Lakes (the first successful disarmament treaty); the 1967 Latin America Nuclear-Free Zone Treaty; and international treaties that ban weapons in space (1967), in Antarctica (1960), and on the ocean floor (1971). Other treaties ban particular weapons, such as the 1972 Biological Weapons Convention and the 1997 Chemical Weapons Convention. The 1987 Intermediate Nuclear Force (INF) Treaty eliminated the U.S. Pershing II and Soviet SS-20 missiles.

Other attempts to bar weapons have not been as successful. The 1970 Treaty on the Nonproliferation of Nuclear Weapons (NPT) included a pledge by the five "official" nuclear weapon states to negotiate a treaty "on general and complete [nuclear] disarmament," but they found nuclear weapons still useful and did not follow through. Cuba, India, Israel, and Pakistan never signed the NPT. Iraq, Iran, and North Korea signed it but ignored it. No one expects nuclear disarmament soon. As a U.S. Defense Department official said, "Nuclear weapons are still the foundation of a superpower."

General and complete disarmament, alas, is either a utopian dream or a fraud as long as security threats exist. Eliminate all security problems and states will disarm. Until then, don't expect states to go defenseless in this world.

A COMBINATION

States use defense, deterrence, détente diplomacy, and disarmament, often in combination. Defense, deterrence, and détente can be combined. Defense and deterrence make the costs of aggression too high, and détente makes the benefits of cooperation enticing. President Nixon emphasized the reinforcing effects of deterrence and détente.

Disarmament, however, conflicts with deterrence and defense. If states are truly disarmed, they can neither deter nor defend. Disarmament also conflicts with détente, as détente presupposes that arms will always exist but that diplomacy can reduce tensions. Disarmament can happen only in a pacific, congenial world.

Mutual deterrence and comprehensive defense may also be incompatible. The opponent's deterrent threat—"If you attack me, I will impose huge costs on you"—becomes incredible if you have an effective defense. This was the problem with SDI and NMD. If they really worked, they could undermine deterrence stability in at least two ways. The possessor of such defensive shields might be tempted to attack, figuring they were invulnerable to retaliation. Or those states without the defensive shields might be tempted to attack before the other side could put their shields into place.

Defense and détente can sometimes be compatible. Well-defended states, feeling secure, can reduce tensions by diplomacy. Détente, however, may undermine one's defenses. Nixon and Carter thought they had a general détente with Moscow and reduced defense spending. When Moscow's expansionist aims became clear with the invasion of Afghanistan in 1979, Carter had to abruptly increase U.S. defense spending. (The Reagan arms buildup actually began under Carter.)

So what is the best way for a state to protect itself? The answer depends on the assumptions you make about the nature of your international rivals. Disarmament works if they are angels. Deterrence and détente work if they are rational and generally keep their agreements. Defense is necessary if they cannot be trusted.

myposcikit EXERCISES

Apply what you learned in this chapter on MyPoliSciKit (www.mypoliscikit.com).

Assessment   Review this chapter using learning objectives, chapter summaries, practice tests, and more.

Menu

Flashcards   Learn the key terms in this chapter; you can test yourself by term or definition.

Flashcards

Video   Analyze recent world affairs by watching streaming video from major news providers.

Videos

Simulations   Play the role of an IR decision-maker and experience how IR concepts work in practice.

Comparative Exercises

KEY TERMS

appeasement (p. 218)

Blitzkrieg (p. 212)

coercive disarmament (p. 215)

credibility (p. 214)

defense (p. 210)

détente diplomacy (p. 210)

deterrence (p. 210)

disarmament (p. 210)

Maginot Line (p. 214)

national missile defense (p. 213)

revolution in military affairs (p. 210)

rogue state (p. 215)

security (p. 210)

strategic bombing (p. 212)

Strategic Defense Initiative (p. 213)

FURTHER REFERENCE

Berkowitz, Bruce. *Strategic Advantage: Challengers, Competitors, and Threats to America's Future.* Washington, DC: Georgetown University Press, 2008.

Cimbala, Stephen J., and Peter Rainow. *Russia and Postmodern Deterrence: Military Power and Its Challenges for Security.* Dulles, VA: Potomac Books, 2007.

Clark, Wesley K. *Winning Modern Wars: Iraq, Terrorism, and the American Empire*. New York: PublicAffairs, 2004.

Croft, Stuart. *Strategies of Arms Control: A History and Typology*. Manchester, UK: Manchester University Press, 1996.

Crowley, Roger. *1453: The Holy War for Constantinople and the Clash of Islam and the West*. New York: Hyperion, 2005.

Dannreuther, Roland. *International Security: The Contemporary Agenda*. London: Polity, 2007.

Doyle, Michael W. *Striking First: Preemption and Prevention in International Conflict*. Princeton, NJ: Princeton University Press, 2008.

Gray, Colin S. *Strategy for Chaos: Revolutions in Military Affairs and the Evidence of History*. Portland, OR: Frank Cass, 2002.

Hill, Charles. *Grand Strategies: Literature, Statecraft, and World Order*. New Haven, CT: Yale University Press, 2010.

Koblentz, Gregory D. *Living Weapons: Biological Warfare and International Security*. Ithaca, NY: Cornell University Press, 2009.

Macgregor, Douglas A. *Transformation Under Fire: Revolutionizing How America Fights*. Westport, CT: Praeger, 2003.

Nichols, Thomas M. *Winning the World: Lessons for America's Future from the Cold War*. Westport, CT: Praeger, 2003.

Omand, David. *Securing the State*. New York: Columbia University Press, 2010.

Owens, William A. *Lifting the Fog of War*. New York: Farrar, Straus, and Giroux, 2000.

Payne, Keith B. *Deterrence in the Second Nuclear Age*. Lexington, KY: University Press of Kentucky, 1996.

Smoke, Richard. *National Security and the Nuclear Dilemma*, 3rd ed. New York: McGraw-Hill, 1992.

Twomey, Christopher P. *The Military Lens: Doctrinal Differences and Deterrence Failure in Sino-American Relations*. Ithaca, NY: Cornell University Press, 2010.

Weinberg, Steven. *Lake Views: This World and the Universe*. Cambridge, MA: Harvard University Press, 2010.

Wirls, Daniel. *Irrational Security: The Politics of Defense from Reagan to Obama*. Baltimore, MD: Johns Hopkins University Press, 2010.

Younger, Stephen M. *The Bomb: A New History*. New York: HarperCollins, 2009.

Zenko, Micah. *Between Threats and War: U.S. Discrete Military Operations in the Post-Cold War World*. Stanford, CA: Stanford University Press, 2010.

CHAPTER 14

The Politics of Nuclear Bombs

Iran has built its missile strength along with its nuclear capacity. In 2009, Iran lofted a small satellite into orbit.
(Parspix/Abacapress.com/Newscom)

Several countries have acquired nuclear technology that is rapidly being turned into bombs. Iran and North Korea, for example, bought tons of nuclear technology from our ambivalent ally, Pakistan. All three countries are defiant toward the outside world, saying, in effect: "For our legitimate self-defense we need and have a right to nuclear weapons. Who are you to criticize? You have lots of them. We will not give up ours!" The attacks of 9/11 turned the nearly forgotten issue of **proliferation** into an urgent concern. According to one expert, 40 countries could, if they wished, develop nuclear warheads. Could the next terror attack be nuclear?

The atomic bomb was developed as a war weapon but evolved into a political weapon. Its political functions appeal to states under threat (Israel, India, Pakistan, North Korea) and those with major-power ambitions (India and Iran). Nuclear proliferation continues. Attempts by the first five nuclear states (the United States, Russia, Britain, France, and China) to stop other states from acquiring "the ultimate weapon" have largely failed. Sooner or later, there's a good chance that some state with deep hatreds will use a nuclear weapon. Concern now focuses on North Korea, but others could use a nuke first.

QUESTIONS TO CONSIDER

1. Is nuclear nonproliferation dead, or can it be restored?
2. How do nuclear weapons confer international prestige?
3. What was "massive retaliation," and what was it designed to do?
4. Which countries have nuclear weapons? Why do others seek them?
5. Why did Iraq resist international inspections of its weapons of mass destruction?
6. Are political uses of nuclear weapons more important than military uses?
7. Do countries have a right to acquire nuclear weapons? How could you talk them out of it?
8. What is Clausewitz's theory of escalation?

WEAPON OF WAR

Just before World War II, Albert Einstein and other scientists advised President Roosevelt that an atomic bomb could be built. During the war, the Manhattan Project—which consumed 30 percent of U.S. electricity during that time—built three. To check that it would work, the first was detonated at Alamogordo, New Mexico, on July 16, 1945. The second and third destroyed Hiroshima and Nagasaki in early August. Truman always said that the decision to drop the bomb was easy. Invading the Japanese main islands would be bloody, and we had spent massive sums to develop the bomb. Truman also believed that in war you can use any weapon not specifically outlawed.

The spectacular new weapon heightened U.S. confidence. Along with the Soviet entry into the war against Japan two days after Hiroshima, it produced the Japanese surrender. But Truman did not order its mass production. He saw no explicit political function for the bomb, such as making the British dismantle their empire or making the Soviets comply with their agreements on East Europe.

The first atomic bomb was tested at the Trinity test site in Alamogordo, New Mexico, on July 16, 1945. (*The New York Times*/Redux Pictures)

proliferation   More states acquiring nuclear weapons.

fissile   Capable of chain-reaction nuclear splitting, namely U-235 and plutonium-239.

Truman in 1946 even proposed internationalizing the bomb: The UN would control all **fissile** material and limit it to peaceful purposes. Proposed by advisor Bernard Baruch, the "Baruch plan" would also prevent a Soviet veto in the Security Council from blocking UN nuclear policy. The Soviets rejected the American plan because it meant an end to their nuclear program before they got their own bomb and gave the United States a permanent lead. Even if it gave up all its nuclear weapons, the United States could make them quickly because it knew how. Furthermore, for the Kremlin, weapons were political tools. Soon Washington came to the same conclusion.

The onset of the Cold War created several political functions for nuclear weapons: nuclear deterrence, alliance building, and international prestige. Others would come later, including those that appealed to nuclear powers of the second rank.

NUCLEAR DETERRENCE

Once the Cold War began, the Truman administration saw the deterrence effect of the atomic bomb, which until 1949 we alone possessed. The Soviets would not attack West Europe, their obvious first target, because that would bring war with the United States and huge costs. But

Truman and Dean Acheson (later secretary of state), thought deterrence would end when the Soviets acquired their own bomb. Then they could deter the U.S. deterrence, and West Europe would become vulnerable.

conventional forces Non-nuclear military strength.

After the Soviets detonated their first bomb in 1949, the Truman administration authorized development of the hydrogen (thermonuclear) bomb and long-range bombers and groped for a way to restore deterrence. In 1950 the famous National Security Council Report 68 (NSC-68) recommended increasing **conventional forces** at home and in West Europe. U.S. divisions under the prestigious General Dwight D. Eisenhower would reassure Europe, which we also pressured to increase their own conventional capabilities. Deterrence, based on conventional forces, would be restored.

Critics said this was a mistake. Huge conventional forces were expensive and unpopular. Nuclear weapons could still deter a nuclear-armed Soviet Union. Strategic theorist Bernard

REFLECTIONS ■ HIROSHIMA

In Hiroshima's Peace Park stand memorials to the bombing of August 6, 1945. A museum shows what residents were doing that morning: working, eating breakfast, going to school. It describes the B-29 bomber, the "Little Boy" bomb, and the attack. A model shows "ground zero." Most of the museum shows the effects of the blast and the radiation on people and objects. There is no politics, just understated horror. Don't miss it if you visit Japan.

—N. O. B.

In Hiroshima's Peace Park this municipal building, which partially withstood the world's first nuclear attack in 1945, was reinforced to stand as a memorial to war's ravages. (Kimimasa Mayama/Corbis)

Hiroshima's Peace Park diorama shows what the city looked like shortly after the 1945 nuclear blast—burnt flesh melted off bones. (John Van Hasselt/Corbis)

extended deterrence Covering allies with your nuclear capacity, as in U.S. promises to NATO.

access One country's ability to be listened to by another.

thermonuclear Powerful release of energy from fusion of hydrogen atoms.

Brodie made this point in 1946, and later Ike's Secretary of State John Foster Dulles promoted it. At this point in the history of the bomb, it is necessary to explore its other political functions.

ALLIANCE BUILDING

Power in international politics comes from many sources, not just from weapons. More important are alliances (see page 258). States form alliances because individually each is weak; together they are strong. Rome's long-lasting power came from its ability to make allies. Nazi Germany was unable to make and keep allies. The United States remained the premier power in the Cold War because it attracted more allies than the Soviet Union.

Both major powers realized early that nuclear weapons helped them build alliances. The Cold War and its arms race increased the threats to medium and small powers, especially those strategically located in Europe and Asia. The major nuclear powers could offer allies **extended deterrence**, protection under the big power's "nuclear umbrella." In addition to NATO, the United States made security treaties with Japan in 1951, Australia and New Zealand (ANZUS) in 1951, and Southeast Asian states (SEATO) in 1954. Nukes gave both superpowers **access** into the foreign policy processes of their allies.

Washington's offer of extended deterrence to its allies was credible for most of the Cold War but started to erode when President Kennedy introduced "flexible response" into NATO strategy. This said NATO will first make a conventional (non-nuclear) response to a Soviet attack and go nuclear later only if absolutely necessary. Kennedy offered it as a way to avoid nuclear war, but it raised doubts in the mind of French President Charles de Gaulle whether the United States would really come to Europe's defense with its nuclear weapons. For de Gaulle, flexible response was a way for the Americans to chicken out. It weakened the credibility of NATO's nuclear deterrence, so he stepped up France's own nuclear program.

CONCEPTS ■ NUCLEAR AND THERMONUCLEAR WEAPONS

A nuclear weapon, like the ones dropped on Hiroshima and Nagasaki in 1945, operates on the principle of fission, the splitting of uranium atoms. Specifically, tiny quantities of the unstable isotope U-235—which gives off many neutrons—are refined and separated from the more plentiful U-238, to a purity of 90 percent or higher, called "weapons grade" uranium. Refined to 5 or 6 percent, uranium can be used to generate electricity but not to make bombs. It can, however, be further enriched until it reaches weapons grade, which many believe is what Iran is doing. In a bomb, a conventional explosion concentrates the U-235, the free neutrons of which smash into and split more atoms, freeing more neutrons and creating enormous heat and energy.

Instead of uranium, modern nukes are made with plutonium, which comes from reprocessing spent uranium from power plants. Plutonium-239 bombs are cheaper than U-235 bombs. A hydrogen or **thermonuclear** weapon uses the heat of a nuclear explosion to fuse deuterium or heavy hydrogen atoms into helium atoms. As the atoms fuse, they release vast amounts of heat and energy. A uranium or plutonium bomb is the starter motor of a hydrogen bomb. Miniaturization technology has so reduced thermonuclear weapons that three or four could fit on a small desk. Most nuclear weapons of the major powers are thermonuclear.

INTERNATIONAL PRESTIGE

Nuclear weapons also enhance **prestige**. In facing a prestigious state, governments are cautious, accommodating, and respectful. Prestige then increases foreign policy successes, producing even more prestige. Security and economic well-being are the most important national interests, but prestige is not far behind. Every major power jealously seeks prestige. De Gaulle practiced the "politics of prestige" to restore France to the front rank. Much of what China does is calculated to boost its prestige. A word from a prestigious state carries weight. States automatically gain respect when they explode their first nuclear warheads, a major reason countries develop them.

prestige Reputation for being successful.

second-strike capability Ability to hit back after a first strike; if credible, promotes deterrence.

CONCEPTS ■ NUCLEAR STRATEGIES

Second-Strike Capability A country has **second-strike capability** if it can absorb a first strike from a foe and have enough nuclear weapons to retaliate and inflict "unacceptable damage" on the enemy. In the early 1960s, Secretary of Defense McNamara estimated that destroying 50 percent of the Soviet economy and 25 percent of its population would be unacceptable to the Soviets. Therefore, the force posture of the United States, after being attacked, had to be able to cause that much damage.

There are four basic ways a state can protect its second-strike capability. It can hide it (submarines), harden it (underground silos), move it (on trucks), or protect it (anti-missiles). The United States still retains its second-strike capabilities by a "triad" of deterrent forces: land-based intercontinental ballistic missiles (ICBMs), submarine-launched ballistic missiles (SLBMs), and air-launched cruise missiles (ALCMs) from long-range bombers. A credible second-strike capability is the crux of deterrence.

First-Strike Capability A state thinks it can attack an enemy first and destroy its second-strike capability, a "disarming" attack that removes the foe's deterrent capability. No one can be confident that a nuclear foe can really be "disarmed" in a first strike; it will still have some second-strike capability. A first strike on a nuclear power would simply invite one's own destruction. It is an unlikely strategy, except for a stateless terrorist group.

Countervalue Attack Targeting the economy and population of the foe, "city busting," common in World War II, is a countervalue strategy. Early Soviet and American strategies emphasized countervalue attacks, but the doctrine faded as too horrible to use.

Counterforce Attack Targeting a foe's troops, bases, and especially missile sites is called a "counterforce" strategy. With more and more-accurate missiles, the superpowers decided to protect their now more vulnerable second-strike capabilities and societies by shifting to counterforce doctrines. It is also more "humane," killing fewer people and cutting the risk of a "nuclear winter." The catch is that counterforce targeting is more likely to be used, precisely because it entails less chance of losing one's own cities to retaliation.

Extended Deterrence A nuclear superpower protects its allies by treating an attack on them as an attack on itself and retaliating on those who attacked them. West Europe was under the U.S. nuclear umbrella during the Cold War, and Japan and South Korea, facing an unpredictable North Korea, remain under it today.

Minimum Deterrence Having even a few nukes for a credible second-strike capability is called *minimum* or *finite deterrence*. This strategy presumes that a few nukes are enough and that arms control agreements would stabilize deterrence. Recent Russian and U.S. strategic arms reduction talks and unilateral cuts have moved both states toward a minimum deterrence posture. China and India claim they seek only minimum deterrence.

On the home front, a policy of prestige can be relatively low-cost and keep leaders and regimes in power. Average Soviets enjoyed the prestige of the Soviet empire and the accomplishments of Soviet science, such as *Sputnik*. They could look beyond their shabby economy and say, "We are equal to the Americans and even ahead in some things." The collapse of the Soviet system left them psychologically impoverished and bitter. The current Russian regime is intent on restoring Russian prestige.

DETERRENCE TRANSFORMED

Deterrence, discussed in the previous chapter, underwent a transformation. In 1952, John Foster Dulles expounded "A Policy of Boldness." The Soviets would not consider attacking, Dulles wrote, if the United States "was willing and able to respond vigorously at places and with means of our own choosing." It did not matter that the Soviets also had nuclear weapons. The United States would inflict horrible devastation on the Soviet Union if it attacked the West. Dulles played down what the United States would suffer. If the Soviets were convinced that the United States had such a capability and doctrine, they would be deterred.

President Eisenhower named Dulles secretary of state and accepted Dulles's nuclear strategy of "massive retaliation." Ike ordered a rapid increase in the production of nuclear weapons and bombers and stepped up the development of missiles to make massive retaliation credible. Ike also shelved the huge conventional-force buildup recommended by NSC-68 and approved a nuclear-deterrence strategy. Large conventional forces were unnecessary and too expensive. Keeping them small would actually enhance deterrence because we'd have no choice but to go nuclear, and the Soviets would know that. American troops in Europe would be only a "trip wire"; an attack on them would set off U.S. nuclear retaliation. Europe would be safe at relatively low cost. It's hard to prove why something did *not* happen, but the Soviets did not invade West Europe, and the 1950s were relatively peaceful. Deterrence, although scary, worked.

NUCLEAR PROLIFERATION

Other states soon noticed the political benefits that come with nuclear weapons, and they began to proliferate. Britain independently developed nuclear weapons and exploded its first bomb in 1952. Britain's forces alone were too small—it currently has some 160 warheads ready

CONCEPTS ■ ACCESS

Alliances give nuclear powers access to the political systems of their allies. A has "access" to B if A can influence the formation of B's policies and affect its foreign policy decisions. Access is a foot in the door. The major nuclear power finds it easier to talk to officials of the dependent non-nuclear country. Access leads to the *responsiveness* of B to A's suggestions and requests. By the same token, a country that develops its own nuclear bomb, such as France and China, can ignore its former protector, the United States and Soviet Union, respectively. For some countries, this is a powerful motive to acquire nuclear weapons.

to be used—to deter the Soviets, but London saw political benefits from nukes. The prestige of being a member of the nuclear club gave Britain access to any negotiations by the superpowers on nuclear arms and to U.S. nuclear policy decisions. France under Charles de Gaulle and China under Mao Zedong came to exactly the same conclusions as Britain. Both leaders sought to break away from their dependence on their respective superpower patrons, to be their own masters.

De Gaulle, as we noted, saw President Kennedy's "flexible response" as weakening deterrence and increasing the chances of war. Accordingly, de Gaulle needed his own nukes to defend France without asking Washington. In 1960 France exploded its first nuclear bomb and then created the *force de frappe* (strike force). De Gaulle argued that his independent nuclear capability strengthened deterrence and pulled France out of NATO's integrated command in 1966. Presidents Kennedy and Johnson opposed de Gaulle's independent nuclear course, which they saw as dividing and weakening the West. They also saw it as eroding their roles as leaders of the free world.

Chinese motives parallel those of France. Mao had major disagreements with the Soviets over nuclear strategy and his radical policies. In the late 1950s, China wanted the Soviets to exploit their space triumphs by getting tougher with "U.S. imperialism." China also wanted to accelerate its own nuclear program. The Soviets refused both demands. China's policies were far too risky and radical, reasoned Moscow. Angry polemics increased between the two Communist lands, and in 1960 the Soviets withdrew their aid funds and personnel.

In 1964 China exploded its first bomb and joined the nuclear club. Nuclear weapons, along with the world's largest standing army, deterred any U.S. or Soviet attack and gave China the status and prestige to attract Communist states and parties to its side of its split with Moscow. Nuclear weapons provided considerable political benefits to China. Khrushchev and Brezhnev opposed Mao's independent nuclear course. They saw it as dividing and weakening the international Communist movement and eroding their roles as leaders of that movement. Notice the close parallel: For the same reasons, Washington did not like France developing its own nuclear force. The Soviets sought to depose Mao and even considered a conventional attack on China's nuclear facilities in 1969. When the Soviets probed President Nixon for the U.S. reaction to such an attack, Nixon replied that it would drive the Chinese into alliance with a very receptive United States. The Soviets abandoned the military option.

CONCEPTS ■ PRESTIGE

Prestige is one of the larger motivators in IR. A has prestige if B believes A usually gets what it wants. Prestige develops as states' economies grow and they obtain their foreign policy goals over time. The immensity of the British Empire brought vast prestige in the nineteenth century. The explosion of the first atomic weapon added to U.S. prestige, while the launching of the first earth satellite, *Sputnik*, in 1957 dramatically enhanced Soviet prestige. States that habitually fail in their foreign policies, such as the Ottoman Empire long before its collapse during World War I—the "sick man of Europe," it was called—see their prestige vanish.

ARMS CONTROL

There are good reasons why countries want nuclear arms even as other countries see good reasons to stop their spread. Faced with nuclear proliferation in the 1960s, Washington and Moscow saw a common interest in stopping it, to preserve their deterrent capability, alliance leadership, and prestige. The United States and Russia still have dozens of times more warheads than anyone else. The newer and smaller nuclear powers are discovering they too have an interest in non-proliferation. If neighboring states get nukes, it negates their own nuclear advantage. A **non-proliferation treaty (NPT)** and other **arms control** agreements do four good things:

non-proliferation treaty (NPT) The 1968 agreement that nuclear powers will not transfer nuclear weapons technology and non-nuclear powers will not acquire it.

arms control Limiting weapons systems, a lesser goal than disarmament.

1. They decrease threats and increase cooperation. Uncontrolled arms races can lead to a surprise attack and prevent cooperation. Agreements that controlled or slowed the arms race led to more agreements. The Antarctic Treaty of 1960, the Outer Space Treaty of 1967, and the Seabed Arms Control Treaty of 1971 kept those places demilitarized. The 1972 Anti-Ballistic Missile (ABM) Treaty froze the number of Soviet and U.S. strategic missiles until Bush 43 abandoned it in favor of a national missile defense (which never materialized). A 1979 treaty cut to 2,250 the nuclear weapon launchers of each side. The Intermediate Nuclear Force (INF) Treaty of 1987 eliminated all Soviet SS-20 and U.S. Pershing II intermediate missiles.

   With tensions lower, especially after the Soviet Union pulled out of East Europe, cooperation increased in three Strategic Arms Reduction Treaties (START)—1991, 2002, and 2010. The last, signed personally by Presidents Obama and Medvedev in Prague, cut the number of deployed strategic nuclear warheads to 1,550 each, a fraction of what it had been. In the right context, arms control can work.

2. They enhance deterrence. With offensive weapons limited, neither side has enough for a first strike, and both preserve their second-strike capabilities, the crux of deterrence. SALT (Strategic Arms Limitation Talks) I and II precluded Soviet and U.S. first-strike capabilities, and deterrence got more stable.

3. They reduce costs. In total, nuclear weapons cost the United States an estimated $1 trillion. After the 1979 Soviet invasion of Afghanistan, Washington put arms control agreements on hold and increased defense spending. This strategy bled the Soviet economy; Moscow could not intervene abroad or sustain domestic consumption. Gorbachev's détente policies—withdrawal from Afghanistan, freeing of East Europe, and reforms at home—led to both Soviet and U.S. defense cuts. The Soviet military burden—some 25 percent of its GDP—was a major factor in its collapse.

4. They stabilize the distribution of power. Early Soviet–U.S. arms control agreements were designed to keep the superpowers in control. In particular, the 1968 NPT (see box on page 232) sought to keep the world bipolar and, it was thought, more stable. Nuclear proliferation brings unpredictable shifts of power and the increased danger that an unstable leader will use a nuke.

CONCEPTS ■ ARMS CONTROL

Disarmament, discussed in Chapter 13, aims at having countries get rid of their weapons, a generally unrealistic goal. Arms control is less ambitious but more realistic. It aims at limiting arms—their type, numbers, testing, deployment, concealment, and transfer. Arms-control treaties aim to slow down arms races and often are part of *détente diplomacy* (see Chapter 13).

No other country wants Iran or North Korea to have nuclear weapons.

5. They try to keep nuclear weapons and materials out of the hands of terrorist groups. Before 9/11, this seemed to be an unreal issue but now is very real. Pakistan now has the world's first and so far only Islamic bomb. A powerful Islamist movement inside Pakistan, the Taliban, supports al Qaeda in a jihad against the West. Pakistan has sold or traded nuclear technology with Iran, Libya, and North Korea. The more countries with nukes, the sooner terrorists will get them. Careful International

President Obama got along well with visiting Russian President Dmitri Medvedev in 2010. The two agreed to cut their strategic nuclear warheads. (Pete Souza/Corbis)

Atomic Energy Agency (IAEA) control of all fissile materials (highly enriched uranium and plutonium) could stop this, but Iran and North Korea hinder IAEA inspections.

CONCEPTS ■ AN ISLAMIC BOMB

Pakistan's detonation of a nuclear device in 1998 brought the world's first "Islamic bomb." Iran could have the second one in a few years. Are both of them sufficiently stable and rational to refrain from using a nuke? Many had doubts. They could quietly transfer them to Islamist terrorists for strikes against Israel, the United States, or India. Such an attack would be difficult to deter because it would not come from a clearly identifiable country. Whom would we nuke in retaliation?

In 2004 news came out that Pakistan had been selling nuclear bomb technology to Iran, North Korea, and Libya (but not Iraq) for years. (Libya abandoned its nuclear program and opened it to inspection.) Muhammad ElBaradei, head of the IAEA, called the revelation "the tip of an iceberg" of a "global black market" and feared nuclear proliferation was accelerating.

Pakistan's government could be overthrown by radical Islamists, including people who aid al Qaeda and assassinated former Prime Minister Benazir Bhutto. Osama bin Laden is likely hiding among sympathetic tribes in Pakistan's untamed northwest along the Afghan border, where government writ does not run. Pakistan is rapidly growing its nuclear arsenal of 80 to 100 warheads. Many worry that it could fall into the hands of fanatics who riot against Danish cartoons. (See box on page 236 for the problem of nukes in irrational hands.)

Iran swears it is developing nuclear technology for the peaceful generation of electricity. Off-and-on, Iran promises international controls and inspections but does not follow through. Meanwhile Iran accelerates its uranium enrichment program. No other country trusts Iran or wants it to have the Bomb. Even Russia, a near neighbor to Iran, joined the West in concern over Iran's nuclear program.

Iranian President Mahmoud Ahmadinejad, elected in 2005 and (crookedly) reelected in 2009, at times seems irrational, as when urging Israel be "wiped off the map." Prominent Israelis said they would be willing to bomb Iran's nuclear facilities, as Israel did to Iraq's in 1981. In 2007 Israeli jets destroyed a Syrian nuclear reactor, constructed with North Korean help. Asked how far he would go to prevent an Iranian bomb, Israel's top air force general, whose parents were from Iran, replied, "2,000 kilometers." Israel does not kid about these things; it preempts.

THE NUCLEAR PROLIFERATORS

Conspicuous among those not signing the NPT were Cuba, South Africa, Israel, India, Pakistan, Brazil, and Argentina. In 1998, India and then Pakistan tested bombs to the cheers of domestic crowds. With them, it's not just prestige; they were born enemies and have fought three wars. Their next, probably starting over Kashmir, could be nuclear. President Clinton visited both countries in 2000 and called the Indian subcontinent "the most dangerous place on earth." He urged both governments to give up nuclear weapons. They demurred. Israel's nuclear program, officially denied, also gives it prestige and the capability to deter an attack.

Argentina and Brazil were in a prestige race to become South America's first nuclear power. In 1991, civilian regimes in both countries recognized that their nuclear programs were expensive and served no purpose, and they ended them. South Africa secretly began a nuclear weapons program in 1974 with abundant local uranium and secret Israeli collaboration. Devices were tested on an island in the South Indian Ocean and in deep abandoned mineshafts. But the end of the Soviet threat and withdrawal of Cuban troops from Angola removed any South African use for nukes. And the white South African government did not wish to pass on nukes to its black successor regime, so South Africa became the first and only state to give up nuclear weapons. By 1991, it dismantled its six nuclear devices and destroyed related technology. South Africa then signed the NPT.

Signing the NPT has not kept some states from building nukes. North Korea exploded a nuclear device in 2006, and Iran may be working on one. After the 1991 Gulf War, an IAEA team in Iraq was astonished at how far along its nuclear program was. Iraq might have had a warhead in another year or two. As part of the 1991 cease-fire, Iraq abandoned development of any WMD but played so deceptively with UN inspectors that the Bush 43 administration believed (wrongly) Iraq had or was working on WMD.

There is also a great temptation to sell nuclear technology. The United States, Russia, Germany, France, Argentina, China, Pakistan, and others have sold "dual-use" technology and fissile material. Peaceful reactors can slowly produce weapons-grade material. Russia sold nuclear

DIPLOMACY ■ THE NUCLEAR NON-PROLIFERATION TREATY

In the mid-1960s, Washington and Moscow feared that many more states would join the nuclear club. According to one U.S. estimate, in 20 years, "peaceful" nuclear reactors worldwide would produce enough plutonium to make 20 bombs daily, greatly increasing the risk of nuclear war.

In 1967 both superpowers submitted identical texts of a draft NPT treaty to the UN. Opened for signatures in 1968, it prohibited the transfer of nuclear material for weapons use, obliged signatories to follow IAEA safeguards in their peaceful nuclear programs, and committed states without nuclear weapons not to develop them and those with nuclear weapons

to make further progress in nuclear arms control negotiations. IAEA inspections are the crux of NPT.

NPT was signed by 170 nations, but not by India, Pakistan, Israel, and several others. The five big nuclear powers committed themselves to eliminating their nukes and not testing them after 1996. Testing is important; without tests, you cannot know for sure if they work. Stopping testing worldwide would mean no new members to the nuclear club. Most countries signed a Comprehensive Test Ban Treaty in 1996, but the U.S. Senate rejected it, saying it couldn't be verified and would block further U.S. nuclear weapons development.

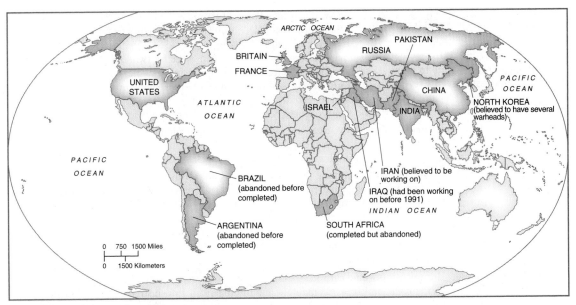

Countries with Nuclear Weapons

reactors to Iran that complied with NPT provisions, but IAEA inspectors in 2003 found traces of weapons-grade materials at the Iranian reactors.

The 1991 Gulf War and disintegration of the Soviet Union in 1991 showed the real dangers of proliferation. China was the last big holdout in limiting and putting conditions on nuclear sales. In the 1990s, China sold nuclear material and technology to Algeria, Argentina, Brazil, India, Iran, Iraq, North Korea, Pakistan, South Africa, and Syria. China now says that buyers must submit to IAEA inspection and pledge not to transfer anything to another country.

Small amounts of nuclear material, mostly from Russia, are smuggled out to the world market. German and Czech police have seized many kilograms of uranium. A "non-proliferation center" tries to track such trade worldwide. The U.S. Nunn-Lugar program paid Russia to reduce its stockpile of nuclear weapons and employ its nuclear scientists in non-military occupations. Another ominous trend is the proliferation of missiles. Some 35 states now have long-range missiles. North Korea developed a crude nuke and has long-range missiles.

WHAT WOULD HAPPEN IF NUKES WERE USED?

1. The political functions of nukes would end. Deterrence would have failed. Alliances would shatter because a non-nuclear ally in a nuclear war would make the most risk-free target for the enemy. Small allies would bail out. Many nonaligned states would treat the combatants as pariahs and not give them access to their markets or their halls of government. There would be no prestige from massive civilian devastation.

decapitation The removal of a country's leadership and ability to direct its war effort.

invasion insurance Ability to deter invasion by possessing even a few nuclear weapons.

2. Disarming attacks would become more likely. Why wait until the other guy is ready? A bit of this already happened with Israel's bombing of Iraq's Osirak reactor in 1981. The raid spurred Iraq's nuclear program, which set the stage for two Gulf wars. Bush 41 and Bush 43 cited the removal of Iraq's nuclear capabilities as one of the prime reasons for invasions. The United States has said repeatedly that it would not let Iran acquire nukes. This motive would become standard once nukes are used.

3. Economies would collapse. A nuclear war involving Israel, for example, would target Gulf oil facilities, producing a sudden 40 percent shortfall in world oil supplies. The world has never experienced anything like that. It could be worse than the Great Depression.

4. The war would escalate, becoming wider and fiercer. One conflict triggers others. A world war is actually several smaller wars strung together. Suddenly seeing new opportunities, other countries join in. Without World War II well under way, Japan would not have seized Southeast Asia from a weakened Britain and France or struck Pearl Harbor. Whoever wins becomes a security threat to other states. If India and Pakistan went to war over Kashmir, China could back its Pakistani friend and the United States its Indian friend.

5. Nuclear **decapitation** would early knock out a country's political leadership and C4I (command, control, communications, computers, and intelligence). British strategist Basil Liddel Hart called it "the shot in the brain." Control of people, defenses, and territory would weaken. Anarchy could break out.

6. Nuclear winter could produce a climatic disaster. Some scientists say detonating many nukes would kick millions of tons of soot into the upper atmosphere, darkening and cooling the earth and cutting photosynthesis, the basis of the food chain. Other scientists dispute the nuclear-winter model, but in geologic time at least three such disasters wiped out most life on earth.

7. The war would be hard to end. With a few nukes in reserve for **invasion insurance**, the horrible costs already absorbed, the burning national hatreds, and the breakdown of international law and organizations, the war could go on for years, even decades. After decapitation, who could negotiate the war's end?

CLASSIC THOUGHT ■ CLAUSEWITZ ON ESCALATION

Carl von Clausewitz (see page 199), a Prussian general with no battlefield victories to his credit, was the first to use "escalation" in its modern military sense. In his book *On War* (German: *Vom Kriege*), he saw escalation as a tendency built into the nature of war: "As one side dictates the law to the other, there arises a sort of reciprocal action, which logically must lead to an extreme." He called this *eine Steigerung bis zum Äussersten*, an escalation to the extreme. The war tries to become absolute or total. The Napoleonic wars, in which Clausewitz fought (against the French), approximated absolute war.

Far from being a lover of such horror, Clausewitz repeatedly cautioned against letting war escalate to an extreme. That would serve no purpose; it would be destruction for its own sake. Civilian authorities, "the Cabinet," must block this tendency by making sure the war serves limited, political objectives. Is escalation automatic or controllable? Clausewitz never came up with an answer, but his book is a warning that escalation can easily spin out of control.

NUCLEAR DOOM?

Do nuclear weapons automatically mean catastrophe? Early in the nuclear age, British Lord Bertrand Russell, a brilliant mathematician, philosopher, and pacifist, predicted humankind would soon

tactical nuclear weapon Small, portable atomic warhead used on or close to the battlefield.

be either annihilated or forced to live under a world dictatorship. About the same time, Albert Einstein said: "Nuclear weapons have changed everything except our way of thinking, and thus we drift toward unparalleled catastrophe." But over time our thinking did change. There is a widespread recognition that nuclear war would be far more dangerous than any conventional war and should be avoided. Slowly, the world gropes to restrain war.

And there are hopeful signs. There is concerted opposition to any country, even the United States, first using nuclear weapons. Nuclear weapons have made deterrence a stable and robust strategy, one that may have made unnecessary the 2003 invasion of Iraq. The prospect of nuclear retaliation so far has inhibited anyone from pressing the button. Major nuclear war is now an obsolete strategy, a realization that alters the conduct of international politics.

The United States has no intention of giving up nuclear deterrence. To be sure, the U.S. nuclear budget is way down, from 24 percent of defense spending in the 1960s to less than 3 percent now. U.S. forces now have few nuclear weapons abroad. Only submarines and land silos have nuclear-tipped missiles. Many **tactical nuclear weapons** have been destroyed. Most nuclear missiles have been "de-alerted" (by removing their warheads) or "de-targeted" (by not inputting any target coordinates).

Nevertheless, the Pentagon gives three reasons to maintain nuclear deterrence: (1) Threats to U.S. and allied security can arise "suddenly and unpredictably." We must be able to counter them. (2) Nuclear weapons remain a "hedge" against renewed Russian hostility and territorial expansion. (3) Rogue states with WMD and missiles must face nuclear retaliation to "give them pause."

Deterrence worked during the long Cold War. It really was, in Winston Churchill's words, the "sturdy child" of the balance of terror. Granted, it could have broken down during the 1961 Berlin Wall and 1962 Cuban Missile Crises. You don't want to test it too many times like that. But even in times of great stress, nuclear annihilation wonderfully concentrates the mind.

Critics rejoin that mutual deterrence might have worked between the United States and the Soviet Union, but they were governed by rational people. Proliferation will eventually put the

---

CONCEPTS ■ INVASION INSURANCE

States believe that with even a few nukes they will not be invaded. Invasions require the massing of forces, and they become a prime target for nukes. This does not necessarily work, however. Egypt and Syria were not deterred from attacking Israel in 1973, even though they knew Israel had nuclear weapons, which, in fact, Israel contemplated using.

Likewise, the possibility that Iraq had nuclear weapons did not deter the 2003 U.S. invasion; indeed, it provoked an invasion that aimed at knocking out Iraq's nuclear program before it actually produced bombs. North Korea and Iran suppose they get invasion insurance by building nukes, but they may be provoking a regional arms race or even a preemptive U.S. strike. Under the threat of North Korean nukes, Japan is reconsidering its nuclear phobia. Ironically, nuclear weapons may make their possessors less secure.

CONCEPTS ■ THE RATIONALITY PROBLEM

Critics of deterrence theory have for decades complained that we cannot always assume an opponent is rational. (Actually, we cannot be sure that all of *our* leaders are rational.) Eventually, in some stressful situation, an excitable chief could press the button. We are merely lucky, warn critics, that it has not happened thus far.

Stalin was calm and cool, but Hitler was noted for flying into rages. Some say he got so mad he chewed the carpet. Often rejecting the advice of his generals, Hitler took risks that doomed his Third Reich. A psychiatrist who examined Hitler in the 1920s concluded he was highly intelligent but psychotic. If Hitler, who obliterated cities with conventional explosives, had had the Bomb he surely would have used it. Fortunately, Nazi anti-Semitism drove many European physicists into U.S. exile, stunting Germany's nuclear program while boosting ours.

Iranian President Ahmadinejad (see Chapter 9) hears voices and calls for the destruction of Israel (which has some 200 nukes), something that surely sounds irrational. North Korea's leaders preach the racial superiority of their people and tell them how lucky they are to live in a well-fed workers' paradise when other countries are starving. Actually, plenty of North Koreans know *they* are starving; their stomachs tell them so. At great risk, many cross into China and live illegally.

Look more closely at alleged irrational leaders, urge defenders of deterrence. Actually, in their situations they may be rational—or think they are rational. Iraq's Saddam Hussein really had to worry about a vengeful Iran. North Korea, alone and isolated, gets far more attention with its few nukes than it could without them. Pakistan, which to this day sees India as its main enemy, could not ignore India's nuclear program. Even Libya's erratic President Qaddafi dropped his nuclear program in the face of Western threats and pressures. To a certain extent, nuclear weapons bring rationality with them.

The rationality question faces its greatest test with the arrival of Islamist extremism. If terrorists could get their hands on a nuclear device—probably from Pakistan, in secrecy and with **"plausible deniability"**—what would deter them from using it? They claim they love death more than we love life. Against whom would we retaliate? Would they really care if we retaliated against Pakistan? Persuading Pakistan to keep its nukes tightly locked up could become a major U.S. mission. Perhaps nuclear deterrence works when balanced but not when power is *asymmetrical* (see page 200).

---

plausible deniability Halfway-believable claim of innocence in the face of uncertain evidence.

bomb into the hands of irrational people so consumed by nationalistic, ideological, or religious hatred that nothing deters them. Today's generation will find out if this is the case. A nuclear war in the Middle East, South Asia, or Korean peninsula is quite possible. The paradox of the post–Cold War age is that now nuclear war—albeit not between the superpowers—is more likely than ever.

my**poliscikit** EXERCISES

Apply what you learned in this chapter on MyPoliSciKit (www.mypoliscikit.com).

 Assessment   Review this chapter using learning objectives, chapter summaries, practice tests, and more.

Menu

 Flashcards   Learn the key terms in this chapter; you can test yourself by term or definition.

Flashcards

Video   Analyze recent world affairs by watching streaming video from major news providers.

Videos

Simulations   Play the role of an IR decision-maker and experience how IR concepts work in

Comparative
Exercises   practice.

KEY TERMS

access (p. 226)

arms control (p. 230)

conventional forces (p. 225)

decapitation (p. 234)

extended deterrence (p. 226)

fissile (p. 224)

invasion insurance (p. 234)

non-proliferation treaty (p. 230)

plausible deniability (p. 236)

prestige (p. 227)

proliferation (p. 224)

second-strike capability
  (p. 227)

tactical nuclear weapon (p. 235)

thermonuclear (p. 226)

FURTHER REFERENCE

Albright, David. *Peddling Peril: How the Secret Nuclear Trade Arms America's Enemies*. New York: Free Press, 2010.

Bernstein, Jeremy. *Nuclear Weapons: What You Need to Know*. New York: Cambridge University Press, 2008.

Brown, Michael E., Owen R. Coté, Jr., Sean M. Lynn-Jones, and Steven E. Miller, eds. *Going Nuclear: Nuclear Proliferation and International Security in the 21st Century*. Cambridge, MA: MIT Press, 2010.

Chubin, Shahram. *Iran's Nuclear Ambitions*. Washington, DC: Carnegie Endowment, 2006.

Cirincione, Joseph. *Bomb Scare: The History and Future of Nuclear Weapons*. New York: Columbia University Press, 2007.

Cooke, Stephanie. *In Mortal Hands: A Cautionary History of the Nuclear Age*. New York: Bloomsbury, 2009.

Cronin, Patrick M., ed. *Double Trouble: Iran and North Korea as Challenges to International Security*. Santa Barbara, CA: Greenwood, 2008.

Delpech, Thérèse. *Iran and the Bomb: The Abdication of International Responsibility*. New York: Columbia University Press, 2007.

Freedman, Lawrence. *The Evolution of Nuclear Strategy*, 3rd ed. New York: Palgrave, 2003.

Ganguly, Sumit, and S. Paul Kapur. *India, Pakistan, and the Bomb: Debating Nuclear Stability in South Asia*. New York: Columbia University Press, 2010.

Harkabi, Yehoshafat. *Nuclear War and Nuclear Peace*. Piscataway, NJ: Transaction, 2008.

Hoffman, David. *The Dead Hand: The Untold Story of the Cold War Arms Race and Its Dangerous Legacy*. New York: Doubleday, 2009.

Langewiesche, William. *The Atomic Bazaar: The Rise of the Nuclear Poor*. New York: Farrar, Straus & Giroux, 2007.

Levi, Michael. *On Nuclear Terrorism*. Cambridge, MA: Harvard, 2007.

Mueller, John. *Atomic Obsession: Nuclear Alarmism from Hiroshima to Al-Qaeda*. New York: Oxford University Press, 2009.

O'Hanlon, Michael E. *A Skeptic's Case for Nuclear Disarmament*. Washington, DC: Brookings, 2010.

Polakow-Suransky, Sasha. *The Unspoken Alliance: Israel's Secret Relationship with Apartheid South Africa*. New York: Pantheon, 2010.

Reed, Thomas C., and Danny B. Stillman. *The Nuclear Express: A Political History of the Bomb and Its Proliferation*. Minneapolis, MN: MBI, 2009.

Rhodes, Richard. *Arsenals of Folly: The Making of the Nuclear Arms Race*. New York: Knopf, 2008.

Rublee, Maria Rost. *Nonproliferation Norms: Why States Choose Nuclear Restraint*. Athens, GA: University of Georgia Press, 2009.

Sagan, Scott D., ed. *Inside Nuclear South Asia*. Palo Alto, CA: Stanford University Press, 2009.

Schell, Jonathan. *The Seventh Decade: The New Shape of Nuclear Danger*. New York: Henry Holt, 2008.

Sheehan, Neil. *A Fiery Peace in a Cold War: Bernard Schriever and the Ultimate Weapon*. New York: Knopf, 2010.

CHAPTER 15

The Challenge of Asymmetrical Conflict

U.S. Marines return fire in Marja, Afghanistan. The long, asymmetrical conflict strained American forces physically and psychologically. (Bryan Denton/Corbis)

America has entered into what military planners call **asymmetrical conflict**, what most people call a war on **terrorism**. The new struggle resembles the Cold War: long, ideological, and focused on gaining and keeping allies. Many ask if "war" is the right word for this struggle because it is a decentralized, free-floating conflict that does not lend itself to invasion and conquest like a normal war. It seldom ends with a surrender; rather, it peters out.

Keeping allies in this struggle is not easy. Most Muslim countries have sizeable Islamist movements that hate America. In some cases—Pakistan and Saudi Arabia, two countries that had sponsored Muslim fundamentalism—these movements could overthrow wobbly governments with devastating consequences. The fall of Saudi Arabia to Islamists could disrupt world oil supplies and plunge the globe into a new Great Depression. Pakistan's fall could deliver nuclear weapons into the hands of terrorists. Our European allies counsel caution, and most parted company with us over the invasion of Iraq in 2003.

The Pentagon abandoned "Global War on Terror" in favor of the "Long War." Few suggest doing anything about Irish, Basque, or Sri Lankan terrorists. There is no general wave of terrorism washing over the world or the United States. There are specific Islamic extremist groups with specific goals: Get the United States out of the Middle East, destroy Israel, and take over Muslim lands. Some envision taking over the world for Islam. Islamists have already taken over Iran, Sudan, and Afghanistan. For the most part, terrorists are not crazy. Osama bin Laden and his organization, al Qaeda (The Base, so called after the computer database he kept of volunteer Muslim fighters against the Soviets in Afghanistan), is composed of militantly committed people, not psychopaths.

The struggle is really over the future of Muslim countries, whether they become modern and moderate or traditional and extremist. A better name might be the "war over Islamic modernization." If we fail, if these lands fall to hate and violence, we may speak of the "Islamic Wars," and they could be nasty.

Success in this war will come if Muslim lands reject bin Laden and his message of hatred and grant him and his kind no succor. Stability will come when Muslim countries combine Islam with modernity, a difficult project but one now under way in some lands. Failure will come if Muslim governments fall into the hands of religious extremists, which is exactly their goal. Then Huntington's "clash of civilizations" (page 147) could become a ghastly "war of civilizations." We must tread carefully; pushing too hard on a shaky Muslim government could topple it.

QUESTIONS TO CONSIDER

1. What is *asymmetrical conflict*? Is it the same as *terrorism*?
2. How do you tell a terrorist from a freedom fighter?
3. How does terrorism relate to *insurgency*?
4. Can a few terrorists really overthrow a government?
5. Why is terrorism so connected to the Middle East?
6. What is "blowback," and how has it hurt us?
7. What is *salafiyya*, and how does it underpin political Islam?
8. Is the United States equipped to fight asymmetrical conflicts?
9. Why do homegrown Islamist terrorists appear in the United States?

asymmetrical conflict One in which the powers of the two sides are very unequal.

terrorism Political use of violence to weaken a hated authority.

insurgency An armed rebellion or uprising.

guerrilla Irregular small-unit, hit-and-run warfare.

counterinsurgency Efforts and methods to put down an *insurgency*.

What makes an Islamic terrorist? There have been several attempts to profile a typical *jihadi*, but no single profile fits all. The 9/11 suicide hijackers, for example, were not poor and ignorant but middle class and educated. Most had lived or studied in Germany and turned into terrorists there rather than in their homelands. None was crazy. (Crazy people make poor terrorists; they can't follow orders.) To get a handle on this complex question, let us divide our consideration into the past, present, and future of the Middle East.

CONCEPTS ■ ASYMMETRICAL CONFLICT

Most people call it "terrorism," but the more professional term is "asymmetrical conflict," because it involves a spectrum of activities of which terrorism is just one. Asymmetrical conflicts are ones in which the powers of the contending parties are way out of balance—lightly armed local volunteers facing regular armed forces, often those of an occupier. Americans have a long connection with asymmetrical warfare; they used it to win their freedom from Britain and fought it against Indians, Filipinos, and Vietcong (see Chapter 4).

When the weaker side knows it's outgunned, it resorts to unconventional tactics. The weaker side's strong point is its ability to live and hide among the local people, who may sympathize and help or, at a minimum, do not snitch. The foreign occupier has great difficulty working among and winning over the local people. If the occupier treats them harshly—a constant temptation—it alienates them even more and harms its own cause.

Terrorism is often the first stage of **insurgency**. By itself, terror never overthrew a government or ousted an occupier. For that, it must grow into a successful insurgency, a long, bloody task. For example, a few militants antagonize authorities by protests, sometimes violent. The authority often overreacts by killing local people, thus creating more recruits for the insurgent cause. On Bloody Sunday in 1972, British paratroopers killed 13 young civil rights protesters in Derry, Northern Ireland. Result: thousands of Catholic youths joined the IRA.

With the right strategy, a small movement can grow into a mass movement—often with an underground terrorist branch—then into a guerrilla army, and eventually into a more-or-less regular army that ousts the occupier or hated government, as it did in China, Cuba, and Vietnam. They do not always win, however. If the occupier or government is clever, it can put down the terrorism and insurrection, as in Malaya, Kenya, and the Philippines.

Guerrilla is simply Spanish for "little war" and was first used in the early nineteenth century as Spanish patriots, civilian "partisans," strove with British help and irregular tactics to expel Napoleon's legions. Napoleon faced similar uprisings in Germany, what Clausewitz called *Volkskrieg* (people's war). Vietnamese peasants used guerrilla tactics against the Chinese, South African Boers against the British, Algerians against the French, and Yugoslav Communists against the Germans. Guerrilla warfare is the method of the underdog.

Counterinsurgency has become a specialized and major branch of U.S. armed forces. General David Petraeus, a Ph.D. and head of Afghan operations, wrote the field manual for counterinsurgency (COIN in Pentagon-speak). Quite different from and more complex than conventional warfare, it involves getting the population on your side by providing what they need, especially security. If you cannot deliver security for ordinary citizens, the insurgents are winning. Counterinsurgency is what we attempted in Afghanistan and Iraq, which U.S. forces took respectively in 2001 and 2003 in less than a month but tried to make secure for years.

THE BACKGROUND OF AN ASYMMETRICAL CONFLICT

The great problem the Middle East inherited from the past is that its great Islamic civilization was brought low, partly by outside forces, and never recovered. Some Muslims believe the West brought them down and now seeks to crush them. They identify strongly with brother Muslims in countries under U.S. occupation, Iraq and Afghanistan. Their rallying cry could be that of Pakistan's founder, Muhammad Ali Jinnah: "Islam is in danger!" The way they see it, they must defend Islam and retaliate for the evils the West has inflicted upon Islam. As noted in Chapter 12, no one is, in their own mind, aggressive.

caliphate Muslim dynasty ruled by *caliphs,* successors to the Prophet Muhammad.

Historically, Islamic civilization was for centuries far advanced over Christian Europe in science, philosophy, medicine, sanitation, architecture, steelmaking, and just about anything you can name. It was through translations from the Arabic that Europe got reacquainted with classic Greek thought, especially Aristotle, which helped trigger the Renaissance and Europe's modernization. A millennium ago Muslims supposed Christianity kept Europe backward.

But Islamic civilization stalled and European civilization modernized. By the sixteenth century, when European merchant ships arrived in the Persian Gulf, the West was ahead of Islam. Why did Islam get stuck? First, there are some specific historical causes. The Mongols in the thirteenth century conquered the great Abbassid **caliphate**, massacred the inhabitants of its capital, Baghdad, and destroyed the region's irrigation systems, something the Arab empire never recovered from. (The Mongols' impact on Russia was also devastating.) Possibly because of the Mongol devastation, Islam turned to mysticism.

Even earlier, however, Islamic teaching had abandoned independent and flexible interpretations of the Koran for a single, set interpretation. Instead of an open and tolerant faith that was fascinated by learning and science, Islam turned sullen and rigid. When the Portuguese first rounded the southern tip of Africa in 1488, they opened up direct trade routes between Europe and Asia, bypassing the Islamic middlemen. Trade routes that traversed the Middle East declined sharply and with them the region's economy.

But more important was the domination of European (chiefly British) imperialists starting in the nineteenth century. Between the two world wars, Britain ruled or influenced a broad swath from Egypt, across Palestine (now Israel and Jordan), Iraq, the Persian Gulf, India, Burma, and Malaya. Imperialism created the same resentment we see in China, the resentment of a proud civilization brought low by arrogant foreigners: "You push in here with your guns, your railroads, and your commerce and act superior to us. Well, culturally and morally we are superior to you, and eventually we'll kick you out and restore our civilization." With this thinking comes hatred of anything Western and therefore opposition to modernity, because that means admitting the West is superior.

MODERNIZATION AND ASYMMETRICAL CONFLICT

Many scholars see the asymmetrical conflicts of the Middle East as the results of failures of modernization. Most Middle Eastern countries have halfway modernized, but this has created big economic, political, and social stresses that can easily erupt into violence. The trick will be to get them to modernize all the way, but many resist on cultural and religious grounds. To oversimplify the situation in the Middle East today:

Islam + imperialism + unemployment + corruption = Islamism

CONCEPTS ■ WHAT IS TERRORISM?

Terrorism is a strategy to weaken a hated political authority. It is a security threat but almost the opposite of the nuclear one: little attacks instead of a huge bang. Terrorism is the beginning stage of guerrilla or irregular warfare and is not a new thing. The Irish Republican Army and Internal Macedonian Revolutionary Organization (IMRO) go back more than a century. The ethnic, nationalistic, religious, and ideological grudges of the twentieth century expanded terrorist activity. Wherever there are groups with grudges, terrorism can start. They are especially prevalent in the zones of chaos of the developing lands.

We look at terrorists as irrational, but they see themselves as rational. Their steps are calm, calculated, and purposeful. They pursue their political goals by gruesome means because the occupier or enemy is much stronger. A "fair fight" means certain defeat, so they must use indirect means. Basques, Kurds, Palestinians, and Tamils desire their own state. Spain, Turkey, Israel, and Sri Lanka, respectively, do not want them to have their own state and repress their movements. Thus were born, respectively, ETA, PKK, PLO, and Tamil Tigers (who did the most suicide bombings). There is always a reason behind every terrorist movement, most commonly national liberation. Afghanistan's Taliban is partly a Pashtun liberation movement.

Terrorism is a group activity, the work of committed believers in political causes. Lone gunmen operating outside of groups, such as John Hinckley, who shot President Reagan in 1981, are simply deranged. Osama bin Laden's al Qaeda bombed U.S. embassies in Africa and a destroyer in Yemen and then flew jetliners into the World Trade Center and Pentagon. Al Qaeda recruits Muslims everywhere for political and religious goals (in Islam, the two are intertwined), to make all Muslim countries fundamentalist and remove U.S. influence from the Middle East. Terrorism today is inseparable from the stresses and strains of politics in the Middle East.

All states officially treat terrorism as criminal, but some—such as Syria, Pakistan, Iran, Libya, and North Korea—quietly engage in "state-sponsored terrorism." The 1981 attempt to kill Pope John Paul II clearly traces back to the Kremlin. The Turkish gunman, an escaped convict, got his money, forged passport, and gun from Bulgarian security police, who were supervised by the Soviet KGB. Terrorists need bases, money, arms, and bombs, and these are sometimes supplied by the intelligence services of one country that wants to undermine another. Lebanon's Hezbollah (see page 139) is sponsored by Iran and Syria. Pakistan, although steadfastly denying it, tries to undermine Indian rule in Kashmir by secretly training and arming Muslim infiltrators, such as those who shot up Mumbai in 2008. Afghanistan also accused Pakistan of aiding a 2008 assassination attempt against President Karzai.

Does terrorism work? Rarely and seldom alone. It is usually one pressure among several. Hezbollah bombings helped persuade both the United States (in 1983) and Israel (in 2000) to leave Lebanon, but those attacks on soldiers were more guerrilla warfare than terrorism. Often terrorism is the first stage of an effort to start mass resistance and guerrilla warfare. Like other types of warfare, terrorism aims to change the enemy's mind. A touch of violence on top of massive political and economic pressures persuaded whites to abandon their monopoly on power in Rhodesia in 1980 and South Africa in the early 1990s.

In many cases, however, especially after terrorists have killed innocent civilians, it stiffens the resolve of the target country. Suicide bombings of Israelis persuaded most to support a giant fence to wall out Palestinians. The horrors of 9/11 convinced most Americans to use armed force to overthrow any regime that might sponsor terrorism against us. Bombings in Europe unified and stiffened the resolve of Europeans. Indians demanded war with Pakistan after the Mumbai massacre. And terrorists want this anger, arguing that the more the target strikes back, the more recruits they will gain—Lenin's revolutionary idea of "the worse, the better."

A subset of the equation is:

$$\text{fast population growth} + \text{slow economic growth} = \text{unemployment}$$

A Muslim country that has tasted Western imperialism and has many unemployed and a corrupt government will likely develop a Muslim fundamentalist movement. Unemployment is predictable from the extremely high birthrate in an economy that is growing only slowly, the case in most Muslim countries. Middle Eastern women bear three times as many children as European women. Until recently, Saudi women bore an average of eight children, helping the Saudi population triple in a generation. Unemployed or underemployed young men are often drawn to extremist politics. The ruling elites' corruption demonstrates to the poor masses that the government is illegitimate. Islamist preaching takes full advantage of this.

The long-term solution is to get these countries modern, with growing economies, jobs, education, small families, and clean government. Much stands in the way. Many economies are *statist* (see page 162) and block the rapid growth that free-market economies can deliver. The oil-producing countries around the Persian Gulf depend on petroleum revenues, much of which they have squandered without provision for long-term growth. Besides, the oil industry requires few workers. Some Arab intellectuals call it the "oil curse" for the way it has skewed

Baath Arab Social Renaissance party, secular and nationalist party that ruled Iraq under Saddam and still governs Syria.

CONCEPTS ■ TERRORISTS OR FREEDOM FIGHTERS?

It has long been said that "one man's terrorist is another man's freedom fighter." If you like the cause, you call him a freedom fighter. If you dislike the cause, you call him a terrorist. The British regarded American patriots and even General Washington as terrorists. Many old Canadian families are descended from Tories who fled the terror of the American Revolution. Northern Irish Protestants call Gerry Adams a terrorist; Northern Irish Catholics do not. Two prime ministers of Israel, Menachem Begin and Yitzhak Shamir, were hunted as terrorists by the British in Palestine before 1948. Millions of Muslims cheered 9/11 as a blow for freedom.

Some thinkers argue that the targets of terrorism separate it from a struggle for freedom. Targeting innocent civilians is terrorism; battling armed soldiers is an act of war. Thus, hurling missiles at Israeli towns is terrorism, but, argue Israelis, Israeli retaliation on the Hamas perpetrators is legitimate self-defense. By this standard, al Qaeda's bombing of U.S. embassies in East Africa (which killed mostly local pedestrians) was terror, but its bombing of the U.S.S. *Cole* in Yemen was legitimate war-fighting.

Such distinctions are irrelevant, and terrorists themselves usually shrug them off, arguing that they, the underdog, must hit the enemy wherever he is vulnerable, and that includes civilians. Chechen terrorists repeatedly hit Russian civilian targets. They once held hostage a crowded theater in Moscow. (Russian police used gas to put the entire theater to sleep, and many died.) The French Resistance in World War II learned to assassinate French collaborators rather than take on the German army. The Germans called them terrorists. The Vietcong terrorized South Vietnamese villages in the name of their liberation struggle. We called them terrorists but roasted whole villages with napalm in the name of a struggle against communism. Remnants of Saddam's **Baath** killed both U.S. soldiers and Iraqi civilians. We called them terrorists. For terrorists, no one who cooperates with the occupier is innocent.

The methods of terrorism help define it. Car and truck bombs, hijacking ships and jetliners, and suicide bombers are the hallmarks of terrorism. The weaker side in an asymmetrical conflict argues that the enemy is equipped with artillery, planes, and tanks, so they must use whatever techniques they can devise, including striking civilian targets.

blowback   Client or junior ally turns on its sponsor.

economic development and made rulers rich and unaccountable. The biggest problems, however, are the cultural and religious attitudes that reject modern life. These factors combine to turn the Middle East into a zone of chaos (see pages 12–13) that threatens the entire world.

The good news about Islamist terrorism is that it has already begun to fade, although it is still strong in Pakistan. Increasingly, Muslim clerics denounce its wanton killing, especially of Muslims, its chief victims. It has no economic doctrine and cannot put food on the family table. Several former adherents have turned against it with harsh words for its un-Koranic extremism. Time may solve the problem.

Most Middle East experts deny there is anything inherent in Islamic doctrine that keeps Muslim societies from modernizing. Looking at cases, though, one finds no Islamic countries that have fully modernized. Atatürk attempted to abruptly make Turkey modern and European between the two world wars, but his measures alienated many Muslims, who are now returning Turkey part way to its Muslim and Middle Eastern roots. The shah tried to modernize Iran but was overthrown by Islamists (pages 147–148). Sadat tried to modernize Egypt but was assassinated by Islamists in 1981. Oil brought some Muslim countries fabulous revenues, making them rich but still not culturally modern.

Does Islam cause backwardness? By itself, probably not. Islamic cultural antipathy toward the West—emphasized by Samuel Huntington (see page 147)—and toward modernity in general slows and often reverses progress in Muslim lands. But modernizing currents are stirring in Islam. As is often the case with religious reforms, going back to the original source can produce a reformation. Some Muslim scholars note that there is nothing in the Koran about suppressing women or blocking progress. The Koran, to be sure, prohibits loaning money at interest, but Muslims work around that by taking equity positions—stocks instead of loans. We are starting to see societies such as Turkey that are both modern and Muslim. One of the best ways to promote this: Educate women. Ironically, this has gone rather far in Iran, where the fundamentalist regime has educated more women than in most other Muslim lands (in separate schools and

CONCEPTS ■ BLOWBACK

One consistent pattern emerges from helping Islamist groups: They turn on their sponsors. Some, including the CIA, call this **blowback**, an action that blows back into your face. Israel, for example, thought it was clever in the 1980s to help Hamas, a religious charity that was supposed to offset Yassir Arafat's secular Palestine Liberation Organization. But Hamas always aimed to destroy Israel and has pushed aside the PLO.

Saudi Arabia, founded in 1932 on the puritanical Wahhabi brand of Islam, used its oil wealth to spread this rigid creed through religious schools in poor Muslim lands, including Pakistan. Now its Wahhabi adherents want to overthrow the House of Saud for drifting away from true Islam and dependence on the Americans.

Pakistan's Inter-Services Intelligence (ISI) invented the Taliban by organizing Afghan refugee students in fundamentalist Koranic academies in Pakistan. Pakistan, with U.S. approval, promoted a Taliban government in Afghanistan to overcome the chaos and lawlessness on its northern border. Pakistan also used Islamist fighters in its own terror campaign to wrest Kashmir from India. Now the Taliban vows a *jihad* against both the Pakistani and U.S. governments. Be careful whom you help in this part of the world.

colleges, of course). These educated Iranian women are now demanding the equality they say is part of the Koran.

In Huntington's terms (see page 171), most Muslim lands are "torn" countries, pulled between Western and Islamic cultures. Many of the educated elite are open to Western values, but most people cling to traditional and even fundamentalist Islamic values. Pakistan's presidents, who know and understand the West and modernization, take big chances by supporting America in overthrowing the Taliban in Afghanistan. Most Pakistanis want it the other way around; some join a jihad against the United States. (Pakistani chiefs also hedge their bets by not cracking down on Islamic radicals.) The governments of Pakistan, Algeria, Egypt, Saudi Arabia, and other Muslim lands are sitting atop rumbling volcanoes of Islamic fundamentalism; they could be overthrown.

Two specific and ongoing causes inflame many Muslims: (1) The existence of Israel and U.S. support for it; and (2) the presence of U.S. forces in Muslim lands. They see Israel as a new type of Western crusader state that seized holy land and must be expelled. They are not interested in compromise. Jerusalem is also holy to Muslims. Israel, however, is but a step to the bigger goal. If Israel did not exist, the region would still be a zone of chaos.

This brings us to Osama bin Laden, seventeenth of 52 children (by multiple and rotating wives) of a Saudi Arabian construction billionaire. Osama bin Laden organized and funded **jihadis** to expel the Soviets from Afghanistan in the 1980s. He never liked and did not work with Americans in this effort and strongly opposed U.S. forces in Saudi Arabia to defend it against Iraq in 1990 and 1991. To him, all of Saudi Arabia (not just the holy cities of Mecca and Medina) is sacred Muslim ground that was defiled by the U.S. troops. Osama bin Laden became furious when a small U.S. force stayed after the 1991 war (removed at Saudi request in 2003) and denounced the House of Saud for allowing it. Saudi Arabia revoked his citizenship in 1996, but he had earlier cashed out his estimated inheritance of $300 million and hidden it in many places. He also continues to get money from relatives, supporters, and Muslim charities in Saudi Arabia. Osama bin Laden is hiding in Pakistan's wild northwest, where tribal inhabitants praise him. Just killing bin Laden won't be enough, as trusted helpers will replace him. One of al Qaeda's chief weapons: the Internet, which carries messages of jihad and instructions on making bombs.

A U.S. Chinook helicopter delivers troops in Afghanistan's Tora Bora, the region from which Osama bin Laden escaped in 2001. (Jeremy Lock/AP Photo)

jihadi   Muslim holy warrior, also called *mujahid* (plural: *mujahideen*).

WHICH WAY FOR U.S. POLICY?

The Bush 43 administration repeatedly rationalized the attack on Iraq by in effect arguing, "We are fighting them over there so that we won't have to fight them here." Critics charge that the war in Iraq made things worse and has been a distraction from getting al Qaeda, which is still in operation. The U.S. invasions stirred up Islamic hatred worldwide. The insurgents in Iraq were mostly home-grown Sunni chauvinists and Islamists divided into dozens of small and hard-to-catch groups. A few foreign jihadis (mostly young Saudis) entered Iraq but soon fell into conflict with Iraqi Sunni groups. They had totally different aims: The Iraqi Sunnis sought to get their share of oil wealth and power; the foreigners wanted a *jihad* (see page 152) against Americans, Shia, and anything secular. A Jordanian fanatic (killed in 2006) set up one group and called it "al Qaeda in Iraq." So al Qaeda did come to Iraq, but only because of the U.S. occupation.

Bush wanted a war in Iraq because he thought wars have clear goals and methods. But asymmetrical conflict is trickier. Al Qaeda is no single enemy country but loosely linked cells in many lands, cells that invent themselves as al Qaeda with little help or guidance from Osama bin Laden. It is a highly international undertaking. Suppressed in one place, it pops up in another. Al Qaeda-affiliated groups recruit in Britain, Nigeria, and the United States, and train in Yemen, Somalia, and Pakistan. On Christmas Day 2009, a young Nigerian Muslim attempted to bring down a jetliner near Detroit with explosives in his underwear. He was the son of one of Africa's wealthiest families, graduated engineering in London, and trained by al Qaeda in Yemen.

What should we do in the face of Islamist terrorism? First, we must remember that bin Laden and his lieutenants want us to overreact, to use our strengths against us, just as his hijackers used our technology against us. The military option is tempting but must be used sparingly, as it tends to provoke Islamism rather than calm it. Few Muslims liked the secular Saddam regime in Iraq, the

CONCEPTS ■ IS ISLAM THE CAUSE?

University of Chicago political scientist Robert Pape vigorously dissents from the widely held view that the prime cause of terrorism in the modern world is Islam. Pape studied suicide bombers worldwide and found little religious influence. The originators and chief perpetrators of suicide bombings were Tamil Tigers, Marxist separatists who fought from 1976 to 2009 for a Tamil state in the north and east of Sri Lanka (formerly Ceylon).

The commonality in suicide bombings in many lands, found Pape, was the desire to rid a country of foreign occupiers, be they Soviets, Americans, Israelis, or Sinhalese (the main nationality of Sri Lanka). The solution, says Pape, is for the foreigners to get out. For example, Israel must leave the West Bank. But Israel did pull out of Gaza in 2005, and Hamas continued its war, demanding not just the West Bank but all of Palestine and the disappearance of the state of Israel. Israel is unlikely to cooperate.

Pape's theory explains suicide bombings of Americans in Iraq but not of the Shia majority in Iraq, who are not foreign occupiers. Far more Iraqi Shia are killed than Americans. Pape's theory does not explain the 2004 Bali bombings unless you define Australian tourists as an occupying force. This theory does not explain the 2005 suicide bombings of three hotels in Amman, Jordan, which killed Arabs. It is also a stretch to say the young Muslims in Madrid (2004) and London (2005) who blew up trains did it to protest the Iraq situation. If Muslims anywhere can commit these acts in support of distant co-religionists, we return to religious and cultural explanations of terrorism. In the Spain and England cases, it is the inability of Muslims to assimilate into European culture and the resultant alienation of unemployed Muslim youth.

least Islamic in the Arab world, but most strongly objected to the U.S. invasion of a brother Arab land. Bin Laden despised Saddam Hussein as a hypocrite and idolater but portrayed the U.S. invasion as a crime against all Muslims.

Bin Laden's immediate target is the "near enemy," his homeland of Saudi Arabia, whose royal house was founded on the puritan Wahhabi faith but now lives quite differently. For decades Saudi officials denied any problems in the Kingdom—they even denied that most of the 9/11 hijackers were Saudis—but now worry that thousands of young *salafis* are ready to overthrow the regime. Saudi Arabia is indeed a prize. The world depends on the flow of oil from the Persian Gulf. Some object that oil is a selfish or greedy cause, but if it is seriously disrupted the entire world will suffer. Anything we do with Saudi Arabia can blow back in our faces. Keeping U.S. troops there aroused much local opposition. Saudi Arabia did not let us attack from its soil in 2003 and asked us to pull out U.S. forces shortly after the war, which we did. Only Saudis can handle the al Qaeda underground in Saudi Arabia.

Our first line of defense is at home—using methods such as improving border and airport controls—and it has worked. It is now much harder for terrorists to enter and operate in the United States, although they keep trying. Credit goes to our front line, Immigration and Customs Enforcement (ICE), which watches U.S. borders and airports and is part of the Department of Homeland Security. A new clearinghouse now lets agencies share information on possible terrorist activity. A major problem has been that, by law and by corporate culture, the CIA shares information with no other agency. There is still not a single computer system or database to link agencies. If all the fragmentary warnings of 9/11 had been put together on a single desk, we might have been able to stop it. The FBI in Washington ignored field reports that young Arab men were taking suspicious flying lessons in which they told instructors they did not wish to learn to take off or land.

salafiyya "The way of the founders," reactionary Islamic puritanism and the basis of current Islamism. Adjective: *salafi*.

sharia Islamic law, drawn from the Koran.

umma The community of all Muslims.

CONCEPTS ■ SALAFIYYA

Islamic fundamentalism's religious root traces back to the thirteenth-century Damascus thinker Ibn Taymiyya, who devised the doctrine of **salafiyya** to combat the terrible Mongol invasion. Although these Mongols converted to Islam, Ibn Taymiyya argued that they were fake Muslims, because they replaced **sharia** with their pagan Mongol laws. Accordingly, they were to be resisted and killed as hypocrites. In the eighteenth century, an Arabian salafi preacher named Ibn Wahhab made a religious alliance with the House of Saud, a combination that took over the peninsula in the 1930s. Saudi Wahhabism and bin Laden's al Qaeda today are forms of salafiyya.

Salafis condemn anything suspicious or modern as hypocrisy or idolatry. Muslim rulers who seek wealth and power are hypocrites. Setting up Western-type states and governments is a form of idolatry. Islam must not be chopped up into separate nation-states—which are idols—but must be preserved as one giant **umma**, as the Prophet Muhammad intended. Salafiyya is an international pan-Islam movement and a permanent undercurrent in Sunni Islamic thought. (It is not found in the Shia branch of Islam, which salafis denounce as pagan and idolatrous.)

Salafiyya can turn its followers into fanatics who seek Islamic purity, reject compromise, and are happy to die as martyrs to the faith. Salafis long to destroy Israel, America, and insufficiently pure Muslim rulers, which means most of them, including the House of Saud. Al Qaeda, a salafi movement, never supported Saddam's secular regime in Iraq or Palestinian nationalism except as ways to arouse Muslims to join a jihad.

radiological   Gives off dangerous radiation.

Patient police and intelligence work rather than military invasion is the better way to curb terrorism while avoiding asymmetrical warfare. We need a sort of international SWAT team with language skills. TV dramas showing such teams in action have been ahead of reality. The FBI does not operate overseas; the CIA has no law enforcement powers; and neither is part of the Department of Homeland Security, which simply shuffled together some existing bureaus of other departments. We are still organizationally unprepared to stop terrorist attacks or deal with their aftermath. The Federal Emergency Management Agency (FEMA), part of Homeland Security, did not inspire confidence in its handling of Hurricane Katrina.

Next, the only way that U.S. law enforcement can operate in other countries is through their police and intelligence agencies, many of which are not completely cooperative or trustworthy.

CONCEPTS ■ TERRORISM PLUS WMD

We earlier discussed weapons of mass destruction—nukes, gas, and bugs. Could terrorists get hold of WMD and use them in spectacular strikes? Some say they already have, that the 9/11 attacks, which killed more than 3,000, were in effect WMD. But what if an organization like al Qaeda gets something far more powerful? America is not safe from nuclear terrorism.

Many experts fear that North Korea could give or sell a nuclear device to Muslim extremists, but Pakistan is unstable and its intelligence agency has an ambiguous relationship to Islamist guerrillas. No fear of retaliation would restrain terrorists from using a nuke once they had one.

Worldwide, there are already more than 30,000 nuclear warheads plus enough fissile material (highly enriched uranium or plutonium) for another 240,000. Much of this material, especially in ex-Soviet lands, is poorly secured and easily stolen and smuggled, giving rise to the term *loose nukes*. A nuclear device would not have to be an advanced or compact model to damage a city. A shipping container would make a good delivery system.

Would a U.S. deterrence threat (discussed in Chapters 13 and 14) be sufficient to persuade potential suppliers to not give or sell nukes to terrorists? Some suppliers might think the bombs could not be traced back to them. The United States could announce that, in cases of uncertainty, it would bomb the three most likely culprits. North Korea in the past performed acts of terrorism with conventional explosives and did not care when they were exposed. The more nations with nukes, the more likely one or more warheads will fall into the

hands of terrorists. Part of the U.S. effort against terrorism, therefore, must include strengthened safeguards against nuclear proliferation, which has not been a U.S. priority until recently (see previous chapter).

Not the same as a nuclear blast, a **radiological** weapon or "dirty bomb" would spew out radioactive dust and contaminate a wide area, such as Wall Street. A radiological weapon is simply waste uranium or plutonium (from hospitals, industries, or power plants) packed around a few sticks of dynamite. It would kill few but might take months to decontaminate. What would be the economic effects of shutting down lower Manhattan? (All the firms there have backup files elsewhere.)

Just after 9/11, letters containing anthrax were mailed out, some to Capitol Hill. Five Americans died from the first instance of bioterrorism. The culprit turned out to be a mad federal scientist, who committed suicide. Initial suspicion focused on al Qaeda, possibly supplied with anthrax by Iraq, but no evidence was found after the 2003 war. Anthrax is not that hard to brew and pulverize and could fall into terrorist hands.

Smallpox is even easier to produce and disseminate—just infect a few dozen volunteers and put them on planes to the United States with instructions to sneeze in crowded places. No Americans have been immunized against smallpox since the early 1970s, but we could quickly crank up an immunization program. Gas is the least likely WMD for terrorists, as it requires large quantities and could quickly be traced to the country that supplied it. As we found in the 1991 Gulf War, nukes deter gas.

Saudi Arabia and Pakistan, for example, have never come clean about extremist activity on their soil; they are scared of Islamists and are reluctant to crack down on them. We must make allies out of moderate Muslim governments by offering them a choice: It's us or the Islamists. Cooperating with U.S. intelligence is better than cooperating with Islamist terrorism, which brings only violence and poverty.

The United States is still vulnerable to terrorist attacks. Computer networks, seaports, oil refineries, and nuclear power plants are weak spots. U.S. controls are lax; an estimated 4 million people are in the United States on expired visas. At least two of them were among the 9/11 hijackers, who had no trouble entering and living in the United States with no one asking what they were up to or how they got their money. The hijackers laughed at how open and easy everything is here. Some of this openness should be tightened. A national identification card should be considered. Both civil libertarians and gun owners cry "police state," but you already carry the equivalent: a photo driver's license with bar code plus a Social Security card. Just combine the two. (Students object, fearing bartenders would ask to see it.) Just such a national ID card has been issued to thousands who daily cross the U.S. borders with Mexico and Canada.

But panicked overreaction and a human need to "do something, anything!" is unwarranted. After 9/11, some Americans bought gas masks and dubious pills. Law enforcement agencies detained men with olive complexions or droopy mustaches. To give in to excessive fear means to give one round to the terrorists, exactly what they want. America's enemies have always assumed that we are a weak and decadent society, one with no deep or spiritual values, dedicated only to money and luxuries and unwilling to sacrifice or sustain casualties. They have failed to understand that America is a highly resilient and adaptive society with great internal strengths.

CONCEPTS ■ HOMEGROWN TERRORISTS

One current puzzle is why some Muslim American citizens turn to Islamist terrorism. Often the children of immigrants, many were born and educated in the United States. That, in conventional thinking, should make them good Americans, and indeed most are. But a small percentage cannot identify with U.S. culture and return to their roots.

The Army psychiatrist who shot his fellow soldiers at Fort Hood in 2009 was born in Virginia of Palestinian parents. The Internet is proving one of al Qaeda's most effective recruiting devices. Its top preacher, Anwar al-Awlaki, was born in New Mexico and graduated from U.S. universities but spews his bilingual hatred from Yemen, his ancestral home.

Most previous waves of immigrants to the United States from Europe had little trouble acculturating and assimilating. More recently, most Asians have done it. The second generation speaks English, and the third often marries outside of the immigrant group. This "three-generation assimilation," however, does not always work with immigrants from a very different culture. Some young Muslims are alienated from U.S. society and embrace Islam more fervently than their parents ever did. A few take personally the suffering and deaths of their co-religionists in Iraq and Afghanistan and feel that Islam as a whole is under attack and they must defend it.

In contrast, Arab Christian immigrants—there are many now from Iraq and Egypt—have no such trouble establishing an American identity; their Christianity helps them acculturate. Indeed, in their home countries Arab Christians are often discriminated against and happy to come to the United States. (U.S. armed forces welcome them for their language skills.) A century ago, the first Arab immigrants to the United States were mostly Lebanese Christians, who acculturated rapidly. Religion matters.

LESSONS OF ASYMMETRICAL CONFLICT

1. Security is a permanent problem. Neither the end of the Cold War nor isolationism gives us security. Hostile forces can disrupt the world and even strike in our homeland.
2. The Middle East is an inexhaustible source of conflict, and we cannot totally withdraw from it or ignore it.
3. Terrorism by itself is rarely an effective strategy. America was enraged but not seriously wounded by 9/11.
4. Huntington's "clash of civilizations" theory looks more plausible (see Chapters 1 and 9).
5. Rapid population growth is a factor in world politics (see Chapter 11). Countries with high unemployment breed conflict.
6. Deterrence doesn't work if your enemy is unafraid of dying. Militant salafis wish to die as martyrs.
7. Invading countries in order to combat terrorism can lead us deep into long-lasting asymmetrical conflicts.

CONCEPTS ■ CYBERWARFARE

Some consider cyberwarfare the latest jump in military technology, possibly as important as airpower and nuclear weapons. Already, criminals attempt daily to hack into banks and businesses worldwide. We've all been hit by computer viruses. Conceivably, a cyberattack could shut down communications and power grids, neutralize air defenses, and unlock top military secrets.

Most cyberattacks so far simply overload target networks, causing them to slow or shut down, producing a "denial of service." Russia preceded its 2008 invasion of Georgia by overloading its computer networks. Far more sophisticated methods that attack a nation's infrastructure are coming, as in 2010 with Stuxnet, a software worm that concentrated on Iran. Many suspected either Israelis or Americans launched it to disrupt Iran's nuclear program. Chinese academic sites—clearly with Beijing's approval—have hacked into U.S. networks, including Google. Very aware of such dangers, in 2010 the U.S. military set up Cyber Command (USCybercom) under a four-star general to guard against attack and prepare countermeasures.

Cyberwar may be particularly suited to asymmetrical conflict, because it gives an underdog an opening to damage a much stronger foe. All one side needs is a computer and a skilled hacker. Cyberwarfare may not, however, be the perfect weapon. It runs the risk of provoking a foe without seriously hurting him.

Cyberattacks can often be traced to their country of origin. Small, probing cyberattacks alert the target to his weaknesses so he can fix them and retaliate. In 2007, Russia, in a dispute with Estonia, attacked Estonia's network. Now Estonia is headquarters of NATO's cyberdefense effort.

Retaliation, especially if mounted by a high-tech power, could do more damage to the attacker's network than he has inflicted. This would give an attacker pause. A cyberattack could rapidly escalate into conventional military exchanges. If someone is trying to destroy your computer and Internet structure, why be nice? A country would likely reserve its Internet retaliatory capability for a major attack; demonstrating it sooner could allow the foe to overcome it. In short, cyberwarfare is no magic weapon but subject to all of the difficulties of conventional warfare: defense, deterrence, retaliation, and escalation.

Be wary of frightening computer stories. As 2000 approached, fearmongers predicted that "Y2K" would bring a massive failure of computers, allegedly because years were listed with only their last two digits, so computers could not distinguish between 2000 and 1900. Systems would crash nationwide, power plants would shut down, and aircraft would fall from the sky—unless, of course, you purchased a special protection plan. Some thinkers suggest that cyberwarfare is also exaggerated.

8. Allies count, both in Europe and the Middle East. The 2003 Iraq War, pursued without regard to the views of allies, isolated America.

9. Terrorists could use weapons of mass destruction. Watching for WMD must be a major objective, but it takes allies.

mypoliscikit EXERCISES

Apply what you learned in this chapter on MyPoliSciKit (www.mypoliscikit.com).

 Assessment Review this chapter using learning objectives, chapter summaries, practice tests, and more.

Menu

 Flashcards Learn the key terms in this chapter; you can test yourself by term or definition.

Flashcards

 Video Analyze recent world affairs by watching streaming video from major news providers.

Comparative
Exercises

 Simulations Play the role of an IR decision-maker and experience how IR concepts work in practice.

Videos

KEY TERMS

asymmetrical conflict (p. 240)

Baath (p. 243)

blowback (p. 244)

caliphate (p. 241)

counterinsurgency (p. 240)

guerrilla (p. 240)

insurgency (p. 240)

jihadi (p. 245)

radiological (p. 248)

salafiyya (p. 247)

sharia (p. 247)

terrorism (p. 240)

umma (p. 247)

FURTHER REFERENCE

Beebe, Shannon D., and Mary Kaldor. *The Ultimate Weapon Is No Weapon: Human Security and the New Rules for War and Peace*. New York: PublicAffairs, 2010.

Bergen, Peter. *The Longest War: The Enduring Conflict Between America and al-Qaeda*. New York: Free Press, 2011.

Berman, Paul. *The Flight of the Intellectuals*. New York: Melville House, 2010.

Bloom, Mia. *Dying to Kill: The Allure of Suicide Terror*. New York: Columbia University Press, 2007.

Bobbitt, Philip. *Terror and Consent: The Wars for the Twenty-first Century*. New York: Knopf, 2008.

Bonner, Michael. *Jihad in Islamic History: Doctrines and Practice*. Princeton, NJ: Princeton University Press, 2008.

Brown, Michael E., Owen R. Coté, Jr., Sean M. Lynn-Jones, and Steven E. Miller, eds. *Contending with Terrorism: Roots, Strategies, and Responses*. Cambridge, MA: MIT Press, 2010.

Calvert, John. *Sayyid Qutb and the Origins of Radical Islamism*. New York: Columbia University Press, 2010.

Clarke, Richard, and Robert Knake. *Cyber War: The Next Threat to National Security and What to Do About It*. New York: HarperCollins, 2010.

Ervin, Clark Kent. *Open Target: Where America Is Vulnerable to Attack*. New York: Palgrave, 2007.

Gardner, Hall. *American Global Strategy and the "War on Terrorism."* Williston, VT: Ashgate, 2007.

Gerges, Fawaz A. *The Far Enemy: Why Jihad Went Global*. New York: Cambridge University Press, 2005.

Giustozzi, Antonio. *Koran, Kalashnikov, and Laptop: The Neo-Taliban Insurgency in Afghanistan*. New York: Columbia University Press, 2008.

Jamal, Arif. *Shadow War: The Untold Story of Jihad in Kashmir*. Brooklyn, NY: Melville House, 2009.

Kepel, Gilles. *Beyond Terror and Martyrdom: The Future of the Middle East*. Cambridge, MA: Harvard University Press, 2008.

Kilcullen, David. *Counterinsurgency*. New York: Oxford University Press, 2010.

Lawrence, Bruce, ed. *Messages to the World: The Statements of Osama·bin Laden*. London: Verso, 2005.

Pape, Robert A., and James K. Feldman. *Cutting the Fuse: The Explosion of Global Suicide Terrorism and How to Stop It*. Chicago: University of Chicago Press, 2010.

Phares, Walid. *The Confrontation: Winning the War against Future Jihad*. New York: Palgrave, 2008.

Riedel, Bruce. *The Search for Al Qaeda: Its Leadership, Ideology, and Future*. Washington, DC: Brookings, 2008.

Sageman, Marc. *Leaderless Jihad: Terror Networks in the Twenty-First Century*. Philadelphia: University of Pennsylvania Press, 2008.

Scheuer, Michael. *Through Our Enemies' Eyes*. Dulles, VA: Potomac Books, 2006.

Shapiro, Ian. *Containment: Rebuilding a Strategy against Global Terror*. Princeton, NJ: Princeton University Press, 2007.

Smith, Paul J. *The Terrorism Ahead: Confronting Transnational Violence in the Twenty-First Century*. Armonk, NY: M. E. Sharpe, 2008.

Whittaker, David J. *Terrorism: Understanding the Global Threat*, 2nd ed. New York: Longman, 2007.

Zulaika, Joseba. *Terrorism: The Self-Fulfilling Prophecy*. Chicago: University of Chicago Press, 2009.

PART V

ECONOMIC BLOCS

International political economy (IPE) is the interface between governments and the world economy. IPE underlies much of IR and helps determine what kind of IR system exists. Does the world now have a new IPE? Are globalization and the Internet transforming the globe into one big market? Or are economic blocs forming—Europe, Asia, and North America, each already producing roughly one-third of the world's economic output—that are less than open? Is the new system likely to be stable? One thing is clear: The IPE does not run itself but requires major-power leadership.

Chapter 16 considers how Europe has grown distant from its Cold War status as a U.S. junior partner. The euro symbolizes the growing power and assertiveness of a united Europe but got a major jolt in 2010 when several members admitted they were running overlarge deficits. NATO, the foundation of Europe's postwar security, has faded in the absence of the Soviet threat. Some European elites would like an EU foreign policy outside of NATO, but the EU is still too fragmented to achieve it. The EU is going its own way, ignoring Washington's pleas to open its markets and follow America's military lead in places like Iraq.

Chapter 17 looks at the amazing shift of world economic growth from West to East, namely, the recent rise of China from communism to state-guided capitalism and the earlier rise of Japan from the ashes of defeat. As China's economy grows, it becomes more assertive, especially in the China Seas. The rapidly growing economies on the Pacific Rim could form a trading bloc with greater production than either NAFTA or the EU. How did Japan's economic miracle happen and then falter? And the biggest question of all, will China turn democratic and open or nationalistic and hostile?

Chapter 18 considers globalization theory in relation to the U.S. economy. How can one find a correct value for the dollar? Is globalization really what's happening to the IPE? Has it already begun to falter, or will it be self-sustaining? What are the complaints of anti-globalists? Can world trade expand without U.S. leadership? Is the United States really interested in an open world economy, or does it too practice trade protectionism? Is U.S. prosperity vulnerable to world shocks that could tumble the dollar and lead to a new Great Depression?

CHAPTER 16

Europe Unifies

Athens rioters protest budget austerity required to shrink Greece's massive debt, which put the euro in doubt. (Pamagiotis Moschandreou/ Corbis)

In 2010 the European Union (EU) learned with horror that it could fall apart. Users of the new euro currency had pledged to limit their government deficits to under 3 percent in order to keep the euro strong and stable, but several of them drastically exceeded that limit. When that came out, starting in Greece, some feared a collapse of the euro that could mean the end of the great postwar project to unify Europe. The project had been making good if unsteady progress.

After years of debate, in late 2009 the Treaty of Lisbon, one of a long series of treaties that slowly pulled Europe toward unity, went into effect. Far from creating a federal democracy, the treaty just streamlined the institutions of the European Union a bit and added a presidency and foreign minister so that Europe could speak with greater unity and authority on the world stage. It was a small step toward creating a Europe that can go its own way.

With the Cold War long over, many Europeans resented America as the new hegemon that tried to mold the world in its image. The resentment came to a head with European opposition to the 2003 Iraq War, which they saw as an example of President George W. Bush's "unilateralism." Europeans seriously disliked Bush 43, and he returned the favor. They liked President Barack Obama initially but soon cooled. U.S. military power is unmatched, but some of its other forms of power are quite limited. Power, remember, is one country's ability to get another to do its bidding, and most of Europe rejects U.S. advice, pressure, warnings, and leadership. Europe forms a weak counterweight to U.S. power (see page 12).

Some French thinkers called America the *hyperpuissance* (hyperpower, stronger than superpower) and vowed to resist it. They were actually expressing the resentment—shared by many Europeans—that is part military, part economic, part cultural, part political, and heavily psychological. Europe fears a U.S. "cowboy mentality" that rejects the UN and international law in favor of military solutions. Europe, after bashing itself bloody in two world wars, has turned strongly anti-war and favors negotiations and treaties. Europe says it will not adopt "savage" U.S. capitalism, with its growing wealth gap, but will build humane (and expensive) welfare states. In health, welfare, and education standards, several European countries are ahead of America.

Culturally, some European elites resent U.S. movies, TV shows, fashions, and music. They fear American junk is drowning out their classical and creative culture, although ordinary Europeans happily consume American movies and fast food. Almost all Europeans think

QUESTIONS TO CONSIDER

1. Will there soon be a "United States of Europe"?
2. What two tracks do NATO and the European Union represent?
3. What did Yugoslavia show about European unity?
4. What areas does NATO cover? Who is a member?
5. Who were the first six members of the Common Market? Who joined later?
6. What is the EU common currency? What are its problems?
7. How are Slovenia and Slovakia similar but different?
8. What political differences have Europe and America developed?
9. What are the difficulties of expanding the EU and NATO?

soft power　Influence through cultural, legal, and moral example.

European Union (EU)　Confederation of most of Europe; began as Common Market in 1957.

America's gun laws and capital punishment are primitive. America is religious; Europe is irreligious (exception: Poland). So-called **soft power** is not a trivial element in IR; it drives long-term shifts of attitude.

Europe tired of depending on the United States for security and always following the U.S. lead. Argue many of Europe's leaders: "We want to be equal to the Americans, the EU equal to the U.S. Our foreign policy will not obediently follow Washington's. And we want our own currency, information technology, major industries, and anything else that gives us independence from the United States." In Washington, Europe declined in importance as China loomed large.

Well before the Cold War ended, the politics of resentment began pulling Europe and America apart. America sees itself as the senior partner and natural leader, the indispensable player. Americans see the Europeans as too divided to play a major role. Europeans had gotten used to America looking after their security, so they never spent enough on defense and now spend less because they face few threats but big budgetary gaps. Europe's big project, however, is not security but the **European Union**, which aims to have its own voice in the world.

EUROPE'S TWO TRACKS

Europe had been working toward unification on two tracks, the security track (NATO) and the economic track (the European Union). During the long Cold War, the two tracks ran closely parallel, one reinforcing the other. With the end of the Cold War—which many date to the fall of the Berlin Wall in 1989—the two tracks diverged until NATO and the EU now have little to

GEOGRAPHY ■ LABELING EUROPE

During the Cold War, Europe was divided into an East and a West. There were some neutrals that were neither in NATO nor the Warsaw Pact (Sweden, Finland, Switzerland, Austria, Ireland, and Yugoslavia). Within East Europe, however, there are two historically and culturally distinct regions: Central Europe and the Balkans.

For our purposes, West Europe is made up of countries that touch the Atlantic, plus Switzerland and Italy. Central Europe is from Croatia north—Croatia, Slovenia, Hungary, the Czech Republic, Slovakia, and Poland, plus Austria. (Do not confuse Slovenia and Slovakia. Slovenia is the northwestern part of old Yugoslavia, next to Austria and Italy. Slovakia is the eastern half of old Czechoslovakia, between Poland and Hungary.)

Central Europe is basically the old Habsburg or Austro-Hungarian Empire (which included southern Poland) and is largely Roman Catholic. This area is more advanced than the Balkans and turned quickly to democracy (Croatia and Slovakia were a little slow) and market economies. Most Central European countries joined the EU in 2004, so that now when we say "Europe" we generally mean West plus Central Europe.

The Balkans (the Turkish word for a mountain chain), long a part of the Turkish Ottoman Empire, is south of Croatia. It includes Serbia, Bosnia, Macedonia, Albania, Greece, Romania, and Bulgaria. The Balkans, largely Eastern Orthodox in faith, are poorer and less democratic than Central Europe and took longer to join the EU. Note how Yugoslavia's attempt to meld its Central European and Balkan elements into one country ended in bloody breakup.

do with each other. Without a main enemy, the forces latent in the Western alliance pulled it apart. NATO had been held together by fear of Soviet expansion; when that vanished, the life went out of NATO. Now West Europe and the United States have an increasingly conflicted relationship over trade, ex-Yugoslavia, Iraq, Iran, and many other questions.

> **UNPROFOR** The 1992–1995 UN Protection Force supposed to keep peace in Croatia and Bosnia.
>
> **IFOR** The 1995 Implementation Force, mostly NATO.

A problem buried at the heart of NATO from its founding helped turn it into a paper alliance: its limited scope. The 1949 North Atlantic Treaty provided that an attack on a member country in Europe or North America would be treated as an attack on all. Places such as the Persian Gulf are "out of area," and genocidal war in ex-Yugoslavia was not an attack on a member. Americans kept expecting their NATO allies to follow the U.S. lead worldwide; Europeans kept saying, "That's not part of NATO, and we aren't following you." This first appeared in the Balkans in the early 1990s when West Europe said it would take the lead in stopping the horrors in Bosnia but then shrank back. Europeans were unwilling to use force to preserve Europe's security. Frustration grew on both sides of the Atlantic.

THE LESSON OF EX-YUGOSLAVIA

Yugoslavia was a rather artificial country that was created and broken by Europe's twentieth-century wars. It was born after World War I, dismembered in World War II, and fell apart after the Cold War. The nationalities of Yugoslavia ("Land of the South Slavs") did not hate each other for centuries; that started under the Nazis in World War II. Tito and his Communists thought they had formed a solid federal system under the slogan "brotherhood and unity." The main language, Serbo-Croatian, is little different from Belgrade (Serbia) to Zagreb (Croatia). Croats, however, are Catholic, Serbs are Eastern Orthodox, and a plurality (but not a majority) of Bosnians are Muslim, having been converted by the Turks.

The breakup of Yugoslavia in the 1990s showed it had been poorly cemented together. Some 100,000 were killed, and West Europe was unable to stop the massacres. In 1991, the leading European powers told Washington they would handle this problem in their own backyard. With the blue helmets and white vehicles of the UN, most West European lands contributed at least a battalion of "peacekeepers" with very limited mandates: Oversee the latest cease-fire but don't get involved in fighting. The United Nations Protection Force **(UNPROFOR)** was ineffective. There was no peace to keep; all sides were willing to fight for what they deemed justly theirs. Serbian forces simply arrested and handcuffed West European soldiers who were in the way.

The Bosnia fighting ended in November 1995 after the United States took an active role. American diplomats arranged for arms to flow in, and recently retired U.S. officers trained Croatian and Bosnian forces. NATO, under U.S. leadership, then enforced a deal made in Dayton, Ohio, mediated by American diplomat Richard C. Holbrooke and Secretary of State Warren Christopher. NATO formed the U.S.-led Implementation Force **(IFOR)**, effective because it came after a cease-fire had been agreed to and because IFOR had orders to shoot.

Next, trouble flared in Serbia's southern province of Kosovo, Serbia's medieval heartland but now populated mostly by ethnic Albanians. These *Kosovars*, Muslim and speaking

KFOR The 1999 Kosovo Force, mostly NATO.

an unrelated language, demanded independence from Belgrade's rule. Underground parties and terrorism appeared, brutally suppressed by Serbian police and soldiers, who drove tens of thousands of Kosovars into neighboring Albania and Macedonia and prepared to massacre the rest.

This time the United States and West Europe, ashamed of having stood by while civilians were massacred in Bosnia, were ready to stop it. In the spring of 1999, under the command of U.S. General Wesley Clark, 78 days of aerial bombardment—no ground troops—persuaded Serbia to pull out of Kosovo. The bombs hit few good military targets, and Serbs killed an estimated 10,000 Kosovars anyway. Kosovo proclaimed its independence in 2008 and was recognized by most countries but not by Russia, China, India, and Spain, who do not wish to encourage their own breakaway movements. The patrols of the Kosovo Force **(KFOR)** try to calm a tense situation. (Eventually Kosovo may join Albania.)

From both Bosnia and Kosovo, Europe learned unhappily that only when America leads do things get done. The United States has the airlift capacity, the satellite intelligence, the communications network, the aircraft, the smart bombs, and the willingness to fight. The message to Europe: Develop your own fighting technology and manpower or stay forever dependent on the Americans. In a tepid response, Europe put together its own small Eurocorps, but it is little more than a headquarters staff in Strasbourg. Ironically, the only times NATO was actually used contributed to its splintering.

THE CRUMBLING OF NATO

Some say the recent eastward expansion of NATO breathed new life into it, but as it expanded it both hollowed out and angered Russia. Fewer and fewer U.S. troops are stationed in Europe; they simply aren't needed. This is to be expected. Alliances are always crumbling; that is their nature. As long as states preserve their sovereignty, they also keep their options for independent courses of action. The new eastern members from the defunct Soviet bloc contribute little to NATO's strength but represent new strategic problems. Russia hates having NATO right on its borders—implicitly, it's still an anti-Russian alliance—and angrily opposes Ukraine and Georgia joining NATO.

NATO no longer faces a Soviet threat and dislikes involvement in the Middle East. Several European countries, with Britain in the lead, contributed a few troops to the efforts in Afghanistan and Iraq, and many have already been withdrawn. Americans and Europeans just don't see the Middle East the same way. Washington sees a region on the brink of chaos that

CONCEPTS ■ ALLIANCES

An alliance is a treaty between two or more countries to come to each other's aid under specified conditions, usually when one member is attacked. Forming alliances is an ancient technique, a natural tendency to band together in the face of threats. When the threats subside, the alliance weakens and falls apart. No alliance is permanent.

The reason for forming an alliance is called the *casus foederis* (literally, "cause for federating," almost the opposite of *casus belli,* reason for going to war). The *casus*

foederis is almost always a security threat. A purely ideological alliance—"Let's get together because we think the same way"—is a nonstarter, an idealistic wish that doesn't get carried out. Many Americans believe alliances are based on mutual liking or shared values. Not necessarily. An alliance is a rational calculation of national interests by the leaders in power at a certain time. Emphasized Britain's Lord Palmerston in the nineteenth century: "Britain has no permanent friends and no permanent enemies; she has permanent interests."

NATO and EU Members

we must stabilize, to ensure the flow of oil, to foster democracy, and to promote an Israel–Palestine compromise. Europeans see a complex region that outside intervention can only destabilize and do not want their troops serving in Iraq or Afghanistan. Americans are generally pro-Israel, Europeans anti-Israel. No amount of diplomacy can bridge these different perceptions.

NATO has always been shaky and dependent on the United States. The traditional European powers exhausted themselves in World War II; afterward, only the Soviet Union and the United States really mattered on the world scene. In 1945 the Soviet Union, too, was drained by the war but still had a large army and major occupation forces in East Europe. The United States, although it quickly demobilized its armed forces, was the only industrial and nuclear power in the world. Europe was prostrate; the necessities of life were in short supply. In France and Italy, large, armed Communist parties threatened to take over. As the Soviets consolidated their hold on East Europe, fear rippled through West Europe that they would be next.

North Atlantic Treaty   The 1949 treaty of alliance that formed NATO.

In a major civil war, Greece tottered on the edge of Communist take-over. Moscow issued tough demands on Turkey, including control of the strategic Turkish Straits.

It was a turning point in U.S. foreign policy. Only ten years earlier, the United States had been isolationist toward Europe. By the spring of 1947, Washington had decided that we had to be deeply involved in Europe. As we considered in Chapter 3, Washington simultaneously produced the Truman Doctrine, the Marshall Plan, and Kennan's "X" article, which defined, respectively, the U.S. military, economic, and theoretical positions in the Cold War.

Two years later, in 1949, the **North Atlantic Treaty** for the first time committed the United States to the defense of foreign lands. NATO was more than a treaty. Its strength was its integrated command structure. Member countries would not decide on their own what to do in the event of attack. At its Paris headquarters, officers from all the member countries devised a joint, coordinated strategy. The top NATO commander—historically an American, although nothing in the treaty requires it—would be able to give orders to the forces of many countries.

NATO worked best when the Europeans were genuinely scared, as in the early 1950s when the North Korean invasion of South Korea suggested Stalin intended to do the same to West Europe. General Dwight D. Eisenhower was NATO supreme commander at this time, and, as skilled a diplomat as he was a soldier, he built the integration of NATO member forces. With Stalin's death in 1953, however, some of the fear that fed NATO subsided. His successors, starting with the flamboyant Khrushchev, launched several "peace offensives" to lull West Europeans into complacency, break up NATO, and reduce the military preparedness of its European members, who never spent much on defense. The crushing of Hungary in 1956 and the Berlin Wall in 1961 reminded Europeans that they still needed a U.S. presence, which Washington was glad to provide. America spent more on the defense of Europe than Europeans did, an inherently unbalanced relationship that had to end. With U.S. protection, Europeans turned their attention to the unification of their continent.

EUROPE GROPES FOR UNITY

Staggering out of the rubble of World War II, most thinking West Europeans understood that they had to overcome their traditional national barriers in order both to avoid future conflicts and to achieve economic growth. The U.S. model was often mentioned: a continental federation with

Who Joined NATO When (Total of 28 Members)

1949	Twelve original signers of the North Atlantic Treaty—the United States, Canada, Britain, France, Iceland, Portugal, Belgium, the Netherlands, Luxembourg, Italy, Denmark, and Norway
1952	Greece and Turkey
1954	West Germany (since 1990 all of Germany)
1982	Spain
1999	Poland, the Czech Republic, and Hungary
2004	Lithuania, Latvia, Estonia, Slovakia, Slovenia, Bulgaria, Romania
2009	Albania and Croatia

free movement of goods and people. Europe, chopped into many countries, each defending its anachronistic economic sovereignty, stunted the continent's political and military capacity to look after itself. Washington understood this early; one of the provisions of the Marshall Plan was for joint European economic planning.

Common Market Early and informal name for European Economic Community, now EU.

tariff Tax on imports.

Economic integration, planned by France's Jean Monnet and Robert Schuman, was to be the engine of European unity. With the 1951 Paris Treaty, they forged the European Coal and Steel Community (ECSC) whereby all the member states—France, West Germany, Italy, Belgium, the Netherlands, and Luxembourg—agreed to pool their coal and steel resources by eliminating tariffs, quotas, and other restrictive practices. The ECSC worked and helped propel West Europe out of its postwar slump.

The next step was more ambitious. The same six countries in the 1957 Treaty of Rome expanded the ECSC concept to include all economic sectors, including labor, hence the name **Common Market**. Members agreed to cut their many **tariffs** with each other by 10 percent a year until they reached zero and to build up a common tariff toward the rest of the world. Workers from one member country could take jobs in another without work permits. With their economies interlocked like those of U.S. states, West Europe moved to an "ever closer union."

The EU was a resounding economic success. Instead of hunkering behind their protectionist walls, European industries had to compete with each other, delivering better products at lower prices. Labor-surplus countries sent their workers to labor-short countries. Standards of living rose dramatically until they now near the U.S. level.

Economics led to integration rather than unification. The economies of Europe's lands meshed, but politics and psychologies lagged behind. A major step forward came with the 2009 ratification of the Lisbon Treaty, which gave the EU something resembling a constitution. In 2005 referendums, the French and Dutch shot down the first EU constitution, which required approval by all members. In 2008, Irish voters did the same but reversed themselves in 2009.

CLASSIC THOUGHT ■ NOW MAKE EUROPEANS

One of Italy's unifiers in the late nineteenth century reflected, "Having made Italy, we must now make Italians." He meant that Italy, unified from the top down, lacked enthusiastic citizens who thought of themselves as Italians rather than as Venetians, Tuscans, or Sicilians. The same applies to Europe now. Europe exists as a set of bureaucratic institutions but not in the hearts of Europeans, who still think of themselves as French, German, or Italian.

Said French Premier Lionel Jospin in 2001: "I want a Europe, but I remain attached to my own nation." Most Europeans still think that way. Zbigniew Brzezinski, a political scientist and President Carter's national security advisor, wisecracked in 2000 that "no 'European' is willing to die for 'Europe.'" (Actually, that was not completely true; dozens of European soldiers—with Spain in the lead—died for Europe in Bosnia.)

Constructing a European patriotism is much harder than setting up complex institutions few understand. Most Europeans go along with the EU but without passion: Okay, if it's a good economic deal. Americans love the United States; Europeans do not love Europe. Building patriotism can take centuries and is helped by facing common threats and problems. We could see a unified Europe before we see "Europeans."

German Chancellor Angela Merkel confers with French President Nicholas Sarkozy. The two clashed on policy and personality. (Georges Gobet/Getty)

Sovereignty, invented in Europe, blocks European unification. Sovereignty's chief—but not only—proponent was Charles de Gaulle of France, who was always a fierce French nationalist. He didn't much like NATO (for its American leadership) or the Common Market (for trying to submerge French sovereignty). He called for a *Europe des patries*, a Europe of fatherlands, countries preserving their traditional powers and distinctiveness, with, of course, France in the lead. De Gaulle also built his version of Europe when he ordered U.S. troops in France and NATO headquarters out of the country in 1966. He withdrew France from the integrated military structure that gave NATO much of its strength. France was still a member of NATO but for

GEOGRAPHY ■ GROWTH OF THE COMMON MARKET

The original six signers of the 1957 Treaty of Rome that created the Common Market, or, as it liked to be called, the European Economic Community (EEC), were France, West Germany, Italy, Belgium, the Netherlands, and Luxembourg. Interestingly, this "Europe of the Six" coincided closely with Charlemagne's original European empire founded in 800, the Holy Roman Empire.

Britain at first chose not to join, preferring its Commonwealth and U.S. connections. The Common Market worked so well, however, that by the early 1960s London decided to apply. This time, in 1963, President de Gaulle of France uttered his famous *Non!* to British entry, arguing that the British were not wholehearted Europeans (he was right). After de Gaulle left office in 1969, negotiations resumed, and in 1973 the Six became the Nine with the addition of Britain, Denmark, and Ireland. Norway was also about to join, but in a referendum most Norwegians voted to keep their sovereignty and oil and fishing rights to themselves.

Greece joined in 1981 and Spain and Portugal in 1986, making an even 12 in what, since 1993, calls itself the European Union. At the start of 1995, Finland, Sweden, and Austria entered the EU. Norwegians again

rejected joining. The East European lands were eager to join but first had to prove they were democracies with market economies. In 2004, after six years of complex negotiations, ten more, mostly ex-Communist countries in Central Europe, joined: Poland, Hungary, Czech Republic, Slovakia, Slovenia (remember, they are not the same), Lithuania, Latvia, Estonia, Malta, and Cyprus. Romania and Bulgaria joined in 2007, making an EU of 27 members. The economic advantages of the EU persuade most European countries to join. Only Norway and Switzerland resist. Turkey has wanted in for years, but Brussels, fearing Turkey is too Middle Eastern and Muslim to be European, has gone very slowly in considering its application.

The EU is not yet a federation like the United States—it is a kind of **confederation**—but it is a single economy, one with a GDP of $14.5 trillion and a combined population of 491 million. The United States has about the same GDP but only 309 million people, so its per capita GDP is higher than Europe's. In 2009, the EU got suddenly richer, but only because the U.S. dollar declined sharply against the euro. Exchange rates change rapidly.

43 years was not integrated into its command structure at its current headquarters near Brussels. In 2009, French President Nicolas Sarkozy put France back into the NATO command. Sarkozy, unlike de Gaulle, was rather pro-American and saw that France could have more influence as a full NATO participant.

confederation Political union looser than a federation.

technocrat Unelected governing official, usually a finance expert.

Like de Gaulle, many Europeans want the EU's economic advantages without losing any of their countries' sovereign political rights. The 1991 Maastricht agreement, for example, aimed for deeper European integration, but some Europeans balked. Their concerns are not trivial. The mammoth 2007 Lisbon Treaty, a sort of constitution, is a completely elite project with no popular input. A united Europe would mean each country giving up much of its sovereignty to distant bureaucrats in Brussels. Polish workers could take jobs in the Netherlands.

A major concern is the top-down, undemocratic EU structure. Europeans rightly complain of a "democratic deficit." The EU is run by remote bureaucrats and **technocrats**, who amass such a complex rulebook (the 90,000 pages of the *acquis communitaire*) that they bore Europeans into obedience. The most important body, the European Commission, both runs the EU's civil service and makes policy. Each member appoints one commissioner; no one elects them, and they became tarnished with fraud and mismanagement. The only elected body—and fewer than half of Europeans bother to vote for it—is the 785-member European Parliament, with limited and uncertain powers.

EUROPE ON ITS OWN?

During the Cold War, America with its big military budget and nuclear weapons defended West Europe. The Soviets kept many divisions ready to strike into West Germany. NATO forces, even with 300,000 Americans in Europe, were not enough. To deter a possible Soviet attack, the United States in the 1960s kept some 7,000 relatively small tactical nuclear weapons—"tac nukes"—in West Europe, now reduced to zero.

Did it work? Sure, say its proponents; there was no Soviet invasion. In logic it's hard to prove why something *didn't* happen. More important was the psychological element to U.S. forces and nukes in Europe: to buck up our European allies as they recovered their political, economic, and military strength, which they did by the 1960s. As Europe got stronger, though, it started talking back

GEOGRAPHY ■ FOUR STAGES OF INTEGRATION

Integration reaches different levels or stages. The lowest is the *free trade area*, where countries simply end their tariff barriers against each other. Example: the North American Free Trade Agreement (NAFTA).

A step higher is the *customs union*, where countries both lower their tariffs to each other and build a common tariff toward the outside world. Example: the *Zollverein* that helped Bismarck unify Germany. Some think NAFTA (see Chapter 18) could move to this level.

Another step up is a *common market*, which does all the above until barriers are zero, even to labor, and takes on some regulatory functions. Example: the original EEC.

The highest stage of integration is the *economic union*, essentially one big economy, with common currency and a quasi-federal structure. Example: the EU, which, if it keeps going, could turn into a federation, what some Europeans urge.

ECONOMICS ■ TROUBLE IN EUROLAND

The **fiscal** imbalances of several European countries in 2010 made some question the future of the **euro**, which was barely ten years old and a major step in European unification. The euro (symbol: €) was adopted by 12 EU countries at the beginning of 1999; now 17 countries use it (Britain, Denmark, and Sweden stand outside the eurozone). The euro has already become a **reserve currency** but much less important than the U.S. dollar. As the dollar grew shaky (see Chapter 18), more trade deals were written in euros.

Before the euro, European countries had to use either their own currencies or **eurodollars** for trade with their neighbors. This meant *transaction costs* of several percent whenever you had to change currencies. Furthermore, eurodollars meant depending on U.S. economic policy, which pushes the dollar up or down with Europe having no voice. And European politicians wanted to have a strong, respected currency of their own. Some problems, dimly perceived at first, came with the euro: Member states cannot set their own interest rates or currencies' values, important elements of sovereignty that they have surrendered.

At Maastricht in the Netherlands in 1991, EU members set up the Economic and Monetary Union (**EMU**) to start the new euro in 1999, supervised by a new European Central Bank (**ECB**) in Frankfurt (equivalent to the U.S. Federal Reserve). At first the euro was used just for accounting and credit cards, but at the beginning of 2002 actual coins and bills replaced older currencies. After initial grumbling, most citizens of Euroland got used to the euro and even like it. Tourists especially like it, as they do not have to change money so often.

Did the euro work? Initially valued at $1.17, it fell to 85 cents in 2001, but as the dollar weakened in response to a massive U.S. budget deficit, the euro climbed to $1.55 in 2008. A "strong" currency is not necessarily good, as it makes it harder for you to export. Worth around $1.30 in 2011, the stronger euro hindered Europe's recovery from the long 2008–2010 slump, and Europeans, like Americans, complained bitterly that China's yuan, which was pegged to the dollar, was way too low.

The euro was not as stable as planned. On paper, the EMU limits a member's fiscal *deficit* (see page 99) to 3 percent of GDP, but, under pressure from unemployment and welfare payouts, virtually all members soon fudged, and the ECB was unable to crack down. Four members' deficits grew especially high—Portugal, Ireland, Greece, and Spain (conveniently dubbed the "PIGS"). When Greece in early 2010 revealed it was running a 12 percent deficit and a national debt bigger than its GDP, it triggered a **sovereign debt crisis**, and Europe-wide panic set in. If Greece **defaulted** it could bring down the whole euro. German Chancellor Angela Merkel warned: "If the euro fails, then Europe fails." Pre-euro, badly indebted countries could **devalue** their currencies; the Greek drachma, for example, would decline in value with little impact on the rest of Europe. But now euro users can no longer individually devalue.

Europe divided over what to do. France wanted stimulus spending to reduce unemployment; Germany wanted *austerity* (see page 289) and deficit reduction to fight inflation. EMU rules forbid **bailouts**, but to save the euro the stronger members put together a €750 ($1,040) billion loan package for the weakest members but made them practice tough austerity. Greeks rioted; Irish and Spaniards sucked it up.

The most bailout money came from Germany, whose taxpayers fumed in resentment, rather like 2010 U.S. Tea Partiers. Some said Germany should drop out of the eurozone and go back to the trusty Deutschmark; others said the PIGS should be kicked out of the eurozone. Calmer economists argue for strengthening the ECB so it can regulate member countries' fiscal balances. That would be a major surrender of member countries' sovereignty. European economists point out that U.S. states cannot run deficits (although California was likened to Greece). The 2010 crisis confronted the EU with a sharp choice: Either move to much deeper union—including an EU treasury ministry that overrides member states' treasuries—or risk falling apart.

to its U.S. big brother. De Gaulle (see previous discussion) withdrew France from NATO's integrated command and built France's own nuclear force. Europe should not rely on the Americans, preached de Gaulle. In 1961, the East German regime built the Berlin Wall, and the Americans made no move to pull it down. West Germans felt let down at the U.S. lack of firmness. Many Europeans began to think de Gaulle might be right.

In the 1970s, the Soviets placed new missiles in East Europe, able to reach anywhere in West Europe. Moderate Europeans worried that the United States would not do enough to counteract the new Soviet threat, whereas radicals and pacifists were afraid the United States was too eager to challenge the Soviets, that U.S. impetuosity, especially under President Reagan, might lead to nuclear war. West European peace movements grew, complaining of "incineration without representation."

The Cold War ended before conflicts within NATO could pull the alliance apart. But now many Europeans and Americans wonder if NATO can or should continue as before. U.S. troop strength in Europe is now a small fraction of what it was and has no clear purpose. We may celebrate NATO's successes—it kept the Soviets at bay, supported European recovery and integration, and established German democracy—but now ask what it is to do. NATO members participate—on a voluntary basis—in out-of-area peacekeeping in Bosnia, Kosovo, and Afghanistan. Some say such missions will give NATO a new reason for being.

Europe, under tight budgetary constraints, is shrinking its armed forces and not modernizing them. By law, some 70 percent of Europe's soldiers cannot serve outside their national territories. The EU's new Eurocorps faces the same problem that has dogged European unity: Who is going to be in charge of it? Twenty-seven countries? Washington did not favor a separate EU force, fearing it would splinter NATO, duplicate effort, and still leave Europe weak. NATO works, said Washington; keep it unchanged.

Considering the resentment that has been building in Europe, Washington might let Europe find out what it can—and cannot—do for itself. Some argue it would be better if they came to us seeking help rather than us hectoring them. We might tell the Europeans, "Go ahead and handle your own security." If they can, so much the better. That will mean that the great postwar U.S. project of making Europe whole and free has succeeded. And if they cannot, they will have to accept U.S. leadership again. It was, after all, not the worst thing that's ever happened to Europe.

fiscal   Balance between taxes and government spending.

euro   Common EU currency; €1 = approximately $1.30 in 2011.

reserve currency   Stable, trusted money of a major country that is used for international trade.

eurodollars   U.S. dollars circulating in Europe.

EMU   Economic and Monetary Union devised at Maastricht in 1991; set up new *euro* currency.

ECB   European Central Bank, the EU's Fed.

sovereign debt crisis   A national government owes so much that it could *default*.

default   Country announces it cannot repay its debts.

devalue   Currency's worth declines in relation to other currencies. (Opposite: *revalue*.)

bailout   Emergency loan to a country or company in difficulty.

quota   Numerical limit on imports.

subsidy   Government payment to prop up an industry.

THE CHALLENGE OF TRADE BLOCS

The United States and the EU quarrel bitterly over trade issues. Europe keeps out several U.S. products by means of tariffs, **quotas**, and **subsidies** designed to protect European farms and industries. Europe sees protection of jobs as its number-one duty. Europe—like Japan—comes

trade blocs   Geographic regions that trade mostly among themselves and keep out non-bloc goods.

comparative advantage   Theory that countries should make only what they can produce efficiently and trade for other products.

up with all manner of excuses to keep out U.S. products, such as claiming hormone-fed beef or genetically modified grain is dangerous. We even disputed whether bananas produced in former French West Africa should get a tariff preference over Central American bananas. The WTO (see Chapter 18) sometimes rules against the EU, and in retaliation Washington slaps high tariffs on certain European products. The disputes do not subside.

The EU's Common Agricultural Policy (CAP) eats nearly half of the EU budget with the biggest chunk going to France. The EU protects its 18 million farmers (far too many) by providing a third of their income in the form of subsidies. The United States helps its 3.4 million farmers (still too many) by providing 15 percent of their income in the form of subsidies. Japan is far worse than Europe; it provides farmers with 55 percent of their income. Australia and New Zealand subsidize farmers very little, resulting in the most efficient farms in the world. But tell a Brussels Eurocrat that Europe has three times as many farmers as it needs; he will shrug and say, "But they get angry and vote when their livelihood is at stake. So the subsidies must continue." The result has been "mountains of butter and lakes of wine" in European surplus food warehouses, all useless and expensive.

Trade blocs can be terribly selfish. In looking after only the needs of their own producers, they keep out the products of others. The earlier selfishness of the individual nation-state just expands to become the collective selfishness of the trade bloc. France no longer keeps out non-French products; now the EU keeps out non-European products. Some fear a world of three major trading blocs—Europe, the Pacific, and North America—that erect trade walls against the rest of the world. Instead of a prosperity that expands until it covers the globe, closed-off trade blocs could lead to escalating rounds of retaliation that leave everyone poorer and angrier. Hitler, at the height of his conquests, dared the United States to invade his "Fortress Europe," implying a sealed-off empire. Could it indeed become such?

The brighter side is that trade blocs may be just temporary as the world progresses from one-country markets to a global market. Blocs may serve their purpose and fade. A trade bloc can be

CLASSIC THOUGHT ■ COMPARATIVE ADVANTAGE

Any product should be produced where it is most advantageous, argued English economist David Ricardo two centuries ago. If Spain grows the best oranges most cheaply—because of climate, soil, and workforce—then it has a **comparative advantage** over England in growing oranges. Spain should concentrate on growing oranges. If England, on the other hand, makes the best cloth most cheaply, then that is its comparative advantage, and it should concentrate on that. Then the two countries trade, Spanish oranges for English cloth, and this maximizes everyone's gain because oranges and cloth are being produced where it is most efficient to do so.

Inefficiency comes when countries, out of an urge to be self-sufficient or protect local producers, try to produce things when they have no comparative advantage, like England growing oranges. How can you tell who has the comparative advantage? Just have free trade with no barriers or subsidies and soon you will see who can produce things best and cheapest. English orange growers will soon go out of business. Americans love this classic argument when it comes to explaining why Japanese should buy U.S. citrus and why Europeans should buy U.S. beef. We do not like it when it explains why Americans should buy Japanese cars.

inward looking (bad) or outward looking (good). If the former, it will lock out foreign competition, damage its own citizens' prosperity, and retard growth worldwide. If the latter, it will be open to foreign competition, help lift up the poorer lands by means of trade, and give its citizens rising living standards. The great task of statecraft in our day lies in keeping trade open. If America does not lead in this task, the world could slide back into protectionism.

ECONOMICS ■ THE RETIRED CONTINENT

The Greek crisis of 2010 forced Europe to look at its fiscal imbalances and conclude that major reforms were overdue. Europe had built itself into an economic box, a series of interlocking problems that are hard to escape and sap the continent of its vitality and ability to play a major world role. Most European countries have the following problems:

1. A large welfare state—the "Europe that protects"—that provides nearly cradle-to-grave benefits, especially for the unemployed. Many argue that Europe can no longer afford the big welfare state; it will have to be trimmed.

2. High taxes to pay for the welfare state, about 40 percent of GDP in contrast to under 30 percent in the United States, Japan, and Australia.

3. Budget deficits—averaging 7 percent of the eurozone's GDP—to cover the shortfall between welfare expenditures and taxes. (The U.S. deficit was 10 percent.)

4. Slow economic growth, much slower than Asia. (The new eastern EU members grow nicely, thanks to their lower wages.) Europeans get long vacations (often a month) and short work weeks (often 35 hours), so that the average American works 350 hours longer a year.

5. High unemployment from slow economic growth, generous unemployment benefits, and "labor-force rigidities," such as anti-layoff laws and geographic immobility. Americans, who have weaker jobless benefits, are less tolerant of high unemployment and vote against any government that doesn't cure it.

6. An aging population that retires early (some at 50) and requires greater and greater pensions. Europe's extremely low fertility rate of 1.3 does not nearly replace Europeans who die. Soon Europe will lack the work force to pay for retirement benefits, pushing governments deeper into debt. By 2050, the average European is projected to be 52 years old, the average American 35. Glumly, Europeans learned they would have to retire later. Germans already work until 67, the same as Americans. In 2010, many French angrily protested a plan to raise the retirement age from 60 to 62.

7. Protected sectors, especially agriculture, that keep out foreign competition to try to hold down unemployment. This has made some sectors of the European economy inefficient.

8. A pacifist mentality. Europeans just don't want war and doubt that any war is justified. Some NATO members send a few forces for peacekeeping but avoid fighting. European opinion massively opposed the 2003 Iraq War.

These factors tend to make Europe preoccupied with domestic affairs and little interested in playing roles elsewhere, in the Balkans or Middle East. European concentration on how to pay for the welfare state also deepens frictions and disagreements with the Americans, who have a more open and flexible economy. The United States and Europe likely will remain on good terms but not true partners.

my**poliscikit** EXERCISES

Apply what you learned in this chapter on MyPoliSciKit (www.mypoliscikit.com).

Assessment   Review this chapter using learning objectives, chapter summaries, practice tests, and more.

Menu

Flashcards   Learn the key terms in this chapter; you can test yourself by term or definition.

Flashcards

Video   Analyze recent world affairs by watching streaming video from major news providers.

Videos

Simulations   Play the role of an IR decision-maker and experience how IR concepts work in

Comparative practice.
Exercises

KEY TERMS

bailout (p. 265)
Common Market (p. 261)
comparative advantage (p. 266)
confederation (p. 263)
default (p. 265)
devalue (p. 265)
ECB (p. 265)
EMU (p. 265)

euro (p. 265)
eurodollars (p. 265)
European Union (EU) (p. 256)
fiscal (p. 265)
IFOR (p. 257)
KFOR (p. 258)
North Atlantic Treaty (p. 260)
quota (p. 265)

reserve currency (p. 265)
soft power (p. 256)
sovereign debt crisis (p. 265)
subsidy (p. 265)
tariff (p. 261)
technocrat (p. 263)
trade bloc (p. 266)
UNPROFOR (p. 257)

FURTHER REFERENCE

Anderson, Perry. *The New Old World*. London: Verso, 2009.

Aybet, Gülnur, and Rebecca R. Moore, eds. *NATO in Search of a Vision*. Washington, DC: Georgetown University Press, 2010.

Benjamin, Daniel, ed. *Europe 2030*. Washington, DC: Brookings, 2010.

Cafruny, Alan W., and J. Magnus Ryner. *Europe at Bay: In the Shadow of U.S. Hegemony*. Boulder, CO: Lynne Rienner, 2007.

Caldwell, Christopher. *Reflections on the Revolution in Europe: Immigration, Islam and the West*. New York: Doubleday, 2009.

Checkel, Jeffrey T., and Peter J. Katzenstein, eds. *European Identity*. New York: Cambridge University Press, 2009.

Dinan, Desmond. *Origins and Evolution of the European Union*. New York: Oxford University Press, 2006.

Giddens, Anthony. *Europe in the Global Age*. London: Polity, 2007.

Judt, Tony. *Postwar: A History of Europe Since 1945*. New York: Penguin, 2005.

Kopstein, Jeffrey, and Sven Sgeinmo, eds. *Growing Apart? America and Europe in the Twenty-First Century*. New York: Cambridge University Press, 2007.

Lundestad, Geir, ed. *Just Another Major Crisis? The United States and Europe Since 2000*. New York: Oxford University Press, 2008.

Mak, Geert. *In Europe: Travels Through the Twentieth Century*. New York: Pantheon, 2007.

Markovits, Andrei S. *Uncouth Nation: Why Europe Dislikes America*. Princeton, NJ: Princeton University Press, 2007.

McCormick, John. *The European Superpower*. New York: Palgrave, 2007.

Menon, Rajan. *The End of Alliances*. New York: Oxford University Press, 2008.

Moore, Rebecca R. *NATO's New Mission: Projecting Stability in a Post–Cold War World*. Westport, CT: Praeger, 2007.

Piris, Jean-Claude. *The Lisbon Treaty: A Legal and Political Analysis*. New York: Cambridge University Press, 2010.

Schnabel, Rockwell A. *The Next Superpower? The Rise of Europe and Its Challenge to the United States*. Lanham, MD: Rowman & Littlefield, 2007.

Serfaty, Simon. *The Vital Partnership: Power and Order; America and Europe Beyond Iraq*. Lanham, MD: Rowman & Littlefield, 2007.

Sheehan, James J. *Where Have All the Soldiers Gone? The Transformation of Modern Europe*. Boston: Houghton Mifflin, 2008.

Thies, Wallace J. *Why NATO Endures*. New York: Cambridge University Press, 2009.

Tiersky, Ronald. *European Foreign Policies: Does Europe Still Matter?* Lanham, MD: Rowman & Littlefield, 2010.

Toje, Asle. *The European Union as a Small Power: After the Post-Cold War*. New York: Palgrave, 2010.

CHAPTER 17

Asia Awakes

Mainland Chinese workers assemble computer boards in a Taiwan-owned factory, an example of the foreign direct investment that sky-rocketed China's economy. Labor unrest in such factories in 2010 brought higher wages. (Imagine China/AP Photos)

"Let China sleep," warned Napoleon, "for when she wakes, she will shake the world." Napoleon's prediction is now coming true. The 2008–2009 recession confirmed a trend underway for years: the shift of economic power from West to East. The West—especially the United States—looked economically incompetent. Great U.S. financial institutions gambled away billions in risky deals. Western economies suffered the biggest recession since the 1930s.

Most of Asia, on the other hand, suffered little and recovered quickly. China, with money to spare, continued to grow, thanks to massive stimulus packages for construction and infrastructure projects. In 2009, China passed Germany as the world's biggest exporter. By 2010, China eclipsed stagnant Japan to become the world's second-largest economy. China is now the world's biggest energy consumer and locks in huge deals for Latin American, African, Persian Gulf, and Central Asian oil, natural gas, and raw materials. China holds a world-record $2.8 trillion in foreign-currency reserves, two-thirds of it in dollars, and much of that in U.S. Treasury debt.

This creditor position gives Beijing political clout. Growing economies with massive surpluses gain power and prestige. Battered, indebted economies lose power and prestige. All countries, including the United States, now speak respectfully to China, and Beijing speaks assertively to other powers. Some admired China as a new and effective system that boosted economic growth without disruption or democracy (see box on page 274). China celebrated the 2008 Olympics, the 2010 Shanghai Expo, and earth-orbiting space launches. Beijing's motive in all this is to show both its own citizens and the world that China is again a great nation—as it was for most of history—and Asia's leading power, its "Middle Kingdom" (*Zhōngguó*), and the second power globally (after the United States).

Beijing's basic policies, both domestic and foreign, are not hard to discern: Nothing gets in the way of China's stable economic growth. Nothing. To complaints of undervalued currency, Beijing replies that it keeps China's economy growing. As for China's environmental degradation, Beijing notes that smokestacks mean industry. As for dealing with unsavory regimes, Beijing claims it does not interfere in other countries' human rights questions but needs their resources to keep growing. Nuclear proliferation? China is reluctant to apply UN sanctions on Iran because China gets much oil from Iran and invests a lot in its energy industries. To calls for democracy, Beijing argues

QUESTIONS TO CONSIDER

1. Is China "rising peacefully"? Or are tensions appearing?
2. Who owns the China Seas? Based on what?
3. Why has East Asia become the center of economic growth?
4. Can China's rapid economic growth continue and serve as a model for others?
5. How have the United States and East Asian countries historically misunderstood each other?
6. Is Taiwan a separate country from China? Should it be?
7. How did Japan handle Western penetration?
8. Was the U.S.–Japanese war inevitable? What steps led to it?
9. What explains Japan's economic growth and later stagnation?
10. Long term, is the Middle East or East Asia our biggest problem?

Shanghai, center of China's rapid growth, has twice as many skyscrapers—most of them new—as New York. (Chang W. Lee/*The New York Times*)

that it is messy and disrupts growth. When an imprisoned Chinese dissident won the 2010 Nobel Peace Prize, an angry Beijing denounced it as outside interference.

China's growth-first policy makes it somewhat predictable, at least in the short term. As long as China keeps growing rapidly, it would be unlikely to endanger that growth by invading Taiwan or starting a trade war with America. But if China's growth is thwarted, say, by a global downturn, protectionism, or disruption of oil supplies, China could turn aggressive and let its military dominate policy, as Japan did in the 1930s. China's military enjoys a growing budget, but so far Beijing's civilian chiefs keep the army on a leash. China's claim to all its nearby seas and support for bellicose North Korea could heighten tension and lead to the formation of an anti-China coalition. Much can go wrong in East Asia, which in the long term could be more dangerous than the Middle East.

Beijing claims its is a "peaceful rise" without wars (see page 204). China's President Hu Jintao in 2005 called for a "harmonious world" where all live in peace. That has not always been the case with China. At one time or another, Communist China has had hostile relations with most of its 15 immediate neighbors. It has fought India, the Soviet Union, Vietnam, and the United States in Korea. As China gets richer it becomes more assertive. Neighboring countries fear China dominating the region. Many countries perceive China as an unfair trade competitor that keeps its currency too cheap. Beijing warns other countries to not sell arms to Taiwan or receive the Dalai Lama. An assertive China is flexing its newly acquired economic, diplomatic, and even military muscles.

China, which has become the "factory of the world," demands and gets respect. Beijing reckons that its "Century of Humiliation" began with defeat in the 1839–1842 Opium War, which Britain fought to sell opium in China, where it was illegal. Superior European firepower turned China into a semicolony. Then in the 1930s Japan began the conquest of China. Understandably, China's defeats and humiliations created nationalist rage, which Beijing now turns up and down as suits it. Resident observers say average Chinese are more nationalistic than the regime, which sometimes has to restrain mass anger at foreign powers. Almost everything China does, from rapid economic growth to nuclear weapons (see Chapter 14) to spacecraft, is an expression of China's deep but wounded sense of nationalism. As Mao Zedong said as he took power in 1949: "Our nation will never again be an insulted nation. We have stood up."

Should China's quest for power and prestige bother us? (What, by the way, does America strive for?) The answer depends on what kind of China will emerge. If China is moving to democracy, great. But China could become rich but not free, a one-party Communist system with aggressive and expansionist designs on the

East Asia

region. Every decade or two, our picture of China alternates. One year we note that China is friendly and cooperative and has adopted pragmatic domestic and foreign policies. A few years later we notice that China uses sweatshop labor, abuses human rights, crushes protests, and claims vast areas of sea.

Modernization theory (see page 181) suggests that a richer China—and it has been growing at around 10 percent a year for decades—will create a large, educated middle class, which will push for

totalitarian Dictatorship that attempts total control.

authoritarian Dictatorial regime but milder than totalitarian.

Standing Committee Top governing body of China's Communist Party.

cadres (from the French "framework"; Chinese *gànbu*) Asian Communist Party members who serve as officials.

Zhongnanhai Beijing center of China's top government offices.

democracy. This is what happened in South Korea and Taiwan; as they became "middle-income countries" (those with per capita GDPs over $8,000), they moved from dictatorship to democracy. China, which could soon reach $8,000 per cap, will not necessarily follow this pattern. China has a **totalitarian** past; South Korea and Taiwan were **authoritarian**. Many authoritarian systems have reformed themselves into democracies, but no totalitarian system has reformed into a democracy; instead, they have collapsed. China is far bigger (population 1.35 billion) and more complex than those two little countries. China has an historical memory of past greatness and nurtures grievances against the foreign powers it believes kept it down. Chief and permanent culprit in Beijing's eyes is Japan, followed by the United States.

China's Communist leaders like the rapid growth of its supervised market economy but refuse to relinquish one-party rule. They permit no organizations or news media not controlled by the Communist Party. Foreigners are watched, and few Chinese discuss controversial topics—such as democracy, religion, or Taiwan—with them. Dissidents and whistle-blowers—including writers, editors, lawyers, medical doctors, and union organizers—are arrested and sent to prison or to "reeducation through labor" camps. China has thousands of Internet watchers to keep out criticism and messages of freedom and democracy. Internet providers

ECONOMICS ■ CHINA'S NEW MODEL

Since Deng Xiaoping took over in 1978, China has developed a new economic model that is neither communist nor capitalist but something in between, a market economy at the lower levels but state-guided at the top. Some call it "market authoritarianism" or "authoritarian capitalism."

Based on the Chinese propensity to save (in contrast to Americans' love of spending), China has plenty of capital to invest. The parts of the economy that we see—bustling export industries, modern cities, and a rising middle class—look like those of a free-market economy. Behind the scenes, however, the state, guided by the Chinese Communist Party, carefully controls major economic activities—banking, investments, and currency parities.

The Party is controlled by its nine-member **Standing Committee**, all very bright and highly educated (most in engineering), which sets China's economic direction in considerable detail. The Standing Committee, it must be said, generally makes sound economic decisions, which let China brush off the 2008–2009 downturn.

Able young Chinese—including businesspeople—are recruited into the Party by educational, business, and career opportunities. Unlike in Mao's day, the only ideology that matters is China's economic growth. The best **cadres** are promoted to lead cities, provinces, and the nation. At the top, the Standing Committee selects China's president and premier, who serve two five-year terms, preventing both lifetime dictators like Stalin or Mao and succession crises.

China is not a federal system, but administration is decentralized to the provincial and local levels with instructions to do whatever it takes to grow the economy. This opens the door for uneven enforcement of law and vast corruption, which a Party commission attempts to halt but barely slows. Corruption is the system's weakest point and the cause of protests. The **Zhongnanhai** can back down in the face of mass discontent before it threatens the regime. Critical individuals or groups are arrested, but when millions of Chinese complain loudly or ignore the law, the regime bends, passing new laws and punishing crooked officials.

China faces problems that could slow its growth. Banks, under Beijing's orders, made dubious loans that fueled a dangerous housing-price bubble. Chinese workers, fed up with low pay and bad conditions, sometimes strike for hefty wage increases, which push up inflation. The Chinese model is not necessarily as stable and effective as Beijing portrays it.

either censor themselves or get closed down. The Zhongnanhai fears that any easing up could unleash dangerous forces, and they may be correct. Peasant protests over crooked officials could get out of hand. In China's west, Tibet and Xinjiang could try to break away. What keeps most Chinese content is their constantly rising living standards. If that tanked, Beijing fears, mass discontent could surface.

America must take China's need for respect into account. China could become the most important problem of the twenty-first century. If things go well, China could move in an open and democratic direction. If things go badly, China could move in a nationalistic and aggressive direction. We should remember that America's involvement in East Asia has been a history of misperceptions, misunderstandings, and tragedies.

Open Door 1900   U.S. policy of China trade open to all and keeping China intact.

trade deficit   Buying more from other countries than you sell to them.

RMB   *Renminbi*, "people's money," China's currency, also known as *yuan*. In 2011 $1 = RMB 6.7.

A HISTORY OF EXAGGERATIONS

Asia did not ask to be "opened" by the West. It was perfectly content with its traditional civilizations when the first Portuguese navigators, sometimes by gunfire, pushed into India, Indonesia, China, and Japan in the early sixteenth century (see Chapter 6). By the early nineteenth century, extensive U.S. trade developed with China, followed by thousands of American missionaries. But the United States never sought a "sphere of influence" or participated in the imperialist carve-up of the China coast. Because of this, Chinese called Americans their "favorite people," and we were proud of that. At the beginning of the twentieth century, U.S. Secretary of State Hay issued the famous **Open Door** notes, telling all powers to keep trade with China open and to preserve China's territorial and administrative integrity.

We saw ourselves as China's big brother and in 1911 supported the new Republic of China and its Nationalist Party. We especially favored Generalissimo Chiang Kai-shek, who was on the cover of *Time* magazine ten times. (Publisher Henry Luce was born and raised in China of missionary parents.) As Japan invaded China in the 1930s, we immediately sided with China and thus collided with Japan. Pearl Harbor grew out of U.S. support for China.

But after World War II and years of fighting the Nationalists, the Chinese Communists under Mao Zedong won power in 1949 and in late 1950 flung their army against us in Korea. McCarthyism looked for someone to blame (chiefly Democrats) for "who lost China?" China went from little brother to dangerous foe; we fought in Vietnam to halt Chinese Communist expansionism, or so we thought. Washington did nothing official with Beijing until Nixon's 1972 visit. Then suddenly U.S.–China ties warmed as both sides used them as leverage against Moscow. Trade, exchanges, and embassies were established. We had reasonable relations again.

But by the 1990s, things turned sour. In 1989 the regime shot prodemocracy demonstrators around Tiananmen Square and gave long prison terms to critics. The Chinese economy boomed, but China (like Japan) sold a lot more to America than it bought; U.S. **trade deficits** soared. Chinese manufacturers ignored U.S. patents and copyrights. The Chinese **RMB** was pegged too low to the dollar, giving China an export advantage. Chinese Christians and Buddhist sects were harassed. Many Chinese, with regime approval, said they were tired of America telling them what to do.

Beijing and Moscow on occasion have said they stand together against the "world hegemonic power," meaning us. They have held joint military exercises, which looked like practice to invade Taiwan. But a strong China scares a weak Russia. Siberia is depopulating, and China could use its resources and lands, some of which Russia took from China long ago by "unequal treaties." A true Sino–Russian alliance is unlikely.

GEOGRAPHY ■ CHINA'S STORMY SEAS

The China Seas—the South China, East China, and Yellow Seas (see map on page 273)—have become contested areas. China claims a wide expanse of them, even far out from its shores (see page 324 on maritime boundaries), and shows little inclination to compromise.

Attention focuses on the South China Sea because it may have much oil and natural gas, in addition to being the major sea lane for all of East Asia. It lies to the south of China and Taiwan, to the west of the Philippines, to the north of a portion of Malaysia, and to the east of Vietnam. Most ships enter it from the south through the Strait of Malacca, passing Singapore, and from the north through the Taiwan Strait (see box on page 278). Beijing calls the South China Sea a "core interest."

Two uninhabited groups of tiny islands in the South China Sea—the Paracel and Spratly Islands—are especially disputed, and not for their land (many are below water at high tide). Their owner gets a 200-mile exclusive economic zone (EEZ, see page 324) around them with undersea drilling rights. The Paracels, equidistant from Vietnam and China's Hainan Island, are claimed by both. In 1974 *South* Vietnam and China fought briefly over them. Unified Vietnam recently attempted to lease out drilling rights to the Paracels, but China warned it not to. Further south, the Spratlys are similarly contested among China, the Philippines, Indonesia, and Malaysia. China claims it has owned both **archipelagos** for centuries, but others reject the claim since no one has ever lived on them.

North of Taiwan, the East China Sea has what Chinese call the Daioyotai and Japanese the Senkaku Islands, also tiny and uninhabited but near seabed oil. Tokyo claims them as part of their Ryukyu Island chain, Beijing as part of Taiwan Province. Interestingly, Beijing and Taipei agree on this. Chinese trawlers—clearly encouraged by the Chinese navy—assert the right to fish in the Daioyotai, and the Japanese coast guard attempts to chase them off. After one such incident in 2010, China stopped exports to Japan of vital rare earth minerals, of which China has a near monopoly. China used its economic leverage to make Japan back down.

Farther north, in the Yellow Sea between China and Korea, North and South Korea occasionally fight over their undefined maritime boundaries. In 2010, a North Korean torpedo sank a South Korean corvette (see box on page 282), but Beijing refused to condemn Pyongyang and denounced U.S.–South Korean naval exercises in the Yellow Sea, most of which is international waters. China, fearful of renewed war on the Korean Peninsula, both supports and tried to calm North Korea. In effect, China claims the Yellow Sea as a security zone.

Amid growing U.S.–China friction in 2010, U.S. Secretary of State Hillary Clinton told an Asian security forum in Hanoi that peaceful settlement of overlapping claims in the China Seas was a U.S. national interest and urged a *multilateral* conference (see page 305). She did not say the seas themselves were a U.S. national interest, just peaceful settlement of them. Clinton was promoting stability and offering to mediate, but China's foreign minister reacted angrily, claiming Washington was trying to "internationalize" what should be a series of *bilateral* talks. One at a time, of course, China would dominate the little countries and take whatever it wanted.

If the analysis at the start of this chapter is correct, though, Beijing's moves are likely to be subdued, to avoid anything that might hurt economic growth. China does not like the informal anti-China coalition that is slowly forming; it would isolate China strategically. Vietnam now seeks U.S. support to stand up for the rights of small Southeast Asian countries in the South China Sea. Not long ago we defined war against Vietnam as a national interest. Is it now in our national interest to help Vietnam?

One big problem is that Washington has never precisely defined U.S. interests in the China Seas. Clearly, they are not American lakes, but are they entirely Chinese lakes? Some urge a U.S. presence to stabilize the region—not as owner but as balancer. With no one to keep competing claims in check, things could destabilize. Despite shrill public rhetoric, Beijing recognizes that with no U.S. forces in the Taiwan Strait and South Korea, tensions would build and hurt China's economic growth. Our hunch: China will calm its stormy seas.

What does the roller coaster in U.S.–China relations mean? We have almost continually *misperceived* China (see page 201), seeing it as a nation for us to either save or destroy, total friend or total enemy. We exaggerated China's friendship and then, after 1949, exaggerated its enmity. Starting with Nixon, we exaggerated it as a friend again. One exaggeration starting in the nineteenth century is the "China market," millions of customers for U.S. products. In truth, we never sold that much to China (it was too poor to buy much) and for decades did far more trade with Japan. Manufacturing in and selling to China still makes portions of U.S. business and agriculture pro-Chinese.

archipelago	Cluster of islands.

WHICH WAY FOR CHINA?

China was actually easier to handle when it was a straight Communist dictatorship. It was revolutionary but isolated and poor, consumed by its latest self-destructive campaign (Great Leap Forward in the late 1950s, Cultural Revolution in the late 1960s) unleashed by Chairman Mao. We were glad when it came out of its shell under Deng Xiaoping in the late 1970s, but that created a new set of economic and political problems.

China's Special Economic Zones, at first in the south and along the coast (in part, aiming to make Hong Kong easier to swallow), encouraged private enterprise and foreign investment. Taking advantage of China's low wages, Japanese, Taiwanese, and Hong Kong capital poured in and was soon producing textiles, clothing, footwear, and consumer electronics. China, starting in the 1980s, scored the fastest economic growth in history, but it cannot boom forever. As Chinese labor costs

GEOGRAPHY ■ CHINA, INDIA, AND THE INDIAN OCEAN

Separated by the Himalayas, China (population 1.35 billion) and India (1.17 billion) are Asia's great rivals. Both were hostile to market economics, but China began opening up in 1979, using foreign direct investment and cheap labor to grow at an amazing 10 percent a year. India began liberalizing its economy only in 1991 but now shows impressive 8 percent growth. Per capita, Chinese are more than twice as rich as Indians. Their economies are different: China concentrates on manufacturing, India on information technology.

India has been a democracy since independence in 1947; the media are free, and power alternates among parties in competitive elections. Indians are famously argumentative. Currently, the founding Congress Party rules India. China has been an authoritarian system since the Communists won in 1949 and keeps tight control of the media, banking, religion, labor, and criticism. China is a unitary system, India a federal system. Both countries have nuclear bombs.

Geopolitics gives China a strong interest in the Indian Ocean, as it depends on Persian Gulf and African oil shipped across it. Much like Britain's "imperial lifeline" to Asia in the nineteenth century, China now develops a "string of pearls" of safe and friendly ports along its oil lifeline, especially with Sri Lanka. China is also building a major navy with a long reach—a "blue water" or "deep water" fleet. India, seeing itself the Indian Ocean's major power, doesn't like this.

China makes increasingly stiff demands on territories it disputes with India, especially Arunachal Pradesh in the very northeast of India. This is not just a remnant of British colonialist borders, but a potential transportation corridor that could link Western China to the Bay of Bengal. A Chinese pipeline through Burma is already under construction. It will (1) open China's inland provinces, (2) shorten shipping distances, and (3) avoid the dangerous chokepoint of the Strait of Malacca. To promote its interests around the Indian Ocean, China invests and never raises human rights questions. Should Chinese influence in the Indian Ocean bother us?

DIPLOMACY ■ WAR OVER TAIWAN?

Beijing demands reunification of Taiwan with the mainland and swears that if Taipei (Taiwan's capital) declares independence, China will invade and reunite by force. Some see a serious threat from Beijing; others see a bluff. China and Taiwan do a lot of business with each other. A forcible takeover would also create an anti-Chinese coalition among other Asian powers. Taiwan's current president improves ties to Beijing. So, for the time being, China holds back from invading. Will it do so forever?

When the Chinese Communists beat the Nationalists in 1949, Chiang Kai-shek's army retreated to the large island of Taiwan with the promise to return soon to liberate the mainland from the "bandit clique of Mao Zedong." For both Nationalists and Communists, there is only one China, a hallowed point of Chinese political culture.

For all intents and purposes, Taiwan really is a separate country. The Manchu dynasty annexed Taiwan in 1683 to stop piracy and a Dutch takeover. It was run by Japan from 1895 to 1945, and elderly Taiwanese still speak Japanese. Their native dialect is quite distinct from Mandarin, and Taiwanese do not much like mainlanders. When the Nationalists took over after World War II, Taiwanese complaints about the new government led to rioting, which Chiang gunned down. Until recently, no Taiwanese were allowed in Taipei's top ranks; those positions were reserved for mainland Nationalists. Many Taiwanese felt like a colony; some formed the opposition Democratic Progressive Party (DPP).

Taiwan was a military dictatorship until 1987, with only one party, the Nationalists, but vigorous economic growth turned Taiwan into a vibrant democracy. Taiwan-born Lee Teng-hui, a Nationalist, won Taiwan's first free presidential election in 1996. In 2000, Chen Shui-bian of the DPP won the presidency and stressed Taiwan's sovereignty, which angered Beijing. The 2008 election of President Ma Ying-jeou, a Harvard-educated Nationalist, calmed things; Ma dropped mention of Taiwan independence and reached a major trade pact with the mainland.

When the United States, under President Nixon, began a **rapprochement** with Beijing in 1972, some Americans talked about a "two Chinas" policy, that is, recognizing that they are two separate countries. Neither Taipei nor Beijing would hear of it, so the United States shifted its diplomatic recognition from the former to the latter. Informally, U.S.–Taiwan diplomatic relations continue (see Chapter 19).

China's standing offer to Taiwan: Come back to China and you can keep your political and economic system for 50 years. This is called "one country, two systems," by which China regained Hong Kong from Britain in 1997 and Macau from Portugal in 1999. Now both are Special Administrative Regions of China with their own governments, currencies, and border controls but under Beijing's sovereignty and quiet veto. Taiwan resists Beijing's offer but in 2010 signed a major free-trade agreement with the mainland. Beijing's aim is to draw Taiwan ever closer.

Should Washington support Taiwan independence? Would threats to cut off China's U.S. trade work? China could simply withdraw its mammoth financial holdings now in the United States, doing serious harm to the U.S. economy. (At the same time, of course, China would harm its own economy; the two economies are intertwined.) Actually, China would not have to *withdraw* anything but simply stop buying any *more* U.S. Treasury bills. We are in hock to China, and that gives Beijing leverage.

China boosts military spending and has some 2,000 missiles—some of them anti-ship—near the 110-mile (175-kilometer) wide Taiwan Strait. China's nationalistic military itches to retake Taiwan and harasses U.S. ships and planes in the China Seas, in effect warning: "America, keep out of our waters!" U.S. policy for years has been to oppose forcible unification; if it's peaceful, no problem. Washington urges Taipei to pipe down about sovereignty or independence and preserve Taiwan's strange status—a country that is legally not a country. As you review the tragedy of U.S.–Japan relations in the last century, ask if the same could happen between us and China. Would the United States really fight for Taiwan?

grow, manufacturing shifts to cheaper Asian lands, such as Vietnam and Indonesia. Massive environmental damage is choking off (literally) China's economic growth.

rapprochement French for "approaching"; two countries drawing diplomatically closer to each other.

The political problem is that China is still governed by a Party elite reluctant to admit that the whole Maoist enterprise—including the death of as many as 50 million of their own citizens—was a mistake. Starting in 1979, Beijing's rulers liberalized China's economy but not its political system, which they still tightly control. Can that last? Or do market economies create pressures for democracy, as they did in Taiwan?

With communism now meaningless, Beijing wins legitimacy by providing higher and higher living standards, especially for the new middle class of businesspeople and urban professionals. China has lifted perhaps half a billion citizens out of poverty. It also deflects citizen discontent into China's very strong nationalism by calling Japan unrepentant and the United States a bully and by staking out territorial claims far into the South and East China Seas. Possible undersea natural gas fields around the Paracel, Spratly, and Senkaku Islands brought China into disputes with Vietnam, Indonesia, the Philippines, Malaysia, Brunei, and Japan. (See map on page 273.) Beijing is uninterested in settling these disputes except on China's terms.

JAPAN ENCOUNTERS THE WEST

The reasons for Japan's success are many. Geography and history helped. The island archipelago was close enough to China to adopt much Chinese culture but sufficiently distant to resist invasion. Two invasion attempts by the Mongol emperor of China, Kublai Khan, in 1274 and 1281, had Japan petrified with fear until a "divine wind" (in Japanese, *kamikaze*) wrecked the invasion fleets. With few natural resources, Japan had to rely on human resources of thrift and cleverness.

Unlike China, Japan did not unify early into a bureaucratic empire but stayed feudal for centuries, until one clan conquered the island chain and founded the Tokugawa Shogunate by 1600. An emperor, virtually a prisoner of the court, served as a symbolic descendant of the sun goddess. Real power was in the hands of a *shogun*, a military chief who ruled by police and by carefully balancing the powers of lesser lords. By the nineteenth century, Japan was a prosperous, highly developed feudal system—with power dispersed among many groups, each with right of veto, and insufficient central authority.

Some thinkers argue that feudalism was so deeply ingrained in Japanese culture that Japan has never come out of it and remains feudal. Tokyo lacks the central authority we take for granted in other modern countries. This is what makes Japanese government so difficult to deal with. Japan's leaders seem to promise one thing, but back home they knuckle under to domestic economic interests. It also means that Tokyo has great difficulty in reforming Japan's ailing financial system.

The arrival of the first Westerners—daring Portuguese navigators in 1542—confused the Japanese. Some traded with the Europeans, and hundreds of thousands embraced the Catholic faith brought to Japan by Jesuits. Others feared the dynamic outside influence would wreck Japan's delicate balance. In 1622 the Tokugawa shogun had the Westerners expelled and Japanese Catholics butchered. Then he firmly closed the door to outsiders; there was little trade or contact for over two centuries.

As the China trade grew, however, the West grew curious and annoyed about Japan. In 1853, the Americans made the opening move as Commodore Perry's black, fire-belching ships entered Tokyo Bay. The worried Japanese officials asked Perry to return next year for their answer. It was no longer possible to keep the foreigners out, so Japan in 1854 exchanged diplomatic recognition with the United States.

What followed was amazing. Officials saw that Japan had to modernize quickly or be taken over, as China was. In 1868, upon the accession of the new Emperor Meiji, vigorous samurai clans

Meiji　Japan's period of rapid modernization starting in 1868.

Manchukuo　Japanese puppet state in Manchuria, 1931–1945.

nonrecognition　Refusal to grant diplomatic recognition.

pushed through a series of reforms called the **Meiji** Restoration, which modernized everything from government and industry through education and clothing. Under the slogan "Rich nation, strong army!" Japan went from the crafts age to the industrial age in one generation. In 1895, Japan beat China, a decade later Russia.

THE ROAD TO PEARL HARBOR AND HIROSHIMA

Economics played a major role in the march to war. Japan depended—as it does today—on exports. Japanese goods, especially textiles, flooded the American market until they were limited by quotas. Japanese felt they were unfairly treated, and this played into the hands of militarists who argued that only imperial possessions could give Japan the economic growing room it needed. As the world economic depression deepened in the 1930s, everyone locked out foreign goods, hurting Japan even more (see Chapter 18). Japan also resented U.S. laws in the early 1900s against Asian immigrants. In California, local laws discriminated against Japanese (and Chinese), and Tokyo felt insulted. Domestic matters have international repercussions.

Like newly unified Germany, Japan began to demand its "place in the sun." If the Europeans could grab colonies, why couldn't Japan? Japanese democrats tried to transplant Britain's constitutional monarchy—with a parliament and cabinet—but they were soon subverted by Japanese ways, a pattern also seen later. The Japanese armed forces were hotbeds of militant nationalism that demanded imperial expansion. They knew this would mean eventual collision with the United States and started quietly thinking about it after World War I. When U.S. Colonel Billy Mitchell demonstrated that airplanes could sink ships in 1926, the Japanese military delegation paid special attention.

The Japanese army in southern Manchuria—there since victory over the Russians—decided on its own to seize all of Manchuria in 1931. They staged a fake bombing and then "punished" the Chinese. Tokyo politicians who opposed this were assassinated. Japan set up the puppet state of **Manchukuo**, but U.S. Secretary of State Henry Stimson did not recognize it. Stimson's **nonrecognition** doctrine showed our indignation in a verbal rather than military way, which Tokyo didn't take seriously. As Stimson recalled later, the Japanese bomb at the Mukden (now Shenyang) railroad tracks in 1931 led straight to Pearl Harbor in 1941 and Hiroshima in 1945. By the mid-1930s, the military owned the Japanese government. In 1937, Japan began the slow conquest of China and was still at it when Tokyo surrendered in 1945. The United States denounced every Japanese move, but words unsupported by power were not taken seriously.

The U.S. military was remiss in not anticipating Pearl Harbor. Many signs pointed to it, but the intelligence was scattered and under no single authority. (One upshot: the creation of the Central

TURNING POINT　■　THE FIRST PEARL HARBOR

Americans did not like tsarist Russia, infamous for its tyranny, Siberian penal colonies, and persecution of Jews. Americans admired Japan, which quickly copied everything Western and embraced dynamic, modern values. In 1904 Japan attacked the Russian fleet at Port Arthur in China, then trounced the Russians on land and sea. President Theodore Roosevelt called them "plucky little Nips" and personally mediated the Treaty of Portsmouth (New Hampshire) that ended the war. Japan's victory in the 1904–1905 Russo–Japanese War convinced other Asians (Chinese and Vietnamese) to copy Japan and resist European takeover. Japan's taste for imperial expansion was only whetted. In 1941, Japan repeated its sneak attack on a naval base.

Intelligence Agency to collate all intelligence data.) Where had the Japanese fleet gone? Why was a special telegram (whose code we had broken) scheduled from Tokyo to the Japanese embassy in Washington on December 7? And the complacent U.S. commanders in Hawaii had depth-charged one Japanese minisub and sighted their air squadrons on radar but didn't understand they were under attack until the bombs fell.

embargo Ban on shipping goods to certain countries.

attaché Military officer serving in an embassy, a legal spy.

Pearl Harbor gave America one major break. By chance, the carriers *Lexington* and *Enterprise* were at sea that day, and carriers were the ships that really mattered in the Pacific war. The battleships and cruisers lost at Pearl were largely irrelevant. Pearl Harbor roused the Americans without seriously harming them. An enthusiastic America was now in the war.

Could the war have ended sooner? A "war party" of extreme militarists—led by the prime minister, General Hideki Tojo—would not consider surrender. One of their arguments was that the Allies would get rid of Emperor Hirohito, still regarded by some Japanese as a living god, which was never the Allies' demand or intention. Again, misunderstanding fed war.

Were the atomic bombs absolutely necessary? No, but we didn't know that at the time. As usual in war, Japan presented an image of willingness to fight forever. Many Japanese soldiers refused to surrender. (The unofficial U.S. policy of executing Japanese prisoners contributed to this.) A U.S. invasion of the main Japanese islands would have been bloody. But the war had become impossible for Japan. American submarines had cut Japanese shipping, and American air attacks had burned cities, industries, and crops. If the war had lasted another year, millions of Japanese would have starved to death. We didn't realize how close Tokyo was to surrender in the summer of 1945.

And the United States had, at great expense, just produced the first atomic bombs. It seemed a waste not to use them. Some radical historians argue that Truman wanted to drop the bombs to show Stalin how tough we were and that we weren't going to put up with his demands. The evidence for this alleged "atomic diplomacy," however, is disputed. Truman ordered the bombings because he

TURNING POINT ■ THE U.S.–JAPAN WAR

Was war between the United States and Japan inevitable? It was as long as we were China's protector. If we had been willing to look the other way as Japan pillaged China—using live Chinese, including babies, for bayonet practice—we could have avoided war with Japan. The entire Far East would be united under a single, hostile hand, which then would have invaded Russia and linked up with Hitler to control all of Eurasia.

Yes, we could have defined our interests narrowly, ending at Midway and Guam, but the world in general and Asia in particular would have been an uncomfortable place for us, to say nothing of those under Imperial Japanese rule. The Japanese view of themselves paralleled the Nazi view of Germans as a superior, conquering race. Recognizing kindred spirits, Hitler put aside his Nordic image of race to declare Japanese "honorary Aryans."

If the United States had had strong forces in the Pacific, Washington might have persuaded the Japanese militarists to desist. But the isolationist United States was lightly armed and uninterested in war, and the Japanese militarists knew it. Instead of firm military steps, Washington used verbal protests and **embargoes** to try to make Japan stop conquering China. The Japanese thought we were bluffing and supposed they would call our bluff at Pearl Harbor.

The calculation omitted the crucial psychological factor—how Americans would react. The brilliant Admiral Yamamoto who planned Pearl Harbor knew he was awakening a sleeping giant and warned Tokyo. He had served several years in Washington as naval **attaché** and knew how Americans would react, but as a good soldier he obeyed orders. The U.S. reaction exceeded his fears. Americans instantly put aside isolationism and rose with vengeful hatred on December 7, 1941.

second-order consequence The later impact of a policy choice.

wanted to end the war. Was it immoral? Would death by starvation of millions of Japanese have been moral? Could we have dropped just the one Hiroshima bomb on August 6, 1945? Tokyo, still torn between war and peace parties, did not reply. The Nagasaki bomb came August 9, the emperor tilted against the war, and Japan asked for peace the next day. Ultimately, the Japanese can blame only their own militarists.

FROM RUBBLE TO RICHES

Japan's cities after the war were gray rubble. A military occupation government under General Douglas MacArthur ran the country but through Japanese bureaucrats. (Too few Americans spoke Japanese.) Hirohito was demoted from living god to ordinary human but stayed figurehead emperor. A new constitution—still called the "MacArthur constitution" because it was drafted by Americans on his staff—set up a British-style system in 1946.

CONCEPTS ■ THE UNFORESEEN CONSEQUENCES OF NORTH KOREA

The world's first Communist dynasty—son and grandson succeed the founding dictator—North Korea got its start in the way World War II ended. Not knowing that the atomic bombs then nearing completion would actually work, Roosevelt at Yalta in early 1945 persuaded Stalin to enter the war against Japan three months after Germany surrendered. (Moscow and Tokyo had adhered faithfully to their 1941 neutrality pact.) When Truman learned that the bomb worked—he was at Potsdam conferring with Stalin after Germany's defeat—he tried to talk Stalin out of entering the war with Japan, but Stalin was happy to grab new territory.

As the U.S. bombs exploded at Hiroshima and Nagasaki in early August of 1945, Soviet forces smashed the Japanese in Manchuria and brought Communist power into North Korea, where Stalin set up a puppet Communist regime under guerrilla leader Kim Il Sung. The expansion of Soviet influence in Northeast Asia, originally meant just to finish off Japan, led to the Korean War in 1950 and to an aggressive North Korea that kidnapped Japanese children (so its spies could perfect their Japanese), practices terrorism, sells missiles to Middle East regimes, and builds nuclear bombs. North Korea engaged in nuclear talks but only as a device to get economic aid.

Policy analysts use **second-order consequence** for an aftereffect, often unforeseen and undesirable, that flows from a policy's initial result. A third-order consequence is the same, only one step later. With

Korea, the initial World War II decision brought an initial consequence of Soviet power in North Korea. A second-order consequence was the Korean War. A third-order consequence is the nuclear impasse and threats of war from a paranoid regime.

In 2010, a North Korean submarine sank a South Korean corvette. Pyongyang denied it but threatened war. Analysts speculated that North Korea's military was positioning itself to dominate the regime after the death of the current dictator, Kim Jong Il, who had suffered strokes. Many North Koreans know their situation is miserable; a rising of the hungry could spin out of control. Several countries fear the sudden collapse of the North Korean regime, which would send starving refugees in all directions. South Koreans are about 20 times richer per cap and, unlike West Germans, are not eager for an expensive reunification.

Beijing, the only regime with good ties to Pyongyang, does not want chaos in its region and quietly tries to persuade North Korea to join multilateral talks, open its economy, and follow China's path. Beijing argues that sanctions just enrage Pyongyang, that quiet diplomacy is best. If China wants to be respected as a major power, however, it had better show some results with North Korea. One possible opening may come when the likely new young dictator, Kim Jong Un, takes over. He had some experience in a Swiss prep school and may know more about the outside world and be willing to calm things. On the other hand, he may be eager to show how tough he is.

Economically, the defeat had certain beneficial aftereffects. The Japanese had nothing else to do but work. Everyone was poor; there was a rough equality. Gone was the dream of imperial expansion; they would have to make do with their little archipelago. Expectations were low; Japanese concentrated on survival and did not ask for much. At first Japanese products were cheap copies of American and European goods made of used tin cans. "Made in Japan" meant shoddy, but quality Japanese goods started appearing with the Korean War. Photojournalists discovered Nikon and Canon lenses and then cameras—at first blatant copies but soon quite original—and Japan replaced Germany in the camera business. A GI took his U.S.-made tape recorder to a Tokyo shop for repair. The owner was inspired to make his own and founded Sony.

Economic desperation gave the Japanese a competitive edge. They had to work harder and smarter, innovate more, and boost productivity. Japan's political culture is cooperative, and Japanese companies accepted **MITI** guidance. Corporations did not feel confined to a single product line; they continually branched out. Japanese growth rates, for many years 10 percent a year, awed the rest of the world. Japan is now the third-largest industrial economy in the world, after the United States and China (Germany is fourth). And it has less than half the U.S. population. Japan's success gives several hopeful lessons: A poor nation can quickly become rich. Low wages give the poor country a competitive edge over rich ones. Natural resources are not the basis for growth; human resources are. Japan's declining population shows once again that rapid population growth in developing lands slows with industrialization.

No economy grows rapidly forever; all eventually slow. In 1990 Japan began two decades of stagnation, bad debts, and depressed stock and property values. Japan suffered **deflation**, which many economists fear more than **inflation**. Some of Japan's once-praised features made things worse: foolish loans, not enough profits, inability to let failed banks and businesses go bankrupt, and (thanks to poor advice from MITI) overexpansion of major industries. Japan has 11 carmakers, most losing money. Japan's wage rates and currency climbed. Now it's cheaper to build a Nissan in Tennessee than in Japan. Japanese corporations turned to **outsourcing** in lower-wage Asian lands, including China, Malaysia, and Vietnam.

MITI   Ministry of International Trade and Industry, guiding hand of Japan's economy; now called *METI*.

deflation   Overall, long-term fall of prices.

inflation   Overall, long-term rise of prices.

outsourcing   Moving production to lower-wage countries.

peg   To fix one currency in relation to another, the opposite of *float*.

yuan   China's currency, another name for *RMB*.

float   To let market forces cause a currency to rise or fall in relation to others.

ECONOMICS ■ YUAN GET FLEXIBLE?

Exchange rates (see next chapter) are a hot topic. Beijing deliberately kept its currency undervalued—by an estimated 20 to 40 percent in relation to the dollar—in order to export more. China for years **pegged** the RMB at 8.3 to the dollar. After much complaint, in 2005 it unpegged the **yuan** in a controlled, managed **float**, but then in 2008 repegged it at 6.8 to the dollar (a 21 percent rise). Many charge China with "currency manipulation" that subsidizes Chinese exports and tariffs imports, but Beijing, fearing any economic slowdown, kept the RMB fixed and low.

With pressures mounting to float the yuan—especially threats from the U.S. Congress—Beijing in 2010 began to make the yuan flexible, but not much and not fast. China gradually makes the RMB usable in more and more international trade deals, apparently aiming to let it grow into a world reserve currency that can compete with or even replace the U.S. dollar. To make that happen, though, the yuan will have to float freely. Fearing harm to its economic growth from Western protectionism, Beijing is likely to get flexible on its yuan.

protectionism   Policy of keeping out foreign goods.

dumping   Selling goods abroad for less than it costs to produce them.

trade surplus   Selling more to other countries than you buy from them.

Japan faces a security dilemma. Long protected by a U.S. treaty and with 47,000 U.S. troops on its soil (most on Okinawa), Japan benefited from holding its defense expenditures to a mere 1 percent of GDP. Japan was a "free rider" but never liked the U.S. bases and subservience to U.S. policy. In 2009, the pro-U.S. Liberal Democratic Party (LDP) was finally ousted by the Democratic Party of Japan (DPJ), which vowed to cut the U.S. presence on Okinawa. Tokyo quickly noticed, however, that without U.S. backup, Japan would face China and North Korea alone. Result: Japan's defense policy changed little, and the U.S. Marines are still on Okinawa.

Things could go wrong with East Asia's economic growth. Heightened by the 2008–2009 global recession, trade **protectionism** grows. More countries slap punitive tariffs on Chinese goods—which, they charge, are **dumped** on the world market—and China retaliates. Some countries have already put up barriers to East Asian products, and American politicians talk about "getting tough" with "unfair" trade competitors. On their part, Asian lands import raw materials but are protectionist on finished goods. They insist on running **trade surpluses**. If trade doesn't roughly balance (over the long term, not necessarily in a given year), eventually it will decline. One of the keys to peace and stability in East Asia is trade.

mypoliscikit EXERCISES

Apply what you learned in this chapter on MyPoliSciKit (www.mypoliscikit.com).

Assessment   Review this chapter using learning objectives, chapter summaries, practice tests, and more.
Menu

Flashcards   Learn the key terms in this chapter; you can test yourself by term or definition.
Flashcards

Video   Analyze recent world affairs by watching streaming video from major news providers.
Videos

Simulations   Play the role of an IR decision-maker and experience how IR concepts work in practice.
Comparative
Exercises

KEY TERMS

archipelago (p. 277)
attaché (p. 281)
authoritarian (p. 274)
cadres (p. 274)
deflation (p. 283)
dumping (p. 281)
embargo (p. 280)
float (p. 283)
inflation (p. 283)

Manchukuo (p. 280)
Meiji (p. 280)
MITI (p. 283)
nonrecognition (p. 280)
Open Door (p. 275)
outsourcing (p. 283)
peg (p. 283)
protectionism (p. 284)
rapprochement (p. 279)

RMB (p. 275)
second-order consequence (p. 282)
Standing Committee (p. 274)
totalitarian (p. 274)
trade deficit (p. 275)
trade surplus (p. 284)
yuan (p. 283)
Zhongnanhai (p. 274)

FURTHER REFERENCE

Bardhan, Pranab. *Awakening Giants, Feet of Clay: Assessing the Economic Rise of China and India.* Princeton, NJ: Princeton University Press, 2010.

Baum, Richard. *China Watcher: Confessions of a Peking Tom.* Seattle, WA: University of Washington Press, 2010.

Dumas, Charles. *China and America: A Time of Reckoning.* London: Profile, 2009.

Emmott, Bill. *Rivals: How the Power Struggle Between China, India, and Japan Will Shape Our Next Decade.* New York: Harcourt, 2008.

Halper, Stefan. *The Beijing Consensus: How China's Authoritarian Model Will Dominate the Twenty-First Century.* New York: Basic Books, 2010.

Hao, Yufan, ed. *Sino-American Relations After Thirty Years: Challenges Ahead.* Burlington, VT: Ashgate, 2010.

Holslag, Jonathan. *China and India: Prospects for Peace.* New York: Columbia University Press, 2009.

Horner, Charles. *Rising China and Its Postmodern Fate: Memories of Empire in a New Global Context.* Athens, GA: University of Georgia Press, 2009.

Hung, Ho-fung, ed. *China and the Transformation of Global Capitalism.* Baltimore, MD: Johns Hopkins University Press, 2009.

Jacques, Martin. *When China Rules the World: The End of the Western World and the Birth of a New Global Order.* New York: Penguin, 2009.

Jha, Prem Shankar. *India and China: The Battle between Soft and Hard Power.* New Delhi: Penguin, 2010.

Kaplan, Robert D. *Monsoon: The Indian Ocean and the Future of American Power.* New York: Random House, 2010.

Kemp, Geoffrey. *The East Moves West: India, China, and Asia's Growing Presence in the Middle East.* Washington, DC: Brookings, 2010.

Khanna, Tarun. *Billions of Entrepreneurs: How China and India are Reshaping Their Fortunes and Yours.* Boston: Harvard Business School, 2008.

Mahbubani, Kishore. *The New Asian Hemisphere: The Irresistible Shift of Global Power to the East.* New York: PublicAffairs, 2008.

Page, Benjamin I., and Tao Xie. *Living with the Dragon: How the American Public Views the Rise of China.* New York: Columbia University Press, 2010.

Pan, Philip P. *Out of Mao's Shadow: The Struggle for the Soul of a New China.* New York: Simon & Schuster, 2008.

Roach, Stephen. *The Next Asia: Opportunities and Challenges for a New Globalization.* New York: Wiley, 2009.

Ross, Robert S., and Zhu Feng, eds. *China's Ascent: Power, Security, and the Future of International Politics.* Ithaca, NY: Cornell University Press, 2008.

Schuman, Michael. *The Miracle: The Epic Story of Asia's Quest for Wealth.* New York: Harper, 2009.

Shirk, Susan L. *China: Fragile Superpower; How China's Internal Politics Could Derail Its Peaceful Rise.* New York: Oxford University Press, 2007.

Steinfeld, Edward S. *Playing Our Game: Why China's Rise Doesn't Threaten the West.* New York: Oxford University Press, 2010.

Sutter, Robert G. *U.S.-Chinese Relations: Perilous Past; Pragmatic Present.* Lanham, MD: Rowman & Littlefield, 2010.

Tay, Simon. *Asia Alone: The Current Crisis and the Coming Pacific Divide.* Hoboken, NJ: Wiley, 2010.

Wasserstrom, Jeffrey N. *China in the 21st Century: What Everyone Needs to Know.* New York: Oxford University Press, 2010.

Wolpert, Stanley. *India and Pakistan: Continued Conflict or Cooperation?* Berkeley, CA: University of California Press, 2010.

Zhu, Zhiqun. *China's New Diplomacy: Rationale, Strategies and Significance.* Burlington, VT: Ashgate, 2010.

CHAPTER 18

The United States and Globalization

Some Americans, horrified at the 2008–2009 financial meltdown and government bailouts, retreated into the simplistic slogans of the Tea Party. (Jacquelyn Martin/AP Photo)

THE GREAT DEPRESSION AND GREAT RECESSION

Economists, a gloomy lot, worried that the **recession** that began in 2008 could last for years. Some compared it to the Great Depression of the 1930s that led to World War II. As in 2008, the **depression** started with a series of U.S. bank failures in 1929, which got much worse with the collapse of the overvalued New York stock market that fall. What made the Great Depression really deep and long, however, was the disastrous 1930 Hawley-Smoot tariff. Other countries immediately retaliated by raising their own tariffs, and world trade shriveled. Factories and banks closed worldwide, and unemployment climbed to over one-quarter of the workforce in the industrialized countries.

Most of the world's governments did the wrong things and made matters worse. They tried to balance budgets to get out of the depression, but these further depressed the economy. The Great Depression did not cure itself. In the United States, Franklin D. Roosevelt's administration cautiously applied the new **Keynesian economics** to reflate the economy. Instead of balancing the budget, the federal government went mildly into deficit to provide jobs, loans, and price supports. Aside from the symbolic lift, however, the U.S. economy stayed depressed.

In Germany, unemployment brought Adolf Hitler to power in 1933. He applied a massive Keynesian solution: gigantic public works projects and large government loans to get industry moving again. He also started World War II, and that cured the Great Depression for all countries by creating factory orders and jobs, many of them in uniform.

Since then, there have been no depressions. Smaller economic downturns are called recessions, informally defined as two or more consecutive quarters (i.e., at least half a year) of a declining GDP. The 2008–2009 crisis, caused by reckless lending (see box on page 293), was dubbed the "Great Recession." **Federal Reserve Board** Chairman Ben Bernanke, a lifelong student of the Great Depression, took steps to prevent another one, but many worried that the recession could last for years.

In 2008–2009 governments worldwide did substantially the same things: lower interest rates, bail out banks, promote car and home purchases, and accelerate infrastructure projects. Did the massive cash infusions work? Well, there was no depression, but it's hard to prove why something *didn't* happen. Conservative critics—few of them economists—complained that much of the spending was wasteful and contributed to staggering national debt, but governments were not willing to risk their citizens' jobs, homes, and pensions by doing nothing. The Great Recession weakened U.S. economic leadership and reheated the debate about currency parities.

QUESTIONS TO CONSIDER

1. How does the 2008 recession compare with the Great Depression?
2. Is a "strong dollar" necessarily a good thing?
3. Can anything replace the dollar as the world's main reserve currency?
4. What international economic institutions try to promote global prosperity?
5. Which countries are the richest? Why is this tricky to calculate?
6. Is globalization still growing, or has it peaked?
7. How does NAFTA differ from the European Union?
8. If free trade is so good, why is it hard to keep it functioning?
9. Is a currency war looming? What can be done to prevent it?

A STRONG DOLLAR?

Americans love hearing that the dollar is "strong." It allows them to travel abroad and import vast amounts of foreign goods. U.S. politicians play to the crowd by affirming they too want a strong dollar, because it means a strong United States. This is not really true, as a too-strong dollar hurts the U.S. economy by exporting jobs and building debt. Many economists urge a weaker dollar to boost exports and manufacturing jobs. At any rate, the dollar has, in spurts, weakened as other countries, alarmed at U.S. indebtedness, bid down the dollar on currency markets. No currency dominates forever. The British pound ruled the nineteenth century and the dollar the twentieth century. What will be the big currency of the twenty-first century?

The dollar is still the world's biggest *reserve currency* (see page 265), but few currencies are steady, and establishing their **exchange rate** involves hard choices. The basic choice is between **fixed** and **floating** exchange rates. China (see page 283) pegs its RMB to the dollar, keeping the yuan undervalued in relation to virtually all other currencies. This gives China an advantage in gaining world markets but infuriates the United States, Europe, and many other lands whose industries are disadvantaged by cheaper Chinese goods.

A floating exchange rate lets the market determine the value of a dollar, euro, or RMB. When foreigners want more dollars, they bid the price up. When they want fewer, they bid the price down. (Beijing, sitting on a mountain of dollars, blocks this process by buying or selling massive amounts of dollars to offset supply and demand and keep the yuan largely constant.) In theory, floating currencies find the right level based on who produces what and which currencies are the safest. In practice, currency markets—like all financial markets—overshoot both ways. All **bubbles** burst. Speculators bet which currency is going up or down, and these billion-dollar bets themselves often make it happen.

The shock of the Great Depression and World War II pushed the major trading countries to fixed exchange rates with the **Bretton Woods** agreement (see box below). The West German mark and

recession Transient, short-term economic downturn.

depression Major, long-term economic downturn; when capitalized as Great Depression, the 1930s.

Keynesian economics The use of government spending to fight recessions.

Federal Reserve Board "The "Fed"; U.S. supervisory bank that attempts to stabilize the economy.

exchange rate How much one currency buys of another.

fixed exchange rate One currency buys a set number of other currencies.

floating exchange rate One currency buys a varying number of other currencies, depending on the market for them.

bubble Market that has gone too high.

Bretton Woods 1944 agreement to fix exchange rates to the dollar backed by gold.

ECONOMICS ■ BRETTON WOODS AGREEMENT

After two years of preparation, the Western allies met at a New Hampshire resort in 1944 to sign an agreement to fix rates of exchange based on the dollar. An ounce of gold was to be worth $35, and other currencies were to be worth a set number of dollars. Bretton Woods was designed to coordinate policy among central banks, which would buy and sell dollars to fine-tune supply and demand. The system was not totally fixed, for if one currency got too far out of line, it could be adjusted downward (*devalued*) or upward (*revalued*).

For about a generation, the Bretton Woods system worked pretty well and aided West Europe's and Japan's postwar recovery. But it was based on the fiction that gold was worth only $35 an ounce, and when that became totally unbelievable, the system cracked. President Nixon ended the gold-backed dollar in 1971.

Japanese yen, for example, went at low rates, respectively 4 and 360 to the dollar. Americans could buy Volkswagens and Sonys at good prices, and German and Japanese industry surged; they became export giants. By the 1960s, pricey U.S. products were losing out to West European and Japanese competition. U.S. corporations and tourists pumped dollars overseas. The United States grew deeper and deeper into debt.

International Monetary Fund (IMF) Makes loans to stabilize currency parities.

World Bank Makes loans to lift up poor countries.

austerity Belt-tightening; major budget cutting.

If we had been under a system of floating exchange rates, the dollar might have devalued itself. But a system of semifixed rates kept the dollar too high. The massive U.S. spending for the Vietnam War, for example, created not only domestic inflation but, when the dollars were sent abroad to pay for our purchases, inflation worldwide. We exported inflation. The Bretton Woods agreement got shakier and shakier. The dollar was clearly too high, and President Nixon finally devalued it in 1971 (see box below), ushering in an era of floating exchange rates.

Over many years a dollar has, with ups and downs, bought fewer euros or yen. Huge U.S. budget deficits (now over a trillion dollars) persuade many that the dollar is unsound, so "speculators" sell them in favor of other currencies. Speculators are not necessarily greedy or gamblers (although they do place multimillion-dollar bets). They can be anyone with currency on hand: corporate executives, bankers, investors, even tourists. If they hear the dollar is "under pressure," that is, more are being sold than bought, they tend to bet the pressure will continue and sell their dollars for other currency. They fear that their dollars will lose value. Thus, even a rumor that a currency is under pressure may bring a wave of speculative selling of that currency that makes the rumor come true. In 1993, financier George Soros bet that the British pound would soon be devalued. He sold pounds for other currencies and overnight made $1 billion. (He has also bet wrong and lost millions.) No currency is completely stable. As the financial crisis that began in 2008 deepened and spread, the dollar weakened. At one point, a euro was worth $1.55.

WHAT TO USE FOR WORLD TRADE?

One area of concern about the U.S. dollar is the mammoth U.S. foreign-trade deficit—7 percent of GDP in 2010—fueled in part by the tremendous debt that America runs at all levels—international, federal, business, and personal. Americans spend money they don't have. Many top economists and businesspeople and even the International Monetary Fund (see below) warned that America's huge debts would lead to a loss of confidence in the dollar—and it did.

ECONOMICS ■ INTERNATIONAL MONETARY FUND

Bretton Woods (see box on page 288) established the **International Monetary Fund** (IMF) to keep exchange rates stable and help countries pay their international debts. IMF headquarters is in Washington, but most countries are members. Funds come from a pool of member countries' contributions. The rich, industrialized countries contribute the lion's share, so they dominate IMF policy.

A sister of the IMF, the **World Bank**, makes low-interest loans to developing countries. Both help countries in need but only if they practice **austerity** and hold down inflation. Some poor countries say these demands are impossible and denounce the IMF and World Bank. Antiglobalists protest the IMF and World Bank and want to abolish them. The weakening of the dollar in the 2008–2009 crisis brought calls to shrink the U.S. role in setting the IMF's agenda.

Special Drawing Rights   (SDRs)
Artificial currency the IMF uses to
make loans.

conventional wisdom   A set of
unexamined but widely believed
assumptions.

Americans consume more than they produce and import about a third more than they export, making the United States the world's biggest debtor nation, owing a trillion dollars. We are still among the world's biggest exporters, but we are even bigger importers. We lived beyond our means, paying for foreign products with overvalued dollars. Chinese do the opposite, saving like crazy, consuming relatively little, keeping their currency undervalued, and building a huge export trade and reserves. The ultimate solution to this imbalance, say economists, is for Americans to save more and Chinese to consume more. This is called "rebalancing."

Oversize U.S. consumption works only as long as our trading partners continue to accept dollars, which they did during the long Cold War. Billions of dollars flowed overseas, and many of them stayed there, becoming the world's reserve currency. This was fun for a while. We pumped dollars overseas and did not have to redeem many of them with our own goods; the foreigners were content to hold the dollars, the origin of the *eurodollar* (see page 265). After many years, though, as foreigners noticed the size of U.S. debts and deficits, they worried that the value of the dollars they held would fall. (The U.S. deficit has recently been about 10 percent of GDP.) In 2008 indebtedness collapsed several old and big U.S. financial institutions and strained Washington's ability to deal with it. So they devalued dollars by selling lots of them for euros, Swiss francs, or yen. The euro, for example, debuted in 1999 at $1.17, fell to $0.85 in 2001, but reached $1.55 in 2008 before declining to around $1.30.

Few see any way to soon replace the dollar as the main reserve currency, the standard money of international commerce and a "safe haven" currency during crises. Two-thirds of world foreign exchange reserves have been in dollars and one-fourth in euros, but some do not trust the dollar as the United States faces banking, budgetary, and foreign-trade problems. Europe offered its euro as an alternative to the dollar, but some question the reliability of the euro, as Europe was in fiscal difficulty, too. China in 2008, itself taking a hit from the weakening dollar, suggested making the IMF's (see box on page 289) **Special Drawing Rights** the new reserve currency. SDRs are not really money but a basket of currencies—mostly dollars, euros, yen, and pounds—that issuing countries loan to the IMF. Using SDRs would cut the dominant role of the dollar in world trade. China could accelerate the shift by making its RMB fully convertible and letting it float (see page 283) but, in fear of hurting its export trade, goes slow. The challenge to the world: If you don't trust the dollar, what do you propose to replace it?

GLOBALIZATION AND ITS ENEMIES

In the 1990s globalization became the **conventional wisdom**: Everyone said it, so it must be true. Corporate executives said: "Think global. There are no more one-country markets anymore. Our products are now made in several countries and sold in many countries. And our competition is doing the same." They told their workers: "Restrain your wage demands, or we'll move this operation overseas." Globalization thus held down wages and inflation, but citizens, seeing their businesses and jobs going overseas, demanded protectionist measures. Consumers heard: "You get the best products at the lowest prices. Never mind where it's made, just enjoy it." The trouble with conventional wisdom, though, is that it's often wrong. There was nothing automatic or inevitable about globalization.

We should be asking three questions about globalization: (1) Is it still the main trend? (2) Is it desirable? (3) Is it stable? Our take: It never covered the entire globe and is now fading. The

Globalization: Tokyo youth get their cholesterol at McDonald's, Japan's biggest restaurant chain. The second biggest is Kentucky Fried Chicken. (Yoshikatsu Tsuno/Getty Images)

2008–2009 recession set it back. It is largely confined to a broad band stretching from West Europe across North America to the Pacific Rim, but even here plenty of barriers block truly open trade. Globalization is great for newly industrializing countries, but most of the poorest countries are only partially involved. Globalization is generally a good thing, provided the rich countries do not mind others catching up with them as jobs flow to the developing lands.

Victorian   Related to reign of Britain's Queen Victoria, 1837–1901.

We now see that globalization is also unstable, vulnerable to banking and currency crises and trade protectionism. Problems from reckless bank loans on one continent soon hit all the others. Globalization depends totally on world markets staying open, and many are now protecting their domestic markets. Only U.S. leadership can keep world trade open, but the United States is turning protectionist, especially after the 2008–2009 recession. Remember what happened the last time world trade constricted: the Great Depression.

Not all countries participate in globalization. The World Bank found that roughly 3 billion people (out of a world population of 7 billion) live in 24 low-income "globalizer" countries (mostly in Asia) that increase their international trade as a percent of their GDP. They enjoy an average of 5 percent a year growth in per capita GDP. But another 2 billion live in countries (mostly in Africa and Muslim lands) where trade as a percent of GDP diminishes—"nonglobalizers"—and they grow poorer by about 1 percent a year. Free trade works, but it needs certain policy and cultural prerequisites that not all countries can provide.

Globalization is not a new concept. Basically, it is another way of saying "lots of trade among countries." A kind of globalization began with the Portuguese and the Spanish voyages of discovery to Asia and to the Americas, which produced a world trade boom during the sixteenth century. Then Great Britain and the steamship led a "**Victorian** globalization" in the nineteenth century, but World War I and the Great Depression ended it. After World War II, a U.S.-led globalization

purchasing power parity (PPP) True worth of a currency; what it can actually buy.

expanded exports as a percent of the world's GDP from 8 percent in 1950 to 28 percent in 2000. There are many reasons for the latest globalization:

1. American corporations invested heavily in West Europe after the war, setting the style for transnational (probably a better name than multinational) firms that were delighted to manufacture and sell anywhere.
2. Tariff barriers fell. Pushed by GATT (now the WTO), tariffs are at an all-time low. (There are still, to be sure, other barriers to free trade.)

ECONOMICS ■ WHO IS RICH?

Who is rich depends on what you mean by "rich." If you mean overall economic clout, you look at a country's Gross Domestic Product (discussed in Chapter 11) at exchange rate, the first column in the table below. This is not "per capita" (divided by population) and is in trillions of dollars. Here even newly industrializing countries—with China in the lead—now have global economic clout. GDP changes from one year to the next. Volatile prices shoot the GDPs of oil exporters up and down.

GDP is now usually expressed in **purchasing power parity** (PPP), which takes cost of living into account. The old way—GDP at exchange rates—misleads, as currencies can get seriously under- or overvalued in relation to each other. To correct for this, PPP notes prices of a standard basket of goods and services in every country. Measured by PPP, China is nearly twice as rich as its exchange-rate GDP indicates, because the yuan is undervalued. So if by rich you mean how well people live, use the second column, per capita GDP (GDPpc) at PPP.

To get a rough idea of PPP and how much over- or undervalued a currency is in relation to the dollar, the British newsweekly *The Economist* publishes its "Big Mac Index," a quick comparison of the cost of the identical hamburger worldwide. The Big Mac is actually a mini-market basket that includes ingredients, rent, energy, and labor. Although it's too urban to rely on, the Big Mac Index generally tracks more-complicated PPP calculations. Big Mac prices go up and down worldwide as currency rates change. In October 2010, a Big Mac in West Europe was more expensive than the U.S. price, indicating that the euro was overvalued. The Big Mac is just a bit high in Japan, suggesting the yen is not, as commonly supposed, much overvalued. (The dollar had fallen against the euro and yen over the previous two years.) Cheap Big Macs, as in Russia and China, indicate their currencies are undervalued. Many countries like to keep their currencies cheap to boost exports and economic growth.

	GDP 2009 at Exchange Rate	GPDpc 2009 at PPP	Big Mac Oct. 2010
United States	$14.4 trillion	$46,400	$3.71
European Union	16.2	32,600	4.79
Canada	1.3	38,400	4.18
Japan	5.1	32,600	3.91
Britain	2.2	35,200	3.63
Mexico	1.0	13,500	2.58
Russia	1.2	15,100	2.39
China	4.8	6,600	2.18

Sources: *CIA World Factbook, The Economist*

3. Transportation became cheap. Thanks to containerization (loading goods at the factory in big metal boxes), it can be cheaper to ship across an ocean than across a country. High-end and perishable goods can be airfreighted at reasonable cost.

subprime mortgage   Risky home loan, one with no money down.

4. Communication became instantaneous and cheap. International phone calls, faxes, and the Internet make your contacts around the world seem as if they're next door. (One by-product of this communication revolution: English is confirmed as the standard world language.)

ECONOMICS ■ THE 2008 FINANCIAL MELTDOWN

For some years, economists and businesspeople believed that the abundant and rapid information of the computer age would prevent economic breakdown. The "efficient market hypothesis" argued that when most investors know all the relevant data, markets behave rationally, like computers playing chess. But the "efficient" machine didn't factor in risk, and banks and hedge funds "tailgated" each other until many of them crashed. Their standard excuse: "Other banks were doing it and making good money, so we had to do it too."

The world crisis began in 2006 with the realization that many American **subprime mortgages** were not going be repaid. But that was just the curtain raiser that revealed the U.S. financial system as "overleveraged," drowning in debt, much of it so complex that giant investment banks were unable to accurately evaluate their assets. In 2008 the entire system unraveled. Banks and rating agencies had assured investors for years that all was well, but suddenly trillions of dollars of loans were "toxic." Unable to come up with capital, many firms failed or were taken over. It soon became clear that the banks of many countries had also loaned recklessly—the worst was Iceland—and they came under similar pressure.

Trends over several years brought on the crisis: (1) U.S. lending standards relaxed to let home buyers get mortgages with no money down and variable-rate (i.e., goes up) interest that started enticingly low. (2) Financial geniuses with MBAs combined these mortgages and sold chunks of the packages like bonds. (3) World buyers thought these "collateralized debt obligations" and other gimmicks were safe, money-making investments and flocked to them. This created demand for ever more subprime mortgages, and U.S. mortgage brokers eagerly issued "liar loans" without due diligence.

It seemed like a magic, win-win-win money machine. Borrowers got homes they could not have afforded before, homes that were supposed to forever increase in value; loan writers collected fat fees; and investors got solid investments in the vast U.S. housing market, which was presumed to be safe. International demand for U.S. mortgages helped drive reckless lending, creating a housing bubble or "asset inflation."

In 2005, variable-rate ("balloon") interest rates started to kick in, making some monthly payments unaffordable. By 2008 the situation was catastrophic, and home foreclosures set records. Win-win-win turned into lose-lose-lose: Borrowers lost their homes; lenders went bust; and investors lost their investments. One big, hidden problem: In these packages of mortgages, no one could tell which were good and which were bad; they were comingled. When things went wrong, banks did not know what their investments were worth, so they could not sell them. Foreclosed subprime homes depressed the overall housing market, so that even "good" loans turned sour when home values declined. Desperate for capital to pay creditors, banks tried to sell off assets, but few would buy assets of unknown value. Their stocks fell, and many banks folded.

Notice the international components in this. Foreign banks and countries put billions into the U.S. mortgage market and their own construction booms, pumping up the bubble. When it burst, America lost some of its world financial leadership. With Wall Street in disrepute, much world financial activity moved to Hong Kong and other Asian banking centers. Technically, the U.S. and European economies recovered, that is, they resumed growing, but at subdued rates that left many still unemployed.

WTO   World Trade Organization, UN-related body, successor to GATT, promotes free trade.

5. Capital flowed across borders. International banking expanded, making transfers and loans quick and easy. This also created a world capital market in which funds seek investments that yield the highest returns.

6. Wages in the Global South were so much lower than First World labor costs that many firms set up shop in China, India, and other newly industrializing lands. Especially burdensome is West Europe's high "social overhead": taxes for medical insurance, pensions, unemployment, and welfare.

Some supporters of globalization, such as *New York Times* columnist Thomas Friedman, got ecstatic, hailing it as a revolution, a new historical epoch. They claimed it would uplift the developing countries, bring down dictatorships, and lead to peace. Said Friedman, only half in jest, "No two countries with McDonald's have ever fought each other." (Actually, India, Pakistan, and Yugoslavia had McDonald's.) Borders become irrelevant, as information, capital, and goods move like an "electronic herd" to wherever there is a market. Governments and banks must offer open, uncorrupt business environments; otherwise investors will stay away. And the whole process is self-enforcing; governments just get in the way. Like the Internet, no one is in charge.

Some thinkers were skeptical. Economist Paul Krugman noted that most goods are still consumed in the countries where they are produced; only a fraction are exported. Globalization in this view is mostly hype. As percentages of GDP, Europe before World War I exported and imported more than now. In those days, thinkers like Norman Angell thought countries were too busy and happy to ever go to war again: Trade interdependence would ensure peace. In 1914, this globalization collapsed and did not revive until after World War II. Does globalization cause peace, or does peace cause globalization? Could war end the recent round of globalization? Could the recent financial turmoil end it?

Some hated and feared globalization and tried to block or reverse it. At the 1999 Seattle meeting of the **World Trade Organization** (WTO), as talks among members stalled over important differences, on the streets protesters denounced the whole enterprise. They saw globalization

ECONOMICS ■ FROM GATT TO WTO

The founders of the IMF (see box on page 289) in 1947 wanted to set up an International Trade Organization (ITO) with enforcement powers, but many feared the ITO would infringe on national sovereignty (a point some Americans still fear). As a weaker substitute, the General Agreement on Tariffs and Trade (GATT) was a treaty among most nations to work for tariff reductions. Headquartered in Geneva, GATT members for decades slogged away at tariff and other trade barriers in a series of "rounds," each lasting many years and with more than a hundred countries haggling. Over half a century, GATT cut tariffs by around 90 percent.

GATT turned into the World Trade Organization (WTO) in 1995. It now has 153 members (including China but not yet Russia) and more power than GATT. WTO has a court to adjudicate trade disputes. Soon there were angry charges of unfair practices, especially between the EU and United States and between the developing and rich countries. The 2003 WTO meeting in Cancún, Mexico, collapsed as Global South delegates walked out in protest over the high agricultural tariffs and huge subsidies—roughly $1 billion a day—that the EU, Japan, and the United States use to protect their farmers (and win their votes). These drive poor countries' products off the world market and keep them poor. Developing lands argue that the rich countries keep saying "free trade" but, especially in agriculture, do not practice it.

as an elite thing guided only by transnational corporations and government specialists. No one votes on it. Workers saw their jobs exported to low-wage countries. Environmentalists saw global pollution. Leftists protested exploitive wages and working conditions in Global South sweatshops. Nationalists feared erosion of U.S. sovereignty. And black-clad "anarchists" just had fun trashing downtown Seattle.

The charge of exploitation of workers in developing lands doesn't hold up. They do not come from a rural idyll; they flee rural poverty and flock to the cities. What are "sweatshops" to us are great jobs to them, vastly better than picking through garbage dumps. Some pay bribes to get a factory job paying $3 a day. If the wages were too low and working conditions too bad, factories in the Global South (or anywhere, for that matter) would get no workers. Actually, multinationals (many U.S.-based) pay above-average wages and introduce new technologies. If workers were paid rich-country wages, their products could not sell on the world market. Their low wages lets poor countries climb to prosperity.

Likewise, First World environmental standards applied now in the Global South would close many industries. It takes a fairly rich country to afford pollution controls. U.S. Democratic candidates sometimes propose minimum wages and environmental standards to "help" the Global South. (More likely, it is trade protectionism to win votes from workers who fear outsourcing of jobs.) Leaders of developing lands say that is no help at all. They know their recent economic growth is based on trade, and any such restrictions hurt growth. "Helping" the Third World by demanding First World wage and environmental standards would pull the ladder away from those trying climb up it.

The real antiglobalist force is old-fashioned trade protectionism, some of it now coming from Washington. As we discussed in Chapter 11, some U.S. jobs are lost. Traditionally, these have been low-paying, low-skilled factory jobs, but recently all manner of jobs, including high-tech professional ones, have also been sent overseas. (See box on page 187.) Although such trends are overstated (especially by Democrats in an election year), they feed American protectionist sentiments, and both parties quickly respond. Bill Clinton was the last free-trade president. Free trade always has rough going.

THE COMING OF NAFTA

West Europe and Japan contrived ways to keep out U.S. goods and services. With U.S. trade deficits getting bigger, Americans grew cranky at what they perceived as trade unfairness across both oceans. In part to combat this alleged trade discrimination, Washington began building its own trade bloc, the North American Free Trade Association. While never calling NAFTA a warning to or retaliation against the EU or Asia, the authors believe that is what Washington had in mind when it formed NAFTA (with Canada) in 1988 and expanded it to Mexico in 1992 (ratified after a hard Senate fight in late 1993). Washington, looking across both the Atlantic and the Pacific, said in effect, "All right, you lock us out of your area and we'll build our own bloc."

NAFTA and the EU are structurally very different. The EU is a highly developed and integrated bloc, one aiming at a single market and European federation. NAFTA has no such aims; it just wants to eliminate tariffs between members, nothing more. The EU has the free flow not only of goods and services but of labor and capital as well. It has a complex governing body, something NAFTA utterly lacks. The EU, since it began as the Common Market, sets up common external tariffs; NAFTA members set their own tariffs with nonmembers.

NAFTA has not had smooth sailing. Although both Canada and the United States benefited from cutting the tariffs between them—they were the world's biggest trading partners before NAFTA anyway—individual industries suffered as production went to the more efficient producers, which is

mercantilism Pre–Adam Smith economic theory that large gold holdings made a nation rich.

precisely what is supposed to happen. American loggers or Canadian retail clerks who have lost their jobs are in no mood to discuss the energizing effects of free trade. Polls indicate that many Canadians would be happy to abolish NAFTA, and it could happen.

American and Canadian workers fear competing with low-wage Mexican workers. Ross Perot campaigned for president in 1992 against

ECONOMICS ■ PROTECTIONISM

In 1776, Scottish economist Adam Smith refuted the old notion of **mercantilism** by arguing that free trade makes everyone more prosperous: "If a foreign country can supply us with a commodity cheaper than we ourselves can make it, better buy it of them with some part of the produce of our own industry." Even unilaterally lowering your trade barriers is good for you.

Few people understand it or believe it; historically, most countries have kept out foreign goods on the theory that they hurt the domestic economy. They build protective barriers in the form of tariffs and quotas (see pages 261 and 265). They give one excuse after another for protectionism. Developing countries say they must protect their "infant industries" from more-efficient foreign competition to give them a chance to take hold. Developed countries say they must protect their mature industries from foreign goods made with cheap labor. Many argue that the country must not grow dependent on foreign supplies of strategic items.

Everybody wants to protect their farmers, and farm subsidies in rich countries—running at $1 billion a day!—are the most egregious form of it. U.S. cotton growers, for example, get $4 billion a year from taxpayers for a crop worth less than that. We then dump our subsidized cotton on the world market at below production cost and devastate struggling Third World cotton growers. Similarly, the EU pays its growers €50 a ton for sugar beets (five times world prices) that nobody needs, and this drives out Global South producers of cane sugar. Thanks to absurd subsidies, Europe is a major sugar exporter. Trying to win the rural vote, neither European, nor American, nor Japanese leaders dare tell their farmers to go into other lines of work. The result is continued Third World poverty and slow economic growth.

Most people instinctively seek trade protection. Americans and Europeans complain about the "export of jobs" to low-wage countries. To stay competitive, companies have to manufacture where costs are low. American presidential candidates proclaim support for free trade in the abstract but add that we must protect jobs in steel, agriculture, manufacturing, and whatever, all based on winning votes. Under George W. Bush, Europe, China, and others brought suits against U.S. trade restrictions before the WTO and threatened retaliation. We could have had—and still may have—trade wars with Europe and China. Whatever you do to protect domestic producers angers foreign producers, and they retaliate.

President Clinton was far more supportive of free trade, but in 2004 and 2008 Democrats denounced the Republican administration for "deindustrializing America," which contained some truth. Over a third of a century, U.S. manufacturing as a percent of GDP fell by half, to 12 percent. Financial services nearly doubled to a quarter of GDP (but started declining in 2008). President Obama put tariffs on Chinese tires and steel pipe, which were allegedly being *dumped* (see page 281).

The shift from manufacturing to services is normal and standard for a mature economy; educated people can benefit from it, but laid-off factory workers cannot. The shift also means that America imports one-third of its manufactured goods, which made Americans uneasy and protectionist. Promotion of free trade inherently comes from elites of corporate executives, economists, and some government officials. Left to the masses—or to politicians chasing votes—tariff and other barriers quickly rise, and everyone is the poorer for it.

NAFTA ratification, claiming "a giant sucking sound" was the drain of U.S. jobs into Mexico. Actually, in the late 1990s U.S. unemployment dropped to a very low 4 percent. Lower-skilled U.S. jobs had been moving to Mexico for years anyway. People tend to get hysterical over trade liberalization. The effects of NAFTA on the gigantic U.S. economy were minute. Its effects on Mexico were at first good and helped pull the Mexican economy out of a crisis. But much industrial growth projected for Mexico went to China, where wages are much lower. For the first decade of NAFTA, Mexico's per capita GDP grew on average only 1 percent a year.

neomercantilism Theory of some nations that big trade surpluses make it rich.

Mexico's slow growth made many wonder if NAFTA should expand to cover the entire hemisphere. If so, how fast? Discussions on a Free Trade Area of the Americas (FTAA) began in 1997, aimed at creating a 34-nation hemispheric market. It would have had fabulous growth potential, but most U.S. administrations and the Congress, frightened of worker and voter backlash, went slowly. Much of Latin America, fearing U.S. domination, opposes a hemispheric trade bloc. Many claim the United States just wants to export freely to Latin America but still protect U.S. agricultural sectors. Brazil complains that the U.S. market for its orange juice—you probably drank some this morning— is unfairly limited to protect Florida growers. With problems like this, efforts to build FTAA flopped at a 2003 meeting at Cancún, Mexico. One big problem with FTAA: It's unpronounceable.

Both NAFTA and WTO aim at lowering import restrictions and expanding trade, but they are at odds over their geographical scope. A trade bloc, such as NAFTA or the EU, says in effect, "We're for free trade in our region, because that is all we can comfortably handle. We limit imports from other blocs because they are threats to our jobs." The WTO says in effect, "Make the whole world one big trade bloc; let all goods and services flow everywhere without hindrance." The more successful WTO is, the less relevant NAFTA or any other trade blocs will be. If WTO really eliminates all trade barriers—something that will take many decades, at best—there will be no point to regional trade blocs that have eliminated barriers between members. If your tariffs and other barriers are already zero with everybody, they cannot be less than zero for your fellow members of NAFTA or the EU.

TRADE WARS?

A basic point of international trade is poorly understood. When two or more countries trade, they are in a win-win situation. They are not in a zero-sum game in which what one wins the other loses. Everybody gains; they all get more and better products at lower prices. If, for example, you tried to keep shirt-making in America for the sake of fellow Americans who make shirts, you would have $50 shirts instead of $15 shirts. If you import most of your shirts and export high-tech, high-value-added goods, such as jetliners and oil rigs, you have more well-paid workers at home and they can buy all the shirts they wish. To be sure, some jobs in the United States are lost; they are mostly in the sectors that compete directly with the imports, such as shirt factories. Usually, though, after a while better jobs are gained.

But suppose some players (such as Japan earlier and now China) practice "**neomercantilism**" by minimizing consumption and maximizing exports. With government encouragement, they become export demons but import far less, thereby building massive trade surpluses. They think this strengthens their economy, but it does them little good and sometimes harm. They have worked hard and accumulated billions of dollars but have chosen to forgo the joy of spending them. They get more respect in the world but live more poorly than they ought to, and, at their expense, Americans live better. They put their hard-earned money into overcapacity and bad loans and then suffer economic difficulties, as Japan has (see Chapter 17).

ECONOMICS ■ CURRENCY WARS?

In 2010, Brazil's finance minister uttered the words "currency war," and the term, loaded with fearful undertones, caught on. He was referring to the efforts of many countries—including Brazil—to prevent their currencies from climbing or, if already too high, bring them down to build or regain their export markets. The big problem was China, which kept the yuan 20 to 40 percent undervalued. Many other countries felt disadvantaged by the low RMB and threatened competitive or even retaliatory devaluations. The trouble is, if many countries devalue, none gain anything, but tensions mount and world trade shrinks.

Billions of foreign investments rushed into newly prosperous Brazil, pushing up the real about 25 percent in relation to the dollar, so Brasilia imposed a tax on capital inflows. In a parallel move, several other countries restricted capital movements. Central banks in Japan, South Korea, and Taiwan tried—by selling lots of their currencies—to bring down their values and recover their big export markets. The U.S. Federal Reserve's "quantitative easing" (in effect, printing more money) to get America out of its slump would also lead to cheaper dollars and thus boost exports. Europe saw how the high euro was harming exports and growth and plotted to lower it.

Much the same happened during the Great Depression as one country after another devalued its currency in the vain hope of boosting exports. It was called "beggar thy neighbor" and just made the depression worse. To prevent another such wave after World War II, the industrialized lands gladly joined the Bretton Woods agreement (see box on page 286) to fix exchange rates. In 2010, worried finance ministers attempted to forge a new agreement to rebalance trade and currencies and prevent competitive devaluations, but it was hard to reach consensus. Currency wars could make the Great Recession resemble the Great Depression.

But politicians and purveyors of "airport economics" (Paul Krugman's term for threateningly titled paperbacks at airport newsstands) persist in telling us that we are in an economic war with much of the rest of the world. It is not a war, however; it is an endless win-win exchange of goods and services. The more barriers that are placed in the way, the slower the gains for all sides. The trouble is that if people and nations as a whole begin to think that they are in an economic war, then they will turn increasingly protectionist. Remember, the road to World War II was paved with high tariffs.

Economic historians point out that global prosperity requires one major country to lead it—to keep trade open, enforce rules, and make its currency the world reserve. Without a strong stabilizer nation, trade constricts and prosperity dims. In the nineteenth century, Britain and the pound sterling were indispensable, but a weakened Britain could no longer play stabilizer after World War I, and the world economy spiraled downward in the Great Depression. After World War II, the United States and its dollars led the world toward ever-freer trade and growing prosperity. But does the United States have the economic strength and political will to continue to lead, or will bankruptcy and protectionism bring down the whole structure? The great tasks of statesmanship have shifted to the economic realm, to keeping the globe open to trade. If we cannot lead, no one else will.

mypoliscikit EXERCISES

Apply what you learned in this chapter on MyPoliSciKit (www.mypoliscikit.com).

 Assessment   Review this chapter using learning objectives, chapter summaries, practice tests, and more.

Flashcards   Learn the key terms in this chapter; you can test yourself by term or definition.

Flashcards

Video   Analyze recent world affairs by watching streaming video from major news providers.

Videos

Simulations   Play the role of an IR decision-maker and experience how IR concepts work in practice.

Comparative
Exercises

KEY TERMS

austerity (p. 289)
Bretton Woods (p. 288)
bubble (p. 288)
conventional wisdom (p. 290)
depression (p. 288)
exchange rate (p. 288)
Federal Reserve Board (p. 288)
fixed exchange rate (p. 288)

floating exchange rate (p. 288)
International Monetary Fund
  (p. 289)
Keynesian economics (p. 288)
mercantilism (p. 296)
neomercantilism (p. 297)
purchasing power parity
  (PPP) (p. 292)

recession (p. 288)
Special Drawing Rights
  (p. 290)
subprime mortgage (p. 293)
Victorian (p. 291)
World Bank (p. 289)
WTO (p. 294)

FURTHER REFERENCE

Bisley, Nick. *Rethinking Globalization*. New York: Palgrave, 2007.

Dumas, Charles E. *Globalization Fractures: How Major Nations' Interests Are Now in Conflict*. London: Profile Books, 2010.

Elkus, Richard. *Winner Take All: How Competitiveness Shapes the Fate of Nations*. New York: Basic Books, 2008.

Friedman, Thomas L. *The World Is Flat: A Brief History of the Twenty-First Century*, rev. ed. New York: Farrar, Straus and Giroux, 2007.

James, Harold. *The End of Globalization: Lessons from the Great Depression*. Cambridge, MA: Harvard University Press, 2001.

Hubbard, Glenn, and Peter Navarro. *Seeds of Destruction: Why the Path to Economic Ruin Runs Through Washington, and How to Reclaim American Prosperity*. Upper Saddle River, NJ: Prentice Hall, 2010.

King, Stephen. *Losing Control: The Emerging Threats to Western Prosperity*. New Haven, CT: Yale University Press, 2010.

Krugman, Paul. *The Return of Depression Economics and the Crisis of 2008*. New York: Norton, 2009.

Mallaby, Sebastian. *The World's Banker: A Story of Failed States, Financial Crises, and the Wealth and Poverty of Nations*. New York: Penguin, 2004.

Mandelbaum, Michael. *The Ideas That Conquered the World: Peace, Democracy, and the Free Markets in the Twenty-First Century*. New York: PublicAffairs, 2004.

O'Brien, Robert, and Marc Williams. *Global Political Economy: Evolution and Dynamics*. New York: Palgrave, 2004.

Phillips, Kevin. *Bad Money: Reckless Finance, Failed Politics and the Global Crisis of American Capitalism*. New York: Viking, 2008.

Posner, Richard A. *The Crisis of Capitalist Democracy*. Cambridge, MA: Harvard University Press, 2010.

Rachman, Gideon. *Zero-Sum Future*. New York: Simon & Schuster, 2011.

Rajan, Raghuram G. *Fault Lines: How Hidden Fractures Still Threaten the World Economy*. Princeton, NJ: Princeton University Press, 2010.

Reinhart, Carmen M., and Kenneth S. Rogoff. *This Time Is Different: Eight Centuries of Financial Folly*. Princeton, NJ: Princeton University Press, 2009.

Schwartz, Herman M. *Subprime Nation: American Power, Global Capital, and the Housing Bubble*. Ithaca, NY: Cornell University Press, 2009.

Smick, David M. *The World Is Curved: Hidden Dangers to the Global Economy*. New York: Penguin, 2008.

Soros, George. *The New Paradigm for Financial Markets: The Credit Crisis of 2008 and What It Means*. New York: PublicAffairs, 2008.

Stiglitz, Joseph E. *Freefall: America, Free Markets, and the Sinking of the World Economy*. New York: Norton, 2010.

Wolf, Martin. *Fixing Global Finance*. Baltimore, MD: Johns Hopkins University Press, 2009.

PART VI

THE POLITICS OF A NEW WORLD

Economic pressures are pushing toward some kind of new world, but economics alone cannot make a better world and can even create new conflicts. The world is trying, imperfectly, to civilize conflicts.

Chapter 19 describes the functions and methods of diplomacy and its changing role. Ambassadors are now largely symbolic, as fast communications and travel increasingly centralize foreign policy. Diplomacy focuses on negotiations and compromise, for which there are some rules for success.

Chapter 20 argues that international law (IL) is generally preferable to war. The foundation of IL is consistency and reciprocity, and laws now exist to regulate state behavior in every area of international relations. The growing volume of exchanges, from economic to the Internet, mean more IL, most of which is based on treaties. With no world police, sanctions used to back laws rely on self-help. Although international courts are limited as long as sovereignty reigns, human rights are increasingly a subject of IL.

Chapter 21 describes the new activism of the United Nations. With the end of the Cold War, Security Council vetoes are now rarer. Many countries now favor the UN, especially for "peace operations." The short, sad League of Nations and its collective security caution us not to expect a world government. Third-party diplomacy increasingly contains and settles conflicts. UN specialized agencies are indispensable in an integrating world. Interestingly, there are now fewer wars; Iraq and Afghanistan are atypical. States tend to fight only if they think they can win, and this is becoming rarer. Part of the reason is that democracies never fight other democracies. Peacekeeping operations also inhibit wars and move them to resolution. There is, indeed, a new world of international relations.

Chapter 22 considers the rise of "transnational" issues, namely the massive and unexpected shortages in our time of F.E.W.—food, energy, and water—and how the earth can cope with them. Energy is the underlying element, for fossil fuels lead to climate change and disruption of food and water resources. Humankind may have to learn to live within the planet's means.

CHAPTER 19

Diplomacy Is Still Alive

The U.S. Embassy in London is not that old—it opened only in 1960—but a new one in a more secure location is due to open in 2016 or 2017. (Andy Rain/Corbis)

Barack Obama pledged to revive U.S. diplomacy, that America's adversaries would find our hand open if they would unclench their fist. Even his predecessor, George W. Bush, better known for waging wars in Afghanistan and Iraq, tried diplomacy on Iran and North Korea—which are actually far greater nuclear dangers. This raised the question: Why go to war when you can open diplomatic contacts, hold multilateral meetings, and devise ways to lower tensions? To be sure, diplomacy cannot solve every conflict; Iran's and North Korea's fists stayed clenched. But with U.S. power stretched thin and domestic and world opinion critical of the U.S. wars, Washington had no immediate desire for new wars, and diplomacy was a convenient way to avoid them. Diplomacy can be useful.

Diplomacy is the putting of foreign policies into practice. A country's diplomats are its eyes, ears, mind, and mouth. They are present at almost every stage of a nation's foreign policy but are often undervalued in the modern world. The Bush 43 administration initially had little use for diplomacy, preferring blunt words and unilateral actions, but by the time Bush left office he was engaged in considerable diplomacy. Barack Obama did more of it, not always with success. **Diplomacy** is the way nations communicate with each other, feeling out their positions and defusing incidents before they get nasty.

For example, in April 2001 a U.S. Navy electronics surveillance aircraft collided with a Chinese jet fighter over the South China Sea and landed on the Chinese island of Hainan. Beijing was furious—or pretended to be—claiming the U.S. spy plane had been in Chinese airspace and had rammed the Chinese jet. Beijing demanded that Washington apologize. The real issue: China's claims to vast areas of the East and South China Seas would be reinforced by a U.S. "apology." Washington's reply was firm but not angry. Said U.S. Secretary of State Colin Powell: "We have nothing to apologize for." The Chinese pilot was to blame, and the U.S. plane was over what most of the world (but not Beijing) called international waters. China held the U.S. crew of 24. In Washington, Congressional anger grew.

Relations could have been damaged, but neither side wanted that. Beijing had too much at stake in its world economic ties, and Washington knew it. After quiet negotiations, an American letter said we were "very sorry" about the Chinese pilot and about entering China's airspace for the emergency landing. The subtleties of the Chinese translation allowed Beijing to claim it

QUESTIONS TO CONSIDER

1. Can diplomacy really calm tensions? In all cases?
2. How did nationalism and democracy hamper traditional diplomacy?
3. Has diplomacy outlived its usefulness?
4. What offices are typically found in a U.S. embassy?
5. How has diplomacy been misused?
6. What are the problems with political appointees as ambassadors?
7. What is the relationship between diplomats and soldiers?
8. What are the various types of third-party diplomacy?
9. How did Morgenthau think diplomacy could be revived?

303

CONCEPTS ■ DIPLOMACY AND FOREIGN POLICY

Diplomacy is the feedback loop by which foreign policy is constantly adjusted. It works like this:

1. An act, usually by a government, starts the process. For example, government B announces it will raise tariffs on imported goods.
2. Government A's embassy in B's capital hears the news and cables A's foreign ministry. A may perceive the act as a threat or opportunity (or both). For example, B's move is a threat if A has an export market in B.
3. Defining the national interest generally takes place in the foreign office (e.g., Department of State) of government A. This is the crux of diplomacy. A's officials decide what they want of country B, in this case, continuation of the export market for A's goods.
4. They establish a goal of trying to get government B to shift its policy, to do

something or not do something. In this example, A wants B to not raise tariffs.

5. They plan a strategy to make B conclude that going along with A's goal is in B's national interest too. The diplomats of A are instructed to suggest promises, threats, punishments, or rewards to government B.
6. They conduct the actual diplomacy by sending A's ambassador to see B's top officials to emphasize that B's goods will enter country A only so long as B does not raise its tariffs on A's goods. This is a threat, but it is presented politely. As a sweetener, ambassador A offers minister B a ten-year trade treaty that benefits both sides.
7. Diplomats monitor and evaluate the policy. If government B takes the deal, A has conducted successful diplomacy. If not, the officials of A would have to go back to points 3, 4, or 5 and try again.

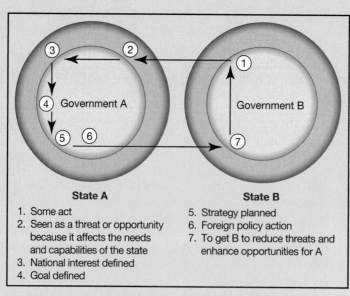

State A
1. Some act
2. Seen as a threat or opportunity because it affects the needs and capabilities of the state
3. National interest defined
4. Goal defined

State B
5. Strategy planned
6. Foreign policy action
7. To get B to reduce threats and enhance opportunities for A

A Model of Foreign Policy

was a "form of apology," and they released the crew. When both sides want it, diplomacy can work. In six months China decided it needed good relations with America and forgot the whole thing. What did China want? Respect (see Chapter 17), and diplomacy delivered that, calming a potentially dangerous crisis.

diplomacy Official political contact among governments.

embassy Chief diplomatic representation of one country to another.

bilateral Two countries.

multilateral Several countries.

THE RISE AND DECLINE OF DIPLOMACY

A crude diplomacy can be found far back in human history, whenever monarchs had contact with each other. At first this involved personal visits, such as the Queen of Sheba's journey to Solomon, probably to arrange trade. The deal was sealed in a way that allowed the Ethiopian emperor, millennia later, to claim he was descended from Solomon. Later, monarchs sent ambassadors, usually court noblemen, for temporary visits to another king to present gifts and make requests. With the rise of sovereignty in the sixteenth century (discussed in Chapter 1) came permanent **embassies**, houses in foreign capitals to report on and influence developments. Bribery was a standard method. Before the French Revolution unleashed nationalism, ambassadors were suave, of noble rank, and spoke French, the language of classic European diplomacy.

From the end of the Thirty Years War in 1648 to the French Revolution in 1789, diplomacy worked moderately well. It didn't prevent wars, but it helped keep them limited because ruling elites shared a common culture and common interests, namely, preserving their power. All players accepted the principle of monarchy, and none tried to overthrow the other. Their quarrels were relatively minor ones, and their wars were not wars of total destruction. Armies were small and professional. Classic diplomacy, operating on the basis of *balance of power* (see Chapter 1), tried to preserve a stable, conservative system by adjusting borders and alliances. Public opinion did not count in this predemocratic age.

CONCEPTS ■ DIPLOMACY

Diplomacy is political contact between national governments. Diplomatic negotiations can be **bilateral** or **multilateral**. Diplomacy is usually carried out by ambassadors, special envoys, or foreign ministers (such as the U.S. secretary of state). *Summit* diplomacy, personal contact by heads of government (such as the U.S. president), is risky and can make things worse. American presidents are especially prone to personalize diplomacy, because that is how U.S. domestic politics works. Lyndon Johnson believed he could persuade anyone he could meet face to face, including hostile foreign leaders.

Things can go wrong in such meetings. Kennedy deepened his Vietnam commitment after he thought Khrushchev looked down on him at their 1961 Vienna meeting. Bush 43 thought he saw Putin's soul by looking into his eyes. He also developed a palsy relationship with the president of Georgia, who then thought Washington would support Georgia's military action to take back breakaway South Ossetia in 2008. Instead, Georgia got quickly booted out, and there was nothing the United States could do.

Diplomacy should not be too personal lest warm feelings cloud rational calculation. Meetings must be prepared in advance and specify the topics to be discussed. Personal meetings should be held only *after* a general understanding has been reached. Some things really are better handled by professional diplomats.

foreign ministry   Branch of national government dealing with IR; called State Department in U.S. and Foreign Office in Britain.

anachronism   Something that no longer fits the times.

recognition   One country's opening of diplomatic relations with another.

symbol   Small thing or gesture that makes a political statement.

Nationalism and democracy changed diplomacy. Gone were the shared values and culture. Conservative monarchs were replaced by nationalistic states. Enthusiasm, the most dangerous of virtues, appeared as nationalistic regimes expanded their borders and colonies. With increased education, mass media, and democracy, public opinion counted for more and more. Politicians now worry that negative public reaction could cost them reelection. It is for this reason that U.S. politicians of both parties emphasize their toughness. It plays well with the voters, at least initially. With the electorate watching, diplomacy became much more difficult.

Particularly difficult for diplomacy to handle were the totalitarian dictatorships of Soviet Russia, Fascist Italy, and Nazi Germany, which used diplomacy as a cover to spread propaganda, subvert other countries, and grab pieces of Europe. Recently, states such as Iran and Libya have used their embassies as bases to carry out terrorist bombings and assassinations. Clearly, diplomacy changed in the twentieth century.

Should we do without conventional diplomacy? It is tempting. Modern telecommunications let **foreign ministries** contact each other directly by e-mail, fax, and telephone without going through embassies. The Washington–Moscow hotline was established in 1963 precisely because normal diplomatic channels were much too slow for the missile age. To understand each nation's position on major questions, all one needs is a mission to the United Nations, the world's greatest listening post (more on this in Chapter 21). For face-to-face meetings, top officials can fly to any capital overnight. Heads of government can meet in "summits," as Presidents Reagan and Gorbachev did in Geneva in 1985. No embassy by itself carries out important negotiations anymore. Some observers say conventional diplomacy has become an **anachronism**.

THE USES OF AN ANACHRONISM

There are still reasons for traditional diplomacy, complete with embassies and titles. Diplomatic **recognition** is an important **symbol**; a country recognized diplomatically by many lands gains legitimacy and sovereignty. If no one recognizes a country, its very existence is dubious. Under apartheid, South Africa granted four of its black "homelands" nominal independence, but no

CLASSIC THOUGHT ■ "SURTOUT, MESSIEURS, POINT DE ZÉLE"

The French "prince of diplomats" Talleyrand, an aristocrat who served both kings and Napoleon with equal aplomb, emphasized, "Above all, gentlemen, not the slightest zeal." Diplomacy must be conducted in calm with a cool head, not with enthusiasm. Zealots make poor diplomats; their commitment leads them to overlook complexity.

Commenting on Napoleon's 1812 invasion of Russia, Talleyrand noted, "It was worse than a crime; it was a blunder." He drew a tongue-in-cheek distinction between a crime, which hurts someone else, and a blunder, which hurts you. Enthusiasts often commit blunders.

other government recognized them. They were considered fake countries and are now again part of South Africa. In 2008 most of Europe and the United States recognized Kosovo, bolstering its independence. (Russia, China, and Spain did not recognize Kosovo, fearing it could encourage breakaway elements in their countries.) Iran, which broke diplomatic ties with the United States in 1979, could not purchase U.S. weapons in its desperate war with Iraq. Iran's mistreatment of American diplomats was a blunder.

Countries can signal their relationship by what they call their diplomatic missions. The highest level is embassy, but other units do the same work without that rank. Israel began relations with West Germany with a "purchasing mission." Later, it became an embassy, indicating full-level diplomatic contact. When the United States opened relations with China in 1972, there was already a U.S. embassy in Taiwan. If we had opened an embassy in Beijing, we would have had to close the one in Taipei, something President Nixon did not wish to do. We finessed the problem by opening "liaison offices" in each other's capital. They did everything embassies do. When, under President Carter, the time was ripe to turn them into embassies, we scaled down the U.S. embassy in Taipei to a "cultural institute" that does everything an embassy does. It is staffed by State Department personnel "on leave" who continue to collect their salaries and benefits. This phony setup got around the question of how to deal with Taiwan when Beijing insists it is the one and only China. Diplomacy must be flexible.

Diplomatic contact continues even when countries get mad at each other and "break relations." They rarely break them all the way, for contacts are still necessary. Instead, they turn their mission into part of the embassy of a third country. The United States broke relations with Castro's Cuba in 1961, but a few American diplomats staffed the "U.S. interests section of the Swiss embassy" in Havana. The Pakistan embassy in Washington houses an Iranian interests section. In this way, hostile countries can both break and maintain relations with each other.

DIPLOMATS

Not everyone who works in an embassy is a diplomat; indeed, only a minority have diplomatic status. Secretaries, drivers, communications people, and other staffers do not have diplomatic status, which is accorded by the host country foreign ministry in limited numbers to embassy officials only. Those accepted have their name, rank, and function printed in a "diplomatic list." They also get diplomatic license plates but still have to pay parking and traffic tickets.

CLASSIC THOUGHT ■ BALANCE-OF-POWER DIPLOMACY

Balance-of-power diplomacy is still around and is often quite useful, although few would say we have a balance-of-power system. Henry Kissinger, a scholar of nineteenth-century balance of power, noted carefully the differences between the eras but added that an "equilibrium of strength" was still necessary and desirable between the United States and the Soviet Union.

President Nixon, who read a great deal of IR, said in 1971, "I think it will be a safer world and a better world if we have a strong, healthy United States, Europe, Soviet Union, China, Japan, each balancing the other, not playing one against the other, an even balance." Nixon's rapprochement with China is a modern example of balance-of-power diplomacy and helped set the stage for a world of several major powers.

persona non grata Latin for "unwanted person"; order to expel a diplomat.

Accredited diplomats enjoy "diplomatic immunity" from arrest, trial, or imprisonment. These immunities developed over the centuries so diplomats could do their job without harassment. They operate on the basis of reciprocity: You treat me well, and I will treat you well. The embassy is considered foreign territory and may not be entered or searched by host-country police. The Soviet bugging and penetration of the U.S. embassy in Moscow, of course, made mincemeat of this tradition. U.S. diplomats there assumed that all their conversations were electronically overheard. The diplomatic pouch and other official shipments are likewise not supposed to be tampered with. The worst a host country can do to those on the diplomatic list is declare them **persona non grata**, an "unwanted person," and order them out of the country within a few days.

In a revolutionary world, some of these niceties have been grossly violated. Iran broke every rule in the book by holding U.S. embassy personnel hostage for over a year. In 1984, when a crowd of anti-Kaddafy Libyans protested at the Libyan embassy in London, an embassy employee shot from a window with a submachine gun, killing a policewoman. The most Britain could do was break relations with Libya, forcing the closure of both embassies. In 1987, French officials learned that a translator at the Iranian embassy was actually supervising terrorism. The man was not covered by diplomatic immunity, but he stayed hidden in the Iranian embassy. French police surrounded the embassy, and the Iranians did the same with the French embassy in Tehran. Here we see the importance of "shared values" in making diplomacy work; when they erode, diplomatic rules collapse.

Ambassadors are treated with deference, a carry-over from the days when most were aristocrats. The new ambassador presents his or her "credentials" to the host country's head of state, not necessarily the head of government. Most countries (but not the United States) split the two functions. A U.S. ambassador appointed to the "Court of St. James" (Britain), for example, presents his or her credentials to Queen Elizabeth, the symbolic head of state, rather than to the prime minister. This is a holdover from the days when an ambassador was a personal representative from one sovereign to another. A new U.S. ambassador in Germany presents his or her credentials to the figurehead president, not the chancellor. Ambassadors are conventionally listed as "extraordinary and plenipotentiary" (full-powered), another carry-over from the days when slow communications meant an ambassador really had the full power to negotiate for his sovereign. Nowadays, foreign ministries back home guide negotiations.

Do ambassadors have any purpose, or are they just for public relations? Much of their activity, of course, is meeting, greeting, and socializing. These are not strictly social occasions, however, for good ambassadors learn a lot from conversations, much of which is reported back to their foreign

DIPLOMACY ■ THE USE OF SIGNALS

In 1971, at an international table-tennis tournament in Tokyo, the Chinese delegation invited the American team to tour China. They did and had great fun. What was dubbed "ping-pong diplomacy" was actually Beijing's signal that they were interested in reestablishing relations. The White House got the signal. Kissinger visited Beijing secretly later that year, and Nixon arrived with great fanfare in early 1972. Good diplomats are quick to notice signals.

office. Some ambassadors, however, do little of substance, and some embassies work perfectly well without them—maybe better. Part of the problem here is the way some countries, especially the United States, fill ambassadorships.

Approximately a third of U.S. ambassadors are political appointees, few with backgrounds in foreign affairs. Often they are prestige-seekers who contribute big money to the president's election campaign. They rarely speak the local language or understand diplomacy. Some flamboyant types think they can solve difficult problems "the way we do back home." The U.S. ambassador to the Vatican, a political appointee, hopped over to Libya to straighten things out with Kaddafy, whom he knew from the oil business. The visit was strictly unauthorized. Shortly thereafter, we bombed Libya and the ambassador resigned. It's no job for amateurs.

Other political appointees, however, have done well. Arthur F. Burns, former chairman of the Federal Reserve Board, was an excellent ambassador to Germany; he spoke both German and economics. Former Senator Mike Mansfield (D-Montana) served as ambassador to Tokyo for years; he had been a professor of Asian studies and knew Japan well. Peter Galbraith, a former Senate foreign-relations staffer, was ambassador to Croatia where he helped settle the Balkan war in the 1990s. But in the main, political appointees have downgraded the importance of the job. If a wealthy person buys an ambassadorship, we in effect tell the host country and our own embassy staff that the position is unimportant.

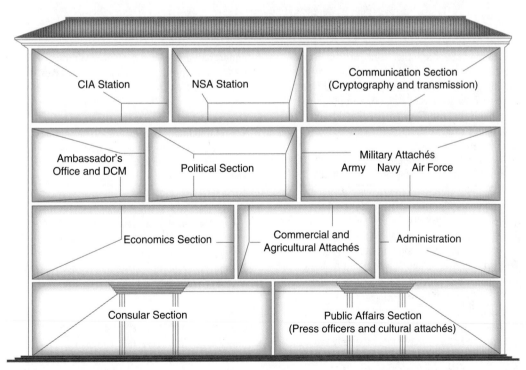

A Typical U.S. Embassy

INSIDE AN EMBASSY

A modern embassy is complex. It monitors its host country's economy, politics, public opinion, military capability, you name it. The embassy cutaway drawing on page 309 represents a typical U.S. embassy, usually a multistory building. Security is tight; all visitors are escorted. A Marine guard behind bulletproof glass carefully scrutinizes your passport. If possible, the building is situated well back from the street, away from car bombs. Large concrete "flower beds" on the sidewalk, actually blast shields, prevent vehicles from getting too close to the building.

The more sensitive offices are on the higher floors. On the ground floor is the consular section, which needs public access. American consuls, assisted by a staff of local employees (they're often cheaper and know the language), screen applicants and issue visas to come to the United States. A tourist visa is quick and easy to get, a student visa more complicated, and a prized immigration visa ("green card") usually requires a long, laborious process. Americans who need help—lost passports, emergency evacuations, lists of doctors and lawyers, registering a birth or marriage—also come to the consular section. The staff does not generally lend you money but can e-mail home.

Also on the first floor might be the public affairs section (formerly U.S. Information Service), which explains U.S. foreign and domestic policies, arranges scholarly, journalistic, and cultural exchanges, sets up exhibits, and sometimes maintains an American library.

REFLECTIONS ■ HOW TO JOIN THE FOREIGN SERVICE

The U.S. Foreign Service, the elite of the State Department, is the closest an American can get to a title of nobility. The 6,000 Foreign Service Officers (FSOs) are carefully recruited, trained, and promoted. Many aspire to join; few are chosen. Should you be interested, here's what to do:

■ Get a really thorough liberal arts education, one heavy on economics, political science, history, and English. Gain fluency in a foreign language. Read good periodicals for background on everything from culture to currency markets.

■ In your senior year, sign up to take the Foreign Service exam, given across the country. Your college career office has information and forms.

■ The exam is difficult, selecting about the top 10 percent of the thousands who take it. All you have to know is everything, especially economics. Don't be too disappointed if you don't pass the first time; you can take it again.

■ Go to graduate school to get the education you should have obtained as an undergraduate. The typical FSO has a master's degree; some have doctorates. The average age of a new junior Foreign Service Officer is 29.

■ Gain relevant work experience in business, banking, journalism, the military, or nongovernmental organizations (NGOs). Experience in developing countries shows you can live and work in the Global South, where many diplomatic postings are.

■ If you pass the written exam, then comes the oral exam, which skims off a minority of those who passed the written exam. To test your smarts and leadership ability, the examiners, veteran FSOs, might ask you anything from U.S. geography to the best fiction you've read lately. They may put you in a group of fellow test-takers to see how you interact and lead.

■ Didn't make it? Don't feel too badly; only a few hundred a year do. And think what a marvelous education and background you now have for private sector international work, which often pays better.

Semipublic offices might be on the second floor. The commercial and agricultural attachés provide information and contacts to help American firms sell their products abroad. The economics section might be here too, keeping tabs on the host country's growth,

> **consulate** Branch of an embassy with limited functions.

interest and inflation rates, and economic policies. The administration section, which distributes paychecks, finds housing, and runs the motor pool, might also be on this floor. Few documents on the first and second floors are classified, and most of the people working there are locals, not Americans.

About the third floor, things get more interesting and more classified. Here might be the ambassador's office and political section. There are few or no local employees. The ambassador or deputy chief of mission (DCM) represents the United States to the host government, conveying its wishes, requests, support, or disapproval. The political section, probably also on this floor, monitors parties, personalities, and policies. If its officers do a good job, there should be no surprises, such as unexpected coups, revolutions, electoral upsets, or wars.

The military attachés—army, naval, and air—may also be on this floor. Their work too is classified. They are considered "legal spies," gathering information on the host country's defenses, size and quality of army, types of weapons, and so on. They may also encourage the host country to purchase U.S. weapons, as this earns foreign currency, spreads out research and manufacturing costs, and ties the country to the United States.

On the top floor are usually the most sensitive and secret offices. The CIA station, whose personnel pass as State Department people, keeps tabs on underground happenings and may try to influence them. Contact with opposition groups, funding of local friends, and surveillance of hostile embassies are part of their duties. When it comes to certain matters, the CIA station chief may know more and be more important than the ambassador.

Nearby might be an electronic eavesdropping office of the National Security Agency. The NSA, which is far more secret than the CIA, conducts signals intelligence ("sigint"), monitoring the radio traffic of other countries and cracking their codes. Probably next door is a conventional communications room that transmits the embassy's reports to Washington, often encrypted. These electronics offices are on the top floor, not only to be close to their antennas but also to give staffers time to destroy files and cryptographic machines should the embassy be attacked.

The embassy is in the capital, but other important cities may have **consulates**, branches of the embassy that perform some of the functions of an embassy, usually in serving visa applicants and Americans abroad. A big consulate is called a consulate general. A consulate general like Hong Kong can be much bigger than a small embassy in an out-of-the-way country.

DIPLOMACY ■ PURGE OF THE "OLD CHINA HANDS"

During World War II, several bright, Chinese-speaking (they had been missionary kids) U.S. diplomats in China predicted that the Chinese Communists would beat the Nationalists after the war. They were right, but when the Communists took power in 1949, Republicans demanded to know "Who lost China?" The U.S. Foreign Service Officers—dubbed the "old China hands" because they had long experience in China—were accused of being pro-Communist (they weren't) and fired. Although later exonerated, their purge warned U.S. diplomats to report only good news. Accurate reporting can get you fired. In this way, political hysteria blinded U.S. policy in Asia for a generation and may have contributed to Vietnam. Politics can wreck good diplomacy.

President Jimmy Carter brought Israeli Prime Minister Menachem Begin, left, together with Egyptian President Anwar Sadat, right, for meetings at Camp David that led to the 1979 Egypt–Israel peace treaty. Personal diplomacy, however, does not always work. (Corbis)

Foreign Service Career corps of professional diplomats.

Only a minority of the people who work in a U.S. embassy are State Department **Foreign Service** Officers. The American secretaries and communications people are a separate category called Foreign Service Specialists. The attachés are from the military, commerce, agriculture, or other departments. Fewer than 30 percent of Americans at our posts abroad work for the State Department. And the local employees typically outnumber the Americans.

DIPLOMACY AND WAR

Many suppose diplomats and warriors are opposites. In some ways they are. Military officers are precise, definite, enthusiastic, can-do types. Diplomats are subtle, cautious, and used to dealing with ambiguities, more likely to tell you why something *shouldn't* be done. The common view is that diplomats work for peace while soldiers practice war, and that the two don't have much in common.

This is not accurate. The two, diplomats and warriors, are, or should be, part of the same foreign policy. One does not make sense without the other. Diplomats from a militarily weak country may have trouble making their point. Those from a militarily strong country are listened to carefully, for if worst comes to worst, they can deliver on their warnings. U.S. diplomats in the 1930s, representing a lightly armed country with no military forces in China, could admonish the Japanese to cease their conquest of China, but the Japanese did not take them seriously. By the same token, military might operating without diplomatic guidance is a blind, raging force that destroys to no good purpose. In the 1930s, Japanese militarists seized control of their government and began the conquest of China, which led them into a devastating war with the United States. The Pacific War

DIPLOMACY ■ THIRD-PARTY DIPLOMACY

One way to settle disputes is to have a neutral **third party** come between the two hostile parties. Third-party diplomacy is often the only way to bring warring nations to the conference table. Their hostility prevents a bilateral (two-party) meeting. The UN often sponsors third-party diplomacy. The Iran-Iraq War, the Soviet occupation of Afghanistan, and the decolonization of Namibia were negotiated under UN auspices. There are three ways a third party may facilitate the resolution of conflict:

Good Offices Here, the third party gets the hostile sides together, providing a meeting place, support services, and security. UN Secretary General Javier Pérez de Cuéllar brought France and New Zealand together under his **good offices** to settle the 1985 sinking of a Greenpeace protest vessel, for example.

Mediation and Conciliation In more-difficult situations, the third party may make proposals and give advice. Presidents Carter and Clinton tried to **mediate** Arab–Israeli conflicts at Camp David. Conciliation goes one step further; the third party, such as U.S. envoy Richard Holbrooke at Dayton in 1995, offers solutions to the disputants.

Arbitration Disputants may agree to let a third party decide the case like a judge. They select arbitrators, who make a decision after hearing the evidence. The parties are supposed to accept the decision, but there is no way to force them, and **arbitration** in IR is rare (but growing in U.S. civil cases).

---

might have been avoided if American diplomats had had military backup and Japanese generals had had diplomatic guidance.

One of the high points of U.S. diplomacy was the 1979 Camp David accords between Egypt and Israel, the first peace treaty between Israel and an Arab country. President Carter mediated personally between President Sadat of Egypt and Prime Minister Begin of Israel, smoothing feelings, suggesting compromises, and not letting his guests leave until they agreed. Notice here how the negotiating was done by heads of government, not by diplomats. A psychological incentive for Sadat and Begin to agree was the fact that the year before they had shared a Nobel Peace Prize. Both were proud of the award, and to have left Camp David without a treaty would have tarnished their reputations as men of peace. Unfortunately, Israelis and Palestinians in 2000 and 2010 were too far apart for, respectively, President Clinton's and President Obama's third-party diplomacy to work.

third party   Someone not party to a dispute.

good offices   Giving disputants a meeting place.

mediation   Suggesting compromises to disputants.

arbitration   Disputants' agreement to obey third-party decision.

CLASSIC THOUGHT ■ WAR BY OTHER MEANS

Some people think Carl von Clausewitz, the early nineteenth-century Prussian military thinker (see page 199), cynically favored war. They take his famous statement that "war is the continuation of diplomacy by other means" as the sort of policy Hitler pursued. Actually, Clausewitz urged that wars be limited to policy goals—set by a civilian government—rather than be allowed to escalate to an extreme, which is what wars might do if left entirely to generals. He is saying don't go to war simply because you have a grudge, but only for clear political goals that cannot be reached otherwise. Do not divorce war from diplomacy.

President Theodore Roosevelt successfully mediated an end to the Russo–Japanese War of 1904–1905. The Japanese trounced the Russians on land and sea but were running short of men and yen. They asked Roosevelt to mediate, and he called Japanese and Russian delegates to New Hampshire where he twisted arms to get the Treaty of Portsmouth that ended the war. For this, Teddy Roosevelt, the most bellicose of all U.S. presidents, won the 1906 Nobel Peace Prize. Roosevelt, too, recognized the importance of military backup in diplomacy. Said he in 1905: "I never take a step in foreign policy unless I am assured that I shall be able eventually to carry out my will by force."

The crux of diplomacy is willingness to compromise. Diplomacy worked best when monarchs played limited games. In a nationalistic world, compromise is hard. Countries may severely distrust one another and fear that giving up anything will be seen as weakness. Public opinion may undermine settlements of serious conflicts. Norwegian diplomats mediated the 1993 Oslo agreement between Israel and the Palestinian Authority, but hotheads on both sides brought the peace process to a standstill by acts of violence. An Israeli fanatic gunned down Prime Minister Rabin for being too willing to compromise. Israeli Prime Minister Ehud Barak's cabinet collapsed in 2000 for the same reasons. Palestinian suicide bombings killed any peace process. In the old days, kings didn't have to worry about public rage.

Could there be a revival of diplomacy in our day? It is possible, and there are a few good signs. The end of the Cold War made some previous antagonists more cooperative. Gone are the ideologies and arms races. Even the most rabidly nationalistic regimes gradually come to their senses after years of the stupendous costs that come with modern warfare. Egypt's Sadat didn't love Israel, but by the late 1970s Egypt was so broke and war-weary that Sadat found it possible to make his historic 1977 visit to Jerusalem, the capital of his archenemy. This dramatic example of "personal diplomacy" paved the way for the 1979 Camp David accords. In 2004, the leaders of India and Pakistan met personally to restart a peace process after years of tension between the two nuclear powers. Germany unified in 1990 with a series of diplomatic agreements that assured its neighbors that Germany would not be a threat. Canada and Spain used diplomacy to calm disputes over fishing rights.

Effective diplomacy, however, depends on the context. In a hostile situation where the parties seriously fear and mistrust each other, as between Washington and Pyongyang, diplomacy can accomplish little. Diplomats can meet and sometimes draft agreements, but they seldom calm hostilities. The Cold War was a long era of extreme mistrust during which only small points could be settled, such as the 1963 hotline agreement. As the Cold War faded, diplomacy accomplished more-serious tasks, such as the 1987 INF treaty that banned intermediate-range missiles. With the end of Cold War hostilities, many questions between the United States and Russia were settled with businesslike diplomacy, as there was no longer much to fear or mistrust.

CLASSIC THOUGHT ■ MUSIC WITHOUT INSTRUMENTS

The expression "Diplomacy without an army is like music without instruments" is attributed to Frederick the Great of Prussia, who ruled from 1740 to 1786. Frederick was both an excellent military commander and a clever diplomat (and fine musician) who helped build Prussia into one of Europe's major powers. He fully understood the military component of diplomacy.

The post–Cold War context prompted a revival of diplomacy in other areas. Third-party diplomats from the UN, the EU, and the United States helped bring together warring sides in Namibia and in the former Yugoslavia. Ethiopians, Eritreans, and Somalis occasionally made some progress in the Horn of Africa. China set up six-party talks to try to get North Korea to drop its nuclear weapons program. Even though it did not work, Washington appreciated Beijing's diplomacy. Turkey, repositioning itself as a Middle East power (instead of a European one), used diplomacy to settle old border and river disputes with Syria and Iraq. Next, Turkey along with Brazil tried to calm the Iranian nuclear problem. Much of the world agreed: "Give diplomacy a chance."

DIPLOMACY ■ MORGENTHAU'S NINE RULES

Hans Morgenthau (see page 24) had a profound impact on the study of international relations in the United States. This refugee scholar from Nazi Germany expounded a *realist* theory (see Chapter 2) that stripped away wishful thinking. He warned against both German and Soviet expansionism but cautioned Americans against indiscriminate use of force. He deplored, for example, the Vietnam War. Morgenthau did not think diplomacy was dead. It could be revived, if these nine rules were observed:

1. "Diplomacy must be divested of the crusading spirit." Ideological or religious doctrines aimed at remaking the world can lead only to war.

2. "The objectives of foreign policy must be defined in terms of the national interest and must be supported with adequate power." Define your interests narrowly, stressing that which really matters, and make sure you have enough power for that purpose.

3. "Diplomacy must look at the political scene from the point of view of other nations." Other countries have national interests, too, and so long as they are limited and rational they are legitimate.

4. "Nations must be willing to compromise on all issues that are not vital to them." If you've observed the first three rules, you will be able to see what is vital and what is not. If your adversary does the same, you can find a middle ground.

5. "Give up the shadow of worthless rights for the substance of real advantage." Don't worry about scoring legal or propaganda points; look to see what you're really getting in terms of national interest.

6. "Never put yourself in a position from which you cannot retreat without losing face or cannot advance without grave risks." Before you enter into negotiations, always ask how they can go wrong and how you can get out gracefully. Don't make unrealistic demands; you may have to back down on them.

7. "Never allow a weak ally to make decisions for you." Countries' national interests are seldom identical, and if you let a smaller ally define yours, you lose your freedom of action.

8. "The armed forces are the instrument of foreign policy, not its master." The military mind is blunt and destructive; the diplomatic mind is "complicated and subtle." With the military in charge, there can be no compromise.

9. "The government is the leader of public opinion, not its slave." Leaders of democracies must, of course, pay attention to public opinion, but they must also inform and educate it.

Source: Hans J. Morgenthau and Kenneth W. Thompson, *Politics Among Nations: The Struggle for Power and Peace*, 6th ed. New York: Oxford University Press, 1985.

mypoliscikit EXERCISES

Apply what you learned in this chapter on MyPoliSciKit (www.mypoliscikit.com).

 Assessment   Review this chapter using learning objectives, chapter summaries, practice tests, and more.

Menu

 Flashcards   Learn the key terms in this chapter; you can test yourself by term or definition.

Flashcards

 Video   Analyze recent world affairs by watching streaming video from major news providers.

Videos

 Simulations   Play the role of an IR decision-maker and experience how IR concepts work in practice.

Comparative
Exercises

KEY TERMS

anachronism (p. 306)

arbitration (p. 313)

bilateral (p. 305)

consulate (p. 311)

diplomacy (p. 305)

embassy (p. 305)

foreign ministry (p. 306)

Foreign Service (p. 312)

good offices (p. 313)

mediation (p. 313)

multilateral (p. 305)

persona non grata (p. 308)

recognition (p. 306)

symbol (p. 306)

third party (p. 313)

FURTHER REFERENCE

Art, Robert J., and Patrick M. Cronin, eds. *The United States and Coercive Diplomacy*. Herndon, VA: USIP Press, 2003.

Berridge, Geoffrey R. *A Dictionary of Diplomacy*. New York: Palgrave, 2001.

Cohen, Raymond. *Theatre of Power: The Art of Diplomatic Signaling*. White Plains, NY: Longman, 1987.

Craig, Gordon A., Alexander L. George, and Paul G. Lauren. *Force and Statecraft: Diplomatic Problems of Our Time*, 4th ed. New York: Oxford University Press, 2006.

Diebel, Terry L. *Foreign Affairs Strategy: Logic for American Statecraft*. New York: Cambridge University Press, 2007.

Dorman, Shawn, ed. *Inside a U.S. Embassy: How the Foreign Service Works for America*, rev. ed. Washington, D.C.: American Foreign Service Association, 2005.

Farber, David, ed. *What They Think of Us: International Perceptions of the United States since 9/11*. Princeton, NJ: Princeton University Press, 2007.

Holbrooke, Richard. *To End a War*. New York: Random House, 1998.

Kessler, Glenn. *The Confidante: Condoleezza Rice and the Creation of the Bush Legacy*. New York: St. Martin's, 2007.

Kissinger, Henry. *Diplomacy*. New York: Simon & Schuster, 1994.

Kopp, Harry W., and Charles A. Gillespie. *Career Diplomacy: Life and Work in the U.S. Foreign Service.* Washington, DC: Georgetown University Press, 2008.

Margalit, Avishai. *On Compromise and Rotten Compromises.* Princeton, NJ: Princeton University Press, 2009.

Ross, Carne. *Independent Diplomat: Dispatches from an Unaccountable Elite.* Ithaca, NY: Cornell University Press, 2007.

Ross, Dennis. *Statecraft: And How to Restore America's Standing in the World.* New York: Farrar, Straus & Giroux, 2007.

Sharp, Paul. *Outlaw Diplomacy: Relations Between Rogues, Pariahs and Polite Company in International Societies.* New York: Palgrave, 2011.

Zamoyski, Adam. *Rites of Peace: The Fall of Napoleon and the Congress of Vienna.* New York: HarperCollins, 2007.

CHAPTER 20

The Uses of International Law

A French frigate steams out of Djibouti to join a multinational fleet combating pirates in the Gulf of Aden. Traditional international law on piracy found new applications in the twenty-first century. (Eric Cabanis/AFP/Getty Images)

For many years, Greece and Turkey glared uneasily at each other. Under the Aegean Sea between them could be oil. Who owns it? Both countries claim the areas are within their territorial waters. Billions are at stake. Wars have been started for less, and the two countries have been bitter enemies for centuries. Instead of reaching for their guns, however, the two countries reach for their lawyers. War is a last resort that neither country wants nor can afford. They hire international lawyers, court law professors, measure their continental shelves, and haggle endlessly. It is better than fighting. By turning an economic and political dispute into a legal and technical dispute, they take some of the tension out of it.

International law (IL) may or may not eventually settle who has undersea drilling rights. More important is the fact that the two states wish to avoid war and find IL a convenient mechanism to do so. Some people who dismiss IL as weak and ineffectual—because it lacks the authority and sanctions of domestic law—fail to grasp its basic purpose. International law regulates exchanges between states in predictable ways, if existing law is followed or new law is created. Bluntly put, IL allows countries to page through law books instead of marching their troops. If both countries use IL, they avoid violence.

If you think about it a minute, this is what domestic law does. Instead of obtaining satisfaction through dueling, disputants obtain it in court. The same anger present in duels is present in lawsuits, but the emotions have been calmed and civilized to eliminate recourse to violence. Much domestic law exists to prevent violence, and this is the case with international law, too. IL, like domestic law, is a calmer-downer. In the post–Cold War era, IL has increased in volume, constraining more state behavior and injecting more lawyers into the foreign policy process.

QUESTIONS TO CONSIDER

1. How is international law (IL) like domestic law?
2. How do consistency and reciprocity over time build IL?
3. If IL lacks the enforcement mechanisms of domestic law, why is it generally obeyed?
4. What is "self help" in international law?
5. What are the several sources of IL? Which is the most important?
6. How can war be legal under IL? And if war is legal, how can "war crimes" be illegal?
7. How far out from its shores does a state extend?
8. Is there an "R2P" that overrides sovereignty?
9. How can piracy law be relevant in our day?
10. How did human rights become prominent in IL?

consistency   Observation of rules with no exceptions for oneself.

reciprocity   Doing to others what they have done to you.

CONSISTENCY AND RECIPROCITY

One of the major—and valid—complaints about IL is that it is used to justify whatever the powerful wish. The major powers are especially prone to cynically cloaking their actions with IL. They are inclined to apply IL to others but not to themselves (see box below). International lawyers, like all lawyers, are for hire.

But even the cynical use of IL is helpful. Once you have asserted, even for self-serving purposes, a point of IL, you find yourself under pressure to observe it consistently. If you denounce a rival for aiding rebels who are trying to overthrow a friendly government, then you are "hoist with your own petard" when you are caught aiding rebels who are trying to overthrow a government. You must either cease complaining about aiding rebels in general or stop aiding your favorite rebels. The U.S. government was in an embarrassing position when several Floridians were charged with breaking U.S. neutrality laws by helping the Nicaraguan *contras*, for that is precisely what the CIA and White House had been doing. Governments try to avoid looking hypocritical.

Another consistency case came when Russian forces broke South Ossetia away from Georgia in 2008. Washington chastised Russia for violating IL by changing borders by force. Moscow in effect replied, "And just what did you do in breaking Kosovo away from Serbia?" Consistency exerts some restraint on decision makers. During the 1962 missile crisis, President Kennedy rejected a surprise air attack on Cuba because it sounded too much like Pearl Harbor, and he didn't wish to be remembered as a "Tojo."

The human mind generally likes **consistency**. One of the surest ways to make people mad is to point out their inconsistencies. If they have claimed one thing in IL, they have some trouble claiming the opposite. Over the centuries, these pressures for consistency build up what is called "customary international law," law that has grown up because most countries preach it and don't want to be caught violating it. Contributing to this is the principle of **reciprocity**: What you do to me, I do to you. Nations, like people, cannot expect to get a whole lot better than they have given. Their obnoxious behavior will soon be returned by offended countries.

Reciprocity tends to be self-enforcing and contagious. Traditionally, cars with diplomatic license plates had been exempt from parking tickets—an extension of diplomatic immunity. Diplomats in Washington often abused the privilege by parking anywhere they liked, even in the middle of the street. In the 1960s, with permission from the State Department, DC police began ticketing diplomatic offenders, and the tickets had to be paid. Soon every country in the world dropped diplomatic immunity for illegally parked cars. (Actually, many other capitals were just itching to do what Washington did first.) Quickly and automatically, law governing diplomats had been modified by the simple principle of reciprocity.

CLASSIC THOUGHT ■ FREDERICK THE GREAT AND IL

It was said of Prussia's Frederick the Great: "First he conquered Silesia, and then he ordered his international lawyers to justify it." The expression epitomizes the cynical use of IL. Unfortunately, the same process goes on in most foreign offices today: First do it, then justify it.

The easiest area in which to apply reciprocity is diplomacy, one of the original topics of IL. Countries that break reciprocity suffer penalties. Obviously, Iran broke every rule in the book when

treaty	Contract between nations.

it held U.S. diplomats hostage in Tehran for over a year. No one retaliated directly against Iran, but most of the world deplored what Iran had done and severely limited diplomatic contacts. Tehran could scoff at this, but it hurt Iran in its war against Iraq. There was a price to be paid for breaking IL. International law is observed, studies show, to about the same degree as domestic law. In fact, law is about as essential in providing order and predictability to international relations as it is for domestic relations.

ORIGINS OF INTERNATIONAL LAW

The great mechanism for constructing IL is the **treaty**, an analog to the contract in domestic law. Treaty-making grew with the rise of the sovereign state in the sixteenth century (see page 17). States and IL were born twins, for IL protects and preserves states. IL also grew with the volume and importance of international exchanges. The opening of the New World spawned colonies, commerce, shipping, piracy, and wars, the worst of which was the Thirty Years War (1618–1648). Indeed, one of the first thinkers on IL, Grotius, wrote during and in horror at that massive war.

The Spaniard Francisco de Victoria (1480–1546), influenced by medieval Catholic thought, wrote that "natural law" from reason and necessity required orderly relations between states. IL transcended the will and consent of kings because states had to recognize the logic and interests of an international community. Another Spaniard, Francisco Suarez (1548–1617), took a more modern view and held that states had to first consent to IL.

TURNING POINT ■ LEGALISTIC EUROPE

One basic point driving Europe and the United States apart (see Chapter 16) is that since World War II, Europeans have become highly legalistic while Americans have rejected legalism in favor of military power. Europeans, after centuries of bloody wars, have come to appreciate governing their relations through treaties, IL, and the United Nations. They look at the many treaties leading to peace in Europe and to the step-by-step building of the EU and say, "See, treaties work." They believe that the expansion of IL through current and new treaties can do the same for much of the world, a view that presumes the rest of the world is eager for peaceful and orderly relations.

America has been going the other way and tends to see the world as violent and disorderly, unripe for treaties and IL. Ironically, from the late nineteenth century through the middle of the twentieth century, American scholars and statesmen, steeped in the classic liberalism of the day (see Chapter 2), concentrated on treaties and IL and denounced "power politics." Woodrow Wilson took us into World War I because German submarines were violating IL. Naively, Washington tried to outlaw war with the 1928 Kellogg-Briand Pact. (It didn't work.) After World War II, realist thinkers such as Hans Morgenthau and George Kennan persuaded Americans to abandon the liberal "legalist-moralist" approach in favor of the restrained application of U.S. power. Some in the Bush 43 administration disparaged IL and treaties and argued they were not binding on us. Europe and America split wide apart on this issue.

ratify   To formally accept treaty as binding.

Bridging both views was the true father of international law, Hugh de Groot (1583–1645), better known as Grotius. (Latin names were fashionable in the seventeenth century.) His 1625 work, *On the Law of War and Peace*, written (in Latin) in reaction to the barbarity of the Thirty Years War, made the case for moderation in warfare and for open, peaceful intercourse between nations. Sovereignty, he said, was limited by divine law, natural law, and the law of nations. The latter arises from both reason and the practice of international relations. Treaties must be obeyed, he said, because it was in the nature of all law that legal commands one has consented to must be obeyed.

With the growth of nationalism and democracy, governments emphasized that IL served state interests in order to sell IL to peoples and parliaments. IL arose in Europe, the birthplace of the modern state, but spread worldwide. Not everyone liked IL. Revolutionary regimes, such as Lenin's in Russia, rejected the state concept and IL. Workers had no country, Lenin argued, and existing "bourgeois" agreements were to be scrapped. It took years before the Soviet Union and then China rediscovered the utility of IL. Nazi Germany never accepted IL and paid for it. More recently, Global South states have denounced IL as something made by colonialists for their own interests, but these lands too have gradually appreciated the value of IL. Eventually, even Iran may get the message.

CONCEPTS ■ HOW TO MAKE A TREATY

Some treaties are bilateral, some multilateral. A treaty can also be called an accord, convention, pact, protocol, agreement, compact, or arrangement. Here's how they make and break them.

1. Negotiation: Any designated representative of a state can negotiate a treaty. Usually this is an official diplomat, but it can be a chief executive, foreign minister, or special representative. Negotiators generally come with proposals prepared by their governments and don't have much leeway to make changes or compromises, which have to be approved back home. Diplomats are not free agents.

2. Signing: Once the negotiators have initialed each paragraph of the text to show they are in agreement, a top figure signs it. If it's an important treaty, presidents may sign it with fanfare. Even unratified, IL stipulates that the parties cannot act contrary to the treaty until ratification has failed.

3. Ratification: Every state has constitutional procedures for its formal consent to treaties. In the United States, two-thirds of the Senate (the House is not involved) must consent to a treaty to allow the president to **ratify** it formally. Technically, the Senate does not ratify, which is done only by the executive. Understandings and reservations may be attached; if important, they have to be renegotiated with the other parties. Failure to ratify releases that state of obligations. Finally, the treaty is registered with the UN Secretariat.

4. Termination. Some treaties are of unlimited duration, some fixed. Some set a time for renewal. Treaties end when one or more parties violate it, when a new treaty supersedes the old one, by war between the parties, and by the disappearance of a state. The Bush 43 administration, desiring to build a national strategic defense, told Moscow that it regarded their 1972 Anti-Missile Treaty as obsolete. Moscow noted that this would end it on both sides, so in effect the 1972 treaty died.

COMMANDS

Like domestic law, international law has both commands and **sanctions**. The command obliges states to behave in particular ways. Maritime law, for example, commands extensive freedom of the seas beyond the 12-mile **territorial limit** but not within it. Diplomatic immunity commands that there be no arrest or trial of accredited diplomats even if they commit a serious crime. In 1986, a South Korean diplomat in New Zealand who habitually drove drunk ran over a pedestrian. All the New Zealand government could do was declare the diplomat *persona non grata* (an unwanted person) and expel him.

sanction Punishment for violation of IL.

territorial limit Extent of sovereignty from states' shores.

executive agreement A commitment of less importance than a treaty.

Because there is no supergovernment to tell states what to do, commands must be those that states impose upon themselves, an important characteristic of IL. States must consent to the commands they will follow. Without consent, there is no IL. Clearly, this is different from domestic law, where citizens may not consent to a law but are under its command anyway. Domestic law occurs within sovereign entities, IL among them.

IL is a direct expression of *raison d'état*, the "reason of the state" or the "interests of the state." Some believe that IL serves and protects the global community, but it is secondary to treaties, which are negotiated among states and command only those who ratify them. Treaties are negotiated by diplomats to get commitments from other states to behave a certain way. They are contracts between states that serve state interests.

Weaker than treaties but still binding are **executive agreements**, widely used by U.S. presidents because Senate approval of treaties is slow and often turns into a political football. The United States now signs few treaties—the Bush 43 administration especially did not like them—but many executive agreements. Critics do not like executive agreements, viewing them as end runs around Senate scrutiny. The early 1950s isolationist Bricker Amendment tried to block use of executive agreements, and the liberal 1972 Case Act required that they be reported to Congress.

Custom creates commands if a particular right or obligation is practiced and not challenged by other states. For example, the United States treats the Chesapeake Bay as its territory, and no one has challenged the U.S. claim. Libya, on the other hand, claims the Gulf of Sidra, but no one accepts that claim because it's too wide. U.S. warships periodically enter it to express lack of consent. Commands based on custom take time to develop and can be ambiguous because they are usually unwritten. The same is true of IL based on reason, morality, and justice. Few states explicitly consent to them. Treaties are a firmer foundation for IL.

CONCEPTS ■ SUCCESSOR STATES

Is Russia the continuation of the Soviet Union and Serbia of Yugoslavia? Most states follow the "continuity rule" and recognize the rights and duties of what are called successor states. Treaties the old government signed carry over to the new. Russia got the Soviet Union's permanent seat on the Security Council but also agreed to existing treaties, such as those on arms control. Serbia stopped calling itself Yugoslavia in 2003 but strove to make sure its treaties, signed under the name Yugoslavia, on the use of the Danube River and its borders with Hungary and Romania were not questioned.

exclusive economic zone Fishing and mineral rights 200 miles from shore belong to that country.

SANCTIONS

Why do states obey international law? Because they benefit from it. Arms control agreements lessen the risk of war, stop arms races, and reduce defense costs. Trade agreements build markets and increase the flow of goods. Extradition treaties remove sanctuaries for criminals. To violate treaties and IL would remove these benefits. When you break a contract, you don't get the benefit of the contract.

DIPLOMACY ■ LAW OF THE SEA

One of the first subjects of IL and one of Grotius's main points is still a hot topic: law of the sea, which continually evolves. Who owns the sea? For most of history it was considered *res nullius* (nobody's thing), so anybody could take its fish. (Big current problem: overfishing.) More recently, some countries, especially poor and landlocked ones, want the sea considered *res omnes* (everybody's thing), so the UN can redistribute profits to them from the vast but unknown amounts of oil, natural gas, and minerals that lie under the seabed.

How far from shore a country's territory extends has been debated for centuries. By the eighteenth century, three miles from shore was defined as a country's territorial limit (sometimes called the "cannonball rule," although old cannons could not shoot nearly that far). Anything beyond three miles was considered international waters. Not every country liked that. The Soviet Union didn't want foreign spy ships getting that close to its shores and proclaimed 12 miles as its limit. Other maritime powers adopted the same view, and now 12 miles is standard. Ecuador and Peru didn't like others fishing so close and proclaimed a 200-mile limit. They even seized U.S. tuna boats.

After many years of negotiation, a UN Convention on the Law of the Sea (UNCLOS) covering territorial limits, **exclusive economic zones** (EEZs), military uses, piracy, environmental pollution, and many other points was concluded in 1982. The United States participated actively in UNCLOS but, fearing infringement on its economic rights, never ratified it. Even so, the United States informally abides by most of its rules.

Now, thanks to UNCLOS, countries agree to a 200-nautical-mile EEZ from their coasts for their own fishing and mineral rights. (A nautical mile is 1.15 U.S. miles, so the EEZ is 230 regular miles or 370 kilometers.) In addition, countries may claim a wider EEZ if they can prove their continental shelves extend beyond 200 miles. Many do so. The EEZ is still open sea for commercial ship movement; it is not sovereign territory.

A problem looms in China's claim to a 200-nautical-mile limit extending deep into the South and East China Seas, including the Taiwan Strait, and the Yellow Sea farther north. The world accepts these waters as China's EEZ, but China sees them also as a security zone with the right to control foreign military ships in them and flights over them. The U.S. Navy traverses these waters well beyond the 12-mile limit in order to survey Chinese military activity, including the possible massing of forces to invade or intimidate Taiwan and submarine bases on Hainan Island. Beijing, citing UNCLOS provisions, calls the U.S. activities in its EEZ prejudicial to China's security and claims the right to bump U.S. ships and aircraft to show it means business. If Beijing wished it, IL could help settle who can do what off China's shores before a major incident blows up.

Global warming is making territorial limits newly relevant. Melting Arctic ice opens up the legendary Northwest Passage to shipping north of Canada. Canada has long claimed a giant Arctic wedge with the North Pole as apex. In 1969 Ottawa passed a law proclaiming a 100-mile Canadian "management zone" extending north of Canada's shores. Any foreign ship, including U.S. ships, must get Canada's permission to transit the zone.

But why do states obey IL when it costs them something and they don't want to obey? No world police force exists to keep states law-abiding, but there are sanctions that make states obey even though they do not want to.

Courts, even at the national level, backed by national police powers, can enforce IL as if it were domestic law. In *Missouri v. Holland* (1920), the state of Missouri did not want to carry out provisions of a treaty with Britain (for Canada) that protected migratory birds. The U.S. Supreme Court ruled the treaty was valid as U.S. law. Now using national courts to sue foreign wrongdoers is a growing trend. A 1993 Belgian law opened its courts to lawsuits over human rights that had nothing to do with Belgium. The cases seemed designed to embarrass leaders rather than actually collect damages. A little-used 1789 U.S. law was dusted off and used to sue the former leaders of Serbia, China, and Britain as well as terrorists and German companies that used slave labor during World War II. The United States has a consistency problem here. We try foreigners in U.S. courts but sometimes reject the jurisdiction of foreign courts to try American wrongdoers, as in the new International Criminal Court. Whichever way we resolve the inconsistency expands the realm of IL.

The UN Security Council can establish special tribunals to try war criminals and human rights violators. Two such tribunals, both with Judge Richard Goldstone of South Africa as chief prosecutor, began functioning in 1995—one in the Hague to try offenders in the wars in the former Yugoslavia and one in Tanzania to judge Hutu and Tutsi perpetrators of genocide in Rwanda. Although faced with questions of how to catch the accused and what laws to employ, they got some convictions and warned future war criminals that they could be brought to justice.

CONCEPTS ■ INTERNATIONAL SANCTIONS

The UN Charter states that "armed force shall not be used, save in the common interest." In 1950 the Security Council charged North Korea with "breach of the peace" and called on it to withdraw from South Korea. Then the UN urged members to assist the South militarily. In 1990, the Security Council authorized war to expel Iraqi forces from Kuwait. Both were examples of international sanctions, which include the following:

1. *Reprisals* include confiscation of property, boycotts, and punitive raids, normally illegal under IL. They become legal when an injured party responds to violations of law. The UN Charter doesn't like any use of force, but it also acknowledges the right of self-defense. Reprisals are far more limited than war. In 1986, the United States bombed military installations in Libya, claiming it was a reprisal to Libyan-sponsored terrorist bombing.

2. A *retorsion* is a milder sanction, a reply against a state that does something objectionable. Iran's support of terrorism and its nuclear program led the United States to cut off all trade with Iran in 1995. In 2010, the UN voted to sanction Iran for its secretive nuclear program, and Iran's exports and imports took a hit.

3. *War* is an acceptable sanction in IL. "Contending by force," Grotius's definition of war, can be used legally against those who start aggressive wars. Defining "aggression," however, is hard; no definition is accepted by all. Often the side that fires first (preempts) is the defender; the aggressor is often the side that mobilizes first.

de facto "In fact"; simplest form of recognition, often informal, without embassies.

de jure "In law"; higher form of recognition, formal and with embassies.

States can take cases against other states to the World Court, but the accused state has to consent in advance. A country cannot be dragged into the World Court. Many states make their participation conditional; the United States is especially cautious. The 1946 Connally Amendment rejects the Court's jurisdiction on "matters which are essentially within the domestic jurisdiction of the United States of America as determined by the United States of America."

SELF-HELP

Injured states can also use a sanction known as "self-help." Weaker states rarely try this against stronger states. The United States indirectly attacked Cuba in 1961, but Cuba did not retaliate by attacking the United States. Some states use extralegal sanctions, such as terrorism and supporting the opposition in the other country.

States that break international agreements have difficulty making new agreements and are isolated diplomatically. For example, Uganda's abuse of foreigners under Idi Amin in the 1970s, Libya's sponsorship of international terrorism in the 1980s, and Iraq's aggression in the Persian Gulf in the 1990s left these regimes shunned in negotiations and reduced their foreign relations.

Worldwide news coverage can damage an offending state. The 1979 Soviet intervention in Afghanistan and the 2003 U.S. invasion of Iraq hurt both on the world scene. No country likes to be called an aggressor; that can lead to realignments and the loss of allies and influence. The Idi Amin regime in Uganda was finally toppled when Tanzania aligned with Ugandan rebels and intervened militarily in 1979. Most of the world cheered.

U.S. action against Panama in 1989 is a dramatic example of extralegal self-help. With not one vote of support in the Organization of American States, the United States invaded Panama, overthrew its corrupt government, and carted off its leader, Manuel Antonio Noriega, for trial and imprisonment in Miami on drug charges. After serving his time, in 2010 Noriega was extradited to France for money laundering and got another seven years. The two Noriega cases set IL precedents.

Self-help, however, often leads to violation of IL. Strong states with important national interests at stake tend to ignore legal commands. It was common during the Cold War. The United States tried to subvert Nicaragua's revolutionary government to preserve its sphere of influence. The Soviet Union invaded Afghanistan to keep a buffer client state. In each case, the injured party either could not or would not employ sanctions to stop the breaking of international law. Lawbreaking states are willing to suffer some long-term costs when violating IL for what their leaders perceive as short-term necessities.

RECOGNITION

Recognition acknowledges the existence of another state and its government. It is important in the lives of countries. If most states, especially the major powers, recognize a country, it buttresses its sovereignty and makes it accepted. Recognition does not necessarily mean diplomats are exchanged. Some poor countries recognize other states but do not maintain embassies there. (They meet at the UN.) Recognition can be **de facto** (in fact) by provisionally dealing with that state's representatives or, at a higher level, **de jure** (by law) upon an official pronouncement to that effect.

When the Chinese Communists, for example, took over the mainland in 1949, the United States continued to recognize the Nationalist government, which had fled to the island province of Taiwan. Then the Korean War, in which Communist China fought the United States, made recognition politically impossible. When the Sino–Soviet rift changed U.S. perceptions of China, President Nixon made his dramatic 1972 trip to Beijing, a form of de facto recognition. In 1979, Beijing and Washington de jure recognized each other. This required Washington to de-recognize Taiwan, as Beijing insists it is the one and only China. U.S. Secretary of State Albright's visit to North Korea in 2000 gave that country de facto but not yet de jure recognition.

Recognition helps make states participants in IL because it gives them certain rights; for example, the right of continued existence, which means the right of self-defense. Article 51 of the UN Charter confirms this right. The duties of states come from respecting the rights of other states. States have a duty to obey treaties. They have a duty not to intervene in another state, although this is widely ignored. Some argue they have the right to protect their citizens in other lands and to render humanitarian service where natural or political disasters "shock the conscience of humankind." In 2003, even the United States sent civilian and military personnel to Iran to help after a terrible earthquake.

The UN Security Council said the international community had a duty to intervene in Haiti in 1994, where a military regime was abusing civil and political rights. Haitians fled in unsafe boats, and hundreds drowned. More interventions are now UN-sanctioned than ever before, and most involve human rights abuses.

TERRITORY

Under IL, conquest and annexation of territory are frowned upon. Disputes over territory can lead quickly to violent conflict. The best way to prevent this is to establish and observe boundaries under IL. First, a border must be agreed upon in a boundary treaty and carefully marked on

REFLECTIONS ■ EICHMANN AND PIRACY

As a young journalist I landed a job with the Associated Press at the Eichmann trial in Jerusalem in 1961. This got me into the meticulously secured building for a firsthand view of this major trial. Adolph Eichmann had been a mid-level Nazi official in charge of rounding up Europe's Jews and shipping them to death camps. He had been living in Argentina under an assumed name when Israeli agents kidnapped him and brought him to Israel for trial.

There was much discussion in the courtroom about the IL aspects of the Eichmann case. How could Israel (1) kidnap someone from another country; (2) try him for crimes committed in distant countries before Israel even existed; and (3) call him a criminal when he was just following orders?

These arguments took weeks and were highly complex, but the main argument of Attorney General Gideon Hausner was piracy. IL had long held that pirates can be tried by whomever catches them; their crimes are not specific to a nation or place. This is now called "universal jurisdiction" but is still controversial. Hausner argued that piracy law set a precedent for other types of international lawlessness. As for Eichmann just following orders, Hausner demonstrated that (1) the orders themselves were illegal, and (2) Eichmann exceeded them in his personal eagerness to kill Jews. Eichmann was found guilty, among other points, of "crimes against humanity" and was hanged in 1962.

—M. G. R.

maps and on the ground, as with concrete pylons and posted signs. Unfortunately, few borders in the world have been so clearly established.

IL tries to move disputes to settlement, often using historic or geographic indicators. There are many boundary questions that IL has tried to solve: the India–Pakistan fight over Kashmir, Venezuela with Guyana, Peru with Ecuador, Argentina with Chile over Tierra del Fuego, Morocco with Algeria over the Spanish Sahara, and Iran with Iraq over the Shatt al-Arab waterway. In this last case, customary IL puts the boundaries between two *riparian* states (see page 363) at the deepest point of the river. In all such cases, IL can work only if the disputants want to settle. Then IL becomes a convenient and sometimes face-saving way to do so.

In a parallel with the law of the sea, states control the air above their territory to the edge of the earth's atmosphere, generally taken to mean as high as a plane can fly. Custom and a UN resolution say that orbiting satellites are outside the state's jurisdiction, like international waters.

WAR

The Kellogg-Briand Pact of 1928 actually outlawed war. Some use this as an example of the irrelevance of IL. Article 51 of the UN Charter allows war for self-defense. In 1625 Grotius wrote that it is lawful "to kill him who is preparing to kill." The difficulty in defining who is the aggressor and who the defender has left international law largely impotent in eliminating the use of armed force. Where IL has been more successful is in limiting the use of armed force. Customary IL prohibits the excessive use of force to defeat an enemy.

Multilateral conventions, going back to the 1864 Geneva Convention, prohibit certain practices and weapons and establish various procedures for the conduct of war. Poison gas, exploding bullets, and shotguns have been prohibited. Neutrals, civilians, and prisoners of war are supposed to have rights and obligations. Victors occupying conquered land have been constrained in their treatment of the defeated. Trials for war crimes are becoming more frequent. Nevertheless, it is safe to say that every side in every war has violated the rules of war.

Attacking harmless civilians is a war crime under the Geneva Convention of 1949, seconded by the U.S. Uniform Code of Military Justice. In 1968, U.S. soldiers slaughtered over 300 Vietnamese civilians in My Lai, South Vietnam. The U.S. military had never instructed its soldiers

TURNING POINT ■ HOLE IN THE OZONE

IL plays a major role in the world's growing awareness of environmental damage. Ultraviolet (UV) radiation from the sun causes skin cancer and other damage. A fragile layer of ozone shields the earth from much UV. Scientists discovered that chlorofluorocarbons (CFCs), chemicals in aerosol sprays and refrigerants, attack and deplete the ozone layer. In 1987 a hole in the ozone layer was discovered over Antarctica. A series of negotiations produced a protocol signed and ratified by many states to reduce the production and use of CFCs. Your air conditioner and hair spray are now different because of that. Discussions are underway to reduce the gases that contribute to global warming.

about war crimes. Now representatives of the Judge Advocate General (JAG) advise all operations and draw up rules of engagement (ROEs), especially important in counterinsurgency operations such as Afghanistan.

Domestic legal systems contribute to IL. The capture of terrorists, for example, raises tricky questions. The Bush 43 administration invented a new category, "unlawful enemy combatants," captives who are neither civilians nor soldiers with no rights as either criminals or prisoners of war. Some were held in Guantánamo for years with no trials, lawyers, or outside contact. In 2008, the Supreme Court ruled that **habeas corpus** still applies even though they were not on U.S. soil. The ruling built pressure to treat the detainees as criminal suspects, which the Obama administration did. A definition like this becomes a precedent for IL worldwide.

habeas corpus   Right of detainee to appear before judge.

human rights   Freedom from government abuse such as torture, jail, or death without due process.

war crimes   Mistreating prisoners or civilians.

precedent   Legal reasoning based on previous examples.

jus ad bellum   Traditional rules on right to go to war.

jus in bello   Traditional rules on behavior in war.

Geneva Convention   Modern rules on behavior in war.

IL AND HUMAN RIGHTS

Before World War II there had been little law on **human rights**; Hitler and the Holocaust changed that. The Nuremberg War Crimes Trials in 1945–1946 established a major precedent by trying the top 21 Nazis and sentencing 11 of them to death. Nuremberg, staffed by U.S., British, French, and Soviet judges, was controversial at the time. There had been no category called **war crimes** before, but Nazi Germany had committed "crimes against humanity" on civilians and prisoners.

Some criticized Nuremberg as "victors' justice" or legalistic revenge that invented dubious laws after the fact and applied them to soldiers who had just been carrying out orders. The legal reasoning against these arguments has been cited ever since. U.S. prosecutor Telford Taylor argued, "There are some universal standards of human behavior that transcend the duty of obedience to national laws." Nuremberg set the precedent for the 1946–1948 Tokyo war crimes trials after Japan's defeat, the 1961 Eichmann trial (see page 327), and recent Bosnian and Rwandan war crimes tribunals. In 2008, the Hague tribunal put Radovan Karadžić, the Serbian chief in Bosnia, on trial for ordering the mass murder of thousands of Muslims (see page 257).

The 2006 trial (and hanging) of Saddam Hussein to some extent continued the concept of war crimes. Where and how to try Saddam—an international tribunal or an Iraqi court? Was he primarily a war criminal or a domestic murderer? He was captured by U.S. soldiers but tried by an Iraqi court, a decision that could serve as a **precedent** for similar cases in the future. Decades earlier, he would likely not have been considered a criminal, merely the head of a defeated state.

These cases continued the Western tradition of trying to limit war and its horrors. Medieval Catholic churchmen expounded **jus ad bellum** and **jus in bello**. The tradition was expanded with the **Geneva Convention**, which is actually a compilation of four conventions held between 1864 and 1949 to which over 150 countries (including the United States) now adhere. It codifies principles on noncombatants, prisoners, wounded, occupation, and permissible weapons. One Geneva-type question: Should terrorist suspects held at Guantánamo be treated as POWs? Torture

civil rights Ability to participate in politics and society, such as voting, free speech, and equality.

R2P Responsibility to protect; theory that outside powers may intervene to stop regimes from abusing their own citizens.

by U.S. soldiers at Abu Ghraib prison in Iraq clearly flunked the Geneva Convention and embarrassed the United States.

Human rights were included in the UN Charter, and the new UN drew up the Universal Declaration of Human Rights in 1948. Although not a treaty, the declaration set the stage for more specific covenants, such as one on **civil rights** (United States ratified in 1992); racial discrimination (United States ratified in 1994); economic, social, and cultural rights; women and children; torture; and most recently (2002) the International Criminal Court. The U.S. delay or failure to ratify these later covenants came from the notion that U.S. sovereignty and Constitution are supreme, to be controlled by no outside power. The new International Criminal Court started without U.S. participation. Congress feared it would bring frivolous charges against American officials and soldiers.

The old IL norm that states can do whatever they wish to their citizens has eroded. In 2001 a new doctrine, **R2P**, advanced the theory that if a state cannot protect its own citizens' human rights, the international community has a responsibility to step in, even overriding sovereignty. The 2003 U.S. invasion of Iraq implicitly contributes to R2P, as the Bush 43 administration argued that dictators are responsible for crimes against their own people. (The Nuremberg and Tokyo trials were for crimes against civilians in *other* countries.) Unwittingly, the Bush administration, hostile to IL, set major IL precedents.

There are problems with R2P. If the Americans assert, say, a responsibility to protect Kosovar Albanians from Serbian massacres (which we did), Russians can assert R2P to protect South Ossetians from a Georgian attack (which they did). Who will decide the proper use of R2P? The UN Security Council? But the United States, Russia, and China have the right to veto Security Council resolutions (see next chapter), so any R2P measure they opposed could be blocked. Aggressive countries could cover their moves as R2P. Critics charge that R2P is a "right to intervene" that powerful lands will use against weaker countries.

Individuals have some rights under various conventions on human rights. Citizens have a right to claim protection by their state. Sometimes they do not get it, and some become refugees. The 1951 Geneva Convention on the Status of Refugees has given refugees some not very clear rights. Criminals can be extradited to the country where the crime was committed, but some states reject extradition and grant foreign political offenders asylum. Criminals committing crimes within the jurisdiction of a foreign state are usually subject to prosecution by that state, as Americans caught using drugs abroad have discovered. So have hijackers, pirates, slave traders, and terrorists.

Treaties on human rights have opened governments to suits in domestic and international courts. In 1996, a Spanish prosecutor charged the former military presidents of Argentina and Chile with killing Spanish citizens. When Chilean general Augusto Pinochet visited Britain for medical treatment in 1998, Spain demanded his extradition, and Britain had to (house) arrest him. Britain skirted the difficult legal issue by letting Pinochet return to Chile for (bogus) health reasons, but the episode showed that ex-dictators are not immune to human rights charges. The European Court of Human Rights faulted Britain for its harsh treatment of suspected IRA terrorists. Britain in 2000 adopted the European Convention on Human Rights as domestic law, thereby giving itself the equivalent of a U.S. Bill of Rights for the first time.

International Court of Justice in the Hague, Netherlands, convenes in 2010 to hear a case between Argentina and Uruguay. (Robin Utrecht/Corbis)

THE FUTURE OF IL

The legitimacy of IL is on the rise in spite of the obvious violations we now see in regional wars, terrorism, and human rights violations. Even the Bush 43 administration was compelled to say it respected IL. The present, unsettled world leaves regional conflicts uncontrolled and with the potential to spread, to disrupt trade, and to lead to massacres. These threats create common national interests for a more stable, orderly world. IL can help.

Half of the world's states are at least approximately democratic and favor rule of law in guiding international relations. Communication and transportation have vastly accelerated exchanges between states, exchanges that have to be regulated. The cyberworld was unhappy in 2000 when the Filipino "love bug" hacker, who caused millions in damage, walked free because the Philippines had no law against it. It does now.

One indicator of the growth of IL is the number of U.S. law schools that teach it. In 1900, only six had such programs. Now, ten times that number exist. One way to produce more law—as Americans well know—is to produce more lawyers. If a new, more peaceful IR system consolidates around the world, there will be a major growth of IL.

EXERCISES

Apply what you learned in this chapter on MyPoliSciKit (www.mypoliscikit.com).

 Assessment   Review this chapter using learning objectives, chapter summaries, practice tests, and more.

Menu

 Flashcards   Learn the key terms in this chapter; you can test yourself by term or definition.

Flashcards

 Video   Analyze recent world affairs by watching streaming video from major news providers.

Videos

Simulations   Play the role of an IR decision-maker and experience how IR concepts work in practice.

Comparative
Exercises

KEY TERMS

civil rights (p. 330)
consistency (p. 320)
de facto (p. 326)
de jure (p. 326)
exclusive economic zone
   (p. 324)
executive agreement (p. 323)

Geneva Convention (p. 329)
habeas corpus (p. 329)
human rights (p. 329)
jus ad bellum (p. 329)
jus in bello (p. 329)
precedent (p. 329)
R2P (p. 330)

ratify (p. 322)
reciprocity (p. 320)
sanction (p. 323)
territorial
   limit (p. 323)
treaty (p. 321)
war crimes (p. 329)

FURTHER REFERENCE

Amstutz, Mark R. *International Ethics: Concepts, Theories, and Cases in Global Politics*, 3rd ed. Lanham, MD: Rowman & Littlefield, 2008.

Armatta, Judith. *Twilight of Impunity: The War Crimes Trial of Slobodan Milosevic*. Durham, NC: Duke University Press, 2010.

Armstrong, David, Theo Farrell, Helene Lambert. *International Law and International Relations*. New York: Cambridge University Press, 2007.

Bass, Gary J. *Freedom's Battle: The Origins of Humanitarian Intervention*. New York: Vintage, 2009.

Byers, Michael. *War Law: Understanding International Law and Armed Conflict*. New York: Grove, 2006.

Donnelly, Jack. *International Human Rights*, 3rd ed. Boulder, CO: Westview, 2006.

Drezner, Daniel W. *All Politics is Global: Explaining International Regulatory Regimes*. Princeton, NJ: Princeton University Press, 2007.

Evans, Gareth. *The Responsibility to Protect: Ending Mass Atrocity Crimes Once and for All*. Washington, DC: Brookings, 2008.

Forsythe, David P. *Human Rights in International Relations*, 2nd ed. New York: Cambridge University Press, 2006.

Gibney, Mark. *International Human Rights Law: Returning to Universal Principles*. Lanham, MD: Rowman & Littlefield, 2008.

Glahn, Gerhard von, and James L. Taulbee. *Law Among Nations: An Introduction to Public International Law*, 9th ed. New York: Longman, 2010.

Goldsmith, Jack, and Eric Posner. *The Limits of International Law*. New York: Oxford University Press, 2006.

Guzman, Andrew. *How International Law Works: A Rational Choice Theory*. New York: Oxford University Press, 2007.

Heller-Roazen, Daniel. *The Enemy of All: Piracy and the Law of Nations.* New York: Zone Books, 2009.

Maogoto, Jackson Nyamuya. *War Crimes and Realpolitik: International Justice from World War I to the 21st Century.* Boulder, CO: Lynne Rienner, 2004.

Moghalu, Kingsley Chiedu. *Global Justice: The Politics of War Crimes Tribunals.* Westchester, CT: Praeger, 2006.

Peskin, Victor A. *International Justice in Rwanda and the Balkans: Virtual Trials and the Struggle for State Cooperation.* New York: Cambridge University Press, 2009.

Rochester, J. Martin. *Between Peril and Promise: The Politics of International Law.* Washington, DC: CQ Press, 2006.

Scott, Shirley V. *International Law in World Politics: An Introduction.* Boulder, CO: Lynne Rienner, 2004.

Shaw, Martin. *What Is Genocide?* New York: Polity, 2007.

Stover, Eric. *The Witnesses: War Crimes and the Promise of Justice in the Hague.* Philadelphia: University of Pennsylvania Press, 2005.

Tuck, Richard. *The Rights of War and Peace: Political Thought and the International Order from Grotius to Kant.* New York: Oxford University Press, 2000.

Walzer, Michael. *Thinking Politically: Essays in Political Theory.* New Haven, CT: Yale University Press, 2008.

CHAPTER 21

The Reach of the United Nations

Under UN supervision, Peruvian peacekeeping forces help Dominican food distributors in earthquake-damaged Port-au-Prince, Haiti, in 2010. (Reuters/Marco Dormino/Minustah/Landov)

The standard approach to the United Nations is to expect too much from it and then denounce it for not delivering. Many look to the UN to solve horrendous problems of war, bloody dictators, genocide, and nuclear proliferation. But the UN has next to no enforcement mechanism—no police or armed forces. It can sometimes borrow—at high salaries—the soldiers of willing countries for peacekeeping missions that the major powers have agreed to in advance. On its own, the UN can do nothing. If anything gets enforced, it's because the major powers, if they are in agreement, want it enforced. In many ways, the UN really is just a big debating society whose conclusions, if they are ever reached, are not always obeyed.

But for every person who denounces the UN for its weakness there are several who would not stand for it infringing on their nation's sovereignty. How many Americans would obey a UN vote requiring the United States to pull out of Afghanistan or cut its emission of greenhouse gases? "No way!" they would say, "We don't knuckle under to any other power." In a world of sovereign states, "world government" is a misnomer. The UN cannot govern much of anything and was not designed to. It was made deliberately powerless because its founding powers did not want anyone else telling them what to do. Voluntary compliance based on reason and national interest is the best it can hope to achieve. The UN was born weak and is likely to stay that way.

The United Nations, however, is still worthwhile. Most countries try to persuade it and work through it. It's a good place to talk, and the talking can sometimes prevent fighting. Few countries totally reject the UN because they do not want to be regarded as international bullies. Even U.S. Republican administrations, which often disdain the UN, do not seriously consider withdrawing from it, for such a move would isolate and weaken the United States. The number of UN peacekeeping operations to settle or contain regional and civil wars has more than doubled since 1987. The major powers want the UN to stabilize world politics. Could the world now be ready, in the words of the Preamble to the UN Charter, for an international organization "to save succeeding generations from the scourge of war"?

QUESTIONS TO CONSIDER

1. Why was the UN designed to have little power?
2. Is Emery Reves's theory of world government valid?
3. Who authored the League of Nations? Why did it fail?
4. What was Roosevelt's concept of the "four policemen"?
5. Who are the permanent members of the Security Council? Should they be permanent?
6. Are peacekeeping operations a legitimate UN function?
7. What is the "democratic peace"? Is it valid?
8. How was functionalism supposed to work?
9. Under what circumstances can peacekeeping work?

THEORY OF WORLD GOVERNMENT

The idea of an international body to prevent war has been around a long time. The Romans proudly spoke of *Pax Romana*, the "Roman peace" that came with being part of the empire, which was, of course, not voluntary. Rome's legions simply crushed those who did not obey and were often at war.

The medieval Roman Catholic Church planted the idea of a unified world—which in those centuries meant Europe—in which kings would acknowledge the supremacy of the pope. The church would provide guidance and try to reconcile conflict among monarchs. The Middle Ages closed, however, with monarchs disobeying the pope; instead, they instituted their own absolute rule, strengthened their kingdoms, and turned them into nation-states. The Protestant Reformation further shattered the tenuous unity of the Middle Ages.

As the Thirty Years War raged early in the seventeenth century, the Frenchman Emeric Crucé proposed a world organization that would promote trade and settle disputes by a majority decision of a council of ambassadors. William Penn, founder of Pennsylvania, proposed a world parliament to settle conflicts by a three-fourths vote and enforce its decisions by armed force. The great Prussian philosopher Immanuel Kant proposed a "League for Perpetual Peace."

In the wake of the Napoleonic wars, Austrian Prince Metternich set up a Concert of Europe in which all the major European monarchs would consult and suppress nationalism and liberalism. This was an international organization based on the balance-of-power theory (see Chapter 1) with a reactionary twist; it fell apart as the forces of modernity made impossible the old order of conservative monarchies. Its final collapse was World War I.

THE SHORT, SAD LEAGUE OF NATIONS

For some observers—especially Americans—World War I, or the Great War, as it was then called, proved the wickedness and perversity of the "balance-of-power" system used by European statesmen to justify the cynical moves that led to the giant conflagration. U.S. President Woodrow Wilson, one of America's first political scientists, slowly and reluctantly brought the United States into the war in 1917 on an idealistic basis, a "war fought to end all wars." Wilson went to the Versailles peace conference insisting that it found a League of Nations to prevent future wars. Britain and France accepted the League idea but set it up to keep themselves in the top spots globally and to retain their vast empires. The Covenant of the League of Nations was part of the Versailles treaty.

CLASSIC THOUGHT ■ LE RÊVE DE REVES

Just as the United Nations was born amid great hopes in 1945, American writer Emery Reves published *The Anatomy of Peace*, a reasoned defense of a supranational entity that would take away each nation's sovereign right to make war. Reves's reasoning:

Wars between groups of men forming social units always take place when these units—tribes, dynasties, churches, cities, nations—exercise unrestricted sovereign power.

Wars between these social units cease the moment sovereign power is transferred from them to a larger or higher unit.

It was a liberal (see Chapter 2), optimistic line of thought, one that suited the times. The historical progression is from smaller to larger units. Logically, the next step is to enroll the nations into a single, large unit: the United Nations. Reves may have been too early with his vision, but was he totally dreaming?

But Wilson couldn't get the Senate to approve the treaty. Slightly more than one-third of the senators found something to object to, and it takes two-thirds to ratify. Some of their objections seemed valid. Could the League Covenant force the United States to go to war, bypassing a congressional declaration of war? Would

> **collective security**   Agreement by all countries to automatically punish aggressor states.

the United States have to keep Britain and France permanently on the victors' throne? Important for Irish-Americans: Did the League mean that Britain could keep Ireland forever? Important for German-Americans: Did League membership mean the United States would assist France in keeping Germany down? In addition, some Republican senators just plain hated Wilson, who was a cold, rigid personality. The treaty failed, and Wilson left office a bitter man. Fed up with Wilson's idealistic rhetoric, America slouched into isolationism.

One of the arguments during and after World War II was whether U.S. participation in the League might have headed off World War II. Most Democrats, certainly Roosevelt and Truman, believed that America's absence from the League had been a terrible mistake—primitive Republican isolationism—that had led to its failure and to war. But passive U.S. membership would have changed nothing, and during the 1920s and 1930s an isolationist America supported only rhetorical peace gestures. An active America willing to contribute military force for "collective security" might have made a huge difference. But that was simply not America in those years.

The League got off to a reasonable start in 1920 with 42 member states (later it grew to 60). All members had one vote in the Assembly, which met about one month a year. (The UN equivalent is the General Assembly.) The Council, consisting of from 8 to 15 members, met more frequently to conciliate disputes. (The UN equivalent is the Security Council.) A permanent Secretariat under a secretary general (just like the UN) ran day-to-day affairs. A magnificent headquarters, the Palais des Nations (Palace of the Nations) opened in Geneva, Switzerland, in 1938, just in time to go out of business.

The crux of the League was **collective security** under Article 16 of the Covenant. Members agreed to leave other states alone. In a dispute, the two sides were to refrain from war for at least three months while the League looked for a solution. If one party turned out to be the aggressor, all League members were required to break economic and political ties with it. If that didn't curb the aggressor, the Council could recommend military actions against it. Surely no would-be aggressor could withstand the combined boycott and military threat of the rest of the world.

The failure of collective security spelled the end of the League. The idea had at least two weaknesses: (1) the difficulty of agreeing on what aggression is, and (2) getting member states to go along with Council requests to apply sanctions.

Aggression is often hard to define. What looks like aggression to some is merely vigorous defense to others. Israelis in the 1967 war, Americans in Iraq, Soviets in South Ossetia, and Iraqis in Kuwait were all convinced they were acting defensively. Even Hitler claimed he was acting to defend Germany against a fiendish threat, and many Germans believed him. In the modern world, everyone is defensive. There are no more "war ministries"; now they are all "defense ministries." The last conqueror to admit that he was practicing aggression was probably Genghis Khan.

Real aggressors often disguise their misdeeds. The beginning of the end for the League came with the Japanese conquest of Manchuria in 1931. The Japanese army set off a small bomb on some railroad tracks and said the Chinese did it. Who could prove otherwise? By the time the League's Council could send a commission of inquiry, the Japanese conquest of Manchuria was complete. The commission noted that the conquest was not ordered by the civilian government and found it difficult to condemn Tokyo. Soon Japan withdrew from the League anyway.

Most of the world didn't care about Manchuria, and a few admired Japan. Britain and France, the leading democracies of the League, were not about to send troops to the other side of the world for an area neither of them valued. There was no point in antagonizing Japan by a boycott, because Britain and France had extensive colonies in Southeast Asia that were vulnerable to Japanese attack. (These colonies were, of course, quickly taken over by Japan early in World War II.) In terms of the national interests of the democracies, Manchuria wasn't worth making a fuss about.

And a few dictators intended to do the same as Japan. Mussolini conquered Ethiopia in 1935, and Emperor Haile Selassie addressed the League's Assembly to warn them with tears in his eyes that Ethiopia may seem far away to them, but soon they too would be victims of aggression. He was right, of course, but Britain, which could have easily ended the Ethiopian campaign by denying Italy use of the Suez Canal, didn't want to risk pushing Mussolini into the arms of Hitler. (He willingly embraced Hitler anyway.)

Hitler noted the League's weak response to the Japanese and Italians. He withdrew Germany from the League and picked up one piece of Europe after another, claiming he was just uniting the German people into one country. Until 1939, nobody tried to stop him. Then Hitler invaded Poland, and it was too late to stop the aggressors with collective security; it took a war. With the outbreak of World War II, the League was effectively dead, although it kept a skeleton staff to hand over its buildings and mandates to the United Nations after the war. (The Palais des Nations in Geneva is now the European headquarters of the United Nations and the site of many important conferences.)

Some say it is unfair to condemn collective security because it was never really tried. Had it not been for the timidity and cowardice of Britain and France (and the isolationism of America), some argue, collective security might have worked. But nations do what they do for good reasons. The democracies couldn't understand at the time the aggressive, world-conquering nature of the dictatorships. They could not foretell the future and feared that sanctions imposed under collective security would only make things worse. And they were in no mood to go to war for distant lands. The trouble with collective security was that it asked nations to be what they aren't: farsighted, altruistic, and willing to let others make decisions for them.

CONCEPTS ■ COLLECTIVE SECURITY

Elements of collective security can be found in ancient Greece and the Middle Ages, but the concept did not come into its own until the League of Nations. The idea, magnificent on paper, offered a middle way between the instability of the balance-of-power system, which had just failed to prevent World War I, and a total world government, which would enforce the peace by a near-monopoly on military power, which was too much to ask for in a world where all nations jealously guard their sovereignty.

The middle way was as follows: All nations would agree to collectively punish any nation that practiced aggression. Like balance of power, collective security was willing to meet aggression by forming an alliance against it. The difference was that collective security was a permanent, standing alliance against any potential aggressor. Each nation would give up some of its sovereignty regarding when to go to war; instead, the League's Council would decide. Any country contemplating aggression would thus know that it would face the combined strength of all other nations. Ergo, there would be no aggression, or so its advocates thought.

Some mistakenly called NATO collective security, but it was simply a defensive alliance. Likewise, the UN effort in Korea does not qualify, as the coalition was voluntary and ad hoc, and the Soviet Union and China were on the other side.

THE RISE OF THE UN

veto   Blocking a measure by just one vote against.

Franklin D. Roosevelt had been assistant secretary of the Navy under Woodrow Wilson and still had some of Wilson's idealism. If America participated in World War II, it must be with an eye toward setting up a United Nations to prevent future wars. FDR saw this as a chance to rectify the tragic failure of the League. In war-time meetings, FDR obtained Churchill's lukewarm support for a postwar UN and Stalin's indifferent consent. The American president was so enthusiastic about the idea, and America was supplying so much war aid, that they felt they must humor the man. Truman continued FDR's hopes for the United Nations when it swung into operation in 1945. This time America was the United Nations' most enthusiastic backer.

As noted, in structure the UN is much like the old League of Nations: a General Assembly (GA) that meets every fall in which all nations have one vote; a 15-nation (enlarged from 10) Security Council that can meet any time to preserve peace; and a Secretariat to run the organization. A secretary general is elected by the GA for renewable five-year terms. The GA has only the power to recommend action. In contrast, the Security Council can order compliance with its resolutions. Each of the five permanent members of the Security Council has the right to **veto** any resolution. That is, if the United States, Russia, China, Britain, or France dislikes some measure, its lone vote—even 14 to 1—shoots the resolution down. The ten nonpermanent members, who are elected by the GA for two-year terms, have an ordinary vote without veto. Nothing, in other words, can go against the wishes of even one of the Big Five.

Problems are immediately apparent. Are these five really the most important or powerful countries in the world? The United States is, but Britain and France have long since been overtaken economically by Germany and Japan, who have both requested permanent seats on the Security Council. China—since 1971 mainland Communist China rather than Nationalist Taiwan—is the most populous country and enjoying rapid economic growth. Russia is big but no longer an impressive force. Some countries are campaigning to add six new permanent seats to the Security Council. Brazil and India, claiming to speak for the Third World, and Egypt, Nigeria, and South Africa, claiming to speak for Africa, each want permanent seats. The Big Five do not like adding permanent members—it would dilute their power—but might consider it if the newcomers have no right of veto. Who is to decide which nations can keep the peace? The Big Five was FDR's wartime notion of who should guide the world. What may have been a reasonable choice then no longer corresponds to power realities decades later. And there is no mechanism for adding permanent Security Council members.

A more basic problem is why any major country should have a veto over the will of the majority. Stalin at Yalta in 1945 insisted on the veto provision, and Churchill and Roosevelt went along. Stalin felt (correctly) that the Soviet Union would be so outnumbered by non-Communist countries that it would suffer permanent condemnation. The UN framers put in the unit veto as a mechanism to enable a major power to stay in the UN and not withdraw over something it didn't like—the way Germany, Japan, and Italy had withdrawn from the League in the 1930s. They understood that the veto could render the Security Council toothless, but better to keep the big powers talking, they reasoned. At first, only the Soviet Union used the veto, but later the Western powers, including the United States, also found it convenient.

In fairness, the veto system has kept the UN alive a lot longer than the League. Without it, one or several of the Big Five powers would long since have withdrawn from the UN. The veto in the Security Council has been likened to a fuse in a house wiring system. If the system overheats, better to have a fuse blow (a veto) than the house burn down. The price for holding the system together in this way, though, is its powerlessness to solve many disputes.

The U.S.-led Kosovo campaign had no UN authorization because Russia and China would have vetoed it. The Security Council did not authorize the 2003 U.S. invasion of Iraq, although Washington claimed that earlier resolutions amounted to an authorization. In 2010 all of the permanent members, even Russia and China, did not veto sanctions on Iran for its nuclear program. Some viewed this as a sign of hope that the Security Council was starting to work as designed. But then China would not support a 2010 resolution naming North Korea as the culprit in the sinking a South Korean navy ship. Only a tepid resolution condemning violence in general in Korea was passed. China did not have to use its veto; the mere threat of one was enough.

THE UN: EARLY IDEALISM

When it began, many people believed in the UN, especially Americans. Washington looked first to the UN to contribute to peaceful solutions to conflicts. In some measure the UN did, but often not in a permanent way. The superpowers rarely agreed to final settlements; they were happy just to end expensive combat in deadlocked Cold War contests. Still, here and there, the UN has helped.

Palestine was one of the UN's first problems (see Chapter 8). The British, who had a mandate to govern Palestine from the old League of Nations, were fed up with Arab–Jewish fighting and announced in 1947 that they would pull out the following spring. They threw the issue to the UN, which devised a partition plan, dividing Palestine into a checkerboard of Jewish and Arab territories. It was probably unworkable, but the General Assembly voted 33 to 13 in favor of partition. The Jews accepted it; the Arabs rejected it.

The 1947 UN partition plan illustrates the difficulty of an outside body trying to settle a local fight. True, a majority of the UN supported the plan, but none of the countries in the immediate region did. Should the vote of a Central American republic (under U.S. pressure) count as much as the vote of a country that would be immediately affected? To the Arabs, the UN vote lacked legitimacy, and they invaded the newly proclaimed state of Israel in the spring of 1948. The UN system didn't work here.

After the Arab attack failed, though, they grudgingly consented to UN mediation. Here the UN was useful, although the result was an unstable armistice rather than a peace treaty.

TURNING POINT ■ THE FOUR POLICEMEN

President Roosevelt saw the possibility of world stability after World War II because the four most powerful nations of the world would cooperate in running the UN. The United States, Soviet Union, Britain, and China would be the globe's "four policemen," each preventing disorder in its area of influence and keeping the peace as the "Big Four" permanent members of the new UN Security Council. (When de Gaulle squawked, France was made the fifth permanent member.)

FDR projected the temporary and illusory unity of World War II onto the postwar future. First, China was big but weak; it had barely resisted the Japanese during the war. With the Communist victory in 1949, China turned into an enemy. Second, FDR, a personally charming man, thought he could charm Stalin into cooperative behavior after the war. FDR was mistakenly projecting his domestic political skills onto the world stage, a common error of American presidents. Britain had been drained by the war and soon lost its colonies. And this was another problem: the rapid growth in number of nations in the world and members in the United Nations, many of them with anticolonial chips on their shoulders. Even if the "Big Four" held together, much of the world would not have obeyed them.

A UN Truce Supervision Organization (UNTSO), staffed by un-armed professional soldiers from neutral countries, helped to keep the peace by reporting violations. The way the truce was reached by Ralph Bunche gives Americans cause for pride (see box below).

proximity talks   Disputants negotiate through a nearby mediator, not face-to-face.

The Korean War, although it was not collective security, gave at least a temporary boost to the authority of the UN. Truman, still a believer in the UN, immediately referred the 1950 North Korean invasion to the Security Council. A resolution urged all UN members to "furnish assistance" to repel North Korean aggression, and it passed. Why didn't the Soviets veto it?

The explanation is half comical. The Soviet delegation had been demanding that Communist China, which had just won a civil war, take the UN seat occupied by Nationalist China, which had retreated to Taiwan. The Security Council, dominated by Western powers, wouldn't comply, so the Soviets showed their displeasure by stalking out. In their absence, the Security Council passed the resolution condemning North Korea and asking for help in resisting aggression. No member has missed a Security Council session since. As the French say, *Les absents ont toujours tort* ("Those absent are always wrong").

DISILLUSION WITH THE UN

Would the right leadership have given the UN strength to solve world problems? This intriguing question can never be settled. The first two secretaries general (see box on page 342) were respected and with that came respect for the UN in general. The next two were weak, indecisive figures, and the UN's reputation as a whole declined.

But was it completely their fault? The UN changed a lot in the 1960s, becoming bigger and more complex. First, membership more than tripled. From 51 founding members—mostly from Europe and Latin America—UN membership ballooned with decolonization in the 1950s and

---

DIPLOMACY ■ RALPH BUNCHE: UN HERO

From black civil rights advocate in the 1930s to world statesman in the 1940s, Ralph Bunche illustrates the American involvement with the founding of the United Nations and how third-party diplomacy can work. Bunche earned a Ph.D. in political science at Harvard, taught at Howard University in Washington, then went into the State Department and served on the U.S. delegation to draft the UN Charter in 1946. Bunche wanted decolonization to be one of the UN's main goals, but his own delegation showed no interest, so Bunche quietly took his draft to the Australian delegation, which got it included in the Charter. Bunche knew how to manipulate procedures, a cardinal diplomatic skill.

Bunche then joined the UN Secretariat as director of trusteeship affairs (i.e., decolonization) and was assigned the delicate task of mediating an end to the first Arab–Israeli war of 1948–1949. With no guidance from superiors and improvising as he went, Bunche finally got the Arabs to agree to **proximity talks** with the Israelis. The Arabs refused to meet the Israelis face-to-face, so Bunche gathered them into a hotel on the Greek island of Rhodes—on separate floors. Endlessly climbing from one floor to another, Bunche carried negotiating points back and forth, deftly adding his own suggestions. In the armistice, all sides agreed to stop fighting along lines that became Israel's borders until 1967. Ralph Bunche won the Nobel Peace Prize in 1950 but was proudest of developing the concept of peacekeeping (see page 346).

1960s. In just two years, 1960 and 1961, most of Africa went from being British, French, or Belgian colonies to independent states, all of which immediately joined the UN. With the addition of former Soviet and Yugoslav republics (Russia blocks admission of Kosovo), there are now 192 UN members, most of them developing countries and poor, some of them ministates.

Poor countries often have a radical perspective on the world economy and demand vast sums for development (see Chapter 11). Organized as the Group of 77 in the GA, they also condemn any situation that looks like colonialism and routinely vote against Israel, Russia, and the United States.

During the Cold War, North–South conflicts merged with East–West conflicts to paralyze the UN. Majorities, especially including the five permanent members of the Security Council, were hard to come by. Sometimes, however, majorities appeared when particular conflicts threatened just about every member's interest. A breakdown in authority in the former Belgian Congo between 1960 and 1963, the 1967 and 1973 Middle East wars, and the ethnic struggles in Cyprus in 1964 and 1974 brought cooperation under the aegis of the UN.

Both the United States and Soviet Union used the UN as a foreign policy tool in the Cold War. They introduced resolutions to embarrass each other and larded their speeches with propaganda. (UN delegates are instructed by their foreign ministries on what to say and how to vote.) During the Cold War, they never allowed the UN to control any conflict in which they had an interest. The Vietnamese and Afghan wars were kept out of the UN, which was unable to fulfill its Charter's peacekeeping purposes.

TURNING POINT ■ GREAT AND NOT-SO-GREAT SECRETARIES GENERAL

The UN's first two secretaries general, Trygve Lie of Norway (1946–1953) and Dag Hammarskjöld of Sweden (1953–1961), were strong personalities who deeply believed in the UN's peace missions. Both stood up for peace even when criticized from East and West, and neither was afraid of committing the UN to difficult situations. Hammarskjöld actually died in the line of duty, in a plane crash while supervising UN forces trying to bring peace to the strife-torn Congo.

Their two immediate successors were lesser men, afraid to use the UN as anything more than a debating society. U Thant of Burma (1961–1971) had such a pro–Third World orientation that he could see no wrong in demands from developing countries. He speedily acquiesced to Nasser's demand to remove UN forces from the Sinai, a step that led to the 1967 Mideast War. Kurt Waldheim of Austria (1972–1981) was a courtly ex-Nazi who hid his past in order to posture as a world leader while doing little.

Stronger leadership returned with Javier Pérez de Cuéllar of Peru (1982–1991). He skillfully projected the UN into conflicts in which the superpowers lost interest as the Cold War faded. UN negotiators mediated a cease-fire in the Iran–Iraq War; the independence of Namibia; the end to the Angolan, Cambodian, and Salvadorean civil wars; and the status of Western Sahara (see Third-Party Diplomacy box on page 313). Boutros Boutros-Ghali of Egypt (1992–1996) inherited a UN at the height of its activity and took a strong leadership role. He sometimes ran afoul of the major powers on the Security Council, including the United States, which vetoed him for a second term for not cutting costs. Kofi Annan of Ghana, the UN undersecretary general for peacekeeping, won U.S. approval and took over in 1997. Annan, with the Rwanda massacres in mind, wanted a more activist UN, but he, too, ran afoul of U.S. isolationism. A bland South Korean diplomat, Ban Ki-moon, took over at the end of 2006 and quietly worked at reforming UN management, inefficiency, and ethics.

THE USES OF THE UN

The UN is an excellent listening post. Diplomats, journalists, and scholars can learn more about what's happening in the world in a few weeks at the UN than anywhere else. Border disputes, regional weather calamities, desperate refugees—often stories that don't appear in the news media—are the standard fare of UN committees. The UN thus serves as an early-warning system for tomorrow's problems and controversies.

The UN is also a diplomatic bargain for small, poor countries that can afford only two or three embassies around the world. At the UN headquarters in Manhattan, for the price of one mission to the UN, they can have diplomatic contact with all nations. Manhattan itself is not a bad location for the UN. There are already so many diverse people in New York City that foreign diplomats don't attract much attention. Even enemies can get together discreetly. Israel could talk to Jordan, Iran to the United States.

The world faces a growing class of problems that require international solutions, the so-called transnational issues, which can include everything from resource scarcity to climate changes (see Chapter 22). Although not yet uniformly appreciated, they are probably the great issues of twenty-first-century politics.

TURNING POINT ■ THE UNITED STATES AND THE UN

The U.S. Congress, especially Republicans from traditionally isolationist states, does not love the UN and deliberately ran up $1.3 billion in UN arrears to get the spendthrift UN to economize. UN officials are very well paid, and some of them are not needed. Congress rejected UN demands as too high and paid less than $1 billion in 1999. (CNN founder Ted Turner personally contributed an even $1 billion to the UN.) Congress also got the U.S. share of the UN budget trimmed from 25 percent to 22 percent. When the UN was founded, argued Congress, the United States was the only rich country in the world, but now there are many rich countries, and they should pay their fair shares.

The Bush 43 White House shared Congress's dislike of the UN. The State Department under Secretary Powell tried to exercise U.S. world leadership within the UN, but Powell was isolated in the Bush administration. The chairman of the Senate Foreign Relations Committee, Jesse Helms (R-North Carolina), wanted the UN greatly trimmed and in 2000 personally warned the Security Council that the United States would withdraw from the UN if it tried "to impose its presumed authority on the American people without their consent." It was the identical argument—don't touch our sovereignty—used by the Republican senators who voted against joining the League of Nations in 1919.

The United States has gone from inventing and supporting the UN to ignoring and distancing itself from the UN. In turn, the United States lost influence in the UN. Before the 2003 Iraq War, many countries urged the United States to operate within the UN framework, but the White House was in no mood for such restraint. U.S.–UN relations dipped lower with the 2005 appointment of John Bolton as U.S. ambassador to the UN. Bolton, an angry neoconservative, trumpeted his disdain for the UN. He demanded major reforms—and many are needed—and threatened to block the UN's budget if he didn't get them. But bullying doesn't work, and the United States found itself isolated in the UN. The Obama-appointed ambassador to the UN, Susan Rice, a Rhodes scholar with NSC and State Department experience under President Clinton, returned to consensus building with some positive results.

REFLECTIONS ■ PAYING ATTENTION TO THE DEEP SEABED

As a journalist for the Associated Press, I covered some of the activities of the 1968 General Assembly. (The GA meets every fall.) Some of the meetings were dull, and many were unintelligible to a newcomer. One meeting I covered seemed pointless until years later. I had actually witnessed an important strategic discussion and didn't know it.

The committee was on the uses of the seabed, chiefly on who owned its mineral rights, but one of the points was on "peaceful uses of the seabed." I thought that was pretty silly, for how could anyone use the seabed for war? Even sillier, I thought, was the quibble between the U.S. and Soviet delegates. The American wanted to prohibit using the deep seabed for "any weapon"; the Soviet wanted to prohibit "any military uses" of the deep seabed. I strained to make a news story out of what seemed to be a dispute about nothing.

Years later, I found out what they had really been talking about. At that very time, in secrecy,

the United States was implanting undersea listening devices on the seabed to monitor the coming and going of Soviet nuclear submarines. Soviet subs were then rather noisy and easy to pick up as they passed the North Cape, Skagerrak, Turkish Straits, and Pérouse Strait (north of Japan). This gave us a terrific advantage.

The Soviets knew what we were doing and hated it. So they tried to use obscure wording in a UN seabed convention to prohibit such devices—"any military uses." The United States knew full well what this meant, so they wanted only a prohibition on weapons (and a listening device is not a weapon). The veiled language used by both sides concealed a major step in the arms race that they wished to keep quiet. If I had known this, I could have had a page-one story. The UN is a great listening post, but you need considerable background to follow its debates.

—M. G. R.

functionalism Gaining countries' cooperation in specialized matters so it spills over into general cooperation.

FUNCTIONALISM

World-order issues may reawaken the **functionalist** dream, a view that waxed and waned along with enthusiasm for the UN. The crux of functionalism is the presumed spillover effect that grows out of cooperation on immediate problems. If Arabs and Israelis, for example, can work together on smallpox eradication, they may temper their hostilities and even learn to live together. There is, alas, scant evidence of any spillover effect.

Nonetheless, many of the specialized agencies linked to the UN do fine work, tasks that would have to be undertaken even if there were no UN. Under the supervision of the World Health Organization, for example, the world wiped out smallpox. In 2010, the UN Food and Agriculture

CONCEPTS ■ FUNCTIONALISM

Political tension prevents the direct building of world authority, but if we can get nations working together on relatively small, "functional" issues—disease, weather, famine, air traffic—gradually they will learn to cooperate, and this will form the basis

of an international community, argues functionalist theory. Cooperation in a narrow area will "spill over" into the broader arena. Americans, who like technological fixes, are often drawn to the functionalist theory.

Organization announced the global eradication of rinderpest, a scourge of cattle. Some of the agencies, such as the Universal Postal Union, long antedate the UN. The UPU makes sure mail flows between countries and keeps tabs on which countries owe postage due. The many agencies also let more countries have an organization in their capital. Geneva, Switzerland, of course, has many agencies, holdovers from the League of Nations.

Some of these agencies became political footballs, especially when Global South members in cooperation with the Soviet bloc took them over and used them as platforms to denounce Israel, South Africa, or the United States. For this reason, the United States and Britain withdrew from UNESCO. (The United States also withdrew for a year from the International Labor Organization, accusing it of subservience to Communist aims.) UNESCO developed a bad reputation as its Senegalese director hired friends at lush salaries to enjoy Paris and politicize the organization. He held office 13 years, immune to criticism because most developing lands supported him.

Major Specialized UN Agencies

Agency	Location	Chief Function
International Court of Justice (ICJ)	The Hague, Netherlands	Adjudicate claims between nations
International Seabed Authority (ISA)	Kingston, Jamaica	Enforce conventions on seabed
International Labor Organization (ILO)	Geneva	Improve labor conditions
Food and Agriculture Organization (FAO)	Rome	Fight famine
UN Educational, Scientific and Cultural Organization (UNESCO)	Paris	Promote exchange of ideas
UN Environment Program (UNEP)	Nairobi, Kenya	Protect environment
UN Children's Fund (UNICEF)	New York	Help world's poorest children
UN Conference on Trade and Development (UNCTAD)	Geneva	Promote economic growth of poor countries
UN High Commissioner for Refugees (UNHCR)	Geneva	Protect refugees
World Health Organization (WHO)	Geneva	Fight plagues
International Monetary Fund (IMF)[a]	Washington	Stabilize currencies
World Bank[a]	Washington	Make loans to poor countries
International Civil Aviation Organization (ICAO)	Montreal	Promote air travel
International Telecommunication Union (ITU)	Geneva	Promote telecom flow
Universal Postal Union (UPU)	Bern	Promote mail flow
World Meteorological Organization (WMO)	Geneva	Share weather information
International Maritime Organization (IMO)	London	Promote world shipping
World Intellectual Property Organization (WIPO)	Geneva	Protect patents
International Atomic Energy Agency (IAEA)	Vienna	Oversee peaceful nuclear development

[a] For more on these agencies, see Chapter 18. The WTO, although headquartered in Geneva, is not part of the UN.

peacekeeping   Third-party military forces to stabilize a cease-fire.

cease-fire   Mutually agreed-upon pause in a war.

ROEs   Rules of engagement, stating when peacekeepers may shoot back.

mission creep   Tendency of modest peacekeeping goals to expand.

GIVING PEACE A CHANCE

Although Iraq and Afghanistan are much in the news, the number of wars is actually down. Even civil conflicts peaked in 1991 and are declining, largely because their U.S. and Soviet sponsors no longer back their favored sides. Problem areas—the Middle East, Eritrea, North Korea—can erupt, but after the Cold War, Russia and America no longer confront each other and abet Third World conflicts. Does *asymmetric conflict* count as war (see Chapter 15)? It is certainly not traditional war between countries. One factor helping peace is the spread of democracies (see box below).

A new type of military activity emerged with the UN, **peacekeeping**. The Middle East, Cyprus, Africa, and elsewhere have seen the blue headgear and white vehicles of more than 40 UN missions to calm hostilities. Their deployments have been growing; currently some 113,000 personnel serve in 18 UN peacekeeping missions that cost $8 billion a year (about 27 percent paid by the United States). The new doctrine of "responsibility to protect" (R2P—see page 330) points to a growing role for international peacekeeping, one that even overrides sovereignty. R2P, however, requires even more money and troops, which few are willing to provide.

Peacekeeping doesn't always work. A firm **cease-fire** is first necessary; without it, failure is almost guaranteed. That was the mistake of UNPROFOR in Bosnia starting in 1992. Equipped with weak and vague **ROEs**, combatants ignored European battalions under the UN and massacred civilians (see page 257). After a U.S.-brokered cease-fire, in 1996 NATO forces in IFOR with "robust ROEs"—meaning ready to shoot—made it stick. In Somalia and other places, UN forces fell into "**mission creep**" and became the target of warlords. The UN is reluctant to send peacekeepers into combat situations, where many shy away from actual shooting or stopping massacres. Peacekeeping requires willingness to shoot.

CONCEPTS ■ THE DEMOCRATIC PEACE

Democracies do not, and seemingly cannot, develop the will to attack other democracies. Yale's Bruce Russett studied all wars since 1816 and demonstrated in his *Grasping the Democratic Peace* that a democratic culture doesn't like to mobilize against another like itself. Democracies prefer to negotiate and compromise. It is hard to demonize another democracy. Democracies fight almost as much as dictatorships, but they only fight dictatorships (and mostly win). And democratically elected politicians know that a long, unsuccessful war will cost them votes, as in 2008.

Democratic elections cannot solve all problems. The 2006 election of the fundamentalist Hamas to Palestinian leadership did not point to peace. Democratic Israel and democratic Palestine sincerely hate each other. The Iranian-sponsored Hezbollah won 11 percent of Lebanon's parliament in 2005 and started a war with Israel in 2006. Iraqi elections have not resolved the murderous tension between Shia and Sunni. The 2005 Egyptian elections gave a major victory to the shadowy Muslim Brotherhood, the original Islamist movement. Perhaps we could insert a Huntington exception to the Russett rule: Democracy brings peace, except in Muslim lands.

A UN convoy, guarded by Bolivian police and Argentine soldiers, delivers food to storm-damaged Haiti in 2008. (Yuri Cortz/AFP/Getty Images)

HUMANKIND'S LAST, BEST HOPE?

NGO Non-governmental organization, international charities and voluntary groups.

Too much was expected of the UN too early. Any international organization (IO) is only as effective as its members make it. If national interests converge, cooperation is likely, as it did with recent resolutions on Iran. The present international system may be leading to a convergence of interests, at least on areas of common concern. No country, not even Russia or China, wants Iran or North Korea to have nuclear weapons. The UN can be the instrument for converting common interests into common policies.

REFLECTIONS ■ NONGOVERNMENTAL ORGANIZATIONS

The term "nongovernmental organization," or **NGO**, was coined when the UN was founded, and now some 25,000 NGOs operate around the globe, especially in famines, disasters, and wars. Going where governments cannot, NGOs include the International Committee of the Red Cross, Save the Children, Médecins Sans Frontières (Doctors Without Borders), World Vision, CARE, and Oxfam. Most religious denominations have an NGO (dubbed RINGO). Real doers, NGOs raise some $6 billion a year and provide more aid than all governments and UN agencies put together and do it far more efficiently. Their downsides: too many of them, wildly decentralized, not always well thought-out, and with overlapping projects that are sometimes public relations for the NGO and culturally at odds with local traditions.

Everyone connected with peace operations has high praise for NGOs. Most focus on food and medical care, but some clear land mines, care for orphans, and foster peace agreements. You might consider a stint with an NGO. By serving humanity, you can learn a language, develop skills, and have an adventure. (Warning: You can also get killed. NGOs are not for the fainthearted.) Such background can help you get into graduate school, government service, journalism, and international business.

The UN and the secretary general depend upon the votes of the members of the Security Council and General Assembly to act in every area. Secretaries general can rarely act on their own. Members' support is essential for peacekeeping operations because they supply the troops, financing, and logistics. Only Australia's push for UN intervention in East Timor (led by Australia) in 1999 made it happen. The effectiveness of the UN reflects members' interest. Australia is close to Timor.

UN resolutions can denounce human rights violations, such as Iraq's in Kuwait or Milošević's in Kosovo. There is a growing consensus among members on human rights. The 1948 Universal Declaration of Human Rights is developing some respect because governments are embarrassed to conduct business with bloody-hand regimes. Even China had to alter its hands-off approach to genocide in Sudan.

The UN does need reform. Its related agencies are sprawling, overstaffed, overlapping, and unaccountable. (There are three UN food agencies, all in Rome.) Some may be corrupt. The dues formula hasn't been updated in decades, and some countries pay too much in relation to their GDPs, others too little. (Biggest overpayer: Japan, which demands a reduction. Biggest underpayer: China.) Security Council membership does not reflect power and wealth realities; Germany and Japan should become permanent members. If General Assembly resolutions are to be respected, the GA will need weighted voting so a microstate does not count as much as a big country. The UN, however, is highly resistant to change because many countries can block reform. If the UN does not reform and slim down to its core competencies—dispute resolution—it could fade before it fully blossoms.

mypoliscikit EXERCISES

Apply what you learned in this chapter on MyPoliSciKit (www.mypoliscikit.com).

Assessment   Review this chapter using learning objectives, chapter summaries, practice tests, and more.

Menu

Flashcards   Learn the key terms in this chapter; you can test yourself by term or definition.

Flashcards

Video   Analyze recent world affairs by watching streaming video from major news providers.

Videos

Simulations   Play the role of an IR decision-maker and experience how IR concepts work in practice.

Comparative
Exercises

KEY TERMS

cease-fire (p. 346)

collective security (p. 337)

functionalism (p. 344)

mission creep (p. 346)

NGO (p. 347)

peacekeeping (p. 346)

proximity talks (p. 341)

ROEs (p. 346)

veto (p. 339)

FURTHER REFERENCE

Bolton, John. *Surrender Is Not an Option: Defending America at the United Nations and Abroad.* New York: Simon & Schuster, 2007.

Gibbs, David N. *First Do No Harm: Humanitarian Intervention and the Destruction of Yugoslavia.* Nashville, TN: Vanderbilt University Press, 2009.

Howard, Lise Morjé. *UN Peacekeeping in Civil Wars.* New York: Cambridge University Press, 2008.

Jolly, Richard, Louis Emmerij, and Thomas G. Weiss. *UN Ideas That Changed the World.* Bloomington, IN: Indiana University Press, 2009.

Kennedy, Paul. *The Parliament of Man: The Past, Present, and Future of the United Nations.* New York: Random House, 2006.

Krasno, Jean E. *The United Nations: Confronting the Challenges of a Global Society.* Boulder, CO: Lynne Rienner, 2004.

Luck, Edward C. *The United Nations Security Council.* New York: Routledge, 2006.

Malone, David M. *The International Struggle over Iraq: Politics in the UN Security Council, 1980–2005.* New York: Oxford University Press, 2007.

Mazower, Mark. *No Enchanted Place: The End of Empire and the Ideological Origins of the United Nations.* Princeton, NJ: Princeton University Press, 2009.

Mingst, Karen A., and Margaret P. Karns. *International Organizations: The Politics and Processes of Global Governance,* 2nd ed. Boulder, CO: Lynne Rienner, 2009.

Muldoon, James P., JoAnn Fagot Aveil, Richard Reitano, and Earl Sullivan. *The New Dynamics of Multilateralism: Diplomacy, International Organizations, and Global Governance.* Boulder, CO: Westview, 2010.

Ramcharan, Bertrand G. *Preventive Diplomacy at the UN.* Bloomington, IN: Indiana University Press, 2008.

Schaefer, Brett D. *ConUNdrum: The Limits of the United Nations and the Search for Alternatives.* Lanham, MD: Rowman & Littlefield, 2009.

Schlesinger, Stephen. *Act of Creation: The Founding of the United Nations.* Boulder, CO: Westview, 2004.

Sitkowski, Andrzej. *UN Peacekeeping: Myth and Reality.* Westport, CT: Praeger, 2006.

Smith, Courtney B. *Politics and Process at the United Nations: The Global Dance.* Boulder, CO: Lynne Rienner, 2006.

Thakur, Ramesh. *The United Nations, Peace, and Security: From Collective Security to the Responsibility to Protect.* New York: Cambridge University Press, 2006.

Weiss, Thomas, David Forsythe, Roger Coate, and Kelly-Kate Pease. *The United Nations and Changing World Politics,* 6th ed. Boulder, CO: Westview, 2009.

CHAPTER 22

Finite F.E.W. (Food/Energy/Water)

The massive 2010 underwater oil spill at a BP drilling site in the Gulf of Mexico underscored the tradeoff between energy and environment. (Petty Officer First Class John Masson/U.S. Coast Guard Handout/Corbis)

As we noted in the previous chapter, the twenty-first century faces several **transnational** issues of growing urgency. Climate change (see box on page 360) can be viewed as a **collective goods** problem. Air, for example, is taken to be free to all; just use it as much and however you want. Factories and cars belch tons of carbon into the air—at no charge—which injures health and may change the environment. Should air then remain "free," or should it come with a price tag? Related to this is the **tragedy of the commons**, what happens when something available to many, such as fish in the oceans, is used without limit: overfishing to depletion, a major current threat.

FINITE F.E.W.

In this chapter, we pay special attention to three growing, interrelated problems—food, energy, and water: F.E.W. According to most scientific opinion, the profligate burning of fossil fuels changes weather patterns, water resources, and harvests. F.E.W. cannot expand infinitely. In our day, all three are starting to plateau off; growth in demand is outstripping growth in supply. This does not mean the end of the planet or a collapse of living standards, but it does force choices in the kind, amount, and pace of resource consumption both at the individual and national level. Asia, as we have seen, is growing rapidly, but it is inconceivable that 4 to 5 billion Asians will live at an American level. The resources simply are not there. Indeed, Americans may not be living at an American level.

Only 11 percent of the earth's land surface is **arable**, and less than a quarter of that is truly fertile, leaving only about half an acre of farmland per human. The **Green Revolution** of the 1960s increased food production, especially in the Global South, by the scientific development of new grains and farming techniques. Farm output has tripled since 1950, faster than population growth, which is slowing. Food became relatively cheap, and most people ate better. India, for example, now produces all the food it needs. Recently, however, world food costs have doubled. Drought hit several major grain-producing countries just as consumption climbed in developing lands. Some problems are short-term, transient blips, but others are long-term, possibly permanent shifts.

Several things hit at once in a way that at first was little noticed. In the first decade of the twenty-first century, grain production went up nicely, but during the same period stocks of grain on hand went *down* sharply, something that sounds contradictory. What happened? Consumption shot up. First, as the developing lands got richer, they ate more grains directly and then began

QUESTIONS TO CONSIDER

1. Will *transnational* issues force greater global cooperation?
2. What was the Green Revolution? Can there be another?
3. Was Malthus wrong or just premature?
4. Are food and energy problems transient or permanent?
5. How urgent a problem is climate change?
6. Has world oil production peaked?
7. Are any alternative energy sources feasible?
8. Has power really shifted to the big oil exporting countries?
9. Would a slightly lower standard of living really hurt us?
10. What can the world community do to control these problems?

transnational   Related to the world as a whole, too big for one country or group of countries to handle.

collective good   Something that all use free, such as air.

tragedy of the commons   Metaphor of overuse of a *collective good*, such as "commons" for sheep pasture.

arable   Usable for food growing.

Green Revolution   The 1960s improvements in plant varieties, especially wheat and rice, boosting output.

feeding grain to cows and pigs to produce meat and milk. (It takes about eight pounds of grain to produce one pound of beef.) Asian cooking traditionally used just a bit of meat for flavoring, but tastes changed with money. Chinese more than doubled their per-capita consumption of meat (from 44 pounds to 110 pounds a year) from 1980 to 2007 and tripled their milk consumption. The rapid growth of McDonald's in China encouraged both hamburger and ice cream consumption. Chinese are eating more like Americans and getting overweight.

But success often undermines itself. Almost 40 years of food surpluses pushed down world prices, driving many farmers out of business. Especially harmful are the subsidies rich nations give their farmers; the cheap surplus food discourages Third World producers from expanding. Agricultural research was cut late in the last century; it no longer seemed necessary. When shortages hit, food production cannot jump up quickly; it is "sticky." It takes a year or two for farmers to see that the increased demand is not temporary and then to plant and harvest crops.

At the same time, possibly related to climate change, harvests faltered for lack of (or sometimes too much) rainfall. Australia, a mammoth food exporter, was in a multiyear drought. Much Australian rice land was turned over to grapes (for wine), which use much less water and yield much higher profits. Other grain-producing lands suffered from weather problems. A massive cyclone inundated Burma, whose military dictators kept out foreign aid. In a few cases—Burma, Cuba, North Korea, Zimbabwe—bad government policies shrank food production.

"Food security" has become a major topic. No country consents to go hungry. Some restrict exports to ensure enough food for the home population. This drives food prices higher and really hurts poor, food-importing countries, where adequate diets slump back to meager diets. Among the very poorest, starvation appears. Hoarding food stocks, economists say, just make things worse for the world overall. Now several countries—including China and Saudi Arabia, both short of arable land and water—are leasing huge tracts in Africa for food production, what critics call a "global land grab" or "agro-imperialism." Defenders argue that improved farming techniques will boost yields and feed both foreigners and hungry Africans.

This was the very time that biofuels became fashionable. Soaring petroleum prices (see our discussion later in this chapter) made getting ethanol from corn seem attractive. Actually, it's

ECONOMICS ■ THE FATHER OF THE GREEN REVOLUTION

Agronomist Norman Borlaug (1914–2009) was an American hero who grew up on an Iowa farm and saved more humans—hundreds of millions—than any other person in history. During the Great Depression he saw how even Americans could go hungry and vowed to fight hunger. With a Ph.D. in plant genetics, Borlaug set up a research station in Mexico, where he personally tilled the soil. There he developed new wheat varieties that boosted Mexico's wheat production tenfold.

He showed Indian farmers how to raise wheat yields from 12 million tons in 1965 to 20 million in 1970. Worldwide, famines were averted and poor countries were able to feed themselves. It was called the "Green Revolution," and Borlaug was its father. For this, he won the 1970 Nobel Peace Prize. Warning of population growth, in 2005 Borlaug predicted the world would have to double food production by 2050 and embrace genetically modified plants.

terribly inefficient and diverts one-quarter of U.S. corn production from food (mostly for animals) to a gasoline replacement. As more farmers saw the price of corn rise and the lush government subsidies, they turned more of their cropland from wheat, soy, and other crops to corn, thus driving up the price of foods made from wheat and soy. Economists, livestock growers, and environmentalists alike denounce corn ethanol. (Ethanol from Brazilian cane sugar, however, is a good bet.)

strategic variable   Major factor that induces systemic change.

barrel   42 gallons, world standard measure for oil.

peak oil   World oil output reaching its maximum and set to decline.

At this same time, energy costs shot up. Petroleum goes into many fertilizers and drives mechanized farming, processing, and transporting, thus raising food production costs. Notice how all three of our topics—food, energy, and water—are related: A problem in one creates problems in the others, and the **strategic variable** is energy. If we solve the energy problem—a difficult undertaking—we solve the food and water problems.

HAS OIL PEAKED?

From 2002 to 2008, the price of crude oil shot from $20 a **barrel** to (briefly) $147. People angrily blamed speculators and oil corporations for manipulating prices, but the market was mostly reacting to supply and demand. Supply is leveling off just as demand, especially from newly industrializing countries like China and India, is climbing.

Some called the drastic climb in world oil prices a "spike," something that shoots up and then down rapidly, forming a spike on a graph. The 2008–2009 global recession cut demand and brought oil prices down for a while. Some experts say we will soon reach "**peak oil**" and can expect no major new finds or breakthroughs to bring supply back above demand. When OPEC says it cannot produce much more, it may be telling the truth. And this is hitting at the very time world energy demand is climbing, chiefly because the developing lands really are developing fast,

ECONOMICS ■ OIL AND US

U.S. motorists hate high gasoline prices and demand the government do something about them. For much of the twentieth century, however, oil-producing countries found prices far too low, which is why they formed OPEC in 1960. By giving each member a quota, OPEC tries to keep petroleum production low enough to keep prices up.

Americans loved cheap gasoline—$1 a gallon in 1998—but might have thought twice. Cheap gas encouraged people to buy more and bigger vehicles and drive them more miles, producing more air pollution, traffic jams, and dependency on foreign oil. Public transportation is scarce. Global warming mounts. Gasoline at $4 a gallon in 2008 made Americans wish they had smaller cars and lived closer to jobs.

America consumes 25 percent of world oil production and imports 70 percent of its oil, a quarter of it from the Persian Gulf. (Our biggest supplier is Canada.) But because oil is one big global market, a disruption anywhere creates shortages everywhere. This is what happened with the 1973 Arab–Israel war and the 1979 overthrow of the shah. It explains why we drove back Iraq in 1991. But should we intervene for oil on a standing basis? It would be trading blood for oil and make us the police force of the Gulf. Can you imagine us fighting in the Gulf so that we can enjoy our SUVs? A better course would be to kick our "oil addiction."

aquifer   Underground water-bearing layer.

consuming much more energy for their factories, homes, and cars. In about ten years, China doubled its energy consumption (chiefly coal), surpassing the United States in 2010.

Those who argue we have reached a peak are not necessarily pessimists. Environmentalists can say, "Finally we'll start getting away from an oil-based economy and its pollution." Scientists can say, "Now high oil prices force us to get serious about alternate energy sources. With enough funding, breakthroughs are likely." And the oil and natural gas exporting countries just grin; they've never been richer or more influential.

Skeptics about peak oil, on the other hand, say that what is hitting the world is not long-term scarcity but price fluctuations, of which we have seen many. The recent fluctuations are the result of several factors, all of which can be offset, they claim. First, the Americans unwittingly took Iraq out of the world oil market with their 2003 invasion. They thought Iraq's oil production would rapidly return and even increase. Instead, Iraq reached its prewar level only in 2008, but now it's climbing nicely. Second, this hit when Nigerian oil production was down by a fourth due to attacks in the

ECONOMICS ■ WAS MALTHUS WRONG OR JUST PREMATURE?

In 1789, Englishman Thomas Malthus, one of the founders of economics, published his celebrated essay predicting drastic limits on the number of humans the earth could sustain. Humans increase their numbers "geometrically" (what we today call "exponentially," at a faster and faster rate) while food supplies increase only "arithmetically" (at a constant rate), he wrote. Eventually, people will outstrip food supplies and die from starvation, war, or disease. You can see where economics got its dismal reputation.

Paul Ehrlich, a latter-day Malthusian, predicted in 1967 that "in the 1970 and 1980s hundreds of millions of people will starve to death." Beware doomsters. There are nine times as many people as at Malthus's birth—the earth's population has doubled just since 1960—and most eat better and live much longer. (Of 7 billion humans, some 1.6 billion are overweight.) Famines have been local and caused by wars and natural disasters, not overpopulation. The problem now is that some developing lands lack money to buy food, a problem solved by economic growth.

Predictions of doom still sell, as with the 1972 book *The Limits to Growth*. A team of academics used computer models to predict that population growth would soon face shortages of food, energy, minerals, and clean air and that standards of living would start declining in the early twenty-first century. Climbing food and fuel prices in our day—due to Asians

getting richer and foolish U.S. subsidies for ethanol—make some wonder whether the *Limits* authors were completely wrong.

Their computer model, however, was based on dubious assumptions and neglected the possibilities of increased supplies and technological change. Brazil, with major programs in scientific agriculture, turned into a food powerhouse. We should have run out of oil long ago, but even after massive usage there is now about the same amount of proven oil reserves as there was a third of a century ago, because new fields and techniques have been developed. Recent high oil prices came from rapid economic growth in countries such as China and India, whose people demand cars and air conditioning and whose governments foolishly subsidize gasoline and diesel fuel, thereby encouraging wasteful consumption.

Factors neglected earlier now loom large: Vast farming areas have been lost to erosion, overuse, desertification, and salinity. **Aquifers** are depleting, especially in the Third World. In China and India, rivers are usable for less and less. Marginal grasslands are drying up and deserts expanding. Global warming is shifting weather patterns to cause droughts in some areas and floods in others. Even the United States is hit by these problems. Perhaps Malthus and the *Limits* people were premature and looking at the wrong factors.

Niger Delta, where environmental damage is severe and angry local people get little of the oil money. With these problems solved, supply will grow and bring prices down, they argue. We've gone through oil-price surges twice before (in the early and late 1970s) but have adjusted. In 1998, oil was $10 a barrel, and gasoline was $1 a gallon. This third time will be overcome about the same way, they suggest.

futures Contracts to sell commodity at certain price in the future, therefore a bet that it will go up or down.

Much of the price jump is due, many claim, to speculators who bid up oil futures in a frenzy that cannot be sustained. When the oil-futures bubble pops, prices fall. In 2008, amid the financial meltdown, oil declined to under $40 a barrel but in early 2011 was around $90. Most economists doubt that speculation plays a big role. **Futures** prices—which are not real oil but simply contracts to deliver oil at a certain price, "paper barrels"—are driven up by the calculation that oil is getting scarcer. Many other commodities—coal, natural gas, iron ore—also climbed without any speculative market but because of very real growing demand from factories, especially in China and India.

The "peakers" say we are reaching the geological limits of oil production. The main producers can add little to their output, and some fields are already declining (such as the North Sea's between Scotland and Norway). All the big, easy oil has been found; new fields are small and expensive to develop, as with floating platforms in deep seas, which, as we discovered in 2010, can become environmental disasters. And this hits just as developing lands slurp up more oil than ever before.

"Non-peakers" agree that oil is at times tight, but point to causes in politics and economics. Investments in oil production and especially in refineries have lagged, often due to exaggerated environmental concerns. America has built no new refineries in 30 years. Oil consumption in the developing lands is soaring. Most oil-rich nations have taken their oil back from giant oil corporations. Now 77 percent of global oil reserves are government owned. The private corporations have an incentive to produce more oil more efficiently, but state-owned oil firms such as those of Russia

---

ECONOMICS ■ THE 2010 GULF OIL SPILL

In 2010 Americans looked at headlines "Crisis in Gulf" and asked which gulf—Persian or Gulf of Mexico? A floating oil drilling vessel was just opening a new well for British Petroleum a mile underwater when the whole rig blew up, killing 11. A gigantic plume of oil and methane then squirted out of the seabed, the worst spill in history, which damaged much of the Gulf of Mexico's fishing, beaches, and wetlands and took three months to stop.

Hypocrisy flowed as thick as tar balls. BP and its contractors had taken reckless shortcuts and had no plan or equipment to contain a blowout; they improvised frantically. The Interior Department issued drilling leases for decades but did not monitor safety. The Obama administration denounced BP but took weeks to get fully involved. Ironically, shortly before the blowout Obama announced an expansion of undersea drilling permits. Gulf states support seabed drilling for its jobs and tax revenues, and few worry about its risks. Legislators and governors, especially in energy-rich states, and presidential candidates get big campaign contributions from the energy industry. They criticized BP but never suggested ending undersea drilling. Senator Mary Landrieu (D-Louisiana) said, "We have to understand we have to continue to drill for oil and gas."

The underlying problem: Americans are addicted to oil (see box on page 356), and Congress is not about to tax it to wean them off it. Ending undersea drilling would make us even more dependent on oil imports. Aside from a few environmentalists, no one said no to seabed drilling.

stagflation   Slow economic growth plus inflation.

and Iran often do not. They lack the high-tech expertise, and high prices give rich oil exporters a perverse incentive to limit production. They need no more cash now, and their oil will be worth even more in the future, so keeping it in the ground is the best bank of all, safer and higher yielding than any investment. That is one reason Russia and Middle East countries do not look very hard for new oil, which geologists say is there.

TECHNOLOGICAL FIXES?

Until the late Middle Ages, most humans heated and cooked with wood. As wood got scarce, coal took over, and *fossil* fuels have dominated ever since. This revolution in energy sources brought modernity and, eventually, pollution. Now may be the time, some argue, for another energy revolution, one that moves humankind beyond fossil fuels. Some countries are taking the idea seriously and developing solar and/or wind power. Germany, Spain, India, China, Japan, and Israel do major export business in "green" energy technology.

The energy problem underlies both the food and water problems. With enough low-priced energy you can desalinate seawater or cleanse polluted rivers for drinking or growing crops. Saudi Arabia, for example, uses waste gas from its oil fields—that otherwise would just be flared off—to desalinate seawater for both households and agriculture. Thanks to free energy, Saudi Arabia grows wheat in the desert.

ECONOMICS ■ ADDICTED TO OIL

Oil plays a mammoth and sometimes destabilizing role in the U.S. and world economy. Through World War II, the United States was the world's biggest oil producer and exporter, but then the Persian Gulf fields came on line, keeping world oil prices low. In response, Americans built energy-inefficient cars, homes, suburbs, and industries. Our main trading partners in Europe and Japan held down oil addiction by taxing oil heavily and encouraging energy efficiency. Europeans pay around $5.50 a gallon for gas ($3 of it in taxes), use a third less fuel per mile, and drive half as many miles as Americans. Overall, an American uses two and a half times as much energy as a European or Japanese, making us vulnerable to oil cutoffs or price hikes.

Americans received a third reminder a few years ago, when oil prices again shot up. The first warning came with the 1973 Arab–Israeli war, after which world oil prices jumped from about $2.50 to $11 a barrel; the second with the 1979 Iranian revolution, which in four years brought oil to $34 a barrel. The result was a **stagflation** that kept U.S. workers' incomes stuck at the 1973 level. Then oil prices slumped in the late 1990s, and Americans purchased many large SUVs and pickups. Later, though, OPEC got its act together and forced the price back up to over $70 a barrel, which many thought was unsustainable and would soon come down.

But increased rich-nation consumption plus China, India, and other developing lands with growing energy appetites pushed oil to $145 a barrel at one point in 2008. Shocked Americans, who import most of their oil, paid more than $4 a gallon at the pump. After several warnings, Americans should have learned about energy vulnerability and efficiency. The oil crisis damaged the U.S. economy and figured in the 2008 election. We could reduce vulnerability to oil-price fluctuations by high gasoline taxes to force Americans to cut consumption. No American politician dares suggest this.

Few countries have such a gift, but could a technological breakthrough hold down energy costs? When petroleum prices pass $100 a barrel, scientists and engineers start taking seriously previous pipe dreams. Some may eventually work, but be warned: Many would produce expensive energy and damage the environment. Only high-priced oil makes these ideas halfway feasible. If oil prices are reasonable, few will be pursued. Another warning: All U.S. presidents since Nixon have urged technological fixes, especially "alternative energy," expensive programs that have yielded little.

1. Oil sands in Canada and oil shale in the U.S. West are abundant. But cooking oil out of them is expensive and leaves mountains of waste and polluted rivers.

2. The world has plenty of coal, but mining and burning it damage the environment. Clean coal technology has been sought for decades with no breakthroughs. "Carbon sequestration," injecting smokestack gas deep underground, has not yet worked in pilot efforts.

3. Ethanol from corn is inefficient—it produces just 1.5 times as much energy as it takes to make—and thrives only because Congress mandates increasing ethanol and subsidizes producers 51 cents a gallon. Diverting some 25 percent of the U.S. corn crop into ethanol contributes to food shortages. Ethanol from sugarcane—Brazil has been running cars on it for decades—produces 8.2 times as much energy as it takes to make, but Congress, to please domestic producers, puts a tariff of 54 cents a gallon on Brazilian ethanol.

4. Biofuels from microbes sound like science fiction but hold promise. Grown like algae in ponds, it could be turned into biodiesel at reasonable cost. Biofuels, whether from ethanol or microbes, do nothing to hold down CO_2 emissions: They're all carbon.

5. Wind power to generate electricity has outpaced production of turbines (many from Japan). Wind farms, however, are often distant from urban areas; major new transmission lines are needed.

6. Solar panels are getting cheaper and may eventually be price-competitive with coal-fired electricity, especially with cap-and-trade incentives. Each home could have solar panels and "live off the grid."

7. Hydrogen, once touted by Bush 43, has so far failed for the simple reason that it takes a lot of energy to create hydrogen, mainly by electrolysis of water atoms.

DIPLOMACY ■ THE GREAT U.S.–SAUDI BARGAIN

Oil has long played a role in U.S. foreign policy. Britain had Iran sewn up with an oil deal before World War I, Iraq just after. When the House of Saud took over Arabia in 1932, however, Americans quickly jumped in with oil exploration that led to commercial finds in 1938. The Saudis never trusted British imperialists, but they trusted us. During World War II, the magnitude of the Saudi fields turned the United States and Saudi Arabia into close partners. In early 1945, President Roosevelt, on his way back from Yalta, met with Saudi King Abdulaziz for a deal: You let us develop your oil fields and buy your oil. We will protect and defend you.

For more than half a century, the bargain benefited both sides. It survived Arab–Israeli wars and the 1980 Saudi buyout of Aramco, the U.S.-owned Arabian-American Oil Company. But can the relationship continue indefinitely? Does not the transfer of wealth from America to Arabia plant the fear that the latter is buying the former? Americans noticed that 15 of the 19 hijackers of 9/11 were Saudis and that Saudi charities support Islamist schools. And what would happen if fundamentalists overthrew the House of Saud? Can the regime forever buy off young Saudis with education and jobs? Can Saudi Arabia modernize without its citizens demanding democracy?

cap and trade   Market-based system to incentivize cutting CO_2 emissions.

8. Geothermal energy looks interesting. Drill down several thousand feet in some places, and the earth can superheat water to run turbines on the surface.

9. Tidal and wave power would be inexhaustible, but machines to capture them break or salt up.

10. Nuclear has been rehabilitated. Now even some environmentalists see it as less bad than fossil fuels, provided the spent radioactive rods can be stored safely for many millennia. After the 1979 accident at the Three Mile Island nuclear power plant in Pennsylvania, no U.S. plants were built for decades, but Sweden, France, and Japan use nuclear power heavily.

One big problem is that the United States has no coherent energy plan. We subsidize the wrong industries and encourage profligate usage. As one critic described U.S. energy policy, "Maximize demand, minimize supply, and buy the rest from the people who hate us the most." Other countries are far more serious and are investing big bucks in alternative energy sources. Washington still coddles the big oil companies and neglects other paths. Meanwhile, we await "Mr. Fusion" (in *Back to the Future*) technology, but cheap, nonpolluting energy and "energy independence" are not likely any time soon, regardless of what politicians promise.

WATER CRISES

Water, according to some, is the new oil but may be even more important. There is precisely as much water on planet earth as there was a century, a millennium, or an ice age ago. It neither increases nor diminishes. Why then is the world in a water crisis? Over 97 percent is salty, and 70 percent of the remainder is ice. Some 70 percent of liquid fresh water goes for agriculture. The distribution and cleanliness of fresh water is shifting. A billion humans live in countries that lack sufficient water. Even parts of America face water shortages; states quarrel over who owns what water. Water, unlike food and energy, cannot be easily transported. It mostly stays in the same rivers it always has. Unfortunately, so much is withdrawn from many rivers that only a trickle reaches the sea.

ECONOMICS ■ WHAT IS CAP AND TRADE?

Environmentalists and economists urge that we partly shift from income, sales, and property taxes to taxes on the carbon in fossil fuels. They argue that this is the only way to cut the dumping of carbon into the atmosphere, which at present is little restrained. The amount of carbon released by burning coal, oil, gasoline, or natural gas is accurately known. (Coal has the most, natural gas the least.) If you burned x tons of coal, you would pay y dollars in taxes, but your other taxes might be lower. Users would have an incentive to burn less fossil fuel, especially the dirtier types. Cars would get fuel-efficient.

Even better, say some economists, is **cap and trade**, a system that creates a market to really incentivize energy producers to watch their carbon output. Each energy producer may belch CO_2 up to a certain level tax-free, the "cap." Above that, the energy producer must buy the unused free amount from a cleaner producer (the "trade" part). Obviously, solar energy produces no carbon, so it has plenty of credits to trade with, say, coal-fired power plants. The dirty producers (coal and oil) start planning how to stay within their caps. Europe has successfully used cap and trade, but the United States, which hates taxes of any sort, holds back. Some envision a global cap-and-trade system, but that would be hard to monitor and enforce.

Diverting rivers—through dams, reservoirs, and canals—can seriously shortchange regions and nations downstream. As cities grow, they comepte with farming areas for water. As countries dam their great rivers, lower downstream levels make nearby wells dry up. Turkey, in order to irrigate its poor southeast, is building 22 dams on the upper reaches of the Tigris and Euphrates Rivers. Downstream, Syria and Iraq got angry, something Turkey attempted to mollify. China diverts the Ili and Irtysh Rivers that flow from its thirsty Xinjiang province into Kazakhstan and is considering diverting the Brahmaputra, which rises in Tibet and flows into India. In Kashmir, India is building a dam on a river that runs into Pakistan, further sharpening tensions. When the British ran much of Africa, in 1929 they allotted Egypt 96 percent of the Nile's water, a percentage that Sudan, Ethiopia, and other upstream countries now mean to rectify.

desiccation Drying out.

Sahel Narrow band south of Sahara, arid but not yet desert.

Industrial waste and fertilizer runoff ruin great rivers, leaving them useless for households or farms. China's rivers are especially polluted. In China, you use only bottled water for drinking and brushing your teeth—and wonder if it is chemical-free. (One advantage of Beijing tap water is that it has few bacteria; waste industrial chemicals have killed them.) Nitrogen in fertilizer runs off into streams feeding "algae blooms" that absorb all oxygen and kill off fish and shellfish. Some of this extends out to sea at river deltas, creating vast "dead zones" devoid of fish. In 2008 Chinese soldiers frantically removed tons of stinking algae and seaweed from such a dead zone for the Olympics sailboat races.

At least partly related to global warming, large areas are subject to **desiccation** and desertification. In Roman times, North Africa was the empire's rich breadbasket; now it is much drier. The Sahara is spreading southward as the **Sahel** dries out from climate change and human overuse, as is China's Gobi desert. Sahelian and Northern Chinese farmers overplowed, dug too many wells, and depleted the fragile aquifer. Competition for scarce water underlay genocidal conflict in Sudan's

Under the impact of global warming, Greenland's massive ice shield is melting and breaking up. (Paul Souders/Corbis)

CONCEPTS ■ THE GLOBAL WARMING DISPUTE

The earth is getting warmer, some scientists say at an accelerating rate. The past ten years are the hottest recorded, the past half century the hottest in 1,300 years. From 2000 to 2007, the earth's average surface temperature rose 1.33 degrees Fahrenheit (0.74° Celsius), a considerable climb. The additional warming expected by the end of this century ranges from a modest 1.1°C to a dangerous 6.4°C.

Arctic ice is melting, allowing ships for the first time to traverse the seas north of Canada and Russia in the summer. Greenland is losing its thick ice cap. Southern species of plants and animals are expanding northward. Glaciers and snowpacks, which supply the river basins where one-sixth of humanity live, have shrunk. Most of Asia's great rivers, including the Ganges, Yangzi, and Mekong, originate in Himalayan glaciers. They provide water for some 40 percent of the world's population, but they are becoming depleted and polluted. Rainfall is shifting in unpredictable ways, increasingly in record downpours, and changing crop patterns. Some regions are getting wetter, others drier. Water determines food production.

Environmentalists, led by former Vice President Al Gore, blame increased carbon dioxide (CO_2) in the atmosphere. At the start of the industrial revolution about two centuries ago, there were 280 parts per million of CO_2, now grown to 380 parts per million, higher than any time in the last 400,000 years, maybe longer. The burning of fossil fuels (chiefly coal and oil) creates a "greenhouse effect" by trapping the sun's heat in the atmosphere, resulting in rising sea levels, climate change, foul air, and refugees, claim environmentalists. Therefore, they urge cutting CO_2 emissions—by carbon taxes, clean technology, lower energy consumption—as an urgent necessity.

But, warn scientists, CO_2 is only half the problem, as methane from cows, natural gas, and decaying plants have strong greenhouse effects. Nitrous oxide compounds have drawn belated concern. NO_x is released from the sea when marine plants and animals cannot absorb all the nitrogen that washes in from fertilizers. It both contributes to warming and destroys the earth's ozone layer.

Treaties to cut CO_2 are difficult. The 1997 Kyoto Protocol limited CO_2 emissions but went hard on the already-rich lands and easy on China (the world's biggest CO_2 emitter), India, and other newly industrializing lands, one of the reasons the United States refused to ratify it. Kyoto expires at the end of 2012, and a 2007 Bali meeting to replace it stalled amid EU–U.S. differences. The Europeans wanted numerical targets; the Americans (and Russians) did not. Al Gore told the meeting: "My own country, the United States, is principally responsible for obstructing progress here in Bali." A 2008 G8 meeting pledged to cut CO_2 output by half, but it had no enforcement provisions. A widely heralded Copenhagen summit in late 2009, attended by President Obama, affirmed lofty aims but reached no deal. The United States and China each produces about one-fifth of the world's carbon emissions, and they especially did not cooperate. Observers spoke of the "Copenhagen fiasco." The underlying reason for all these failures: No country is willing to harm its economy.

Ensuring compliance with international protocols is hard, and many of the signing countries exceeded Kyoto's limits. Unless you are immediately threatened by rising sea levels—such as small island states and low-lying regions—you tend not to worry. When the major powers get scared, we may see some progress. China, for example, now learning that poisoned air kills people and slows economic growth, claims to be ready to do something. In the meantime, China builds hundreds of new coal-fired power plants a year. As noted in Chapter 17, Beijing lets nothing get in the way of China's economic growth.

Some skeptics doubt that global warming is human-made. They emphasize that warming episodes reappear across geological time, and this one too may be normal and natural. If that is the case, the rise in atmospheric CO_2 does not necessarily cause global warming; therefore, curbing CO_2 will have little or no effect, they argue. Skeptics point out (correctly) that people tend to get swept up in *conventional wisdoms* (see page 290) that turn out to be wrong, and that global warming could be one of them. In their view, there's too much alarmism and not enough science. Atmospheric physics is exceedingly complex and takes much time to investigate. Environmentalists worry that we do not have much time.

Darfur region. West Africa's Niger River is shrinking from lower rainfall, deforestation, and silt. In Australia, the Horn of Africa (Somalia, Ethiopia, and Kenya), North China, and North India, failure of sufficient rain has devastated agriculture. Badly needed: water conservation and irrigation systems.

sovereign wealth funds Big pots of government money invested abroad.

Economists tell us that water—like air—is underpriced and therefore cannot be rationally allocated. In some places water is scarce but free, an absurd combination. With no or a low price tag, farms and industries just help themselves—the tragedy of the commons again.

F.E.W. AND HUMAN SECURITY

We now learn that human security goes beyond preventing wars and promoting human rights. It means that on a finite planet we must pay attention to the scarcity, costs, and distribution of resources. At present, no international body can regulate these transnational problems. There are several talking shops, but they have little authority. We may have to invent something that can supervise global scarcities before they become deadly. Columbia economist Jeffrey Sachs proposes a new U.S. Department for International Sustainable Development to coordinate tangled aid investments.

Consider the recurring problem of high oil prices. They drastically shift money (perhaps $1 trillion a year) and therefore power from the rich countries into the hands of the oil exporters. In return, many of the oil exporters build **sovereign wealth funds** that give them leverage on U.S. and European economic and foreign policies. Would Washington take tough steps against, say, Saudi Arabia, which could, with a phone call, withdraw billions from the U.S. economy? These big pots of government money sloshing around the earth looking for investments destabilize the world economy, creating unsustainable debt in everything from developing countries to the U.S. housing market.

This shift of oil money means Russia, Iran, Venezuela, Saudi Arabia, and others see no reason to accommodate the big oil importers. Tehran asks itself: Would the Americans risk a sudden shortfall of several percent of world oil output by invading or bombing Iran? Tehran figures they would not, so they brazenly continue their threatening behavior. Iran deters America without nukes. (This logic might not work with Israel, which Iran's President Ahmadinejad has vowed to "wipe off the map." If Iran produces nukes, Israel will strike.) Thinks Tehran, Moscow, and Caracas: "We've got the upper hand, so why be nice?" There is little we can do about it.

Some call this divide between oil exporters and oil importers "OPEC versus OECD." The Organization of Economic Cooperation and Development is a think tank supported by 31 mostly rich capitalist countries, most of them oil importers. Headquartered in Paris, the OECD compiles the only reliable economic statistics. Russia, Mexico, Norway, and Canada, although oil exporters, are not members of OPEC but often go along with OPEC output quotas.

The rich countries have problems with expensive oil, but the really devastating consequences are felt by industrializing lands that also must import oil. China, India, and much of the Global South saw their newly robust economic growth slow because of high oil prices. Oil exports do not promote democracy or fight corruption; they make them worse. Oil concentrates wealth in the hands of a few and locks autocrats into power.

Could oil scarcity lead to the *resource wars* mentioned in Chapter 1? Considering that petroleum played a role in the 1991 and 2003 wars with Iraq, maybe we've already had a resource war. Defenders of those wars angrily deny it, pointing out that seizing and keeping oil fields was never a U.S. goal. In fact, both wars for a time *decreased* the amount of oil available on the world market. War is a counterproductive method for securing oil, because oil is easy to sabotage, and occupation

cyclical   Changes that come and go, like a pendulum swing.

secular   Long-term change that goes only one way.

of an unruly land is a political and military mess. The planners of the 2003 Iraq War admit that they drastically underestimated the difficulties of occupying Iraq.

A bigger cause of war comes from concern over what the oil-exporting country is *doing* with its new wealth. We already mentioned the destabilizing impact of *sovereign wealth funds*, many of them from the Persian Gulf. Oil revenues enabled Saddam Hussein to build one of the biggest armies in the world and use it twice against neighboring countries, Iran and Kuwait. Fear that he was building weapons of mass destruction—even if unfounded—persuaded President George W. Bush for war. Now oil pays for Iran's nuclear program, giving Israelis and Americans similar fears. Israeli air strikes on Iranian nuclear facilities would be a war caused indirectly by oil but not a war for oil. It would still have a catastrophic effect on the world's oil supply. Saudi oil revenues enable elements within the Kingdom to fund Islamic charities that are fronts for terrorist groups.

How will food affect world politics? Here the United States, Canada, Brazil, and Australia have the advantage. They are the "Arabs of food," major exporters with (mostly) the right combination of soil, temperature, and water. Lose one of those—the way Australia has lost water—and their exports shrink. Climate change may actually improve Canadian farm output.

Roughly one person in seven in the world is hungry, almost all of them in the Global South. Food is generally available, but at prices too high for the poor to afford. The World Bank estimates that climbing food costs pushed some 100 million people into the ranks of the poor in 2007. Food riots have broken out in recent years in Haiti, Cameroon, Egypt, Cote d'Ivoire, Bangladesh, Afghanistan, Mozambique, and Gabon. Third World governments fear the anger of consumers and try to hold down food costs, sometimes by foolish subsidies that do nothing to increase the amount of food available. For the middle class, higher food prices mean giving up health care. For those on $2 a day, it means no meat. And for those in absolute poverty, on $1 a day, it means eating only the cheapest cereal grains, such as millet. For those even poorer, it means hunger. The poor in Haiti eat fried mud pancakes; they have no nutritional value but quiet the hunger pangs.

These countries are the sources of desperate immigration we discussed in Chapter 11. Haitians and West Africans attempt to reach the United States and Spain, respectively, in rickety boats; many perish. Those who make it are often arrested and deported. The Third World is trying to sneak into the First, and the First World doesn't welcome them. "Economic refugees" have become a major problem. How forceful should the rich countries be in keeping them out? Even South Africans rioted and drove out economic refugees from Zimbabwe who, they feared,

CONCEPTS ■ CYCLICAL OR SECULAR CHANGE?

Global warming illustrates the two kinds of change that analysts deal with. **Cyclical** change is repetitive; certain historical phases follow one another like a pendulum swing. Cycles of global warming and cooling are examples of cyclical change; there is change, followed by change back again.

Secular change means a long-term shift that does not revert back to the old pattern. The contention that the earth is undergoing one-way warming is an example. One of the problems faced by historians, economists, and political scientists is whether a change they are examining is secular—a long-term, basic shift—or cyclical—something that comes and goes repeatedly. China's change of dynasties every couple of hundred years is an example of cyclical change. The earth's population growth is an example of secular change.

would take their jobs. A 2008 U.S. Defense Department study on the security impacts of global warming noted that one of the biggest was environmental refugees.

Refugees can cause wars. The underlying element of Arab–Israeli wars is the displaced Palestinians. Millions of Bengali refugees fled into India from repression in East Pakistan. In 1971, India decided it was cheaper to fight a war with Pakistan in order to create the new nation of Bangladesh out of Pakistan so the refugees could go home. Darfuris from Sudan fleeing into Chad have sharpened border tensions there. Some 2 million Iraqis fleeing into Syria and Jordan become a fertile recruiting ground for Islamist terrorism.

Water can cause tension, too. Israeli–Syrian claims to the Sea of Galilee helped trigger the 1967 war. Israel's subsequent takeover of the West Bank's aquifer enrages Palestinians. The United States pulls water out of the Colorado River until just a trickle reaches Mexico, which protests strongly. Under international law, all **riparian** countries have certain rights, but the more powerful riparian powers usually dictate who gets how much water. The big problem with water scarcity is that it generates environmental refugees.

Can the United Nations or other international bodies take collective action in the F.E.W. questions? Cooperation does not come naturally, and many of the problems intensify nationalism. Oil and food producers want maximum income. In a time of food scarcity, foreign aid in food tends to dry up. The United States gave food aid when it had massive surpluses in order to support domestic farmers, but with less surplus food, that could change.

Could an international body order, beg, or persuade nations to behave cooperatively, for example, in giving up tight supplies of food to those who have none? Or can we leave the global

BTC Baku-Tbilisi-Ceyhan, pipeline from Azerbaijan through Georgia to the Turkish coast.

riparian Country along and with rights to a river.

GEOGRAPHY ■ PIPELINE POLITICS

The Caspian area and Central Asia (see page 144) have plenty of oil and natural gas, but how to get it to the outside world forms one of the twenty-first century's geopolitical problems. The region's pipeline corridors can basically run along the four points of the compass, but all of them are trouble-plagued:

North, through Russia, is the traditional corridor, one that links up with the much-bigger Siberian gas lines that feed Europe a third of its natural gas (expected to rise to half by 2030). Moscow therefore has a huge incentive to keep this corridor primary and under its control, as it gives the Kremlin both wealth and a voice in European foreign policies. But many Western countries fear giving Russia so much power. The northern corridor is also one big reason Russia crushed Chechnya so brutally: a major pipeline runs through it.

West, across Azerbaijan, Georgia, and Turkey, is what the United States strongly (but quietly) prefers,

precisely to offset Russia's pipeline power. Major U.S. private funds went into the new Baku-Tbilisi-Ceyhan (pronounced "jayHAHN"), or **BTC**, oil pipeline. A natural gas line is planned to follow this route all the way into Europe. Naturally, Moscow opposes this corridor, one of the reasons it dismembered Georgia. The BTC is also vulnerable to Kurdish separatist sabotage in southeast Turkey.

East, through the "stans" into China, is what China needs to feed its zooming energy appetite. China, now building a major pipeline along this corridor, is the net winner from problems in the north and west corridors.

South, through Iran, the logical choice, is blocked by U.S.–Iranian hostility. It is short, could be built quickly, and would yield Iran and the world major benefits. We suspect that eventually mutual gain will persuade both Tehran and Washington to realign their policies in a rational direction.

allocation of food to purely market forces? Atlantic bluefin tuna, for example, are overfished. The 2010 Gulf oil spill damaged their breeding ground. The large fish, prized by ancient Phoenicians and Greeks, gets rarer and more expensive. Some countries propose international limits on the bluefin tuna catch so it does not disappear. Extinction is easy; cooperation is hard.

Actually, by cutting fats and sugars for a simpler, less-caloric diet, Americans would be healthier and live longer. But few see it that way. Your grandparents (or great-grandparents) in the Great Depression and World War II lived a modest lifestyle, consuming far less meat, sugar, oil, and electricity than today. And life was not bad. Families typically had one car, not one car for each family member. Phones were scarce during the war, and many families had none, let alone five. The global economy may be giving us a chance to relive the spare but adequate lives of the 1930s and 1940s.

While it is hard to imagine international collective action that could manage the big transnational problems, the situation may require it. Even Americans, who are maniacs about their sovereign independence, demand that something be done when prices climb and gobs of spilled oil start washing onto wetlands and beaches. One country or a few cannot solve such problems, neither can current international organizations like the UN and its related specialized agencies, which were set up to have minimal authority. The globe may just be getting started in organizing itself. We, the authors, won't see it, but you may.

mypoliscikit EXERCISES

Apply what you learned in this chapter on MyPoliSciKit (www.mypoliscikit.com).

Assessment   Review this chapter using learning objectives, chapter summaries, practice tests, and more.

Menu

Flashcards   Learn the key terms in this chapter; you can test yourself by term or definition.

Flashcards

Video   Analyze recent world affairs by watching streaming video from major news providers.

Videos

Simulations   Play the role of an IR decision-maker and experience how IR concepts work in practice.

Comparative Exercises

KEY TERMS

aquifer (p. 354)
arable (p. 352)
barrel (p. 353)
BTC (p. 363)
cap and trade (p. 358)
collective good (p. 352)
cyclical (p. 362)

desiccation (p. 359)
futures (p. 355)
Green Revolution (p. 352)
peak oil (p. 353)
riparian (p. 363)
Sahel (p. 359)
secular (p. 362)

sovereign wealth
    funds (p. 361)
stagflation (p. 356)
strategic variable (p. 353)
tragedy of the commons
    (p. 352)
transnational (p. 352)

FURTHER REFERENCE

Bakker, Karen. *Privatizing Water: Governance Failure and the World's Urban Water Crisis*. Ithaca, NY: Cornell University Press, 2010.

Bower, Tom. *The Squeeze: Oil, Money and Greed in the 21st Century*. New York: Harper, 2009.

Bryce, Robert. *Gusher of Lies: The Dangerous Delusions of "Energy Independence."* New York: PublicAffairs, 2008.

Chamberlain, Gary. *Troubled Waters: Religion, Ethics, and the Global Water Crisis*. Lanham, MD: Rowman & Littlefield, 2007.

Chasek, Pamela S., David L. Downie, and Janet Welsh Brown. *Global Environmental Politics*, 5th ed. Boulder, CO: Westview, 2009.

Collier, Paul. *The Plundered Planet: Why We Must—and How We Can—Manage Nature for Global Prosperity*. New York: Oxford University Press, 2010.

Connelly, Matthew. *Fatal Misconception: The Struggle to Control World Population*. Cambridge, MA: Harvard University Press, 2008.

Cribb, Julian. *The Coming Famine: The Global Food Crisis and What We Can Do to Avoid It*. Berkeley, CA: University of California Press, 2020.

Egeland, Jan. *A Billion Lives: An Eyewitness Account from the Frontlines of Humanity*. New York: Simon & Schuster, 2008.

Freidman, Thomas L. *Hot, Flat, and Crowded: Why We Need a Green Revolution—and How It Can Renew America*. New York: Farrar, Straus & Giroux, 2008.

Gore, Al. *Our Choice: A Plan to Solve the Climate Crisis*. Emmaus, PA: Rodale Books, 2009.

Houck, Oliver A. *Taking Back Eden: Eight Environmental Cases that Changed the World*. Washington, DC: Island Press, 2009.

Hulme, Mike. *Why We Disagree About Climate Change: Understanding Controversy, Inaction and Opportunity*. New York: Cambridge University Press, 2009.

Kerry, John, and Teresa Heinz Kerry. *This Moment on Earth: Today's New Environmentalists and Their Vision for the Future*. New York: PublicAffairs, 2008.

Klare, Michael T. *Rising Powers, Shrinking Planet: The New Geopolitics of Energy*. New York: Metropolitan, 2008.

Lomborg, Bjørn. *Smart Solutions to Climate Change: Comparing Costs and Benefits*. New York: Cambridge University Press, 2010.

Lovell, Bryan. *Challenged by Carbon: The Oil Industry and Climate Change*. New York: Cambridge University Press, 2010.

Maass, Peter. *Crude World: The Violent Twilight of Oil*. New York: Knopf, 2009.

McKibben, Bill. *Eaarth: Making a Life on a Tough New Planet*. New York: Times Books, 2010.

Nordhaus, William. *A Question of Balance: Weighing the Options on Global Warming Policies*. New Haven, CT: Yale University Press, 2008.

Orr, David W. *Down to the Wire: Confronting Climate Collapse*. New York: Oxford University Press, 2009.

Pearce, Fred. *When the Rivers Run Dry: Water—The Defining Crisis of the Twenty-First Century*. Boston: Beacon, 2007.

Pielke, Roger, Jr. *The Climate Fix: What Scientists and Politicians Won't Tell You About Global Warming*. New York: Basic Books, 2010.

Ridley, Matt. *The Rational Optimist: How Prosperity Evolves*. New York: HarperCollins, 2010.

Roberts, Paul. *The End of Food*. Boston: Houghton Mifflin, 2008.

Rogers, Peter, and Susan Leal. *Running Out of Water: The Looming Crisis and Solutions to Conserve Our Most Precious Resource*. New York: Palgrave, 2010.

Sachs, Jeffrey D. *Common Wealth: Economics for a Crowded Planet*. New York: Penguin, 2008.

Simon, Christopher A. *Alternative Energy: Political, Economic, and Social Feasibility*. Lanham, MD: Rowman & Littlefield, 2006.

Singer, Clifford. *Energy and International War: From Babylon to Baghdad and Beyond*. Hackensack, NJ: World Scientific, 2009.

Smil, Vaclav. *Global Catastrophes and Trends: The Next Fifty Years*. Cambridge, MA: MIT Press, 2009.

Solomon, Steven. *Water: The Epic Struggle for Wealth, Power, and Civilization*. New York: HarperCollins, 2010.

Steiner, Christopher. *$20 Per Gallon: How the Inevitable Rise in the Price of Gasoline Will Change Our Lives for the Better*. New York: Grand Central, 2009.

Stern, Nicholas. *The Global Deal: Climate Change and the Creation of a New Era of Progress and Prosperity*. New York: PublicAffairs, 2009.

Sweet, William. *Kicking the Carbon Habit: Global Warming and the Case for Renewable and Nuclear Energy*. New York: Columbia University Press, 2008.

Zedillo, Ernesto, ed. *Global Warming: Looking Beyond Kyoto*. Washington, DC: Brookings, 2008.

Photo Credits

Chapter 1

p. 2: Pete Souza/Corbis; p. 18: Reuters/Nickola Solic/Landov

Chapter 2

p. 20: AP Photo

Chapter 3

p. 40: Bettmann/Corbis; p. 51: Ernie Sisto/*The New York Times*/Redux Pictures

Chapter 4

p. 56: Bettmann/Corbis; p. 69: AP Photo

Chapter 5

p. 72: Bettmann/Corbis; p. 86: Ozier Muhammad/*The New York Times*/Redux Pictures

Chapter 6

p. 96: Jim Watson/Getty Images; p. 106: Pete Souza/Corbis

Chapter 7

p. 112: Greg English/AP Photos; p. 114: Hulton Archives/Getty Images

Chapter 8

p. 126: AP Photos; p. 138: Richard Wainwright/Corbis

Chapter 9

p. 142: Patrick Baz/Getty Images; p. 153: Capt. Rory Quinn/U.S. Marines/*The New York Times*/Redux Pictures

Chapter 10

p. 160: Werner Rudhart/Corbis; p. 169: Jack Manning/*The New York Times*/Redux Pictures; p. 173: Gustavo Amador/Corbis

Chapter 11

p. 176: Brian Lee/Corbis; p. 185: Luis J. Jimenez/*The New York Times*/Redux Pictures

Chapter 12

p. 194: William G. Vanderson/Hulton Archives/Getty Images; p. 201: Pierre Bessard/Redux Pictures

Chapter 13

p. 208: Tom Stoddart/Getty Images; p. 217: Bettmann/Corbis

Chapter 14

p. 222: Parspix/Abacapress.com/Newscom; p. 224: *The New York Times*/Redux Pictures; p. 225 (left): John Van Hasselt/Corbis, p. 225 (right): Kimimasa Mayama/Corbis; p. 231: Pete Souza/Corbis

Chapter 15

p. 238: Bryan Denton/Corbis; p. 245: Jeremy Lock/ AP Photo

Chapter 16

p. 254: Pamagiotis Moschandreou/Corbis; p. 262: Georges Gobet/Getty

Chapter 17

p. 270: Imagine China/AP Photos; p. 272: Chang W. Lee/*The New York Times*

Chapter 18

p. 286: Jacquelyn Martin/AP Photo; p. 291: Yoshikatsu Tsuno/Getty Images

Chapter 19

p. 302: Andy Rain/Corbis; p. 312: Corbis

Chapter 20

p. 318: Eric Cabanis/AFP/Getty Images; p. 331: Robin Utrecht/Corbis

Chapter 21

p. 334: Reuters/Marco Dormino/Minustah/Landov; p. 347: Yuri Cortz/AFP/Getty Images

Chapter 22

p. 350: Petty Officer First Class John Masson/U.S. Coast Guard Handout/Corbis; p. 359: Paul Souders/ Corbis

Index